AF352676

Jewish Temple Theology and the Mystery of the Cross

Jewish Temple Theology and the Mystery of the Cross

Atonement and the Two Goats of Yom Kippur

Richard J. Barry IV

The Catholic University of America Press
Washington, D.C.

The paper used in this publication meets the minimum requirements of
American National Standards for Information Science—Permanence of Paper
for Printed Library Materials, ANSI Z39.48-1992.

∞

Cataloging-in-Publication Data is available from the Library of Congress
ISBN : 978-0-8132-3717-6
eISBN : 978-0-8132-3718-3

for Federica

Contents

Acknowledgments

This is a book about the cross of Jesus Christ. How can I acknowledge anything if I do not first acknowledge that I take this same cross to be my single hope and my only boast? What I can offer here is, certainly, only a small drop of scholarship in that vast ocean of divine mercy, but I am thankful that the Lord has given me the strength and support to give what little I have.

The strength and support that God has given me has taken the form of a thousand faces, a beautiful cloud of people who have surrounded me with love and friendship throughout my life, and in a special way over the last few years as I have carried out this work. I begin with my family. My dad, Richard Barry III, and my mom, Judith (Hall) Barry, have been unfailing in their love and encouragement, and I cannot begin to express my gratitude for the fact that they gave me the gift of a happy home throughout my childhood, the gift of guidance and friendship in adulthood, and unconditional love always. What's more, my parents gave me the gift of a beautiful sister, Jennifer, and through her a wonderful brother-in-law, Erik Arvidson, and through *them* the joy of a nephew and two nieces, Jacob, Hailey, and Zoe. Thank you, all, for the immeasurable gift of family.

As this project began to take form in my mind and in my heart, our family endured our greatest tragedy when my cousin Michael P. Barry died at the very young age of twenty-six. Mike himself knew both the joy of God's intimate presence—he indeed radiated that goodness and love that comes only from God's indwelling grace—and the mournful agony of the wilderness of mental illness. Mike has been present to me in a million ways as I have worked on this book; he has been an inspiration and a companion as I have meditated on the full landscape of

Christ's saving work, which encompasses the highest highs and the lowest lows, making all things new. I am thankful to Mike, and all of my wonderful cousins, uncles, aunts, and grandparents, who have been a constant source of love and encouragement every step of the way.

There are so many others who have been such constant friends throughout this process. The present text has its roots in my dissertation, and I could not have asked for a better dissertation director. D. Stephen Long has been an extraordinary guide and an academic role model. I am grateful for all of his helpful advice and encouragement.

This book is also the continuation of a hundred conversations that I've had over the years around campfires and on running trails with friends that I've had—in some cases—since kindergarten. These friendships mean the world to me; I am a much clearer thinker, and far better man, for them. I especially think of Greg Seiders, Matt Izzi, Noah Shier, Joe Nawrocki, Dan Sammartino, Marcus Verduchi, Dan Geary, Kyle Vander Meulen, Matt Thollander, and many others at George Washington, the Witherspoon Fellowship, Notre Dame, and Marquette.

I am thankful for John B. Martino, and the entire editorial staff at Catholic University of America press, for their extensive efforts to improve this book. It has been a great pleasure working with you.

Over the last eight years, I have had the joy of teaching at Providence College in Providence, Rhode Island. As tempting as it is to elaborate on my appreciation for each of my friends here at PC, the list of names would be too long; I will simply say that I am truly thankful for all the friendships I have formed here, and the many ways I have grown intellectually and personally through fellowship with these colleagues. A special word of gratitude, however, is owed to Stephen A. Long and Andrew Geist, each of whom have read (or heard read to them) extensive portions of this text, and who have provided outstanding suggestions for improvement. Even more, they—along with our other great colleagues—have given me the gift of intellectual fellowship and true friendship. I consider myself extraordinarily blessed. I am also grateful to Kathryn Long for her wonderful help in the final stages of editing this manuscript.

As if all of that wasn't enough, the Lord, the giver of all good gifts, has seen fit, in recent years, to multiply his blessings yet more extravagantly. In the midst of writing and rewriting these pages, I met Federica Wade. Soon after meeting, we found ourselves at the Commons Neighborhood Eatery in Foxborough, where she asked me about the book I was writing. This being only our second date, I gave my short "elevator pitch," and thought we'd quickly move on to some other topic less focused on Levitical goats. But her beautiful eyes sparkled, and she followed up with more detailed questions, and then comments connecting these ideas to things she had been reading, and ideas she had been thinking, and her brilliant insights sparked new ideas in me, and back and forth it went. We continued on excitedly, full of laughter and joy, prayer and thanksgiving, and a year later we were married. This book is now complete, but the conversation continues and bears new fruit every day. Thank you, Federica, for helping me to see the world anew, in all its beauty, and especially for helping me to draw closer to our Lord every day. I dedicate this book to you; in so many ways, it has been inspired by you, even when I did not yet know your name. Thank you for this inspiration, thank you for our beloved son, Richie, and thank you for the joy of being by your side every day.

RICHARD J. BARRY IV
Providence, RI
February 2, 2023
Feast of the Presentation of the Lord

Introduction

Tree of Life, First and Last

> We shall not cease from exploration
> And the end of all our exploring
> Will be to arrive where we started
> And know the place for the first time.

> —T.S. Eliot, *Little Gidding*[1]

If the tree is known by its fruit, what kind of tree was planted on Mount Calvary? Its tragic fruit, its only fruit, seems to be death: the lifeless body that descends into the arms of a heart-pierced mother. Yet Christians see this same tree as the icon of love, the only source of life for a sin-torn world. Day by day, year by year, they return to this tree with faith in its ability to heal and bind, soothe and revive; many have found upon this tree the only fruit able to fill the hungry soul. If we know the tree by its fruit, how then do we classify the cross of Jesus Christ?

There is a tree mentioned in the opening paragraphs of the first book of the Christian Bible, mentioned again in the final chapter of the last book, and virtually ignored in the hundreds of intervening pages. The return of the "tree of life" in Revelation seems as sudden as its disappearance after the third chapter of Genesis, yet attentive readers can hear the rustling of its leaves on every sacred page. According to Peter Thatcher Lanfer, this tree creates an *inclusio*, a bracket that surrounds and ultimately orients the entire Christian canon toward the center of the lost garden Eden.[2] The tree of life, then, is always strangely present in Scripture because it remains the human soul's most basic and intimate goal. The great drama that unfolds between Yhwh and Israel should thus be depicted as a narrative of return, an invitation to begin again on the journey for which we were made.

In its concluding verses, Revelation blossoms into a vision of the New Jerusalem, the glorious dwelling place of God, descending from the sky. In communicating this vision, the author weaves scattered threads from

---

1. T. S. Eliot, "Little Gidding" in *T. S. Eliot: Collected Poems, 1909–1962* (New York: Ecco, 1991), 208.

2. Peter Thacher Lanfer, *Remembering Eden: The Reception History of Genesis 3: 22–24* (Oxford: Oxford University Press, 2012), 34.

the Hebrew Bible together into a scriptural garment fit for the resurrected messiah. Most notably, the author uses Eden's basic landscape, but infused with major cultic imagery drawn from the Jerusalem temple and configured according to the pattern of the eschatological temple in Ezekiel. Hearing the prophet Ezekiel echoed in John is no surprise; both are given visions of a new Jerusalem after a tragic period of "Babylonian" exile. Ezekiel emphasizes the water that flows East from below the "threshold of the temple," and reports that "All kinds of trees for food will grow up on both banks of the stream. Their leaves will not wither nor their fruit fail; they will yield new fruit every month, because the water for them flows from the temple. Their fruit will serve for food and their leaves for healing" (47:12).[3]

Compared to Ezekiel, John's eschatological vision is harmonious, and different. He starts by saying, "I saw no temple in the city, for its temple is the Lord God the Almighty and the Lamb." (21:2). It would be a mistake to stop reading at the words "no temple," to imagine that the center of Jewish worship is eradicated in the new creation. John is saying something more profound: the reality of the temple is elevated beyond what mind had conceived, for the enthroned God Almighty and the Lamb eternally *are* the eschatological temple.[4] Indeed, key features of the earthly Jerusalem and its focal point, the temple, are preserved, including gates that remain always open (Rv 21:25; cf. Ezek 46:1), purity laws in the temple precincts (Rv 21:27), and a great river of living water which flows from the center, "from the throne of God and of the Lamb" (Rv 22:1). Where Ezekiel envisages trees lining the temple-river's banks, John sees something more specific. He sees the great tree of Eden: "On either side of the river is the tree of life with its twelve kinds of fruit, producing its fruit each month; and the leaves of the tree are for the healing of the nations" (Rv 22:2b). For John, the final blessing promised to those who are "victorious" (Rv 2:7) and who "wash their robes" (Rv 22:14; cf. Rv 7:14) is access to this boundlessly fruitful and healing tree. The glory prepared for Adam and Eve, the fullness of life hidden since

3. For biblical citations, unless otherwise noted, I will use the New Jewish Publication Society translation (NJPS) when quoting the Hebrew Bible, and the New Revised Standard Version (NRSV) when quoting the New Testament.

4. On this point, see Gregory Stevenson, *Power and Place: Temple and Identity in the Book of Revelation* (Berlin: de Gruyter, 2001), 268–69; Robert A. Briggs, *Jewish Temple Imagery in the Book of Revelation* (New York: Peter Lang, 1999), 107, note 203. This observation from Revelation is anticipated in the Gospels, as they report Jesus' claim that the destroyed temple would be "rebuilt" in three days. This already implies that Jesus' resurrected body would be the eschatological temple.

the foundation of the world, is now the gathering point of a restored and deified humanity.

The tree in John's vision may initially come as a surprise because of its apparent absence since Genesis 3, but its very description reveals to us that this tree has always been there, even when our eyes were dim to its presence. In his book, *The Genesis of Perfection*, Gary Anderson highlights how the opening pages of a novel, or the first minutes of a movie, are often fully understood only after seeing how the story ends.[5] From a canonical perspective, the primordial account of the creation and fall of Adam and Eve is more perfectly understood as the drama unfolds. Anderson says, "*Religious readers know where the story is heading before they have glossed even one word,*"[6] and therefore believers inevitably interpret key persons and symbols in a way that respects the "narrative unity"[7] of the inspired text's final form. In Revelation, we discover how the Garden of Eden and the Jerusalem temple inform one another, and how the eschatological "New Jerusalem" elevates them both. As we read these texts together and watch symbolic landscapes overlap throughout the canon, overlooked details reveal theological depths.

The first link between Eden's sacred geography and the floorplan of YHWH's temple is the location of the tree of life in Genesis: "And from the ground the Lord God caused to grow every tree that was pleasing to the sight and good for food, with the tree of life in the middle of the garden, and the tree of knowledge of good and bad" (Genesis 2:9). This is a garden oriented around a sacred center: the same God who breathes life into dust offers yet more life, a super-abundance of life, in the form of a fruitful tree. The expulsion narrative in Genesis 3 makes it clear that, after sin, what was initially a free gift and an implicit goal must now be veiled and guarded. "Now that the man has become like one of us, knowing good and bad, what if he should stretch out his hand and take also from the tree of life and eat, and live forever!" (Genesis 3:22). The Life eternal, for which Adam and Eve were made, has suddenly become a threat to their wellbeing. Therefore, cherubim are stationed at the garden's easterly entrance, with a flaming sword preventing trespass.

Gordon J. Wenham has argued that several features of the garden intentionally allude to temple imagery, making the garden an "archetypal

---

5. Gary A. Anderson, *The Genesis of Perfection: Adam and Eve in Jewish and Christian Imagination* (Louisville, KY: Westminster John Knox Press, 2001), 8–13.

6. Anderson, 8, emphasis in the original.

7. Anderson, 11.

sanctuary."[8] For example, cherubim, as the traditional guardians of holy places, are especially associated with the temple in the Hebrew Bible.[9] Images of cherubim appear on its curtains and walls, and two are stationed above the ark of the covenant. The temple faces east just as Eden's cherubim were stationed to the east. Water flows from each sacred space, and both are notable for their "good gold" and precious gems. This connection was well understood by ancient readers of scripture. Anderson shows how early Jews and Christians developed the idea that Eden and the temple had corresponding layouts. According to the second-century BC *Book of Jubilees*, for example, Noah "knew that the garden of Eden was the holy of holies and the dwelling of the Lord."[10] St. Ephrem the Syrian further suggests that the tree of life is found in the "inner region of Paradise," and that the tree of knowledge serves as a kind of curtain protecting the most sacred tree, which is the primordial holy of holies. Anderson explains that, for Ephrem, "if [Adam and Eve] hadn't disobeyed God's command, they would have been given access to the Inner Sanctum."[11] Instead, with a reach, they fall into exile.

This brings us to the other geographical landmark, the place of exile outside the garden walls: "the Lord God banished him from the garden of Eden, to till the soil from which he was taken. He drove the man out. . ." (Genesis 3:23–24a). This is the first mention of wilderness, the land of exile, the lonely desert landscape of a pilgrim people. It is the place called "Godforsaken," seemingly outside God's providence. Desert. Chaos. Here in its first three chapters, the entire geography of the Hebrew Bible is summarized: what follows is a human drama that occurs in the space between

8. Gordon J. Wenham, "Sanctuary Symbolism in the Garden of Eden Story," in *I Studied Inscriptions before the Flood* (Winona Lake, IN: Eisenbrauns, 1994), 399–404. Other research that explores this connection includes G. K. Beale, *The Temple and the Church's Mission: A Biblical Theology of the Dwelling Place of God* (Westmont, IL: IVP Academic, 2004), 66–80; Joshua Berman, *The Temple: Its Symbolism and Meaning Then and Now* (Northvale, NJ: Aronson, 1995), 21–34; Jon D. Levenson, *Resurrection and the Restoration of Israel: The Ultimate Victory of the God of Life* (New Haven, CT: Yale University Press, 2008), 82–90; L. Michael Morales, *Who Shall Ascend the Mountain of the Lord?: A Biblical Theology of the Book of Leviticus* (Downers Grove, IL: IVP Academic, 2015), 39–74.

9. Cf. Rachel Elior, *The Three Temples: On the Emergence of Jewish Mysticism in Late Antiquity* (Oxford: Littman Library of Jewish Civilization, 2005), 75–76.

10. James H. Charlesworth, ed., "Jubilees," in *The Old Testament Pseudepigrapha*, trans. O. S. Wintermute, vol. 2 (New York: Doubleday, 1985), bk. 8.19; cf. J. T. A. G. M. van Ruiten, "Eden and the Temple: The Rewriting of Genesis 2: 4–3: 24 in The Book of Jubilees," in *Paradise Interpreted: Representations of Biblical Paradise in Judaism and Christianity*, ed. Gerard P. Luttikhuizen (Leiden: Brill, 1999), esp. 75–79.

11. Anderson, *Genesis of Perfection*, 80; cf. 46–47, 56–57.

the inner sanctuary and the place of exile. Israel repeatedly finds herself in the wilderness, outside the gates, banished from her promised home, but never fully: hope for the holy of holies, the tree of life, never dies.

These themes are meticulously drawn together in Revelation 21–22. John describes a city of open gates, where there is nothing "unclean" (nothing touched by death and decay), and where the tree of life stands at the center. "Then he showed me a river of the water of life, clear as crystal, coming from the throne of God and of the Lamb, in the middle of its street. On either side of the river was the tree of life [*xúlon zōēs*], bearing twelve kinds of fruit, yielding its fruit every month; and the leaves of the tree were for the healing of the nations. There will no longer be any curse; and the throne of God and of the Lamb will be in it (*autē*). . ." (Rv 22:2–3, NASB). Lanfer notes that it was not uncommon in early Jewish literature to merge the images of the tree of life and the throne of YHWH,[12] thus making the tree *itself* in Revelation 22 the very throne of God and the Lamb.[13] In other words, in the final chapter of Christian scripture, the imagery of the garden of Eden and the temple's holy of holies—the tree of life and the throne room of YHWH—are fused and embodied in the image of a lamb standing as slain (cf. Rv 5:6). This is the culminating depiction of perfect holiness, around which all history spirals.

Revelation also says, "there will no longer be any curse." Above all, this puts an end to the curse of exile that began in Genesis 3, which was recapitulated throughout Israel's history, and is also felt as a strange alienation in every human heart. With the final unveiling of the tree of life, Revelation vividly portrays our homecoming, a glorious return after an impossibly long journey.

When the sacred tree is fully revealed at the end of history, it is leafy, fruitful, and crimson-stained.[14] When the Christian imagination looks

12. Lanfer, *Remembering Eden*, 55. Cf. Andrei Orlov, *Dark Mirrors: Azazel and Satanael in Early Jewish Demonology* (Albany: State University of New York Press, 2011), 22–23. Orlov draws attention to a number of relevant passages. For example, in the *Life of Adam and Eve* (which is roughly contemporary with Revelation) it says, "And the throne of God was fixed where the Tree of Life was" (22:4). Similarly, 2 Enoch says, "And in the midst (of them was) the tree of life, at that place where the Lord takes a rest when he goes into paradise. . ." (8:3).

13. This idea is further supported, Lanfer says, by the fact that the pronoun *autē* in verse three could easily point back to the tree of life: "The only other singular referents in which the throne could be placed are the river or the street and neither of these seems likely, whereas the *singular* Tree of Life could be the "seat" of God's presence, as it is so frequently elsewhere" (63).

14. 2 Enoch also notes the crimson coloring of the tree: "And that tree [of life] is indescribable for pleasantness and fine fragrance, and more beautiful than any (other)

closely at the tree's bark, it seems that the tree has been bloodied, coated in the ancient symbol of life. We discover that this same tree has been the site of a death which is the ultimate source of everlasting life. While scripture primarily refers to Christ's death on "the cross," *staurós*, five New Testament verses call it "the tree," *xúlon*.[15] The influence of Deuteronomy 21:22–23 for this choice of words is universally recognized and mentioned explicitly in Galatians 3:13: "Cursed is everyone who is hung on a tree."[16] But the earliest theologians, geniuses at drawing theological connections, also associated Christ's "tree" with the tree of life. Ephrem the Syrian sang, "Very sad was the Tree of Life / that saw Adam hidden from him. / Into the virgin earth he sank and was buried, / but he arose and shone forth from Golgotha."[17]

The ultimate revelation of the tree of life is the cross of Jesus Christ. It is creation's most beautiful tree, the sacred center of the universe, the greatest icon of love, the very throne of YHWH, and something that should never have happened. The cross is the form that the ancient tree must take in the context of sin—perhaps only the eyes of faith can see how this cursed death can be the very picture of triune love—yet the fruit has been the same from the beginning: the gift of a Life so overflowing that it cannot be circumscribed by time: life immortal, everlasting and eternal. This offer of immortality can be nothing less than participation in the divine nature: the original promise unsatisfied in the first generation but abundantly fulfilled in the last. The narrative arch of the entire Christian Bible is brought into focus, and we realize that to receive the fruit of Christ's cross is to arrive again where we started.

---

created thing that exists. And from every direction it has an appearance which is gold-looking and crimson, and with the form of fire." James H. Charlesworth, ed., "2 (Slavonic Apocalypse of) Enoch," in *The Old Testament Pseudepigrapha*, trans. F. I. Andersen, vol. 1 (New York: Doubleday, 1983), sec. 8.4 (long version), pg. 114.

15. Acts 5:30, 10:39, 13:29; Galatians 3:13; 1 Peter 2:24.

16. See chapter eight, below, for further analysis of this verse.

17. Ephrem, *Ephrem the Syrian: Hymns* (Mahway, NJ: Paulist Press, 1989), 332. Similarly, John of Damascus says, "The tree of life which was planted by God in Paradise pre-figured this precious Cross. For since death was by a tree, it was fitting that life and resurrection should be bestowed by a tree," "An Exposition of the Orthodox Faith," in *Nicene and Post-Nicene Fathers, Second Series*, vol. 9 (Buffalo: Christian Literature Publishing Co., 1899), 80. And, in the West, Hilary of Poitiers says, ". . . but now, thanks to the redemption wrought by the tree of Life, that is, by the Passion of the Lord, all that happens to us is eternal and eternally conscious of happiness in virtue of our future likeness to that tree of Life," "Homilies on the Psalms," in *Nicene and Post-Nicene Fathers, Second Series*, vol. 9 (Buffalo: Christian Literature Publishing Company, 1899), 241.

We arrive again, but we do not start over in a way that renders the intervening chapters irrelevant. Rather, it is now clear that the promise of Eden, and of the tree that stands at its center, is the hidden hope behind the deepest mysteries of Israel, whose history is shaped by the steady rhythm of Promised Land, exile, return, and longing still. Between Eden and the New Jerusalem of Revelation, we find the centering symbolism of the Ark of the Covenant, the Holy of Holies, and the Jerusalem Temple. And one cannot speak of the Temple without acknowledging the sacrificial practices that brought life to Mount Zion day and night. The cross must be understood in the rich analogical context of Tree and Temple, with their accompanying liturgical and sacrificial symbols; to misread this network of symbols would be to introduce significant distortions.

With the Tree of Life, the Holy of Holies, the Throne of God and the Lamb, Scripture proclaims the hope for a return to the center in the midst of Israel's reoccurring expulsion to the outside. This simultaneous movement in and out finds its greatest expression in Israel's most profound liturgical act: the once-yearly Day of Atonement, Yom Kippur. This is the day on which the high priest, representing the nation, goes beyond the veil and is permitted to worship before the throne, at creation's cosmic center. This is the day when all impurity and sin are eradicated and banished from the holy city. This is the day that attempts to knit together a nation perpetually caught between Zion and wilderness, caught in sin, hoping for Eden. For Christians, the work of Yom Kippur is perfected in the death, descent, and resurrection of Jesus Christ. But to *really* embrace the priestly word "atonement," and approach the meaning of Christ's cross from a thoroughly biblical perspective, one must learn to think with the mind of ancient Israel. It is, in the end, the only way to arrive at the beginning.

* * * * *

This book is a study of the Tree of Life, which comes finally to be planted outside the city walls. This cross is *both* the center and displaced, the point at which two extremes are embodied simultaneously, in a remarkable mystery—the most holy and the least, Zion and the wilderness. The central argument is simple: first, an adequate Christian soteriology, an adequate interpretation of the cross, must maintain the distinction between these two movements—to the center, to the periphery—and second, these movements are expressed with unequaled profundity on Yom Kippur, when two identical goats prefigure a single atoning work. One, as spotless sacrifice, the other as sin-bearer: *two* goats, without collapsing the difference—or should we nevertheless say one goat looked at with crossed eyes? The cross of Jesus Christ should be interpreted as a fulfillment of *this* form, outlined in Leviticus and faithfully observed yearly in Jerusalem until the destruction of the Temple. The newness of Christ is a trans-figuring newness, and thus the shape of atonement for the ancient covenant remains the proper shape of atonement in the new, only now (according to Christian conviction) illuminated from within by the glory of the incarnate and resurrected Son. It is this unique liturgical action at the "center" of Israel's cult which reveals the fuller meaning of the Temple, discloses the deep theology of the Tree of Life, and helps us contemplate the Cross of Jesus Christ.

The argument of this book will be developed in three major sections. In parts one and two, I will argue that to really understand the theology of "atonement" as it develops within Scripture—starting with the ancient Jewish roots of that word—and thus to understand the meaning of the cross more fully, we must seek "total immersion" in the biblical world. This means seeking to be oriented within biblical "space" and synchronized within biblical "time." The study of soteriology ultimately grapples with the promise: "See, I am making all things new." The "all things" of creation in Genesis 1 are ordered spatially and temporally, and so the restoration anticipated by Israel and perfected in Christ is a restoration of spatial and temporal peace. Thus, we will focus on the "Space of Atonement" (part one) and the "Time of Atonement" (part two) in the Jewish theological imagination, before turning ultimately (part three) to the way Christ takes up and reconfigures the space and time of atonement in his definitive saving work.

Part one, the "Space of Atonement," will explore sacred geography. Since the drama of scripture takes place between the extremes of Zion and wilderness, we will begin with a meditation on Zion. To begin with a theology of the temple is to emphasize what is positive first; the temple is not just a remedy for sin, but an expression of what is eternally beautiful, or as I've already suggested, a recapitulation of Edenic joy. One might even say that, through temple theology, Israel embarks on her own rich meditation on the beautiful, the true, and the good (the "transcendentals" in Greek philosophy); thus, our pilgrimage to Zion consists of three chapters that study the site from these three vantage points: chapter one will demonstrate that the temple itself is the site of transforming glory (beauty); chapter two will explore the temple as the site of sacrificial right-action (goodness); chapter three will show how the temple is the site where the theo-logic of creation is made manifest (truth). Chapter four, then, will bring together these temple reflections to show how, with its sacrificial cult, we reach the pinnacle of creation at Zion, an icon of the peace and harmony between heaven and earth that God is bringing into being through Israel. But as Israel comes to know the perfect goodness of God, she becomes more acutely aware of the reality of sin and the surrounding wilderness. She must go through this desert as she flees Egypt and she will return to this wasteland on occasion as she struggles to live up to her covenantal promises. Therefore, chapter four is also a meditation on the geographical extremes, a complex geography that shapes biblical theology and is especially foundational to Levitical thought.

Part two, on the "Time of Atonement," shifts to the liturgical and cosmic action that restores all temporal reality to its proper rhythm, the Day of Atonement. To understand this liturgy, one must understand Israel's sacrificial cult more broadly, which is quite foreign to many modern readers. A key component is the ancient priests' "hamartiology," their theology of sin. Chapter five will explore the multifaceted crisis of sin, and the surprising ways that "sin itself" was seen to "besiege" the temple. This way of imagining things lent itself to a dramatic vision of sin that made it possible for the priests to see themselves as warriors on the liturgical front lines of a great cosmic struggle: they, along with the nation they represented, were defenders of the beautiful, the good, and the true against the chaos and horror of an ever-encroaching wilderness.

Building on Israel's distinctive theology of sin, chapter six will seek a sophisticated understanding of Israel's "sin offering" (or, in Jacob Milgrom's terms, the "purification offering"), which requires reflection on the word "kipper" and on the symbolism of blood in Leviticus. Then, with the rich theological foundations for priestly soteriology established, chapter seven will grapple with the logic and rhythm of Yom Kippur itself. Here we will trace the distinct movements of the two goats brought before YHWH on this holiest of holy days and reflect on why *both* goats are needed if the nation—and the cosmos—are to be thoroughly healed. These reflections will ultimately reveal the complexity, and profundity, hidden in the simple priestly term "atonement."

In chapter eight, we move from a primary focus on the Jewish contexts for key theological terms to a consideration of how these terms are taken up in Christian theology. I will first discuss how the Day of Atonement shaped the earliest Christian interpretations of Jesus Christ and his cross, both in the New Testament and in patristic theology. Drawing on the previous two chapters, we will see how each goat embodies a distinct lexicon, and how learning to clearly differentiate the "goats" (the twin movements necessary for atonement) clarifies crucial New Testament passages that have sometimes been misread. We will then see how common it was in the early church to interpret Christ's saving work explicitly in terms of both the YHWH-goat *and* the Azazel-goat (often translated as "scapegoat"). Finally, we will assess the advantages and disadvantages of the unique way the church fathers interpreted Christ in light of Yom Kippur.

Building on the extended analysis of atonement in space and time in both ancient Jewish and early Christian theology, part three will turn at last to a consideration of how this approach to soteriology might be fruitfully taken up again in contemporary theology. In chapters nine and ten, I will show how two major figures in modern Christian theology—David Bentley Hart and Hans Urs von Balthasar—provide remarkable yet potentially incomplete accounts of Christ's saving work. Each account would be incomplete insofar as it might be read to emphasize only half of the work performed on the Day of Atonement, either focusing on the YHWH-goat or the Azazel-goat. Chapter nine will focus on the "goat for the Lord," the pure and spotless gift of love that recapitulates the original pattern of creation. The connection between recapitulation and Jewish sacrificial theology has been beautifully developed in modern times by Hart, and thus his work will represent the best of contemporary YHWH-goat soteriology.[18] I will also briefly suggest how the satisfaction model developed by Anselm and Aquinas—which is the most typical approach in Catholic theology—puts its emphasis in the same place. Chapter ten will turn to a very different approach, which has also found advocates in modern theology and has been especially controversial. This section will deal primarily with the disputed soteriology of Hans Urs von Balthasar but will also draw from the related teachings of Karl Barth and Sergei Bulgakov. I will show that Balthasar ultimately articulates a theology that perfects the work of the "goat for Azazel," and I will explain why this movement is also necessary for a comprehensive soteriology.

Finally, I will wrestle in chapter eleven with the question of how the one Christ, in his single passion, death, and resurrection, can and does fulfill the work of the two distinct goats. More strongly, I will argue that the two "movements," represented by the two goats, actually require each

18. When I speak of "YHWH-goat soteriology" and "Azazel-goat soteriology," here and in what follows, I am using these terms as shorthand for "a soteriology that predominantly focuses on the themes associated with the YHWH-goat (or Azazel-goat), as expounded in this book." No theologian has written or presented a theology that they have explicitly labeled a "YHWH-goat soteriology" or "Azazel-goat soteriology," but I will argue that such a thing is identifiable when we are deeply familiar with the theology of Leviticus, and especially the theology of Yom Kippur in Leviticus 16.

other in a comprehensive account of Christian salvation. By insisting that Christ fulfills the work of the Yhwh-goat *and* the Azazel-goat simultaneously on Mount Calvary, even though their movements appear to be opposite extremes, I will try to articulate the paradox proper to Christian soteriology. All of this will provide the context needed to consider how Yom Kippur soteriology relates to other approaches to the theology of the cross, with special emphasis on Khaled Anatolios' soteriology of "doxological contrition" along with other well-known approaches: penal substitution, feminist critiques of traditional theories of atonement, and Girardian "scapegoating."

In the epilogue, at last, we "arrive where we started," at the tree of life, to contemplate how a Yom Kippur soteriology might help us better understand that biblical mystery planted at the origin and culmination of the Christian canon.

Before setting off on our pilgrimage to Mt. Zion, a final word on "methodology" is in order. Throughout this book, I rely as heavily as possible on the insights of the best modern Hebrew Bible scholarship. I strive to ensure that historical-critical research on the book of Leviticus (which is often written by Jewish scholars keen to overcome the anti-priestly prejudices of earlier liberal Protestant scripture scholars) informs my understanding of biblical soteriology. While my overarching theological goal is a fuller interpretation of the cross in Christian systematic theology, a major underlying conviction is that recent historical research is indispensable in helping us to see the full shape and texture of the ancient priestly word "atonement," and that proper contextualization of this word makes possible a more nuanced interpretation of Christ's saving work, within his own Jewish context. Because this is a work of systematic theology, I will also make theological connections across texts, and occasionally critique historical-critical scholarship when it downplays the theological questions within the text or otherwise seems excessively narrow.[19] I hope to remain sensitive throughout to the basic historical

---

19. At the beginning of his own book on Christian soteriology, Peter Leithart identifies the many fields he draws from as he contemplates the saving work of Jesus Christ, including: "Old Testament studies, particularly on Leviticus and the Levitical system of the temple, purity, and sacrifice," "historical Jesus studies," and "dogmatic studies of soteriology." *Delivered from the Elements of the World: Atonement, Justification, Mission* (Downers Grove, IL: IVP Academic, 2016), 17. Then Leithart observes: "I *use* the scholarship of various disciplines, responsibly I hope, to construct an argument that does not fit neatly into any of them." Leithart, 18. The one who strives to intelligently weave together the insights of specialists in various areas so as to draw nearer to the theological mystery at the heart of it all will inevitably take steps and draw conclusions

shape of ancient Jewish thought, especially priestly thought, while hopefully also showing that systematic theologians can contribute to a deeper
understanding of these texts by using the "tools" proper to our field of
study. A theologian is to pick up notes of resonance across varied theological traditions, especially within scripture, and sing the eternal melody
once again. The Bible is not a repository of fragments, but an invitation
into the great drama which at last brings us to that holy Tree which alone
brings eternal life.

---

that specialists would never consider or imagine (sometimes because of the specialist's
greater understanding, sometimes due to their narrowed horizons). There is risk here,
but it can be rewarding. Leithart shows how fruitful it can be to think beyond the sub-
fields. But by casting a wide net, one also quickly confronts his own limitations as the
catch becomes unmanageable. Facing this reality, Leithart admits: "I am sure that there
are dozens of highly relevant works in each of these fields of which I am utterly ignorant.
For reasons that may be clear by the end of this book, I have tried to learn to be cheerful,
even giddy, in my limitations." Leithart, 18. In this work, I have tried to follow Leithart's
example.

Part I

The Space of Atonement:
Temple Theology

Section Introduction

Total Immersion in Sacred Geography

Christian theology is inescapably incarnational—strangely attentive to the history, to the drama, of dust—but incarnational predispositions are not a Christian innovation. Jewish theologian Michael Wyschogrod has shown that incarnational theology has its roots in the Hebrew Bible. These ancient scriptures make a claim that is anathema to deists and pantheists alike: God takes up a spatial, earthly *dwelling*.[1] Without denying omnipresence, Wyschogrod insists that in the Bible, "God also has an address. . . . He dwells in Number One Har Habayit Street. Number One Temple Mount Street."[2] Wyschogrod recognizes that opposition to idolatry—especially the worship of fabricated gods—coupled with later Jewish commitments to apophatic theology—exemplified in Maimonides' philosophical resistance to anthropomorphism—have contributed to a negative attitude toward the idea of divine incarnation in Jewish thought.[3] And yet, he says that these convictions should not blind us to other themes that are in no way marginal to biblical theology: "The whole history of the tabernacle and of the temple in Jerusalem is a history of a concept of a home for God in the world, a dwelling place for God."[4] The very word *dwell* suggests the intimacy, the weight, of God's presence *in this place*. The God of the Bible may not be limited, but he also does not abhor the notion of spatial location:

1. The verb *shakhan*, to dwell, is the root of the noun *shekinah*, the important rabbinic concept emphasizing God's dwelling presence. The Hebrew word "tabernacle," *mishkan*, simply means dwelling place.

2. Michael Wyschogrod, "Incarnation," *Pro Ecclesia* 2, no. 2 (1992): 210.

3. Michael Wyschogrod, "A Jewish Perspective on Incarnation," *Modern Theology* 12, no. 2 (1996): 199–201.

4. Wyschogrod, "Incarnation," 210. Wyschogrod says that there is a "temptation to lift God above spatiality," Wyschogrod, "A Jewish Perspective on Incarnation," 203; many feel they are honoring God, exalting God, by refusing to entertain the idea that God should be committed to a physical location. Without disrespecting the genuine concern not to limit God (a concern that is also fully expressed in scripture—the dialogical sophistication of the Hebrew Bible is seen in Solomon's speech at the dedication of the temple, where God's real dwelling in the house is simultaneously acknowledged and questioned; 1 Kings 8, vv. 13 and 27), the truth is that we limit God more when we predetermine what sort of behavior is appropriate to the Lord.

in making himself present to a people, he locates himself in their world to draw them to his.[5]

As we saw in the introduction, Israel's emphasis on spiritual geography begins in the first verses of Hebrew scripture and remains a persistent focus throughout the Jewish theological tradition.[6] This same emphasis swells in the book of Revelation as ancient biblical symbols are layered up to suggest a fulfillment beyond imagination. In the final chapters of Revelation, biblical geography is not set aside, but it is developed and transfigured: our vision is centered on the slain Lamb, the Tree of Life, the great throne, all illuminated by divine glory and bathed in living water. What we see in the descending Jerusalem is a people brought back from exile, washed clean, and gathered finally into the eternal holy of holies. We have the open gates inviting in and orienting all creation toward worship in unity, but we also have the "outside," the place of those who will not wash their robes. The coordinates are the same as ever before, but they are intensified here as salvation history crescendos toward the final "amen!"

To appreciate Yom Kippur within Israel's mature sacrificial theology, we must place ourselves within the sacerdotal geography that structured Jewish thought and prayer. Upon this spiritual landscape, the drama of Christ's life and death plays out. As Christianity spread through the Mediterranean and across the world, the original landscape was left behind, literally and figuratively. Names and places mentioned in the Bible no

---

5. For Wyschogrod, it is even more important to say that "The Jewish people, as a people, in some degree and in some form is the dwelling place for God in the world." Wyschogrod, "Incarnation," 212; cf. Wyschogrod, "A Jewish Perspective on Incarnation," 204–8. This, he says, is the "seriousness of the election of Israel." Wyschogrod, "Incarnation," 212.

Of course, to speak of God's incarnation in the people of Israel, or to speak of God's incarnation in the temple, is to use the word analogously, especially compared with the Christian affirmation of the doctrine of incarnation. The word "homoousios" remains the great challenge, as does the definition of Chalcedon. Gary Anderson has said that there are good historical reasons why sustained reflection on Jesus' incarnation in light of the temple theology of indwelling is rare in the Christian tradition: Theodore of Mopsuestia used this very temple theology to argue that the divine presence abandoned Christ on the cross, just as the Lord abandoned the temple before the Babylonian exile. For Nestorius too, "the indwelling of God in Jesus' body, like a temple, is a *wholly extrinsic affair.*" Gary A. Anderson, "Mary in the Old Testament," *Pro Ecclesia* 16, no. 1 (2007): 47. Anderson shows that temple imagery did not simply disappear from Christian theology, however, but it migrated to the person of Mary, the Theotokos, in whom divinity was pleased to tabernacle. Anderson, 49 ff.

6. Michael A. Fishbane, "The Sacred Center: The Symbolic Structure of the Bible," in *Texts and Responses*, ed. M. A. Fishbane and P. R. Flohr (Leiden: Brill, 1975), 9.

longer beckon the senses; descriptions of the temple no longer cause the Christian heart to strangely warm. It quickly became possible to write expansive atonement theologies with only cursory reference to the temple or the sacrificial cult, and then for these references to take on a decidedly negative tone.

Certainly, one can understand why later theologians drew upon images and ideas closer to hand in attempting to understand the mystery of salvation. Such pragmatic catechesis is already seen in the teaching of Paul,[7] so there can be no question about its validity in Christian discourse. Yet it *would* be misguided for Christian theology to forget its Jewish roots. The *Gestalt* of the old covenant (even if for Christians it is a teleological form, ordered toward further revelation) must shape our perception of the new, even as Christians maintain that the revelation of Jesus Christ transfigures the old, from glory to glory. Failure to maintain this connection makes it possible for modern theologians and sociologists to casually depict and dismiss Zion as a mountain of violence, cruelty, and punishment.[8] Compare this mentality to the theophany of Psalm 50: "The mighty one, God the LORD, speaks and summons the earth from the rising of the sun to its setting. Out of Zion, the perfection of beauty, God shines forth" (vv. 1–2, NIV). Certainly, this same psalm also challenges any superficial sacrificial theology,[9] and it emphasizes the theme of YHWH's judgment against the wicked,[10] but all of this work is done in the overarching context of beauty and intimacy, the basic theme of Zion's

7. This point is well made by Stephen Finlan, *The Background and Content of Paul's Cultic Atonement Metaphors* (Atlanta: Society of Biblical Literature, 2004), 1–2.

8. Among modern Christian writers, the association between temple, ritual sacrifice, and violence is all too common. Whether one is reading defenders of penal substitutionary atonement—like John Stott, J. I. Packer, or the authors of *Pierced for our Transgressions*, Steve Jeffery, Michael Ovey, and Andrew Sachs—or critics of traditional Christian soteriology—ranging from Rene Girard, Raymund Schwager, S. Mark Heim, J. Denny Weaver, Joanne Carlson Brown and Rebecca Parker, Rita Nakashima Brock, Delores S. Williams, Darby Kathleen Ray, Margaret Daphne Hampson, or Stephen Finlan—one finds Jewish cultic places and practices associated primarily or exclusively with wrath, punishment, and death. For example, in his defense of penal substitution, Thomas R. Schreiner looks at the temple cult and says, "But reflect on the violence of the activity: the blood, the entrails and the goriness of it all. The death of the animals shows that the penalty for sin is death. When we are told that the sacrifices are a soothing aroma, the image indicates that they satisfy God's wrath, that they appease his anger." "Penal Substitution View," in *The Nature of the Atonement: Four Views*, ed. James Beilby and Paul R. Eddy (Westmont, IL: IVP Academic, 2006), 83. This is just one example, but it could be multiplied many times over. See chapters eight and eleven for more.

9. See vv. 8–14.

10. See vv. 16–22.

holiness. Therefore, the first step in encouraging a Christian Yom Kippur soteriology is to walk in the footsteps of our ancient Jewish fathers and mothers—including the holy family, Mary, Joseph, and Jesus—and set out for Zion, the mountain of God.

Our pilgrimage will unfold in three chapters. It will more or less explicitly attempt to sustain a dialogue between modern biblical scholarship (especially recent Jewish research into priestly theology) and contemporary Christian systematic theology (especially the work of Hans Urs von Balthasar) all to better understand the mystery of the Jerusalem temple. The primary contribution of Christian theology in these three chapters is structural: just as Balthasar organized his *magnum opus* in three parts, corresponding to the three transcendentals—beauty in *The Glory of the Lord*, goodness in *Theo-Drama*, and truth in *Theo-Logic*— these chapters might be seen as a mini-trilogy reflecting specifically on the mystery of the temple. Thus, chapter one will consider the temple as Israel's doxological center, the place where God is encountered in glory. Chapter two will consider "the action," the drama between God and his chosen one, Abraham, which forever marks this space as holy ground. Chapter three will consider the temple as the space of divine truth, where creation points toward heaven, and heaven comes down to earth.

Overall, we will see that Balthasar can help modern historical-critical research into Jewish temple theology, and vice-versa. Balthasar offers scholars of biblical theology a way to systematically consider the various themes that gather around the temple. At the same time, Balthasar's theology can benefit from recent biblical research. Balthasar wrote his impressive study on the "old covenant" in 1967, and the scripture scholar he relied on most was the Lutheran Gerhard von Rad. This penultimate volume of the *Glory of the Lord* series—along with its companion on the "new covenant"—demonstrates the depth and the seriousness of Balthasar's lifelong engagement with scripture and with serious biblical scholarship. Nevertheless, biblical research has advanced significantly in the last fifty years, especially when it comes to a sympathetic reading of ancient Jewish theology generally, and priestly theology specifically. It is most appropriate, therefore, to continue to clarify, sharpen, and strengthen the biblical foundations of Balthasar's work in dialogue with updated research. While arranging the material through the help of Balthasar, the substance of what follows is drawn primarily from critical scholarship on the theology of ancient Judaism.

CHAPTER 1

From Zion, Perfect in Beauty, God Shines Forth (Theo-Aesthetics)

While Christian theologians have often linked the institution of the temple with the terms appeasement, propitiation, violence, and death, this offers, at best, a radically truncated understanding of Israel's most sacred space. Such words fail to capture the awe and joy inspired by Zion for those who lived in the shadow of its wings. For these people, the temple was synonymous with worship, praise, beauty, and peace; it was the source and summit of the nation's liturgical life, the one place where life was lived well: "the world as it ought to be."[1] As the doxological center of Israel, it stood as a permanent invitation to sing God's glory. Here the nation's weak voices practiced harmonizing with the angelic choir. Here they learned the movement of worship in spirit and truth. Here they joined the liturgy of praise for which the world was created.

It is necessary, therefore, to more deeply understand how the temple was a positive and transformative reality in ancient Jewish thought. Hans Urs von Balthasar's approach to "theological aesthetics," which is ultimately an extended meditation on the biblical theme of glory in scripture and tradition, offers modern readers a framework to approach temple theology more sympathetically. Insofar as divine glory streams from the temple in Jewish priestly theology, and insofar as the temple is the definitive place of humanity's doxological-liturgical response, it is rightly a place of extraordinary significance for theological aesthetics. From a Balthasarian perspective, this raises profound questions: what *form* does this space take in the biblical imagination? How is this mountaintop sanctuary *uniquely* related to themes such as revelation and encounter, desire and transformation? How can *this* structure, *this* cedar house, communicate divine glory in an especially transparent way? And perhaps most importantly, is the Jerusalem temple ultimately a form of beauty and life, or is it a monument to the deformation of violence and death? To better

---

1. Jon D. Levenson, "The Jerusalem Temple in Devotional and Visionary Experience," in *Jewish Spirituality, Vol 1* (New York: Crossroad, 1986), 53.

understand the place of the temple in the rich symbolic theology of ancient Israel, it is helpful to review some of Balthasar's key concepts.

Contemporary Theological Aesthetics: A Resource for Temple Theology

As mentioned, the spirituality of the temple was incarnational and sensual. Perhaps there are spiritualities in the history of human culture that are strictly otherworldly, that are "excarnated" and almost angelic, but such a religion seems far from the pilgrim's experience in Jerusalem. Their faith, their prayer, took advantage of all the senses; perhaps more than anything, it was a feast for the eyes.[2] With this observation, we stand at the threshold of theological aesthetics—where the place of sight has been prominent though precarious. The world has been darkened by idolatrous gazing since the time of Eden ("the tree was good for eating and a delight to the eyes. . ."), and the eye was considered so perilous that it might be better to pluck it out than be led astray. To approach such matters with care, it is important to apprentice oneself to a sure guide. Balthasar is equal to the task.

Balthasar begins with the traditional aesthetic terms, "splendor" and "form"; in the inaugural volume of his trilogy, *Seeing the Form*, he unpacks these terms through the analogous concepts of interiority and communication (and then soul and body).[3] That which is interior, which is most intimate, shines forth in its exterior expression, as the self-revealing form which that interior life takes. Balthasar asks, "What is a person without a life-form, that is to say, without a form which he has chosen

---

2. For an excellent recent overview of how the pilgrim's senses were engaged on Mount Zion, see Christine Elizabeth Palmer, "The Jerusalem Temple: A Sensory Encounter with the Sacred," in *The Routledge Handbook of the Senses in the Ancient Near East* (London: Routledge, 2021).

3. Balthasar works with these philosophical categories without, of course, suggesting that they pre-determine the shape of Christian revelation. He critiques the "aesthetic theology" of the Romantic period extensively. Hans Urs von Balthasar, *The Glory of the Lord: A Theological Aesthetics, Vol. 1: Seeing the Form* (San Francisco: Ignatius Press, 1982), 79–104. Nevertheless, these concerns do not detract from his conviction that philosophical reflection can augment Christian contemplation: attention to form and splendor makes a fruitful contribution so long as these philosophical concepts remain open to correction or expansion in the light of Christ. Thus, for example, Neoplatonic attention to harmony must not be used to flatten out the concrete drama of Christ's life, including especially the cross and descent, with all of its ugliness and formlessness. Cf. Cyril O'Regan, *Anatomy of Misremembering: Von Balthasar's Response to Philosophical Modernity. Volume 1: Hegel* (Chestnut Ridge, NY: The Crossroad Publishing Company, 2014), 457–58.

for his life, a form into which and through which to pour out his life, so that his life becomes the soul of the form and the form becomes the expression of his soul?"[4] What is especially true for the human being, whose interior depths are fathomless, is true also of all creation: no being can fail to express something of its own inner light, the essence that shimmers in and through this concrete, embodied existence.

As that inner light finds expression, it is perceived as splendor, and it is captivating because it communicates the basic goodness and truth of *this* being's interiority. Or again in Balthasar's words, "The appearance of the form, as revelation of the depths, is an indissoluble union of two things. It is the real presence of the depths, of the whole of reality, and it is a real pointing beyond itself to these depths."[5] That which appears truly communicates itself, but without exhaustion. The "depths" are genuinely expressed in the concrete form, and yet the depths remain evermore profound such that the form can only "point beyond itself" toward even greater mysteries.

This is the nature of "symbol,"[6] which is a mode of discourse that does not despair of communication, even as it remains aware that a gap between expression and comprehension (mastery) always remains. But this "gap" is no ugly ditch. It is not the torment of the finite soul, but the cause of finitude's greatest joy: the space between expression and com-

---

4. Balthasar, *GL1*, 24.

5. Balthasar, 118. In the same section, Balthasar says, "The form as it appears to us is beautiful only because the delight that it arouses in us is founded upon the fact that, in it, the truth and goodness of the depths of reality itself are manifested and bestowed, and this manifestation and bestowal reveal themselves to us as being something infinitely and inexhaustibly valuable and fascinating." Balthasar, 118. Notice, this *manifestation* is a *bestowal*—with this word "bestowal" we are brought into the domain of gift-giving. The concrete form makes present the gift that this being bestows. In other words, then, when being, precisely through its unique form, communicates its inner depths as gift, it creates wonder and fascination in the perceiver.

6. This word should be understood in the context of "sacramental ontology." David Bentley Hart has articulated useful guidelines for better and worse uses of the term "symbol." David Bentley Hart, *The Beauty of the Infinite: The Aesthetics of Christian Truth* (Grand Rapids, MI: Eerdmans, 2004), 26–28. He finds, for example, that Paul Tillich's semiotics are finally inadequate precisely because the concrete form is disrespected. While Tillich says "the symbol participates in the reality of that for which it stands," a formula that has promise, in practice Tillich uses symbols as diving boards into deeper waters. Hart: "Of course, the advantage of vague talk concerning 'symbol' is that it allows theology to prescind from the difficult details of particular narratives to the more governable realm of abstractions. . . ." Hart, 26. A proper theological aesthetics, Hart insists, never gets around or behind the concrete form, and thus any talk of symbol must be understood "in terms of sacrament, icon, or real presence." Hart, 28; cf. Balthasar, *GL1*, 124, 438–39.

prehension is the space of wonder, which never fails to delight and satisfy precisely because it is never mastered. In this context, we must speak also of mystery, the mystery that gives itself to our perception fully, inexhaustibly, drawing us in rapture, and moving us toward song.[7] Form communicates depth—not a submerged depth that trickles out here and there, like clues in a whodunit, but rather a depth that is entirely present on the "surface" of form, depth which the form expresses entirely, but never finally, because the depth cannot be exhausted. This is because such "depth" of existence is—referring now to Erich Przywara's *Analogia Entis*—participation in an essence that always exceeds us. Being is "suspended" by that "in-and-beyond" rhythm called *analogia*, meaning each created thing truly expresses what it cannot fully express.[8]

Therefore, in theological aesthetics, the space between expression/ existence and interiority/essence is a valley of splendor, where every encounter inspires delight and longing (*eros*) in the human subject. The perceiver rejoices in the gift of such beauty and longs for deeper communion with this self-revelation. The result is rapture: the encounter with splendor draws the subject out of herself toward the self-communicating other. Again, in Balthasar's words, "We are 'enraptured' by our contemplation of these depths and are 'transported' to them. But, so long as we are dealing with the beautiful, this never happens in such a way that we

7. Cyril O'Regan helpfully specifies that Balthasar emphasizes "positive mystery," which is "the superlative presence of the divine as glory, or the superlative manifestation of the divine glory." Cyril O'Regan, "Newman and von Balthasar : The Christological Contexting of the Numinous," *Eglise et Théologie* 26, no. 2 (1995): 166. Here mystery has content (especially Christological content) which "invites participation." O'Regan, 188. Positive mystery is distinguished from "negative mystery," a merely privative understanding of mystery that serves only to specify "the limit of the competence of cognition to inquire into and grasp the nature of divine reality" (166).

8. Erich Przywara's philosophy is foundational in this chapter, and for this entire book. His watershed *Analogia Entis* has only recently been translated into English, eighty years after it first appeared. Erich Przywara, *Analogia Entis: Metaphysics: Original Structure and Universal Rhythm* (Grand Rapids, MI: Eerdmans, 2013). In this book, Przywara attempts to articulate a "creaturely metaphysics," an approach in which metaphysics *has no solid resting place*, but is a movement, a dance, a joyful restlessness that resists every closure and silence. Creaturely metaphysics is a suspended tension in which each element (for example, being and consciousness) can find itself and define itself only by moving toward the other . . . but at the same time, this movement is not the monotonous back and forth of the metronome, because there is a certain directionality, a "becoming" that keeps the dance going in ever new movements and variations. At the heart of metaphysics, for Przywara, there is incompleteness, openness, and ambiguity which can never be rounded off, but which at the same time is not chaotic movement hither and thither, but somehow always ordered toward greater fullness. It is for this reason that being can articulate a mystery that is nevertheless infinite.

leave the (horizontal) form behind us in order to plunge (vertically) into the naked depths."[9] It is important to underline again the fact that the appearing form of the beautiful is not a husk to be discarded in pursuit of a disembodied, wholly spiritual essence, but that external form and inner splendor are interrelated such that the expressive form is never left behind.

The theme of rapture brings attention to two related points that are also crucial. Aesthetic delight—first of all—depends upon, and celebrates, distance and difference; if the "other" is mastered, devoured, or otherwise eliminated, there is no space left for appreciation or desire. Second, the other must genuinely communicate itself and make itself available to be received: if the "object" is maximally incomprehensible or absolutely formless or purely imperceptible, it would fail to arouse desire and enkindle delight. Theological aesthetics, therefore, requires the distance of otherness, and also the hopeful joy of unity-in-difference. From this perspective, the need for both kataphatic and apophatic moments in theological expression is fully protected.[10]

The main point to emphasize here is how the place of aesthetic splendor and rapture is the space of rejoicing. As Balthasar describes it, the "objective evidence" of the appearing form draws out a response from the subject, who, in being drawn toward the object, is transformed by it. The object becomes part of the subject; it leaves its mark on the subject as it elevates her and invites her to participate in its beauty. Beauty is not selfish, but it streams forth to gather others to itself, drawing them in peace toward unity. To more fully receive the gift, the subject must often be transformed to make space for this new beauty: certain internal boundaries must be removed, certain new faculties must be developed, certain prejudices must be reevaluated, and a certain vulnerability must be risked. Openness to beauty necessarily implies openness to change, because beauty always involves an "other," and aesthetic otherness inevitably implies new possibilities for growth and expansion. As D. C. Schindler put it, "in love, the soul is 'tuned,' as it were, or 'adapted' (*coaptatio*) to the particular good it encounters as something suitable to it and for it."[11] Beauty (and the love it elicits) has the profound ability to tune our hearts to reality.

9. Balthasar, *GL1*, 119.

10. For the analogical relation between apophatic and kataphatic, Hart is especially clear: *Beauty of the Infinite*, 310–11. O'Regan's articulation of Balthasar's defense of the kataphatic against modern critics is also helpful here. O'Regan, *Anatomy of Misremembering*, 446; cf. 240 f.

11. D. C. Schindler, *Love and the Postmodern Predicament: Rediscovering the Real in Beauty, Goodness, and Truth* (Eugene, OR: Wipf and Stock Publishers, 2018), 100.

If this is true for beauty generally, it is supereminently true of "glory" (Hebrew *kavod*, Greek *doxa*), the biblical word for divine radiance (as Wholly Other) making itself perceptible to human subjects, and drawing them in to partake of and be transformed by it.[12] For Balthasar, "response" is, therefore, an important word. One is not given the grace to perceive divine glory so as to become a dumb spectator but to be transformed and empowered to act and live as a partaker of this glory, which is to say: glory inspires, and requires, a doxological response. Encountering glory, receiving glory, we are glorified, brought into the communion of glory, and thus our lips are opened to proclaim God's praise. Those who sing quickly discover that even their song is a gift; speaking specifically of the Christian experience, Balthasar says, "The believer cannot consider his answer to the light of God's witness to be a second, autonomous word existing alongside Christ's word, even though it is true that the believer never yet felt himself taken so seriously as a person and so fulfilled as when he spoke this word. He knows that both he and the word of faith he gives in reply are taken up into the trinitarian witness."[13] The doxological response—in both its contemplative and active dimensions—is a genuine response emerging from the worshipper's own heart. She experiences this as a grace that is given unexpectedly by a surpassing generosity.

Therefore, Balthasar's theological aesthetics raise crucial issues that would be essential to a nuanced, sympathetic temple theology. First, there is the emphasis on sense experience, and especially vision. What role does visual experience play in temple theology? Second, there is an emphasis on "beauty," including the relationship between inner essence, or "splendor," and exterior communication, or form. What is the innermost essence of the temple, and how does its embodied form communicate that essence? From a biblical and early Jewish perspective, is the sanctuary of Zion experienced as beautiful, with a form expressing an inner radiance? Third, our review of theological aesthetics emphasized the way form simultaneously communicates, and fails to communicate, the expressed splendor. The "depths" that are expressed in the beautiful form are still more profound than their expression, and this "more" is the space

12. The Hebrew word *kavod*, Balthasar points out, "initially connotes what is physically heavy or weighty, but then it can refer to everything which gives any living being . . . an external force or impetus (*gravitas*) that makes it appear imposing. . . ." Balthasar, *GL1*, 33. As with any other attempt to predicate a human reality to God, Balthasar acknowledges the analogical nature of divine Glory. Cf. Hans Urs von Balthasar, *The Glory of the Lord: A Theological Aesthetics, Vol. 6: Theology: The Old Covenant* (San Francisco: Ignatius Press, 1991), 33–34.

13. Balthasar, *GL1*, 191.

of mystery. How does the temple express itself in a way that points toward further depths, or heights, inviting the worshiper deeper into the theological mystery? Fourth, when we encounter the beautiful, the result is delight, longing, and rapture. Beauty brings joy, enflames desire, and draws the subject out of himself. Is this the experience of Israel with respect to the temple? Was this place associated with dread and disgust, or hope and delight? Fifth, closely related, the encounter with beauty is transformative. The experience of being drawn toward the beautiful form involves an elevation and re-formation of one's own soul. How does the temple transform the lives of those who are drawn to it? Sixth, one must insist upon the uniqueness of theological Glory and the glorified response. While beauty generally reveals the truth and goodness of being, divine glory invites one to a more immediate encounter with Being-itself. As Aidan Nichols explains:

> Every beautiful form possesses an openness to the infinite, but some beautiful forms possess this more than others. Beautiful form is heterogeneous, differentiated, qualitatively variable, or more or less significant in terms of focusing the totality of being at large. . . . Every form is a contraction of the totality of being, and some are more contracted than others. This should remind us that it is for *God* to provide the norm by which he will interpret himself. . . . Only God can fashion a form that could be a comprehensive revelation of himself, the world and our relation to both of these.[14]

Therefore, is the temple, as it is described in the Bible, uniquely associated with the revelation of divine glory? How does it transform humanity in a distinctly theological way as it draws Israel into communion with God? In what sense is it depicted as a "form," given by God, as a means of God's self-revelation?

These are major topics in a theological aesthetics of the temple. Some of these questions will be addressed in this chapter, and all of them will be addressed over the course of the next three.

The House of Glory, the Joy of Israel

Having reviewed key terms in Balthasar's theological aesthetics, we can turn more fully to Zion. Without question, the temple is the preeminent doxological space in the Hebrew Bible. Admittedly, there is a major

---

14. Aidan Nichols, *A Key to Balthasar: Hans Urs Von Balthasar on Beauty, Goodness, and Truth* (Grand Rapids, MI: Baker Academic, 2011), 27.

drawback to associating divine glory too closely with the temple: it may seem to diminish glory by giving it too narrow a context. God is not parsimonious with his glory. In the Bible, all the earth is filled with God's glory (Numbers 14:21 and Psalm 19:1–6) and is called upon to sing his praise (Psalm 66:1–4). Nevertheless, sometimes this terrific "weight" is present in a more particular way: glory settles on Sinai (Exodus 24:16), it blazes at the tent of meeting (Leviticus 9:23–34), it fills Solomon's temple (1 Kings 8:11), and it characterizes the eschatological temple (Ezekiel 43:1–5); in the New Testament, it is made incarnate in Jesus Christ (John 1:14). A celebration of divine immanence is a central biblical theme.[15]

Although the philosophically sensitive reader might wish to accentuate divine transcendence, Benjamin Sommer argues that biblical writers were not shy about speaking even of God's immanent *bodily* presence; for the priestly writer specifically, "*kabod* refers to God's body and hence to God's very self."[16] From this perspective, the full wonder of the last verses of Exodus can be appreciated: "And then the cloud covered the tent of meeting. YHWH's *kabod* had filled the tabernacle!"[17] For the most

15. This is especially true in P: "*Indeed, a central theme of priestly tradition—perhaps, the central theme of priestly tradition—is the desire of the transcendent God to become immanent on the earth this God has created.*" Benjamin D. Sommer, *The Bodies of God and the World of Ancient Israel* (Cambridge: Cambridge University Press, 2011), 74, emphasis in original. As we will have occasion to note below, many scholars have claimed that this is less true of D, and the tension between these different approaches is theologically productive.

16. Sommer, 68. Sommer's book opens with a shocking claim, "The God of the Hebrew Bible has a body." Sommer, 1. He goes on to show that, in some of the oldest strands of biblical tradition, God even has "bodies"—that there is "fluidity" in divine selfhood—a fact that is seen with greater clarity when the text is read in its broader ANE context. The priestly writers, he says, reject the idea of fluid divine selfhood and multiple embodiments, but they do not reject embodiment outright. For them, the *kabod* is the divine body, it has "a particular shape" even though "it is not clear that it has a permanent size." Furthermore, Sommer borrows a Newtonian distinction to suggest that, in priestly writings, "the *kabod* is made of energy but not matter." Sommer, 71. Cf. Moshe Weinfeld, *Deuteronomy and the Deuteronomic School* (Winona Lake, IN: Eisenbrauns, 1972), 198–206.

17. Translation of Exodus 40:34 in Sommer, *Bodies of God*, 73. Sommer insists that here, and in many other priestly texts, "the identity between the *kabod* and God" is clear. Sommer, 73, cf. 222 n.65. This view does not represent a scholarly consensus; while Michael B. Hundley acknowledges that "the [*kavod* YHWH] is an especially appropriate metonym for YHWH himself," he hastens to nuance this position: "although the glory is inextricably linked with the divine presence, the glory does not encapsulate that presence." Michael B Hundley, *Keeping Heaven on Earth: Safeguarding the Divine Presence in the Priestly tabernacle* (Tübingen: Mohr Siebeck, 2011), 43. Hundley will later refer to glory as "connected to yet distinct from Yhwh himself. . . . Yhwh's glory thus functions like a garment, or more particularly, a cloak, which shrouds his immediate presence in light,

ancient priestly tradition, it seems, God is truly, bodily here, ablaze in the tabernacle, in the midst of his people Israel. The priestly writer, therefore, has a vivid sense of indwelling where God becomes "locally" present, and perceptible, in his sanctuary.

If God is God—if God is not a being among beings—it seems inconceivable that divine glory or presence could be limited to a point on a map.[18] But circling back to the basic affirmations of theological aesthetics, the self-revelation of God to man involves God's glory manifesting itself in creation, which does not ensnare God in finitude but draws creation to God through the particular. Furthermore, while the most ancient idea that God has a "body" will certainly be interrogated in the unfolding Jewish and Christian theological traditions, that there is "shape" to God's indwelling luminosity and splendor—that God is not sublime formlessness, but "infinitely *formosus*, the supereminent fullness of all form"[19]—contains an insight worthy of appreciation and preservation. One therefore finds the first stirrings of theological aesthetics in the priestly texts insofar as there is an emphasis on vision, beauty, form, and splendor; for modern Christian theology, this remains a significant achievement.

From the perspective of philosophical materialism, the finite cannot ultimately give access to the infinite, but can only trap our gaze in the idolatry of beings. By contrast, an analogical, sacramental approach (as seen in Balthasar's theological aesthetics) makes it possible to imagine unfathomable depths being present in the appearing form as an icon that heals and elevates the mind and heart of the perceiver. As Cyril O'Regan points out, Balthasar's view is well summarized in the title of his 1963

---

simultaneously revealing and concealing him." Michael B. Hundley, "Divine Fluidity? The Priestly Texts in Their Ancient Near Eastern Contexts," in *Text, Time, and Temple: Literary, Historical and Ritual Studies in Leviticus*, ed. Francis Landy, Leigh M. Trevaskis, and Bryan D. Bibb (Sheffield: Sheffield Phoenix Press, 2015).

18. This is, Sommer explains, the Deuteronomist insight, where "God dwells in heaven and nowhere else. On earth, God places His *shem*, in the one place he chooses for it (viz. the Jerusalem temple). . . . [T]he *shem* is only a sign of the divine presence, not a manifestation of God Himself." Sommer, *Bodies of God*, 62; cf. R. E Clements, *God and Temple*, (Philadelphia: Fortress Press, 1965), 90–91, 94–96, 100. Thus, Solomon says, "But will God really dwell on earth? Even the heavens to their uttermost reaches cannot contain You, how much less this House that I have built!" (1 Kings 8:27, NJSV). The interpretation of the divine name as "only a sign" in D has also been debated; see the discussion in chapter three, below.

19. Hart, *Beauty of the Infinite*, 177. Speaking of the form of revelation, Balthasar insists that the God who is revealed is not "an infinite non-form (*ápeiron*), but the appearance of an infinitely determined super-form." Balthasar, *GL1*, 432. Cf. Balthasar, 117–19.

book: *Das Ganze im Fragment* ("The Whole in the Fragment")[20]: "For Balthasar, a fragment is a particular, irreplaceable seeing of a whole."[21] This idea of the capacity of the fragment to communicate the whole is true of being generally, but the symbols of revelation have a privileged transparency to the whole—maybe the best way to say it is, in these icons, the whole is especially to the surface.[22] In the context of the Jewish covenantal religion, then, the temple is that "fragment" and "symbol" which expresses the truth of the divine "whole" in an unparalleled way. This is readily apparent through the attention to detail given to the tabernacle, its furnishing, its construction, and its liturgy, found in the second half of Exodus through the first half of Leviticus. To repeat what Nichols said in summarizing Balthasar's position: "Only God can fashion a form that could be a comprehensive revelation of himself, the world and our relation to both of these."[23] The fact that the priestly writers have God himself giving, and often repeating, remarkably precise instructions on how to construct the tabernacle suggests that they understood this holy space to be of particular divine concern; in the context of priestly theology generally, it becomes clear that the tabernacle is the inimitable site of divine revelation, a place where the intimacy between Israel and her God, as well as all creation and its God, finds its unique expression. *This* is the form that *God gives* to express his presence and his infinite beauty.

Recent scholarship has increasingly shown the importance of vision in biblical temple theology. For example, Gary Anderson has described the iconic role of the temple in his article "To See Where God Dwells: The Tabernacle, the Temple, and the Origins of the Christian Mystical Tradition." Anderson first reviews several biblical texts that associate seeing the temple or the ark of the covenant with actually seeing God; in an interesting example, Anderson says that even though the vowel markers for Exodus 23:17 in the Masoretic text suggest that Israel must "*appear before* the face of the Lord" three times a year, it can be argued that the verbal stem has been wrongly vocalized and that the original requirement was that Israel visit the temple three times a year "*to see the*

---

20. O'Regan, *Anatomy of Misremembering*, 500. *Das Ganze im Fragment* was translated as *A Theological Anthropology* (Eugene, OR: Wipf & Stock, 2010).

21. O'Regan, *Anatomy of Misremembering*, 510–11.

22. For Balthasar, "The revelation of grace is not the establishment of a new form within the created world; it is but a new manner of God's presence in the form of the world, a new intimacy in our union with him, an intimacy to which the child of God has access and in which he participates." Balthasar, *GL1*, 452. See also the Aidan Nichols quote in the previous section.

23. Nichols, *A Key to Balthasar*, 27.

face of the Lord."[24] Other texts express the importance and seriousness of seeing the temple and its furniture more straightforwardly. Consider the importance David places in seeing the ark and its dwelling (2 Samuel 15:25), or how adamant the author of Numbers is that the Kohathites not see the temple furniture "lest they die" (4:20). Psalm 48 is also presented as an outstanding example of this emphasis on the visual. The psalm first focuses the singer's attention on the "holy mountain," "beautiful in elevation," which is "the joy of all the earth," before identifying it as Mount Zion in "the city of the great King" (vv. 1-2). It is here, "in the midst of [God's] temple" that worshipers "ponder [God's] steadfast love" (v. 9). Then the psalm culminates with a remarkable invitation to the pilgrim in Jerusalem:

> Walk about Zion, go all around it,
> > count its towers,
> consider well its ramparts;
> > go through its citadels,
> that you may tell the next generation
> > that *this is God*,
> our God for ever and ever.
> > He will be our guide for ever. (vv. 13–15, emphasis added)[25]

This is remarkable. Anderson quotes Amos Hacham, who says that "the one who sees the Temple in its splendor and glory feels within himself as if he saw, face to face, the glory (*kavod*) of the Lord. He cries, 'this [this building] is God, our God.'"[26] Thus, according to Anderson, "these texts exhibit ancient Israel's deeply held view that God really dwelt in the Temple and that all the pieces of that building shared, in some fashion, in his tangible and visible presence."[27] After then reviewing extra-biblical evidence, Anderson concludes that to gaze upon the temple and its fur-

---

24. Gary A. Anderson, "To See Where God Dwells: The Tabernacle, the Temple, and the Origins of the Christian Mystical Tradition," *Letter & Spirit* 4 (2008), 15. An updated and expanded version of this article has appeared more recently: "Christology: The Incarnation and the Temple" in Gary A. Anderson, *Christian Doctrine and the Old Testament: Theology in the Service of Biblical Exegesis* (Grand Rapids, MI, Michigan: Baker Academic, 2017). For a similar argument, see Anderson, "Mary in the Old Testament," 2007, 43–46. For Anderson's argument on the vocalization of the stem *ra'ah*, see Anderson, "To See Where God Dwells," 15, note 6. Balthasar also reflects on the call "to see" the face of YHWH: Balthasar, *GL*6, 70–72.

25. This is Anderson's translation at "To See Where God Dwells," 18.

26. Anderson, 18.

27. Anderson, 18.

niture was often associated with actually seeing the face of God. This, then, is the significance of the psalmist's instruction that the pilgrim walk about, go around, go through, count, and consider well the details of the building and its surroundings, and ultimately go forth and tell future generations of the architectural theophany: "this is God." In biblical priestly theology, God's glory so permeates this place, and shines through it, that it serves as an icon most worthy of contemplation. God himself has become the splendor of the Zion sanctuary, and the pilgrim has access to this inner mystery through a sensory, visual encounter with the form of the building itself.

Michael B. Hundley has similarly explained that, while holiness is a quality peculiar to God as transcendent of the created world, "elements"—such as the temple and its furniture—"closely associated with the deity may absorb some of the divine essence."[28] God does not dwell in creation like a ghost in an old house, a wispy presence that leaves the physical surroundings unaffected. Nor is God's tabernacling destructive, as if divinity is in conflict with the material creation itself. Rather, in the theological imagination of the ancient cultic writers, God's indwelling draws material creation up so that sanctuary furniture, priestly rites, and the temple as a whole, communicate God's real presence to the worshipers who gather in Jerusalem.

The Hebrew Bible scholar Walter Brueggemann has also drawn attention to the emphasis on beauty in priestly literature, on the corresponding attention to visionary experience, and on the connection between these themes and divine holiness. Brueggemann argues that, while the "Deuteronomic-covenantal-prophetic traditions," which emphasize hearing and obedience, typically get more attention in biblical scholarship (especially Protestant biblical scholarship), "Less recognized is a second perspective on obligation, stemming from the tradition of tabernacle-

---

28. Michael B. Hundley, "Sacred Spaces, Objects, Offerings, and People in the Priestly Texts: A Reappraisal," *Journal of Biblical Literature* 132, no. 4 (2013): 753. In this article, Hundley is exploring the nature of "holiness" in ancient Israel and comparing Israel's concept of holiness to the way certain objects are divinized in surrounding ancient Near Eastern cultures. He says that, for ancient Israel, ". . . no person, place, or object is intrinsically holy. For example, on its own, the ark is simply a pretty box. Rather, holiness is derived exclusively from its source, YHWH, and roughly connotes belonging to the deity and thus to the divine sphere. As we will see, holiness is more than just a label; it likewise seems to carry some of the dangerously potent divine essence." Hundley, 753. After looking at how certain objects are divinized in surrounding polytheistic cultures, Hundley returns to Israel: "Although the Priestly terminology and ancient Near Eastern terminology are different, the effects are similar; sacralized and divinized elements belong to the divine realm and are imbued with some of its essence." Hundley, 754.

temple-Priestly tradition: that Israel is to see, to look on the splendor and beauty of Yahweh."[29] Brueggemann later expands on this point in a passage that is worth including in full:

> Israel is summoned to worship YHWH in a holy place of unspeakable splendor (Pss 29:2, 96:9; 1 Chr 16:29; 2 Chr 20:21). The old, familiar translation of the recurring phrase in these texts is "the beauty of holiness." The NRSV prefers to render "holy splendor," thus accentuating the awe, which precludes any ease or artistic coziness. What interests us in this recurring formula, rendered either way, is that the visibly powerful sense of presence in the shrine has a mark of holiness to it, which variously reflects symmetry, proportion, order, extravagance, awe, and overwhelmingness. This is a sense of the "surplus" of Yahweh, situated at the center of Israel's life, which is experienced as visual and which from its central and dominant position resituates and recharacterizes everything in Israel's mundane world in relation to this center of occupying holiness.

At the center of the priestly literature, Brueggemann finds a theological aesthetics that accentuates many of the points that Balthasar also emphasizes. These texts present an aesthetic experience that is visual, that is beautiful, and that—even more importantly—is a direct encounter with divine holiness. This is an experience of the splendor of God, which takes more familiar, philosophical aesthetic categories (symmetry, proportion, order) and interweaves them with concepts that suggest the glory of the tabernacling Lord (extravagance, awe, overwhelmingness).

Furthermore, such encounters with glory are transformative in ancient Israelite religion. Just as surely as the temple and its furniture—constructed of acacia wood, gold, and bronze—conveys divine glory, the human worshiper is also taken up into, and then herself communicates, this indwelling *kabod*. As we have seen, for Balthasar, beauty is indispensable to a well-rounded theology because of the way it draws the perceiver toward contemplation and enkindles a desire for unity. Beauty, in sharing itself, inspires the viewer's full responsive participation. This phenomenon is experienced in a yet more profound way when divine glory is communicated: the invisible God condescends to human perception, elevating the believer's vision to see what infinitely surpasses the power of mortal humanity's weak eyes, and strengthens our voices to join the doxological refrain known only to the angels—"Holy! Holy! Holy!" Bal-

---

29. Walter Brueggemann, *Theology of the Old Testament: Testimony, Dispute, Advocacy* (Minneapolis: Fortress Press, 2005), 421.

thasar says, "There is no dodging this paradox, which begins with the self-communication of the Wholly Other and ends with the thanksgiving of the creature that has been overtaken."[30] Balthasar makes clear that, for biblical religion, all initiative exists on God's side, and through our participation in glory we receive what remains always beyond us: our glorified existence in God is at every moment a gift of God's grace, and our response is one of humility and desire.

This is the story of the temple: the humble worshiper, invited to dwell in God's house, is enflamed with a desire for greater and greater intimacy. Who can forget King David's plea: "One thing I asked of the Lord, that will I seek after: to live in the house of the Lord all the days of my life, to behold the beauty of the Lord, and to inquire in his temple" (Psalm 27:4). We also find in scripture an awareness of how the encounter with God is transformative. The most famous example of this in the Old Testament—which, within the biblical narrative, is chronologically before tabernacle or temple, but not unrelated—is the glorification of Moses after his encounter with God. "Moses came down from Mount Sinai . . . [he] was not aware that the skin of his face was radiant, since he had spoken with [the LORD]" (Exodus 34:29). The glory that was proper to God now shines through the human being who has drawn nearest to him. Crispin Fletcher-Louis points to another passage in Ezekiel, where God explains how he had rescued Israel from utter despair, entered into a (marital) covenant with her, and clothes her with beauty. God says, "Your fame spread among the nations on account of your beauty, for it was perfect because of my splendor that I had bestowed on you, says the LORD God" (Ezekiel 16:14, NRSV). Fletcher-Louis explains that, for Ezekiel, "Israel *really* is the genuine bearer of divine presence and, as queen to her king, the rightful wearer of God's glory. This is why the first half of the piece climaxes with the statement that Israel's beauty was perfect because God bestowed his own splendor on her."[31] It is clear that transformation in divine glory is not specific only to an isolated few, but it is a gift given to the nation. Later, we will also see how an analogous glorification was, in late-biblical and extra-biblical literature, associated with the appearance of the high priest ministering in the temple, making the visual encounter with the priest a type of theophany that transforms the

---

30. Balthasar, *GL6*, 10.

31. Crispin HT Fletcher-Louis, "God's Image, His Cosmic Temple and the High Priest: Towards an Historical and Theological Account of the Incarnation," *Heaven on Earth: The Temple in Biblical Theology*, ed. T. Desmond Alexander and Simon J. Gathercole (Carlisle: Paternoster, 2004), 88.

worshipers gathered at the temple. In any case, the important theo-aesthetic themes of the craving for union with God, in his great and fearsome beauty, and the transformation that comes through such intimacy, are both prominent in the priestly tradition.

The promise of the temple, Jerusalem, and the holy land is the promise of hospitality; the elect are invited into a space that is not properly their own, a space for which they nevertheless were most intimately made.[32] It is the space of God's own life that must become a permanent home for the chosen people, and this eternal space is iconically present in Israel. As the psalm says, "You who live in the shelter of the Most High, who abide in the shadow of the Almighty, will say to the Lord, 'My refuge and my fortress; my God, in whom I trust.' . . . Because you have made the Lord your refuge, the Most High your dwelling-place, no evil shall befall you. . ." (Psalm 91:1–2, 9–10, NRSV). When God dwells in Zion, and Israel draws near in worship, they are not merely dwelling in proximity to God in the promised land, but the psalmist goes so far as to say that they dwell *in* God himself.[33] What we see in temple theology, therefore, is the drama of a people invited to live in the space that God opens *within himself*; to be housed in God. Such intimacy also brings risk and judgment when the covenant people turn away, giving up their share in God's glory. To turn from holiness is to close the self off from freedom and love, and therefore to truly live within the "space" of God's holiness, human beings must make "space" for God in themselves, through openheartedness, to live ecstatically *in* God (without, of course, collapsing the metaphysical distance between finite and infinite). Such transformation and mutual indwelling between heaven and earth, God and humanity, is the great hope of priestly theology.

This discussion of communal intimacy and transformation brings us into the liturgical sphere. In scripture, the heavenly realm is a realm of praise and thanksgiving, and it is our highest dignity to mirror that way of being. Zion, in Second Temple Judaism, exists to both echo and embody this heavenly praise in song and silence,[34] what Balthasar calls a

32. See the section entitled "A dwelling place in God's life" for this theme in Balthasar: Balthasar, *GL6*, 178 ff.

33. Cf. N. T. Wright, *The Case for the Psalms: Why They Are Essential* (New York: HarperCollins, 2013), 98–99.

34. Many Levites (minor clergy) were charged with the responsibility of singing the Psalms. Describing the movements of the high priest during a temple service, Ben Sira says, "Then the sons of Aaron the priests sounded forth / On trumpets of turned metal-work: / So they sounded and made heard the glorious noise. . . / And the singers gave their voice. . . ." Robert Hayward, *The Jewish Temple: A Non-Biblical Sourcebook* (London: Routledge,

"dialogue of mutual blessing: man sends God's blessing back to him . . . Israel wanted to be pure answer and pure light reflecting back light. . . ."[35] When Balthasar develops the theme of covenant in the sixth volume of the *Glory of the Lord*, he emphasizes—without diminishing the wholly unanticipated and perfectly free initiative of God—the dialogical nature of Israel's covenantal relationship with God. The relationship is simultaneously one-sided and mutual: the God who speaks the word elicits an answer.[36] Mount Zion is that place where the covenantal answer is given rightly and justly, and thus where Israel is realized as a doxological reality. Balthasar makes this point powerfully:

> Israel's true 'originality' lies in the fact that it is able to transform everything into praise, to invite everyone to join in its song of glorification, and even to draw them into this whether they wish to take part or not. . . . Here, in giving back the word, Israel best understands its universal mission to give back to God, in the name of the world, God's word which goes forth to the world as a whole.[37]

When the liturgical mission of Israel is accentuated, the centrality of Zion is again reinforced, because the temple is unquestionably the principal site of Israel's liturgical life in the Second Temple period.

David Fagerberg says, "Liturgical theology is the faith of the Church in ritual motion"[38]—along the same lines, the liturgical life of the temple is

---

2002), translation of Hebrew Sirach 50:16a, 18a on pages 42–43. Hayward points to how the importance of the singers is already clearly seen in 1 Chronicles 15:16–22; 25:1–31; 2 Chronicles 29:25–30. Hayward, 58–59; cf. E.P. Sanders, *Judaism: Practice and Belief, 63 BCE-66 CE* (London: SCM Press; Trinity Press International, 1992), 62, 78, 80, 81.

At the same time, the temple was also known for its orderly movements and profound contemplative silence, a feature emphasized by Aristeas, writing around 150-100 BC. He says, "And a complete silence reigns, with the result that one might suppose that there was not a single person present in the place, even though there are around 700 ministering priests present and a great number of men bringing up the sacrifices; but everything is discharged with awe and in a manner worthy of the great Godhead." Hayward, *The Jewish Temple*, Aristeas 95, on page 29. Cf. 33–34, where Hayward suggests biblical parallels such as Habakkuk 2:20 and Zechariah 2:13.

35. Balthasar, *GL6*, 207.

36. Cf. Balthasar, 155.

37. Balthasar, 209. Notably, Anderson shows that "praise" is not a private, individual action in the Hebrew Bible, but it is a cultic reality, and "the location of praise is none other than the cultic sanctuary itself." Gary A. Anderson, "The Praise of God as a Cultic Event," in *Priesthood and Cult in Ancient Israel*, ed. Gary A. Anderson and Saul M. Olyan (Sheffield: Sheffield Academic Press, 1991), 18–19.

38. David W. Fagerberg, *Theologia Prima: What Is Liturgical Theology?* (Chicago: Hillenbrand Books, 2012), ix.

the faith, hope, and love of Israel in ritual motion. As the nation gathers in this space to join in the continual flow of rituals, the covenant is reaffirmed and realized. But, crucially, this liturgy is wholly rooted in its place. As Crispin Fletcher-Louis has said, "The temple is theatre. The high priest is an actor on a cosmic stage."[39] While the scriptures painstakingly spell out the specifications for the tabernacle, this dwelling place of God, this liturgical "stage," it is every bit as detailed concerning the daily and yearly rituals that were dramatically performed here alone. With surprising regularity, modern scholarship will speak *either* of the temple as a physical structure *or* of sacrifices as ritual practices, without bringing the two themes together. But the physical structure is at all times alive with sacrificial ritual. The beauty of the place and the drama of its liturgy are inseparable.

Why Zion? Concluding Reflections

Mount Zion is uniquely *the* mountain of worship because it is the very address of YHWH.[40] But why this mountain? If God is Lord over all creation, what theological reason could there be for privileging one mountain over another? How are we to believe that the great and glorious God of ancient Israel arbitrarily chose a modest hill in an unremarkable landscape as his earthly home? Why should this "mountain" merit Israel's attention, why was it seen as uniquely revelatory, and how could it possibly claim our attention today—especially given the well-known fact that the ancient world was rife with such "sacred mountains"?[41] To answer this question, we must turn to the theo-drama that, in the Jewish theological imagination, definitively establishes Zion as the true cornerstone of creation and mirror of heaven. To know why this *really is* the mountain of God—earth's highest point and source of all beauty—to know what sets this temple apart, over and above every other structure that claimed to house the gods—we must meditate on the binding of Isaac.

39. Crispin Fletcher-Louis, "Jesus' Divine Self-Consciousness: A Proposal" (Manchester, 2014), 4, https://www.academia.edu/8211442/Jesus_Divine_Self-Consciousness_A_Proposal_British_New_Testament_Conference_2014_.

40. Gary Anderson has drawn attention to the way that praise and joy, in the Hebrew Bible, are specifically cultic realities. He says, "In Hebrew as well as in the other Semitic languages of the ancient Near East (Hebrew, Jewish Aramaic, Syriac and Akkadian) the term 'joy' is not so much a general term of emotional happiness, but rather a term which connotes particular pleasures associated with the observation of specific rituals." Anderson, "The Praise of God as a Cultic Event," 25. Thus, from the perspective of priestly theology, to say all life is ordered toward praise is precisely to say it is ordered toward the temple and liturgy.

41. Cf. Mircea Eliade, *The Sacred and the Profane: The Nature of Religion*, trans. Willard R. Trask (New York: Harcourt Brace Jovanovich, 1987), 36–41.

But before approaching that topic, some provisional conclusions can be drawn from this first foray into temple theology in light of theological aesthetics. What is most clear is that priestly theology put immense emphasis on the importance of a visual encounter with God in the temple; indeed, at Zion, Israel gathers to see God through the experience of the temple, its rituals, its furniture, the high priest, and other sensory experiences. This rich "form" is precisely the means by which the splendor of the indwelling Lord became manifest to the chosen people. In the Hebrew Bible, his glory finds its complete liturgical and iconic expression here alone. Balthasar's approach to theological aesthetics suggests that we must not conceive of the concrete "form" of the temple as a husk that can be discarded so that we can "plunge (vertically) into the naked depths."[42] The vast theological meaning of this place, so absolutely central to the ancient Jewish covenants, is neither voided nor overcome by the new covenant; it is the irreplaceable context in which Christ's own saving work takes place. In fact, his saving work cannot be adequately understood or explained within any other context. Balthasar strictly condemns the view that "all that God has instituted for our salvation, culminating in his incarnation, is in the end only something preliminary which must finally be transcended by either a mystical or an eschatologico-celestial immediacy that would surpass and make superfluous the form of salvation, or, put concretely, the humanity of Jesus Christ."[43] The indissoluble prominence of the temple is entailed in this claim.

Furthermore, from this theological perspective, we have seen that the covenant people are elevated and transformed through aesthetic visual experiences. As the psalms so often suggested, this experience enflames Israel's desire: "How lovely is Your dwelling-place, O Lord of hosts. I long, I yearn for the courts of the Lord. . . . Better one day in Your courts than a thousand [anywhere else]; I would rather stand at the threshold of God's house than dwell in the tents of the wicked" (Psalm 84:2–3, 11). What is most clear of all, perhaps, is that Mount Zion is associated repeatedly and consistently with beauty, awe, bliss, and glory. In approaching a biblical understanding of atonement, temple, and sacrifice, these are the first and most important words. At the center of priestly theology, that which orients all else is splendor and peace, not wrath and violence. And yet, the great liturgical act by which this "peace" is expressed is sacrificial; it involves slaughter and blood and immolation. How can a ritual of slaughter be associated with a place known for its otherworldly beauty? This will be a key question moving forward.

42. Balthasar, *GL1*, 119.
43. Balthasar, 301–2.

CHAPTER 2

The Action on the Mountain Stage (Theo-Drama)

Toward the end of the Abraham cycle in Genesis, the narrative seems to accelerate, and events of remarkable theological importance are described with stunning concision. In the twenty-first chapter of the book, Isaac is conceived, born, circumcised, and weaned in eight swift verses, then the focus shifts suddenly to the dismissal of Ishmael, which is described in thirteen verses. The writer or compiler of Genesis then interrupts the fascinating family drama with an account of the establishment of Beersheba, before once again shifting gears with a hazy transition: "Some time afterward. . . ." What follows in the first nineteen verses of the twenty-second chapter—only about three hundred Hebrew words—is a narrative that has inspired and challenged interpreters for millennia. There have been Jewish rabbis and commentators who have identified this drama—the *Akedah*, the binding of Isaac—as the central mystery of their covenant faith. In modern times, others have identified this same story as exemplifying the dangerous religious roots of violence and fanaticism. As we will see, theological interpretation of both Mount Zion and the sacrificial rites of the temple are intimately tied up with this debate over the nature of Abraham's greatest test. The theological coherence of Yom Kippur, and similarly, of the sacrifice of Jesus Christ on the cross, rises or falls with the coherence of Abraham's response to Yhwh as recorded in Genesis 22.[1]

In Genesis 22:2, God issues that famous command: "Take your son, your favored one, Isaac, whom you love, and go to the land of Moriah, and offer him there as a burnt offering on one of the heights that I will point out to you." The question that invariably presses on commentators today is, how should Abraham have responded? The traditional response for Jews and Christians has been to see Abraham's "readiness" as exemplary of covenantal obedience and faithfulness. With Immanuel Kant, however, new questions were raised:

1. While I will refer to "Genesis 22" throughout this chapter, my focus will be on the first nineteen verses, the narrative of the binding of Isaac and the subsequent blessings.

> Even though something is represented as commanded by God,
> through a direct manifestation of Him, yet, if it flatly contradicts
> morality, it cannot, despite all appearances, be of God (for example,
> were a father ordered to kill his son [*Sohn töten*], who is so far as
> he knew, perfectly innocent [*ganz unschuldigen*]).[2]

The principle that this passage articulates is brilliant in its moral clarity
and theological coherence. After all, only the most doctrinaire voluntarist
would suggest that God could command a moral evil and that it would
be right to do evil if a higher power commanded it. Kant seems to merely
reproduce, in a philosophical idiom, the fundamental truth proclaimed
by John: "This is the message we have heard from him and proclaim to
you, that God is light and in him there is no darkness at all" (1 John 1:5).
At first sight, then, it seems that Kant has completely undermined the
moral integrity of both the (alleged) divine tester and the (alarmingly)
obedient Abraham in this foundational narrative.

Yet, the situation with respect to Genesis 22 may not be as straightforward as Kant suggests. First, we should immediately point out that
while the German Bible correctly translates the Hebrew as "*opfere* ihn
daselbst zum Brandopfer"—offer him there as a burnt offering—Kant
has reinterpreted the key word of this command as a demand "to kill,
töten." Second, Kant emphasizes that the son in question is "completely
innocent, *ganz unschuldigen*"—in other words, morally spotless—suggesting that the killing would at least be more justifiable if the son were
not so pure. The relevance of these observations should become clear in
what follows, but for now, we can simply flag the questions: are "to offer"
and "to kill" straight synonyms? And within the biblical mindset, how
does the innocence of the son relate to God's command?

I mentioned that, with Kant, "new" questions are raised about Genesis 22. This is only partially true. As far back as the first century, and
probably earlier still, this story was the subject of polemic. Philo, for
example, angrily denounced Abraham's "quarrelsome critics."[3] Early
Jewish apologists were aware of the need to argue in defense of their
patriarch. But anxieties over Abraham's actions have certainly intensified

2. Immanuel Kant, *Religion within the Limits of Reason Alone* (New York: Harper
Torchbooks, 1960), 81–82. That Kant has Abraham in mind in making this argument is
even more explicit in a later book, *The Conflict of the Faculties*; see R. W. L. Moberly, *The
Theology of the Book of Genesis* (Cambridge; New York: Cambridge University Press,
2009), 181–82.

3. See Edward Kessler, *Bound by the Bible: Jews, Christians and the Sacrifice of Isaac*
(Cambridge: Cambridge University Press, 2004), 38.

since the Enlightenment. After Kant, we are not surprised to find modern authors who allege that any god who would issue such a command is in fact Satan,[4] and who classify the man who would follow through with the act as a "sacred monster."[5] If the moment of Abraham's greatest theological triumph—according to the mainstream tradition—is now despised by modern thinkers as a moment of violence, fundamentalism, and irrationality, are the Abrahamic faiths—Judaism, Christianity, and Islam—permanently undermined?

Kant's approach, of course, is to contrast an unalterable ethical maxim with a historically contingent narrative or event, thus severely undercutting the account in Genesis. Unless the biblical interpreter is willing to retreat into theological voluntarism to salvage the legitimacy of God's command and Abraham's obedience—and even here Kant offers a solid retort, virtually echoing the warning of St. Paul that "Even Satan disguises himself as an angel of light" (2 Cor 11:14; cf. Gal 1:8) to say that the ethical maxim is unambiguous while the legitimacy of a supposed divine "apparition" is much less clear—it seems that the narrative must be dismissed as a relic of ancient savagery. But as I've already begun to suggest, despite all his moral certitude, Kant has little interest in, or time for, the theological or narrative context of this story within the Abraham cycle, the book of Genesis, the Hebrew scriptural canon, or ancient Jewish thought generally.

A careful reading of Genesis 22 indicates that—whether or not the narrative can ultimately be received as morally acceptable—something far more subtle and interesting is occurring in the text than a cruel test of loyalty. Walter Moberly, a scholar of the Hebrew Bible who has defended and developed the theological interpretation of scriptural texts, has argued that the proper interpretation of Genesis 22 demands contextualization of the story that pays close attention to the use of certain theology-rich terms: interpretation must be attentive to the meaning of these words in their historical and canonical context.[6] Following this method generally, I will focus on five key words in the Hebrew text that at least complicate the dismissive reading that is common today, and that

4. See, for example, Moberly's review of the work of feminist theologian Bobbie Groth in R. W. L. Moberly, *The Bible, Theology, and Faith: A Study of Abraham and Jesus* (Cambridge: Cambridge University Press, 2000), 168–69.

5. Richard Holloway quoted by Moberly, *The Theology of the Book of Genesis*, 182.

6. Moberly describes and justifies his method of "contextualization of the story within the Old Testament" in *The Bible, Theology, and Faith*, 75. The words Moberly emphasizes are: "test" (*nissah*), "fear of God" (*yere' 'elohim*), "provide/see" (*ra'ah*), and "bless" (*barek*). With one exception, my focus will be on a different set of words.

will also suggest that the story is most illuminating when read in the context of temple theology.[7]

The First Word: Abraham/hinneni

In establishing the drama that will be recounted in this pivotal Genesis chapter, the first verse opens with a two-word dialogue that immediately captures the reader's attention with its beauty, simplicity, and profundity: God (*Elohim*) says "*'abrāhām*," and Abraham responds, "*hinnēnî*." The whole theology of the Akedah has already been communicated in this two-word dialogue—and, actually, no dialogue could better capture the mature theology of both Sinai and Zion. This is the entire mystery of Israel in embryonic form: the joy and the sorrow of the one called and the one learning to say *hinneni*. In a short essay on Christian ethics, Balthasar reflects on Abraham as a "moral subject" and says that he "is constituted by the call of God and by obedience to this call (Heb 11:8)."[8] These two themes, call and obedience, are expressed with outstanding clarity in this opening exchange.

---

7. It is difficult to determine the *original* historical context for this narrative, and it seems at this point that there is no consensus. While it was once said that the text has an Elohist origin, which would suggest that the earliest setting for the narrative preserved in Genesis 22 is the Northern Kingdom, many today question whether E, as a separate source, even existed, or whether this "document" is a modern scholarly construction (see, for example, David M. Carr, "No Return to Wellhausen," *Biblica* 86, no. 1 [2005]: 107–14.) Plus, even those who assigned this text to E recognized a variety of additions and redactions, weaving in material from J and revising the document in a number of places. Claims about what is original and what is redaction are rooted in presuppositions concerning the text's earliest form; as Levenson points out, "the efforts by adherents of the [Elohist] consensus to excise YHWHistic features are circular at best. . . ." Jon D. Levenson, *The Death and Resurrection of the Beloved Son: The Transformation of Child Sacrifice in Judaism and Christianity* (New Haven, CT: Yale University Press, 1995), 122; cf. John van Seters, *Abraham in History and Tradition* (New Haven, CT: Yale University Press, 1975), 229–231, 239–240.

A review of all the different theories on date, province, authorship, and redaction history of this text would be a massive undertaking that would not ultimately get us very far. For our purposes, I will proceed on the conviction that the research of Levenson, Anderson, Moberly, and others—research that revives and bolsters the ancient rabbinic insight that this narrative is an etiology for the Jerusalem temple and the sacrificial cult— is persuasive. One helpful study that emphasizes the priestly elements in Genesis 22, and argues that this text is redactional, drawing together a number of biblical traditions, is Konrad Schmid, "Die Rückgabe der Verheißungsgabe: Der 'heilsgeschichtliche' Sinn von Gen 22 im Horizont innerbiblischer Exegese," in *Gott und Mensch im Dialog: Festschrift O. Kaiser*, ed. M. Witte (Berlin: de Gruyter, 2004), 271–300.

8. cf. Hans Urs von Balthasar, "Nine Propositions on Christian Ethics," in *Principles of Christian Morality*, ed. Heinz Schurmann, Joseph Cardinal Ratzinger, and Hans Urs von Balthasar (San Francisco: Ignatius Press, 1986), 89.

It starts, therefore, with the profound reality of a God who speaks, and more remarkable still, the God who addresses this man by name— and not just any name, but the name that God himself gave specifically and personally to the chosen one: *'abrāhām,* or *'ab-hamon,* "Father of Many" (Genesis 17:5). This is important. The first word of the unfolding drama *immediately recapitulates and reaffirms everything that came before* in the Abraham cycle by the simple confirmation of a name. Significantly, this name is a vocational name, and equally, a promissory name. Simply by saying the name, the God-fearing Abraham can hear the message: "be not afraid; you are the father of many." Perhaps this helps us to understand the surprising peace and confidence that pervades the drama of Genesis 22; Father-of-Many knows who he is and who he is becoming by grace. He knows that his name is a promise from a God who has proved himself faithful, and thus he is ready to listen to his Lord's command.

But it also seems that, in speaking this name, God is not merely recognizing Abraham, but he is opening a space for Abraham's response. God makes room for genuine dialogue and real action, for humanity's participation in the unfolding drama.[9] Just as much as there is a hidden reassurance in this opening address, there is also a hidden question: are you with me still? Do I still have a partner in the saving work I have begun? As Balthasar insists, true drama fully engages the actor's freedom, and so God asks the aged Abraham, his covenantal partner, if he is ready for one more adventure, if he is willing to set out again.[10] All at once, therefore, God announces his presence, recognizes his chosen one by name, reinforces Abraham's unique vocation, and invites a response.

In responding to this personal call, Abraham inevitably expresses himself: there is a type of condescension wherein Abraham, standing

9. This differs from Gordon Wenham's reflections on the verse: "the narrative could simply begin 'Abraham, please take. . .' (cf. [Gen] 12:1, 15:1, 16:8, 17:2). Yet this prolongation is suggestive. Is God hesitating before giving his awful order? The text does not say so, but the break in the address raises such questions." Gordon Wenham, *Genesis 16-50,* Word Biblical Commentary (Dallas: Thomas Nelson, 1994), 104. In contrast, Balthasar says, "All biblical ethics is based on the call of the personal God and man's believing response." Balthasar, "Nine Propositions on Christian Ethics," 89. Understanding this "prolongation" as a reflection of God's making room for Abraham's participatory response— rather than the hesitation of a god who is preparing himself to make an unethical request—seems more appropriate to biblical theology generally.

10. For the echo of Genesis 12:1 in Genesis 22:2, through the use of the term "*lek-lĕkā,* go forth," see Levenson, *The Death and Resurrection of the Beloved Son,* 127; Nahum M. Sarna, *Genesis: The Traditional Hebrew Text With the New JPS Translation* (Philadelphia: Jewish Publication Society, 1989), 150.

before God, successfully communicates his own depths in language. He might have responded in a million ways, but he chose one word: *hinneni*. The usual English translation is "Here I am,"[11] but others have preferred "yes"[12] or "ready."[13] Jon Levenson says, "There is no good English equivalent for the [Hebrew] 'hineni.'. . . The term indicates readiness, attentiveness, receptivity, and responsiveness to instructions."[14] With the word *hinneni*, the idea of responsive obedience is in play, and therefore, for many modern readers, *hinneni* casts a shadow over the entire episode—indeed, over the entire biblical tradition—because the way of obedience and submission is seen as dehumanizing. Modern thought generally, and modern theology specifically, is extremely sensitive on this point: the need to protect individual autonomy is seen as paramount. This is not a marginal issue. Most post-Enlightenment readers of the text will approach the questions raised by the word *hinneni* with a strong (even if implicit) apprehension of anything that undermines the idea of personal sovereignty as promoted by magisterial Enlightenment thinkers. According to Cyril O'Regan, critique of classic biblical/Christian anthropology is fundamental to modernity's self-understanding. He says that, from the perspective of the Enlightenment, ". . . Christian forms of life are shown to be pathological in that they represent attacks on human integrity, autonomy, and legitimate self-regard."[15] Again, for

11. NJPS, NRSV, NIV, KJB, ESV, etc.

12. Victor P. Hamilton, *The Book of Genesis: Chapters 18-50* (Grand Rapids, MI: Eerdmans, 1995), 97.

13. E. A. Speiser, *Genesis: Introduction, Translation, and Notes* (Garden City, NY: Anchor Bible, 1964), 162.

14. Jon Levenson, "Genesis Introduction and Annotations," in *The Jewish Study Bible. Tanakh* (New York: Oxford University Press, 2004), 45. The Brown-Driver-Briggs *Hebrew and English Lexicon of the Old Testament* similarly says that *hinneh* "in response to a call, indicates the readiness of the person addressed to listen or obey," quoted in Hamilton, *The Book of Genesis*, 97. Or again, "It is close to saying, 'I am willing to execute everything I am about to hear.' This is a 'confession of readiness.'" Mishael Caspi and John T. Greene, "Prolegomenon," in *Unbinding the Binding of Isaac* (University Press of America, 2007), xiii. Nahum M. Sarna agrees: "*hinneni* expresses an attitude of attentiveness and receptivity. It is the only word Abraham utters to God in the entire episode." Sarna, *Genesis*, 151.

15. Cyril O'Regan, *Anatomy of Misremembering: Von Balthasar's Response to Philosophical Modernity. Volume 1: Hegel* (Chestnut Ridge, NY: The Crossroad Publishing Company, 2014), 7. The conflict between pre-modern vs. Enlightenment anthropologies is carried out in biblical commentaries; Moberly reviews the work of some modern Jewish biblical interpreters who contrast Abraham's "ethically engaged" boldness in challenging God on the destruction of Sodom and Gomorrah (Gn 18:16–33) with the "submissive" Abraham of Genesis 22, who prefers "devotion to ethics"; Moberly, *The Bible, Theology, and Faith*, 155. As Moberly points out, when the issue is cast in these terms, the "questioning" Abraham is often seen as the true father of (modern) faith.

many modern readers, any force or figure external to one's own conscience that would claim authority or demand obedience is framed in terms of power struggles and vulnerability to abuse. If traditional Judaism and Christianity have exalted Abraham's *hinneni* as the very perfection of creaturely being,[16] many post-Enlightenment thinkers consider the promotion of passivity and obedience, which might be implied by this word, to be religion's original sin.

Abraham's *hinneni*, in other words, is radical and divisive. It certainly does not help—from the perspective of those who might want to defend biblical *hinneni/fiat* anthropology—that the "test" that immediately follows Abraham's declaration of readiness is the command to offer his beloved son as a sacrifice. That Abraham appears to move forward without hesitation seems to confirm our worst fears, reinforcing the awful dangers lurking in this word. While a comprehensive reflection on this problem is impossible here, something more must be said about *hinneni* because the moral coherence of the entire temple cult hangs on the strength or weakness of this idea. Can Abraham's "readiness, attentiveness, receptivity, and responsiveness" before God be defended, especially in a post-Enlightenment context?

Just as Balthasar's unparalleled reflection on the theological concept of glory assisted us in the last chapter, so also his work on vocation, obedience, and freedom is highly relevant here. Overall, as O'Regan explains, Balthasar is engaged in a symphonic "remembering" of Christianity's premodern beliefs, practices, and forms of life, which requires him to challenge the unquestioned supremacy of human autonomy in modern thinkers.[17] Balthasar can be a resource for biblical interpreters insofar as he helps us appreciate a pre-modern social imaginary that is (at least plausibly) closer to these texts than post-Enlightenment perspectives. This certainly comes into play as we consider the question of whether Abraham's *hinneni* is a dehumanizing form of slavery, or whether it can be genuinely celebrated as an icon of true freedom and flourishing. In approaching this question,

---

16. In Christianity, this same concept is more often discussed under the term *fiat*; Mary's *fiat* ("let it be done") should be read as a recapitulation and perfection of Abraham's *hinneni*. The word used to translate the Hebrew in LXX is *idoú*, which is also the first word of Mary's response to the angel in Greek in Luke 1:38, "*eîpen dè Mariám Idoú.* . . , Mary said, 'Behold. . . .'" Joel Green has shown the many parallels between the opening chapters of Luke and the Abraham cycle, Joel B. Green, *The Gospel of Luke* (Grand Rapids, MI: Eerdmans, 1997), 52 ff. Green also, notably, translates Mary's *Idoú* as "Here am I." Green, 82.

17. This is seen in his critique of figures such as Hegel (O'Regan, *Anatomy of Misremembering*, 193–94) and Moltmann (O'Regan, 342–43).

therefore, we should turn to the second volume of Balthasar's *Theo-Drama*, where he explains the "two poles" of finite freedom: (1) autonomy of movement (*autexousion*) and (2) freedom of consent (that is, consent to the Good). Over millennia, philosophers have staked out diverse positions between these two poles, some leaning in one direction, others leaning the opposite way; this philosophical debate seems interminable.

From the theological perspective, the loud and stormy philosophical arguments about "freedom" are interrupted by the words "*Go forth from your native land...*" (Genesis 12:1). Another Freedom has communicated itself, and so our reflection must now grapple not only with the creaturely poles identified above, but also with that Freedom who is wholly beyond what finitude conceives: infinite Freedom, a Freedom who is in no way contingent or restricted. With the revelation of the biblical God, the two poles of our finite freedom are suspended in the always-greater-difference of infinite freedom, and—Balthasar argues—this suspension does not rob us of freedom (it is not the suspension of a marionette); rather, it opens up the possibility that we might be free indeed. To argue this point, Balthasar shows that each of the creaturely extremes, left to themselves, becomes corrupt: on the one hand, the emphasis on autonomy inclines toward the illusion that the hubristic, titanic striving of the individual will can achieve self-fulfillment through power, wealth, honors, or earthly pleasures. This catalyzes a cycle of desire that, in attempting to augment the self to achieve self-fulfillment, paradoxically diminishes the human soul. As Balthasar says, this trajectory leads to the twisted mindset that "everything—including God—would be a means (*uti*) enabling finite freedom to enjoy its own self (*frui*),"[18] and thus, finite freedom becomes increasingly enslaved to finitude[19] such that, over time, "freedom" becomes smaller and smaller until it virtually disappears. On the other hand, the freedom of consenting to the Good, insofar as "the Good" is identified as an otherworldly ideal—an escape from the quotidian into pure contemplation, a rapture from the self, an abandon into One or Nothing—itself does violence to genuine freedom insofar as the person and the personal melts away. This is a form of despair, finitude's forlorn self-mutilation, and such violence can hardly represent true freedom. In either case, the machinations of finite freedom to establish and protect itself result in its diminishment.

---

18. Hans Urs von Balthasar, *Theo-Drama, Vol. 2: Theological Dramatic Theory: The Dramatis Personae: Man in God* (San Francisco: Ignatius Press, 1990), 228.

19. Balthasar says that, from this perspective, even "God" becomes an object of one's grasping; this "God" is therefore necessarily a god insofar as it is instrumentalized, it becomes a finite object fitted to the perceived needs of the finite soul.

For Balthasar, with the revelation of infinite freedom—again, "Now the LORD said to Abram, 'Go. . .'" (Gn 12:1)—the hopeless philosophical polarities are brought into a new, liberating suspension. The freedom of autonomy is discovered to be a participation in infinite freedom, and the freedom of consent—now not just to a philosophical good (which ultimately remained a creaturely ideal), but the Good who calls by name— is made personal: each pole is shown to be ordered toward the other, both poles together are shown to be ordered toward personal communion. True autonomy is true consent to personal relationship with God and neighbor. With the calling of Abraham, one already hears the whisper of creation's most profound truth: freedom is love and love is freedom.

For theologians like Balthasar and David Bentley Hart (both of whom are students of St. Gregory of Nyssa), the human being is finite, but nevertheless a finite *spirit*, and thus—according to this anthropology—we are not grounded in ourselves—nor are we armored souls—but we are open and vulnerable (ultimately, to love and be loved).[20] This openness makes it possible to say that our beatitude is to love with ever greater depth and delight; we are made for a fullness that never ceases flowing over.[21] This is because—and here we come to the central point— to truly "possess" relational joy, one can never close their fist on the object, but must always remain open in a relationship of *mutual* possession. In such a form of life, one's "self" is found only in handing oneself over, in forever returning oneself to the beloved even as one receives themselves from the beloved. The joy of love involves giving love away, and thus the soul rich in beatitude is the soul who practices poverty in spirit. For Balthasar, the biblical tradition suggests that it is this mode of life *alone* that corresponds to what human beings *truly* are: persons suspended in God, made to mirror God's self-giving way of being. And thus, every form of idolatry is resisted with the greatest possible force precisely because such practices kill the human spirit through suffocation.

It is not as if an open, self-giving, kenotic way of life is simply more "personally fulfilling." It is not as if the sense of being suspended in

---

20. As Hart says: "The Christian understanding of the soul is, of necessity, dynamic, multifarious, contradictory; no one more profoundly expressed this dynamism than Gregory of Nyssa, for whom the soul could be understood only as an *èpéktasis*, an always outstretched, open, and changing motion, an infinite exodus from nothingness into God's inexhaustible transcendence. . . ." David Bentley Hart, *The Beauty of the Infinite: The Aesthetics of Christian Truth* (Grand Rapids, MI: Eerdmans, 2004), 114–15.

21. For analysis of Balthasar's own endorsement of Gregory of Nyssa's *epektasis*, and the corresponding anthropology which describes "the human subject as constitutively erotic and ecstatic," see O'Regan, *Anatomy of Misremembering*, 141–45.

God—not grabbing one pole or the other in a bid for grounding and permanence in created being but realizing one's freedom by letting go *in* infinite freedom—simply has more utilitarian value, all things considered. Rather, pre-modern theologians were convinced that this is the only way of being that reflects the truth of who we are as creatures who have their being and freedom only and always through participation in Divine Being and, therefore, obedience to this way of existence is a matter of life or death for the created spirit. In opposition to the shrunken lives that generally characterize the human condition, the "mansions" that dwell in the Father's house are the great souls, open and free.

What we can conclude, then, is that human freedom is fully autonomous when it enters into communion with infinite freedom, and thus, when finite freedom comes to resonate with infinite freedom in love. In this way (and only in this way), the created soul has achieved perfect authenticity insofar as it is obedient to its own great mission to "become . . . what you are"[22]—where "what you are" is precisely openness to "becoming" as the created spirit allows herself to be open to the always-greater freedom that calls her forward.[23] Insofar as this call to magnanimous living reflects the basic structure of created existence in its integrity, it is the very image of peace. There is no violence to this reality, even though it may require real ascetical effort, powered by grace, to strengthen and train the heart to love.

When God speaks, Abraham says *hinneni*. Admittedly, the theology of freedom that we have briefly summarized in this section, with the assistance of Balthasar, Hart, and Przywara, may have a Catholic and Orthodox *Sitz im Leben*: Maximus the Confessor's post-Chalcedonian meditation on the two wills of Christ has been a major impetus for this understanding of human being in Christian thought. At the same time, I argue that, in the opening dialogue of Genesis 22, the basic shape of a theology of interpersonal freedom and vocation is already revealed.[24] And

---

22. Cf. Erich Przywara, *Analogia Entis: Metaphysics: Original Structure and Universal Rhythm* (Grand Rapids, MI: Eerdmans, 2013), 124.

23. For an excellent discussion of the themes we are considering in this section in conversation with Thomistic philosophy, see D. C. Schindler, *Love and the Postmodern Predicament: Rediscovering the Real in Beauty, Goodness, and Truth* (Eugene, OR: Wipf and Stock, 2018), 49–63.

24. Balthasar claims that the old covenant establishes a pattern of relation between infinite and finite freedom, but it nevertheless remains inadequate:

This confronts us with the problem which Old Testament theology cannot solve. Here genuine infinite freedom and genuine finite freedom are joined in a covenant, but, in the form in which it is made, this Covenant cannot attain fulfillment; it can only point

these ideas are not marginal in Jewish thought; Jon Levenson has shown in his introduction to the theology of Sinai (that is, the theology of covenant) that "The ancient Near Eastern covenant was not an impersonal code, but an instrument of diplomacy founded upon the personal relationship of the heads of state. The essence of the covenant lies in the fact that the latter pledge to be faithful to one another."[25] The biblical notion of obedience to law or command, therefore, was not the impersonal "rule of law" characteristic of the modern sovereign state, but rather it is the call and response of persons in communion: "At the heart of Israel's relationship with YHWH lay a dialogue of love."[26]

This Balthasarian reflection is meant to help us appreciate the theology behind the two-word dialogue that opens the biblical account of the Akedah, especially as modern readers. Is *hinneni* the appropriate posture before God? Did Abraham respond rightly? Remember, according to the narrative beginning in Genesis 12, by the time Abraham says *hinneni* ten

---

toward it. . . . in biblical terms, it was necessary for the Spirit of God to be implanted in the hearts of the Covenant partners (Jer 31:31), and this, for the present, remained but a promise. Therefore the Sinai Covenant itself must undergo mediation so that ultimate immediacy can be attained: and this takes place precisely through the christological paradox, according to which, without confusing the freedoms (*asunchutōs*, in the Chalcedonian expression), infinite freedom indwells finite freedom, and so the finite is perfected in the infinite, without the infinite losing itself in the finite or the finite in the infinite.

(Hans Urs von Balthasar, *Theo-Drama, Vol. 2: Theological Dramatic Theory: The Dramatis Personae: Man in God* [San Francisco: Ignatius Press, 1990], 201). For Balthasar, the fullness of deification—our partaking of the tree of life—requires a perfection that can only be achieved by the concrete *analogia entis*, Jesus Christ, who is the personal realization of finite and infinite freedom without confusion and without division. But, from the perspective of temple theology as I am developing it in this chapter and in this book, I am convinced that we can re-frame the more negative assessment of the Old Testament in this particular quote. A magnifying glass can be used to study insects or scorch them to death, and Christocentrism can be similarly double-sided. It can be used to depreciate the "yes" of Abraham and other Old Testament saints—including even the "yes" of Mary—or it can magnify the goodness and glory of Israel which, by grace, establishes the pattern that Jesus uniquely fulfills. The latter approach seems to me more promising.

25. Jon D. Levenson, *Sinai and Zion: An Entry into the Jewish Bible* (San Francisco: HarperOne, 1987), 28.

26. Levenson, 75. Levenson reflects further on the problem of obedience and freedom in terms of the "dialectic of covenantal theonomy." Levenson explains, "Because his commandments are grounded in the history of redemption, they are not the imposition of an alien force, but rather the revelation of a familiar, benevolent, and loving God, and the ethic is not one of pure heteronomy." Jon Levenson, *Creation and the Persistence of Evil: The Jewish Drama of Divine Omnipotence* (Princeton, NJ: Princeton University Press, 1988), 144.

chapters later, trust and mutual faithfulness have been solidly established. Abraham may be obedient, but there is no reason to call his obedience blind. Abraham is responding to something he has *seen*, something he has experienced powerfully in his own history. He is responding to a God who has proved faithful again and again, beyond his and Sarah's greatest expectations. The sights and sounds of his household, no doubt, were entirely upended by the coming of his son—a child born to a woman who was long past menopause, an heir born to a couple who suffered decades of infertility. Can there be any doubt that Abraham had pondered this mystery in his heart, day and night, for many years? Father-of-Many's very name was a permanent reminder of his incredible vocation, one that had come to him by God's grace alone, and one that was to be realized through his obedience. At this point in his life, Abraham's whole field of vision has been completely, astonishingly filled with living icons of God's faithfulness and goodness. To say that his *hinneni*—his readiness, attentiveness, receptivity, and responsiveness—is blind or unthinking, especially at this point in the narrative, is an unfair reading of the story.

Therefore, when God calls, Abraham responds. The harmony of infinite and finite freedom communicated in this two-word narrative is analogous *not* to the violent external obedience of master and slave, but to the intimate and trusting obedience of dance partners. What is exceptional about Abraham is how naturally and easily this old man moves in the world. He exemplifies fluidity of movement. Experienced dance partners do not struggle against one another; they respond to even a slight shift, they get lost in their shared gaze, they feel each other's rhythm, they anticipate one another, and seem even to breathe together, spontaneously and freely. This is obedience according to the word's etymology: the Latin word *obedientia* comes from ob-audire, which suggests an intensified hearing or listening. Dancers listen to the music in and through their partners, and in their bodies, they act out a drama that unifies without violence. Abraham has learned to dance, and therefore he is fully engaged and truly alive.

All of this comes even before the command is made, but, as I've said, the entire theology of the Akedah has been expressed proleptically in two words—or, rather, in a single word, because these two words are really one: the (objective) identity given by God to Abraham, Father-of-Many, is (subjectively) expressed in his identity *Hinneni*, Ready-Receptive-Obedient. In Israel, true patriarchy—if I may use the word—is receptive-readiness to fulfill one's vocation. In the divine economy, to be a spiritual father or mother is to be free of idolatry and responsive to divine movement. This is the humility necessary to be great. For all the world, greatness comes from seizing, grasping, claiming, conquering. *Veni, vidi, vici!* Abraham already, at the outset, is aware of the fact that his greatness is nothing like worldly greatness, his fatherhood has nothing to do with his virility, but that his whole identity and his entire hope is a gift. Abraham is already called Father-of-Many because Abraham has learned to let go and really listen. Balthasar asked, "What is a person without a life-form? . . ." *Hinneni* is Abraham's life form, and through this form, splendor shines.

The Second Word: ʿaheb

I have spent an extra amount of time on the word *Abraham/hinneni* due to the conviction that the entire narrative of Genesis 22, and consequentially the whole drama of Mount Zion, is here expressed in embryonic form. This foundation will shape the interpretation of the other key words. The next verse, which brings us finally to God's astonishing, dreadful command, contains three of these words: "And he said, 'Take your son, your favored one, whom you *love* (*ʾahavta*), Isaac, and go forth to the land of *Moriah* (*hammōriyyāh*), and offer him there as a *burnt-offering* (*leʿōlāh*) on one of the heights that I will point out to you."[27] First is the word "love," the Hebrew word ʿaheb.

As we saw at the beginning of this chapter, the Akedah has been at the center of a philosophical polemic for centuries, and Kant himself drew a line in the sand when he said that, "were a father ordered to kill his son"—even if the order ostensibly came from God—the moral agent should refuse. Reading the biblical narrative, the modern imagination can hardly avoid being influenced by the frequent depictions, in movies and television, of wild-eyed cult leaders, or glassy-eyed cult followers, or the grim, legalistic severity of so many religious parents as depicted in popular culture. And without a doubt, these Hollywood depictions are not merely imagined; history bears witness to the existence of "true believers" whose hearts are hardened, who are a danger to family and society, and who can be abusive, irrational, inhumane, and cruel. Equally tragic is the fact that some people do suffer from mental illnesses that cause them to "hear voices," and there are those rare and terrible instances when such "voices" drive the afflicted person to do monstrous things.

Along with all this, we inevitably confront an early modern anti-Christian polemic that compounds the unease many feel when reading Genesis 22. As O'Regan says, "In a variety of Enlightenment rhetorics

---

27. This is the NJPS translation with Levenson's slight modifications. *The Death and Resurrection of the Beloved Son*, 127.

and disparate chronicling of deviance, church tradition is blamed for obscurantism, authoritarianism, fanaticism, and its ultimate conclusion, that is, war."[28] One of the great questions of the day is whether all religious belief is, at root, a kind of violence. And so, when we are confronted by those horrifying news reports of parents who "hear a voice" and actually do massacre their children, coupled with daily news coverage of holy war declarations and religious justifications for every imaginable brutality, the situation certainly seems bleak.

Against this cultural backdrop, we read of a God who says, "Take your son. . . ," and a father who subsequently "rose early. . . ." For many, the only sensible question to ask today is whether Abraham had a mental illness, or whether perhaps he is one of these stone-faced "believers" who are more prepared to slit his son's throat than to question his beliefs. There is no getting around the fact that, for most of us, something is chilling and unjustifiable here, and by gilding the story with reflections on infinite and finite freedom, along with breezy paeans to obedience, perhaps this will all come across as a desperate apologetic for a narrative best left in the iron age. Immanuel Kant's suggestion that the "God" of the Akedah is a false god seems to be the only acceptable conclusion.

By the same token, it is necessary to again insist on attempting to read the story in its own context, allowing it to speak and, perhaps, to surprise. When teaching the story of creation in Genesis 1 and 2, theologians regularly insist that these chapters be read with attention to genre and historical setting—they point out that the author would not have intended for these passages to be approached with the same mindset as we approach, say, a modern physics textbook. But then, some of these same teachers will dismiss, or denounce, the events of Genesis 22, as if it was written to be a handbook for modern family ethics, or as if it should be read primarily in a twenty-first-century judicial context where the phenomenon of "hearing voices" is solid evidence in an insanity defense.

Attention to the portrait of Abraham presented in the biblical canon simply does not support the notion that this person is best understood in the context of modern concerns about religious fanaticism or (religiously-tinged) criminal insanity. Abraham is consistently depicted as a responsible, thoughtful, peaceful man. Consider, for example, his generous handling of his conflict with Lot: "Let's not quarrel. . . . If you go to the left, I'll go to the right; if you go to the right, I'll go to the left" (Gn 13:8–9), or the way he begs for Sodom and Gomorrah (Gn 18:16–33). Abra-

---

28. O'Regan, *Anatomy of Misremembering*, 12.

ham has flaws, but to paint him as a monster is inconsistent with the biblical portrait.

An important element of God's command in Genesis 22:2 is the way Isaac is identified, his name coming only after a series of descriptors: "Take, pray, your son, your only one, whom you love. . . ."[29] Edward Kessler says that for both the rabbis and the early church fathers, "the purpose of the drawn-out description of Isaac was to increase Abraham's affection."[30] Abraham's love of Isaac is called upon, and intensified, as God issues the command. In fact, some of the earliest recorded interpretations of the Akedah strongly emphasize the strength of Abraham's love and devotion toward Isaac. For example, according to Philo,

> The wife of [Abraham] bore to him in full wedlock his only and dearly cherished son, a child of great bodily beauty and excellence of soul. For already he was showing a perfection of virtues beyond his years, so that his father, moved not merely by a feeling of natural affection but also by such deliberate judgement as a censor of character might make, cherished for him a great tenderness.[31]

Josephus similarly begins his retelling of Genesis 22 by saying,

> Now Isaac was passionately beloved of his father Abraham, being his only son and born to him "on the threshold of old age" through the bounty of God. On his side, the child called out the affection of his parents and endeared himself to them yet more by the practice of every virtue, showing a devoted filial obedience and a zeal for the worship of God. Abraham thus reposed all his own happiness on the hope of leaving his son unscathed when he departed this life.[32]

Whereas the perfect innocence of the son compounds the disgust Kant feels toward this story, both Philo and Josephus emphasize not merely the child's innocence, but even this child's perfection in virtue. Such virtue only served to increase Abraham's love, beyond the attachments of natural affection, into true adoration. Thus as God calls for "your son, your favored one, your beloved," waves of affection grow and reach their peak

---

29. This is Robert Alter's translation. Robert Alter, *Genesis* (New York: W. W. Norton & Company, 1997), 103.

30. Kessler, *Bound by the Bible*, 48; Cf. Levenson, *The Death and Resurrection of the Beloved Son*, 127–27.

31. Philo, *On Abraham. On Joseph. On Moses.*, trans. F. H. Colson, Loeb Classical Library (Cambridge, MA: Harvard University Press, 1935), 85.

32. Josephus, *Jewish Antiquities, Books I–IV*, trans. H. St. J. Thackeray, vol. 4, Loeb Classical Library (Cambridge, MA.: Harvard University Press, 1967), 109–11.

with the pronunciation of the name, Isaac—a name which itself means Laughter. In identifying this person, God identifies everything that is good in Abraham's earthly life, and he singles out the very personification of Abraham's joy.

Yes, Abraham loves his son. With natural affection—as would any father—and with moral affection (according to Philo and Josephus)—as any good person would love an exemplar of perfect virtue—Abraham loves his son. But then there is also a "self-interested" affection insofar as Isaac embodies the *entirety* of Abraham's future, as Josephus himself recognized when he said that "Abraham thus reposed all his own happiness on the hope of leaving his son unscathed when he departed this life."[33] This point cannot be emphasized enough: Abraham has nothing else. His entire life, his every hope, every one of his precious, promised children—more numerous than the stars of the sky—all of it is to be found in Isaac and nowhere else. For ancient Jewish readers, the death of Isaac would be Abraham's own eternal death.[34] There is no alternative, no "plan B." David Bentley Hart put it especially well: ". . . all of Israel slumbers in [Isaac's] loins, because he is the child of Sarah's dotage who cannot be replaced, because he is the whole promise and substance of God's covenant. . . ."[35]

Therefore, we are not at liberty to read this story in isolation, as if it is a thought experiment designed for a philosophy class. Rather, it is the story of a man called out of obscurity and promised unimagined bless-

33. 4:111.

34. The extent to which Abraham put his hope in Isaac is brought out clearly by Kevin Madigan and Jon Levenson, who explain that the ancient Hebrew sense of hope in children goes beyond the "truism" that children bring consolation that life goes on. This is still a fairly individualistic way of thinking about things, whereas Israel's perspective was different: "If, in fact, individuals are fundamentally and inextricably embedded within their families, then their own death, however terrifying a prospect, may not be thought to have the finality that death carries in a culture with a more individualistic, atomistic understanding of the self, like the culture of the modern West." Jon D. Levenson and Kevin J. Madigan, *Resurrection: The Power of God for Christians and Jews* (New Haven: Yale University Press, 2008), 107. The relative fluidity between individual and family in an ancient culture like Israel's helps to explain how the "self" really does survive for the person rich in children, whereas it does not for the one who is childless. This accentuates the degree to which Abraham's own identity and future hang in the balance.

35. Hart, *Beauty of the Infinite*, 351. Moberly is also very good on this point; see Moberly, *The Bible, Theology, and Faith*, 130–31. This point was earlier emphasized by von Rad, who argued that the combination of Genesis 21 (the loss of Ishmael) and Genesis 22 (the offering of Isaac) constitutes Abraham's "road out into Godforsakenness"; cf. Konrad Schmid, "Abraham's Sacrifice: Gerhard von Rad's Interpretation of Genesis 22," *Interpretation: A Journal of Bible and Theology* 62, no. 3 (July 1, 2008): 270–71.

ings—land, wealth, status, and most importantly, descendants—the story of a family that suffered the agony of infertility for nearly an entire lifetime, and a family that continued to endure an excruciating wait after the promise had been made, and after covenants were sealed. And then: a child, whose name is synonymous with joy, the very embodiment of a lifetime of prayers, a family's single chance at life after death.[36] The slender word "love"—*'aheb*—cannot possibly bear the weight of what this father felt toward his boy, but it is the only word we have. And then God breaks in again with the familiar command, "go forth." The first time Abraham heard these words, he was told to "go forth *from*," leaving behind everything he knew, on the strength of a promise. Now, at the end of his life, Abraham is instructed to "go forth *to*," to set his eyes on the mountains, and to bring with him the promised one, to be offered back in sacrifice. Abraham's love must now pass through a purifying fire.

The Third Word: Moriah

Returning to the key verse in which God gives the command, it says, "Take your son . . . and go forth to the land of *Moriah* (*ham-mōriyyāh*). . . ." We have already emphasized the importance of sacred geography in biblical theology, and now as we arrive at the defining moment of Abraham's life, we are told of a specific destination. Various etymologies have been offered for the word Moriah, but one popular option is to understand this name as foreshadowing the title that Abraham gives to the site, "YHWH-*yireh*, the Lord will see" (22:14). The Hebrew verb *ra'ah*, see or provide, is used repeatedly throughout the chapter, and therefore it is at least plausible that the name Moriah already alludes to the vision, and provision, that is so crucially important to understanding the story.[37]

As important as the earliest etymology of the word may be, from the perspective of intra-biblical theological development, the canonical history of the word "Moriah" is also very important. The word is used on only one other occasion, by the priestly author of Chronicles, and he uses it almost in passing—no special attention is drawn to the word—but this

36. This is not to ignore the person of Ishmael, but, of course, at this point in the Genesis narrative, the son of Hagar is long gone.

37. For the notion that "Moriah" anticipates Abraham's vision, see Wenham, *Genesis 16-50*, 104–5; Sarna, *Genesis*, 391. Moberly also sees the verb *ra ah* in Moriah, but he points out that the missing aleph in Moriah is a possible problem; *The Bible, Theology, and Faith*, 111–12.

should not blind us to the brilliant theological argument that the chronicler is making. The author says, "Then Solomon began to build the House of the Lord in Jerusalem on Mount Moriah, where [the LORD] had appeared to his father David, at the place which David had designated, at the threshing floor of Ornan the Jebusite" (2 Chronicles 3:1). In this verse, there is once again an emphasis on God's appearing, *ra'ah*, but this time with reference to his appearance to King David as described in 1 Chronicles 21. In that chapter, David decides to order a census, which was understood to be a grave sin (perhaps because it suggests the idea that the king was putting faith in numbers, rather than in God alone). As punishment, the nation falls under a pestilence that kills many, and an angel of destruction approaches Jerusalem, the new royal city. One imagines the angel raising his sword, about to strike, when there is an interruption: "God sent an angel to Jerusalem to destroy it, but as he was about to wreak destruction, the LORD saw (*rā'āh* YHWH) and renounced further punishment and said to the destroying angel, 'Enough! Stay your hand.' The angel of the Lord was then standing by the threshing floor of Ornan the Jebusite" (1 Chr 21:15). *The* LORD *saw*. The angel is standing on the threshing floor, ready to strike, when *the* LORD *saw*. The LORD saw—*what*? The narrative does not explain, suggesting that these two words are meaningful in themselves. In Genesis 22:14, as we will discuss below, Abraham names the mountain in the land of Moriah YHWH *yir'eh*, the place where God will see. Many years later, an angel stands ready to crush Jerusalem, and *ra'ah* YHWH, God sees. Knowing that a few chapters later this very site will be explicitly identified by the Chronicler as Mount Moriah, it seems reasonable to suggest that God sees the obedience of Abraham and Isaac at this place, he sees their sacrifice, and for Abraham's sake, God saves Jerusalem.[38]

The passage continues: "David *looked up* and *saw* the angel of the Lord standing between heaven and earth, with a sword drawn in his hand directed against Jerusalem" (1 Chr 21:16a). Once again there is an emphasis on seeing, and here the parallel between Abraham and David is quite explicit. Genesis 22:4 reports that, after a three-day journey, "Abraham looked up and saw"—the *only* difference between this verse and 1 Chr. 21:16, in the Hebrew, is the use of the name Abraham rather than David. In both cases, the men *look up*—suggesting the height of the site—and *saw*. While Abraham saw the site of his greatest test, David sees an angel standing between heaven and earth with a sword raised, but stayed. This sight causes David to fall to the ground in repentance.

---

38. Cf. Levenson, *The Death and Resurrection of the Beloved Son*, 180–82.

All of this occurred at an elevated threshing floor, a place where wheat was processed, separating the grain from the chaff. David, and with him the entire city of Jerusalem, will be spared on account of what God saw, but not without coming to the threshing floor, a place linking heaven and earth, where the chaff will be removed and where the grain will be made ready to become life-giving bread.

While we are briefly exploring the theology of Chronicles, it is worth pointing out the generous attitude of Ornan himself, who is the owner of the threshing floor. When King David tries to buy the site, Ornan immediately offers to give it to him as a gift, along with oxen for burnt offerings and the wheat for grain offerings, and ends by saying "I give it all." In response to the Jebusite's generosity, David articulates an important principle for sacrificial theology, while explaining why he must pay for the site himself: he says, "No, I will buy them at the full price. I cannot make a present to the LORD of what belongs to you, or sacrifice a burnt offering that has cost me nothing" (1 Chr 21:24). The importance of the costly "free gift" is fundamental to sacrificial theology, and both the former owner and the new owner of the threshing floor exemplify this attitude.[39] All this is met with divine approval: after David builds an altar, God responds "with fire from heaven on the altar of burnt offerings [cf. Lv 9:24]. The LORD ordered the angel to return his sword to its sheath. At that time, when David *saw* that the LORD answered him with fire from heaven at the threshing floor of Ornan the Jebusite, then he sacrificed there. . ." (1 Chr. 21:26–28). The angel returning his sword to its sheath certainly refers to the averted punishment, and it probably also alludes to the way Abraham's hand also was stayed on the height in the land of Moriah, but maybe it isn't too much of a stretch to suggest a subtle allusion to the cherubs with their flaming swords protecting Eden. What *is* this mountain that David bought for sixty pieces of silver?

Without a doubt, the author of Chronicles wants us to imagine that we, with David, have returned to an ancient place with profound theological meaning. Given the various ways 1 Chronicles 21 seems to echo Genesis 22, the explicit reference to Moriah in connection with the threshing floor a few chapters later (2 Chr 3:1) now seems quite natural.

---

39. Also significant here is Klawans observation that the prophetic critique of the temple cult is often driven not by disgust toward sacrifice itself, but by the phenomenon of the rich stealing from the poor and thus offering a sacrifice that has cost them nothing. Jonathan Klawans, *Purity, Sacrifice, and the Temple: Symbolism and Supersessionism in the Study of Ancient Judaism* (Oxford: Oxford University Press, 2006), 84 ff.

This elevated place—the final destination of the tabernacle of Moses after its long journey—is founded on the vision and the offering of both Abraham and David, patriarch and king, and this offering somehow links heaven and earth. The covenants of Abraham, Moses, and David, are now brought together at the heart of the new capital city: from Zion, perfect in beauty, God shines forth. Whether or not the author of the Akedah had Jerusalem in mind when it was first written, it is a fact that by the time the books of Chronicles were written, a hermeneutic circle had been drawn around Moriah and Zion, such that one could not be interpreted without the other.[40] Thus, when a second temple Jew heard the words of Genesis—"Take your son . . . and go forth to the land of Moriah"—and as she contemplated the three-day journey that the father and son took, she imagined a pilgrimage to Mount Zion, perhaps not unlike the one she herself had made on occasion. She can interpret her own spiritual journey to "Moriah" in light of Abraham's *hinneni*-mission, and she is also able to interpret Abraham's sacrifice in the context of then-contemporary temple theology. She believes that the place where Abraham handed over what was most precious to him is the place where she makes her own sacrifices, thus she can understand that on Mount Moriah she is participating in something that brings all the generations of Israelites together in a unified movement of love and trust.

The Fourth Word: ʿolah

With the fourth key word, we return one last time to Genesis 22:2—"Take your son . . . and offer him . . . as a burnt offering (ʿolah). . . ." This word, ʿolah, appears repeatedly in the chapter—five times between

40. Without a consensus on the date, provenance, or redactional history of Genesis 22 (as mentioned in footnote 7 above), it is not possible to assertively claim exactly when the "land of Moriah" became associated with the Jerusalem temple, but it can at least be said that the scholarly opinion of Isaac Kalimi and others—that the association had already been made in the first temple period, only to be reinforced by the Chronicler; Kalimi, "The Land of Moriah," 350, 362—is at least plausible. From this perspective, it is similarly conceivable that early temple theology could draw upon Abrahamic traditions, and vice-versa. It is indisputable that later second temple theology, and then post-temple rabbinic theology, took the connection between Abraham, Isaac, and Zion as axiomatic. In *Jubilees*, after following the biblical account of Abraham naming the place "the LORD has seen," the author straightforwardly adds, "It is Mount Zion." James H. Charlesworth, ed., "Jubilees," in *The Old Testament Pseudepigrapha*, trans. O.S. Wintermute, vol. 2 (New York: Doubleday, 1985), chap. 18.13. Similarly, after Josephus says that Abraham set out for the "Morian Mount," he adds that Abraham "proceeded with his son alone to that mount whereon king David afterwards erected the temple," Josephus, *Jewish Antiquities*, 4:111–13.

vv. 2–8, and again at verse 13.[41] Many today will skim over the word since the nuances of cultic sacrifice are lost on us. It is as if a baseball reporter substituted the generic word "hit" for the words home run, grand slam, base hit, sacrifice fly, and bunt—all of the detail, color, and texture would be removed from his story. Similarly, when we come to the biblical word ʿolah, burnt offering, many will substitute the generic word "sacrifice" in their minds, and then further shrink the word sacrifice to mean "kill." Thus we have Immanuel Kant thousands of years later using the extremely broad verb "töten, kill" to characterize God's command before denouncing it. The Hebrew word harag (to kill) does not appear in Genesis 22, nor does the word ratsach (to murder), but instead the word ʿolah. Once again, overlooking the details of the narrative, in their historical context, is an unjust reading of the text.

That the word ʿolah appears six times in this short passage is all the more striking when one considers the fact that the same root word is used only one time in the rest of the book of Genesis; after the flood it says, "Then Noah built an altar to the Lord and . . . he offered burnt offerings (ʿōlōt) on the altar" (8:20). The word is used often in Exodus— especially in the sections attributed to P—and then abundantly in Leviticus—over sixty times. It is therefore quite remarkable to find in Genesis 22 the clustered repetition, in a very small space, of this key word from the cult's technical vocabulary.[42]

We should, therefore, turn to the first chapter of Leviticus to achieve greater insight into the meaning of God's command. Much more will be

41. Here are the places where the term is used:
- Genesis 22:2: . . . and go to the Land of Moriah, and offer him there as a **burnt offering.** . .
- Genesis 22:3: . . . He split the wood for the **burnt offering.** . .
- Genesis 22:6: Abraham took the wood for the **burnt offering** and put it on his son Isaac. . .
- Genesis 22:7: And Isaac called to his father Abraham, ". . . where is the sheep for the **burnt offering?**"
- Genesis 22:8: And Abraham said, "God will see to the sheep for his **burnt offering,** my son.". . .
- Genesis 22:13: . . . So Abraham went and took the ram and offered it up as a **burnt offering** in place of his son.

42. In a fascinating observation—one that is highly significant for this book—L. Michael Morales says, "The binding of Isaac on Mount Moriah in Genesis 22 contains cultic terminology clustered together elsewhere only for the ordination of the Levitical priesthood (Lev. 8–9) and for the Day of Atonement (Lev. 16), and probably served to prefigure the entire cultic economy—even as the foundation of the Jerusalem temple." L. Michael Morales, *Who Shall Ascend the Mountain of the Lord?: A Biblical Theology of the Book of Leviticus* (Downers Grove, IL: IVP Academic, 2015), 73.

said about the Levitical sacrificial texts in upcoming chapters. Here we'll just introduce the key ideas that are most useful for interpreting Genesis 22. By the end of the book of Exodus, Moses has exactly followed God's instructions in erecting the tabernacle, and then the tabernacle, its furniture, and the priests are consecrated with oil. With this, Moses' work is finished—then the cloud of God's glory settles on and fills the tabernacle. Transitioning to the book of Leviticus, God immediately calls to Moses from the tent of meeting and gives instructions on how to perform various sacrificial rituals, starting with the burnt offering. There are actually five major categories of sacrifice described in Leviticus: the burnt offering (ʿōlâ), grain or cereal offering (minkâ), thank offering or well-being offering (zebaḥ šĕlāmîm), sin offering (ḥaṭṭāʾt) and guilt offering (ʾāšām). That the burnt offering is listed and described first, here and in nearly every other place where sacrifices are enumerated, is striking and surely significant.[43] James W. Watts says that this pattern suggests "rhetorical preeminence," which can be explained in various ways.[44] In explaining the prominence of the burnt offering, Jacob Milgrom, who will be introduced more formally in the fifth chapter, mentions "its hoary antiquity, popularity, versatility, and frequency."[45] The burnt offering is also the first and last sacrifice offered each day: the Tamid, in which a year-old lamb is offered every morning and evening (cf. Exodus 29:38–42; Numbers 28:1–8), is the temple's opening and closing liturgy; thus it seems to frame and orient the various other sacrificial practices that occur at the tabernacle or temple throughout the day.[46] Furthermore, L. Michael Morales points out that "the most honorific detail concerning the ascension offering [the ʿolah]" is often missed: "the altar itself derives its name from it—the altar is, more fully, called 'the altar of the ascension offering.'... Even when other sacrifices are being legislated, this title for the altar ensures that the ascension offering 'upstages' them."[47] For these reasons, it seems that the ʿolah was especially meaningful in ancient Israel.

43. This is true in P, Deuteronomy, the prophets, Psalms, and in Chronicles: James W. Watts, *Ritual and Rhetoric in Leviticus: From Sacrifice to Scripture* (Cambridge: Cambridge University Press, 2007), 64–65.

44. Watts, 64.

45. Jacob Milgrom, *Leviticus 1-16. A New Translation with Introduction and Commentary*, The Anchor Bible (New York: Doubleday, 1991), 146.

46. Drawing on the work of John Kleinig, Morales points out: "all sacrifices were 'virtually incorporated into [the Tamid],' making the ascension offering [the ʿolah] 'the fundamental sacrifice.'" L. Michael Morales, "Atonement in Ancient Israel: The Whole Burnt Offering as Central to Israel's Cult," in *So Great a Salvation: A Dialogue on the Atonement in Hebrews*, ed. Jon C. Laansma, George H. Guthrie, and Cynthia Long Westfall (London: T&T Clark, 2019), 30.

47. Morales, 30.

This suggests that there might be special theological and symbolic significance to the burnt offering. Within the literature, however, there is a continuing debate about the feasibility of determining the symbolic interpretation of ancient sacrificial practices. Are we still able to access the symbolic or theological meaning of ancient liturgical texts? A figure like Jacob Milgrom tries to understand the symbolism of ritual acts; earlier scholarship was sometimes marked by its blatant contempt for priestly texts, and ancient Jewish sacrificial practices were frequently dismissed as "superstition and empty ritualism."[48] In response to such a flippant approach, one that was even more common in early historical-critical research—seen most explicitly in Wellhausen[49]—Milgrom veers in the opposite direction, and says, "I assume the Priestly Code makes sense . . . it is a self-contained system—logical, coherent, and whole. A system is built on postulates, but, in our case, they are nowhere stated."[50]

Watts, while sympathetic to Milgrom's goals, has raised several concerns about the tendency of interpreters to try to explain what these rituals "really mean." He points out that such explanations are almost

48. Watts, *Ritual and Rhetoric*, 6.

49. Julius Wellhausen's (1844–1918) influence on the trajectory of modern biblical interpretation has, of course, been monumental, but not always positive. When Christian biblical interpreters and theologians in the modern period disparage the priestly tradition as an inferior theological strand, they are following the path forged by Wellhausen. Jonathan Klawans finds an anti-Semitic bias in Wellhausen's work, a bias that is reflected in Wellhausen's claim that the Jews squandered a pure religion of "ethical monotheism" in favor of law and ritual. *Purity, Sacrifice, and the Temple*, 50; Cf. Lou H. Silberman, "Wellhausen and Judaism," *Semeia* 25 (1982): 75–82. Klawans says, "Wellhausen's contempt for priests, their rigidity, and the cult goes hand in hand with his reverence for the prophets, their spirit, their authentic religion, and their ethics." Klawans, *Purity, Sacrifice, and the Temple*, 75. Crispin Fletcher Lewis, in a section entitled "The Priesthood: A Pariah of Biblical Scholarship," similarly criticizes Wellhausen's "brazen derision of the Priestly material in the Pentateuch" and says that he is "a clear example of the commitments and values of a certain (liberal) Protestantism that has dominated biblical scholarship for the majority of the modern period." "Jesus as the High Priestly Messiah: Part 1," *Journal for the Study of the Historical Jesus* 4, no. 2 (2006): 156. More broadly, Jon Levenson protests that "the dominant impression one receives from the literature, especially in America, is that the Temple, its traditions, and its personnel are an embarrassment to those who wish to present the Old Testament sympathetically. Their sympathy stops at the foot of a certain hill in Jerusalem." "The Temple and the World," *The Journal of Religion* 64, no. 3 (1984): 282. For the subtle ways in which an academic tradition of "anti-Judaism" continues to infect biblical scholarship, see Benjamin D. Sommer, "Dialogical Biblical Theology: A Jewish Approach to Reading Scripture Theologically," in *Biblical Theology: Introducing the Conversation* (Nashville: Abingdon Press, 2009), 8–12.

50. Jacob Milgrom, *Cult and Conscience: The Asham and the Priestly Doctrine of Repentance* (Leiden: Brill, 1976), 2; quoted in Watts, *Ritual and Rhetoric*, 3–4.

always imposed on the text from beyond the text. While Leviticus offers detailed rubrics for ritual action, it says little about the symbolic or metaphorical significance of these acts. Watts believes that Milgrom's last point—that the postulates that make sense of sacrifice are nowhere stated—calls our attention to the main problem in his method. Watts stresses that "ritual practices, such as animal offerings, are usually far older than their interpretation by ancient texts, not to mention by modern ethnographers and interpreters. It is difficult to show that any one symbolic interpretation of them is widely shared by those who participate in the rituals themselves."[51] So far as Watts is concerned, Milgrom succeeds in showing that there is at least one symbolic system that makes coherent the ritual acts described in Leviticus, and it is possible that *some* ancient people had a theological perspective similar to what Milgrom describes. The next question, Watts says, is "who did so, and when?"[52] A "unified and static symbolic system,"[53] like the one suggested by Milgrom, is probably a historical illusion, Watts thinks. In any case, insofar as suggested symbols "are not explicitly stated in the text" and therefore "they impose a theology on [Leviticus] that the book does not express,"[54] historians should be more modest in their interpretation.[55]

51. Watts, *Ritual and Rhetoric in Leviticus*, 8; cf. Hundley, *Keeping Heaven*, 27.
52. Watts, *Ritual and Rhetoric*, 10.
53. Watts, 7.
54. Watts, 6–7, footnote 17.
55. For his own part, Watts wants to see what rhetorical studies might contribute to the interpretation of Leviticus. He is keen to point out that the book of Leviticus does not in fact present a ritual, but a text (which happens to describe certain ritual acts). People write to persuade, and so the question becomes, why did the author of Leviticus 1–5 write this detailed section on sacrificial rites in the way he did? Overemphasis on the search for a text's "meaning" easily misses its "broader function as an instrument for persuasion." Watts, 30. Reading the text with an awareness of rhetorical concerns can be helpful, as Watts proves throughout the study.

One apprehension I have, however, is the way in which the text can easily be diminished, becoming only a window into (reconstructed) ancient power conflicts—and thus, Leviticus is seen as an effort to persuade worshippers to embrace new sacrifices (the sin and guilt offerings) that, it so happens, are economically beneficial to the priests themselves. This type of reading echoes Wellhausen's own highly political interpretation of the ancient Jewish cult, even if Watts is *far* more nuanced and sympathetic toward priestly motives: see especially Watts, chaps. 7, "The Rhetoric of Priesthood." Watts makes many fascinating and helpful observations, and I will refer to his study often below, but his desire to find a setting for the text within some intramundane struggle remains nevertheless inadequate to an interpretation of these passages as scripture. In fact, the effect of such a reading is to take the text and turn it on its head: what seems on the surface—and what has been received for millennia—as an invitation to true worship of the one God becomes the remnant of an ancient but prosaic bid for control. The call to worship is just a pretense

Jonathan Klawans is also critical of Milgrom, but this time for being *inadequately* attentive to the symbolic meaning of sacrificial practice.[56] In his groundbreaking book, *Purity, Sacrifice, and the Temple*, Klawans challenges scholars to consider their presuppositions about the origins of sacrifice. Klawans finds that most modern reconstructions of the history of sacrifice interpret the ancient practices as reflecting primitive ideas that are increasingly spiritualized over time as the religion evolves. This interpretive framework tends to undermine the relevance of ancient sacrificial practices, seeing them as a transitional stage in social development or religious consciousness, thus making it easy to conclude that the earlier stage is now, in itself, theologically unimportant.

Klawans points out that an analogously critical or dismissive attitude was also taken toward purity laws until the work of Mary Douglas, who pointed out that such cultural regulations are not primitive (using the rules of modern hygiene to show the persistence of not-always-strictly-rational "avoidance behaviors" in modern society), and that they symbolically communicate core societal values. Klawans appreciates the way Milgrom, when it comes to interpreting Levitical impurity laws, has taken the ball from Mary Douglas and run with it: his interpretation of these laws is nuanced and profound, generally respecting the foundational theological convictions that are expressed through such laws.[57] But on sacrifice, Klawans concludes that Milgrom takes a step back, reverting to a focus on evolutionist reconstructions of how Israel's sacrificial cult might have developed—and he generally expresses relief that even more primitive ideas have at least been demythologized—rather than paying full attention to "what is going on in the text itself."[58]

As an alternative to these evolutionist approaches to interpreting ancient sacrificial practices, Klawans invites scholars to read the text in its current form[59] to see how sacrifice interacts with purity rules to form

---

to the demand for earthy submission. In the end, a wall forms between the reader and the text; the new "literal" meaning is remarkably obscure, even esoteric, where words that seem to refer to God actually refer to human maneuvering, once you have the eyes to see. For more on this concern, see Moberly, *The Bible, Theology, and Faith*, 179 ff.

56. Watts himself says that Klawans' critique of Milgrom is "virtually the opposite" of his own. Watts, *Ritual and Rhetoric*, 6, footnote 17.

57. See chapter five, below.

58. Klawans, *Purity, Sacrifice, and the Temple*, 29. This tendency in Milgrom is especially evident in his essay, "On the Theory of Sacrifice," where he, for example, calls the remnants of the idea that sacrifice is food for the gods in the Bible "fossilized vestiges from a dim past. . . ." Milgrom, *Leviticus 1–16*, 440.

59. Because he is suspicious of the idea that scholars are competent to splice up sources within Leviticus and then order them by what is more or less primitive, Klawans

a complex but coherent symbolic system. The goal is not to find a single "theory" that can exhaustively explain sacrifice, but instead to identify "organizing principles" that will help illuminate the basic presuppositions that shape the priestly imagination. Klawans says that these "organizing principles will need to be concerns central to the priestly traditions of the Pentateuch, which will help us understand better the dynamic between the systems of sacrifice and defilement."[60] He identifies two: (a) a desire to imitate God and (b) a hope to attract and maintain God's presence in the temple. These themes will be a point of focus in the chapters on the theology of Yom Kippur later in this book.

It seems to me that Klawans, by inviting us to think symbolically, and even analogically, draws us into the theological universe of the priestly writers more profoundly and consistently than Watts does; in fact, Klawans imposes less on the text even though he requires more imagination from the reader, who must embed himself or herself in a very different culture with a distinct theological vocabulary. As Benjamin Sommer points out, studies that never get past reconstructing and arguing about the supposed "geo-political conditions" that may lay behind the text are poorly attuned to the theological dimension of the ideas presented, and they thus "avoid grappling with these ideas' deep humanistic significance."[61] Klawans' symbolical reading is less guilty of this weakness which is all too common in modern biblical studies. Whether or not there may have been interest in achieving greater financial security or communal authority on the part of a possible author, I take all of this as secondary to the real message of these scriptures, which also happens to be the surface meaning: training in the sacrificial worship of the living God in the tabernacle.

Understanding this debate between Watts, Milgrom, and Klawans helps us to approach the crucial question of this section in a more sophisticated way. The question is this: why does the burnt offering have priority in priestly theology? What does this offering signify? In closely reading Leviticus 1, we can identify three primary themes relevant to

---

favors a "synchronic readings" of the text in its current form, "and as an integral part of the Pentateuch as a whole," as advocated by Rolf Rendtorff and Joseph Blenkinsopp. See Klawans, *Purity, Sacrifice, and the Temple*, 49–52. This does not mean that Klawans denies that the text has a history—that more than one hand has contributed to its composition—but only that reconstructions of that pre-history, given the extremely limited evidence we have, frequently draw on assumptions that say more about the interpreter than the people she is describing.

60. Klawans, 48.

61. Benjamin D. Sommer, *The Bodies of God and the World of Ancient Israel* (Cambridge: Cambridge University Press, 2011), 96–97.

these questions. First, the idea of "drawing near," second the emphasis on spotlessness, and third the concept of "ascending." Thus, turning to the first point: the description of this offering begins with Leviticus 1:3, which says, "If an *'olah* is his offering. . . ." The word for "offering" is *qorbān*, which means "that which is brought near"—the root is *k-r-b*, "to draw near"—and is translated in the LXX by the Greek word *dōron*, "gift."[62] The term *qorban* is used 34 times in the first sixteen chapters of Leviticus, and it is an umbrella category for the different kinds of gifts that the Israelites might bring. It is important to point out that using the word *qorban* puts the emphasis on a movement toward something or someone, without any violent connotations (unlike the connotation of the English word sacrifice today).[63] The sense of this opening phrase, therefore, is, "If it is by a burnt offering that you draw near. . . ," and the presupposition would seem to be that God *wants* Israel to draw near to him in the tabernacle and that the rituals described in Leviticus are *intended* to promote such communion—without losing sight of God's holiness and otherness.[64] In Exodus 40, God's Presence, God's Glory, descends and tabernacles at the Tent of Meeting—God has drawn near to his people—and now in Leviticus 1, God instructs Israel on how to draw near to him. David Fagerberg says "liturgy is the trysting place of God," and this is very much true of the tabernacle/temple and its liturgy.[65]

When Israel draws near, what shall she bring? If it is a burnt offering, the chapter specifies the acceptable type of animal—whether it is from the herd (cattle) or flock (sheep or goats)—"a male without blemish (*tāmîm*)" (Leviticus 1:3, 10).[66] Thus, the second key element is that the gift shall be spotless. For Milgrom, along with most other modern commentators, the understanding of spotlessness in this text pertains to

---

62. Milgrom, *Leviticus 1-16*, 145. Cf. Christian Eberhart, "A Neglected Feature of Sacrifice in the Hebrew Bible: Remarks on the Burning Rite on the Altar," *Harvard Theological Review* 97, no. 4 (October 1, 2004): 491; Christian Eberhart, *The Sacrifice of Jesus: Understanding Atonement Biblically* (Minneapolis: Fortress Press, 2011), 71; Morales, *Who Shall Ascend?*, 214–15.

63. For a nice overview of the ways in which the Latin term "sacrifice" and the Hebrew word "*korban*" are similar and different, see Joshua Berman, *The Temple: Its Symbolism and Meaning Then and Now* (Northvale, N.J.: J. Aronson, 1995), 114–16.

64. David Bentley Hart spells out the theological implications when he says, "Before all else, though, sacrifice is *qurban*, a drawing nigh, an approach in love to the God who graciously approaches his people in love." Hart, *Beauty of the Infinite*, 350.

65. Fagerberg, *Theologia Prima*, 108. Fagerberg borrows this poetic imagery from G. K. Chesterton.

66. It is also possible to bring a bird as a burnt offering (a turtledove or young pigeon), but the requirement for spotlessness is, in these cases, not repeated.

physical perfection specifically.[67] Klawans approaches this requirement from an interesting perspective: the need to provide a spotless animal is demanding on the offerer. She or he must pay careful attention to the herd or flock, diligently protecting the animal from injury, and carefully inspecting each one to see whether it is suitable.[68] There is a call to excellence, one that is demanding on the offerer as well, and therefore it is perhaps no surprise that the same word also came to characterize human perfection. An especially significant text that uses *tāmîm* in reference to human spotlessness is Genesis 17:1, which is generally identified as a Priestly text. It reads, "When Abram was ninety-nine years old, the Lord appeared to Abram and said to him, 'I am *El Shaddai* [God Almighty]. Walk in my ways and be blameless (*tāmîm*)." Similarly, in Deuteronomy, God tells his people not to mimic the disgraceful behaviors of the surrounding people: "You shall be perfect (*tāmîm*) before YHWH your God" (18:13). Both the Priestly writer and the Deuteronomist use the cultic term "without blemish" to describe how Abram's descendants must be before God; the word expresses the high moral demands made on the covenant people. By the time of Philo, the requirement of an unblemished sacrifice was understood as a "figure" that expresses what God seeks from us: "they must come with no infirmity or ailment or evil affection in the soul, but must endeavour to have it sanctified and free throughout from defilement, that God when He beholds it may not turn away His face from the sight."[69] As Klawans suggests, the offerer's careful inspection of the sacrificial animal comes to be seen as an imitation of the way God carefully inspects us to see if we have remained spotless. There is no doubt that the repeated emphasis on the notion that the offering must be without blemish is hugely significant in the Levitical cult, and profoundly shaped the interpretation of biblical sacrifice.[70]

67. Leigh Trevaskis argues against this general consensus that the use of *tāmîm* in Leviticus 1 pertains only to physical criteria without ethical implications. In cognitive linguistic terms, Trevaskis says that physical wholeness is clearly intended within the cultic domain, which is primary. Nevertheless, the ancient interpreter would have access to a secondary domain for interpreting the word *tāmîm*, and thus the need for ethical integrity is already suggested by the priestly writer. *Holiness, Ethics and Ritual in Leviticus* (Sheffield: Sheffield Phoenix Press, 2011), chaps. 5 and 6.

68. Klawans, *Purity, Sacrifice, and the Temple*, 63–64.

69. Philo, *On the Special Laws, On the Virtues. On Rewards and Punishments*, trans. F. H. Colson (Cambridge, MA: Harvard University Press, 1939), I.167, page 195. See Klawans, 120–21.

70. Notably, the connection between sacrificial spotlessness and the demands of virtuous living carries over into the New Testament. The Septuagint goes in two directions with the term *tāmîm*. In the cultic texts, the word is nearly always rendered *ámōmon*

Third, the word *'olah* itself literally means "that which ascends," from the root word *'alah*, "to ascend, go up." Once again, we should notice the directionality of the cultic practices; returning to Leviticus 1:3, the hyper-literal rendering of "If his offering is a burnt offering. . ." would be, "If by 'that which ascends' he 'draws near.'. . ." The horizontal imagery of drawing near to God is linked with the vertical imagery of ascension.[71] The *'olah* is the paradigmatic ascending sacrifice. It is the only offering where "the animal is completely incinerated on the altar."[72] This explains why it is called a "burnt offering" in English, even though the word *olah* does not actually derive from the verb "to burn."

But again, just *why* is this type of offering repeatedly given priority? Watts offers a convincing suggestion: "the biblical writers regard this offering as most representative of Israel's worship, as best expressing the proper worship of God."[73] Unlike other offerings, in which a token portion of the gift is consumed by fire while the rest is consumed by the offerer or the priest, the burnt offering represents complete "letting go," absolute freedom from grasping; it is economic foolishness, wild exuberance, an absurd excess. Every morning and every evening, the temple would open and close with this symbol: I hand life over completely.[74]

That's easy enough to do, one might respond, when the "life" being handed over is not your own! Here it is the poor bull, or ram, or goat which is the gift, and a person's livestock rarely constitutes his or her entire life. But, returning to Moriah, the situation was different for Abraham: remember, God identifies Isaac, points toward Moriah, and says,

---

(spotless, immaculate) while Deuteronomy 18:13 is translated *téleios* (perfect, complete). Thus, Jesus insists, "Be perfect (*téleioi*), therefore, as your heavenly Father is perfect (*téleiós*)" (Matthew 5:48), while Paul exclaims that the Father "chose us in Christ before the foundation of the world to be holy and blameless (*amōmous*) before him in love" (Ephesians 1:4). Here we have two tributaries stemming from the same Hebrew cultic word, *tāmîm*. Other texts that refer to human spotlessness include Ephesians 5:27, Philippians 2:15, Colossians 1:22, Jude 1:24. There are additional texts that even more explicitly link Christ to the spotless sacrificial animal: Hebrews 9:14 and 1 Peter 1:19.

71. With this in mind, Morales translates *'olah* as "ascension offering." See *Who Shall Ascend?*, 60, 62; 133–137.

72. Milgrom, *Leviticus 1-16*, 172. There is an exception to this; Leviticus 7:8 mentions that the hide goes to the priest who offers the burnt offering.

73. Watts, *Ritual and Rhetoric*, 71.

74. As Joshua Berman puts it, with reference to the Akedah, "[The *'olah*] symbolizes our willingness to devote our entire existence to the service of God . . . it is a vivid symbol of [the offerer's] own dedication to God in the entirety of his essence." Berman, *The Temple*, 123–24. See also Leigh Trevaskis' argument for why the burnt offering is "P's 'most holy' offering *par excellence*." *Holiness, Ethics and Ritual in Leviticus*, 260; cf. 251–61.

"offer him there as a burnt offering"—in Abraham's cultural context, this *does* represent the handing over of his entire life, as we have seen. Abraham is invited to "draw near" to God by giving up his beloved son. He is told that his son should ascend to God on that great mountain, in smoke and ashes. The theme of ascension is especially prominent in Genesis 22:2, when Abraham is told "to offer him there as a burnt offering on one of the heights"—the word translated "to offer" has, in Hebrew, the very same root as the word "burnt offering"—the root ʿ-*L*-*H*—and so the sense of going up or ascending is doubly emphasized.

In the section describing Abraham's love for Isaac, we reviewed the belief that Philo and Josephus held that Isaac was a moral exemplar. Philo speaks of Isaac's "great bodily beauty," his "excellence of soul," and his "perfection of virtues."[75] Josephus agrees that Isaac practiced "every virtue" and showed "zeal for the worship of God."[76] Of course, none of this is mentioned in Genesis 22, and it could be dismissed as a nationalistic exaltation of ancestors. But in this case, in this context, an argument can be made that their claim is rooted in the text precisely because Abraham was called to offer Isaac as an ʿ*olah*. That word carries with it the *t mîm* requirement: Isaac's moral spotlessness is strongly implied in the fact that God identified him as a suitable offering.

The rabbinic tradition continued to build on this connection, as they insisted more and more forcefully that Isaac fully participated in the offering of his life. This interpretation, again, was not unrelated to the text. As Jon Levenson points out, most guesses on Isaac's age put him in his 20s or 30s. After putting the wood for the fire on Isaac's back and leaving behind the servants, it says Abraham and Isaac "walked together" (v. 6). Isaac next asks his father where the animal was for the offering, and Abraham says, "God will see to it. . . ," and the text again affirms, they "walked together" (v. 8). According to Levenson, "the first time these words appear ["the two walked together"], Abraham has just assured his two attendants that he and Isaac will, after an act of worship, return to them. But by the second time, Isaac has accepted his mandated role as a victim. And the two of them still walked together, or to render the Hebrew *yahdāw* more literally, [they walk] 'as one.'"[77] As the union of purpose between father and son became a greater focus in later interpretations, Isaac's faith seemed to soar even higher. For example, Josephus has Abraham explain to Isaac that he has been chosen as a sacrifice, and then Josephus reports:

---

75. Philo, *On Abraham*, 85.
76. Josephus, *Jewish Antiquities*, 4:109–11.
77. Levenson, *The Death and Resurrection of the Beloved Son*, 134.

The son of such a father could not but be brave-hearted, and Isaac received these words with joy. He exclaimed that he deserved never to have been born at all, were he to reject the decision of God and of his father and not readily resign himself to what was the will of both . . . and with that he rushed to the altar and his doom.[78]

This chapter began with a discussion of the word *hinneni*, Abraham's readiness before God, and now the interpretive tradition has found that Abraham and Isaac are "as one" in this attitude. One can plausibly maintain, given the connections we have been tracing, that this story constitutes the definitive illumination of the full meaning of the crucial word "without blemish" in the Jewish tradition, and it also represents the quintessential example of ʿolah.

The Fifth Word: raʾah

After the journey, Abraham and Isaac arrive together at the place chosen by God, and the scriptures describe how Abraham builds an altar there. And then, "Abraham picked up the knife to slay (*lišḥōṭ*) his son" (Genesis 22:10).[79] With these words, the original disposition that Abraham articulates in verse 1 (*hinneni*) is brought to fulfillment by father and son on the mountain of Moriah. Here we are meant to find a freedom of the will before God that clings to nothing, that hands back everything—even that which is most precious.[80] God[81] interrupts again: "Abraham! Abraham!," and the patriarch responds, "*hinneni.*" The dialogue that frames this entire drama is repeated after the act, the only difference being that this time the old man's name is spoken twice, effectively

78. Josephus, *Jewish Antiquities*, vol. 4, bk. I:232; quoted in Levenson, *The Death and Resurrection of the Beloved Son*, 191.

79. To emphasize once more the cultic context for these words, I should point out that the word *shachat*, to slay, is used thirty-three times in Leviticus by P, always in reference to the ritual slaughter of the sacrificial animal. The same word is used elsewhere in the Bible for killing more generally, but given the centrality of ʿolah terminology in Genesis 22, *shachat* would be the most natural verb to use. Compare Leviticus 1:5, 1:11, 16:15, etc.

80. Nahum Sarna uses a word that has a rich history in the mystical tradition: "disinterested." He says, "The totally disinterested nature of his devotion to God must be established beyond any doubt." Sarna, *Genesis*, 393.

81. The text indeed says that it is the "*mal ʾakh* YHWH, angel of the LORD" who calls out to Abraham. According to Benjamin Sommer, the word *mal ʾakh*, which literally means "messenger," in J and E often refers to "a small-scale manifestation of God's own presence, and the distinction between the messenger and God is murky." Therefore, he says, the term is more similar to an "avatar" (an idea from Indian religion) than what we today think of when we say "angel." Sommer, *Bodies of God*, 40.

affirming and re-affirming his vocational identity. Father-of-Many! Father-of-Many! The truth of this name is doubled through the action that epitomizes its true meaning: "readiness, alertness, attentiveness, receptivity, and responsiveness."

The theme of vision weaves through the narrative from beginning to end, with the word *ra'ah* appearing numerous times. We have already observed that the very name Moriah may gently allude to the importance of seeing. The word is used explicitly three times in the course of the story. First, on the journey, Abraham looks up and *sees* the place where God is sending him.[82] Second, after Isaac asks why they had not brought a sacrificial animal, Abraham says that God will see (to) it.[83] Third, after Abraham's hand is stayed, he *looks up* and sees a ram caught in the thicket.[84] More will be said below about the substitution of the ram for Isaac, but for now, we will focus on the most important use of the Hebrew word *ra'ah* in Genesis 22. After offering the ram as an *'olah*, Abraham names the sacred mountain. It says, "And Abraham named that site *Adonai-yireh*, whence the present saying, 'On the mount of the Lord there is vision'" (Genesis 22:14). Note the emphasis on *vision*. The previous chapter of this book featured a Balthasarian meditation on the theme of glory, the divine splendor that communicates itself—gives itself—as revelation to human beings: God making himself available to our perception. Especially in priestly theology, the temple on Mount Zion is at the center of this aesthetic and visionary experience. The claims made for this location are extravagant, even though by all accounts, the hill on which the temple stood is quite modest. Additionally, anthropologists have shown that the idea of a sacred mountain was pervasive in the ancient world. So, to reiterate a central question from the previous chapter on theo-aesthetics: why should *this* particular site in Judea have any claim to our attention today? Why focus on this seemingly arbitrary peak?

These questions have motivated this extended meditation on Genesis 22, an episode that could be called—from the perspective of temple theology—"the action." It is one of the central dramas of the Hebrew Bible, and within the canon itself, it is offered as the foundational narrative of

---

82. "On the third day, Abraham looked up and *saw* (*way-yar*) the place. . ." (Genesis 22:4).

83. "And Abraham said, 'God will see to the sheep for His burnt offering, my son'" (Genesis 22:8). The word here translated "sheep" is *seh*, and it is a more general term, meaning "one of the flock," and could be in reference to a sheep or a goat. Cf. Moberly, *The Bible, Theology, and Faith*, 107, footnote 52.

84. "When Abraham looked up, his eye fell upon a ram, caught in the thicket by its horns" (Genesis 22:13).

the temple site. Now, immediately after the climax of the story, the site is named, and with that name, we return to the aesthetic theme of vision. The name given by Abraham, *YHWH-yir'eh*, can be read in a few different ways, each of them with its own theological significance. First, the name echoes verse 8, when Isaac asks about the burnt offering animal, and Abraham says " *'elohim yir'eh lo*, God will see for himself" the sheep for the offering.[85] Moberly explains that "The context seems to require that 'see' here has the sense not merely of sight but of sight leading to corresponding action. . . ."[86] There is a link between vision and provision, when God "sees," God "sees to it," God ensures that the vision is fulfilled. With this in mind, Abraham's ultimate name for the place, "*YHWH-yir'eh*," is often rendered as "the LORD will provide" by translators. Then the text's commentary on the name—*behar YHWH yērā'eh*—is translated, "On the mountain of the LORD it will be provided."

The only problem is, these translations hide the significant theme of vision (though the Latin etymology of "provide" does maintain the nod to vision: *pro-videō*). It would be as accurate to say that Abraham names the place "the LORD sees," and then say, "On the mount of the LORD there is vision."[87] But another valid way to read Abraham's original name for the site is, "the LORD is seen,"[88] and thus, "On the mountain of YHWH, he can be seen."[89] In other words, the name could suggest that at this place, both God sees, and God is seen. The place where God sees is equally the place of theophany.

Jon Levenson has analyzed the common rabbinic explanation for the origin of the name of Jerusalem. The rabbis said that the name nods to the fact that the land was both the site of Abraham's test, *YHWH-yir eh*, and home to Melchizedek (king of Salem; cf. Psalm 76:2). Thus the two names for the land were put together: Yireh-salem, Yĕrûšālaim.[90] Acknowledging that this is an "unscientific" etymology for the word Jerusalem, Levenson goes on to explore whether or not the emphasis on sight

85. See the note on Alter, *Genesis*, 105.

86. Moberly, *The Bible, Theology, and Faith*, 107–8.

87. Or, for Alter, "On the mount of the LORD there is sight." *Genesis*, 106.

88. Cf. Stanley Walters, "Wood, Sand and Stars: Structure and Theology," *Toronto Journal of Theology* 3, no. 2 (September 1, 1987): 310; Hamilton, *The Book of Genesis*, 114; Wenham, *Genesis 16-50*, 110–11.

89. Levenson, *Sinai and Zion*, 95; Jon D. Levenson, "The Jerusalem Temple in Devotional and Visionary Experience," in *Jewish Spirituality, Vol 1* (New York: Crossroad, 1986), 44.

90. This explanation is spelled out in *Genesis Rabbah* 56:10; cf. Levenson, *The Death and Resurrection of the Beloved Son*, 119.

in Genesis 22 could have been, for the author of the narrative, an intentional "pun" on the word Jerusalem, and thus an allusion to the temple.[91] All of this can be added to our earlier review of the word "Moriah" to further suggest that the drama of Abraham and Isaac was always intended to speak to the theological origins of the temple. Thus when we emphasize that "Mount Zion is a place of visionary experience,"[92] the action of Abraham and Isaac at that location is an integral part of the vision.

We can press the issue one more time: just what is it that God sees at Moriah? There is a preposition used in the narrative that may help us address this crucial question. At Genesis 22:13, we read that the ram is offered *in the place of* (*tḥt*) Isaac. Some later rabbinic interpreters, turning to a secondary meaning of the word *tḥt*, argued that the ram was sacrificed *after* Isaac. This interpretation was used to suggest that Abraham and Isaac really did carry out the sacrifice, Isaac's blood really was shed, and his flesh was even reduced to ashes, but then God resurrected him.[93] While this interpretation constitutes a rather dramatic elaboration of the biblical text itself, it also represents a profound theological insight that is true to the letter of the text. The fact is, Isaac really was given over completely—even assuming, as the obvious reading suggests, that the knife did not touch him—and the slaying of the ram indeed occurs both *after* the total sacrifice of Isaac, and also *in that same place*: in the same location, geographically, but also as a sacramental sign that shares the same theological-symbolic space.[94]

As the rabbis insist again and again, based partly on their expansion of the Genesis story, what God sees on Mount Moriah is Isaac's blood. In

91. Levenson says, "Given the centrality of Jerusalem to the history of Israel from the tenth century B.C.E. on, it is striking that the name of the city appears in the Pentateuch not once. . . . Whatever its explanation, the reticence about naming Jerusalem may account both for 'Salem' in chapter 14 and for 'Adonai-yireh' in chapter 22. In each instance, the text may be deliberately employing a term that only suggests Jerusalem and does not name it." Levenson, 123. Compare van Seters, *Abraham in History and Tradition*, 238.

92. Levenson, *Sinai and Zion*, 95.

93. Kessler, *Bound by the Bible*, 126–28.

94. Kessler shows that the rabbinic and patristic interpretations are somewhat different here: "Thus, in contrast to the church fathers who described the ram as ransoming Isaac, *the rabbis described the ram as representing Isaac.* The ram's importance is dependent upon its association with Isaac." Kessler, 144, emphasis added. The Jewish tradition refers more and more to "Isaac's blood" and "Isaac's ashes," while it is the ram that dies. Perhaps it is appropriate, from the perspective of the later tradition, to imagine Isaac looking upon the ram's blood and ashes and saying, "This is my blood, these are my ashes." The sacrifice of the ram is increasingly understood as significant because it is in fact the sacrifice of Isaac.

a couple of chapters we will explore the fact that, in priestly theology, blood is not the portent of death, but the great symbol of life. Isaac truly is "the boy who lived"; for the early interpreters, his life is characterized by total freedom, abandoning even what is most precious to him, in radical obedience before the God who has proven his faithfulness. In all of this, Isaac mirrors the remarkable *hinneni*-freedom of Abraham, who offered everything he had, his single hope in life and death. Father and son truly walk as one. Together, called by God, they put into motion a self-giving that becomes synonymous with the word "life," which in principle reverses the cursed death of Adam's clenched fist, and therefore establishes this site as truly the new Eden, the place of superabundant life.[95] In a unique way, both Abraham and Isaac are totally given up, they ascend together through the fire of a heart that "fears God." The gift given to Abraham and Sarah, the beloved son, is reverently returned, and then YHWH confirms his perfect mercy and goodness *again* by giving *even more*. David Bentley Hart puts it best. Isaac, he says, "is the entire gift, returned before the gift has been truly given; but then God . . . gives the gift again. . . . Henceforth Israel is doubly given, and can know itself only as gift, imparted by God and offered ceaselessly back to God, in the infinity of love's exchange."[96]

The main theme of Jon Levenson's great book is found in its title: *The Death and Resurrection of the Beloved Son*. Levenson notices the key pattern in the Hebrew Scriptures: the beloved son belongs to God, the son endures some kind of death (often a humiliation), and the son is restored and elevated. Isaac, therefore, is the icon of a redeemed life, a type of life that passes through death into an even greater abundance. The blood that courses through his veins has indeed been given as a burnt offering, but without final loss, and therefore Isaac has a type of resurrection life. As Hart so brilliantly emphasizes, *this very same blood* is shared by all of Israel—from that day to today—because Isaac is the source of the bloodline. All Israel must live up to the identity that is already most intimately hers, from her beating heart to her every limb. Yes, Israel, especially when she lives as Abraham and Isaac did, is the resurrection people—perhaps, from a Christian perspective, not yet the full consummation of this identity, as the events of Good Friday and Easter deepen and expand the mystery already present on Mount Moriah, but this fact does not at all diminish the true goodness, great beauty, and pure grace that is at the foundation of Israel's life.

95. For the connection between Adam and Abraham in Genesis, see N. T. Wright, *The New Testament and the People of God* (Minneapolis: Fortress Press, 1992), 262–66.
96. Hart, *Beauty of the Infinite*, 352.

This is the mystery of Moriah, and the Jewish theological tradition has meditated on it deeply. We have already mentioned that the morning and evening burnt offering, the Tamid, is a liturgical *inclusio* that contains all other sacrifices at the temple. Exploring the meaning of this practice, the rabbis were as perceptive and creative as ever. They said, "when Israel would sacrifice the daily offering on the altar and recite this verse ['on the ṣ-p-n-h side of the altar'], the Holy One (blessed be He!) would remember the binding of Isaac."[97] This is in reference to Leviticus 1:11, which specifies where the burnt offering is to be sacrificed: "It shall be slaughtered *before the Lord* on the *north side* (ṣāpōnâ) of the altar. . . ." As you can see, the vocalized Hebrew in this verse is the word ṣāpōnâ, which does mean north side. But another possible vocalization for the same Hebrew consonants is ṣĕpûnâh, which means "hidden," or even, "treasured up" (cf. Psalm 119:11). By "playfully misreading" the text in this way, the words recited morning and evening are "hidden (ṣĕpûnâh) before the Lord,"[98] as if the priest calls to mind a mystery treasured up in the heart of God. What is it that God sees when these words are spoken? It is the blood, the life, of Isaac, given by Abraham and given again by God. In this way, the entire temple cult is, first and foremost, rooted in the mystery of the Akedah, a binding which is true liberation for those who follow in the footsteps of the ones who said *hinneni*.[99]

This is what God sees, and somehow in this vision, *God also is seen.* Certainly in the burnt offering, there is the God who provides the ram, who is faithful to his covenant, and who freely gives and gives again. Perhaps also, there is here a glimmer of the truth that will unfold with greater clarity in the history of revelation. God, we have said, in calling Abraham and awaiting his response, is the God who makes space for the freedom of the other, who desires genuine and free communion. There is

---

97. *Leviticus Rabbah* 2.11, quoted in Gary A. Anderson, *Sin: A History* (New Haven: Yale University Press, 2009), 201; cf. Levenson, *The Death and Resurrection of the Beloved Son*, 185; Kessler, *Bound by the Bible*, 143.

98. Anderson, *Sin*, 201.

99. ". . . in the rabbinic mind, Israel's daily sacrificial service was a way of memorializing the heroic self-offering of the patriarch Isaac. Every time Israel made her sacrifice on earth, God contemplated Isaac's merits that were stored in heaven." Anderson, 201. Similarly, ". . . we must see in the name 'Moriah' an effort to endow Abraham's great act of obedience and faith with ongoing significance: the slaughter that he showed himself prepared to carry out was the first of innumerable sacrifices to be performed on that site." See also Levenson, *The Death and Resurrection of the Beloved Son*, 174. Peter Leithart refers to "the role of the Aqedah as the foundation and background for all sacrifice. . . ." Peter J. Leithart, *Delivered from the Elements of the World: Atonement, Justification, Mission* (Downers Grove, IL: IVP Academic, 2016), 317, footnote 56; cf. 113.

vulnerability and self-giving in this love. Abraham's response, in word and act, signifies an analogous self-giving that comes to exemplify life's core meaning: not to cling to the self, but to hand oneself over in freedom and love in God. In the fullness of time, the tradition stemming from Mount Moriah would come to understand that such self-giving in fact captures the inner mystery of the triune God who is Love. God is glimpsed on this mountain because Abraham, Isaac, and Jacob[100] radiate the divine glory of the human being fully alive. In other words, perhaps the mutual-self-sacrificial motion of the three patriarchs on Moriah is, itself, one of YHWH's most luminous theophanies in the Hebrew Bible.

A Final Word: Akedah

In a delightful twist, the story that captures that paradox of true freedom and life through self-giving is remembered as "the binding," *akedah*. Despite the way this particular drama is so often denounced and dismissed in modern thought, the Abrahamic religions remain bound to the mystery of Moriah, and rightly so, because, despite the critics' rush to distance themselves from the events described in Genesis 22, Abraham's *'olah* and the re-presentation of this one sacrifice in the priestly liturgical service on Zion contains one of the most profound truths of the Jewish and Christian faith. Even if, in Genesis, this truth is still somewhat hidden, like a shadow that captures the reality only in blurred outline, nevertheless the truth is here, and thus we must return again and again to Moriah/Zion to meditate on its meaning.

One of the primary goals of this book thus far has been to critically assess the notion that the temple is the site of divine anger and retribution, violence, and death. It is necessary to highlight the fact that the story of Abraham and Isaac has nothing whatever to do with punishment: there is not even the slightest hint that God calls for Isaac's life to punish Abraham, or anyone, for anything. This story is more analogous to the tempting of Adam and Eve in Eden, but unlike our first parents, Abraham succeeds in establishing the pattern for paradisiac life—his *hinneni*, which calls forward toward Mary's *fiat*, becomes the first word in the new creation. It is as if Genesis 22 provides the basic coordinates for finding the way back to the sacred center, the place where humanity and God dwell in peace.

By the same token, this affirmation does not eliminate the difficulty that the "offering" demanded involves separating body and blood, letting lifeblood empty out from the flesh. Why should this be part of the com-

---

100. Jacob/Israel as present already in Isaac's loins, as Hart says.

mand? Even though I just argued that there is no mention of sin in the narrative of Isaac's binding, perhaps this aspect points to the vast difference between Genesis 2–3 and Genesis 22. One remembers the shattering words of Jesus Christ: "Whoever comes to me and does not hate father and mother, wife and children, brothers and sisters, yes, and even life itself, cannot be my disciple" (Luke 14:26). These words seem uncharacteristic and absurd. But it is apparently necessary: something about the human condition is so tied up in the attitude of craving, of clinging, of self-centeredness—analogous to the state of Saṃsāra, in Buddhist terms—that the medicine seems for us like violence and death. To give up the self-destructive hold on finite things, to hand them over completely, even to die to them and "hate" them, and to finally allow oneself to be suspended in divine freedom and love requires something radical, something seemingly impossible, but there is no other way.[101]

Neither Abraham nor Isaac is called to die in the story as punishment—there is certainly no sense of propitiation here—but they are called to hand themselves over because *this is what it means to live*. The goodness of the covenant is not in growing in number or in wealth, but in living with God, and such life is characterized by giving, not taking. Abraham had Isaac truly only after letting him go, giving him back, and recognizing what it means to be in communion with God. It is so often said that God "calls off" the sacrifice on the mountain, that God did not *actually* want Isaac's life, but this seems like an inadequate interpretation. God does in fact want Abraham to live out the truth of *hinneni*, to express in his actions the truth that to receive grace, one cannot cling to it but must enter into a relationship of giving, even as it relates to that which is most precious to us. This becomes the cornerstone of the covenant. Abraham passes the test because he does give up what is most precious to him in this world, and God again proves trustworthy because nothing is lost but the gift is returned. The total gift of Abraham and Isaac is then sacramentally realized and recapitulated in the offering of the ram. This should not be read as a retreat but as the joyful commemoration of what actually occurred: "Abraham! Abraham!" "*Hinneni*." These words sum up the entire drama, and they represent that basic truth that is repeated at both the beginning and the end of the story.

Finally, to reiterate, the abounding faithfulness of God to the covenant is shown vividly in the fact that Isaac is twice-given: he is not lost

---

101. For an illuminating reflection on the meaning of "hate" in such contexts, see David W. Fagerberg, *On Liturgical Asceticism* (Washington, D.C: The Catholic University of America Press, 2013), 66–67.

but given super-abundantly. If this were not the case, the story of Israel would have reached its grim end that day, and the accusation that the commanding "deity" was demonic would be well supported. It would be a story of violence and death, and that's it. Instead, the maxim concisely articulated by C. S. Lewis finds dramatic expression: "Put first things first and we get second things thrown in: put second things first and we lose both first and second things."[102] This is not to minimize the life of one's child, or anybody's life, as a mere "secondary" thing of ambiguous importance—any more than Christ shows disdain for parents or spouses or siblings or the self. The point, rather, is that the moment any one of these things is idolized as if it were ultimate, everything is lost. On the flip side, Balthasar says, "Grace . . . can belong internally to the creature to the extent that the latter is ready to return the gift: thus, Abraham never possessed his son more intimately than after he had gone through the ultimate renunciation."[103] The covenant is fully ratified when the covenant partner is unspoiled by ego, the son is truly received when the father's hands are unclenched. This is the truth that Abraham seems to perceive, almost intuitively, and therefore Abraham really is not blind in his obedience, but more perceptive than anyone. When we perceive the theologic at the root of the story—an understanding of reality that runs at cross-grains with everyday assumptions, but that nevertheless results in an even greater freedom and joy than we anticipate—it is easier to explain why this story has stood the test of time and remains the spiritual center of the Hebrew Bible.

102. This concise statement is from a letter Lewis wrote to Dom Bede Griffiths in 1951, *The Collected Letters of C. S. Lewis, Volume 3: Narnia, Cambridge, and Joy, 1950–1963* (New York: HarperCollins, 2007), 111; cf. Lewis's essay, "First and Second Things" in *God in the Dock: Essays on Theology and Ethics* (Grand Rapids, MI: Eerdmans, 1972), 278–81.

103. Hans Urs von Balthasar, *The Glory of the Lord: A Theological Aesthetics, Vol. 6: Theology: The Old Covenant* (San Francisco: Ignatius Press, 1991), 147.

CHAPTER 3

On Earth as in Heaven
(Theo-Logic)

We have seen that the temple is the place toward which Israel journeys to enjoy a personal, experiential, even visual encounter with the transforming glory of God. It is the place of praise and glorification. We have also seen that this vision of glory finds its definitive shape in the *hinneni*-act of Abraham (and Isaac) on the mountain top; that Abraham's free movement in response to the divine call helps to establish this space as holy ground, the dwelling place of the *kabod-YHWH* (the glory of God). True human freedom is seen in the person ready to respond positively to his or her God-given vocation, and true divine freedom is seen in the God who gives and gives again in abundance. For Israel, therefore, Zion is the site of aesthetics and ethics, glory and freedom. Our meditation on the theology of the temple cannot be complete, however, until we critically assess the logic of this mystery: how can this space iconographically represent the truth of creation and the truth of God? In other words, as we have already seen in both of the previous sections, there is an assertion that God is distinctively *present* in this place, that infinite divine Being and finite creaturely being somehow intersect and inter-dwell here. But is it not the case that infinity and finitude are mutually exclusive? How can they come together at Zion? The theological tradition cannot avoid these questions.

In the long history of Jewish meditation on the mystery of God's earthly dwelling place, we find several approaches to temple theology that attempt to conceptualize the relationship between God and creation in the sanctuary. In this section, I will briefly touch on two main ideas that are introduced in embryonic form in the Bible, but then develop much further in post-biblical literature: (1) the idea that the temple is a microcosm, and (2) the idea that the temple is the mirror of heaven. As Jonathan Klawans has noted,

> it is imperative to distinguish carefully between those sources that describe the temple as representing cosmos and those that describe a temple *in* heaven to which the Jerusalem temple constitutes an earthly analogue. While the two ideas are not contradictory, there

are many tensions between them, and, we will see, it is a general rule that ancient Jewish sources will articulate only one or the other of these approaches, and not both.[1]

While this is the general rule, it is not hard and fast. Distinguishing the "poles," to borrow a "Przywaraian" term that we have drawn on already in earlier chapters, may help us better notice and appreciate two tendencies in temple theology, but hopefully this schematic will not blind us to the nuances of the texts themselves.

The central question in this section is how God relates to creaturely being, and the two ways of understanding the temple outlined above correspond with two perspectives on God's relation with the world. (1) As the early Israelite theologians developed the notion that the temple is a microcosm, they wrestled with the question of God's immanence, the mystery of "God-in-creation." Similarly, (2) as early Israelite theologians reflected on the idea that the earthly temple reflects God's heavenly temple, they pondered the question of God's transcendence, the mystery of "God-beyond-creation." Notably, therefore, around the time when Plato and Aristotle were writing their respective metaphysics, striking the matches that would ignite Western philosophy, the ancient Jews were confronting analogous questions through theological meditation on a central symbol of their faith. When Jerusalem and Athens enter dialogue, Zion is the perfect place to host the conversation. In any case, anticipating the conclusion of this chapter, we should look back to the introduction of the first part of the book, which began with an awareness of the fact that the theme of incarnation has a pre-history in temple theology; now we will push this claim one step further to consider how the temple should rightly be seen as a rough-draft "concrete analogia entis." In other words, climbing Mount Zion from opposing banks, the temple themes of "God in creation" and "God beyond creation" will find each other at the peak, producing the formula "God beyond-and-in creation."[2] This is ultimately a Christological affirmation, but it is not without anticipation.

At the Center of Creation

As we have already discussed, one of the difficulties in interpreting ancient religious institutions and practices is that the symbolic worldview that animated these cultures is rarely described explicitly or systemati-

---

1. Klawans, *Purity, Sacrifice, and the Temple*, 111.
2. Cf. Przywara, *Analogia Entis*, 159–60.

cally, especially in the oldest material. The idea that the temple is a microcosm seems to be of first importance in understanding its theological significance in ancient Israel, and no temple theme has received more attention in modern academic literature,[3] even though the Greek word *mikrókosmos* obviously does not appear in the Hebrew Bible. The idea that the temple epitomizes and makes present in miniature the reality of the entire cosmos is a key idea, especially in the priestly writings.[4]

One of the reasons why modern scholars have been more attuned to the relationship between creation and temple building in priestly theology is the fact that there is now a much greater familiarity with the broader cultural and theological landscape. Since the nineteenth century, scholars of ancient Hebrew religion have had ready access to Mesopotamian creation myths like the well-known *Enuma Elish*, which bears a faint family resemblance to biblical creation accounts, like lost cousins raised in different worlds. This Babylonian story offers a general theogony, but focuses on the hero Marduk, who achieves preeminence by conquering Tiamat, the ocean goddess, bringer of chaos. From her defeated corpse he constructs our world, and from the blood of Tiamat's consort, Kingu, he creates human beings who, through their toil, will bring relief to the gods. In gratitude for Marduk's triumph, the other gods build him a temple; they say, "You have freed us, / Therefore, we must glorify you. / We will construct a House for Marduk known throughout the land / Its

---

3. There is now an extensive body of literature on this issue. See especially Klawans, *Purity, Sacrifice, and the Temple*, 113–23; Hayward, *The Jewish Temple*, 9–10; Levenson, "The Temple and the World," 284–88, 295–97; Levenson, "The Jerusalem Temple," 138–45; Levenson, *Sinai and Zion*, 138–45; Levenson, *Creation and the Persistence of Evil*, 78ff; Beale, *The Temple and the Church's Mission*, 32–36; Clements, *God and Temple*, 65–67; Andrei Orlov, *Divine Scapegoats: Demonic Mimesis in Early Jewish Mysticism* (Albany: SUNY Press, 2014), 37 ff.; Crispin H. T. Fletcher-Louis, *All the Glory of Adam: Liturgical Anthropology in the Dead Sea Scrolls* (Leiden: Brill, 2002), 62–66, 74–75; Crispin H. T. Fletcher-Louis, "Jesus, the Temple and the Dissolution of Heaven and Earth," in *Apocalyptic in History and Tradition*, ed. Christopher Rowland and John Barton (Sheffield: Sheffield Academic Press, 2002), 122–29; Fletcher-Louis, "God's Image, His Cosmic Temple and the High Priest," 82–83, 88–89; Elizabeth Bloch-Smith, "'Who Is the King of Glory?' Solomon's Temple and Its Symbolism," in *Scripture and Other Artifacts*, (Louisville, KY: Westminster/John Knox Press, 1994), 18–31; Yves Congar, *The Mystery of the Temple, or, The Manner of God's Presence to His Creatures from Genesis to the Apocalypse*, trans. R. F Trevett (Westminster, MD: Newman Press, 1962), 94–100. For Mesopotamian and Egyptian parallels to the cosmic symbolism in the Jerusalem Temple, see Bernd Janowski, "Der Tempel als Kosmos—Zur kosmologischen Bedeutung des Tempels in der Umwelt Israels," in *Egypt—Temple of the Whole World* (Leiden: Brill, 2003), 163–86.

4. Levenson defines "microcosm" succinctly when he says the temple is an "*eikōn*. . . . It is not one of many items in the world. It is the world *in nuce*, and the world is the Temple *in extenso*." Levenson, "The Temple and the World," 285.

precincts will be our place of comfort and rest."[5] Soon after receiving this promise, the gods build the temple and Marduk is enthroned in his new dwelling. What is notable here is the pattern, which has parallels in other ancient cosmogonies, of the god who is victorious over chaos, who establishes the world, and who commemorates the victory by building a temple, establishing a throne, and there receiving tribute.

The story of Genesis seems to depart from this pattern in numerous respects. No story of God's origin is given or implied. The idea of a cosmic war to defeat chaos hardly registers.[6] And then, in the priestly account of creation, while God rests upon completing his work, no temple is mentioned. This series of dissimilarities between *Enuma Elish* and Genesis 1 could imply that—against the surrounding cultural norms—the creation of the world and the establishment of God's tabernacle are very distinct in the biblical tradition, thus undermining the cosmic relevance of the temple, as if the themes of creation and covenant worship are unrelated in Israel. Over the last forty years, however, biblical scholars have started to notice long-forgotten parallels in the priestly materials that have catalyzed new interest in the temple as a cosmic reality.[7] In 1976, Joseph Blenkinsopp detected key formulas that appear

---

5. Victor Harold Matthews and Don C. Benjamin, *Old Testament Parallels: Laws and Stories from the Ancient Near East* (New York: Paulist Press, 2006), 19.

6. Jon Levenson's investigation of the *Chaoskampf* theme in the Hebrew Bible is a modern classic. He suggests that the memory of a war between YHWH and the sea god/chaos is retained in a number of passages—references to Yam, Leviathan, Amalek, and Gog all nod in this direction. Remnants of this ancient concept are retained even in the opening chapter of Genesis, he says, where the creation of the waters is not mentioned, and the goal might be understood as bringing order to the primordial abyss. Nevertheless, Levenson admits that the theme of cosmic war has largely been removed from the priestly account of creation. Levenson, *Creation and the Persistence of Evil*, esp. 1–13. Sommer has defended Kaufmann's affirmation of God's sovereignty in the Bible against Levenson; see Sommer, *Bodies of God*, 271–72 n.106. A different, useful approach to the questions raised by Levenson is found in Matthew Levering, *Scripture and Metaphysics: Aquinas and the Renewal of Trinitarian Theology* (Hoboken, NJ: Wiley-Blackwell, 2004), 77ff.

7. Jon Levenson identifies rabbinic passages where the building of the sanctuary is already correlated with the creation of the world. Levenson, *Creation and the Persistence of Evil*, 96–99. Even further back, one finds creation and temple repeatedly paired in priestly literature. In *Jubilees*, God "said to the angel of the presence, 'Write for Moses from the first creation until my sanctuary is built in their midst forever and ever. . .'" (1:28). The text then speaks of how the angel communicates to Moses "the division of years . . . from [the day of creation until] the day of the new creation when the heaven and earth and all of their creatures shall be renewed according to the powers of heaven and according to the whole nature of earth, until the sanctuary of the Lord is created in Jerusalem upon Mount Zion" (1:29). It seems that for the author of *Jubilees*, first creation and "new creation"—the creation of the sanctuary—go together.

frequently in the priestly texts: the "solemn conclusion," which marked the successful completion of a work, and the "execution-formula," which affirmed that the work was carried out exactly according to God's command.[8] By tracking the use of these formulas, Blenkinsopp identified three key moments in the priestly narrative: the creation of the world, the consecration of the tabernacle at Sinai, and the installation of the tabernacle in the land promised to Israel.[9] Looking carefully at the linguistic parallels between the creation and the sanctuary building "conclusion formulas" in P, Blenkinsopp finds that the consecration of the tabernacle is "the climax of creation."[10]

One year later, Moshe Weinfeld published a paper that made the important observation that the priestly account of God's creation in Genesis and the story of the building of God's sanctuary in Exodus both end in the same way: with a theology of Sabbath (Genesis 2:2–3 and Exodus 31:12–17). There are also a number of verbal echoes between these passages emphasizing "satisfactory completion of the enterprise commanded by God."[11] The goal, in both cases, is the same; as Levenson puts it, "the cosmogonic and the historical myths are not to be distinguished: their end point is the same, Yhwh and Israel at rest in His sacred precincts."[12] Later that same year, Peter J. Kearney published similar findings that linked creation and tabernacle.[13] He noticed that there are seven speeches in Exodus 25–31, each beginning with the words "The Lord said to Moses," and the seventh speech (as Weinfeld also said) focused on keeping the Sabbath. The first six speeches give precise instructions on how to set up the tabernacle, and even these speeches seem in some way to parallel the days of creation. The command to construct the lampstand is given in the first speech, which corresponds to the separation of light and darkness. The third speech addresses the fabrication of the "laver of bronze," which is elsewhere called "the Sea" (1 Kings 7:23), which could parallel God's separation of the dry land and the sea. The sixth speech, which would be

8. Joseph Blenkinsopp, "Structure of P," *Catholic Biblical Quarterly* 38, no. 3 (1976): 276.

9. Blenkinsopp, 278.

10. Blenkinsopp, 286.

11. Weinfeld's paper was published in Hebrew in 1977; it appeared in English a few years later. "Sabbath, Temple, and the Enthronement of the Lord: The Problem of the 'Sitz Im Leben' of Genesis 1: 1–2: 3," in *Mélanges Bibliques et Orientaux En l'honneur de M. Henri Cazelles*, ed. A. Caquot and M. Delcor (Kevelaer: Butzer & Bercker, 1981), 503.

12. Levenson, "The Jerusalem Temple," 52.

13. Peter J. Kearney, "Creation and Liturgy: The P Redaction of Ex 25–40," *Zeitschrift für die alttestamentliche Wissenschaft* 89, no. 3 (1977): 375–87.

associated with the creation of human beings, focuses on the craftsman Bezaleel, who is filled with the Spirit so as to carry out the work.[14]

Therefore, in the mid-1970s various lines of evidence for the connection between creation and tabernacle emerged, which helped spur renewed interest in the idea that the Jerusalem temple[15] was a cosmic institution. Due to the recent, more sympathetic readings of priestly texts, it is now regularly argued that, within this theology, the work of creation is not properly complete until the tabernacle is erected and God's glory dwells with his people. But perhaps this is putting it badly because, according to this approach, the tabernacle is not the final piece of the puzzle that must be added before creation is whole—it is, rather, the very same creation in miniature, with one notable distinction: at Sinai, God invites and empowers his creatures to partake in the work of establishing the cosmos.[16] The rhythm of Exodus is command and precise execution, and in some ways, even this mirrors Genesis, which reads similarly: "God said, 'Let there be an expanse in the midst of the water . . .' God made the expanse. . ." (Gn 1:6-7).[17] But now the execution is carried out by

14. While this work has been well received overall, some argue that a few of the parallels described by Kearney are a stretch. For an example of such a critique, Levenson, *Creation and the Persistence of Evil*, 83. As a result, efforts have been made to offer alternative explanations for how the seven days of Genesis are symbolically connected to the construction of the tabernacle of Exodus. Margaret Barker relates the days of Genesis to the assembly of the tabernacle in Exodus 40:17–32, where the execution formula "as the Lord had commanded Moses" is repeated seven times; Margaret Barker, "Time and Eternity: The World of the Temple," *Month* 34, no. 1 (2001): 16–17; Margaret Barker, *Temple Theology* (London: SPCK, 2004), 17–19. For a scholar who thinks the persuasiveness of Kearney's elaborate theory of correspondences has been underplayed, see Crispin Fletcher-Louis, "The Cosmology of P and Theological Anthropology in the Wisdom of Jesus Ben Sira," in *Of Scribes and Sages: Early Jewish Interpretation and Transmission of Scripture*, ed. Craig A Evans (Sheffield: Sheffield Academic Press, 2004), 11–14.

15. Notably, the sevenfold pattern from the passages on the wilderness sanctuary is carried over into temple building, too; 1 Kings 6:38 points out that it took Solomon seven years to build the temple. It was dedicated in the seventh month (1 Kings 8:2) during a seven-day festival (1 Kings 8:65). Thus, just as there are parallels between creation and building the tabernacle, something similar can be said with respect to the temple. Cf. Levenson, "The Temple and the World," 288–89.

16. Gary A. Anderson, *The Genesis of Perfection: Adam and Eve in Jewish and Christian Imagination* (Louisville, KY: Westminster John Knox Press, 2001), 201. Jonathan Klawans ties this in with the idea of *imitatio Dei*; Klawans, *Purity, Sacrifice, and the Temple*, 115–16. See also Frank Gorman, "Priestly Rituals of Founding: Time, Space, and Status," in *History and Interpretation: Essays in Honour of John H. Hayes*, ed. M. Patrick Graham, William P. Brown, and Jeffrey K. Kuan (Sheffield: Sheffield Academic Press, 1993).

17. Cf. Gary A. Anderson, "As We Have Heard So We Have Seen," *Conservative Judaism* 54 (2002): 55.

free human beings, invited to respond to God's word and (with the help of the Spirit; Exodus 35:31) themselves build the sanctuary where God will dwell. In so doing, they recapitulate the divine work of establishing order. Emphasis on establishing order is crucial for Levenson as well: "The concern of creation theology is not *creatio ex nihilo*, but the establishment of a benevolent and life-sustaining order, founded upon the demonstrated authority of God who is triumphant over all rivals."[18] A "benevolent and life-sustaining order"—this is key. True enough, Levenson says, this order is kept primarily through maintaining boundaries,[19] but are such boundaries the heart and soul of this "order"? What is at the very center of the "life-sustaining order" that is the hallmark of priestly creation theology?

According to Gary Anderson, the completion of the work of Moses is not simply in building a structure. The work is complete, instead, with the lighting of the sacrificial pyre, or in other words, with the inauguration of the Tamid sacrifice, the morning and evening burnt offerings. He says, "when the daily sacrifices began (Exodus 29:38–42 = Leviticus 9) *the goal of all creation would be consummated.*"[20] It is important to again emphasize, therefore, that tabernacle and sacrifice go together. The divine presence which is enjoyed at the tabernacle, and the corresponding cosmic order associated with the tabernacle, are inseparable from the burnt offerings that would open and close each day.[21] Therefore, the concept of cosmic order must be read in light of the Akedah theology that we explored in the previous chapter. If Levenson is indeed correct that the goal of creation is to establish a "benevolent and life-sustaining order," and if Anderson is right that the work of creation is consummated with the lighting of the sacrificial pyre, then it can rightly be argued that this order is ultimately characterized by the mysterious word *hinneni*: true freedom, true readiness before God.

18. Levenson, *Creation and the Persistence of Evil*, 47.
19. Levenson, 65.
20. Anderson, *Genesis of Perfection*, 202.
21. One finds hints of this idea already in the Greek translation of Sirach, which says that at the culmination of the Tamid sacrifice, the priests would lead the congregation in shouts and song: "Then all the people hastened together / And fell to their faces, to the ground. . . / And the people besought the Lord Most High / In prayer before the Merciful One, / Until the order (*kosmos*) of the Lord was completed." Sirach 50:17, 19 in Hayward, *The Jewish Temple*, 74. Hayward notices that in the translator's choice of words, "we are invited to see the implication that the *kosmos*, the universe, is somehow 'completed', Greek *suntelesthêi*, in the Tamid." Hayward, 79. It is sacrificial praise that brings the *kosmos* to completion.

Levenson continues by suggesting that order was "founded upon the demonstrated authority of God who is triumphant over all rivals," but again, if triumph over chaos is commemorated in the temple, in the microcosm, then it must be a triumph that works itself out through the self-giving posture that characterizes the sacrificial practices that bring life to the sanctuary. After all, God is seen, YHWH-*yireh*, specifically at the place where the *Abraham-hinneni* relationship is brought to act; somehow this way of being must itself be the undoing of every chaotic and demonic force. If the theology of the Akedah and the theology of Mount Zion are interrelated, and if the temple consummates and re-presents creation in its most essential form, then it must be the case that the very essence of the mystery of creation itself was somehow re-expressed on Mount Moriah.

Stemming from the widely recognized relationship between creation and temple-building in the ancient Near East, and the specific priestly interconnection between Genesis 1 and Exodus 25–40 as it has been described in recent studies,[22] one might well expect to find that the temple is rich with iconic, cosmic features. This expectation is heightened given the profound attention to detail expressed in the priestly texts on the construction of the tabernacle in Exodus, or the analogous way in which Ezekiel exhaustively describes exact temple measurements (Ezekiel 40–42); it seems clear that every room and piece of furniture is of utmost significance. It should therefore come as no surprise that the early interpretative tradition poured over each aspect of the temple in an attempt to understand its cosmic meaning.

The Psalmist says that YHWH "built His Sanctuary like the heavens, / like the earth that He established forever" (78:69).[23] For those able to interpret the symbols, the temple on Mount Zion is homologous, it has a like structure, to heaven and earth. Certainly, Philo and Josephus had such vision.[24] According to Josephus, if one studies the construction of the tabernacle, the priest's vestments, and the furniture, "every one of these objects is intended to recall and represent the universe, as [the observer] will find if he will but consent to examine them without prej-

---

22. Leviticus 8 and 9 should be included as well. See Gary A. Anderson, "Inauguration of the Tabernacle Service at Sinai," in *The Temple of Jerusalem: From Moses to the Messiah: In Honor of Professor Louis H. Feldman*, ed. Steven Fine (Leiden: Brill, 2011), 1–15.

23. See Levenson's commentary on this verse: *Creation and the Persistence of Evil*, 87.

24. The teachings of Philo and Josephus on the temple are extensively summarized in various places. See Hayward, *The Jewish Temple*, 108–53; Klawans, *Purity, Sacrifice, and the Temple*, 114–23.

udice and with understanding."[25] The general approach taken by both Philo and Josephus was to observe that the tabernacle or temple is subdivided into three areas of increasing holiness—the outer court (altar), the holy place (shrine), and the holy of holies (adytum or *debir*)[26]—and to correlate this tripartite structure with the threefold cosmos—earth and sea, the visible heavens, and the highest heaven. With this superstructure in place, the fixtures located in each realm were symbolically associated with the appropriate cosmic elements. Josephus and Philo focus on the shrine (symbolic of the visible heavens), and describe the menorah as a symbol of the "seven planets";[27] the twelve loaves of the bread of presence call to mind the twelve months of the year or the signs of the zodiac; and special emphasis was given to the veil, in which four colored materials are woven together, which are said to represent the four elements that make up the universe.[28] Modern scholars, using ancient Near Eastern parallels, have identified numerous other possible cosmic symbols. To pick just a couple of examples: as mentioned, the copper basin in the outer courtyard is called "the Sea," and the altar of burnt offerings may well have been related to the earth.[29]

Then, of course, there is the symbolism of the holy of holies, that perfectly square, windowless, innermost chamber of the temple. In Solomon's temple, this room contained the ark of the covenant with its

25. Josephus, *Jewish Antiquities* Book 3, Paragraph 7, Line 180.

26. On the "grades of sanctity in the tabernacle," see Menahem Haran, *Temples and Temple-Service in Ancient Israel: An Inquiry into the Character of Cult Phenomena and the Historical Setting of the Priestly School* (Oxford: Clarendon Press, 1977), 175–88; cf. Michael B. Hundley, "Sacred Spaces, Objects, Offerings, and People in the Priestly Texts: A Reappraisal," *Journal of Biblical Literature* 132, no. 4 (2013): 749–67; Rachel Elior, "The Jerusalem Temple: The Representation of the Imperceptible," *Studies in Spirituality* 11 (2001): 131–32; Mary Douglas, *Leviticus as Literature* (Oxford: Oxford University Press, 1999), 57–59.

27. Beale makes an interesting observation: the generic word "lights" (*me'ōrōt*) is used five times in Genesis 1 to identify the lights in the sky, whereas more expected words, like sun and moon, do not appear. Beale, *The Temple and the Church's Mission*, 34–35. Another common suggestion is that the menorah represents a "cosmic tree," or more specifically, the tree of life. Levenson, *Creation and the Persistence of Evil*, 84.

28. "The tapestries woven of four materials denote the natural elements: thus the fine linen appears to typify the earth, because from it springs up the flax, and the purple the sea, since it is incarnadined with the blood of fish; the air must be indicated by the blue, and the crimson will be the symbol of fire." Josephus, *Jewish Antiquities* Book 3, Paragraph 7, Line 183. Emphasis on the veil grows in apocalyptic literature, where one perceives in it the entire history of the world. Orlov, *Divine Scapegoats*, 44–50; Barker, *Temple Theology*, 27–32; Margaret Barker, *The Great High Priest: The Temple Roots of Christian Liturgy* (Edinburgh: T&T Clark, 2003), 188–228.

29. Beale, *The Temple and the Church's Mission*, 33.

kappōret (sometimes translated as "mercy seat," 1 Kings 6:19), and two large cherubim with a wingspan as wide as the room itself (1 Kings 6:23–28; 2 Chronicles 3:11–13). On the walls of both the shrine and the holy of holies, Solomon instructed the workers to carve "reliefs of cherubim, palms, and calyxes" (1 Kings 6:29); 2 Chronicles also mentions palm trees (3:5), precious stones (v. 6), and chains decorated with pomegranates (v. 16). Absolutely everything was overlaid with pure gold. The room, it seems, was filled with lush greenery, the fragrance of blooming flowers, and the whirl of cherubim in flight. It was the *Shabbat*-space,[30] the *shalom*-place,[31] the very throne room[32] of the glorious God of Israel.

The imagery of the room undoubtedly calls to mind a peaceful, fertile garden. As we saw in the introduction of this book, readers of Hebrew scripture have repeatedly connected this space to the garden of Eden, and many parallels invite and justify that connection.[33] The temple is the truth of creation in miniature, and at its innermost heart—hidden, but nevertheless present—it is paradisiacal. For Margaret Barker—who definitely favors a strong mystical theology which she associates with the first temple—the high priest who steps beyond the veil, into the holy of holies, steps "outside matter and time, and rituals in the holy of holies were deemed to take place in eternity. . . ."[34] She associates this with "original unity," which she con-

---

30. The connection between holy space and holy time, especially the ideas of sanctuary and Sabbath, is of profound importance for early temple theology. For a helpful introduction to this connection, see Berman, *The Temple*, 10–19.

31. The idea that the holy of holies—and, indeed, the entire temple complex—is the great icon of peace is a central argument of this first part of the book. Therefore, the claim found in the *Book of Similitudes* (1 Enoch 37–71) is of utmost importance. In the throne room of God, an angel says to Enoch, "[YHWH] shall proclaim peace [*shalom*] to you in the name of the world that is to become. For *from here* proceeds peace [*shalom*] since the creation of the world, and so it shall be unto you forever and ever and ever." (1 Enoch 71:15, emphasis added)

32. Analogous to an intimate private "bedchamber"; Michael B. Hundley, "Before YHWH at the Entrance of the Tent of Meeting: A Study of Spatial and Conceptual Geography in the Priestly Texts," *Zeitschrift Für Die Alttestamentliche Wissenschaft* 123, no. 1 (2011): 22.

33. Levenson, "The Temple and the World," 297–98; Levenson, *Sinai and Zion*, 128–33; Beale, *The Temple and the Church's Mission*, 66–80. For a recent study that does an exceptional job of emphasizing this idea, see Morales, *Who Shall Ascend?*

34. Barker, *Temple Theology*, 24. Barker is one of the most fascinating and unconventional voices in contemporary biblical scholarship. Crispin Fletcher-Louis, in a recent account of his intellectual debts, says his thought includes "a sprinkling of Margaret Barker (a muse to many of us. . .)" *Jesus Monotheism: Volume 1: Christological Origins: The Emerging Consensus and Beyond* (Eugene, OR: Cascade Books, 2015), xiii. Indeed, Barker is attractive for her bold, paradigm-shifting vision, but she also raises concerns with some of her idiosyncratic or brazenly unorthodox beliefs. Therefore, many who work with

strues in terms of "the One." While one might fairly critique Barker for advancing a reductively monistic understanding of God in her temple theology, it is indeed true that Eden is the icon of original unity, the garden where the all-unity of love was broken and where Adam and Eve were made incapable of the Tree of Life by a clinging desire to take what had not been given. Abraham and Isaac exemplify the exact opposite way of being, the route to true life through freely handing oneself over in a bond of trust. This at last points humanity back toward what is most original, and thus it is fitting that (again, according to the priestly Chronicler) the mountain of the Akedah would become the site of the temple, and that the central, most sacred precinct of the temple would once more be a garden sanctuary where God and his creatures might live together in joy, peace, and oneness.

This notion of dwelling *together* raises one other central feature of the temple that has been largely neglected thus far: the priests themselves,

---

Barker feel compelled to make some kind of statement about her highly original perspective. Here's mine.

Those who minimize the importance of priestly theology reduce the polyphonic richness of the Bible. To her credit, Barker has been way out in front of the movement to give temple theology the respect and esteem that it deserves. Before it was popular, she emphasized the centrality of temple themes in both canonical and extra-canonical works, Jewish and Christian. However, in her own way, Barker exemplifies similarly divisive tendencies. Like so many biblical scholars, her reading of the scriptural text is highly partisan; as if separating the goats from the lambs, she deems large blocks of the Bible unsatisfactory due to the influence of later, ostensibly decadent theological movements, while other textual strands are isolated, scrubbed of corruption, and celebrated as the true theology of early Israel. (You might say she is Wellhausen in mirror image.) What sets Barker apart is that, for her, it is the ancient temple traditions that are retrieved as profound and fruitful—those texts that can be traced back specifically to the practices of the pre-Josiah first temple (as she reconstructs it)—while the villain in her account is the Deuteronomists who set themselves against the vibrant, cosmic, symbolic, and ancient faith of Abraham, Isaac, and Jacob, and in its place impose the grim, philosophical, and novel "'Moses' religion." Barker, *Temple Theology*, 6, cf. 78. The glorious world of first temple theology can and must be reconstructed only with help of those texts that the Deuteronomists, later rabbis, and then "orthodox" Christians, have suppressed. Barker, cf. 9. Therefore, while Barker is often delightfully provocative, and while her black-and-white approach has the advantage of being clear and forceful, the systematic marginalization of *huge* swaths of biblical material, exemplifying utter disinterest in the notion of a shared "canon," cannot finally represent a way forward for Christian theology. At best, she makes us aware of voices in the Bible that have been inadequately understood or appreciated, but these voices still must come into dialogue with other biblical traditions, including the Deuteronomists and redactors. Scholars such as Levenson and Sommer model a more subtle and nuanced approach to minority biblical traditions. For a similar critique of Barker, see D. Stephen Long, *Hebrews*, Belief: A Theological Commentary on the Bible (Louisville, KY: Westminster John Knox Press, 2011), 153–56; cf. Stratford Caldecott, *All Things Made New: The Mysteries of the World in Christ* (Tacoma, WA: Angelico Press, 2011), 201–6.

and especially the high priest. After all, human beings were not typically admitted to God's private chamber in the old covenant, except for the high priest, and then only once a year on Yom Kippur. Israel enters into God's most intimate space in the holy of holies only through the mediation of the high priest, and thus appreciation for the significance of this office is an important aspect of temple theology. In fact, insofar as the instructions for building the tabernacle and its furniture, designs for priestly garments, rubrics for priestly ordination, and guidelines for the sacrificial rites are completely intertwined in Exodus 25 through Leviticus 9, it must be said that the office of the priesthood and the institution of the temple are interpenetrating realities.[35]

This concept can be seen by reflection on his vestments. From the biblical perspective, the correct design and usage of the priestly vestments is crucial, and the parallels between the High Priest's garments and the tabernacle itself are very significant.[36] As Gary Anderson points out, because only priests were allowed in the inner sanctuaries of the tabernacle, the rest of Israel did not have direct visual access to these spaces, but when they saw the high priest adorned in glory—his turban with the name of YHWH written on a gold plate, his breastplate with its many precious gems, his clothing woven from the same materials, with the same cosmically significant colors, as the temple's sacred veil[37]—they reacted with awe and joy: "To catch sight of the High Priest is to glimpse the

35. As Leigh Trevaskis says, ". . . the holiness of the high priest and the sanctuary share a degree of interdependence so that to remove one detracts from the holiness of the other." *Holiness, Ethics and Ritual in Leviticus*, 222; cf. 226. Peter Leithart describes the intimacy between priest and temple in this way: "In Hebrew, architectural terminology overlaps with anatomical, and this along with other hints suggests that the tabernacle is humaniform. In particular, the tabernacle is an architectural replica of the high priest, and vice versa. . . . Both the tabernacle and the priestly garments are made after the pattern of glory that Moses glimpses on Sinai, so that the tabernacle is an architectural depiction of a glorified man." "'We Saw His Glory': Implications of the Sanctuary Christology in John's Gospel," in *Christology, Ancient and Modern: Explorations in Constructive Dogmatics*, ed. Oliver D. Crisp and Fred Sanders (Grand Rapids, MI: Zondervan Academic, 2013), 123.

36. Brant Pitre puts this especially clearly: ". . . it is critical to note here that in ancient Judaism, there was one person who was viewed as embodying in himself both the Temple and the cosmos. That person was the Jewish High Priest, whose liturgical vestments were meant to replicate both the Temple and the universe." Brant Pitre, "Jesus, the New Temple, and the New Priesthood," *Letter & Spirit* 4 (2008): 61.

37. See Beale, *The Temple and the Church's Mission*, 39–45. According to the description of the high priest in Wisdom of Solomon, "on his long robe *the whole world was depicted*, and the glories of the ancestors were engraved on the four rows of stones, and your majesty was on the diadem upon his head" (18:24, NRSV, emphasis added).

inner recesses of the divine chamber."[38] In other words, the high priest, resplendently vested, mediates to Israel the inner mysteries of the temple, even as he personally represents all of Israel, and indeed all of creation, to God in the holy of holies on Yom Kippur.[39] This latter view is clearly expressed by Philo, for whom the priest also "represents the world" and is a "small cosmos."[40] The high priest and the temple interrelate in profound ways, perhaps pointing toward and requiring one another.

One additional microcosm theme which finds expression in biblical and early Jewish literature bears mentioning; this theme is something of a corollary to everything we have discussed in this section. For ancient Israel, the temple was truly the center—the "navel"—of the universe, it is the axis that unites the spheres, and it is the "foundation stone" that secures cosmic order. There is no second temple text that more clearly expresses this theme than Jubilees: "And [Noah] knew that the garden of Eden was the holy of holies and the dwelling of the LORD. And Mount Sinai (was) in the midst of the desert and Mount Zion (was) in the midst of the navel of the earth."[41] This idea likely goes much further back in

38. Anderson, "As We Have Heard So We Have Seen," 55; cf. Anderson, "Inauguration of the Tabernacle Service at Sinai," 14. The intense language used to describe visions of the high priest is most striking, especially in the Hebrew version of Sirach (The Wisdom of Jesus Ben Sira), which uses an immense range of natural and cultic imagery to describe the high priest: "When he covered himself with the garments of glory / And clothed himself in garments of beauty." Sirach 50:11, translated by Hayward, *The Jewish Temple*, 42. Equally incredible is the "astonishment" of *Aristeas* when he sees the high priest Eleazar, "both as regards the form of his robe and his splendor which consisted in the dress which he wore, a tunic and the precious stones upon it." Paragraph 96, translated by Hayward, 29. Aristeas then describes the "royal diadem" on the priest's head, upon which God's sacred name was embossed, and he concludes, "The overall appearance of these things created awe and confusion, so as to make one think that he has come close to another man from outside the world. . . ." Paragraph 99, Hayward, 30.

39. Fletcher-Louis, "Jesus' Divine Self-Consciousness: A Proposal," 4. The priest's "dual" role as mediator between God and Israel has been emphasized in three recent studies: Carmen Joy Imes, "Between Two Worlds: The Functional and Symbolic Significance of the High Priestly Regalia," in *Dress and Clothing in the Hebrew Bible*, ed. Antonios Finitsis (London: T&T Clark, 2019), 29–62; Christine Palmer, "Israelite High Priestly Apparel: Embodying an Identity between Human and Divine," in *Fashioned Selves: Dress and Identity in Antiquity*, ed. Cifarelli Megan (London: Oxbow Books, 2019), 117–27; Christophe Nihan and Julia Rhyder, "Aaron's Vestments in Exodus 28 and Priestly Leadership," in *Debating Authority: Concepts of Leadership in the Pentateuch and the Former Prophets*, ed. Katharina Pyschny and Sarah Schulz (Berlin: de Gruyter, 2018), 45–67.

40. Philo, *Life of Moses*, 2.135. Quoted in Beale, *The Temple and the Church's Mission*, 47. Elsewhere Philo also says that each rational soul is a temple; Hayward, *The Jewish Temple*, 110–11.

41. Charlesworth, "Jubilees," 8:19. Other extra-biblical examples include *Sibylline Oracles* 5.249-51; *1 Enoch* 26.1; *Aristeas* 83; Philo's *Legatio ad Gaium* 294; and Josephus'

the priestly tradition than Jubilees, at least as far back as Ezekiel, where there are references to Jerusalem as "the center (*bĕtôk*) of the nations,"[42] and even "at the very navel (*ṭabbûr*) of the earth."[43] To associate this location with the navel points to its centrality, yes, but also to the idea that it is the place from which creation originated, the true source of our world. The same theological community that saw Zion as the source of the world would also celebrate this Judean hill as a mountain of unmatched elevation; thus, Mount Zion truly was the source and summit of Israel's spiritual life.

There was nothing more crucial for Israel than to maintain good order at the microcosmic center. The priests were convinced that they had a vocation, on behalf of the whole people, to carefully fulfill their ritual duties, believing that the entire cosmos was protected and sustained by their work. According to Levenson, their successful efforts were considered the ultimate "bulwark and guarantee against chaos,"[44] and failure would thus be devastating for heaven and earth. As Fletcher-Louis says, "There is much to suggest that they thought that temple service was 'sacramental' and that because it guaranteed the stability of its symbolic referent, the real physical world, its destruction would logically mean the real destruction of that world."[45] And so they would return, day and night, to Mount Moriah, continually grafting themselves into the self-giving faithfulness of Abraham and Isaac through their sacred rites, convinced that by this humble work they were establishing for Israel and the world a lasting cosmic peace.

Temple as Microcosm: Philosophical Implications

By interrelating the phenomenon of the temple with the mystery of creation itself, priestly theology invites a conversation between philoso-

---

War of the Jews 3.52–5, which is another nice clear text: "The city of Jerusalem lies at its very centre [of Judaea] for which reason the town has sometimes not inaptly been called the 'navel' of the country." For a general review of this material, see P. S. Alexander, "Jerusalem as the Omphalos of the World : On the History of a Geographical Concept," *Judaism* 46, no. 2 (1997): 147–58; Fishbane, "The Sacred Center," 14; Levenson, "The Temple and the World," 282–84.

42. For a defense of the translation of *bĕtôk* as "in the very center of," see Levenson, "The Temple and the World," 284.

43. Ezekiel 38:12. For a defense of the rare word *ṭabbûr* as "navel," see Levenson, *Sinai and Zion*, 115–17.

44. Levenson, 154.

45. Fletcher-Louis, "Jesus, the Temple and the Dissolution," 128.

phy and theology. Here there is already a meditation on how creaturely truth may point toward a yet deeper divine truth. The temple is a complex symbol that shows how different cosmic orders relate to one another, all pointing toward and centered in the immanent presence of God. In the outermost sphere, the courtyard, there were symbols of land and sea. This is the realm where priests moved freely, performing their everyday work, with their regular rhythms of guarding and keeping the sacred space, fueling the fire, and offering sacrifices. The holy place was next, one sphere closer to the center, and it included symbols associated (originally or eventually) with light, cosmic trees, nourishing bread, the four elements, the seven planets, and the twelve months. Priests of the house of Zadok also performed rituals in this space—keeping the lamps lit, the bread fresh, sprinkling blood before the veil—but less frequently, more solemnly. This sphere came to represent cosmic order, indicated by the references to the heavenly bodies which teach Israel how to properly keep Sabbaths and festivals. At the very center of the (micro-)cosmos is the paradisiacal peace and perfect unity of Israel's one God. This space was open to the high priest alone, and only once a year. Yet even though this realm was hidden—veiled—it was by no means neglected or forgotten. Every action performed in the temple was directed toward the throne room where the God of Israel dwelled, and thus what was most hidden was also most real in the theological imagination of the ancient Jews.

Notice that, according to the microcosmic interpretation of the temple, God's *immanent presence* in creation is highlighted. One passes from sphere to sphere, closer and closer to God, who is invisibly present in the holiest sphere of creation. Granted, we have already alluded to the fact that in the priestly system the presence of God is not simply inevitable; God's presence is contingent on the maintenance of order. Cosmic order, represented by the symbols of the shrine, was like a "bridge" between the inmost presence of God, the holy of holies, and quotidian life, represented by the earth and sea of the outer court. Understanding the importance of "order" also helps clarify the theology of purity and impurity: like the God who separates light and darkness, land and sea, Israel is called to distinguish pure and impure. Only that which is pure—untouched by "dirt," by death or decay[46]—can draw near to the temple, a place thoroughly aligned with Edenic life. Humanity's vocation on earth is to carry forward God's creative work of preserving life-sustaining order, and in so doing maintain creation as a suitable

---

46. See discussion in chapter five.

sanctuary for God. As noted above, Jonathan Klawans sees two "organizing principles" behind temple and sacrifice, one of which is "concern with attracting and maintaining the presence of God within the community."[47] The idea of preserving (micro-)cosmic order in the temple was, within this mode of thought, essential to maintaining a place suitable for and attractive to God.

Therefore, the temple was a sophisticated aid toward philosophical reflection on the inner truth of creation, one in which the mind is drawn, by reflection on well-ordered cosmic realities, toward the God who dwells in glory at the inmost center of all creaturely being. Earlier, in the chapter on the theological aesthetics of the biblical temple, one of the major questions we asked was, what *form* does this space take? And also, how does the temple express itself in a way that points toward further depths, or greater heights, such that it invites a journey into greater and greater mysteries? The reflections in this chapter have, I hope, helped to fill out possible answers to those questions. With respect to the second chapter of this book, the theme of "temple as microcosm" also includes an implicit ethic: the role of humanity in creation is to maintain and embody the order necessary for life to flourish and for God to dwell peacefully with his creation. This includes sacrificial practices that show a continual recommitment to the openheartedness of the Akedah.

After looking at this traditional understanding of temple theology, one can conclude that, overall, the emphasis is on a God who is wholly descended. That's the strength, and also the weakness, of the tradition of seeing the temple as a microcosm. *If* this were the *only* paradigm for understanding the temple, *if* God's throne were located within the cosmos, in one sphere among others[48]—albeit one of unparalleled holiness—God is nevertheless diminished, limited, made finite. At least two problematic understandings of God could result from this view, and each stems from an interpretation of how the holy of holies relates to the

---

47. Klawans, *Purity, Sacrifice, and the Temple*, 48.

48. This, Sommer indicates, was an early priestly view. See *Bodies of God*, 74–77. Furthermore, according to Sommer, there is no suggestion in priestly texts that after descending to dwell in the tabernacle, God remains also in heaven; Sommer, 98. Unsurprisingly, one can find alternative readings of P. Compare, for example, Robert S. Kawashima, "The Priestly Tent of Meeting and the Problem of Divine Transcendence: An 'Archaeology' of the Sacred," *The Journal of Religion* 86, no. 2 (2006): 226–57. None of this should suggest that those sources that develop the microcosm tradition much later—Philo and Josephus above all—had a view of God as strictly immanent. That is clearly not the case. As I will emphasize below, all later interpreters in the Jewish tradition drew from a canon that included texts that emphasize both immanence and transcendence.

other spheres in the temple. The first sees the holy of holies as the highest sphere: just as the macrocosmic sky is higher than the earth, so also is God's heaven higher than the sky. Problematically, this picture accentuates the way that the microcosm tradition can easily imply that God's realm is merely a privileged place within the universe—perhaps more perfect, but nevertheless in univocal continuity with the rest of creation. This is a polytheistic ontology, or what David Bentley Hart calls "monopolytheism" because it involves "a view of God not conspicuously different from the polytheistic picture of the gods as merely very powerful discrete entities who possess a variety of distinct attributes that lesser entities also possess, if in smaller measure. . . ."[49] With this frame of mind, "heaven" is seen as a spatial location in the cosmos where the gods live—or, what is more pathetic, where the sole god and his created angelic servants live—and from which they (or he) interact with human beings. By correlating the areas of the temple with earth, sky, and "highest heaven," the microcosm tradition suggests an ontologically horizontal understanding of the relationship between the domain of the god and the domain of humanity, with the former existing perhaps just beyond the firmament.[50]

The second, more sophisticated application of the divine immanence implied by the cosmic symbolism of the temple is based on a picture of sacred spheres as more and more intimate, more and more interior, easily leading to a pantheistic perspective that ultimately sees the world as an expression of God. According to Przywara, "Pan-the-ism" means "proceeding fundamentally 'from below to above,' the all becomes God."[51] Aspects of Margaret Barker's temple mysticism—which, she claims, faithfully reflects the first temple theology—seem to fit this category. For her, the holy of holies signifies "Day One," which was remembered by the rabbis "as the Day (or the state) in which the Holy One was one with his universe. Day One was thus the state of unity underlying (rather than preceding) all the visible creation. . . . Those who entered the holy of holies understood how the original unity had become the diversity of the

49. David Bentley Hart, *The Experience of God: Being, Consciousness, Bliss* (New Haven, CT: Yale University Press, 2013), 127.

50. See J. Edward Wright, *The Early History of Heaven* (Oxford: Oxford University Press, 2002), 55–57. Wright sees the ancient Canaanite religions, including early biblical traditions, taking the architecture of the tripartite universe—here depicted as netherworld below, earth, and heaven above—quite literally. With such reconstructions of ancient cosmology, however, it seems appropriate to refer back to Klawans' critique of modern scholarship, which underestimates the ability of early cultures to think metaphorically.

51. Przywara, *Analogia Entis*, 165.

visible creation."[52] Elsewhere she says, "It was not 'the first day' [in Genesis 1:5] but the state beyond the temporal and material world; it was the eternal present. Just as the holy of holies was in the midst of the temple, so too the eternal presence of God was in the midst of creation. . . . The holy of holies behind the veil symbolized God in the midst of creation."[53] The unity of Day One is the invisible, veiled divinity, the state that underlies the entire visible creation. This conception of a hidden divine unity beyond the veil of material creation serves as a foundation for various esoteric traditions, and one can certainly see why the ancient priestly tradition became so enamored with number mysticism as a way of passing through the material toward the inner "holy of holies" of God's immanent presence. Closed off from this view, it would seem, is the true freedom of God in relation to the world, and the otherness of God and creation which is the condition for genuine revelation and relationship. It's no surprise that Barker is antagonistic to the Deuteronomist's "historical covenants,"[54] strongly favoring immutable cosmic mysticism coupled with primal temple mythology, which she associates with the priestly tradition. But does such Parmenidean stasis really capture the truth of divine and creaturely being?

The concept of the temple as microcosm has many advantages. By highlighting the intimacy of God and creation and the theological relevance of the 'book of nature,' and even by developing a style of mysticism that foreshadows Proclus, the use of temple symbolism to contemplate the mysteries of earth and heaven has had a lasting, positive effect in Judaism and Christianity, one that is sometimes neglected in some academic circles, especially at times of narrow historicism. Then again, the sardonic words of God, recorded by Isaiah and cited by St. Stephen the martyr, must not be forgotten: "Yet the Most High does not dwell in houses made by human hands; as the prophet says, 'Heaven is my throne, / and the earth is my footstool. What kind of house will you build for me, says the Lord, / or what is the place of my rest?'" (Acts 7:48–49; cf. Isaiah 66:1). The philosophy of the temple as microcosm is

---

52. Barker, *The Great High Priest*, 24–25. For parallel ideas in Philo and 2 Enoch, see Martha Himmelfarb, *Ascent to Heaven in Jewish and Christian Apocalypses* (New York: Oxford University Press, 1993), 84–86.

53. Margaret Barker, *Temple Mysticism: An Introduction* (London: SPCK, 2011), 56.

54. For example, "The priestly theology saw the pattern of history as a whole, revealed in the holy of holies as past, present, and future. It was the Deuteronomists who made 'history' an interpretation of the *past* events, made Moses the centre of their scheme. . . ." Barker, *Temple Theology*, 36.

finally inadequate to fully capture the relationship between divine and human truth, and in fact, on its own, it can only be a distortion.

Mirror of Heaven

There is a second strain of thought that, as mentioned above, is substantively distinct from the idea that the temple is a microcosm. While the priestly writers, along with late figures like Josephus and Philo, extensively develop the idea that the temple is the microcosm of the world, others draw attention to an idea that—at first—may seem to be quite opposite: the Jerusalem temple and the temple cult are earthly imitators of a transcendent heavenly temple.

As we transition to this theme, a preliminary note. When historians of biblical literature or ancient Judaism come across a new theological concept, they often attempt to explain the idea purely in terms of some then-contemporary controversy, some societal crisis, as if all religious reflection is, at its root, a sectarian reaction to the daily headlines. For Feuerbach, theology is anthropology in disguise; for many others, theology is power politics in disguise. Everything comes down to acrimonious political posturing. If ancient people were anything like modern politicians (or modern academics!), then a perpetually discordant setting for theological reflection is not unthinkable. Still, historians do not always adequately appreciate how theological ideas grow and develop not only through war but also through dialogue and reflection, by contemplating the perennial theological mysteries in continuity with one's forbearers.[55] In this section, we will be looking at the idea that the earthy temple mirrors a heavenly temple. As we will see, it is often assumed that such an idea was provoked by some crisis or dispute: the Babylonians have reduced the holy temple to rubble, or a faction has been bitterly excluded from the temple, or purists have removed themselves, believing that this

---

55. For example, Tryggve N. D. Mettinger quotes R. P. Carrol: "dissonance gives rise to hermeneutic." *The Dethronement of Sabaoth: Studies in the Shem and Kabod Theologies* (Lund: CWK Gleerup, 1982), 17. While this is true, shouldn't it also be said that the human spirit aspires to reflective interpretation and understanding in diverse circumstances? Doesn't prayer give rise to hermeneutic? Conversation? Love and happiness? Dissonance may be a powerful motivating factor, but so are "moments of experienced fullness, of joy and fulfillment," as Charles Taylor puts it. *A Secular Age* (Cambridge, MA: The Belknap Press of Harvard University Press, 2007), 5. For a critique of the interpretive/dating presuppositions of Mettinger and others, see Benjamin Sommer, "Dating Pentateuchal Texts and the Perils of Pseudo-Historicism," in *The Pentateuch: International Perspectives on Current Research*, ed. Thomas B. Dozeman, Konrad Schmid, and Baruch J. Schwartz (Tübingen: Mohr Siebeck, 2011), 85–94.

temple (and/or the priesthood that ministers in this temple) has become apostate and therefore must be rejected.[56] Without a doubt, such fracturing occurred in ancient Israel—as in probably any human community of two or more thoughtful people. But it is also quite possible that the idea that the earthly temple mirrors the heavenly temple could develop in a more irenic setting.

Benjamin Sommer has summarized the notable distinction between the Priestly interpretation of God's presence in the tabernacle and the Deuteronomic interpretation. As emphasized in the previous section, according to Sommer's study of the priestly tradition, God himself (God's own glorious body) fully comes to rest in the tabernacle over the ark of the covenant. God is intimately and assuredly present to his people. For whatever reason—perhaps stemming from perfectly legitimate theological concerns over limiting God in time and place—the Deuteronomists are said to have articulated a different vision for God's relation to the tabernacle. They insisted, according to Sommer, that God *does not* descend to earth, but remains always enthroned exclusively in heaven, and rather makes the divine *Name* (*shem*) dwell in the temple. Sommer says, "So insistently do deuteronomic traditions maintain that God is not on earth that it becomes clear that for them the *shem* is only a sign of divine presence, not a manifestation of God himself."[57] The parade example of this phenomenon is Solomon's speech in 1 Kings 8, which is consistently directed toward God *in heaven* (vv. 22, 23, 30, 32, 34, 36, 39,

---

56. For example, Barker emphasizes the Josiah-Deuteronomistic reforms in her account of how ancient priestly theology was marginalized. Others will find a more proximate historical setting in the Maccabean displacement of the Zadokites.

57. Sommer, *Bodies of God*, 62. Sommer's interpretation of "Name theology" is neither idiosyncratic nor a consensus. An early advocate of a similar view is von Rad, and his arguments have been developed and supported by many scholars of the book of Deuteronomy. Mettinger's articulation of "Name theology" is especially clear and well-known; *The Dethronement of Sabaoth*, 38–79. More recently, however, a number of dissenting studies have been published which argue that the lack of divine "presence" in the temple in D has been overstated, and a false dichotomy between transcendence and immanence has been imposed. See Ian Wilson, *Out of the Midst of the Fire: Divine Presence in Deuteronomy* (Atlanta: Scholars Press, 1995); Sandra L. Richter, "The Place of the Name in Deuteronomy," *Vetus Testamentum* 57, no. 3 (2007): 342–66; Michael Hundley, "To Be or Not to Be: A Reexamination of Name Language in Deuteronomy and the Deuteronomistic History," *Vetus Testamentum* 59, no. 4 (2009): 533–55. For Sommer's response to some of these critiques, see *Bodies of God*, 218 n.47. In this section I am following the scholarship of Mettinger and Sommer while recognizing that there are no "ideal types." Just as there are ample resources within priestly theology to prevent the immanence of God from becoming domestication, there are resources within the D tradition to prevent transcendence from becoming absence.

etc.), where Solomon says repeatedly that the temple is for God's *shem* (vv. 16–20, etc.), and where he famously exclaims, "But will God really dwell on earth? Even the heavens to their uttermost reaches cannot contain You, how much less this House that I have built!" (v. 27) If God is uncontained by even the highest heaven, claims of God's immanent presence in the temple are quickly tempered. The concept of an uncontained God "in heaven" certainly bursts through any concept of heaven as a discrete inter-cosmic sphere.

One therefore finds in the Deuteronomists a "theology of transcendence,"[58] and thus symbols of the temple find a less theophanic, more historical interpretation in D. For example, rather than seeing the ark of the covenant as God's throne or footstool, the site of God's indwelling glory, the Deuteronomic school sees it as a chest which stores the covenant tablets (1 Kings 8:9). The ark thus serves as a reminder of the Mosaic covenant, it is "educational," "it now houses symbols rather than divinity."[59] Generally, this perspective highlights the fundamental discontinuity between God and the world, and according to Sommer, it bears some resemblance to what we today call nominalism.[60] God is transcendent, and the temple is more a pedagogical conduit of prayer, helping to draw the worshiper into relationship with the otherworldly God of the Sinaitic covenant.

Here we have one tradition celebrating God's immanence and another celebrating God's transcendence. Wonderfully, these traditions did not live out their days in opposing war camps but were brought together in a single name: Moses. *None* of the ancient commentaries we have speak of Priestly and Deuteronomic sources. They speak of Moses, who communicates to Israel the word of God. This drawing together of profound theological perspectives in a single peaceful household has been a catalyst for reflection that has continued for millennia.[61] Believers have

58. Sommer, *Bodies of God*, 64.

59. Sommer, 100; cf. Mettinger, *The Dethronement of Sabaoth*, 50–51. For a more extensive analysis of the ark as either throne or chest, including consideration of how the ark and the *kappōret* are distinct, see Menahem Haran, *Temples and Temple-Service in Ancient Israel: An Inquiry into the Character of Cult Phenomena and the Historical Setting of the Priestly School* (Oxford: Clarendon Press, 1977), 246–59.

60. Sommer says, "The *shem* is merely a name in the sense that Western thinkers regard names: a symbol, a verbal indicator that points toward something outside itself." Sommer, *Bodies of God*, 65. Again, for an alternative view, see Hundley, "To Be or Not to Be," 547–51.

61. On the theological significance and veracity of the "Mosaic authorship" of the Pentateuch, see Brevard S. Childs, *Introduction to the Old Testament as Scripture* (Philadelphia: Fortress Press, 1979), 132–35. Jon Levenson argues that what is ultimately

read that God is truly present in the tabernacle, and they have read that God dwells in heaven, and they have contemplatively pondered how these affirmations relate to one another.[62]

It thus seems plausible, returning to the meditation that opened this section, that the idea of a transcendent heavenly "temple," an ontologically distinct divine reality upon which the earthly temple is analogically patterned, could develop in this fertile dialogical soil, without strictly requiring an acute historical crisis or bitter factional hostility to the Jerusalem cult or its priesthood. As Sommer points out, the problem of immanence and transcendence is a perennial philosophical and theological problem, and thus it is not necessary to locate a sectarian or sociopolitical setting to understand how it is a single complex theological symbol—the temple—came to be a locus for reflection on both God's truth in creation, and God's truth beyond creation.[63] This is not to say that individuals or groups who were separated from the Jerusalem temple—either due to the temple's destruction by Babylon or divisions within the community—did not gravitate toward the claim that the earthly temple is a pale reflection of a much greater reality—certainly, this idea could be very useful in holding the community together during exile, and useful also for polemicists, giving them a way to swear continued fidelity to the (eternal) temple while rejecting the earthy institution. Still, the important thing is, whether or not one gravitates first and last toward a narrowly historical explanation for how these ideas originated, the theological insight is still significant, and its significance persists to this day.

Like the idea that the temple is a microcosm, the ancient belief that the Jerusalem temple mirrors the heavenly temple has received extensive scholarly attention in recent years.[64] Because the material is well covered,

---

intended in the ancient affirmation of Mosaic authorship is "the unity and divinity of the Torah" in "The Eighth Principle of Judaism and the Literary Simultaneity of Scripture," *The Journal of Religion*, 1988, 208. Levenson arrives at a position analogous to Childs' by defending the "simultaneity of all parts of the Bible" through an awareness of "divine authorization," 213.

62. Levenson points out that, insofar as the Torah includes different perspectives, it is "bipolar" and "the tension between perspectives yields a spiritual dynamic that neither perspective alone could have produced." Levenson, "The Jerusalem Temple," 37.

63. See Sommer, *Bodies of God*, 96–97, 240 n.66; Sommer, "Dating Pentateuchal Texts," 91, 101–8. To take a more specific example, for arguments that 1 Enoch—which is at the headwaters of much later reflection on the heavenly temple—is not sectarian, see Fletcher-Louis, *All the Glory of Adam*, 21–25.

64. See Klawans, *Purity, Sacrifice, and the Temple*, 128–38; Hayward, *The Jewish Temple*, 10–13; Himmelfarb, *Ascent to Heaven*, 9–28; Martha Himmelfarb, "Apocalyptic Ascent and the Heavenly Temple," *Society of Biblical Literature Seminar Papers*, no. 26

I will only briefly review some of the key primary texts in this tradition. Without a doubt, the prophet Ezekiel's chariot vision has an unparalleled influence, and it may represent an early example of what happens when priestly and Deuteronomic theologies come together. If the priestly tradition asserts that God has established his (mobile) throne here on earth, located at the heart of Israel in the holy of holies,[65] and if the Deuteronomists focus on God's *heavenly* dwelling place while also affirming Jerusalem as God's chosen city,[66] what happens when these views come together? Risa Levitt Kohn argues that Ezekiel uses terms and concepts drawn from *both* priestly *and* Deuteronomic sources, and that "Ezekiel fuses P and D material to create a unique synthesis."[67] Perhaps this fascinating synthesis can be seen in the first chapters of Ezekiel's book, where he portrays the divine throne both in heaven and on earth, both transcendent and locomotive.

As the book opens, the exiled Ezekiel, abandoned in enemy territory along a Babylonian canal, looks up and sees: "the heavens opened and I saw visions of God" (1:1). What follows is an elaborate account of God's heavenly dwelling place, with special emphasis on the "living creatures"—later identified as cherubim (10:20)—all portrayed using terms traditionally associated with the glory of God: fire, lightning, clouds, radiance, fear, and awe. The chapter culminates with a description of the throne, and what's more amazing, of the one who is enthroned. Ezekiel says, "Above the expanse over their [e.g. 'the living creatures'] heads was the semblance of a throne, in appearance like sapphire; and on top, upon this semblance of a throne, there was the semblance of a human form. . ." (1:26). With the heavens opened, as if a veil has been pulled aside, Ezekiel is given visual access to the eternal holy of holies.

This is not the first time God's heavenly throne room has been described in the prophetic literature; already in Isaiah there is a descrip-

---

(January 1, 1987): 210–12, 216; Elior, *The Three Temples*, 14–15, 29–31, 63–66, 71; Clements, *God and Temple*, 65, 68; John J Collins, *Jerusalem and the Temple in Jewish Apocalyptic Literature of the Second Temple Period* (Ramat Gan: Bar Ilan University, 1998), 13–16; Levenson, *Sinai and Zion*, 122–25, 140–41; Weinfeld, "Sabbath, Temple, and the Enthronement of the Lord," 505–6.

65. Sommer calls this perspective "*locomotive*: There is a center, but it moves." Sommer, *Bodies of God*, 87–90.

66. Sommer, 101.

67. Risa Levitt Kohn, "A Prophet Like Moses? Rethinking Ezekiels Relationship to the Torah," *Zeitschrift für die alttestamentliche Wissenschaft* 114, no. 2 (2006): 247. Of course, to enter this conversation is to plunge into the tense debates over how to date P, Deuteronomy, the Deuteronomic history, Ezekiel, and proposed redactions of each of the above.

tion of the Lord "seated on a high and lofty throne; and the skirts of His robe filled the Temple" (6:1). Here God is surrounded by six-winged seraphs who sang "holy, holy, holy!" (v. 3). In this vision, temple iconography has become animate and Isaiah sees the living realities that they convey, but it is not clear that Isaiah is visualizing anything more than the reality of God's presence in the *earthly* temple.[68] In other words, the book of Isaiah does not necessarily indicate that the prophet enjoys a vision of a heavenly temple that transcends the earthly.

This is why the revelation to Ezekiel is so significant. According to Martha Himmelfarb, "Ezekiel's visions of the chariot throne mark the beginning of a trend to dissociate God's heavenly abode from the temple in Jerusalem."[69] There is truth in this, but maybe we can nuance the point in this way: while Deuteronomic theology had already dissociated God's heavenly abode from the temple,[70] Ezekiel begins the process of imagining the—so to speak—"two temples" together. In his first chapter, Ezekiel locates God firmly and resplendently in heaven, but in chapter 8 the prophet is brought, in a vision, to the Jerusalem temple, to the inner courts, and "the Presence of the God of Israel appeared there, like the vision that I had seen in the valley" (v. 4). Unfortunately, Ezekiel's tour of the Jerusalem temple is not a happy one; he is confronted with numerous abominations in the holy space, and thus in the tenth chapter Ezekiel sees God depart from the temple, here again, enthroned above the cherubim, carried aloft in a wheeled angelic chariot. Notice: the priestly teaching that the *kabod* YHWH dwells immanently in the temple is reaffirmed by the fact that, according to Ezekiel himself, what he saw in Jerusalem was like what he had seen in heaven. Similarly, God's "locomotive" presence is also reaffirmed; God is free to abandon Zion. But then, the Deuteronomic insistence on God's transcendent heavenly dwelling is also supported by the opening vision. Undeniably, these two traditions together create an ever more complex theological symbol; it has inspired mystical theology ever since.

When it comes to reflection on the heavenly temple, Ezekiel is groundbreaking and unavoidable, but the classic biblical text for the later tradition comes much earlier in the canon, in a bizarre comment within an otherwise straightforward genealogy: "All the days of Enoch came to 365 years. Enoch walked with God; then he was no more, for God took him" (Genesis 5:23–24). Every other entry in the genealogy, from Adam to Lamech, father of Noah, ends with the words "and he died," but Enoch

---

68. Cf. Levenson, *Sinai and Zion*, 123.
69. Himmelfarb, *Ascent to Heaven*, 11.
70. As Himmelfarb fully recognizes: Himmelfarb, 12.

lives 365 years (note the cosmic significance) before being "taken" by Elohim. This caught the attention of ancient readers, to say the least. With Deuteronomic and prophetic texts, as well as several psalms (viz. Ps 11:4; 103:19), speaking of God enthroned in heaven, and now with some prophets also recording detailed revelations of God enthroned in the holy of holies, increasingly intimate knowledge of heavenly realities were starting to be described, and Enoch was the most logical narrative vehicle for visionary journeys, precisely because Genesis can be read to suggest that he experienced a heavenly rapture.

And thus the phenomenon of the *Book of the Watchers* (1 Enoch 1–36) emerges in Hebrew religious literature by at least the third century BC.[71] The story of the fall of the watchers, and especially the account of Azaz'el's punishment, will be significant for our understanding of Yom Kippur in the next chapters. In our current context, however, the fourteenth chapter of the book is most important, because here Enoch describes his visionary journey to heaven. Many familiar theophanic motifs are used in describing heaven: fire, ice,[72] clouds, lightning, cherubim, immensity, fear, desire, and of course, glory. As Enoch travels through the heavenly landscape, he passes through three houses which, it has been noted, seem to correspond to the three increasingly holy sections of the earthly temple.[73] Enoch ultimately approaches the inner house, built "with tongues of fire" (14:15) and excelling in "glory and greatness" (v. 16). And then:

> I observed and saw inside it a lofty throne—its appearance was like crystal and its wheels like the shining sun; and [I heard] the voice of the cherubim; and from beneath the throne were issuing streams of flaming fire. It was difficult to look at it. And the Great Glory was sitting upon it—as for his gown, which was shining more brightly than the sun, it was whiter than any snow. (vv. 18–20)

Here, for the first time in the extant record, there is an unambiguous visionary tour of heaven. Enoch's description of the three houses insinuates that the heavenly temple has roughly the same structural form as the

71. Chapter and verse references below are from James H. Charlesworth, ed., "1 (Ethiopic Apocalypse of) Enoch," in *The Old Testament Pseudepigrapha*, trans. E. Isaac, vol. 1 (New York: Doubleday, 1983), 5–89.

72. The peculiar relationship between fire and ice in the heavenly house says something about the odd nature of the place: "And I entered into the house, which was hot like fire and cold like ice. . ." (1 Enoch 14:13).

73. Himmelfarb, *Ascent to Heaven*, 14–15.

earthly equivalent, and he reconfirms the vision of Isaiah and Ezekiel when he describes God enthroned in glory.

In another early Enochic text, *The Book of Similitudes* (1 Enoch 37–71), Enoch's vision of the heavenly temple is even further developed. Here again Enoch "ascended into the heavens," but now there is a greater emphasis on esoteric knowledge: "[the angel Michael] showed me all the secrets of the extreme ends of heaven. . ." (71:4). There is also much more attention to the presence of the angels, dressed in white garments (v. 1), along with the "seraphim, cherubim, and ophanim[74]—the sleepless ones who guard the throne of his glory" (v. 7), thus reinforcing the importance of the cherubim in the holy of holies. Enoch sees "the Antecedent of Time," whose clothing is indescribable (v. 10), and in response, "I fell on my face, my whole body mollified and my spirit transformed. Then I cried with a great voice by the spirit of the power, blessing, glorifying, and extolling" (v. 11). The vision of God in the heavenly holy of holies causes the worshiper to respond with humility and to undergo a spiritual transformation that culminates in joyful praise.[75]

Temple as Mirror: Philosophical Implications

After the temple in heaven and the temple on earth were distinguished, the next obvious question is, how do these temples relate? Early on, a passage from the book of Exodus became indispensable in reflecting on this question. In Exodus 24, Mount Sinai seems to be divided into three zones. At the bottom of the mountain, a sacrificial altar is built around which the whole people gather and commit themselves to the covenant. Then Moses, Aaron, Aaron's sons Nadab and Abihu, along with the seventy elders, are told to ascend the mountain. At a certain point, they see God above but are instructed to go no further. Only Moses is invited to continue toward the top, to the cloud-covered peak, where

---

74. *Ophanim* is the Hebrew word for the "wheels," which are emphasized in Ezekiel 1, cf. Elior, *The Three Temples*, 63–64.

75. For more on the increasingly important theme of spiritual transformation through heavenly ascent, see Himmelfarb, *Ascent to Heaven*, 29–46; Christopher R. A Morray-Jones, "Transformational Mysticism in the Apocalyptic-Merkabah Tradition," *Journal of Jewish Studies* 43, no. 1 (1992): 1–31; April D. DeConick, "What Is Early Jewish and Christian Mysticism?," in *Paradise Now: Essays on Early Jewish and Christian Mysticism*, ed. April D. DeConick (Atlanta: Society of Biblical Literature, 2006), 18–24; Fletcher-Louis, *All the Glory of Adam*. For additional visions of the holy of holies in early Judaism (in texts preserved by early Christians), see *Apocalypse of Abraham* 18:1–3, 12–14; *The Life of Adam and Eve* in Greek, chap. 33; *The Testament of Levi* 3:4–7, 5:1.

the "Presence of the Lord abode on Mount Sinai" (24:16); on the seventh day God appears as a "consuming fire" (v. 17) and speaks. One of the primary instructions God gives is the design of the sanctuary: "Exactly as I show (*mar'eh*) you—the pattern (*tabnît*) of the Tabernacle and the pattern (*tabnît*) of all its furnishings—so shall you make it" (25:9; cf. 26:30, 27:8). It is possible that the original author's intention for the word "pattern" was the equivalent of a modern-day blueprint.[76] Nevertheless, as the heavenly temple was gradually distinguished from the earthly temple, commentators returned to the word "pattern" to help clarify the relationship between heaven and earth.

The idea that God gives a "pattern" or "form" for the temple reoccurs in scripture. It is mentioned again in 1 Chronicles 28, where David charges his son Solomon to build the temple. We find, starting at verse 11 and running through verse 18, a massive run-on sentence in which David describes the temple and its furniture. The sentence begins, "David gave his son Solomon the plan (*tabnît*) . . . the plan (*tabnît*) of all that he had by the spirit. . ." (28:11, 12). At the very end of the long sentence, it says, ". . . and the gold for the figure (*tabnît*) of the chariot—the cherubs—those with outspread wings screening the Ark of the Covenant of the Lord. [David says to Solomon:] 'All this that the Lord made me understand by His hand on me, I give you in writing—the plan (*tabnît*) of all the works" (vv. 18–19). It is incredible to think that this use of the relatively rare word *tabnît*, specifically in the context of temple building, is coincidental. Here we have the claim that the pattern was given to David in the spirit, and that he passes it on to Solomon. This includes the crucial details for the chariot throne, which was by this time, as we have seen, especially associated with heavenly realities. Later, the writer of the Wisdom of Solomon goes even further when he has Solomon say, "You have given command to build a temple on your holy mountain . . . a copy (*mímēma*) of the holy tent that you prepared from the beginning" (9:8). From here it is a short step to the teaching of the Book of Hebrews, in which the author explains, "They offer worship in a sanctuary that is a sketch (or figure, *hupodeígmati*) and shadow (*skia*) of the heavenly one; for Moses, when he was about to erect the tent, was warned, 'See that you make everything according to the pattern (*túpon*) that was shown you on the mountain'" (8:5; cf. Heb 9:23–24).[77] Finally, in a Jewish work

---

76. Cf. Fletcher-Louis, *All the Glory of Adam*, 267 ff.; Levenson, *Sinai and Zion*, 140–41; Klawans, *Purity, Sacrifice, and the Temple*, 129.

77. Also, in the New Testament, see Acts 7:44, where Stephen says that Moses built the tabernacle "according to the pattern (*túpon*) he had seen."

written soon after the fall of the second temple, God explains that the Temple was with him "from the moment that I decided to create paradise" (2 Baruch 4:3).[78] God showed this temple to Adam, then to Abraham, and finally to Moses "on Mount Sinai when I showed him the likeness of the tabernacle and all its vessels. Behold, now it is preserved with me. . ." (vv. 5–6). The earthly copy may crumble, but the heavenly tabernacle does not fail.

In these texts, we see an effort to conceptualize a relationship between two interrelated dwellings, one heavenly and the other earthly. Various Hebrew and Greek words are used to describe the relationship: *tabnît* (plan, form, figure), *mímēma* (imitation, copy), *hupodeigma* (model, figure, sketch), *skia* (shadow), *typos* (type, copy). Also, the LXX translates the Hebrew word *tabnît* in Exodus 25 and 1 Chronicles 28 as *paradeigma* (pattern, model, paradigm). All of these metaphors, drawn from different fields, point in the direction of a relationship of dependence. The heavenly reality is more actual, more essential, and the earthly structure is shaped in conformity with its heavenly counterpart, which is the "true" (cf. Hebrews 8:2, 9:24). Is this Platonism? Certainly, the Greek words listed above have platonic resonance, but it is possible to see an authentic priestly/Deuteronomic trajectory of thought which seems to travel in a similar direction, thus creating a very comfortable space for a fruitful dialogue between Moses and Plato.

Here we stand at the origins of a movement that will forever after remain profoundly influential in Jewish theology; it will shape later apocalyptic, Merkavah, Hekhalot, and Kabbalistic approaches to the mystery of God. The conviction that there is an inviolable heavenly temple was a crucial support for Israel after the Jerusalem temple is destroyed in AD 70. For our purposes, what is most important is to see how the theological symbol of the temple facilitated reflection on the relationship between divine and creaturely truth. The creaturely reality was increasingly understood as a reflection of what is unchanging and most holy, the eternal sphere of God's presence. If we were to translate this into scholastic philosophical terms, we might say the "essence" of the temple is *beyond* its creaturely "existence" in Jerusalem, just as, analogously, God is beyond creation; God is transcendent. Appreciation for the true transcendence of God opens possibilities for participatory metaphysics: creaturely

78. From James H. Charlesworth, ed., "2 (Syriac Apocalypse of) Baruch," in *The Old Testament Pseudepigrapha*, trans. A. F. J. Klijn, vol. 1 (New York: Doubleday, 1983), 5–89.

being—and the temple before all else—does not subsist in itself but imperfectly manifests eternal Truth.[79]

In its most pure form, this philosophical perspective would imply a wholly transcendent understanding of truth: Truth belongs to heaven, not to the creature, and thus it must "come down" to us from without. There is something inescapably alien about divine truth, and thus we can only await what we do not innately possess. The temple is given by God on Mount Sinai, or the prophet is chosen by God and ascends in the spirit to the heavenly throne, but in either case, the gift is unanticipated and seemingly detached from the here and now. The response, again and again, is that the seer falls on his or her face, overwhelmed by the splendor of God's uncreated light; if he or she is to survive the encounter with God, there must be a spiritual transformation. Put more strongly, the worshiper must, through grace, become more like God to withstand God's all-holy, wholly-other presence in the heavenly realm. Returning to the two "organizing principles" articulated by Klawans in reference to temple theology and sacrifice, a strong understanding of God as transcendent can encourage, perhaps counterintuitively, an *imitato dei* theology (or, at least, *imitatio angeli*[80]). The implicit ethic suggests that the temple community (or the ecclesia) must receive from heaven a mode of being that is perhaps, by the world's standards, foolishness. Liturgically, then, it is not a surprise that the worshiping community sometimes came to see itself as raptured, joining the heavenly choir, imitating and being initiated into an eternal reality that surpasses the limitations of time and space.[81]

From a Christian or Jewish perspective, which so strongly emphasizes the fact that God's love is unmerited and that grace is a free gift, the theological value of this approach is obvious. But there are also definite drawbacks. Just as we saw that the understanding of temple as microcosm could result in either (mono)polytheism or pantheism, there are at least two significant dangers to be found in this alternative trajectory of thought if it is unchecked. First, while God's glory is rightly celebrated as wholly other, the danger remains that God will become entirely extrinsic to creation and that the relationship between creature and creator will be seen as arbitrary

---

79. According to Jon Levenson, "In short, what we see on earth in Jerusalem is simply the earthly manifestation of the heavenly Temple, which is beyond localization. The Temple on Zion is the antitype to the cosmic archetype. The real Temple is the one to which it points, the one in 'heaven,' which cannot be distinguished sharply from its earthly manifestation." *Sinai and Zion*, 140.

80. Klawans, *Purity, Sacrifice, and the Temple*, 143.

81. Cf. Fletcher-Louis, *All the Glory of Adam*; DeConick, "What Is Early Jewish and Christian Mysticism?," 23–24.

and imposed. The total otherness of God eventually becomes the irrelevance of God, opening the way to deism, culminating in atheism.[82]

Alternatively, second, the earthly temple could become, not a symbol of joy, but despair: so pale and pathetic is the imitation when compared to the heavenly/eschatological reality that the earthly institution is despised in favor of the otherworldly. Himmelfarb calls this a "desacralization of the earthly temple in favor of the heavenly. . . ."[83] The emphasis on divine Truth—which is unmarred by time, impermanence, and the dustiness of earth—can become so absolute that it eclipses all else, and creaturely truth becomes devalued or annihilated. It is not hard to see how such an attitude could promote pietistic sectarian movements like the Essene community. In Przywara's terms, this is the danger of "Theo-pan-ism." He says, "'Theo-pan-ism' means that, proceeding fundamentally 'from above to below,' God becomes the all."[84] Such a pessimistic, otherworldly, starkly dialectic theology might encourage believers to abandon their worldly responsibilities, and thus provoke a reaction-formation (for example, political theologies that move headlong in the opposite direction, toward a revolutionary obsession with creating heaven on earth). Acclaiming God's transcendent glory may start as a celebration of God, but it runs the risk of ultimately collapsing into hatred of God's good creation and/or hatred of God's crushing perfection. Once again, the theology of temple as mirror of heaven is finally inadequate to capture the relationship between divine and human truth, and in fact, on its own, it can only end in distortion.

The Concrete Analogy: First Draft

The two tendencies we have investigated in this section—temple as microcosm and temple as mirror of heaven—represent distinct modes of thought. Once again, Przywara provides some guidance for understanding each of these "poles," and what is fascinating, as I have suggested on a few occasions, is how closely the different temple traditions correspond with Greek philosophical movements, *mutatis mutandis*. Przywara schematizes this as two interpretations of the prefix in *ana-logia*. It could be read as the Greek word *ánō* (ἄνω), which means "from the above and

82. For reflection on the negative effects of such "extrinsicism," see Henri De Lubac, "Internal Causes of the Weakening and Disappearance of the Sense of the Sacred," in *Theology in History*, trans. Englund Nash Anne (San Francisco: Ignatius Press, 1996), 223–40.

83. Himmelfarb, *Ascent to Heaven*, 13.

84. Przywara, *Analogia Entis*, 165.

back to the above," or it might imply the word *aná* (ἀνά), which means "intrinsically ordered."[85] Each of these understandings of *analogia* finds a champion in Greek philosophy in Plato and Aristotle.

According to Przywara, Plato and Aristotle each attempt to avoid the extreme positions represented by Heraclitus—for whom everything is change—and Parmenides—for whom change is an illusion and everything is one. Thus, Plato and Aristotle seek to critique the extremes and instead put "fundamental emphasis upon the *meson* [middle] between them."[86] Simplifying things as much as possible, Przywara essentially says that, for Plato, the formula "archetype and image" helps to guide the philosopher toward the "in-between" which is the "'in-stantiation' of the archetypes in nature."[87] The real in this system, Przywara says, comes "from above" because the image mirrors the timeless archetypes[88]—it is a philosophy, in other words, of icons which make present "the radiance of what lies beyond the heavens: figurality as participation."[89] A major problem for Plato, however, is that he "does not actually aim at the ideal 'through' the real, but 'away from' the real,"[90] and this problem goads Aristotle. It is one of the inspirations of the latter's own attempt to mediate between Heraclitus and Parmenides. Aristotle wants to highlight the "inner completeness of the world of sensible particulars," arguing not for "participation," but "indwelling" which "unites idea and reality."[91] One finds the "middle," for Aristotle, "within" the order of nature.

Przywara celebrates the insights of Aristotle and Plato, but he also shows how each of their philosophies reaches a limit, beyond which they come undone. Neither finds peace on its own terms. The problem, he says, is that "they betray a 'desperate longing' for the divine: a variously accented 'delirium,' reeling between intoxicated unity with the divine and defiant distance from it. . . ."[92] This is where the parallel reflections in Jewish temple theology represent a significant contribution, because now the themes of indwelling and transcendence were developed in relationship with the covenantal God whose name was revealed to Moses, and whose personal love and concern was repeatedly encountered in history. Drawing the covenantal faith together in a single cultic center also helped

85. Przywara, 238–39.
86. Przywara, 239.
87. Przywara, 239–40.
88. Przywara, 241.
89. Przywara, 241.
90. Przywara, 245.
91. Przywara, 246.
92. Przywara, 259–60.

to make otherwise abstract philosophical discussions not just personal but concrete: this one institution represents *both* the summary truth of creation *and* the highest truth of heaven. Somehow the longing of the intrinsically ordered creation finds its answer in the blazing revelation of heavenly glory: in this one theological symbol, the highest transcendence finds its most intimate indwelling. Both immanence and transcendence find concrete expression in a single, complex, unified theological mystery.

The temple was the subject of two distinct discourses, but these discourses never fully came together in second temple Jewish theology. From one perspective, the temple represented the perfection of creation, the Edenic purity that God called into being from the start, and from the other perspective, the temple pointed toward the splendor of the uncreated heaven, the place from which the angels eternally cry out in delight, "Holy! Holy! Holy!" From one perspective, the temple was a monument to humanity's great vocation and dignity, our calling to partake in the creative ordering of the world, and from the other perspective, the temple was the place where the visionary is overwhelmed, falls down in worship, and experiences his unworthiness before God. From one perspective, the temple is the locus of God's free and immediate indwelling at the very heart of creaturely being, and from the other perspective, it only vaguely mirrors a reality that so far surpasses creaturely competence that the prophet is reduced to ecstatic stammering about palaces of fire and ice. For one, the truth of God is found most intimately in and through the peaceful order of the good creation, for the other, God's truth is an apocalyptic interruption that shakes the foundations of the world. The ultimate site of hospitality, the temple hosts both modes of reflection, and there are even premonitions that the two views are called to recline together like lion and lamb, but the path toward this harmony is not yet clear.

As we have emphasized, Przywara's great contribution is the understanding of the *analogia entis* as the suspended tension between poles. Balthasar insists that the *analogia entis* is not merely a philosophical rule, but it is revelation proper to Christian theology: because Jesus Christ, the incarnate *logos*, is the "ultimate union of divine and created being," Balthasar says that he "must constitute the final proportion between the two and hence must be the 'concrete analogia entis' itself."[93] Especially in light of the definitions of Nicaea—which affirms that there is difference in divine unity—and Chalcedon—where Christ's divinity and humanity are undivided and unconfused—Christians have a long tradition of reflec-

---

93. Hans Urs von Balthasar, *Theo-Drama: Theological Dramatic Theory, Vol. 3: The Dramatis Personae: Persons in Christ* (San Francisco: Ignatius Press, 1993), 222.

tion on how the infinite might fully and peacefully come to expression in the finite without the destruction of either. The claims made about Jesus of Nazareth were, undoubtedly a stumbling block for many ancient Jews, but from the perspective of temple theology, it must be said that this reflection on the ontological relationship between divine and creaturely truth was not unanticipated.

To introduce a topic that will be the focus of the eighth chapter: in the New Testament, Jesus Christ is the fulfillment of the temple. This affirmation is now receiving greater attention, catalyzed by researchers associated with what is sometimes called the "third quest" in New Testament scholarship, which has sought to interpret the biblical accounts of Jesus of Nazareth within a Second Temple Jewish context. N. T. Wright has led the way in this research, arguing that Jesus understood his vocation in terms of finally enacting a "real return from exile,"[94] the long-awaited realization of "the great healing, the great restoration, of Israel,"[95] which is inseparable from the idea of "the return of YHWH to Zion."[96] Jesus does this by "a necessary reordering of Israel's symbolic universe"[97]— including symbols like temple and Torah—"reconstituting" these symbols around himself.[98] As Wright points out, "Jesus acted as if he thought he were the reality to which the Temple pointed, or even the one who had authority over the Temple. . . ."[99] Ultimately, Wright says, the themes of "the return of YHWH to Zion, and the Temple-theology which it brings into focus, are the deepest keys and clues to gospel christology."[100]

Insights like these have encouraged other scholars to focus on the centrality of the temple as they reread the gospels and other early Christian texts.[101] In some crucial verses, Jesus does not merely replace the

94. N. T. Wright, *Jesus and the Victory of God* (Minneapolis: Fortress Press, 1996), 127. In the background here is Wright's claim that there was a widespread conviction in the Second Temple period that the Babylonian exile never truly ended, that Israel was never fully restored, and even now awaited a new exodus. Cf. Wright, 126–31.

95. Wright, *Jesus and the Victory of God*, 130.

96. Wright, 612.

97. Wright, 472.

98. Wright, 473.

99. Wright, 647.

100. Wright, 653.

101. The literature here is now extensive, especially as it pertains to the book of John. Important studies include Mark Kinzer, "Temple Christology in the Gospel of John," in *Society of Biblical Literature 1998 Seminar Papers 37*, 1988, 447–64; Briggs, *Jewish Temple Imagery in the Book of Revelation*; Stevenson, *Power and Place*; Alan Kerr, *The Temple of Jesus' Body: The Temple Theme in the Gospel of John*, vol. 220 (Sheffield: Sheffield Academic Press, 2002); Cyprian Robert Hutcheon, "'God Is with Us': The Temple

temple, he *is* the temple. Consider these two passages from the opening pages of the Gospel of John. "And the Logos became flesh and tabernacled (*eskēnōsen*) among us and we beheld his glory (*dóxan*), glory as the only begotten from the Father" (1:14).[102] As many have pointed out, by drawing together a key LXX word for God's indwelling in the temple and the theme of divine glory, this passage undoubtedly associates Jesus with the priestly tabernacle. Then, in the next chapter, while standing in the Jerusalem temple, Jesus announces: "Destroy this temple, and in three days I will raise it up" (2:19). The gospel writer then clarifies that Jesus was speaking of "the temple, which is his body" (v. 21).[103] The big question here is, of course, whether Christ is *replacing* his temple-body with the Jerusalem temple, or whether he is suggesting a more organic "fulfillment," one in which the truth of the temple is elevated through its non-contrastive relationship with Christ. As it will become clear in forthcoming chapters, I read the texts in the latter sense; the fate of the temple and of Jesus Christ are intermingled, the type and the antitype conspire, they breathe together, in such a way that when one gives up his spirit (Mt 27:50), both do (Mt 27:51).[104] In the overall narrative arch of the Synoptics, Jesus journeys toward Jerusalem and the temple, but in the overall arch of the Christian biblical canon, Jerusalem and the temple journey toward Christ. Like the high priest, but more so, Jesus is the personified, vivified, and enfleshed recapitulation of the most holy sanctuary in its whole history from Eden to Moriah, Sinai to Zion.

Over many years, Christians have reflected on the notion that Jesus is the truth of the Father who both descends from heaven as an unanticipated gift and gathers up, orders, and perfects all creation from the bottom up. While some will claim that this type of Christology is a Hel-

---

in Luke-Acts," *St. Vladimir's Theological Quarterly* 44, no. 1 (2000): 3–34; Beale, *The Temple and the Church's Mission*, 169–334; Fletcher-Louis, "Jesus as the High Priestly Messiah"; A. L. A. Hogeterp, *Paul and God's Temple: A Historical Interpretation of Cultic Imagery in the Corinthian Correspondence*, Biblical Tools and Studies 2 (Leuven: Peeters, 2006); Paul M. Hoskins, *Jesus as the Fulfillment of the Temple in the Gospel of John* (Eugene, OR: Wipf & Stock Publishers, 2007); Pitre, "Jesus, the New Temple"; Nicholas Perrin, *Jesus the Temple* (Grand Rapids, MI: Baker Academic, 2010); N. T. Wright, *Paul and the Faithfulness of God* (Minneapolis: Fortress Press, 2013), 711 ff.; Leithart, "'We Saw His Glory'"; Kathleen Troost-Cramer, *Jesus as Means and Locus of Worship in the Fourth Gospel* (Eugene, OR: Wipf and Stock, 2017).

102. As translated by Joseph R. Greene, "The Realization of the Heavenly Temple in John's Gospel: Jesus and the Spirit" (Diss., Southeastern Baptist Theological Seminary, 2012), 112.

103. Greene, 144.

104. Cf. Pitre, "Jesus, the New Temple," 63.

lenistic intrusion, in fact, these ideas are profoundly anticipated in temple theology; insofar as Jesus associates himself with the truth of the temple, the themes of temple as microcosm and temple as mirror of heaven immediately become available for interpreting the mysterious identity of the Nazarene. On that note, N. T. Wright has asked, "What might it do to our systematic Christologies to make the Temple, rather than theories about natures, persons and substance, central to our reflection? I do not know. But I do know that if we were to try we might find all kinds of new themes opening up before us."[105] Based on our research in this chapter, it seems that, when one digs deep into temple theology, one finds that some of the great philosophical questions that captivated the ancient Greek philosophers were also to be found in Jewish reflections on the temple, just in a different idiom. Perhaps we will discover, in response to Wright's question, that Christologies that make the temple central will not look radically different from Nicaea and Chalcedon after all.[106] In fact, it may be the case that the rules of faith established by the ancient church represent the legitimate continuation of temple reflection in a new key, one in which the two strands of temple theology explored in this chapter are perichoretically interrelated for the first time, thus opening the way for significant philosophical and theological development.

105. N.T. Wright, "Jesus' Self-Understanding," in *The Redemption: An Interdisciplinary Symposium on Christ as Redeemer*, ed. Stephen T. Davis, Daniel Kendall, and Gerald O'Collins (Oxford: Oxford University Press, 2006), 58.

106. Cf. Long, *Hebrews*, 153. Another theologian who has taken up Wright's challenge and offered at least the beginning of an answer is Peter Leithart. See "'We Saw His Glory.'"

CHAPTER 4

The Extremes of Sacred Geography

Weaving the Strands of Temple Theology: Beauty, Goodness, and Truth

Throughout the chapters of this opening part of the book, this "mini-trilogy" developing a systematic theology of the temple, we have focused primarily on priestly theology, but of course, Zion and its house of worship were also a royal institution. In the Old Testament, it is emphasized again and again: David was the favored one. According to the book of Psalms, he was the poet who wrote songs of praise, melodies that could be heard in Jerusalem for hundreds of years as awe-struck pilgrims climbed the mountain of God. David is the one who brought the ark at last to Jerusalem, leaping for joy before God and making sacrifices. David was the one who came to the threshing floor, saw the angel standing between heaven and earth, and fell to the ground in repentance. He knew that this was holy land, so he bought it from Ornan the Jebusite at full price, and he intended to build the house of God. David was the favored one, he was beloved, and yet he was not allowed to fulfill his dream and build the temple. Why?

According to the Chronicler, God came to David and said:

> You have shed much blood and fought great battles; you shall not build a House for My name for you have shed much blood on the earth in My sight. But you will have a son who will be a man at rest, for I will give him rest from all his enemies on all sides; Solomon (*Šelōmōh*) will be his name and I shall confer peace (*šālôm*) and quiet on Israel in his time. (1 Chr. 22:8–9).

It was not fitting that the house of God should be built by a man of war. In fact, as Levenson points out, in the book of Exodus, "an old law forbids the altar in any shrine to be made of dressed stone, 'for you have struck your sword against it and thus profaned it' (Ex. 20:25)."[1] No wars, no swords: the temple was to be an icon of peace, sabbath, and life.

---

1. Levenson, *Sinai and Zion*, 96. Cf. Berman, *The Temple*, 73–75.

As I have mentioned a few times, one of the leading goals of this mini-trilogy has been to push back against the common assumption that the temple was a place of violence, punishment, and death. Whatever modern Western theologians or sociologists might think, this assumption could not be more different from the presuppositions which formed the foundation of early Jewish temple theology. In the minds of those who actually worshiped in this space, who revered it and loved it, Zion truly was perfect in beauty, and to approach the altar of God was to personally encounter surpassing joy and delight. Even in a time of sin, *especially* in a time of sin, the people would crawl back to the one place where they knew they could find forgiveness and new life. Here was the hope of resurrection, established at the very heart of the nation.

I have argued that the temple was, in the ancient covenant, an uncommonly powerful theological symbol that draws together and correlates many aspects of Jewish religious life. It is the icon that, in both its complexity and simplicity, best captures what it means "to be" Israel. To appreciate the theological mode of "being" specific to Israel and exemplified by the temple, I have meditated on this mystery in terms of its beauty, its goodness, and its truth. In the first chapter, therefore, the emphasis was on the idea that, for ancient Israel, the temple was the site of God's indwelling glory, the place where divine splendor took form and allowed itself to be perceived. Visitors to the temple were invited to contemplate the structures of Jerusalem as an icon of God; this God wholly surpasses finite representation, but nevertheless makes himself available to the worshipers' loving gaze in the sacrament of his dwelling place. The nation's response to this great splendor was to be drawn forward in praise and worship. In other words, it was the place of communal and personal conversion and sanctification in God's light.

In the next chapter, the mystery of Zion was approached again, but this time in terms of "the action" that caused the mountain to be renamed *YHWH-yireh*, "The LORD is seen." The drama of Genesis 22 really comes down to the meaning and the challenge of a single word: *hinneni*. When God calls Abraham, Abraham responds with that one word which implies openness, readiness, and freedom before God. Hearing this word, God effectively asks, "Will you live out this identity? Will you carry it through to the end? Would you even offer back the gift that I have given you, your only hope in the world, that which you love best, your very son, Isaac?" It is a difficult and sobering story, but no narrative in the Hebrew Bible better communicates the radical claim that God makes on his people: they must fully let go of every clutching desire, and they must fully die to self if they want to know the true meaning of life. Israel has nothing unless Israel gives up everything; Israel must again learn to stand naked before God. In the narrative, God also reaffirms that he is the God of life and superabundant, extravagant grace. Here is the basic truth of the Jewish covenant put into astonishing action: YHWH is the God who is seen where there is mutual self-giving in love.

In the previous chapter, the mystery of the temple was approached a third time, but now with a focus on the way temple theology addresses the question of truth, the problem of the relationship between God's "logic" and creaturely "logic," that is, the *Logos* and the *logoi*. What we discovered is that the temple was the focal point for two distinct ways of conceiving the relationship. On the one hand, the priestly tradition especially emphasized God's immanent presence in the temple,[2] and also the idea that the temple is a microcosm, the place where all creation was gathered and represented in ideal harmony. The sense, then, was that the indwelling presence of God was intimately hidden at the heart of creaturely being, and humanity was called to help order, sustain, and protect the good creation. On the other hand, influenced by the Deuteronomic school, a second perspective seemed to emphasize that God is wholly other, utterly transcending the created world, and that the empty temple represents, or perhaps participates in, God's heavenly dwelling. From this perspective, the revelation of God interrupts creation, and human beings are in need of a transformation that comes through an ascent beyond worldly finitude. Taken together, these views imply a "suspended middle," God beyond-and-in creation, the creaturely rooted in a Truth that fully surpasses it.

Having contemplated the temple from each of these three perspectives, one final clarification is in order. According to Balthasar, in Greek philosophy, as it is received in Christian tradition, "Truth, goodness, and beauty are so fully transcendental properties of being that they can be grasped only in and through one another."[3] As Balthasar says in the first volume of the *Glory of the Lord*, without beauty and splendor, the call to the good—the *hinneni* form of life—can appear brutal and cold, and the demonstration of truth can become impersonal and irrelevant.[4] But then, without goodness, the *eros* of beauty can degrade into self-absorbed covetousness and lust, and the logic of truth lacks personal

---

2. But, again, see Sommer's point that this emphasis is not without nuance. Even within P, there is an implicit critique of divine immanence. Cf. Sommer, *Bodies of God*, 119–20.

3. Hans Urs von Balthasar, *Theo-Logic, Vol. 1: Truth of the World* (San Francisco: Ignatius Press, 2000), 225.

4. Cf. Balthasar, *GL1*, 19.

concern and moral direction. Finally, without truth—without appreciation for the analogous nature of creaturely being suspended between logical poles—beauty can be reduced to either a univocal symmetrical order or the equivocal sublime, and goodness might be reduced to either a univocal categorical imperative or equivocal divine volunteerism. Each "transcendental" protects its fellows from disfiguration, and thus first three chapters of this book must be read together.

Applying these observations, then, we can say that the beauty of the temple is in the way it communicates to the worshiper the goodness of covenantal grace and the goodness of self-giving, and also in the way it reveals the truth of the God who dwells most intimately in creation and draws creation toward transcendent life. The goodness of the temple is driven by that Glory who shines fearfully and wonderfully upon the sons and daughters of Abraham, ecstatically moving them to set out toward a way of being that is both different from the nations and is the hope of the world. The goodness of the temple is also clarified by the truth that creaturely being is suspended in God, that the reason why self-abandonment in God is good for the human being is that it corresponds to the reality of what it means to be a creature. Finally, the truth of the temple is clarified by the realization that Zion is the *hinneni*-place, the fountain of beauty. This truth ultimately points toward an ontology of love.

Hopefully we have now answered the questions that were introduced in chapter one: why does this small hill in Jerusalem take on such significance, why is it seen as the very center and heart of creation? Holding together our discoveries in the chapters on beauty, goodness, and truth in temple theology, we find that the biblical tradition advances a rich and sophisticated answer to these questions, one that is far more than nationalistic special pleading. This is the site of a truly unique revelation, for it is the site where the true God of creation, the God of Abraham, Isaac, and Jacob, meets his people face to face. We can now see how everything works together—the grades of holiness, the diverse liturgical practices, the profound symbolism of the furniture, the Edenic holy of holies, the chariot throne—all of it serves to draw Israel more and more into relationship with Yhwh, a relationship that transfigures the people of God and culminates in the great cosmic liturgy, the heavenly doxological song:

> "Holy, holy, holy!
> The Lord of Hosts!
> His presence fills all the earth!"[5]

5. Isaiah 6:3.

Interruption. An Empty, Howling Waste: Israel's Hell

Tragically, that's not all.

How good and lovely it would be, that the creation were spoken into existence, the temple constructed in obedience, and that God should dwell with the people in harmony forever. But any cursory look at biblical geography since Genesis 3—or any passing familiarity with "current events" at any point in human history—will remind us that Mount Zion is not the only topographical marker. In fact, Israel is surrounded on all sides by its antithesis: wilderness, chaos, and death. It is a vicious terrain that is always storming the gates. In the biblical story, Israel's position is precarious, vulnerable to the darkness, and sometimes she even abandons herself to the night. To speak at such length—as I have done—about the beauty, goodness, and truth of the temple, to celebrate its status as perfect peace and rest, may come across as willful ignorance or a massive deception. Is it not the case that the temple is very small compared to the wilderness, which stretches in every direction, as far as the eye can see? Is it not the case that the most characteristic situation for Israel is not paradisiacal peace, but judgment, and even exile? What place is there for such idyllic fairy tales in the chaos of this world, which features an abyss of ruined lives, of compounding miseries, where no two stones are left one upon the other?

Balthasar himself might be critical of some aspects of the temple theology that I have developed in this first part of the book, especially those places where I draw upon extra-biblical second temple literature. In the sixth volume of the Glory of the Lord, his *Theology of the Old Covenant*, Balthasar refuses to look away from or gloss over one of the central themes of the Hebrew Bible: God's judgment on Israel and his just wrath.[6] As Balthasar says in the introduction to that volume,

> It is not possible to enjoy a reposeful aesthetic contemplation of the divine glory, a contemplation that would consider God 'in himself' and thus could dispense with the opposition between God's holiness and the unholiness of the world, of which the contemplator is the mathematical exponent, as it were. Glory is the intruding lordliness of him who comes to confront the world, both judging it and gracing it. It is this that distinguishes the biblical reality from the epiphanies of gods outside the Bible.[7]

6. See, for example, Balthasar, *GL6*, 218, 301.
7. Balthasar, 14.

Keeping this in mind, one can understand the reserve Balthasar shows for late second temple literature, especially the extra-biblical apocalypses. These texts, he says, fall under a category made infamous by Luther: they are "*theologia gloriae*, theologies of glory." It is not a compliment. Balthasar believes that in the second temple period the prophets vanish and God falls silent. Confronted with this "long twilight," some attempts were made to force the return of lost glory. This is how Balthasar interprets (1) messianic literature (which promotes glory in history through political revolution), (2) intertestamental apocalyptic (for example, the books of Enoch), and (3) Hellenizing wisdom literature (like Sirach or the Wisdom of Solomon). Balthasar's negative assessment of these texts is not absolute—he recognizes that this literature is an indispensable "mediator" without which the New Testament would be impossible to conceive—but on a hierarchy of theological value, Balthasar is *much* more appreciative of the canonical prophets of old.

The main problem for *theologia gloriae* is stated directly: "it is a theology that has somehow put the nights and terrors of the judgment behind itself, without integrating them in depth."[8] In this context, Balthasar is consistently negative toward apocalypses like *1 Enoch*. It is not the case that such texts simply ignore evil: in fact, personified evil forces play a major role. Nevertheless, unlike the proclamations of the great prophets, which were "double-sided," offering both "judgment *and* salvation" to the same community,[9] on Balthasar's reading the non-biblical apocalypses often suggest blithely that the allegiance with evil is a problem for "them," the damned masses, while the minority of unstained chosen ones is saved. The lines are neat and clean, black and white.[10] This is very different from the *biblical* crisis of God's wrath—which rips through Israel itself and is not reserved only for "the nations," nor does it bypass a spiritual elite.[11]

8. Balthasar, 304.

9. Balthasar, 339.

10. Cf. Balthasar, 339–43. For further reflection on Balthasar's positive and negative approaches to apocalyptic literature, see O'Regan, *Anatomy of Misremembering*, 87–91 and chapter 6, esp. 383–94.

11. A critical note on Balthasar's approach to second temple literature: to his credit, he takes the idea of the biblical canon seriously. As illuminating and helpful as non-canonical texts may be, and while the deuterocanonical books have authority, he certainly prioritizes the foundational biblical texts in interpreting the theo-drama of ancient Israel. He also quite rightly points out some real theological weak points in these books. Nevertheless, without allowing the apocalyptic or pseudepigraphal texts to become a substitute canon (*pace* Margaret Barker), it is not necessary to read second temple literature flatly

This point is crucial because it also marks the difference between the covenantal faith, in which sin is an infidelity that strikes at the heart of Israel, and the ancient mythologies of the surrounding cultures. As we have seen, in those creation myths, the world is established as the result of a cosmic battle in which the creator god defeats an evil power, a chaos monster, often depicted as a sea god. Here the "us vs. them" duality seems to be written into the foundations of the created world: good and evil are absolutes and they are locked in violent confrontation. Levenson discerns echoes of this old myth throughout the Hebrew Bible; for him, the result is a theodicy in which chaos has not yet been fully conquered, God's absolute sovereignty is unproven, and thus God must be roused again and again to action through prayer. When God is deprived of a worthy cosmic opponent, as in theologies of *creatio ex nihilo*, and when evil becomes mere privation of the good, as in developed metaphysical traditions, Levenson believes that the battle imagery loses its potency.[12] This loss makes it harder to understand the vitality of priestly theology, where the priests are on the front lines of the cosmic war, YHWH's primary soldiers in a liturgical battle to defeat once again the chaos demon and to protect the throne of YHWH against all pretenders.

There are understandable reasons why Levenson's approach to the problem of evil has found supporters in contemporary theology. But Balthasar says that, despite any advantages that may accrue by giving up ideas like divine omnipotence, "there is no possibility of seeing evil as rooted anywhere in the divine sphere: neither in Yahweh himself, since he is all-holy, nor in any divine powers hostile to him, for no such powers

---

or dismissively, which is sometimes the case in Balthasar. This is one area in which recent scholarship—including biblical research by Jewish theologians, and the nuanced studies catalyzed by E. P. Sanders—can help to overturn bad habits too often found in some of the earlier studies. Sometimes it seems that Balthasar over-emphasizes the weaknesses of these books, perhaps partly to highlight the *novum* of Christ Jesus. For Catholic theology, the *novum* is not in doubt, but, certainly, it is not necessary to denigrate one good (like second temple Jewish theology) to recognize the perfection of another (Jesus Christ). Balthasar knows this well, of course, but after reading his interpretation of some texts in *GL6*, it seems pertinent to emphasize this point. In any case, it is possible to read a text like *The Book of the Watchers* as an entirely licit and illuminating theological meditation on biblical themes without ignoring how the text nevertheless falls short.

12. As Levenson says, "[YHWH's] victory is only meaningful if his foe is formidable, and his foe's formidability is difficult, perhaps impossible, to imagine if the foe has long since been vanquished." *Creation and the Persistence of Evil*, 27. Again, Levenson intends to employ these marginal biblical traditions in developing a modern theodicy, especially after the Shoah. Cf. Levenson, xxiii.

exist. . . ."[13] From this perspective, evil instead emerges from within the struggle to maintain the covenant, thus it is an interpersonal drama between God and his people. There are real benefits to Balthasar's approach. For primeval mythologies about the divine triumph over chaos, the victory is merely a matter of power, which is actually not that interesting. The mightier force wins every time. But in biblical theology, the problem of wilderness and chaos is not "out there," it is a problem for each human heart. The biblical struggle is therefore fundamentally different and more precarious: it's the struggle of freedom and love. It is the easiest thing in the world to kill an opponent, and the hardest thing to bring the enemy into a relationship of mutual loving-kindness.

At the same time, the imagery that Levenson alerts us to remains illustrative: Israel is in fact engaged in a struggle against what is fundamentally opposed to God's good creation: "disorder, injustice, affliction, and chaos"—and we could add exile, darkness, and above all else, death—"which are, in the Israelite worldview, one."[14] As we will see in the next chapter, Israel is aware of the fact that such evil has an existence of its own, one which must be confronted and overcome by the power of life and light. Such evil was represented in Israel by a series of theological images, and perhaps not surprisingly, given the importance of "the land" in biblical theology, many of these symbols are geographical. Thus the concepts of wilderness, desert, pit, and sea often represent the forces that oppose the treasured priestly concept of "life-sustaining order." The primary Hebrew word that is translated as "wilderness," or sometimes "desert," is *midbār*. In various places, this wilderness is described as "vast and dreadful" (Dt 1:19, 8:15), "an empty howling waste" (Dt 32:10), a place where there is no water (Dt 8:15) but only desolation (Is 64:1, Jer 12:10, Joel 2:3). The wilderness is the place of abandonment and destruction (Nm 32:15), it is where frightening wild beasts such as "seraph serpents and scorpion" roam (Dt 8:15), and where the people are exposed, "ungathered and unburied" (Ezek 29:5). Finally, the wilderness is associated with hardship and death, as seen in the people's protest that they have been brought "to die in the wilderness" (Ex 14:11; cf. Nm 21:5, 32:13–15).[15]

13. Balthasar, *GL6*, 215.

14. Levenson, *Creation and the Persistence of Evil*, xix.

15. Cf. Robert Barry Leal, "Negativity towards Wilderness in the Biblical Record," *Ecotheology* 10, no. 3 (2005): 368–75. Significantly, many of the most starkly negative depictions of wilderness come from the Deuteronomist. The importance of Jerusalem as God's chosen city is emphasized in D, whereas P's *tabernacle* tradition speaks more of a

This geographic imagery has the advantage of clearly distinguishing the wilderness from the theological meaning of Jerusalem. In fact, the difference between Zion and wilderness could not be greater. These two geographical markers remain irreducible, and actually, incomparable. But with respect to Balthasar's concerns, this obviously does not mean that "wilderness" is no longer a problem for Israel. "Wilderness" is always looking for a weakness so as to penetrate the holy city, and that the chaos of sin is successful in breaching the gates of Jerusalem is undoubted. But the breach does not destroy the distinction between Zion and wilderness. Israel's position foreshadows the paradoxical complexity that will be a hallmark of the church as well: Israel gathered around the temple is already the salvation of the world, the personification of God's loving order, the real presence of life, beauty, goodness, and truth. But it is precisely in light of this exalted identity that Israel's sin is so great.[16] This is the problem of chosenness; the God who reveals himself actually expects perfect holiness from his people, defined in terms of justice and love. He expects them to leave the wilderness behind, completely and forever.[17] That Israel fails—running after finite idols, treating the poor unjustly, refusing to embrace the call to holiness and communion—provokes the great national tragedies that the prophets confront.

The problem of exile is so profound precisely because it is the impossible, catastrophic victory of wilderness over God's holy city. Babylon succeeded in destroying heaven and earth when it unleashed its chaos on Mount Zion. Consider the starkness of the book of Lamentations. "Alas! The Lord in His wrath has shamed Fair Zion, has cast down from heaven to earth the majesty of Israel. He did not remember His Footstool on His day of wrath" (2:1). Here and elsewhere there is some ambiguity about God's involvement in the destruction, but wrath is often associated with abandonment, removal of protection, the loss of the life-sustaining order

---

"wandering center," as Sommer often puts it. This perhaps makes priestly theology especially well-suited to contemplate the strange interaction of holiness and sin in the sacred house of YHWH, the fruit of which is the theology of Yom Kippur.

16. According to Balthasar, "The glory of the God who disclosed himself always reveals his holiness as well . . . and thus it also discloses the full unholiness of the person beholding the glory," Balthasar, *GL6*, 13. Similarly, "for Israel, the central concept of evil . . . is derived from its fundamental experience of God and concept of God." Balthasar, 215.

17. I think of Lewis' sobering line: "If we insist on keeping Hell (or even earth) we shall not see Heaven: if we accept Heaven we shall not be able to retain even the smallest and most intimate souvenirs of Hell." C. S. Lewis, *The Great Divorce* (San Francisco: HarperOne, 2009), viii–ix.

resulting in death and decay.[18] Life without God, excluded from the tree of life, the holy of holies, is simply a living-death. It is hell. When you appreciate the positive theology of the temple, and the theological distinction between temple and desert, the full horror of the exile comes into stark relief. Nothing worse could happen to Israel.

The words "exile" and "death" are interchangeable; this is plainly stated in many places, and it is especially clear in the book of Deuteronomy. Kenneth J. Turner's study of exile in the book of Deuteronomy focuses on how the words *avad* (destruction, to perish, to be destroyed) and *shamad* (destruction or annihilation) are frequently used to denote exile.[19] For example, the author writes,

> When you have begotten children and children's children and are long established in the land, should you act wickedly and make for yourselves a sculptured image in any likeness, causing the Lord your God displeasure and vexation . . . you shall soon perish [from *avad*] from the land that you are crossing the Jordan to possess; you shall not long endure in it, but shall be utterly wiped out [from *shamad*]. (Deuteronomy 4:25–26)

Notably, the same root words are used in Leviticus 26, the passage from the priestly Holiness Code that articulates the blessings and curses associated with obedience or disobedience to God's commandments, but here there is a greater emphasis on the destruction of the cult site:

> I will destroy [from *shamad*] your cult places and cut down your incense stands, and I will heap your carcasses upon your lifeless fetishes. I will spurn you. I will lay your cities in ruin and make your sanctuaries desolate, and I will not savor your pleasing odors. . . . [You] shall perish [from *avad*] among the nations; and the land of your enemies shall consume you. (Leviticus 26:30, 38)

18. It is also surely true that in this verse and many others, God's wrath is portrayed as not simply the passive allowance of evil, the removal of protection, but God's active punishment. The major question is whether this represents a change in God or merely a change in humanity. This question is far too large to say anything significant about it here. Let this brief comment suffice: it may be the case that Israel, when she is secure in covenantal grace, is blessed by the encounter of God's blazing glory, but when the covenant is broken by infidelity, that same glory that was a blessing becomes a curse. The discussion of the sin of Nadab and Abihu in the next chapter will shed some light on this issue.

19. Kenneth J. Turner, *The Death of Deaths in the Death of Israel: Deuteronomy's Theology of Exile* (Eugene, OR: Wipf & Stock Pub, 2010), 47–61.

It is not the case that every single Israelite dies on account of the exile, just as it is not the case that Adam stopped breathing the moment he sinned. But to be removed from the land—and for priestly theology especially, to lose the tabernacle—was to undergo annihilation as a covenant people. Exile is death.

The interaction between wilderness and Zion is complex. On the one hand, the eschatological ideal is the final triumph over wilderness and death, a time when all nations will be gathered safely in worship at Zion. At this point, the wilderness will no longer be a threat to the life of God's people; it is permanently set apart and removed. On the other hand, the "immanent" threat is represented by the terrifying word "exile," which describes the unspeakable scenario where the temple is overrun by wilderness, desecrated, and utterly destroyed. It is the triumph of ugliness, evil, and lies; it is the undoing of creation. Most of the time biblical Israel lives between these poles, ordered toward that final peace which is "now and not yet," while also struggling with the ever-intrusive threat of wilderness.

Reflecting on the contrast between eschatological peace and worldly turmoil, it is clear that the *Chaoskampf* (the struggle against the anti-order of sin) is not a skirmish that is limited to the edge of society—if only sin were such a marginal problem for humanity!—but rather, sin must be confronted from the inside out.[20] The prophets never stop insisting that the line of sin runs right down the middle of Israel, and if it runs down the middle, it hits the center: the temple is not undisturbed by sin. If the world is affected, so is the microcosm in Jerusalem.[21] The work of "atonement" in the temple is therefore necessary, and this work is both offensive and defensive. It is offensive insofar as it reaffirms and reestablishes the eschatological reality of peace that the temple already makes present in the world. It is defensive because it rebuilds the boundaries,

---

20. There is, of course, a problem with using battle imagery to speak of the "conflict" between holiness and sin: isn't holiness necessarily nonviolent? This is a special problem for the Christian book of Revelation. I will only note the problem here without fully exploring it, but notice how the great issue of "judgment," and Balthasar's insistence that judgment not be prematurely set aside, is certainly at issue. If wilderness is not *just* an illusion, how does Love engage it? Can non-violence "confront" violence non-violently, yet mightily? An affirmative answer seems plausible, but it needs development. For an (ultimately) non-violent read on the book of Revelation, see Hans Urs von Balthasar, *Theo-Drama: Theological Dramatic Theory, Vol. 4: The Action* (San Francisco: Ignatius Press, 1994), 45–58; cf. J. Denny Weaver, *The Nonviolent Atonement* (Grand Rapids, MI: Eerdmans, 2011), 20–35.

21. Barker makes this point as well, *Temple Theology*, 62–63.

distinguishing and vigorously separating the temple from its opposite, the wilderness.

In this book thus far, I have focused primarily on the temple as a symbol of joy in response to the dismissive and negative treatment of the temple that is too common in Christian theology. Plus, it is surely not wrong to find our orientation in that symbol of life and light, for these realities are true in a way that death and darkness never can be. It is possible to overplay the importance or power of violence and evil;[22] as the psalmist says, "Weeping may last for the night, but a shout of joy comes in the morning" (Psalm 30:5, NASB). Nevertheless, this epilogue is also necessary to prevent imbalance. For the biblical writers, the temple is not merely an untouched oasis, a resort to which one might flee to "get away from it all." The temple, while remaining the icon of life and hope, is ground zero in the struggle against sin. That is precisely why Yom Kippur is necessary.

22. This is where the privation theory of sin is most helpful, and Hart is especially persuasive on this point, as we will discuss in chapter nine.

PART II

The Time of Atonement:
Yom Kippur

Section Introduction

Learning the Rhythms of Atonement

As David Fagerberg said, "Liturgical theology is the faith of the Church in ritual motion . . . [it is] a genuine theology, but one manifested and preserved in the rite as *lex orandi* even before it is parsed systematically."[1] Up to this point, I have spent all my time on the "systematic side," surveying the mystery of the temple three times, from the perspective of beauty, goodness, and truth. Now we must emphasize again that this sacred space is liturgical space: the temple was not just contemplated as an abstract symbol, but it was alive in ritual motion. The last chapters of Exodus, which describe the physical structures of the sanctuary in detail, and the first chapters of Leviticus, where rubrics for the sacrificial rites are outlined, are interrelated. As I've mentioned, it is not difficult to find studies of Israel's sacred space that overlook the sacrificial rites, and vice versa. While academic specialization is inevitable, we must nevertheless be attentive to the fact that the theology of the temple undoubtedly emerges from Israel's ancient liturgical practices, even as this life of prayer was enriched by the various schools of theological reflection on the cosmic and theological significance of the space itself.

Our focus therefore now shifts to the holy mountain as liturgical space, with an emphasis on the most sacred of the holy rites performed on Mount Zion. To quote Fagerberg again, "The starting point for liturgical theology must be real liturgies, and they do not exist in the abstract. Actual liturgies exist."[2] Yes, actual liturgies exist, both today and three millennia ago, but unfortunately our knowledge of ancient temple liturgies is relatively sparse. The Bible is not silent on the matter, but it is taciturn. Leviticus 16 stands out as an unusually detailed description of a specific temple liturgy. With Yom Kippur, we have the Bible's most elaborate and detailed liturgical rubrics.[3] Therefore, anyone interested in the

---

1. Fagerberg, *Theologia Prima*, ix.
2. Fagerberg, 40.
3. As Daniel Stökl Ben Ezra says, it is "the most detailed description of any ritual in the Bible." *The Impact of Yom Kippur on Early Christianity: The Day of Atonement from Second Temple Judaism to the Fifth Century* (Tübingen: Mohr Siebeck, 2003), 18. The nature of the relationship between this text (as a text) and the actual liturgy that occurred

relationship between *lex orandi* and *lex credendi* in ancient Israel generally, and in priestly temple theology specifically, must spend some time with this unusual text. On this holy day, the theology of the temple is *lived*, it is put into *living practice*, even before systematic theologians have a chance to reduce it to definitions. What's more, by shifting our attention specifically to Yom Kippur, we shift our attention to Israel's most holy *day*, and another key element of priestly theology comes into focus: priests were concerned not only with sacred space, but sacred time. On "the Day," on this "Sabbath of Sabbaths,"[4] space and time are made holy; here is *the* liturgy that brings multidimensional cosmic renewal.

If the only goal were to understand temple theology, then attention to the liturgy of Yom Kippur would be a vital component of any comprehensive study. But our interest is more precise. Christians routinely claim that Christ's cross effects atonement, but this affirmation is not always paired with an adequate appreciation for the fact that the word "atonement"—the Hebrew *k-p-r*—is inextricably linked to temple theology, and especially, to priestly temple theology. That helps explain the amount of time we have invested in unpacking temple theology: a biblical theology of atonement requires "total immersion" in temple modes of thought. Given the fact that the Jerusalem temple was destroyed almost two millennia ago, and that seismic cultural differences separate us from this ancient institution, it is necessary to plunge ourselves into the most recent scholarship to appreciate the meaning of the temple as sympathetically as possible.

Now that we see that the temple is the center of Israel's life of praise and the place where she is glorified in God's Glory, now that we have considered that the theological foundation of the temple is *hinneni*-life, and now that we have reflected on the strange truth that the temple is simultaneously the microcosm of creation and the mirror of heaven, a new question emerges: what becomes of this place when it is entangled in lies, besieged by evil, and suffers ugly disfigurement? Does the priestly theological tradition deny that even the sacred mountain is vulnerable to such corruption? To the contrary! Addressing the unique vulnerability of Zion was constantly at the forefront of priestly concern. The Levites were

---

in the temple (as a ritual) is widely debated. For discussion and literature reviews, see Watts, *Ritual and Rhetoric*, 27ff; Hundley, *Keeping Heaven*, 17ff; Trevaskis, *Holiness, Ethics and Ritual in Leviticus*, 27–39.

4. Morales says, "the Day of Atonement is dubbed a *šabbat šabātôn* (Lev. 16:31; 23:32), a Sabbath of solemn rest or, with he LXX translation, 'the Sabbath of Sabbaths.'. . ." Morales, *Who Shall Ascend?*, 167–68.

given the vocation to "serve and protect" this mountain (cf. Gn 2:15; Nm 18:5–6), and this charge led to a spiritual confrontation with all things unholy. On the Day of Atonement, everything came to a head: the forces of life and light engage in a great liturgical battle against the powers of death and darkness. The survival of the temple, the survival of the world, stood in the balance.

In this section, we will begin in chapter five by turning to the biblical narrative that is identified as the immediate impetus for the first Day of Atonement, the story of Nadab and Abihu, before considering the problem of sin and impurity more broadly. After gaining a better understanding of the nature of the "problem," from the perspective of temple theologians, we will then consider in chapters six and seven the detailed liturgical solution which is prescribed in the sixteenth chapter of the book of Leviticus. Here we will encounter the theology of the two goats, one serving as a spotless "purification offering," the other serving as a sin-bearing goat. The distinction between these vocations, as we will see, is crucial. Much of the focus in these chapters will be on the work of the high priest and the two goats, but one should not think that this is a private activity: we will also see how all Israel joins in the work of atonement. Finally, in chapter eight, we will consider how the theology of Yom Kippur continued to inform the earliest Christian reflections on the saving work of Jesus Christ, both in the New Testament and among the earliest post-biblical Christian theologians. We will find that there is ample justification, in both scripture and in early Christian tradition, to pursue a Christian Yom Kippur soteriology.

CHAPTER 5

The Wages of Sin: A Multifaceted Crisis

The Original Sin: Nadab and Abihu

Ask any Christian familiar with the basic doctrines of the faith about the origin of sin according to the biblical narrative, and nearly everyone would blame the tragic newlyweds, Adam and Eve.[1] Because modern scholars assign this disheartening story to the Yahwist source, perhaps we could say that the priestly account of Genesis 1 ends on a much more positive note: "And God blessed the seventh day and declared it holy. . ." (Genesis 2:3). The "very good" creation is left in restful peace; doesn't this imply an optimistic anthropology, in welcome contrast to the Adam story with its curses and exiles, and especially in contrast to the subsequent interpretive tradition with its dogmatic focus on original sin?

The question is, does creation really reach its end, according to priestly theologians, in the first verses of Genesis 2? In chapter three, we explored why the answer to that question must be "no." Recall how the building of the tabernacle parallels the creation of the world in priestly theology. This discovery was made after biblical researchers started focusing on the similarities and differences between the creation story in the priestly tradition and the analogous myths of neighboring cultures, especially the *Enuma Elish*. In that Mesopotamian myth, we saw how the Babylonian temple was built to celebrate the victory of Marduk over the chaos demon; the consecration of the temple and the beginning of sacrifices to the enthroned god was the capstone of that victory, the beginning of a blessed period of peace and prosperity. Despite the stark differences between Genesis 1 and the story of Marduk—especially in terms of divine theogony—we also saw some similarities between the divine work of creation in Genesis and divinely commissioned tabernacle building in Exodus 25–40,

---

1. Some of the material in this section first appeared in Richard J. Barry IV, "'They Feasted Their Eyes': Nadab, Abihu, and the Original Sin." *Journal of Theological Interpretation* 17, no. 2 (2023): 145–165, https://doi.org/10.5325/jtheointe.17.2.0145.

all of which suggests that it is actually the building of the sanctuary that is the culmination of creation, or maybe better said, the recapitulation of cosmic creation in a way that engages human freedom.

Therefore, the purpose of creation, from this priestly perspective, is to draw human freedom into God's just ordering of the world, or even to draw human freedom into the life-giving cycle of glory and praise. It is thus easy to understand Gary Anderson's argument (which we discussed in chapter three) that, from the perspective of the priestly theologians, with the completion of the tabernacle and the inauguration of the morning and evening Tamid sacrifice, "*the goal of all creation would be consummated.*"[2] God had a reason for speaking into existence globes of dirt to whirl around spheres of fire. The purpose, it seems, was to breathe life into the dust and invite it into the communion of love through songs of praise. The Sabbath described in the passage from Genesis is not wholly consummated until humanity freely enters such rest, and this, Anderson argues, is what finally occurs when the sacrificial pyre is lit and the morning and evening Tamid begins. In a way never before possible, it can now be said, "there was evening and there was morning," an eighth day,[3] and it was very good indeed.

If this were the *Enuma Elish*, the enthronement of the god in the temple would usher in a period of uninterrupted peace and victory. When

2. Anderson, *Genesis of Perfection*, 202. Benjamin Sommer makes the same claim. He says, "These eight days of dedication, described in Exodus 40–Leviticus 10, represent Israel's true beginning. For P, the Israelites became a nation, truly deserved the name Israel, only when God arrived in their midst and they responded accordingly—that is, when the tabernacle was complete and they initiated their worship. . . . We can go one step further. The events at the beginning of the first month of the second year represent the culmination of creation, for until then the world had been incomplete. . . . " Emphasizing the cosmic significance of this moment, Sommer says this section in Leviticus represents the "inaugural ceremonies for the world itself." Sommer, *Bodies of God*, 111.

3. According to Leviticus 9:1, the inauguration of the tabernacle takes place on the "eighth day," after a week of preparation during which the Aaronic priesthood and the tabernacle are consecrated and the new priests wait before the Lord in obedience (Lv 8). The eighth day is a new first day, one that is both "integrally connected with the previous seven" and yet "not like the previous seven." Milgrom, *Leviticus 1-16*, 571. This sense of both continuity and newness applies to the relationship between Leviticus 8 and 9, but following Anderson's suggestion, the theological interpreter would do well to also see this eighth day as the epitome of the seven days of creation from Genesis 1:1–2:3. As Christophe Nihan says, "while the seven days of Lev 8 echoed the creation of the world in Genesis 1:1–2:3, in Lev 9, the offering of the first sacrifices on the *eighth* day somehow takes the place of the *first* day *after* the creation." Christophe Nihan, *From Priestly Torah to Pentateuch: A Study in the Composition of the Book of Leviticus* (Tübingen: Coronet Books Inc., 2007), 233.

the gods finished building his house, Marduk says to them, "This, too, is your House. Take your seats and enjoy its pleasures!"[4] This they gladly do, swearing oaths of fidelity to Marduk, and curses on all traitors. With reference to ancient Near Eastern stories like this one, Anderson says, "the moment of temple building *always* ushers in an age of peace and tranquility."[5] And at first, something similar seems to occur in Leviticus 9. After a series of offerings were made to God, the chapter concludes with Aaron blessing the people. And then, "the Presence of the LORD (*kĕbôd-YHWH*) appeared to all the people. Fire came forth from before the LORD and consumed the burnt offerings and the fat parts on the altar. And all the people saw, and shouted [for joy[6]], and fell on their faces" (Lv 9:23–24). Now, the tabernacle has been constructed, the priests have been vested, all have been consecrated, all as God has commanded. At long last, with the concluding verses of Leviticus 9, the great work which began in Exodus 25—or perhaps even, the great work begun at Genesis 1:1—comes to its apogee: the tent blazes with the glory of God.[7] As the offerings are accepted in a burst of divine brilliance, the people shout with joy and fall in worship. On this eighth day, one would not be surprised if the angelic choir sang once more the ancient refrain, "The heaven and the earth were finished, and all their array" (Genesis 2:1).

Within the next two verses, the sanctuary is profaned and Aaron's eldest sons are dead. This is the unbelievable honesty of the Hebrew Scriptures. In a book written by priests, in a book celebrating priestly service, the high priest's own family defiles the tabernacle immediately upon its sacred inauguration. According to the text, "Now Aaron's sons Nadab and Abihu each took his fire pan, put fire in it, and laid incense on it; and they offered before the LORD alien fire, which He had not enjoined upon them. And fire came forth from the LORD and consumed them; thus they died at the instance of the LORD" (Lv 10:1–2). There is no millennium of peace or time for feasting in God's kindly presence; the revelation of glory is instantaneously coupled with human sin, and with sin, death.[8] From this vantage point, who could say that the P source is

---

4. Matthews and Benjamin, *Old Testament Parallels*, 20.

5. Anderson, *Genesis of Perfection*, 202.

6. Cf. Milgrom, *Leviticus 1-16*, 591.

7. This is not the only account of God's glorious descent to the tabernacle; a similar narrative can be found at the conclusion of Exodus 40. The question of how to relate these two texts has been a topic of conversation since rabbinic times. For a modern reflection on the problem, see Anderson, "Inauguration of the Tabernacle Service at Sinai."

8. Anderson suggests that the "immediacy" of this sin may be the result of the work of a redactor, and that the initial narrative spanning from Exodus 19 to Leviticus 9 may

more optimistic than J? In fact, it's just the opposite: while for Genesis 2–3, the sin of the first humans is provoked by the tempter, in Leviticus the first sin after the completion of heaven and earth (the tabernacle) appears without any prompting or warning.

While some modern readers are uncomfortable with the story of Adam and Eve—wondering why God would even make the commandment against partaking of the tree of knowledge, and further questioning why there would be so severe a punishment for such a seemingly minor sin—the story of Nadab and Abihu might cause even greater discomfort if it were widely known. What does it mean? What is an "alien fire," and why was the divine response so shockingly lethal? One answer is simply to echo Anderson: "We are left completely in the dark about the motivation of these two wayward priests and the specific nature of their sin."[9] All that is certain is that this story underscores the fact that God's indwelling presence is not just a source of blessing—what Bonhoeffer might call "cheap grace"—but it also introduces high risk.[10] The demands are greater and the margin for error is much narrower.[11] Certainly, the fate of Nadab and Abihu would have communicated that message to the nation of Israel as it gathered around the tent of meeting.

---

have more in common with the significantly more triumphant creation myths of the surrounding cultures. Cf. Anderson, *Genesis of Perfection*, 205–7. The same impulse to highlight the immediate threat of sin that caused one redactor to add the story of Nadab and Abihu, Anderson says, may have inspired yet another redactor to add the narrative of the Golden Calf immediately after God gives Moses the covenant tablets in Exodus. With each redaction, the propensity to sin is emphasized more and more. Other commentators have also emphasized the connection between the Golden Calf and the sin of Nadab and Abihu; for example, Mary Douglas, *Leviticus as Literature* (Oxford: Oxford University Press, 1999), 205.

9. Anderson, *Genesis of Perfection*, 204. Anderson has recently elaborated on this answer: "'Through Those Who Are Near to Me, I Will Show Myself Holy': Nadab and Abihu and Apophatic Theology," *Catholic Biblical Quarterly* 77, no. 1 (January 2015).

10. Sommer especially excels at emphasizing this point. He argues that this narrative serves as a valuable self-critique in priestly theology; while P does indeed advocate a vision of divine immanence (as we discussed in chapter three), priestly writers were not ignorant or flippant about the difficulties of this view, and the "alien fire" of Nadab and Abihu only serves as a reminder of the strangeness of the priestly conviction that God truly dwells in the tabernacle. Sommer says, "Yet precisely at the moment in which the domestication of the *kabod* climaxes, and specifically among those who have direct access to that divine presence, it becomes brutally clear that holiness cannot be contained." Sommer, *Bodies of God*, 120. For another worthwhile meditation on the danger and ambiguity of the cult, Bryan D. Bibb, "Nadab and Abihu Attempt to Fill a Gap: Law and Narrative in Leviticus 10.1–7," *Journal for the Study of the Old Testament* 26, no. 2 (2001): 83–99.

11. As Wenham says, "the closer a man is to God, the more attention he must pay to holiness and the glory of God." Gordon J. Wenham, *The Book of Leviticus* (Grand Rapids, MI: Eerdmans, 1979), 156.

Other commentators, however, have attempted to understand exactly what went wrong on the eighth day. For as long as there has been biblical commentary, a range of possible liturgical and moral errors have been discussed.[12] James Watt has emphasized the rhetorical goals of the priestly author: the author specifically wants to convince the hearer of the absolute importance of *obedience* or *compliance* to the divine command. Watts points out that "after two chapters [Lv 8–9] of repeating *ka'ăšer tsiwwāh* Yhwh, 'as Yhwh had commanded,' 10:1 announces that Nadab and Abihu did *ăšer lō tsiwwāh*, 'what had not been commanded.' The intrusion of the negative, *lō*, 'not,' in the familiar refrain comes like a thunderclap. . . ."[13] According to Watts, the implicit claim of the priestly rhetorician is that the very fact that this lethal outbreak of divine fire has not occurred *since* Nadab and Abihu is proof that the priests are doing their job well, and must continue in their diligent obedience.[14]

As is so often the case, Watts helpfully draws our attention to the way words are being used to persuade. From this perspective, the possible motivations of Nadab and Abihu are irrelevant; the whole point is simply that priests are charged with the task of perfect obedience, which they have since observed. But as theological readers, the story merits further reflection,[15] and the historical-critical and redactional discoveries outlined above provide an excellent opportunity for theological interpretation. Narratively and theologically, *within P*, as we have seen, this story follows *immediately* upon the completion of creation, and thus within this frame of thought it really is "an event of cosmic scope."[16] Canonically, however, the story arrives *long after* the creation accounts. The redactor puts the narrative of Adam and Eve immediately after the priestly account of creation, which serves in its own way to communicate the crisis themes of disobedience, death, and exile. Bringing all of these strands together,

12. For a review of early Jewish reflections on the sin, see Robert Kirschner, "The Rabbinic and Philonic Exegeses of the Nadab and Abihu Incident (Lev. 10: 1–6)," *The Jewish Quarterly Review* 73, 1983, 375–93; Milgrom, *Leviticus 1-16*, 633–35.

13. Watts, *Ritual and Rhetoric*, 106.

14. Cf. Watts, 111–12.

15. In saying this, I don't mean to downplay that faithful exercise of ritual rubrics is, from an ancient Near Eastern perspective, important in and of itself. As Michael Hundley says, "correct performance of a ritual is much more important than understanding how or why it works." *Keeping Heaven*, 66. This does not mean for Hundley, however, that the rituals are wholly without "underlying rationale." Hundley, 36. As mentioned in chapter two, an adequate analysis of Biblical ritual neither rips away the liturgical husk to get to the pure spiritual kernel, nor assumes an allegedly primitive "empty ritualism."

16. Sommer, *Bodies of God*, 112.

it seems very appropriate for theological readers to understand that there is a genuine parallel, or at least echo, in the diverse stories of "Original Catastrophe."[17] My interpretation of Nadab and Abihu will therefore consider whether these corresponding stories communicate something similar about human nature.

Watts is certainly right that, at some level, the issue of obedience is prominent in both stories, and that disobedience leads to crisis. If we were to follow a divine command theory, it might be adequate to stop here: "because God said so" would be an acceptable explanation for why a certain action is sinful. For those who are persuaded that divine law is ordered toward participation in God through growth in holiness, virtue, and love, however, there will always be an attempt to better perceive where the human actors went wrong. Because the drama of Nadab and Abihu depicts not just individual disorder, but the source of cosmic-temple disorder, it becomes *especially* critical to consider whether this was only a failure to follow the jots and tittles. Even though Leviticus 10:1–3 is concise—much more so than Genesis 2–3—I argue that both stories seem to operate under a common warning: "as soon as you eat of it, you shall die" (cf. Gn 2:17).[18] What is this devouring sin that leads so instantly to death?

Several modern scholars have suggested that the sin of Nadab and Abihu was a form of idolatry.[19] Many of these explanations suggest that the narrative is designed to support the larger goals of centralizing worship in Jerusalem and maintaining the distinctions between Israel and her neighbors. As plausible as these theories may be in terms of historical reconstruction, there is reason to believe that there is yet more to say.

---

17. As Sommer describes the story of Nadab and Abihu, 112. In fact, Sommer's reading of Adam and Eve is more ambiguous than his reading of the story of Nadab and Abihu; cf. 112–18. Compared to Sommer, Anderson is more straightforward in drawing the comparison.

18. For an expanded version of the argument presented here, see Barry, "They Feasted Their Eyes."

19. For example, according to Jacob Milgrom, the text is designed to oppose the syncretistic "private incense offering," which he argues was a common and often idolatrous practice among the ancient Jews even after sacrificial worship was isolated to the Jerusalem temple. Cf. Milgrom, *Leviticus 1-16*, 628–33. Milgrom translates "alien fire" as "unauthorized coals" (598) which are coals not taken from the tabernacle altar. By eliminating the use of unauthorized coals, the priestly writer is in effect removing the possibility of private incense offerings. Analogous arguments are presented by Richard S. Hess, "Leviticus 10: 1 Strange Fire and an Odd Name," *Bulletin for Biblical Research* 12 (2002): 187–98; cf. John E. Hartley, *Word Biblical Commentary: Leviticus* (Waco, TX: Word Books, 1992), 131–33.

One hint comes from Leviticus 16, the chapter on the Day of Atonement, which begins with these words: "The Lord spoke to Moses after the death of the two sons of Aaron who died when they drew too close to [*bĕqorbātām*, encroached upon][20] the presence of the Lord" (v. 1). In other words, the guidelines for Yom Kippur are understood very explicitly as an emergency response to the tragedy that occurs on the eighth day, and that tragedy is described in terms of the way Nadab and Abihu "drew near."

The word that Milgrom translates as "encroach" is already familiar to us: the root of *bĕqorbātām*, q-r-b, is the verb *qarab*, "approach, draw near." As we discussed in the second chapter, the nominal form of the same stem, *qorbān*, is often translated "an offering," and the overall connotation of these words is that we are dealing with questions about *how* human beings are to draw near to God. As we saw, the entire book of Leviticus opens with a description of the *ʿolah*, the burnt offering, as one mode—perhaps the most fitting mode—of drawing near to YHWH. Now with Nadab and Abihu, there is another mode, a kind of "drawing near" that is not commanded and causes immediate death: both Leviticus 10:1 (*wayyaqribû*)[21] and Leviticus 16:1 (*beqārebātām*) depict the sin of Nadab and Abihu as an inappropriate mode of drawing near to the Lord.

The rabbis explored this problem from all angles and developed a long list of possible sins committed by Nadab and Abihu, and indeed, one of their concerns was precisely the brothers' mode of approaching God. It is important to remember that, according to the broader biblical narrative, Nadab and Abihu already enjoyed a privileged relationship with YHWH. Exodus 24 describes how Moses, Aaron, Nadab, Abihu, and the seventy elders ascended Mount Sinai, where they "saw the God of Israel" (v. 10). With this story in mind, the *Pesikta de-Rab Kahana*—an early fifth-century collection of rabbinic homilies tied primarily to the calendar of Jewish feasts, says:

And further proof of the arrogance of Aaron's sons, said R. Phinehas, is to be had from the following verse: *And upon the nobles of the children of Israel He laid not His hand*, etc. (Exod. 24:11) from which it may be inferred that they deserved to have a hand laid upon

---

20. "Encroached upon" is Milgrom's revealing translation; *Leviticus 1-16*, 1011–12.

21. This instance of the word is almost always translated "they offered," but Baruch Schwartz prefers "presented, 'brought near'." Baruch J. Schwartz, "Leviticus, Introduction and Annotations," in *The Jewish Study Bible. Tanakh* (Oxford: Oxford University Press, 2004), 227; cf. Baruch A. Levine, *The JPS Torah Commentary: Leviticus* (Philadelphia: The Jewish Publication Society, 2003), 59.

them. For, as R. Hoshaia said, when Scripture tells us that at Sinai *They beheld God, and did eat and drink* (ibid.), are we to understand that food and drink went up with them at Sinai? No, what the verse is telling us is that <u>they feasted their eyes upon the Presence</u> in the manner of a man who is eating and drinking without restraint. . . . [A]ccording to R. Tanhuma, Exodus 24:11 teaches that <u>Aaron's sons stood and stared in a gross way, feasting their eyes boldly on the Presence</u>.[22]

Those inclined to see rabbinic exegesis as wholly fanciful could easily dismiss this claim as remote from what can be positively shown in the slender verses that describe Nadab and Abihu's actions in Leviticus. But I argue that, whether or not the rabbis' reading of Exodus 24 can be defended, this passage *is* successful in capturing the central vices that lead to the brothers' fall in Leviticus 10: arrogance and greed. The brothers are the types of men who stand and stare, who ravenously consume what has not been given. Where do we see this in Leviticus?

Consider how, in the last verse of Leviticus 9, the divine glory appears and "all the people saw, and shouted, and fell on their faces" (v. 24). The entire nation falls before the awesome splendor of God. Based on biblical expectations, one cannot imagine a more appropriate or promising response than this. But *the very next word* in Hebrew shatters the scene immediately: *wayyiqḥû*, "and they took" (Lv 10:1). The root word is *laqach*, and it is a very common word, but perhaps it is theologically illuminating to notice how the word is used in Genesis 3. The famous verse reads, "When the woman saw that the tree was good for eating and a delight to the eyes, and that the tree was desirable as a source of wisdom, she took (*wattiqqaḥ*) of its fruit and ate. . ." (v. 6). This was, undoubtedly, an unauthorized taking, the attempt to seize a good that would have otherwise been freely given. It is a biblical pattern that sometimes something delights the eyes and seems to promise happiness, and the instantaneous response is: "take," "seize," "devour."

Nadab and Abihu had already been blessed with a vision of God on Mount Sinai, and now with the rest of their people, they are blessed again. But when everyone falls in reverence, they take up their fire pans. The usual interpretation is that they take their fire pans to *offer* some-

22. This is found in the 26th *Piska*; see William G. Braude, ed., *Pesikta De-Rab Kahana*, trans. Israel J. Kapstein, 2nd Revised ed. (Philadelphia: Jewish Publication Society, 2002), 542. Italics in original, underlined texts for emphasis. This chapter from the *Pesikta* is effectively reproduced in the roughly contemporary *Leviticus Rabbah* (chapter 20); it is then picked up in other commentaries across the centuries.

thing, which seems well-meaning even if misguided. But Baruch Schwartz has provided another interpretation that potentially unlocks the rabbinic insight that they "fed their eyes," and also unlocks the parallel with the other great fall narrative of Adam and Eve. Schwartz agrees with Milgrom that the word typically translated as fire ('ēš) should be translated as "coals"—hence, "each took his pan, put coals in it, and laid incense on it; and they offered before the Lord unauthorized coals."[23] But while these are understood to be live coals for Milgrom, who emphasizes an illicit incense offering, Schwartz argues that the word should be interpreted as "kindling material" which Nadab and Abihu placed in their pans "in order to attract the divine fire to light them." Therefore, while "God intended that the manifestation of His presence would ignite the altar fire, marking His acceptance of His people's devotion, [Nadab and Abihu's] intent was for the divine fire to ignite their own pans; that is, they were attempting to arrogate control of the deity to themselves."[24] If this interpretation has merit, it corresponds beautifully with the rabbinic concern that the brother's illicitly "fed their eyes" on the glory of God; in other words, rather than opening themselves to receive God with humility and joy, they sought to reach out to domesticate God as their own. This is the great priestly temptation, and the brothers are at special risk because they have been so abundantly blessed.

In the second chapter, I meditated at length on some of the key words from Genesis 22, the story of the binding of Isaac. In our current context, one more word can be added to the mix. When God gives his command in the second verse of the chapter, it begins "qaḥ, take." "Take your son. . . ." This is a fundamentally different kind of taking, one stemming from total openness and presence before God. I have called it "hinneni-life," a form of being exemplified in Abraham and Isaac that represents a reversal of the grabbing of Adam and Eve, and thus a return to Edenic peace. Nadab and Abihu represent a parallel tradition describing the origin of cosmic disorder; here again, sin is introduced into "the heavens and the earth," the tabernacle. It is much shorter than the drama of the patriarch and matriarch, and because it is heavy with cultic terminology, it does not feel as universal. But it nevertheless communicates something all too familiar: the instantaneous desire to "take," even to reach out to possess God himself, through force. The temptation to arrogate divinity so as to elevate oneself is at the heart of pride, and it is the polar opposite of the way of humility and love. Perhaps a Christian parallel can be found in John's warning about the things of "the

23. Milgrom, *Leviticus 1-16*, 595.
24. Schwartz, "Leviticus," 227.

world," which are "lust of the flesh, lust of the eyes, and pride of life" (1 John 2:16). Such distorted, egocentric desire is the way of death, something that Nadab and Abihu discovered with unusual swiftness.[25]

After sin, Adam, Eve, and the serpent, each receive their respective curses. Amid the curses, there is also the well-known protoevangelium, the first hint of the one to come who will crush the serpent's head. Nadab and Abihu also receive their curse—they are struck, so to speak, by the angel's flaming sword as they approached the new Eden[26]—and this leads to a number of chapters that describe purity laws and the disposal of impurity. Then, finally, the liturgy of Yom Kippur is described in great detail, and it is narratively placed immediately after the death of the brothers. This is the good news of Leviticus, the promise of forgiveness and purification in the time of sin. As Anderson says, after the cosmic catastrophe of Nadab and Abihu, "the Day of Atonement served to set creation aright."[27]

Misbegotten: What Sin Introduces

As we begin to grapple with the theology of Yom Kippur, therefore, we start with the premise that the goal of this great liturgy is to restore creation after Nadab and Abihu introduced corruption. The central liturgy described in Leviticus 16 has two fundamental moments: an ascetic moment that removes sin, and a unitive moment that restores covenantal harmony. Before describing these moments (or movements) which bring restoration, the nature of the crisis within the priestly theological imagination must be clarified, because the ancient cultic perspective on these issues will be foreign to most contemporary readers of the Bible. From a modern, more individualistic perspective, once Nadab and Abihu received their punishment—once they had died before the LORD—it seems that the problem is solved. Justice is satisfied: there is sin, there is punishment. If the sin is the failing of the individual, then the problem of this person's sin is resolved upon his or her death. What more could be required? What good is "atonement" in this situation?

A close reading of the text of Leviticus 16 creates problems for an individualistic understanding of sin and atonement. After describing how blood is sprinkled in the holy of holies (see below), the priestly writer makes the

25. Again, I dive much deeper into the surprising parallels between Leviticus 10 and Genesis 2–3 in Barry, "They Feasted Their Eyes."

26. Cf. Trevaskis, *Holiness, Ethics and Ritual in Leviticus*, 95.

27. Anderson, *Genesis of Perfection*, 204.

motive for this action explicit, and it is not what we would expect: "Thus he shall purge (*wekipper*) the Shrine of the uncleanness and transgression of the Israelites, whatever their sins; and he shall do the same for the Tent of Meeting, which abides with them in the midst of their uncleanness" (Lv 16:16). Who is the object of this "purgation"? Amazingly, it is not, in the first place, the Israelites, but the tabernacle itself. For the modern reader, it makes no intuitive sense to say that a tent should be the subject of purgative rites when the Israelites sin—especially not the holy of holies, which no human has yet entered. What is the theo-logic behind this ritual?

To approach this subject, let us return one more time to the tragic fall of Nadab and Abihu. Even though the text says that the divine fire "consumes" them, their corpses nevertheless remain: "Moses called Mishael and Elzaphan, sons of Uzziel the uncle of Aaron, and said to them, 'Come forward and carry your kinsmen away from the front of the sanctuary to a place outside the camp'" (Leviticus 10:4). Two things to notice: first, sin creates a "something." In this case, the "something" is especially vivid: it is the human corpse, that dead weight, the tragic remainder of sin. Second, that remaining "something" pollutes the sanctuary and must be removed from the camp. Death is the ultimate impurity, and it is in principle antithetical to the life of the tabernacle and the One who dwells therein. The purgation of the tabernacle of any pollutants, impurities, or sins is therefore the urgent priority of the priests who, as we saw, stand on the front lines in the conflict between Life and death. Recent research has made rapid progress in understanding the theological background behind the two convictions that undergird the Jewish priestly theology of the Day of Atonement: (1) sin is a "something" and (2) sin pollutes the sanctuary. A summary of these findings will make it possible to appreciate the work of the two goats more fully.

The "Thingness" of Sin

In his book, *Sin: A History*, Gary Anderson argues that to understand a theologian's soteriology, it is essential to pay attention to the imagery she or he uses for sin. The image used to describe the problem generally correlates with the terms used to describe the solution. Thus, he points out that "stained hands are *cleansed*, burdens are *lifted*, and debts are either *paid off* or *remitted*."[28] Through metaphor, words and images are given on loan to abstract subjects like "sin" so that we might discuss what

28. Anderson, *Sin*, 4.

is unspeakable. Building on this observation, Anderson tracks the metaphors for sin within the Bible itself, showing that the preferred images
for describing sin in scripture change over time. Therefore, Anderson
shows that there is a transition from an earlier emphasis on the concept
of sin as a burden to a latter emphasis on the concept of sin as a debt.
This shift was due in part to the growing influence of Aramaic in the
Second Temple Persian period; the earlier Hebrew idiom "to bear [the
weight] of sin" over time gave way to the parallel Aramaic idiom, which
is literally "to assume a debt."[29]

Because we are dealing with relatively early priestly material, our
focus is on Anderson's description of the most ancient biblical images for
sin. Anderson says, "What is most striking is the frequency of the idiom
'to bear [the weight of] a sin' within the Hebrew Bible; it predominates
over its nearest competitor by more than six to one. For Hebrew writers
in the First Temple period, therefore, the most common means of talking
about human sin was to compare it to weight."[30] Most people, Anderson
says, are surprised when they learn that this idiom is so common. The
Hebrew words *nāśā'* (to bear) *'ăvōn* (iniquity) present problems for translators, and thus they often settle for translations that obscure the weight-
iness of the words. The difficulty is that the very same phrase, *nāśā'* +
word for sin (whether it is *'ăvōn*, or, elsewhere, *ḥaṭṭā't* [wrongs] or *pesă'*
[transgressions]) appears in two seemingly opposite contexts: one which
emphasizes the culpability of the guilty party, and the other which suggests that the sinner is forgiven. Anderson draws on the work of Baruch
Schwartz to show that there is logic in using the same phrase to communicate both culpability and forgiveness: it all comes down to who is
bearing the sin.[31] When the sinner himself bears the sin, when he carries
the weight, he suffers on account of the sin, but when another party, such
as God, bears the sin, the sin is thus *carried away* from the sinner, and he
is relieved of the burden, or, in other words, he is forgiven. In either case,
the imagery is that of bearing loads, but this is usually obscured because
the Hebrew phrase "to carry away (the weight of) sin" (*nāśā' 'ăvōn*) is
rarely translated literally. Instead, translators render it simply "to forgive
a sin." According to Anderson, "Crucial to this discussion is the notion

29. Anderson, 27–28.
30. Anderson, 17.
31. Baruch J. Schwartz, "The Bearing of Sin in the Priestly Literature," in *Pomegranates and Golden Bells: Studies in Biblical, Jewish and Near Eastern Ritual, Law, and Literature in Honour of Jacob Milgrom*, ed. David Pearson Wright, David Noel Freedman,
and Avi Hurvitz (Winona Lake, IN: Eisenbrauns, 1995), 3–21.

that sin in biblical thought possesses a certain 'thingness.' Sin is not just a guilty conscience; it presumes, rather, that some-'thing' is manufactured on the spot and imposed on the sinner."[32]

Anderson's findings build on Jacob Milgrom's earlier studies into ancient priestly terminology. Jacob Milgrom (1923–2010) was an American rabbi and long-time professor of Near Eastern Studies at the University of California, Berkeley, who retired in 1992 and lived the rest of his life in a beautiful home in Jerusalem, located almost exactly one mile from the Temple Mount, the site of the sacred rituals he had spent his entire academic career studying. It was Milgrom who led the way in clarifying the ancient understanding of sin and impurity. One of Milgrom's most important claims was that priestly theology presupposes that wrongful acts generate a dangerous pollution. Beginning in the early 1970s, Milgrom published a series of articles that reconsidered the purpose of the *ḥaṭṭā't* sacrifice (cf. Leviticus 4:1–5:13), which is one of the five major types of sacrifice cataloged in the early chapters of Leviticus, and which is also the primary offering required on Yom Kippur (Leviticus 16:6, 9).[33] One thing that distinguishes these sacrifices from other ancient Israelite temple rituals was the fact that they usually featured rites of blood manipulation. In other words, rather than dashing or pouring the sacrificial blood directly on the sides of the altar (which was the practice for burnt offerings—cf. Lv 1: 5, 11, 15; Lv 8:19—well-being offerings— cf. Lv 3:2, 8, 13—and guilt offerings—cf. Lv 7:2), the "purification offering"[34] alone requires that the victim's blood be either sprinkled toward, or rubbed on, the cultic furniture itself. On Yom Kippur, the high priest takes the blood of two *ḥaṭṭā't* offerings, a bull and a goat, and sprinkles it on the *kappōret*, which is the "solid gold slab . . . atop the Ark."[35] Then, in another phase of the ritual, the blood is apparently sprinkled in the shrine,[36] and then it is both rubbed on the "horns" of the burnt offering

32. Anderson, *Sin*, x.

33. For more on the five types of sacrifice described in Leviticus, see chapter two.

34. This is the most common translation for *ḥaṭṭā't* in modern scholarship, see footnote 7 in chapter seven for reasons why Milgrom and others prefer this to the traditional translation, which is "sin offering."

35. Milgrom, *Leviticus 1-16*, 1014. Older translations called the *kappōret* "the mercy seat," a translation Milgrom rejects.

36. Leviticus 16:16, after describing the rituals in the Holy of Holies, says ". . . [Aaron] shall do likewise for the Tent of Meeting. . . ." Milgrom is comfortable claiming that this is in reference to the "shrine," the space before the holy of holies that contains the incense altar, menorah, and the table for the bread of the Presence. Support for this view is found in Exodus 30:9–10, which suggests that "once a year" the incense altar is purified through the application of blood to its horns, and Leviticus 4:7 and 4:18 describe a similar ritual.

altar in the courtyard[37] and sprinkled toward the same altar (Lv 16:18–19; cf. Lv 4:25, 30, 34). The question for Milgrom is, what is the significance of these unique and elaborate blood manipulations?

Milgrom's answer is ultimately rooted in a sophisticated understanding of two key words: *ḥaṭṭā't* (again, traditionally translated as "sin offering") and *kipper* (often translated as "atonement"). Milgrom argues for a clean break from the conventional translations and argues that the words mean "purification offering" and "purgation." Below we will explore the reasons why Milgrom opts to translate *ḥaṭṭā't* and *kipper* as he does, but right now, let's assume his translation is correct. Milgrom's idea was that, when the blood is smeared and sprinkled on the cultic furniture, the priest is purging and decontaminating the holy space with the blood. Yet again, this is counterintuitive; why should the ark of the covenant, the incense altar in the shrine, or the altar of burnt offerings in the courtyard, need to be purified? These items are each known for their outstanding holiness.

To answer this question, Milgrom provides a window into the theological convictions of the ancient Near East. As we have seen, ancient temples were often considered centers of cosmic warfare: monuments to the victorious god but also the main battleground where the victory is continually being won against demonic opponents. For the surrounding cultures, a sophisticated demonology accompanied these ideas. David P. Wright, in *The Disposal of Impurity*, collects a bricolage of Hittite[38] and Mesopotamian[39] ritual texts that provide guidelines for removing and banishing demonic forces from both individuals and sacred spaces.[40] A key aspect of the rituals collected by Wright is that the evil forces to be exorcised have personal, preternatural vitality, insofar as they are *demonic*. Milgrom, analyzing similar sources, says that these texts "are

---

37. Ancient Near Eastern altars characteristically featured "right-angle tetrahedra projecting from the four corners," and these protrusions resembled animal horns. The Hebrew word *qeren* refers both to the horns of an animal and this architectural feature found on both the incense altar and the burnt offering altar. See Milgrom, *Leviticus 1-16*, 234–36.

38. David P. Wright, *The Disposal of Impurity: Elimination Rites in the Bible and in Hittite and Mesopotamian Literature*, Society of Biblical Literature Dissertation Series 101 (Atlanta: Scholars Press, 1987), 45–60.

39. Wright, 60–72. See also Hundley, *Keeping Heaven*, 124–34.

40. Wright points out that there are more examples of rites for removing demonic impurity from individuals than from sacred spaces in the surviving ANE literature, but that both types of removal were nevertheless known and practiced. Wright, *The Disposal of Impurity*, 276. The best example of the latter is the purification of the temple on the fifth day of the Babylonian *Akītu* festival: Wright, 62–65.

grounded in the axiom, common to all ancient Near Eastern culture, that impurity is the implacable foe of holiness wherever it exists; it assaults the sacred realm even from afar."[41] The priests and priestesses of the ancient world were watchmen, charged with the responsibility of protecting and purging the sacred realm from wild impurities that lay in wait, ready to storm the gates and ransack the temple.

Looking at priestly theology against this backdrop, Milgrom recognized that the ancient Israelites matched their neighbors in their level of concern for purging the sacred precincts from impurity. And yet, even with this common concern, an even greater difference appears: by the time the Levitical priestly texts were written, the demon-gods had already been exorcised from the temple, and from the world, not by rites, but by shifts in doctrine. Levitical monotheism, Milgrom says, left no space for the possibility that there are columns of chaos monsters on the march against Zion. The priestly theologians needed to develop a new understanding of impurity and sin, one which was consistent with both Israelite monotheism and long-standing convictions about the importance of purgative cultic rites to protect the temple, which is to say, to protect the cosmos.

The result is what has been called the "miasma theory" of impurity and sin. As early as 1971, Milgrom explained that within priestly theology "sin is a miasma which whenever committed is attracted to the sanctuary."[42] Sin, therefore, is conceived using images of a polluting vapor that is drawn toward the tabernacle, contaminating the holy space. Milgrom's overall theory was fully articulated for the first time in his groundbreaking 1976 article, "Israel's Sanctuary: The Priestly 'Picture of Dorian Gray.'" Here Milgrom expands and clarifies his earlier claims. He says that "for both Israel and her neighbors, impurity was a physical substance, an aerial miasma which possessed magnetic attraction for the realm of the sacred."[43] Similarly, impurity is a "dynamic and malefic

41. Milgrom, *Leviticus 1-16*, 257. Milgrom's claims in this area have been bolstered by Yitzhaq Feder's research into Hittite and Israelite parallels. He says "Hittite oracle and ritual texts make frequent reference to various forms of depersonalized evil such as curse. . . , bloodshed. . . , oaths. . . , and impurity. . . ." *Blood Expiation in Hittite and Biblical Ritual Origins, Context, and Meaning* (Atlanta: Society of Biblical Literature, 2011), 111.

42. Jacob Milgrom, "Kipper," in *Encyclopaedia Judaica*, 1971, 1040. The word miasma is defined as a "noxious vapour rising from putrescent organic matter . . . which pollutes the atmosphere. . . ." *Oxford English Dictionary*, third edition, 2001.

43. Jacob Milgrom, "Israel's Sanctuary: The Priestly 'Picture of Dorian Gray,'" *Revue Biblique* 83 (1976): 392.

power," and it is "the implacable foe of holiness wherever it exists; it assaults the sacred realm even from afar."[44] Then, in his celebrated three-volume Leviticus commentary, the first volume of which was published in 1991, Milgrom repeats and again expands on his theory. Impurity is analogous to "electromagnetism" where the "minus charge of impurity is attracted to the plus charge of the sanctuary. . . ."[45] From this perspective, the greater the impurity or sin, the more profoundly it pollutes the temple because "sancta contamination varies directly with the charge (holiness) of the sanctuary and the charge of the impurity. . . ."[46]

As mentioned, the surrounding cultures understood such dynamic, airborne impurity to be demonic. The Jewish Bible scholar Yehezkel Kaufmann, who believed that Israel was fully monotheistic, saw only discontinuity between Israel's priestly cult and the neighboring presuppositions. In 1960 he argued that "'the domain of impurity' is a state of being or a situation, and not 'an active force'"[47] On the other side of the spectrum, Baruch Levine argued that ancient Jewish cultic beliefs were in greater continuity with neighboring theologies/demonologies. Writing in 1974, Levine said that for ancient priestly theology, to become impure—which for him includes becoming impure through sin—introduces "a kind of demonic contagion into the community."[48] Furthermore, the "forces of impurity" were "unleashed by the offenses committed";[49] apparently, each offense weakens the community's defenses, making it vulnerable to demonic attack. The emphasis on actual demons is notable here: Levine accepts the idea that sin and impurity denote literal demonic activity against the residing god.

Milgrom's perspective on impurity and sin in ancient Israel charted a narrow path between these two views. First and foremost, with Kaufmann, he is adamant that impurity is not demonic. He says that Israel's monotheistic convictions are so strong by the time Leviticus is finalized, the demonic has been "expunged" from its thought-world.[50] With that

---

44. Milgrom, 392–93. More recently, see Liane M. Feldman, *The Story of Sacrifice: Ritual and Narrative in the Priestly Source* (Tübingen: Mohr Siebeck, 2020), 73–74.

45. Milgrom, *Leviticus 1-16*, 270.

46. Milgrom, 980–81.

47. Levine summarizing Kaufmann's view in Baruch A. Levine, *In the Presence of the Lord: A Study of Cult and Some Cultic Terms in Ancient Israel* (Leiden: Brill, 1974), 79.

48. Levine, 75.

49. Levine, 78. Jon Levenson also promotes the anti-Kaufmann view that evil retains demonic vitality for ancient Israel; *Creation and the Persistence of Evil*. See also Hundley, *Keeping Heaven*, 124–25.

50. Milgrom, "The Priestly 'Picture of Dorian Gray,'" 397; Milgrom, *Leviticus 1-16*, 259–60, 289, 766, 976–77, 981–82, 1068–69. Wright took the same position as his teacher

said, Milgrom then challenges Kaufmann's belief that impurity is "completely devitalized"[51]—this pushes things too far in the opposite direction. Like Levine, he believes that sin and impurity are dynamic and dangerous. To hold these views together, Milgrom argues that the priestly writers advanced a revolutionary idea:

> The demons have been expunged from the world, but man has taken their place. This is one of the major contributions of the priestly theology: man is 'demonized.' True, man falls short of being a demon, but he is capable of the demonic. He alone is the cause of the world's ills. He alone can contaminate the sanctuary and force God out.[52]

According to this picture, there is only humanity and God, face to face, and those impurities and sins that pollute the temple, even from a distance, are "generated"[53] by human beings, by human actions. "Anti-God forces," Milgrom insists, "do not inhere in nature"[54]—thus, they are a pollution emanating from us, endangering God's presence as they gather in the sanctuary, like nitrous oxide attacking the ozone.

Since introducing the idea of sin and impurity as "miasma," Milgrom's theory has been widely discussed in the secondary literature. He has supporters and detractors. An important early supporter is Baruch Schwartz, an Orthodox Jewish scholar who earned his doctorate at Hebrew University in Jerusalem in 1988 while Milgrom was hard at work on his Leviticus commentary a few miles away. When it came time to honor Milgrom with a festschrift in 1995, Schwartz's contribution was listed first on the long table of contents; the article, "The Bearing of Sin in the Priestly Literature," is a milestone in the reception of Milgrom's work. As it pertains to the concept of sin or impurity as a "something" generated by human beings, Schwartz expands the range of terms used to describe what the ancient priests may have had in mind. He refers to this "something" as "a sort of metaphysical spontaneous generation. Though invisible, defilement is believed to be quite real; though amorphous, it is substan-

---

Jacob Milgrom, *The Disposal of Impurity*, 50, 273. Mary Douglas provides a concise overview of the role of demons in ancient religion, ultimately agreeing with Kaufmann and Milgrom that such demonic activity is conspicuously absent in the Hebrew Bible: Douglas, *Leviticus as Literature*, 10–11, 147–48.

51. Milgrom, "The Priestly 'Picture of Dorian Gray,'" 397.

52. Milgrom, *Leviticus 1-16*, 260, cf. 982, 1068–69.

53. Milgrom, 1069.

54. Milgrom, "The Priestly 'Picture of Dorian Gray,'" 82; cf. Milgrom, *Leviticus 1-16*, 260. Hundley agrees; *Keeping Heaven*, 193.

tive."[55] Again, for Schwartz, "The entire priestly system of impurity and its disposal rests on the postulate that impurity is not simply a condition, a ritual 'state'; it is the defilement itself. It is *real*."[56] He refers to it elsewhere as "objectified" transgressions, as "odious, foul objects that come into present existence,"[57] and precisely *because* it has this bizarre existence, or an "independent nature,"[58] the priestly writers insist that sin must be intentionally removed from the sanctuary.

The problem is, the means by which such a "metaphysical" object is generated from creaturely impurity or sin is never explained.[59] As we saw earlier, Anderson claims that the "thingness" of sin is "manufactured on the spot"—he elsewhere suggests that, when it comes to the burden of sin, "we must presume that the offending item has been, as it were, manufactured ex nihilo upon completion of the forbidden act."[60] An obvious follow-up question would be, who is "manufacturing" this burden from *nothing*? It would seem that such creative power would have to come from God, but does this mean that God (together with human beings?) creates this metaphysically weighty sin? That would be a hard pill to swallow. Mary Douglas, while remaining generally supportive of Milgrom's approach to sin and impurity, cautions that "one can notice that the language of dirt and ablution is unnecessarily materialist."[61]

55. Schwartz, "The Bearing of Sin," 5. Later in the same article, Schwartz calls "objectified sin" a "metaphysical" object. Schwartz, 19. Similarly, Hundley calls impurity a "stain" and says that the stain "is perceived to be real. As in the ANE, it is a malevolent force that harms whatever it comes into contact with and thus must be removed." *Keeping Heaven*, 179. Joshua Vis also supports and defends Milgrom's concept of sin and impurity as a "material reality," one which "materialize as stains on the sancta." Joshua Marlin Vis, "The Purification Offering of Leviticus and the Sacrificial Offering of Jesus" (Ph.D. diss., Duke University, 2012), 9.

56. Schwartz, "The Bearing of Sin," 5, emphasis in original.

57. Schwartz, 7.

58. Schwartz, 19.

59. The lack of clarity about how Milgrom's miasma theory actually works is one of the critiques advanced by Hyam Maccoby, who is generally unpersuaded by the idea that impurity pollutes the temple from a distance. See Hyam Maccoby, *Ritual and Morality: The Ritual Purity System and Its Place in Judaism* (New York: Cambridge University Press, 1999), 169ff. Milgrom offers a comprehensive answer in "Impurity Is Miasma: A Response to Hyam Maccoby," *Journal of Biblical Literature* 119, no. 4 (January 1, 2000): 729–46. See also Klawans' critique of Maccoby: "Rethinking Leviticus and Rereading 'Purity and Danger,'" *AJS Review* 27, no. 1 (April 1, 2003): 98–99.

60. Anderson, *Sin*, 19.

61. Douglas, *Leviticus as Literature*, 148. Roy Gane also critiques Milgrom for being unnecessarily focused on physical realities. *Cult and Character: Purification Offerings, Day of Atonement, and Theodicy* (Winona Lake, IN: Eisenbrauns, 2005), 159–60. Gane prefers to say impurity is "quasi-physical," and accepts the idea of miasma as a metaphor

Perhaps so, but one might also call it helpfully "fleshy," keenly aware of the physical effects of our crooked actions. When it comes to sin, the priestly perception of its "thingness," the way it can hang around long after the action itself is forgotten, and the way in which this ugly "reality" demands an equally concrete response, is a theological insight worthy of continued consideration. And yet, it is also right to acknowledge that there are many outstanding questions about the nature and origins of the "metaphysical" something that burdens the sinner and invades the temple in priestly thought. All we know at this point is that the priests were concerned about it and that it was perhaps considered vital but not (strictly speaking) demonic. One does not expect the ancient priests to have answers to all the questions we might want to ask about substantive sin,

---

"provided it is clear that in our ritual context they do not refer to literal physical substances subject to physical constraints in the material world. . . ." Gane, 160. I would be surprised if Milgrom didn't accept this qualification in general. See also Isabel Cranz, who presents the argument against Milgrom's miasma theory, but does conclude by saying, "In ritually enacting the removal and/or neutralization of these sins or pollutants, the latter take on a quasi-material nature as exemplified, for example, in the dispatch of sins of the Israelites into the desert in Lev 16:21–22." *Atonement and Purification: Priestly and Assyro-Babylonian Perspectives on Sin and Its Consequences* (Tübingen: Mohr Siebeck, 2017), 112.

Along similar lines, but pushing further, James A. Greenberg has recently produced a revisionary account of atonement in Leviticus that pits itself consistently against the "pollution and purge" view—which Greenberg associates with Milgrom and his followers—in favor of what he calls the "relationship view." See *A New Look at Atonement in Leviticus: The Meaning and Purpose of Kipper Revisited* (Winona Lake, IN: Eisenbrauns, 2020). Throughout his book, Greenberg opposes the now mainstream view that the sanctuary is somehow polluted, and thus he thoroughly disagrees with the "miasma" theory in all of its forms. Those who find that Milgrom is still highly persuasive, at least in his most basic claims—as I do—will need to confront Greenberg's arguments; this is not the place for a full critique of his "new look." I'll simply say this: for Greenberg, the temple is *either* perfectly holy *or* it is incoherent. How can it be most holy and polluted simultaneously? I fully appreciate how consistent Greenberg is in acknowledging the temple's holiness—I hope to be similarly consistent—but I worry that his approach sometimes flattens priestly temple theology, where Zion (as microcosm) is indeed experienced as the summit of holiness *and also* ground-zero in the liturgical battle against the forces of darkness. Therefore, I find that figures like Jacob Milgrom and Mary Douglas still do a better job of communicating to modern readers the analogical, sacramental, and theological perspective of the ancient priests, who were able to imagine the temple as simultaneously all-holy *and* burdened, as purified by the worshipers' offerings *and* still in need of purification. If we imagine impurity as a substance analogous to salmonella, such an approach will not make sense; in that case, a surface is either contaminated or it is not. But again, as I will argue below, understanding that the temple is a microcosm opens up richer theological possibilities. I hope that my arguments below will show that Milgrom's core discoveries remain persuasive.

but those questions nevertheless deserve answers if temple theology is to
have contemporary relevance. Here we will continue to explore the fine
points of ancient priestly thought on the miasma of sin so as to understand the background of the Yom Kippur liturgy with as much nuance
as possible, but in the tenth chapter, below, we will need to directly wrestle with the immense metaphysical difficulties created by this biblical idea.

Distinguishing Sin and Impurity

In the previous section, when discussing the pollutants that attack
Israel's all-holy sanctuary, I referred to the "thingness" of impurities and
sins interchangeably. To more fully appreciate the richness and sophistication of priestly ethical thought—and also to more fully appreciate how thoroughly the Day of Atonement restores creation—this should be clarified. In
priestly thought, while impurity and sin are analogous concepts, they are
not synonymous. In fact, the failure to distinguish between the two has
weakened Christian interpretation of Jewish purity laws and, correlatively,
the temple cult; it is important that we not repeat those errors here.

This Body of Death: Impurity

Jonathan Klawans has traced the history of anthropological
approaches to purity laws in the nineteenth and early-twentieth centuries.
Pioneering scholars such as William Robertson Smith and James Frazer
were inclined toward "antiritualism," "the common-place critique of
ritual as empty formalism,"[62] and thus their interpretations of biblical
purity laws were largely critical. According to Klawans, Mary Douglas
was the one to provide a badly needed intervention, arguing that "purity
rites should not be understood as empty vestiges or irrational obses-
sions,"[63] and instead showing how Jewish purity laws ultimately promote
a sophisticated symbolic/theological system.[64] Emboldened by Douglas's
work in social anthropology, Milgrom articulated his own interpretation
of priestly purity codes, showing that the concern for purity was intended
to reinforce perhaps *the* central theme of the Hebrew Bible, which the
Deuteronomist expressed with special force: God says, "I have put before

62. Klawans, *Purity, Sacrifice, and the Temple*, 19.
63. Klawans, 19.
64. In *Purity and Danger*, Douglas showed that, far from being meaningless vestiges,
purity laws serve not only to express an idea but also to impose or reinforce it." See the
excellent summary of Douglas's key findings in Klawans, 19.

you life and death, blessing and curse. Choose life—if your offspring would live—by loving the Lord your God, heeding His commands, and holding fast to Him." (Dt 30:19–20). *Choose life.* In the previous chapters, we discussed how the temple was the summit of Israel's life, the place where Life himself dwelled among his people, and where Israel would gather to hold fast to the true source of life.[65] Zion was ultimately the main battleground where the forces of life and the forces of death met; with the sound of the shofar, the whole nation of Israel took its position on the mountain of God, ready to engage the enemy under the banner that read, "choose life."[66]

For Milgrom, the purity laws were all about this great battle between life and death, all about this basic command to choose life. After all, the first step in choosing is distinguishing; in our world, the forces of death are everywhere, like tares that strangle the wheat. Purity laws train the chosen people to remain vigilant. They are honest about the world: it is true that in our daily lives, our "quotidian" existence, there is both death and life as surely as there is night and day. At present, it is impossible to avoid death and its co-conspirators; the wisdom of Koheleth is not denied.[67] But even in this setting, *especially* in this setting, Mount Zion represents an offer and an opportunity. It says, *choose life.* Return again to YHWH, the source of hope, the one who breathes life into dust. For Israel, the final victory over death has not yet appeared, yet it is sacramentally offered in anticipation on Mount Zion, the place of Edenic presence and promise.

To approach this place, therefore, requires self-reflection and preparation. As a kingdom of priests, a holy nation, each person is called upon to distinguish between the forces of life and death in their own lives, an assessment which includes an inventory first of moral actions, certainly,

---

65. Levenson captures the way life and temple were identified: "Psalm 133 and its kindred literature offer a paradigm that is spatial: death is the norm outside Zion and cannot be reversed, but within the temple city, death is unknown, for there God has ordained the blessing of eternal life. To journey to the Temple is to move toward redemption, to leave the parched land of wasting and death for the fountain of life and the revival and rejuvenation it dispenses." Levenson, *Resurrection and the Restoration of Israel*, 92. Purity laws are meant to symbolically reinforce this theological landscape.

66. As Reuven Hammer points out, "life" is the central theme of the High Holy Days overall: "Indeed, life and death are the overriding concerns of these days. Rosh Hashanah emphasizes life and its renewal; Yom Kippur deals with death and renunciation, but only so that we may return to life purified and reinvigorated." *Entering the High Holy Days: A Complete Guide to the History, Prayers, and Themes* (Philadelphia.: Jewish Publication Society, 2005), 36.

67. "That is the sad thing about all that goes on under the sun: that the same fate is in store for all." Ecclesiastes 9:3.

but which also includes the inevitable ways in which our bodies are vulnerable to the intrusion of death. The thing that must be underlined is this: the second category need not imply moral condemnation. It is *expected* that every human being, from the best to the worst, will suffer the forces of death in their body from time to time as they journey through life. Israel does not look away from this bodily reality, and Israel also recognizes that our fragility distinguishes us from the holy God who is the source of all life. In this context, "unclean" (*ṭāmēʾ*) was a word that identified the basic truth that human beings often find themselves ensnared by death. It did not mean disgusting, and it was not shocking.[68] It was usually not even avoidable. "Unclean" did not make you wicked,[69] it did not make you a social outcast. It was just a reminder that, alas, we are dust and to dust we will return. Someday, even *I* will be the corpse that makes another unclean, and there will be evening and morning, there will be bathing and waiting, and all those who plant my poor flesh in the ground will—in due time—gather once again on Mount Zion, believing that Life is greater than death even still. There is an honesty to the impurity system: recognition of the sorry truth of this world and confidence in the yet greater truth of the one who brought Israel out of the land of Egypt once before and, someday, once again.

Therefore, in a way analogous to the priest in the temple, the everyday Jew was called upon to make distinctions in their own lives, separating the clean and unclean, and engaging in the appropriate rites when the normal rhythms of life bring them face to face with the reality of their own mortality and their existence "in territory held largely by the devil."[70] This, in any case, is Milgrom's general interpretation. He admits seeking

---

68. This point is clearly emphasized by Jonathan Klawans, *Impurity and Sin in Ancient Judaism* (Oxford; New York: Oxford University Press, 2004), 23–24; *Purity, Sacrifice, and the Temple*, 53–55. Mary Douglas also says, "Unclean is not a term of psychological horror and disgust, it is a technical term for the cult. . . ." Douglas, *Leviticus as Literature*, 151. This does not mean that it is wholly insignificant whether one is ritually clean or unclean. It is still better to be in God's more immediate presence, which is not possible while in a state of impurity, but in any case, one does not have a "right" to the temple; as Leigh Trevaskis points out, graduated access to God's presence is the universal rule. Only the high priest is invited to the Holy of Holies itself, and even this invitation is scrupulously regulated. Trevaskis, *Holiness, Ethics and Ritual in Leviticus*, 89 n. 176. Moderation and mediation is the rule for Israel after Eden, and thus there is a tolerance for and realism toward quotidian ambiguity.

69. As Milgrom succinctly says, "contracting impurity is no sin!" Milgrom, *Leviticus 1-16*, 298.

70. To borrow a phrase from Flannery O'Connor; *Flannery O'Connor: Spiritual Writings* (Maryknoll, NY: Orbis Books, 2003), 129.

a "comprehensive theory" that explains the impurity laws as "a system governed by a priestly rationale,"[71] and his ultimate conclusion is this: "The bodily impurities . . . focus on four phenomena: death, blood, semen, and scale disease. Their common denominator is death."[72]

In priestly texts, the most obvious example of this symbolic attentiveness to death is the first phenomenon mentioned by Milgrom, the uncleanness that comes from corpses and carcasses themselves. Numbers 19:11–22 describes how those who touch a corpse, or enter the tent where a person has died, or who touch a human bone, or even a grave, are unclean for seven days. Of course, in ancient society, it would be nearly as hard to completely avoid all contact with corpses as it would be to prevent becoming a corpse. Even though uncleanness is associated with dead bodies, priestly law also *requires* that human remains be treated with respect and reverently buried, not avoided at all costs out of fear of uncleanness. This is true even for priests; while those who serve the temple were generally encouraged to avoid impurity, making sure that close family members are properly buried takes precedent in the Holiness Code (Lv 21:1-4).[73] The woman or man who becomes unclean by touching a human corpse is unclean for seven days and must perform a bathing rite on the third and seventh day to be made clean. Because of the impurity, the person would not be able to visit the tabernacle (or later, the temple), and thus you might say they suffered a kind of exile in solidarity with their deceased loved ones.[74] Nevertheless, again, these moments of abstinence from the tabernacle were a "normal" part of life, insofar as death is, unfortunately, still the norm in this world.[75]

71. Milgrom, *Leviticus 1-16*, 46.

72. Milgrom, 1002; cf. 46–47, 732–33. For a good overview, Jacob Milgrom, "Rationale for Cultic Law: The Case of Impurity," *Semeia* 45 (1989): 103–9. Schwartz agrees: "The Bearing of Sin," 4–5. Milgrom is not the very first to associate impurity with death; for precedent, see Klawans, *Purity, Sacrifice, and the Temple*, 57. For a good overview of various "rationale" for impurity laws, including Milgrom's suggestion, see Joe M. Sprinkle, "The Rationale of the Laws of Clean and Unclean in the Old Testament," *Journal of the Evangelical Theological Society* 43 (December 1, 2000): 637–57. For a critique of such comprehensive theories, see T. M. Lemos, "Where There Is Dirt, Is There System? Revisiting Biblical Purity Constructions," *Journal for the Study of the Old Testament* 37, no. 3 (March 1, 2013): 266.

73. The high priest is the exception; he is not allowed to touch any corpse, even close family. This certainly suggests how the high priest, like the sanctuary itself, is held to the very highest standard of holiness. See Leviticus 21:10–12.

74. Trevaskis explores the connection between impurity and post-Edenic exile. See Trevaskis, *Holiness, Ethics and Ritual in Leviticus*, esp. 101–6.

75. Contact with animal carcasses also brought impurity, but such impurity only lasted until evening. See, for example, Leviticus 11:39.

Because Milgrom believes that each of the phenomena that make men and women impure symbolize death, he must also explain the connection between death and skin disease (Lv 13–14), semen (Lv 15:1–18), menstrual blood (Lv 15:19–33), and blood loss during childbirth (Lv 12). The first connection, death and skin disease, is probably the easiest to justify. The disease described in Leviticus 13 and 14 caused the skin to lose color and become scaly, making the victim look like a living corpse.[76] Milgrom says, "The main clue for understanding the place of *ṣāraʿat* [scale disease] in the impurity system is the fact that it is an aspect of death: its bearer is treated like a corpse."[77] As evidence, Milgrom points to Numbers 12, where Aaron and Miriam murmur against Moses, and Miriam is afflicted with *ṣāraʿat* as punishment, becoming "white as snow." Aaron pleads with Moses, saying, "Let her not be like a corpse" (v. 12).[78] Therefore, it seems that the connection between "scale disease" and death is strongly suggested in scripture.

Milgrom recognizes that the link between, say, delivering a child and death, or between other phenomena associated with reproduction (semen and menstruation) and death, is counterintuitive. But in defense of his "comprehensive theory," Milgrom argues, "The loss of vaginal blood and semen, both containing seed, meant the diminution of life and, if unchecked, destruction and death. . . . [I]n the Israelite mind, blood was the archsymbol of life ([Lev]17:10–14; Deut 12:23. . . . Its oozing from the body . . . was certainly the sign of death."[79] This includes also the par-

---

76. This disease (Heb: *ṣāraʿat*) was first translated as "leprosy" in the Septuagint, but commentators agree that it is not the disease today known as Hansen's disease, and it may be an illness that is unknown in the modern world. Cf. Milgrom, *Leviticus 1-16*, 816–18. Milgrom calls it "scale disease." While I will focus here on *ṣāraʿat* in human flesh, it is notable that the same word is used for mold or fungus in fabrics (Lv 13:47–58) and on building materials (Lv 14:33–53) that apparently had a similar appearance. Even inanimate objects, then, are susceptible to the forces of death, and thus these objects can also carry and transmit impurity.

77. Milgrom, 819.

78. Milgrom, 819. Milgrom also points to Job 18:13 as further evidence: here, with apparent reference to Job's "malignant boils" (Job 2:7; cf. Lv 13:18–23), it says "Death's firstborn consumes his limbs."

79. Milgrom, 767; Cf. 46, 732–33, 1002. Weaknesses have been identified in Milgrom's theory on this point in particular, and therefore his approach has been amended by other scholars. It is noted that one does not become ritually impure if he loses pints of blood through, say, severing a limb. Blood loss is impure only in association with the reproductive organs, which raises the question of whether sex itself is associated with impurity. Therefore, a number of scholars have argued that symbolic death alone is inadequate to explain the various impurity laws, but rather, "both death *and* sex figure in the ritual purity system of ancient Israel, and that the system serves to highlight the differences between

turient, the new mother, who in the course of delivery loses a large amount of blood. Thus, in Lv 12 the period of impurity after childbirth seems related to such extreme blood loss (surely the association between delivering a child and death was stronger in the ancient world when delivery was so great a risk to mother and child).

In any case, the association between these perfectly natural human processes—and indeed, regarding the blessing of new life through delivery, something that is commanded ("be fruitful and multiply") and celebrated—again illustrates that to be "unclean" was not to be wicked or disgusting,[80] but it was an ordinary feature of life in this world. It represented a moment of exile from the more perfect form of existence exemplified by the glorious temple, and this temporary exile was soon relieved through the purification that normally comes through rest, adulation, and sacrifice. In each home, in each heart, the reality of death is both acknowledged and confronted through the regular rhythms of priestly purity law. Therefore, priestly theology did not ignore death, as if the reality of God's indwelling presence in the temple immediately actualized the final peace envisioned by the prophets (for example, Isaiah 11), nor did it obsess over death, as if despair is the final word, but rather it soberly acknowledged the weakness of the flesh while returning again and again to the source of life.

Now, for Milgrom, not every instance of impurity has the power to automatically create defilement in the sanctuary; one knows that the

---

persons and God." Klawans, *Purity, Sacrifice, and the Temple*, 57–58; see 266 n.39 for references to other scholars who earlier argued for something similar, including Tikva Frymer-Kensky and David P. Wright. See also Gane, *Cult and Character*, 201. In other words, the fact that we both die and that we sexually reproduce distinguishes us from God, and therefore the symbols of these realities make us less suited to the perfect intimacy with God realized in the heavenly sanctuary. A major point of emphasis throughout Klawans' work is that the priestly theology of holiness and sacrifice is shaped by the goal of *imitatio Dei*. As evidence, he points to the principle that is mentioned a few times in Leviticus, where God says "you shall be holy, for I am holy" (Lv 11:45, cf. Lv 19:2). Klawans, *Purity, Sacrifice, and the Temple*, 58.

If this dual model for interpreting impurity is correct, one might say that the temple foreshadows the evangelical counsels, and in this case, especially celibate chastity. Sex was certainly not forbidden in ancient Israel, nor denigrated, but the temple represented an even higher form of life which might be called heavenly, angelic, or divine. This proposal would be worth pursuing, but for simplicity's sake, in this chapter, I am going to stick with Milgrom's explanation, which is powerful in itself and which does not necessarily contradict the emendations of other scholars.

80. It is unfortunately true that traditions developed around the biblical text in which menstruating women were treated harshly and cruelly. Milgrom says that compared to these extra-biblical traditions, priestly theology is "remarkable" in its moderation. Milgrom, *Leviticus 1-16*, 952–53.

sanctuary itself has been polluted by an impurity if a purification offering (*ḥaṭṭā't*) is required at the end of the cleansing process. According to Milgrom's theory, impurity affects the sanctuary in a "graded" way: first, less severe pollution contaminates the outer courtyard (which is the place of the burnt offering altar); second, more severe pollution has enough malevolent power to push through to the shrine (which houses the altar of incense, the menorah, and the showbread table); and third, the most wicked evils penetrate the holy of holies itself (the place of the ark of the covenant, God's very dwelling place).[81] When one is a victim of, or comes into contact with, uncleanness, this seems to produce a "defilement" that has the potential—depending on its severity—to pollute the sanctuary.[82] Therefore, after a certain period of time, and sometimes after mandated washing rituals, the Israelites were required to bring a purification offering to the temple to purge *the sanctuary* of the major defilement. For example, according to Leviticus, the woman who has given birth must bring a pigeon or a turtledove as a purification offering after her period of uncleanness (Lv 12:7); the cleansed victim of scale disease must bring a ewe lamb as a purification offering (Lv 14:10, 19); and men and women who have suffered abnormal genital discharges must bring a pigeon or a turtledove, again as a purification offering (Lv 15:14–15, 28–30). It is also sometimes necessary to bring purification offerings for less severe impurities *if* the person has forgotten to perform the required purification rites.[83]

Everything we have discussed thus far deals with the problem of ritual *defilement* and the need for *purification*, both for the individual and for the sanctuary. But this is only half of the problem. Let us turn again to the key verse from Deuteronomy: "I have put before you life

---

81. See Milgrom, 254–61; 980–85; Milgrom, "The Priestly 'Picture of Dorian Gray.'" Milgrom uses the analogy of Oscar Wilde's novel *The Picture of Dorian Gray*, which is about a handsome libertine who engages in the full spectrum of sin. His external appearance remains pristine, but a hidden portrait of him becomes more disfigured with every transgression. For Milgrom, in an analogous way, the sins of Israel scar and deface the sanctuary, making it foul and ugly, and less and less suitable for Israel's all-holy God.

82. Leviticus 15:31, for example: "You shall put the Israelites on guard against their uncleanness, lest they die through their uncleanness by defiling My Tabernacle which is among them."

83. See Leviticus 5:2, 3, 5–6. This occurs when a person touches the carcass of an impure animal, or touches (for example) a bed that has been made unclean by genital discharge, *and* the person does not perform the required purification rite. For these relatively minor impurities, the purification rite is generally as simple as bathing in water, but if the person forgets to perform the rite, they produce a more serious defilement in the sanctuary because "prolonged impurity will increase in its vitality. . . ." Milgrom, *Leviticus 1-16*, 310–11.

and death, blessing and curse. Choose life . . . by loving the Lord your God, heeding His commands, and holding fast to Him." (30:19–20) Here we see a special emphasis put on obedience, on moral action—in other words, the Deuteronomistic command puts us in the realm of sin. But as Milgrom put it, "contracting impurity is no sin!"[84] As we have seen, ritual impurities, these symbols of death, are generally a "normal" part of life, at least in the world as we know it.[85] But there is a second kind of death that *is* avoidable, and that the covenantal people are obligated to avoid, and that occurs when the will is turned toward sin.

Choosing Death: Sin

The Levitical purification offering could decontaminate the sanctuary of both pollution from both ritual impurity *and* the pollution of sin itself. The problem of sin in the sanctuary is the main focus of Leviticus 4, the chapter that describes the purification offering in the greatest detail. But it will surprise many modern readers that the problem addressed in Leviticus 4 is *unintentional*, or *inadvertent*, sin. According to Milgrom, an inadvertent sin can occur in two ways: first, if the person intends to follow the law but breaks it accidentally (say, unintentional homicide), or second, when the person did not know the law when they acted in violation of the law. Thus, inadvertent sins are due to "negligence or ignorance."[86] Traditional Catholic moral theology would say that an act is not a "mortal sin" if it is unintentional or if one is unaware of its wrongness,[87] and therefore the expansive Jewish concern for inadvertent sin may seem misguided.[88] However, given the overarching goal of "choosing

84. Milgrom, 298.
85. A more complete discussion of the priestly system would include an analysis of dietary laws, which occupy a middle position between unavoidable impurity and sinful acts. The literature on the possible symbolic meanings of dietary laws is a library unto itself, but in any case, dietary laws do not figure heavily into the logic behind the high priest's actions on Yom Kippur, so they are not as important to our analysis here.
86. Milgrom, *Leviticus 1-16*, 228. The word translated "unintentional" is *šegāgāh*; see Nobuyoshi Kiuchi's overview of various translator's views: *The Purification Offering in the Priestly Literature: Its Meaning and Function* (Sheffield: JSOT Press, 1988), 25–31.
87. The *Catechism of the Catholic Church* unambiguously states that sins committed in ignorance or without complete consent of the will are not mortal sins. CCC 1859.
88. Ephraim Radner points out that the priestly category of "inadvertent sin" has a remarkable parallel to the Catholic concept of venial sin, which was developed in medieval theology. Ephraim Radner, *Leviticus* (Grand Rapids, MI: Brazos Press, 2008), 59 n. 1. Thomas Aquinas notes that the word "venial" comes from the word "pardon" (Latin: *venia*)—these are pardonable sins. This, for Aquinas, is analogous to disease and death: a person sick in bed can be healed, a person dead in a casket cannot. Some sins are a sickness

life" that animates priestly theologians, the value and even the wisdom of this concern can be defended today, and actually, there are noteworthy analogies in modern moral theology.

For example, an analogy might be drawn between "inadvertent sin" and the recent attention to social or structural sin. Structural sin, for the individual, is typically a matter of ignorance or negligence—sometimes a mix of both. Often one does not intend to participate in such sinful arrangements, and corporate sins are usually so pervasive that one can hardly avoid being compromised in one way or the other, whether it be systemic racism, or a pornographic culture, or indifference to the poor, or consumerism and materialism, or throwaway culture, or dehumanizing crudeness and meanness, or sexism, or the culture of death, or cynicism, or any other communal sin.[89] How should the individual respond when they are made aware of such ubiquitous and unintentional sins, including even his or her own inadvertent participation in these sins? It seems appropriate that the response should be different from one's response to "brazen sin"—what the Catholic might call mortal sin—since unintentional sins are in fact unintentional; to feel profound personal guilt and remorse may prove to be a debilitating distraction, especially when we are also victims of structural sins insofar as we are inevitably born into broken cultures. At the same time, for someone to rest comfortably in one's previous negligence or ignorance would be to fail to take responsibility for how each person perpetuates systemic sin, whether or not it is intentional. We are responsible for each other, and when we tacitly allow social sin to shape our own secret thoughts and resulting behaviors, we have contributed to the brokenness of this world—again, intentionally or not.

---

in the soul, others are death for the soul. For Aquinas, sins are venial when the sinner is not fully and personally responsible for the act; for example: "a sin committed through weakness or ignorance" (*ST* 1–2, q. 88, a. 2). This is very similar to "inadvertent sin," as Milgrom describes it.

Another fascinating parallel can be seen when, in the same article, Aquinas quotes Ambrose: "penance makes every sin venial"—in Catholic theology, mortal sins are also certainly pardonable through the grace of Christ in the sacraments. Milgrom argues that in ancient priestly theology, "there can be no sacrificial expiation for the brazen sinner" Jacob Milgrom, "The Priestly Doctrine of Repentance," *Revue Biblique* 82 (1975): 186—in medieval Catholic terms, such a sinner's acts are not "venial" (that is, forgivable). However, with remorse and verbalized confession, the brazen sinner "reduces his intentional sin to an inadvertence, thereby rendering it eligible for sacrificial expiation." Milgrom, 199. This interesting parallel deserves greater attention.

89. Cf. Jacob Milgrom, *Leviticus: A Book of Ritual and Ethics* (Minneapolis: Augsburg Fortress, 2004), 32–33.

The priestly theology of unintentional sin seems to be another facet of a sophisticated investigation into the complex and inexorable ways in which we are ensnared by death. It isn't just the death that comes "naturally" to our bodies in this fallen world, but it is also the innumerable subtle ways in which we find ourselves shaped by the forces of death in our presuppositions and misguided actions due to unintentional sin. Such sin is real, it is damaging to social peace and justice, it is degrading, it wrecks our ability to love God and neighbor, and it requires (among other things) a theological response because even inadvertent sins are an affront to the God of love, justice, and peace.[90] Unsurprisingly, for the priestly theologians, the right response is to accept responsibility for one's own contribution to the polluted moral community, to positively "choose life" precisely at the moment when the reality of one's own inadvertent alliance with moral death becomes apparent, and to therefore draw near to God again in the temple. Only through this continual commitment—individually and collectively—to drawing near to the God of life again and again will these structures of sin start to wobble and fall.[91]

Not every sin, of course, can be explained by ignorance or negligence. There is also the brazen sin, the most horrifying reality of all because here the member of the covenant community freely chooses "death" in their actions toward God and neighbor. In priestly theology, this kind of sin is identified with the words *ăvōn* and *pesă*'. These two words come together in an important Yom Kippur verse, one that we will analyze more fully in chapter seven: "Aaron shall lean both of his hands upon the head of the live goat and confess over it all of the iniquities (*ăvōn*) and transgressions (*pesă*') of the Israelites, including all of their sins, and put them on the head of the goat. . . ."[92] These are the sins that the much later Christian tradition will call "mortal"—they are grave and they are intentional.

90. Radner's theological discussion of inadvertent sin is valuable and in many ways consonant with what I have argued in this section. *Leviticus*, 59–65.

91. Priestly theologians are also attuned to the fact that there are varying levels of responsibility for unintentional sin. Thus, priests and chieftains, the religious and political leaders, who have greater responsibility for a just and harmonious society, also have greater culpability when they are guilty of inadvertent sin. In Leviticus 4:3–12 the priest who sins inadvertently must bring an unblemished bull as a purification offering, the most valuable of the offerings, and its blood is applied in the shrine, suggesting that the pollution generated by the high priest's sin penetrates more deeply into the temple. This graduated response to unintentional sins shows that the priests believed that those with greater responsibility for leading Israel—especially the priests themselves—also have greater power to endanger Israel through their sin.

92. Leviticus 16:21, translated by Milgrom, *Leviticus 1-16*, 1010.

What is the distinction between "iniquities" and "transgressions"? According to Milgrom, "The rabbis define 'iniquities' as *zĕdônôt*, deliberate wrongdoing. . . , whose gravity is one notch below that of 'transgressions.'"[93] "Transgression"—*pesă*ʿ—is therefore the word for the gravest conspiracy with death humanly possible. Notably, this is not a word that calls to mind general human wrongdoing, but it points very specifically to *covenantal* violation: the word means "rebellion." Milgrom says, "Its usage originates in the political sphere, where it denotes the rebellion of a vassal against his overlord (e.g., 1 Kgs 12:19, 2 Kgs 1:1; 3:5, 7; 8:20, 22); by extension, it is transferred to the divine realm, where it denotes Israel's rebellion against its God (e.g., Isa 1:2; 43:27; Jer 2:8; 33:8)."[94] The connection between the sins of vassals against their suzerains and the sins of Israel against YHWH certainly calls to mind the way in which ancient Jewish covenant theology parallels Hittite suzerainty treaties.[95] These covenants established a personal relationship, with personal obligations, between unequal parties. Violation of the terms of the covenant was indeed rebellion.[96] If such an intimate personal context is implied by the use of *pesă*ʿ in Leviticus 16, it seems that the sin that pierces the heart of the sanctuary most deeply is Israel's coldblooded violations of its covenant promise to the Lord—or in Milgrom's words, "open and wanton defiance of the Lord."[97]

Impurity and Sin: An Analogous Relationship

Priestly theology, therefore, depicts a broad spectrum of ways in which human beings encounter the forces of death. In trying to capture the full breadth of the problem that humans face in this world, one might

93. Milgrom, 1043. Compare Kiuchi, *The Purification Offering in the Priestly Literature*, 50. Other interpreters favor "culpability" for *ʿăvōn*: Hundley, *Keeping Heaven*, 167; Gane, *Cult and Character*, 101–2, 294.

94. Milgrom, *Leviticus 1-16*, 1034.

95. Levenson, *Sinai and Zion*, 26ff.

96. Admittedly, the word *pesă*ʿ does not refer exclusively to covenant unfaithfulness in biblical literature. In Amos 1–2, for example, the same word is used to describe the sins of "the nations."

97. Milgrom, *Leviticus 1-16*, 1034. The Holiness Code, Leviticus 17–26, is identified by historical-critical scholars to be a priestly text that is written in a different time period than Leviticus 1-16. In the Holiness Code, one finds an inventory of the types of sins that the author of Leviticus 16 may have had in mind when he spoke of "iniquities and transgressions." As Klawans summarizes it, "These defiling acts include sexual sins (e.g., Lev. 18:24–30), idolatry (e.g., Lev. 19:31; 20:1–3), and bloodshed (e.g., Num. 35:33–34). These three sinful behaviors are also frequently referred to as 'abominations' (תועבות)." Klawans, *Impurity and Sin in Ancient Judaism*, 26.

say that the priests worry about the incursions of death in both "being" *and* "act." In other words, these theologians knew, simply because we are beings in the world, we are subject to the powers of death. To communicate this fact—to "raise awareness" we might now say—the books of Leviticus and Numbers articulate a complex symbolic system of purity laws. The purity system also reinforced the great truth that we are not God, that God is holy, and that Zion, the mountain of Life, can have no association with the valley of death.

But of course, the kingdom of death advances not only in the realm of material being but also in the realm of our very actions. Well aware of this, the priestly theologians, therefore, engage in a comprehensive investigation into how our actions can be corrupt. They do not limit themselves to the egregious sins—those towering evils forbidden by the Ten Commandments—but they dwell instead on our "unintentional" failings, the ways in which the power of death weasels its way unannounced into our everyday dispositions and habits, the varieties of brokenness that become apparent only in retrospect. In many ways, it is the slow encroachment of a *culture* of death that has the greatest power to undo creation. Therefore, Leviticus trains the chosen people to turn again and again toward the temple to combat those unintentional sins that endanger the nation.

At the lowest rung of this great chain of un-being, there are the brazen sins, the horrifying possibility of human beings freely choosing death over life. These are moments of rebellion, where men and women take up arms against the good creation, and where men and women willingly enlist on the side of chaos. As Milgrom says, in priestly theology, it is no longer the demons who attack the divine realm—who needs demons when humans choose to be demonic? It is us, it is I, who generate the sins that fly screaming toward Yhwh's dwelling place, desperate to drive God from the world, eager to watch the whole thing burn. As we have seen, this confrontation takes place on Mount Zion: here is the true axis of creation. If the forces of evil can drive God from the holy of holies, they have driven God from all creation. Zion is the site of this great drama: life and death, light and darkness, true God and false.

This section opened with the claim that the dual pollutants that attack the sanctuary—physical impurities and sins—are related but different. There is now a vast secondary literature attempting to express the similarity and difference between these two "realities" which attack the sacred space.[98] In

---

98. For literature reviews of different approaches taken to the relationship, and/or the distinction, between sin and impurity, see Klawans, *Impurity and Sin in Ancient Judaism*, 4–20; and Lemos, "Where There Is Dirt, Is There System?," 274–83.

contemporary research, Klawans has been a leading voice; he has clearly articulated the differences between what he calls "ritual impurity" and "moral impurity."[99] One major clue that we are dealing here with two different phenomena is the fact that sacrifices intended to address ritual impurity result in "purification" (to be made clean, *taher*), while sacrifices meant to combat sin result in "forgiveness" (*sālaḥ*).[100] But while it does seems that these two kinds of pollution are distinct, they are not wholly separable phenomena. As David P. Wright has pointed out, both kinds of impurity are intimately connected to the life of the temple, and both potentially require a purification offering for final healing.[101] But without denying the connection, Klawans remains eager to highlight the distinction, because it is important to avoid conflating the two spheres of pollution into a "single symbolic system"—which had occurred with Hellenistic Jews like Philo: for understandable apologetic reasons, ritual impurity laws were justified as always ultimately ethical. Such a monochromatic interpretation, however, drains the fine details from priestly engagement with the forces of death. Klawans believes it is important not to reduce the ritual to the moral, or vice-versa, and he therefore insists that these are *"two distinct but analogous conceptions of contagion."*[102] For Klawans, the two must

99. These are not biblical terms, he acknowledges. But Klawans argues that they are better than other attempts to label the distinction, such as Levitical vs. spiritual/ritual defilement (Büchler), "contagious pollution" vs. "danger beliefs" (Frymer-Kensky), and tolerated vs. prohibited defilements (Wright). See Klawans, *Impurity and Sin in Ancient Judaism*, 5–17.

100. Milgrom, "The Priestly 'Picture of Dorian Gray,'" 391–92; Schwartz, "The Bearing of Sin," 7; John Dennis, "The Function of חטאת Sacrifice in the Priestly Literature," *Ephemerides Theologicae Lovanienses* 78, no. 1 (2002): 121; Watts, *Ritual and Rhetoric*, 134–35.

101. Wright summarized by Klawans, *Impurity and Sin in Ancient Judaism*, 36–37. Thomas Kazen also points to ways the two systems overlap: "Dirt and Disgust: Body and Morality in Biblical Purity Laws," in *Perspective on Purity and Purification in the Bible*, Library of Hebrew Bible/Old Testament Studies 474 (New York: T&T Clark, 2008), 44, as does Jay Sklar, *Sin, Impurity, Sacrifice, Atonement: The Priestly Conceptions* (Sheffield: Sheffield Phoenix Press, 2005), 149.

102. Klawans, *Impurity and Sin in Ancient Judaism*, 38, emphasis in original. Cf. Schwartz, "The Bearing of Sin," 7, 21; Hundley, *Keeping Heaven*, 180. Klawans use of the word "analogous" brings to my mind Przywara's own fascinating interpretation of the relationship between the "ontic" and the "noetic"—being and consciousness. From this perspective, perhaps we could say that ritual impurity points to a "privation" in being, or material brokenness (especially if we follow Milgrom in saying that impurity relates to death). But then, moral impurity, or sin, points to a "privation" in act, or spiritual brokenness. Perhaps Przywara's observation about the mutuality of being and consciousness-in-act might clarify what Klawans has discovered: that there are two *analogous* conceptions of impurity, one which is not sinful but which is associated with bodily decay,

not be conflated, but they also cannot be wholly divided, because they are together related to a common story of cosmic woundedness, and because these two forces of decay surely influence each other in diverse ways.

Before moving on to the question of how Yom Kippur addresses human brokenness as described in Jewish priestly theology, one final clarification is in order. We must return one more time to the "something" that pollutes the sacred space as a result of ritual impurity and sin. Now that these two types of impurity have been distinguished, we can clarify how the sanctuary is affected by their corresponding pollutants. On this question, the breakthrough article was written by Schwartz. In "The Bearing of Sin in the Priestly Literature," Schwartz points out that these alleged metaphysical substances, these "miasma," which pollute the sanctuary, are often seen as equivalent in modern literature, as if ritual and moral impurity generate the same kind of contamination. But a close reading of Leviticus 16 suggests that this is not actually the case. Verse 16 of that chapter reads: "Thus he shall purge the adytum of the pollution (*miṭṭum ʾōt*) and transgressions (*pĕšāʿim*) of the Israelites, including all of their sins. . . ."[103] For Schwartz, it is important to notice that two different categories of pollution are identified here: the first indicates "bodily impurities" (or ritual impurity), and the second, sin (or moral impurity). Meditating on the fact that *two* categories are here mentioned, Schwartz concludes that the high priest is combatting two analogous phenomena through his blood manipulations in the sanctuary. Schwartz says, "Only bodily impurities generate defilement; sin does not. When the Israelite sins, what penetrates the realm of the sacred is not defilement but rather the transgressions themselves; on Purgation Day [Yom Kippur], *both* are expunged by the blood of the goat of purification."[104]

This difference is further illustrated in verse 21, which describes how sins are transferred to the Azazel-goat. The heart of this verse generally mirrors v. 16, but there is an important change that makes a big difference. Again, the verse reads, "Aaron shall lean both of his hands upon the head of the live goat and confess over it all of the iniquities (*ăvōn*) and transgressions (*pesăʿ*) of the Israelites, including all of their sins. . . ."[105] Notice that there is no longer reference to "pollution"—the problem of ritual impurities has disappeared, and now both words point to the prob-

---

and the other which is sinful and which is associated with misdirected acts. These are distinct, but not unrelated, realities.

103. This is Milgrom's translation; *Leviticus 1-16*, 1010.

104. Schwartz, "The Bearing of Sin," 7.

105. Leviticus 16:21, translated by Milgrom, *Leviticus 1-16*, 1010.

lem of brazen sins. Reflecting on this change, Schwartz argues that the reason ritual impurities are not mentioned is that they were eliminated instantaneously by the blood manipulation ritual in the sanctuary. But then, sins, as an analogous yet different kind of substance, are not simply destroyed by the blood; they are merely released from the sanctuary and must still be removed from the temple. Schwartz says,

> Only after having purged the adytum, shrine, and altar of the impurities *and sins* may the priest place the latter on the head of the scapegoat. . . . The inference is clear: the sins can be transferred to the scapegoat at this point and not before, because only now has the priest acquired them himself. They have been accumulating in the adytum and the shrine, and he has just released them: now he transfers them to the head of the goat in order to dispose of them for good.[106]

This idea is extremely important. The defilement created by ritual impurity dissolves immediately through the blood ritual. Schwartz says the blood "eradicates" them.[107] Why this should be the case will be discussed later, but for now, it is important to simply see that such impurities are no longer a factor and that such impurities are not relevant to the Azazel-goat ritual.[108] The "something" of sin, however, is a different type of problem. It is not simply destroyed or eradicated by the blood ritual; for whatever reason, the metaphysical density of sin—whatever that might mean—is such that it requires a second step for its total removal. It must be genuinely, ritually loaded onto a sin-bearing creature and driven away. Again, more will be said about this below, but here the point is simply that the complex Yom Kippur liturgy addresses two analogous problems: "*eradicating* impurity and *driving away* sins" and thus both goats are necessary to fully purge the sanctuary.

A Desecration Where It Does Not Belong: Conclusion

After this review of recent research into impurity and sin in ancient Israel, the full tragedy of the sin of Nadab and Abihu is clear. Whatever

---

106. Schwartz, "The Bearing of Sin," 17.

107. Schwartz, 15.

108 This point was made by Milgrom on numerous occasions. For example, ". . . the sacrificial animals of Lev 16 also suffice to purge the sanctuary [of ritual impurities]. This leaves the live goats [*sic*] to function in an entirely different sphere: the elimination of Israel's sins . . . the live goat has nothing to do with the sanctuary's impurities but, as the text emphatically and unambiguously states, it deals with *ăwōnōt* 'iniquities. '. . ." Milgrom, *Leviticus 1-16*, 1044.

the brothers might have done wrong, this original sin of priestly theology resulted in an absolute crisis. Immediately upon consecrating the most sacred space, immediately upon receiving the ineffable blessing of God's true indwelling presence in their midst, an event occurs that is a total tragedy and absolute corruption. Not only that but this tragedy was caused by the eldest sons of Aaron himself: for the priests, the blame rested squarely on their own shoulders. It was a humiliating moment, one that undoubtedly haunted future generations as they heard the story recounted.

We can now say that it was a cultic crisis for two related reasons. First, the tragic sequence of actions directly resulted in two corpses in the sanctuary itself. Now that we have seen how serious the ancient Israelites were about protecting this holiest space from such defilement, one can better imagine how disturbing it would be to hear about two dead bodies lying in the very courtyard of God's dwelling. Second, as if that were not enough, the dead bodies were a direct result of grave sin.[109] The perverse action, therefore, produced a "something" that violently attacked the space that was intended to communicate life and peace. The physical corpses of Nadab and Abihu are an appropriate symbol of the way sin produces a burdensome substance that needs to be physically borne from the sacred precincts. Such sins, it seems, cannot be destroyed. Once they come into existence, they can only be banished, sent outside the camp, much like Nadab and Abihu's corpses need to be physically removed. Ever since this first moment, the priests and laypeople of ancient Israel remained aware of their own responsibility for keeping the sanctuary free from all stain so that it would remain a suitable dwelling place for the God who is the creator of the universe and redeemer of Israel. In this fallen world, it was impossible to avoid death altogether, and so everyone worked together to stay vigilant, "to guard and to keep"[110] the new Eden free from the slithering sins that corrupt creation.

There are many ways for modern men and women to read this material. One possible approach would be to see it as a testament to a primitive, magical way of thinking. As such, it may be interesting to historians and anthropologists, and perhaps it could be more generally educational insofar as it opens our eyes to the primitive superstitions that still plague human societies, but it does not have much positive content. With such

109. Milgrom makes the same point. He says, "Nadab and Abihu had polluted the sanctuary doubly in life by their sin and in death by their corpses." Milgrom, 1011.

110. It is widely argued that when God told Adam "to cultivate and to keep" (Gn 2:15) the garden, the words ʿābad and šāmar allude to Adam's priestly responsibility to serve God and guard/keep the law. See Beale, *The Temple and the Church's Mission*, 66–70.

a mindset, one would not be inclined to press priestly theologians with many follow-up questions, because one could hardly imagine that these ideas communicate anything substantive or edifying. If such an attitude was more common before, today, thankfully, we find many writers who take the priests much more seriously as profound thinkers and true theologians, and in fact genuine contributors to Scripture. Therefore, it is now possible to imagine that there is, in fact, a theo-logic in even these materials. It is now possible to treat the Levitical priests as great thinkers worthy of hard questions.

The priestly materials offer a sophisticated analysis of the problem of sin. It is not systematic in the way that St. Thomas Aquinas is systematic in the *Secunda Secundæ Pars* of the *Summa*, but it is nevertheless sophisticated and elaborate, and Milgrom makes a strong case that, far from being an alternative to the prophetic emphasis on ethical obligations, Levitical thought anticipates and supports the prophetic impulse. In priestly theology, each individual's sins polluted the sanctuary that stood at the center of the nation, thus endangering the entire community should YHWH flee from his dwelling place in response to the accumulating pollution. Sin is never an entirely private affair, and thus priestly theology developed a doctrine of "collective responsibility."[111] In other words, the twelve tribes should understand themselves to be the "keepers" of their brothers and sisters; each person has a certain responsibility to the community to pursue the shared covenantal goal of being "a kingdom of priests and a holy nation" (Ex 19:6). With this in mind, Milgrom says, "It was the genius of Israel's priesthood, as reflected in this sacrificial ritual, to give a national dimension to ethics, to make ethical behavior an indispensable factor in determining Israel's destiny. . . . Israel's priests are the precursors of its prophets."[112]

In Leviticus, we do not merely find a mature reflection on the problem of sin and death, but more importantly, we also find the solution that God established: the liturgy of Yom Kippur. Therefore, we now turn our full attention to this great liturgy, the highest holy day on the Jewish calendar, to see how the chosen people pursued healing and forgiveness in the midst of sin.

---

111. The revolutionary priestly idea of collective responsibility—and its less popular sister doctrine, "collective retribution"—is a theme that Milgrom emphasizes again and again in his various works. Cf. Milgrom, "The Priestly 'Picture of Dorian Gray,'" 398; Milgrom, *Leviticus 1-16*, 260–61; Milgrom, *Leviticus: A Book of Ritual and Ethics*, 32.

112. Milgrom, *Leviticus 1-16*, 231.

CHAPTER 6

To Heal the World: Foundations for Priestly Soteriology

How Aaron Shall Enter: A Better Way

The sixteenth chapter of Leviticus describes the most important and the most sacred liturgy on the Jewish calendar.[1] It is the "acme of all temple rituals,"[2] and in fact "the inner sanctum of the Torah."[3] This is the day that liturgically conveys and realizes the greatest intimacy possible between YHWH and humanity. After recalling the way Nadab and Abihu improperly "encroached upon the presence of the Lord," God says to Moses: "This is how Aaron shall enter the adytum. . . ."[4] With these words, God invites Israel, in the person of the high priest, into the divine bedchamber,[5] the most private and vulnerable space of God's dwelling, the "trysting place" of heaven and earth.[6] This is a terrifying and exhilarating proposal; in this simple verse, the full weight of the *tremendum et fascinosum* should be felt, not least of all because, within the narrative, as these words are being spoken, two lifeless bodies are being carried away from the tent. And yet the psalmist pleads, "One thing I ask of the Lord, only that do I seek: to live in the house of the Lord all the days of my life, to gaze upon the beauty of the

---

1. Hammer, *Entering the High Holy Days*, 107; Thomas Hieke and Tobias Nicklas, "Introduction," in *The Day of Atonement: Its Interpretations in Early Jewish and Christian Traditions* (Leiden: Brill, 2011), vii.

2. Daniel Stökl Ben Ezra, *The Impact of Yom Kippur on Early Christianity: The Day of Atonement from Second Temple Judaism to the Fifth Century* (Tübingen: Mohr Siebeck, 2003), 28.

3. Gane, *Cult and Character*, xix. In fact, Leviticus 16 is the middle chapter of the middle book of the Torah: Rolf Rendtorff, "Leviticus 16 als mitte der Tora," *Biblical Interpretation* 11 (2003): 255. Morales argues that Leviticus 16 is the "literary and thematic centre" of the book of Leviticus *and* the Pentateuch. *Who Shall Ascend?*, 28.

4. Leviticus 16:1, 3. Milgrom's translation, *Leviticus 1-16*, 1009.

5. This is Michael B. Hundley's helpful analogy, "Before YHWH," 20–21.

6. Cf. Fagerberg, *Theologia Prima*, 108. Peter Leithart echoes this comment in a charming observation about the Levitical sacred calendar: "Yahweh comes near to establish times of communion with his people, to set up a calendar of trysts with his bride." *Delivered from the Elements of the World*, 96–97, footnote 12.

Lord, to frequent His temple" (Psalm 27:4). It may not be safe, but there is nothing better.

Garments of Glory

"This is how Aaron shall enter." The text identifies two essential conditions that must be met by any high priest who would pass beyond the veil. The first pertains to the offerings that he brings, and the second pertains to his vestments. For convenience, let's review the second condition before turning toward a more thorough review of the first. The high priest is known for his elaborate, highly ornate vestments, which include a rich blue robe, a multi-colored ephod (similar to an apron), and a golden breastplate with shimmering gems representing the twelve tribes. The specifications for these vestments are given in Exodus 28 and 39, alongside the specifications for the tabernacle itself, and both the vestments and tabernacle are described in similarly precise detail. In Leviticus 8, the washing and vesting of Aaron and his sons is the first step in the inauguration of the cult. As briefly mentioned in the last chapter, the high priest's garments are especially notable because the very same materials are used in constructing both the tabernacle and adorning Aaron. For example, the sash—which is worn by all priests—is woven using blue, purple, and crimson woolen threads; these are the same colors and the same style of weaving (*rōqêm*) as the curtain which serves as the outer entrance of the tabernacle.[7] The high priest, however, also wears the ephod, which has the same colors and is woven in the same more elaborate style (*ḥōšēb*) as the *parochet*, the veil through which the high priest must pass to enter the holy of holies.[8]

In this way, it seems that the garments the priests wear are "indexed" to particular sections of the tabernacle.[9] Because all priests are called to minister in the shrine, each wears vestments that are similar to the curtain that divides the outer courtyard from the shrine. But only the high priest wears vestments similar to the *parochet* because he alone is summoned into the holy of holies on Israel's behalf. The high priest serves as a mediator between God and Israel; the whole nation is elevated with him as he ascends to the holy of holies, and the glory of God likewise shines through

7. Compare Ex 26:36 (the curtain) and Ex 39:29 (the sash). See Milgrom, *Leviticus 1-16*, 502.

8. Compare Ex 26:31 (the veil) and Ex 28:6 (the ephod). See Milgrom, 502.

9. For the concept of "indexing" in relation to other modes of analyzing ritual, see Hundley, *Keeping Heaven*, 29–37.

him when he is fully vested such that, by gazing upon him, Israel is given a glimpse at the veil that both conceals and reveals the indwelling God.[10]

Despite the grandeur that is unique to the high priest, what is most significant about the opening verses of Leviticus 16 is that, to enter the holy of holies, Aaron must first be *stripped* of these glorious garments and approach in the simple linen tunic. There is an almost kenotic impetus here; for the high priest to stand before Israel in glory, he must stand first before God in humility.[11] Additionally, however, Milgrom endorses the idea that, already in Leviticus, the high priest's plain white tunic represents angelic worship, pointing to Ezekiel 9:2–3, 11, Ezekiel 10:2, and Daniel 10:5 as parallel passages where angels are described wearing linen vestments.[12] The office of the high priest, without a doubt, is a complex symbol: throughout the Yom Kippur liturgy, the high priest moves in and out of the different sacred spheres, performing rituals on behalf of different groups of people, and changing vestments on several occasions,[13] all of which highlights the fact that the high priest is called upon to simultaneously embody earthly and heavenly realities, representing Israel and the whole cosmos in heaven, and representing heavenly glory on earth.[14]

10. See the discussion in chapter three (footnote 38), where I mentioned the remarkable way in which the worshipers respond to the high priest in the *Letter to Aristeas*. As a parallel, one thinks of the way Moses' face beamed when descending Mount Sinai in Exodus 34:29–35. Furthermore, Exodus itself explains the purpose of the vestments: they "are made 'for glory and beauty.'. . ." Exodus 28:2, 40, quoted by Fletcher-Louis, *All the Glory of Adam*, 44. Much more can be said about the vested high priest as mediator and icon, especially when the cosmic and heavenly symbolism emphasized by Josephus and Philo is factored into the discussion. For example, Brant Pitre makes the suggestive point that the high priest "was viewed as embodying in himself both the Temple and the cosmos." "Jesus, the New Temple," 61–62.

11. Milgrom articulates a similar argument. *Leviticus 1-16*, 1016.

12. Milgrom, 1016. For additional second temple reflections on white linen garments as representing an elevation to angelic status, see Andrei A Orlov, *Heavenly Priesthood in the Apocalypse of Abraham* (Cambridge: Cambridge University Press, 2013), 130–33; Ina Willi-Plein, "Some Remarks on Hebrews from the Viewpoint of Old Testament Exegesis," in *Hebrews: Contemporary Methods—New Insights*, ed. Gabriella Gelardini (Leiden: Brill, 2005), 31; Himmelfarb, *Ascent to Heaven*, 18.

13. In Leviticus 16, he changes his clothing once, but by the time of the *Mishna Yoma*, the high priest is depicted as changing garments numerous times.

14. Concerning the latter, an especially important part of the high priest's wardrobe is the gold "plate" that is fastened to the high priest's turban/mitre. This plate is inscribed with the words "Holy to the Lord" (*qōdeš laʾdōnāi*), and according to Exodus 28:36–38, the inscribed plate was related to the high priest's ability to bear sins. Cf. Milgrom, *Leviticus 1-16*, 623–24; Schwartz, "The Bearing of Sin," 16. That the high priest wore the divine name on his forehead (a point emphasized by *Aristeas* 98–99 and Philo in *Life of Moses* II.114) became increasingly important in later Jewish mystical traditions. See Orlov, *Divine Scapegoats*, 25–34.

The Purification Offering

The other condition of the high priest's entrance into the holy of holies pertains to the offering he must bring. We read: "This is how Aaron shall enter the adytum: with a bull of the herd as a purification offering _and a ram for a burnt offering_. . . . And from the Israelite community he shall take two he-goats for a purification offering _and a ram for a burnt offering_."[15] From the theological perspective, these words should again be read in the context of Nadab and Abihu's trespass. While they unquestionably approached in the wrong way, and while their movement is best labeled "encroachment," this does not mean that God intends for there to be an inviolable barrier between his Presence and his people. Much to the contrary. But this begs the question: how _should_ Israel approach her God? Turning to this question, the message of Leviticus 16 becomes more positive, despite its tragic setting: the goal is to articulate the appropriate way of drawing near to the LORD, and from the perspective of the priestly authors, this is ultimately a question of appropriate sacrifices.

With that in mind, it is striking that the high priest is instructed to draw near with two offerings: with a purification offering _and_ a burnt offering. This sequence is repeated twice—the first offering is for the priests the second is for the whole community—but in each case, the purification offering and burnt offering go together. This is surprising, and it has not been emphasized enough in previous studies. Aaron is told to enter "with a bull . . . for a _ḥaṭṭā't_ and a ram for a _ʿolah_," yet when entering the holy of holies, the high priest brings _only_ the blood of the _ḥaṭṭā't_. The _ʿolah_ ram has not yet been slaughtered, and even after it is slaughtered, its blood is never brought into the tent. _Why_ does the author of Leviticus suggest that the purification offerings are paired with burnt offerings, and how is it that the _ḥaṭṭā't_ and _ʿolah_ are together related to the high priest's movement toward God?

The _ḥaṭṭā't_ is the only offering described in Leviticus that involves red-handed blood manipulations on or toward cultic furniture. The blood of the burnt offering is also separated from the body, but it is dashed or drained upon the sides of the courtyard altar,[16] signifying the fact that life is being given or returned to God via the altar. In this section, I will argue that the purifying use of the blood in the context of sin, signified

---

15. Leviticus 16:3, 5 translated by Milgrom, _Leviticus 1-16_, 1009, emphasis added.
16. For a full investigation of the _ʿōlāh_ blood rite and its various interpretations, see William K. Gilders, _Blood Ritual in the Hebrew Bible: Meaning and Power_ (Baltimore: Johns Hopkins University Press, 2004), 61–84.

by the blood manipulations, is *the* significant difference between the *ḥaṭṭā't* and the *'olah*, but otherwise, the *ḥaṭṭā't* draws on the same theological principles as the *'olah*, and is ordered toward and completed in the *'olah*. The important implication of this is that both of these sacrifices are rooted in the underlying theological principles articulated in chapter two's meditation on the offering of Isaac. In other words, my most important claim is that it is finally the blood of Isaac, the *life* of Isaac, that overcomes the impurity and sin that pollutes the temple.

I admit at the outset that this is a canonical and theological interpretation. Many critical scholars have done outstanding work tracing the (possible/plausible) historical evolution of the priestly texts, and many have also issued strict warnings against imposing symbolic interpretations on ritual texts.[17] As we saw in the debate between Klawans, Watts, and Milgrom about the possibility of symbolically or theologically interpreting biblical sacrifices, priestly ritual texts are quite austere when it comes to theological explanations for the rites they describe: very little is stated explicitly, and therefore to answer the "why" questions requires us to augment what is said with ideas from parallel sources. But profound respect for the particular—particular authors, particular texts, particular times and places—makes it difficult for some to accept interpretive strategies that bring in ideas from other contexts. While such restraint is surely appropriate for strict historians, it may artificially limit the theological realities that are communicated by these texts and across these texts. After all, we know with theological certainty that these texts *together* constitute inspired scripture. For that reason alone, tracing how the Spirit might be drawing together truths from originally isolated historical moments in the history of Israel is, in itself, theologically justifiable. We can look to Przywara's helpful epistemological rule: "truth in-and-beyond history." As creatures, we do not have access to an unmediated Truth-beyond-history, or Truth-beyond-creatureliness, but at the same time, history is not fragmentation and isolation and meaninglessness. Historical criticism on its own, if given a historicist inflection, finds a single meaning in each text or fragment— the meaning intended by the author at the time of composition as best as that can be discerned through historical reconstruction—but there is no unifying element across the fragments. Everything becomes compartmentalized; it becomes *so* particular that it is at risk of losing meaningful value. In so many cases, the text becomes nothing but a collection of

17. A good summary of such concerns can be found in Gilders, 2–11.

veiled and ambiguous mementos of the power struggles of a long-lost people. Of course, on the flip side, most modern readers are aware of the dangers associated with reading scripture without regard to its historical shape and development. Among many other problems, the text can become otherworldly, a kind of oracle communicating mysteries from beyond, which can quickly collapse into a dehumanizing and violent fundamentalism. Thus, Przywara gives us a framework for understanding how it is possible to insist with maximal robustness on the two "extremes" that are often pitted against each other in popular theological discourse: historical-critical *and* theological interpretation, practiced with attention to "truth in-and-beyond history."

What's more, it has also been argued that an analogical mode of reasoning is *especially* appropriate to priestly theology. For example, William Gilders has noticed that "many biblical scholars seem intent on identifying a single authoritative meaning, a one-to-one referent, for each discrete symbolic act or object," which is imprudent because "ritual acts are characteristically multivocal symbols, with multiple levels of meaning. . . ."[18] Similarly, Mary Douglas' research also encourages us to think about priestly theology more integrally and imaginatively. At the beginning of *Leviticus as Literature,* she stresses the fact that this theology is aesthetic, analogical, and mythopoetic. In contrast to linear, discursive logic she associates with Deuteronomistic texts and traditions, Douglas argues that

> Leviticus' literary style is correlative, it works through analogies. Instead of explaining why an instruction has been given, or even what it means, it adds another similar instruction, and another and another, thus producing its highly schematized effect. The series of analogies locate a particular instance in a context.[19]

This is, for sure, a more aesthetic way of reasoning. It is the skill of seeing how apparently disparate ideas correspond in an elaborate tapestry of interconnected spheres. Therefore, without ignoring or disrespecting the pre-history of these different texts—their most original setting, the possible identities and motivations of the original authors, the way they might have evolved through redaction, etc.—there is something about priestly theology that especially invites and encourages drawing reasonable connections, and that resists artificial constraints on the text, as if it's meaning is univocal.

---

18. Gilders, 3.
19. Douglas, *Leviticus as Literature*, 18.

Even with those admissions and caveats, I have tried to prioritize the shape of "truth in history" here, and I hope to remain as close as possible to recent critical discoveries, to allow those discoveries to serve as the steel frame for broader theological reflections. In fact, returning to my main point in this section, there are outstanding historical and textual reasons for associating the purification offering and the burnt offering. As we saw regarding Leviticus 16, vv. 3 and 5, the purification offering and the burnt offering are frequently paired (Lv 5:7; 9:2–3, 7; 10:19; 12:6, 8; 14:19–20, 22, 30; 15:15, 30; Nm 6:11, 16; 8:12). When they appear together, the purification offering is always performed first, the burnt offering second. That the *ḥaṭṭā't* precedes the *'olah* could indicate that the first prepares the way for the second. In his description of the historical development of the purification offering, Milgrom argues that it in fact emerges as a development of the burnt offering. He shows that the burnt offering has varied motivations in scripture; it is sometimes given out of joy, other times to entreat, and in the earliest texts, to expiate. Based on this, he concludes:

> The fact that the burnt offering answers every conceivable emotional and psychological need leads to the inference that it may originally have been the only sacrifice offered except for the *šĕlāmîn* [the well-being offering], which provided meat for the table. . . . With the advent of a tabernacle/temple, however, it became imperative to devise specific sacrifices to purge the sacred house and its sancta of their contamination and desecration. Thus the purification and reparation offerings, respectively, were devised. These two sacrifices, once introduced into the sacrificial system, became the expiatory sacrifices par excellence and ultimately usurped the expiatory function of the burnt offering for the individual.[20]

This historical connection between the burnt offering and the purification offering may help to explain the similarities between them. First of all, the ritual structure of the two sacrifices is parallel. In each case, an animal "without blemish" is selected. Both are initially brought "to the entrance of the Tent of Meeting . . . before the Lord" (1:3, cf. 4:4). In each case, the offerer must lean his hand upon the head of the animal that he has brought, the animal is slaughtered, there are blood rites, and finally rites

---

20. Milgrom, *Leviticus 1-16*, 176; cf. 267–68, 288, 1049, 1083. With this history in mind, Gary Anderson says that the burnt offering for expiation, which is mentioned in Leviticus 1:4 and 16:24, is "a vestigial usage," *Sacrifices and Offerings in Ancient Israel: Studies in Their Social and Political Importance* (Atlanta: Scholars Press, 1987), 878.

for burning/disposing of the flesh; only after each of these identical steps do the rubrics diverge in any significant way.

These parallels are notable, but it is also true that the well-being offering (*šělāmîm*) shares many of these same features. There are, however, conspicuous elements that set the burnt offering and purification offering apart from the well-being offering. First, one of the hallmarks of priestly literature is the demarcation of graded spheres of holiness—we have had occasion to remark on this phenomenon many times already. To distinguish the different spheres, the priests use the words "holy" and "most holy."[21] The well-being offering falls into the first category, while the *ʿolah* and the *ḥaṭṭāʾt* are in the second, more rarified category.[22] Trevaskis argues that "the 'burnt offering' is P's 'most holy' offering *par excellence*," and thus the purification offering's holiness is measured against the standard of Israel's most precious sacrificial gift.

Additionally, in the description of the *ḥaṭṭāʾt* ritual, the author insists that the animal "shall be slaughtered at the spot where the burnt offering is slaughtered before the Lord" (Lv 4:24, cf. 4:29, 33; 6:18). Recall that this "spot" is identified as the "northside" of the altar in Leviticus 1:11, which the rabbis whimsically revocalized as "hidden before God" when associating the burnt offering's life with the life of Isaac.[23] The *ʿolah* and the *ḥaṭṭāʾt* thus share the same "space," both in terms of physical location and degree of holiness.

With this in mind, it is finally and most importantly worth noting that, unlike other sacrifices, the offerer him- or herself receives no material benefit from either the burnt or purification offering. In both cases, the worshiper relinquishes the gift completely. This is different from the well-being offering, where the offerer receives back a large portion of the meat to enjoy with family and friends. As we have seen, the burnt offering was considered the characteristic Jewish sacrifice because it ritually expressed a most complete selflessness in love. The entire gift was submitted to the altar of the Lord. With the purification offering, there is a similar sense of total abandonment. Whether the offering is bought by a priest or layperson, the blood is used to purge the tabernacle, and the

21. For this phenomenon, see Philip Peter Jenson, *Graded Holiness: A Key to the Priestly Conception of the World* (Sheffield: JSOT Press, 1992); Hundley, "Sacred Spaces, Objects, Offerings, and People in the Priestly Texts: A Reappraisal."

22. For a defense of the claim that the burnt offering is "most holy," see Trevaskis, *Holiness, Ethics and Ritual in Leviticus*, 251–61. The purification offering is specifically called "most holy" in Leviticus 6:17.

23. For further reflection on the meaning of "northside": Milgrom, *Leviticus 1-16*, 164–65.

excess blood is poured out at the altar's base. Then certain holy parts of the animal (the fat, the kidneys, the loins, etc.) ascend through immolation. What remains of the animal has one of two destinations. If the animal is offered on account of a priest's sin, the remains are carried "to a clean place outside the camp, to the ash heap, and burn it up in a wood fire; it shall be burned on the ash heap" (Lv 4:12). But if the offering is brought by a layperson, then the priest who performs the sacrifice "shall eat of it; it shall be eaten in the sacred precinct, in the enclosure of the Tent of Meeting" (Lv 6:19–23).

The disposal ritual for the sin offering is, therefore, both similar and different from the burnt offering. The important similarity is that nothing is retained by the offerer; both have a fundamentally ascetic, open-handed orientation. For the priest and the layperson who must bring a sacrifice due to their own sin, neither gets to partake of the meat that results from their twisted actions.[24] At the same time, perhaps because there is something inevitably mournful about the sin offering, its remains are not given the dignity of total immolation in the temple's divine fire. Instead, the vivid ritual requires, in the case of priestly sin, that the animal's poor body be removed from the tabernacle, removed entirely from camp, and burned at an ash heap—albeit in a "clean" place. By combining the sorrowful image of the sacrificial body carried beyond the walls and the dignified concept of a clean place, the text suggests the fundamental ambiguity of this offering, which both partakes of the Edenic holiness of the burnt offering, but which nevertheless is instigated by modes of being that cause our exile. The liminality of a "clean ash heap" outside the camp is a perfect expression of the tragic yet sacred nature of this offering.[25]

24. As Douglas points out: "a person may not profit from his ill-doing." *Leviticus as Literature*, 76.

25. For less severe sins or impurities, especially for purification offerings brought by individual laypersons, the meat is consumed by the priest who performs the sacrifice. This eating must take place "in the sacred precinct, in the enclosure of the Tent of Meeting" (Lv 6:19). As others have argued (see citations listed below), the reason for this consumption need not be overly esoteric: with the blood manipulations, the priest has performed a service for the offerer and for Israel, a service which should theologically be seen as an inconvenience. That the sacred space is polluted with sin and impurity is always an abnormality, even if it has become commonplace in this world. If we recall the *Chaoskampf* theme and the notion that the priest is a warrior on the front lines, defending against evil encroachments, as discussed above, then the fact that he will require sustenance to strengthen him for this work is understandable. The meat—which is in fact "most holy" (Lv 6:22) and thus worthy of dignified disposal in a holy place, even the digestive "fire" of a holy person—helps to invigorate the priests for their essential work, without in any way rewarding the sinner.

In the time before the tabernacle was constructed, and before the introduction of the *ḥaṭṭā't* as a distinct offering, when the *'olah* apparently performed "double duty" as a joyful gift and as expiation for sin, there was inevitable ambiguity over the nature of sacrifice. Is Israel's cultic duty merely an accommodation to sin, a regrettable payment to an angry god? The fact that priestly theology comes to clearly distinguish the *'olah* from the new *ḥaṭṭā't* is a theological advance of profound importance. After this distinction, the fundamentally positive and thankful (*eucharistia*) nature of the burnt offering is reinforced,[26] and the secondary nature of sacrifice in response to sin is clarified. This clarification within priestly theology should correct the tendency in some Christian interpretations to see all sacrifice as punitive. As James Watts says, "Early Christian rhetoric depicted the *ḥaṭṭā't* and the *'āsām* offerings of Leviticus 4–5 as paradigms of Israel's whole system of worship. . . . Christian interpreters regarded atonement for sin and guilt as the essential goal of all Jewish offerings."[27] To the extent that this is true, this mode of thought, by accentuating what is secondary, lost the overarching positive orientation of the Jewish cult.[28]

There is another interpretation. Some claim that the impurity or sin, which the blood of the *ḥaṭṭā't* purges, is itself transferred to the sacrificial carcass, and that this transfer of pollution necessitates the elimination of the now contaminated flesh—either by removing it from camp or consuming it. This speculation seems unnecessary and theologically untenable. The problem is that this interpretation requires commentators to say that a sin-infested carcass is simultaneously "most holy" and polluted with sin, a sin which is eliminated precisely when the (holy) priests consume it. Such action involves the *intentional* mingling of the holy and the impure in a way that is fundamentally at odds with the vocation of those men whose entire mission is to "distinguish between the sacred and the profane, and between the unclean and the clean" (Lv 10:10). It is true that the most pure temple *is* miasmically attacked by what is most corrupt (the *something* of sin). In priestly theology, this is a tragic fact of fallen life. (I emphasized this point in supporting Milgrom against Greenberg's critiques; chapter five, note 61.) But the priest's role is to untangle these realities and restore—as often as necessary—the unspeakable purity of God's dwelling. That this untangling should occur by means of an *intentional* mingling or confusion of holy and polluted things strikes me as unlikely.

For discussion of the idea that the flesh of the offering becomes impure, and that priestly consumption of the flesh is an elimination rite, see Wright, *The Disposal of Impurity*, 131–33; Milgrom, *Leviticus 1-16*, 622–25; Gane, *Cult and Character*, 91–105. Alternative views, which are similar to my view, are articulated by Kiuchi, *The Purification Offering in the Priestly Literature*, 46–52, and more recently, with persuasive force, Vis, "The Purification Offering," 243–47.

26. See Klawans, *Purity, Sacrifice, and the Temple*, 71–72 and references at 271 note 118.

27. Watts, *Ritual and Rhetoric*, 79.

28. In this context, I think of the helpful distinction made by Andrew Louth between two arches, a "greater arch" that stretches up from creation to deification, and a "lesser

The fact that the burnt offering is not intrinsically associated with sin is similarly suggested in the narrative tradition, and here we should turn again to the Akedah of Genesis 22. As mentioned above, in chapter two, the story as we have it today does not even hint at the notion that God requires the life of Isaac on account of any wrongdoing. The narrative only serves to establish what is good—the proper way of being, the proper way of drawing near to and seeing God on Moriah—not to respond to what is evil. The purification offering, then, is a burnt offering forced into a strange new world, one in which death lurks like a lion, corrupting every aspect of our lives. In such a context, it would be naive or even deluded to carry on as if we remain in paradise still. No, in *this* world it is necessary to take concrete steps to guard against evil, intentionally choosing life over death. Therefore, I argue that in the distorted context of sin and death, the ʿ*olah* assumes a new form: it is the *ḥaṭṭā't*, where life is not only freely given, but it is re-applied specifically to purge the stain of sin. This is still primarily a positive movement toward God, but one intentionally designed to combat the impurities and sins emanating from human brokenness.

The Yom Kippur liturgy poignantly suggests that where there is a purification offering, the burnt offering is implicitly present. That is why, going back to the opening verse which launched this reflection, Aaron enters the holy of holies "with a bull of the herd as a purification offering *and* a ram for a burnt offering"—even though the ram is not yet slaughtered and its blood is never literally brought into the adytum. The *ḥaṭṭā't* already contains, and points toward, the ʿ*olah*, which is both its historical and theological origin *and* goal. Despite everything else, the openhearted freedom of Isaac remains Israel's most basic truth, and in the moment of crisis, her only hope.

The Life of Isaac on Yom Kippur: The Theological Context

A Controversial Word

After the preparatory comments on the priest's vestments and the description of the *ḥaṭṭā't-*ʿ*olah* offering—the means by which Aaron "shall enter"—Leviticus 16 turns its focus on the purification offering itself, which

---

arch" from the fall to redemption, which is ultimately intended "to restore the function of the greater arch." "The Place of Theosis in Orthodox Theology," *Partakers of the Divine Nature: The History and Development of Deification in the Christian Traditions*, 2007, 35. The purification offering belongs to the "lesser arch," but the burnt offering is characteristic of the "greater arch" in priestly theology.

includes the bull offered for the priests, and the *two* goats offered for all Israel. The text specifies the purpose of these offerings: "*kipper*," which Milgrom translates "to effect purgation" (v. 6). Here we have arrived at the word *kipper*, a word that has launched a thousand interpretations. Watts explains why this word is so crucial and controversial: "the priestly writers of Leviticus give virtually no interpretation of the rituals they describe and prescribe. There is, however, one exception to this generalization. The P writers offer one explanation, or rather one word of explanation, rather frequently. The word is *kipper*, and it appears forty-nine times in Leviticus."[29] Because the purpose of the entire ritual is shaped by the interpretation of this one difficult word, a few comments are in order.

In general, Milgrom has been my starting point throughout this part of the book, and I will continue that precedent here. In a short essay on the word *kipper*—the concluding article of his massive commentary on *Leviticus 1-16*—Milgrom explains why he moves away from the common translations of "atone" or "expiate," favoring "to purge" instead.[30] Philology is at the heart of his argument. Milgrom believes that the most likely Semitic cognate for the Hebrew *kipper* is the Akkadian *kuppuru*.[31] This latter word in Akkadian ritual texts refers—in the more literal sense—to the action of "rubbing off" or "wiping," and then—as an "abstraction of the literal meaning"[32]—to the general action of purging or purifying. Milgrom provides examples of this word being used in Akkadian "wiping rites," rites that involved wiping a small area to symbolically

29. Watts, *Ritual and Rhetoric*, 130.

30. See Milgrom, *Leviticus 1-16*, 1079–84. Christian theological skirmishes stand behind some of these interpretive debates and influence interpretations on all sides. For example, questions about the distinction between "expiation" and "propitiation" with respect to Christian atonement have been very contentious. Schwartz provides a very helpful overview of the debate in Protestant scholarship, especially between Charles Dodd and Leon Morris, which largely shaped the discussion in the twentieth century. "The Prohibitions Concerning the 'Eating' of Blood in Leviticus 17," in *Priesthood and Cult in Ancient Israel* (Sheffield: JSOT Press, 1991), 53 n. 3.

31. Milgrom continues the trend of critiquing earlier commentators who tried to link *kipper* to an Arabic cognate *kafara*, meaning "to cover over." For those interested in arguing that the blood "covers" the sins, this is an appealing option, but Milgrom cannot find a clear example where the blood is "rubbed on" (in the sense of "cover") in the Biblical texts, and numerous other arguments have been raised against using a relatively late Arabic word to interpret the earlier Hebrew. See Milgrom, *Leviticus 1-16*, 1080–81; Schwartz, "The Prohibitions Concerning the 'Eating' of Blood in Leviticus 17," 54 n.1; cf. Levine, *In the Presence of the Lord*, 56–60; Sklar, *Sin, Impurity, Sacrifice, Atonement*, 44 note 2; Watts, *Ritual and Rhetoric*, 130–31; Feder, *Blood Expiation in Hittite and Biblical Ritual Origins, Context, and Meaning*, 168.

32. Milgrom, *Leviticus 1-16*, 1080.

represent general cleansing. In other words, if your goal was to remove all the dust from your home, you would physically wipe down every exposed surface, but these ancient rites were often content to apply the purging agent to "key locals" that symbolized the whole according to the principle "*pars pro toto*": a part taken for the whole. This is very much like the phenomenon of applying blood simply to the horns of an altar or sprinkling it toward key locations, rather than meticulously scrubbing every square inch of sacred space. Akkadian and Hebrew ritual acts are rooted in concrete analogies (such as the physical action of wiping a contaminated space to clean it) but they nevertheless remain rituals, meaning they communicate something that is more-than-merely-physical.

In any case, Milgrom follows the tradition of scholarship[33] that hears an Akkadian accent in the verb *kipper*, suggesting that the physical act of "wiping" something off is in the earliest background of the developing priestly theology of temple "purging." Simply stated, the sins accumulating in the temple needed to be purged with the blood of the purification offering; this blood somehow removed the sins through the action of rubbing the blood onto the contaminated sacred objects. Milgrom believes that from this most ancient etymological starting point, the word *kipper* continued to evolve to take on additional figurative meanings. In fact, the consonantal root of the verb *kipper* is K-P-R, which is also the root of the noun *kōfer*, which translates "ransom." The two ideas are linked (in Milgrom's reconstruction) by the fact that, in ancient cultic rites, it was very important to properly eliminate the "wiping material" after it "absorbed the impurities," and thus the now-contaminated wiping material became—so to speak—a substitute through which the evil was removed. From there the concept of ransom is only a relatively short step away: one thing is lost, a price is paid, that life might be (re-) gained. God's wrath is averted by substitution of some kind.[34] In the very last stage, Milgrom says, the word becomes a general theological principle, analogous to the English word "atonement."[35]

---

33. Milgrom did not originate this reading; the discussion dates back to the early 20th century. See references in Levine, *In the Presence of the Lord*, 56–57; Watts, *Ritual and Rhetoric*, 131, note 2; and for an argument that is critical of Milgrom's view, see Yitzhaq Feder, "On *Kuppuru, Kippēr* and Etymological Sins That Cannot Be Wiped Away," *Vetus Testamentum* 60, no. 4 (January 1, 2010): 535–36.

34. Milgrom, *Leviticus 1-16*, 1082.

35. The English word "atonement" was created in the early sixteenth century to express the state of restored "at-one-ment" between God and humanity. Thus, for Milgrom, the meaning of the word shifts from the priestly action—purifying polluted spaces— to the result of the purification—at-one-ment, renewed communion, with God.

While Milgrom does admit some etymological connection between *kipper* and *kofer*, he has been criticized for *understating* the importance of the concept of "ransom" in properly interpreting the priestly term *kipper*. This is much more than a debate about etymology; at its heart, this is a debate over whether the "purification offering" of Leviticus is fundamentally punitive, and whether the sacrifice ultimately has its "power" because it delivers a required death. If the *ḥaṭṭā't* is significant because it provides the punitive death that God allegedly requires, if God is appeased by the cessation of life, and if it is God's will that such death occur on his holy mountain, then the entire symbolism of Mount Zion discussed throughout this book is overturned. The temple is then the site of wrath and punitive death, and everything Edenic, beautiful, good, and true about this place is compromised by the claim that violence is ultimately needed to overcome violence.

The view that *kipper* should be understood with reference to "ransom" has been argued by Jay Sklar. In his book, *Sin, Impurity, Sacrifice, Atonement: The Priestly Conceptions*, Sklar basically says that Milgrom is correct in affirming a purgative element in the verb *kipper*, but that the concept of "ransom" is equally important for an accurate interpretation of the priestly term, and that both elements must be held together.[36] Sklar ultimately translates *kipper* as "to effect [*kofer*]-purgation"—in other words, the object that purges the sacred space (generally, blood) is effective because it pays an acceptable price, it appeases God's anger. There are a few steps in this argument. First, Sklar establishes a "sin-disaster connection" in biblical theology. Sklar explores the various types of "disaster" that might result from sin according to Leviticus, and these include death (as in capital punishment), *kārēt*,[37] sin-bearing, and guilt-bearing. Sklar reads each of these in terms of "punitive consequences" for sin. This may or may not be correct in every case, but overall, the most important point is that each of these realities is anathema to the fundamental truth of the temple, which is Life. Each of the "disasters" mentioned is associated with the mournful state of exile, the grey land beyond the gates, symbolic of chaos and death. In my view, the civil penalties articulated in various biblical sources have lasting spiritual

---

36. For a more concise summary of his argument, see Jay Sklar, "Sin and Impurity: Atoned or Purified? Yes!," in *Perspectives on Purity and Purification in the Bible*, ed. Baruch J. Schwartz (New York: T&T Clark, 2008), 18–31.

37. Which means "to be cut off"—this may mean "excommunication," or it may point to the person's death. For a full discussion, see Sklar, *Sin, Impurity, Sacrifice, Atonement*, 15–20.

significance (especially for Christians) primarily to the extent that they are markers that give insight into the theological landscape which is the "stage" for the basic drama of Israel.

The second step of Sklar's argument is an analysis of the word *kofer*, which is generally translated as "ransom" or "appeasement." To reach his definition of *kofer*, Sklar engages in a close reading of various texts; one of the most important is Exodus 30:11–16, partly because it is one of the few texts that use *kofer* that is widely identified as being P, and partly because it is a text where the noun *kofer* is related to the verb *kipper*. Here God says that when Moses performs a census, the people being counted must pay a "ransom" (*kofer*) of "half a shekel" (30:12–13) so that they might "make atonement" (*kipper*) for themselves (v. 15, 16). It does seem that the author is implying that this monetary payment to the priests somehow protects Israel from the negative effects of a census. Yet at the same time, it is not clear that sin has been committed in this case; in fact, in another place (the opening verses of Numbers) God *commands* Israel to take a census.[38] Similarly, as Vis points out, in this passage "there is no objectified guilt and the context is not sacrificial."[39] Therefore, however *kipper* is being used,[40] there is reason to doubt that this passage illuminates the *cultic* meaning of *kipper* in Leviticus.

38. Sklar assumes that the action of census taking is somehow sinful: "While it is not as clear as in Exodus 21 [the case of the goring ox] why the deed is wrong (reasons of pollution? infringement upon the property of the LORD?), the end result is the same: one party has offended another and is liable to severe consequences at the hand of the offended." Sklar, 53. But again, the text itself seems to imply that the census is permissible yet dangerous, and thus requires an extra layer of protection; the concepts of sin and offense may be extraneous here.

39. Vis, "The Purification Offering," 177.

40. For Milgrom, as we saw above, when *kipper* is used in the context of "ransom," it is a "denominative" use of the word—that is, the verb *kipper* is here being derived from the noun *kofer*, and thus in these cases it means not "to purge" but "to ransom." This would be a secondary definition of the verb, one that may not be *wholly* separate from the primary sense (to purge, from the Akkadian), but one which is nevertheless "sharply distinguished" from the cultic understanding of the word. Milgrom, *Leviticus 1-16*, 1082–83. Levine speaks of this distinction as *kippēr* I and *kippēr* II. Levine, *In the Presence of the Lord*, 67ff. The distinction is emphasized even more strongly by Schwartz, who says, ". . . it seems most likely that the previously held view, that [*kofer*] 'ransom', and [*kipper*] 'purge', are etymologically and/or semantically related with each other, is false—these are unrelated homographs." Schwartz, "The Prohibitions Concerning the 'Eating' of Blood in Leviticus 17," 54. Sklar reviews and responds to these kinds of arguments in Sklar, *Sin, Impurity, Sacrifice, Atonement*, 4–7; cf. 47 n.14. He says that it is generally not "purge" or "ransom," but both elements are in each use of *kipper*. The reason why ransom is so important for him is because of his understanding of the relation of sin and punishment. My disagreement with this view will become increasingly clear in what follows.

Other texts analyzed by Sklar are even more specifically in the realm of civil legislation. They deal with the possibility of payments or punishments to resolve tensions between humans (in other words, they are "horizontal" in nature). One text that heavily influences Sklar's analysis is the (non-P) legislation in Exodus 21 addressing what happens in response to a fatal ox goring. If there is previous evidence that the ox was prone to this kind of behavior, its owner could be put to death, according to this law. The injured party (it is not entirely clear who, in this case, since the goring was fatal) can, however, demand a monetary payment in exchange for the ox owner's life: "If ransom [*kofer*] is laid upon [the owner], he must pay whatever is laid upon him to redeem his life" (Ex 21:30). While this passage does help to clarify the concept of *kofer*, it does not establish a link between ransom and temple theology. In yet another text (attributed to H), the possibility of a ransom in the case of murder is precluded: "You may not accept a ransom for the life of a murderer who is guilty of a capital crime; he must be put to death" (Nm 35:31). After this stipulation, the text shifts into an explanation of how the spilled blood "pollutes the land," and that this polluting blood can be "purged" (*kūppar*) only by the blood of the murderer—in other words, capital punishment (cf. Nm 35:33–34). Here again, it seems unlikely that this text explicates the meaning of cultic sacrifice, for numerous reasons. First, it is almost certainly later than the main body of Leviticus 1–16, and thus the priestly concept of *kipper* was already established. Similarly, while this passage *is* playing with the concepts of pollution and purgation (and certainly there are interconnections between land and sanctuary in H), it is impossible to imagine that this law is intimately connected to literal cultic practice. To isolate just one problem: Leviticus repeatedly requires that the sacrifice be "unblemished." Could a murder's lifeblood ever be associated with that term? Such a criminal could never be seen as an acceptable offering to God (even leaving aside the issue of human sacrifice), and there are obviously no rites associated with the blood of a murderer. Thus, it is far more likely that the established cultic language of *kipper*, which does not imply ransom in its original setting, is being extended to analogously support an "eye for an eye/life for a life"-type logic (cf. Lv 21:19–21). Further still, the discussion here seems rather remote from the statement, a couple of verses earlier, that a murderer cannot be ransomed. Isn't it possible that the use of the term *kofer* followed by the shift to the concept of *kipper* is done for stylistic reasons (repetition of homographs) without implying a profound theological connection between words?

After reviewing these texts (and a few others from outside the Torah), Sklar defines the biblical concept of *kofer* as:

. . . a legally or ethically legitimate payment that delivers a guilty
party from a just punishment that is the right of the offended party
to execute or to have executed. The acceptance of this payment is
entirely dependent upon the choice of the offended party [to accept]
a lesser punishment than was originally expected, and its acceptance
serves both to rescue the life of the guilty and to appease the
offended party, thus restoring peace to the relationship.[41]

Thus, *kofer* includes the concepts represented by the English words
"ransom" and "appeasement." It is "ransom" insofar as it is a price or
penalty that has been set and that must be paid to save someone who is
(in this case, justly) imperiled—this penalty may be painful, but it is more
desirable than the alternative. It is "appeasement" insofar as *kofer*
reflects a situation where one party has been offended and rightly
demands propitiation. For Sklar, then, this is a legal arrangement in
which an offended party accepts a "mitigated penalty . . . in place of a
much harsher, yet deserved, penalty" to restore a broken relationship.[42]
It is precisely this type of arrangement that, Sklar argues, stands behind
the Levitical theology of *kipper*. Thus, when we read Leviticus 16:6—
"Aaron shall bring forward his own bull of purification offering *to effect
purification* for himself and for his household. . ."—Sklar would say that
the blood has the power to purge because sacrificial blood is the *kofer*-
payment demanded by God in exchange for one's life.[43] To put it more
plainly, God demands the life of the animal (read: death) as the ransom-
payment required in place of the life (read: death) of the sinner. At the
very heart of this argument is the question of what sacrificial blood symbolizes, and thus the debate largely boils down to competing interpretations of Leviticus 17:11.

Life is in the Blood

Just as the word "*kipper*" must bear the burden of being the mono-
logical explanation for the goal of the purification offering, Leviticus
17:11 is the primary text for understanding the meaning of blood in the
temple cult. This passage is ascribed to the Holiness Code, and thus it

41. Sklar, *Sin, Impurity, Sacrifice, Atonement*, 60. This is the "positive" definition of
the word. There is another "negative" definition, meaning bribe, which Sklar does not
associate with the cultic *kipper*.
42. Sklar, 83.
43. The concept of a "ransom payment" is mentioned frequently throughout Sklar's
text. To give just one example, see Sklar, 139.

was very likely written after Leviticus 16,[44] and yet it has been argued that this text makes explicit the theological principles that are in fact inherent in earlier priestly tradition.[45] If this is right, then Leviticus 17:11 is a key text for understanding the theo-logic of temple ritual. It reads: "For the life of the flesh is in the blood,[46] and I have assigned it to you for making expiation for your lives[47] upon the altar; it is the blood, as life, that effects expiation."[48] Several sticky interpretive issues have arisen around this sentence. First, is this verse offering an interpretation of sacrificial blood generally, or the well-being offering narrowly (cf. 17:5)? Second, what is intended by the Hebrew word "*nephesh*" here (frequently translated as "life" in this context)? Finally, third, what about *kipper*? Understanding this verse will help us to assess the argument of those who insist that the punitive element is a central feature of the priestly purification offering.

In the discussions of Leviticus 17:11, these three questions are interrelated. This becomes clear in reviewing Jacob Milgrom's argument for a narrow reading of the verse. He claims that this verse is dealing *only* with the well-being offering—the joyful type of sacrifice that provides meat for the table (cf. Lv 3)—which is mentioned explicitly a few verses before the text in question (v. 5). As evidence for this interpretation, Milgrom points to the fact that verse 11 is giving a rationale for the command decreed in the previous verse: you shall not "eat" an animal's blood (v. 10) because the *kippering* life is in the blood (v. 11). Because the well-being offering alone is consumed by the offerer, it makes sense to say that the priestly legislator must have that type of sacrifice in mind.

But wait a minute: if this verse is about the well-being offering, why does it use the verb *kipper* at all? The well-being offering (*šĕlāmîm*), after all, has nothing to do with purging the temple. To explain this ambiguity, Milgrom must argue that the very act of killing an animal for meat is,

44. I have assumed the dating promoted by Milgrom, along with Israel Knohl, which has won substantial support in subsequent scholarship. See Milgrom, *Leviticus 1-16*, 13–35.

45. A good example of such an interpretation is Vis, "The Purification Offering," 204ff.

46. Hebrew: *nep̄eš habbāśār baddām hî.*

47. Hebrew: *leḵappêr ʿal-napšōtêḵem.* Schwartz dislikes the NJPS translation here, and says that this second clause of the verse is meant to communicate God's assertion that "It is not you who are placing the blood on the altar for me, for my benefit, but rather the opposite: it is I who have placed it there for you—for your benefit." Schwartz, "The Prohibitions Concerning the 'Eating' of Blood in Leviticus 17," 51. This has appeal; it seems to recall Abraham's response to Isaac: "God will provide the lamb."

48. Hebrew: *kî-haddām hū bannep̄eš yeḵappêr.*

implicitly, a type of wrongdoing (cf. vv. 3–4); it is a kind of murder! Such wrongdoing is acknowledged and addressed when the blood of that animal is placed on the altar: the "murderer's" life—the one who has killed the animal for food—is "ransomed"—that is, rescued from God's wrath—by the blood of the animal. Notice that while Milgrom argues consistently that *kipper* means "to purge" in Leviticus 1–16, he believes that the same word must mean ransom (now derived from *kofer*) in Leviticus 17 because "purge" wouldn't make any sense in the context of the *šĕlāmîm*.[49] For Milgrom, this view is further supported by the fact that, when the phrase "*lekappêr ʿal-napšōtêkem*" is used elsewhere, it clearly means "to ransom your lives";[50] in each case, something has occurred to stir God's wrath, and therefore a ransom must be presented to assuage God.[51] Milgrom reasons that killing animals must spark divine anger and thus a ransom is required to save the offerer's life. The approved ransom price is the blood of the animal.

By restricting the interpretation of Leviticus 17:11 to the context of the *šĕlāmîm*, Milgrom attempts to make a very precise argument: the word *kipper* in Leviticus 17 *must* be translated "ransom," and thus it must derive from *kofer* because this is the only way to understand why the verb *kipper* would be used in the context of worshippers partaking of the meat. However, ransom does not make sense in the context of the purification offering (as described in Lv 4–5), because their blood acts as a "ritual detergent" and not as a ransom. Thus, Leviticus 17:11 must not be a general statement about the nature of sacrificial blood, but rather it refers *only* to the well-being offering; it is, in other words, an isolated case.[52] Milgrom seeks to segregate the more common priestly concept of blood as purifying agent and the more innovative "Holiness Code" development of blood as ransom. Schwartz supports Milgrom in depicting the argument in Leviticus 17 as idiosyncratic. He says, "It is the only place in the Priestly code, or for that matter in the Bible, in which sacrificial blood is said to be a ransom for human life. This is the only place in which the [*kipper*]-action attributed to blood has the sense of ransom

49. See Milgrom, *Leviticus 1-16*, 707–13; Jacob Milgrom, *Leviticus 17-22: A New Translation with Introduction and Commentary* (New York: Doubleday, 2000), 1474–78.

50. The verses identified are Exodus 30:15, 16. Milgrom, *Leviticus 17-22*, 1474. Schwartz (among others) also points to Numbers 31:50. "The Prohibitions Concerning the 'Eating' of Blood in Leviticus 17," 55 n.1. See also Julia Rhyder, *Centralizing the Cult: The Holiness Legislation in Leviticus 17-26* (Tübingen: Mohr Siebeck, 2019), 219.

51. Or so the argument goes—but see the doubts I raised in footnote 38 above with reference to the census in Exodus 30.

52. Milgrom, *Leviticus 17-22*, 1475.

rather than purification."[53] By bracketing this verse, Milgrom and Schwartz are protecting their more nuanced and sympathetic "Picture of Dorian Gray" theology of Levitical sacrifice against typical Christian interpretations that hyper-focus on wrath, punishment, and propitiation. On the one hand, they'll allow that ransom is an operative concept in the cult, but on the other hand, they'll insist that the concept is chronologically late, secluded to this single text, and relevant to a single offering: the less contested well-being offering. It is *not* relevant to the theology of the purification offering. In other words, and finally, this verse is not ultimately relevant to the theology of Yom Kippur since there is no well-being offering on Yom Kippur.

This high-wire balancing act of conceding a "ransom" interpretation of the *kipper*-blood in one case and isolating it from priestly theology more generally has been controversial. The weak link in the argument is the claim that verse 11 addresses the *šĕlāmîm* exclusively; unlike many of Milgrom's other discoveries, this proposal has been frequently critiqued.[54] The main problem for Milgrom is that, while the well-being offering is mentioned early in the chapter, the immediate context for verse 11 is more general. It says, "And if anyone of the house of Israel or of the strangers who reside among them partakes of *any* blood, I will set My face against the person. . . ."[55] The verse is explaining why *all* blood is forbidden for consumption, which would include hunted game that is not offered at the tabernacle (vv. 13–14). Thus, Sklar gives a persuasive interpretation of the scope of v. 11:

> In short, then, v. 10 takes its eyes off of the peace offering to make a general prohibition against the consumption of the blood of any animal, sacrificial or not. Verse 11 then provides two grounds for this general prohibition: (1) the blood of animals contains its life, which may not be consumed, and (2) there is only one purpose that the LORD has allowed the Israelites to use animal's blood for, namely, making atonement.[56]

---

53. Schwartz, "The Prohibitions Concerning the 'Eating' of Blood in Leviticus 17," 55–56. He elsewhere calls H's theory "new and unique," one that is articulated as an alternative to P's theory. Schwartz, 59. This view is supported by Gilders, *Blood Ritual in the Hebrew Bible*, 170–76.

54. See the list of critical citations Milgrom himself mentions in Milgrom, *Leviticus 17-22*, 1474–75. See also Kiuchi, *The Purification Offering in the Priestly Literature*, 102–3. More recently, Sklar (see below), Gilders, *Blood Ritual in the Hebrew Bible*, 22; Vis, "The Purification Offering," 210–11; and Rhyder, *Centralizing the Cult*, 221.

55. Leviticus 17:10, emphasis added.

56. Sklar, *Sin, Impurity, Sacrifice, Atonement*, 177–78.

If v. 11 is not specific to the *šĕlāmîm*, if it articulates a theology relevant to cultic blood rites generally, then the separation that Milgrom tries to create between this verse and the rest of priestly theology is substantially weakened. When that dam bursts, suddenly the ransom-mentality floods everything else: at least from the perspective of H, if we accept the notion that the author intends for us to interpret *kipper* here as ransom, then the logic of ransom is operative in all sacrifice. In her recent book *Centralizing the Cult*, Julia Rhyder also accepted the interpretation of *kipper* as "ransom" in Leviticus 17 but says the introduction of the ransom idea is a new and unprecedented interpretation created by H.[57] Sklar goes further: he claims that H is merely making explicit what is everywhere else implicit: blood is the ransom price of the cultic economy. In other words, by undermining the idea that Leviticus 17:11 is an isolated case, but retaining Milgrom's concession that *kipper* here means "ransom," Sklar insists that throughout Leviticus the purificatory use of the blood works because it operates as a *kofer*-arrangement. It appeases God's wrath because the animal's death is an acceptable substitution for the offerer's death. God, as the offended party, consents to accept one punishment in the place of another.

To reiterate my concern: such a result manifestly undermines the consistent overarching theology of the temple—which, we have seen, is the site of paradigmatic beauty, goodness, and truth—and it would compromise priestly theological insight substantially. It takes a striking affirmation—"it is the blood, *as life*, that effects expiation"—and turns it on its head, suggesting that the meaning of the word life is "death." If this is true, the implications seem to be as follows: Israel's cult is indeed a system in which God must collect his pound of flesh for human wickedness. That animal sacrifices can be interpreted as a lesser punishment may suggest a degree of magnanimity on God's part, and yet the arbitrariness of God's penalties is perhaps most frightening of all. Is it really possible, theologically, that for *unintentional* sins, and even for impurities stemming from motherhood, God demands death . . . but will generously settle for the spilled blood of an animal, so long as there is death in one form or another? If this were the heart and soul of priestly theology, supersessionist attitudes toward the cult really do have aesthetic and moral advantage.

In light of these pressing theological concerns, a recent proposal advanced by Joshua Vis offers an appealing and persuasive alternative. Vis does not attempt merely to reconstruct the wall between Leviticus

---

57. Rhyder, *Centralizing the Cult*, 220.

17:11 and the purification offering—in fact, Vis agrees with Milgrom's critics that this verse *does* express the general symbolic meaning of blood in priestly (H) theology—but he then takes aim at the recent scholarly commonplace that *kipper* in this case idiosyncratically means "ransom." In other words, he thinks Milgrom is wrong on both counts, and thus a new interpretation of this key verse is needed. He offers the following translation of the Hebrew: "For *the spirit* of the flesh is in the blood, and I have placed it for you upon the altar *to purge your spirits*; for it is the blood that *purges by means of the spirit*."[58] For our purposes, it is important to emphasize that the key choices Vis makes are to translate *nephesh* as spirit and *kipper* as purge.

As for the first word, *nephesh* is one of those fantastically rich words that defies easy translation. Often, in the context of Leviticus 17, it is translated "life," but Vis' choice of spirit is understandable. As Charles Owiredu says, "The range of meanings given to the term [N-P-š] expresses the psychophysical unity of the person. It can be understood as the 'principle of life', the animating force joined together with the body in a human being or an animal."[59] In other words, as Vis points out, while the concept of "soul" is not in view (if by that we mean a disembodied consciousness), this word does point to one's living essence, dynamic interiority, "animating force,"[60] perhaps even—this is my own suggestion— the spiritual holy of holies at the center of one's life. From this perspective, one can see how the English word "spirit" might help to capture aspects of the Hebrew that remain untouched by the word "life." Neither is adequate, but both are accurate.

For Vis, the important point is that it is this "spirit," this inner essence, that is both *in* the sacrificial blood,[61] and is purged *by* the sacrificial blood. In other words, it is the presence of living spirit in the blood that has the power to purge the human spirit, who is burdened by sin. Whereas Milgrom, Schwartz, Sklar, and Rhyder all understand the second

58. Vis, "The Purification Offering," 205. Emphasis added.
59. Charles Owiredu, "Blood and Life in the Old Testament" (Durham University, 2004), 5–6.
60. Vis, "The Purification Offering," 204.
61. There is an extended discussion of what type of *beth* is being used in Leviticus 17:11a: *essentiae* or *locale*. Vis thinks the "spirit"/life is *in* the blood, but it is nevertheless distinct from the blood, and thus he prefers the locative reading. Vis, 206–9. Milgrom generally interprets the phrase to mean "blood-as-life," and thus he takes it to be a *beth essentiae*. Either interpretation is apparently possible, and in terms of the theological symbolism of blood, it is not clear to me that a definitive choice in one direction or the other makes a decisive difference.

clause to say that God gives the sacrificial blood "to ransom your lives," Vis says that God gives the blood "to purge your spirits," and he perceptively associates this phrase with the culminating passage of Leviticus 16, which is also attributed to the author of the Holiness Code. Leviticus 16:30 says, "For on this day, he [the priest] shall purge you to purify you of all of your sins; you shall be declared pure before YHWH."[62] For Vis, when the blood of the purification offering is manipulated in the temple, an effect of this action is to purge the "life/spirit" of the offerer of the sins that he or she bears. The blood of the offering has the power to purge because of the spirit/life within it. There are, of course, plausible counterarguments to this reading; the possibility that *kipper* in Leviticus 17 is associated with the noun "ransom" (*kofer*) is not completely eliminated. Nevertheless, Vis has offered a persuasive alternative that does not require a theological perspective that is idiosyncratic compared with typical priestly doctrine (*pace* Milgrom, Schwartz, and especially Rhyder), and it does not imply that the logic of the purification offering is inseparable from a "*kofer*-arrangement," which is steeped in a questionable theology of appeasing God through death (*pace* Sklar). Instead, it affirms that life purifies lives, spirit purifies the spirit, and that blood is the theological symbol of the spiritual life that overcomes death, not by taking up the strategies of death, but by simply reaffirming the commitment to true life.[63]

This is Milgrom's usual position as well, and it is this insight that makes his work so profound: even though he finds it necessary to speak of ransom in Leviticus 17, when it comes to the theology of P in the early

62. Vis's translation, 224. Apparently independently, Liane Feldman argues for a similar translation. See Feldman, *Story of Sacrifice*, 189.

63. As an aside, I should acknowledge that this point has also been highlighted more and more by Christian scholars in recent years, especially in interpreting the book of Hebrews. David Moffitt's book is an excellent example. He draws on a number of studies that show that the centerpiece of the *ḥaṭṭā't* offering is not the death of the animal but the identification of blood as life, and he applies this research to Hebrews effectively. This has been massively helpful in advancing Christian soteriology. Moffitt does rely in large part on Sklar's book without noting how his ransom theory is in tension with the blood-as-life model. I hope this present work is useful in establishing a better foundation for the biblical theology of blood. See David M. Moffitt, *Atonement and the Logic of Resurrection in the Epistle to the Hebrews* (Leiden: Brill, 2011), 256–77; David M. Moffitt, "Blood, Life, and Atonement: Reassessing Hebrews' Christological Appropriation of Yom Kippur," in *The Day of Atonement: Its Interpretations in Early Jewish and Christian Traditions*, ed. Thomas Hiek (Leiden: Brill, 2011), 211–24. Similarly, see Christian Eberhart, "Characteristics of Sacrificial Metaphors in Hebrews," in *Hebrews: Contemporary Methods, New Insights* (Leiden: Brill, 2005), 39–43; Eberhart, *The Sacrifice of Jesus*, 94–101; Vis, "The Purification Offering," 256ff; and especially Willi-Plein, "Some Remarks on Hebrews," 33.

chapters of Leviticus (1-16), Milgrom is clear: "It has been established that the animal's blood is the ritual detergent in the *ḥaṭṭaʾt* sacrifice. . . . Impurity (*ṭumʾâ*) is the realm of death. Only its antonym, life, can be its antidote. Blood, then, as life is what purges the sanctuary. It nullifies, overpowers, and absorbs the Israelites' impurities that adhere to the sanctuary, thereby allowing the divine presence to remain and Israel to survive."[64] Blood, in this eidetic system, is the sacrament of what is most pure and holy, that *nephesh* shared by God and living creatures,[65] and thus it has absolute priority over the realm of death, which is a usurper that can only weakly mimic the intrinsic authenticity and splendor of the beauty, the goodness, and the truth of YHWH's *nephesh*.[66] In fact, the idea that the hosts of heaven wage a great battle against the storming brigand from the outer darkness, that the mountain of peace is the site of the *Chaoskampf* described by Levenson, is also recognized by Milgrom. Through the liturgical ministry of the priests, he says, "holiness-life has triumphed over impurity-death."[67]

---

64. Milgrom, *Leviticus 1-16*, 711–12. As he elsewhere notes, the equation of blood and life is also affirmed by P, with the obvious example being Genesis 9:4. Milgrom, 46.

65. Vis, "The Purification Offering," 227, 254.

66. Contrast this with Gane's very different interpretation of the sacrificial blood. He argues that when worshippers bring their *ḥaṭṭāʾt* offerings to the sanctuary throughout the year (as described in Leviticus 4–5), and when they lay their hand on the animal, the animal's sacrificial blood actually becomes a carrier of that person's sin. Then the priest intentionally brings this sin-laden blood *into* the sacred sphere to deposit it there, at least for a time. See Gane, *Cult and Character*, 172–81. For Gane, then, the blood is not simply a detergent (176), but it is a means by which "imperfection removed from offerers is transferred to YHWH's sanctuary" (177) and thus "sacrificial purification of the offerer necessarily involves transfer of his/her evil to YHWH" (180). Gane unambiguously states that "YHWH mandate[s] the defilement of his sanctuary through outer-altar and outer-sanctum purification offerings" (179). The goal is that these evils, brought into the sacred space throughout the year, would ultimately be removed on Yom Kippur. Given what I have argued in this chapter, it is probably clear that I find this idea unlikely from the perspective of priestly sacramental thought, as I understand it. Just as blood should not be interpreted as a symbol of death, neither should it be perceived as a carrier of sin or evil. Each of these theories takes priestly symbolic action and reverses its meaning: blood becomes a sign of both death and evil! As Milgrom says, Gane's interpretation seems "untenable." "The Preposition מן in the חטאת Pericopes," *Journal of Biblical Literature* 126, no. 1 (April 1, 2007): 162. For Gane's response to Milgrom, see Roy E. Gane, "Privative Preposition מן in Purification Offering Pericopes and the Changing Face of 'Dorian Gray,'" *Journal of Biblical Literature* 127, no. 2 (July 1, 2008): 220–22. See also Vis's critique at "The Purification Offering," 189–91; and also Christophe Nihan, "The Templization of Israel in Leviticus: Some Remarks on Blood Disposal and Kipper in Leviticus 4," in *Text, Time, and Temple: Literary, Historical and Ritual Studies in Leviticus,* ed. Francis Landy, Leigh M. Trevaskis, and Bryan D. Bibb (Sheffield: Sheffield Phoenix Press, 2015), 116–18.

67. Milgrom, *Leviticus 1-16*, 47.

In using the words "sacrament" and "liturgy" above, I intend to call into question another assumption that is commonly seen: the idea of blood as a "ritual detergent" must denote a belief in blood's magical properties, and thus priestly temple actions are ensnared in primitive superstitions.[68] In an article that highlights the sacramental nature of priestly theology, Crispin Fletcher-Louis points out that "in her worship, her sacrifices and her construction of sacred space and time, Israel shares ancient Near Eastern assumptions about the efficacy of ritual and the need for signs that mediate the divine presence."[69] He later refers to priestly theology as an "iconographically rich and sacramentally centered world. . . ."[70] If a participatory and incarnational concept analogous to Christian sacraments can be detected in the Hebrew Bible, then the question becomes: what is being "made present" in the temple's sacrificial rites? I argue that the purpose of the temple, and especially of the sacrificial rites, is for Israel to be (re-)grafted into the life of Abraham, Isaac, and Jacob by (re-)presenting the self-giving that is at all times the foundation of Israel's existence. Jacob-Israel (father of the twelve) is already present in Isaac on Mount Moriah, and Isaac is the twice-given son, the superabundance of God's grace.[71]

The blood that pulses through Isaac is the very same blood that he will pass on to his children. All Israel carries that blood, that graced *life*, and it is this life that is to be given again to the God who was "seen" on Mount Moriah—that is, the true God who is known not for destruction but for giving life and giving it again in abundance. As I've argued, had Isaac died physically that day, his life-blood would not continue to run

68. For the claim that some Levitical cultic rituals rely on a belief in magic, see Levine, *In the Presence of the Lord*, 55–56, 90–91. Even more polemically, Christian theologian Stephen Finlan frequently uses the word "magic" in describing atonement theologies as part of his argument that such sources represent a primitive mindset that should be overcome. Cf. Stephen Finlan, *Problems with Atonement: The Origins of, and Controversy about, the Atonement Doctrine* (Collegeville, MN: Liturgical Press, 2005), 35, 84, 89, 101.

69. Crispin H. T. Fletcher-Louis, "The Image of God and the Biblical Roots of Christian Sacramentality," in *The Gestures of God: Explorations in Sacramentality*, ed. Geoffrey Rowell and Christine Hall (London: Continuum, 2004), 73–89.

70. Fletcher-Louis, 86. Consider also Sommer's suggestion that P's theology is analogous to Catholic sacramental theology: Sommer, *Bodies of God*, 135, 256 n.57.

71. In using the word "sacrament" or "quasi-sacrament" here and below, I am admittedly relying on Christian theological concepts in an attempt to better understand the mysteries of Jewish temple rites. In the context of Christian theology, there is precedent for the concept of the "sacraments of the Mosaic law." An updated consideration of this theological idea is needed, but it is beyond the scope of our discussion here. For now, see Matthew Levering, *Christ's Fulfillment of Torah and Temple: Salvation According to Thomas Aquinas* (Notre Dame, IN: University of Notre Dame Press, 2002), 121–22.

in the veins of Israel, but instead, he dies sacramentally through the ram so that his blood can, at the same moment, give life to the nation and be poured out for God. Through this sophisticated symbol, the worshiper pours him- or herself forth without diminishment precisely because such self-giving is the greatest possible fullness. Blood truly is the sacrament of life, and Israel must see herself as a Blood of Life people. Therefore, she understands that she is handed over to God with abandon, with trust, but without loss. The sacrament in Isaac makes this theological truth present.[72]

72. I appreciate that this particular symbol involves an animal's physical death, an action that can be out of step with modern sensibilities. Many modern men and women, far removed from pastoral life, find it difficult to see past the apparent violence. A few reflections. First, even while acknowledging distaste for blood sacrifice, we should be mindful of the fact that this attitude is in many ways driven by the fact that, in the modern West, we have simply outsourced the task of animal slaughter; this makes the sense of moral superiority suspect. Other cultures, including ancient cultures, were forced to be attentive to animal life and death in a way that is less common today. That they may not have formed mawkish bonds with these creatures, unlike some modern people, is partly a reflection of economic realities. That these cultures also showed greater respect and care for the flock and herd than modern "factory farm" societies, however, seems indisputable. Second, there is sometimes a sense that it is wasteful to sacrifice an animal. The best justification for such an argument is found in Psalm 50, where God says: "For Mine is every animal of the forest, the beasts on a thousand mountains. . . . Do I eat the flesh of bulls, or drink the blood of he-goats?" (vv. 10, 13). These verses show that the Israelites did not have a simplistic theology about the need to feed God; they knew that ultimately everything belonged to YHWH and that YHWH did not benefit from sacrifices in any material way. Yet even with this conviction, they continued to sacrifice! This seems to support the idea that such sacrifices really were quasi-sacramental for Israel. If the act became rote, or if Israel ever developed the childish notion that God depended *on them* for sustenance, then the truth of the rites would be lost, and the prophets would rightly speak out. Even though God does not "need" sacrifice in any mythological way, this does not mean the animal is wasted. On the one hand, it must be acknowledged that in most cases the meat of the animal was consumed by either the priests or the family and friends of the one who brought the offering. But on the other hand, and more importantly, there is a subtle secular assumption here that a life set apart for religious purposes is a waste. From Israel's perspective, the animal chosen to be offered to God has a far greater dignity. What more honorable life for a sheep or a goat than to be chosen for the Lord? Such creatures were to be "spotless," and they would have received greater care and attention from their owners on account of their great vocation. Cf. Klawans, *Purity, Sacrifice, and the Temple*, 58–62. Plus, is it better to be eaten by a human (or by a wolf), or to be life in the temple? Remember again the song of David: "One thing I ask of the Lord, only that do I seek: to live in the house of the Lord all the days of my life, to gaze upon the beauty of the Lord, to frequent His temple" (Ps 27:4). We must at least entertain the notion that an ancient society's hierarchy of values differs from our own—we can discuss whether these values are better or worse, but the difference must first be acknowledged—and thus what seems like a terrible "waste" for a modern person may be seen as the greatest excellence for those who engage in this practice.

Lifeblood: Concluding Reflections

We can now summarize the major arguments that I have made with respect to the symbolism of the first goat's blood. In chapter two, I defended the permissibility of reading Genesis 22 and Leviticus 1 together. I also pointed out that the theological interconnectivity between these two texts was explicit at least as early as the books of Chronicles, and that, for Levenson at least, it is plausible to imagine that Zion was already in mind when Genesis 22 was written. In this chapter, I advanced the argument by pointing to the well-established theory that the purification offering historically develops from the burnt offering. Whatever theological insights were contained in the earlier offering surely persisted, to some extent, in the latter. While there are both similarities and differences between the two, the primary difference is that purification offerings require far more elaborate blood manipulations. If the burnt offering was recognized as quintessential for Israel insofar as it expressed the ideal of total (*hinneni*) self-giving, and if this mode of being was articulated with exquisite eloquence in the primordial action of Abraham and Isaac—an action that expressed, in principle, Edenic peace between God and humanity—then the purification offering is that same joyful movement repurposed to address the tragedy of sin. The purpose, in other words, is to return to the primordial posture dramatically established by Israel's father and son, but to fully realize this freedom, the flotsam of sin must first be straightforwardly addressed. Because, according to Milgrom and others, sin and impurity create a "something" that pollutes the sacred space, it is not possible to simply return to the burnt offering as if nothing happened. The pollution of Nadab and Abihu must be addressed first on the way to full enjoyment of the holy burnt offerings.

The way those sins and impurities are counteracted is through blood as a "ritual detergent" in the sacred spaces, and now we can see that it is the blood of Isaac-Israel that sacramentally has this purging power.

Third, and finally, it is certainly acceptable to acknowledge—from the Christian perspective—that the transition to the "unbloody sacrifice" of the Eucharist is a positive theological development for a variety of reasons, including the fact that it does not require an animal's death. But this concession should not prevent us from interpreting Jewish sacrificial practices sympathetically and with appreciation. A theological development need not—should not—rely on disdain for what came before, because in Christ these ancient mysteries are seen in their fullest glory. Correlatively, the more we can perceive and value the theo-logic in the ancient cult, the more we will perceive the glory of Christ crucified and risen. Therefore, modern distaste for blood rituals mustn't bar us from seeing what is good and profound in temple theology.

Again, because the life of Isaac is the very life of the offerer (who is in the same chosen and covenantal bloodline), in re-presenting the life of Isaac sacramentally in the sacrifice, the offerer presents her or his own life in him. It is a matter of conforming oneself again, even in the time of sin, to the pattern of the Akedah, which is the doubly graced[73] foundation of Israel's entire existence. Such a way of life overcomes sin and death, and it is incomprehensible to sin and death. Therefore, when the priest ritually applies blood to the temple furniture, he is applying the blood of Isaac as the one adequate antidote to the miasma of death. In doing so, he has taken sides in the cosmic conflict, advancing the cause of order and harmony and driving out the forces of chaos and division by reiterating the peace of Eden (which is *hinneni*).

In these many pages, we have been meditating on the mystery of "how Aaron shall enter the adytum" after the illicit encroachment of Nadab and Abihu. This entering is double-pronged: (1) it represents the proper mode of *qorban*, "drawing near" to God, in contradistinction to the brothers' approach, and (2) it serves a new, mournful purpose, to remove the sin that now accumulates at the heart of Israel's sacred space, which was the dwelling place less and less suitable to an all-holy God and thus must be remedied at once. In the extended meditation on the wages of sin (chapter five), we have seen that the realm of death pollutes creation at every level; in the priest's sophisticated system, much of this corruption is unintentional and unavoidable. This represents the thoughtful realism of the priests, who recognize that disorder and decay are now an ineluctable quotidian reality. But whatever the cause, the cult offers Israel an opportunity to return repeatedly to the foundation stone of selfless devotion to God, upon which the nation is built. In this way, and in this way only, death is overcome. This movement toward God is Israel's vocation morning and night, but the movement is epitomized and made perfect on Yom Kippur.

73. Cf. Hart, *Beauty of the Infinite*, 352.

CHAPTER 7

Making All Things New: Yom Kippur in Leviticus

The Two Goats: A Theological Interpretation

Now that we have, in chapter five, established the basic problem of "miasmic" sin invading the sanctuary, and in chapter six explained the notion of life-blood as a purifying agent, the foundational theological infrastructure for the high priest's movements on the highest holy day are in place. From here we can contemplate the ritual itself, and especially consider why there are two goats rather than just one. Thus, we read in Leviticus 16: "Aaron shall bring forward his own bull of purification offering to effect purgation for himself and for his household; and he shall take the two he-goats and set them before the Lord at the entrance of the Tent of Meeting."[1] Three comments come to mind. First, priestly purification is the initial step. The priest, who is called to mediate between God and Israel as he moves between realms in the tabernacle, and especially the high priest, who is a complex symbol representing the repentant nation before God and heavenly glory before the nation, must embody exceptional holiness. Given this calling, priestly sin represents an especially acute threat to the entire nation. Just as the air in a war camp is still and heavy the night before the battle, the high priest felt the weight of his sacred responsibility. His campaign would be precarious; the seared remains of priestly sons might haunt his thoughts in the hours leading up to his embarkment. The high priest is sent, remember, on a journey to the center of the world, to the throne room of highest heaven, to stand as a representative of *all* creation before I Am. In the process, he would be stripped of his beautiful robes, essentially naked before God, with nothing but the blood of life to protect him.

Anticipating the moment when he will stand alone before God, the high priest trembles and feels his unworthiness. The traditions associated with Yom Kippur thus describe the solemn preparations in the hours leading up to his liturgical expedition. There are seven days of regular

---

1. Leviticus 16:6–7, as translated by Milgrom, *Leviticus 1-16*, 1009.

195

sacrifice and duties in the shrine, as if he is preparing himself to withstand the weight of glory in the holy of holies—and at the same time, to bear the weight of sin away from that place. The night before the high feast, his priestly *aides-de-camp* would ensure that he remained awake all night—a vigil intended to prevent an invalidating nocturnal emission— and they would read to him from the scriptures: from Job, from Ezra, from Chronicles, from Daniel.[2] The tremendous gravity of the moment is eloquently expressed in the *Mishnah Yoma*, which describes how the elders of the priesthood would address the high priest as the Day arrived: "'We abjure you by Him who caused his name to rest upon this house, that you will not vary in any way from all which we have instructed you.' He turns aside and weeps. And they turn aside and weep" (*mYoma* 1:5).

The awe-filled solemnity of this moment reflects the basic joy and trepidation of being the chosen people, the ones called to an intimate relationship with an all-holy God. The relational nature of this crisis— and this is the second point to notice in the passage cited above—is expressed in the simple phrase "before the Lord." In the prayerful presence of the whole nation, the priest brings the ox and the two goats "before the Lord." Drawing upon built environment studies, Michael Hundley points out that an ancient temple "provides cues to elicit proper behavior, to which people respond automatically and appropriately."[3] With this in mind, he suggests that the walls of the tabernacle represent spheres of intimacy, leading ultimately to a room analogous to a bedchamber. When the author of Leviticus instructs Aaron to bring his offerings "before the Lord," therefore, this commandment is "both a location and an evocative reference point"; it speaks to the threshold that distinguishes the divine sphere and the human, which is also the point at which the two meet.

2. From time to time, I will rely on the *Mishnah Yoma* for color commentary. These details come from *Mishnah Yoma* 1:6–7 translated by Jacob Neusner, trans., *The Mishnah: A New Translation* (New Haven, CT: Yale University Press, 1988). I will use Neusner's translation throughout.

This rabbinic account of the Day of Atonement was put to paper in redacted form, many think, in the early third-century AD. There is naturally debate over whether this document reproduces temple realities accurately. For a discussion of this issue, see Stökl Ben Ezra, *Impact of Yom Kippur*, 19–28; cf. Günter Stemberger, "Yom Kippur in Mishnah Yoma," in *The Day of Atonement: Its Interpretations in Early Jewish and Christian Traditions*, ed. Thomas Hieke and Tobias Nicklas (Leiden: Brill, 2011), 121–37. Stökl Ben Ezra takes the nuanced position that the historicity of the actions described in the *mYoma* needs to be assessed case by case. Milgrom finds the details of the high priest's preparation plausible; *Leviticus 1-16*, 1015–16.

3. Hundley, "Before YHWH," 18.

Standing at the threshold, one must be *invited* into another's home, and then invited into the more private areas within the home. The themes of humility and gift, contrasted with pride and plunder, have been fundamental throughout this book, and the theology of the temple generally, and the Day of Atonement especially, underlines how—by means of space and time—God prepares his people for a personal relationship. True relationship includes waiting, listening, being hospitable, and receiving hospitality. It is not that Israel is excluded from the holy of holies because God is—strictly speaking—threatened by her presence. God is not an introvert who needs ample "alone time." The issue, since the exile of Adam and Eve, since the death of Nadab and Abihu, is learning how to be a people "before the Lord," that is, having the openness of heart and the greatness of spirit to be genuinely in Love.[4] Such profound intimacy does cause the heart to shudder because it requires absolute vulnerability, which is the ultimate risk, but it is also the only true freedom. Israel is invited. She is given a place, a time, and even a means by which she might approach: the life of the beloved son, the firstborn who dies and, behold, lives even still.

This leads to the third observation about the opening verse: Israel is invited to take the "two he-goats," which are together described as a *ḥaṭṭāʾt* (v. 5), and set them before the Lord. Here we have arrived at a most pressing question: why *two* goats? Let's read further: "Aaron shall place lots upon the two goats, one marked 'for the Lord' and the other 'for Azazel'" (v.8). With a casting of lots, a different purpose or vocation is assigned, and each vocation is associated with a name, and each name is associated with a place. One is called to the center, the holy of holies, and the other will be sent out, to the wilderness. Even though the goats will move in opposite directions, another tradition clarifies that these two goats were identical in appearance. *Mishnah Yoma* puts it like this: "the religious requirement concerning them is that the two of them be equivalent in appearance, height, and value. . ." (*mYoma* 6:1). That the goats should look alike is also attested in even earlier Christian sources. *Barnabas* says the goats shall be "beautiful and similar"—or again, "similar, beautiful, and equal."[5] Perhaps because they look so similar and therefore

---

4. As L. Michael Morales says, the central theme of the Pentateuch—seen most especially in the Day of Atonement—is "*YHWH's opening a way for humanity to dwell in the divine Presence.*" *Who Shall Ascend?*, 38 (emphasis in original).

5. This is Stökl Ben Ezra's adaptation of Kirsopp Lake's 1912 *Loeb Classical Library* translation of the *Epistle of Barnabas* 7:6a and 7:10a. See Stökl Ben Ezra, *Impact of Yom Kippur*, 152–53.

need to be differentiated, another early tradition indicates that a "crimson thread" shall be tied upon the horns of the Azazel-goat after he receives his lot.[6] Therefore, as we proceed to discuss the distinct mission of each goat in the next few pages, it is also worth remembering their initial correspondence. Although each has a unique destiny, they are together a single *ḥaṭṭā't*, a single work of purgation, and their roles are interrelated.

The Goat for the Lord

The Azazel-goat is left standing at the entrance of the tabernacle after it receives its lot, and it is momentarily forgotten; all of the emphasis turns to the purification offering blood manipulations for the priests (using the blood of the ox) and for the people (using the blood of the YHWH-goat). A section of precise rubrics detailing the movements of the high priest in the sanctuary comes next, and here we find a reminder of the primary themes we've been discussing. The section begins: "Aaron shall bring forward (*wĕhiqrîb*) his own bull of purification offering (*haḥaṭṭā't*) to effect purgation (*wekipper*) for himself and his household. . ." (v. 11). There is beauty here, as the priest begins his journey into the heart of God's glorious presence, but there is also a mournful quality to this movement because the priest here has a mission to undo what should never have been. The priest comes to "de-sin" (*ḥaṭṭā't*) the sanctuary, to remove the impurity that pollutes God's dwelling, thus the higher goal of contemplative unity with God in the holy of holies is distracted by the immediate demands of purgation (*kipper*) and re-consecration.[7]

---

6. See *mYoma* 4:2, and also the earlier reference in *Barnabas* 7:8, 7:11. See Orlov, *Divine Scapegoats*, 26ff for an overview of the tradition of the crimson thread and its relation to the *Apocalypse of Abraham*; and Orlov, 90ff. for possible parallels between the crimson thread tradition and the *Book of the Watchers*.

7. While we have discussed the *ḥaṭṭā't* throughout this part of the book, we have only alluded to the dispute over whether this word should be translated as "sin offering," which is traditional, or "purification offering," which Milgrom advocates. Ever since the early 1970s, Milgrom has strongly and repeatedly defended his choice of "purification offering." He made a few key arguments. First, contextually, he points out that, while the verb *ḥaṭṭā't* in the basic "*Qal*" (a verb stem in Hebrew) can mean something like "to sin," the *ḥaṭṭā't*-offering is prescribed in a number of situations that have nothing to do with "sin" as we understand the word in English. For example, the *ḥaṭṭā't* after childbirth, or the *ḥaṭṭā't* to consecrate the altar. In these contexts and others, the word sin is "theologically foreign." Milgrom, *Leviticus 1-16*, 253. Second, there is a grammatical argument. When in reference to the offering, *ḥaṭṭā't* is a nominalized *pi'el* derivative—in Hebrew, the *pi'el* is an intensified form of the verb. Milgrom understands *ḥaṭṭā't* to be a privative *pi'el*, which means the word would more properly translate as "to de-sin, to remove sin," or in Milgrom's translation, "to cleanse, expurgate, decontaminate." Jacob Milgrom, "Sin-

The text mentions in passing that the bull shall be slaughtered,[8] but then moves quickly along to the rituals that most interest the priestly community: the blood manipulations. After the blood has been collected, the priest makes his first procession to the heart of creation, the holy of holies, this time carrying a blazing censor in which he would add "finely ground perfumed incense," consisting of frankincense and spices. As with neighboring cultures, incense was held in high esteem, and it seems quite natural that beautiful aromatics should be associated with this new Eden.[9] Every faculty was used to communicate the glory

---

Offering or Purification-Offering," *Vetus Testamentum* 21, no. 2 (April 1, 1971): 237. Therefore, the more appropriate translation for *ḥaṭṭā't* in Leviticus is "purification offering," not sin offering (a mistranslation that allegedly goes all the way back to the LXX). Because many scholars of Leviticus follow Milgrom's translation, and given its explanatory power with reference to Leviticus 16, I have generally followed his translation in this book. On the other hand, I will continue to call Yom Kippur "the Day of Atonement" rather than "the Day of Purgation" (the latter being Milgrom's choice) because at-one-ment better captures the overall result of the holy day, which undoubtedly includes purgation but is not limited to it.

There have also been critiques of Milgrom on his translation of *ḥaṭṭā't*. Watts' makes the argument that by translating *ḥaṭṭā't* as "purification offering," and interpreting this word as a technical term, the rhetorical impact of Leviticus 4–5 is lost. He says, "These chapters deliberately and repeatedly juxtapose verb, common noun, and offering name of the same root, especially *ḥṭ'*, in patterns that are quite redundant. . . . For example, the refrain 'sin that he sinned . . . as sin' appears eight times. . . ." Watts, *Ritual and Rhetoric*, 87–88. Watts says modern readers miss the rhetorical impact of the Hebrew words when *ḥaṭṭā't* is translated "purification offering."

8. Leviticus 16 does not specifically mention the "hand-leaning ritual," but all agree that the ritual was performed. According to the guidelines for the *ḥaṭṭā't*, which were described in detail in Leviticus 4, the high priest shall bring the bull forward, "lean his hand upon the head of the bull, and slaughter the bull before the Lord" (Lv 4:4; the procedure is the same for other sacrifices. See Leviticus 1:4 for the burnt offering and Leviticus 3:2 for the well-being offering). The text's lack of clarity on the meaning of this action has generated a lively conversation. For an especially comprehensive review of the literature, see Trevaskis, *Holiness, Ethics and Ritual in Leviticus*, 178–96.

Milgrom argues in favor of those who say that the ritual designates ownership; by leaning one's hand upon the animal, the offerer affirms that the offering is truly his to give. This is in contrast to other scholarly approaches, which claim that sin is transferred to the animal and the animal is substitutionally punished, or even theories in which the offerer's soul is united with the animal's and brought into God's presence through the animal. But the issue of rightful ownership was, in fact, quite serious: a primary impetus for the prophetic critique of the cult was that stolen goods were being offered. See Klawans' discussion on hand-leaning in the context of prophetic concerns: *Purity, Sacrifice, and the Temple*, 85. In chapter three we heard David articulate a key principle: "I cannot . . . sacrifice a burnt offering that has cost me nothing" (1 Chr 21:24). Ownership may seem mundane, but it is integral to the symbolism of the entire liturgy.

9. This is supported by other ancient Jewish texts, such as the *Book of the Watchers*, which describes one of Enoch's journeys: ". . . there was one tree such as I have never at

of God's presence, and the nose is not excluded from the lavish banquet of the senses.

After the first fragrant approach, the high priest would exit the holy of holies and return to the courtyard, where he would receive the blood of the bull, which had been slaughtered earlier (*mYoma* 4:3 further adds, quite realistically, that someone was charged with the task of stirring the blood so that it would not congeal). The text of Leviticus says, "He shall take some of the blood of the bull and sprinkle it with his finger on the *kappōret* on its east side; and in front of the *kappōret* he shall sprinkle some of the blood with his finger seven times" (v. 14). What does it mean to "sprinkle?" As Milgrom notes, the text itself is not clear, but the rabbis explain that the high priest would move his hand "like one who cracks a whip,"[10] thus flinging blood in the direction of the ark, the Lord's earthy footstool on earth. After this movement was complete, the priest would retreat once more to the courtyard where he would slaughter the goat for the community, the YHWH-goat, collect its blood, and return yet again to the holy of holies where he would repeat the blood ritual.

After these back-and-forth movements between spheres, after the sprinkling ritual for priests and people in the holy of holies, an explanation is offered. This passage has been cited a couple of times before, but hopefully it will be more meaningful now: "Thus he shall purge (*wekipper*) the adytum of the pollution and transgressions of the Israelites, including all of their sins. . . ." Milgrom's insights make sense of this passage: when the high priest sprinkles the blood about the ark—and then, just after, when he continues the process by performing blood manipulations in the shrine (cf. Lv 16:16b, Ex 30:10, Lv 4:3–7) and upon the burnt offering altar in the courtyard (vv. 18–19; cf. Lv 4:30)—that

---

all smelled; there was not a single one among those or other (trees) which is like it; among all the fragrances nothing could be so fragrant. . ." (1 Enoch 24:4). The passage goes on to speak of a tall mountain which is God's throne, and it further explains that this "tree of life" is preserved for the righteous, that it will be planted in the "holy place," and that the elect "shall enter into the holy (place); its fragrance shall (penetrate) their bones. . ." (1 Enoch 25:6).

The research of Cornelis Houtman helps bolster the aesthetic reasons for the emphasis on incense. He draws attention to the prominent but overlooked role of smell in the Hebrew Bible—including the deathly stench of corpses—and makes an interesting comment: ". . . it is plausible that for an Israelite odours were not only either pleasant or unpleasant, but also carriers of either life or death." "On the Function of the Holy Incense (Exodus XXX 34–8) and the Sacred Anointing Oil (Exodus XXX 22–33)," *Vetus Testamentum*, 1992, 460–61. As he approaches God's presence, the priest seeks to be holy as God is holy, to embody life as God embodies life, and thus he is swaddled in heavenly aromatics.

10. *Mishnah Yoma* 5:3. See Milgrom, *Leviticus 1-16*, 1032–33.

blood purifies the temple from the sins and impurities that have accumulated there. The presence of sin, this putrid miasma, makes the temple ill-suited for the indwelling presence of an all-holy God, but when the priest draws near with the *ḥaṭṭāʾt* blood, the ritual detergent of the cult, he purifies and re-consecrates (v. 19) the space to fully restore its radiance as the center of the Lord's covenantal presence to Israel.

The Beauty of Atonement: The Theo-logic of the Priest's Action

Let's step back and ask: if we could glimpse the mystical realities behind this liturgy, as deeply as possible, what is really happening through the priest's actions? We know from earlier chapters that the temple in general, and the holy of holies as its epitome, is a physical manifestation of God's tremendous glory. It was toward this place that the desire of Israel was oriented, as the psalms repeatedly suggest, and the meeting of desire and pure beauty at Zion opened the door to transformation into new life. That said, the temple is not merely a place for stagnantly contemplating the glory of God, but for the right action that emerges from, and is ordered to, that vision. It is the place where human beings learn to say *"hinneni"* with all their heart, soul, and strength. Such readiness before God is the essence of life for those called to communion with the one who is Life itself. This indeed is the truth: the truth of God, the truth of creation. Mount Zion is the world's source and essence, it is the microcosm that encapsulates the most profound harmony of earth and sky, land and water. Here the proper rhythms are measured so that the macrocosm is preserved in peace. The temple is a reminder that there is a mysterious depth to all creation and that glory dwells most intimately at the heart of creaturely being. Then again, this sacred mountain is a mere shadow of heavenly Truth; God's glory is greater still. The temple follows the contours of heaven but cannot wholly capture its essence. As the high priest climbs the stairs to the holy of holies, he ascends to a realm that is truly other, and thus the apophatic note of later traditions is appropriate.

Thus, the high priest, ministering in the holy of holies, draws near to establish true unity between the chosen people and the God of splendor and mystery. But we also know that the movement toward the perfect peace which is appropriate to this paradise is obstructed by an appalling reality. The gravest wickedness of Israel has pierced the holiest place in creation, violence has been unleashed on the earth by human cruelty, and these jolts of discord fling themselves upon the mountain of God with one objective: drive out the holy one of Israel so that the world might return to the primordial abyss. Therefore, the high priest's mission is not one of pure bliss as he elevates creation and communicates divine life, from glory to glory. Instead, now the call to unity (at-one-ment) involves a struggle against powers and principalities. The priest must engage in a movement of purgation, he must bear away the transgressions, to restore right order to the world. In this liturgical battle, most importantly, the high priest does not take up the weapons of this world, he does not meet violence with violence. Moriah is indeed named *YHWH-yireh*, both "The Lord is Seen" and "The Lord Will Provide." It is God who has provided the right response to the encroaching death on his holy mountain, it is God who provides the antidote. It is God who gives the blood, which is life. It is he who breathed life into the dust, he who brought stirrings of hope to Sarah's barrenness, it is he who provided yet again when Isaac was preserved through faith. Blood is the sacrament through which Israel draws near, open-heart to open-heart, and it is this form of life that overcomes every attempt at destruction.

When Aaron, the high priest, descends to the holy of holies, the blood he bears overcomes the darkling stains simply through its own vitality. In chapter five, we saw how the pollution in the temple exists in two basic forms. One is the remnant of ontological decay, the brokenness of the physical world, and thus is associated with the elaborate symbolism of Israel's impurity laws. The other is more terrible; it is spawned from disordered actions—idolatry, murder, lustful sexual acts—and it leaves behind a more serious wound in creation. We've heard Schwartz call this residue a "metaphysical spontaneous generation . . . though amorphous, it is substantive," and Gary Anderson says the offensive object is "manufactured ex nihilo upon completion of the forbidden act." In Milgrom's system, this "miasma" is drawn to the sanctuary through a sort of electromagnetic attraction; what is least holy impulsively propels itself against what is most holy. We have reviewed the evidence that impurity and sin are analogous, creating similarly cursed substances, but not identical. Schwartz advances this discovery by showing that these two basic types of "death" respond to the healing lifeblood differently. Schwartz explains that there is a

> . . . dual process of eliminating, by means of the purification sacrifice, the two distinct types of contaminating substances, sins and impurities, which have been accumulating in the sanctuary. Just as the blood of the [*ḥaṭṭāʾt*] purges impurity, it *removes* sins—not from, but *of*, the community; not of, but *from* the sanctuary, the abode of the divine Presence. . . .[11]

11. Schwartz, "The Bearing of Sin," 16.

Here's the basic distinction: the blood "purges" impurities, it "removes" sins. Schwartz later clarifies that "the blood of the [*ḥaṭṭāʾt*] not only removes [impurities] from the sancta, it *eradicates* them. With sins it is otherwise. They need to be driven away even after they have been removed from the sancta; purification alone does not eliminate them."[12] One further statement helps to accentuate the difference: "Only the deliberate sins stubbornly maintain their independent nature, and only they need to be driven away."[13]

From these passages, we can conclude that, when it comes to the unavoidable workings of death in material creation itself (as seen in the rich symbolic system of impurity), life simply overcomes death. When life-blood is applied to the holy of holies and the outer spheres, it eradicates impurity. The spiritual life represented in the self-giving love of Abraham and Isaac, through which YHWH himself is seen, overcomes the decay of creation—one of the curses of Genesis 3—without struggle. With the spirit's breath, dry bones are ready to spring back to life without hesitation. When it comes to intentional sin, however, something has been generated that is more difficult to overcome. A severe wound in the flesh may heal, but ever after a scar remains. Similarly, when it comes to open rebellion against God, when it comes to a man or woman who hears God's word— "I have put before you life and death, blessing and curse"—and freely chooses death, something demonic has spawned, something that can be overcome but not simply eradicated. In such cases, Schwartz explains, the blood (of Isaac) loosens the sin, but a residue remains that must be driven away. At this point, the unique mission of the second goat emerges.

The Goat for Azazel

The first part of this book featured long meditations on the peace and joy of Zion, and then at the end—almost as an afterthought—attention turned to the wilderness which surrounds and attacks Israel. This was not to minimize sin or to downplay the expansiveness of the surrounding desert, but rather it is a reflection of the fact that beauty, goodness, and truth is infinitely *more* than the darkness, so much worthier of contemplation and song. In fact, the wilderness is coherent or describable only to the extent that it inversely mirrors goodness, which alone has true being. Nevertheless, in the Babylon of our lives, it is not infrequent for us to find the words of King David on our lips: "For I know my transgres-

---

12. Schwartz, 17–18. Milgrom says much the same, cf. *Leviticus 1-16*, 1043–44.
13. Schwartz, "The Bearing of Sin," 19.

sions, and my sin is ever before me. . ." (Psalm 51:3, NRSV). With this in mind, it can be said that even though the goat for the Lord, as fundamentally positive and joyful, is theologically primary, the goat for Azazel has special significance for those who journey through this vale of tears.

The last time we saw the second goat, it had received the lot "for Azazel," and thus it is "stationed alive before the Lord," awaiting its sorrowful mission "into the wilderness to Azazel" (v. 10). Before continuing with a meditation on the ritual associated with this goat, a few comments about the meaning of the word "Azazel" might help to set the scene. The debate over the meaning of the Hebrew word ʿăzāʾzēl has continued since rabbinic times. The most popular position in scholarship today (and the one defended by Jacob Milgrom himself) is that in the misty prehistory of ancient Israel—before the doctrine of monotheism solidified, when *Enuma-Elish*-style gods and demons still roamed the world—there was a demonic power associated with the wilderness named Azazel (which may have meant "fierce god"[14]). Milgrom insists that, by the time of priestly theology, the belief in such preternatural beings dissipated in favor of strict monotheism. Nevertheless, the name Azazel became something of a place-marker, referring to the wasteland beyond, "the land of Azazel" . . . just as even the most level-headed materialist might refer to Ireland as the "land of leprechauns" today. In any case, Milgrom is quite insistent on a demythologized name: ". . . Azazel is the name of a demon who has been eviscerated of his erstwhile demonic powers by the Priestly legislator."[15]

14. According to David Wright, "though the etymology of the name is not certain, it is best explained as a metathesized form of ʿzz-ʾl meaning something like 'fierce god' or 'angry god.'" *The Disposal of Impurity*, 22; cf. Milgrom, *Leviticus 1-16*, 1021; Hayim Tawil, "Azazel, the Prince of the Steepe: A Comparative Study," *Zeitschrift für die alttestamentliche Wissenschaft* 92, no. 1 (January 1, 1980): 43–59.

15. Milgrom, *Leviticus 1-16*, 1021. Milgrom follows Kaufmann here. Many have since agreed with Milgrom's position that Azazel is the name of a demon who has been utterly declawed. See especially Wright, *The Disposal of Impurity*, 21–25; Douglas, *Leviticus as Literature*, 9–11; Jan Heller, "Der Name Asasel," *Communia Viatorum* 40 (1998): 126–30; cf. Tawil, "Azazel, the Prince of the Steepe." Others have agreed that Azazel was a demon, but they reject the idea that he has been "eviscerated" of demonic powers in Leviticus. For example, Baruch Levine disagrees with Kaufmann's claim that "'Azazel was a virtual non-entity, a passive recipient of the sins of the Israelites," and he says to the contrary that the demon Azazel would have resisted the coming of the sin-bearing goat, and thus the high priest must have exercised "potent powers in compelling ʿAzazel to admit the goat into its domain." *In the Presence of the Lord*, 81–82. Milgrom finds no evidence that Azazel has "any active role" in the Levitical rite; seemingly in response to Levine, he points out that Azazel "neither receives the goat nor attacks it." Milgrom, *Leviticus 1-16*, 1021; cf. Milgrom, 1042-43, for a direct response to Levine's theory. If it is true that Azazel is demythologized in Leviticus, mythology certainly came roaring back in second temple

Whether or not priests, or the larger Israelite community, actively believed in the existence of desert demons, the fact that the destination of the second goat was still associated with the primordial monsters is adequate to suggest the dreadfulness of his mission. Christophe Nihan also highlights the profound symbolic significance of naming Azazel as the demon of the wilderness. Nihan says that naming this demon:

> *actually serves to highlight the general division upon which the entire system of P in Lev 1–16 is construed.* While Yahweh is located inside the sanctuary and is associated with order, culture, and a coherent society, Azazel is associated with the wilderness, a symbol of chaos, anomy, and *anti-culture*. The opposition between Yahweh and Azazel in Lev 16 personifies the antinomy between two extreme poles: the sanctuary on one hand . . . and the wilderness on the other. In the course of the ceremony, all forms of transgressions against the social and moral order devised by the creator God are sent back to Azazel, and therefore transferred outside the boundaries of the community, which is thus also represented as standing on the side of order as opposed to disorder.[16]

Therefore, by introducing the "Azazel" figure, the priestly theologian is orienting the reader using coordinates drawn from the most basic symbolism of the cult. This only reinforces our earlier argument that the high priest is responsible for recapitulating the order and peace of the sanctuary through the blood rites. Now, with the Azazel-goat, the Yom Kippur liturgy acknowledges the tragic reality of the "empty, howling waste."

Back to the text. After the high priest has used the life-blood of the Yhwh-goat to both purge the sanctuary of impurities and release the sins for removal, ritual attention turns fully to the fate of the lonely goat waiting at the tent's entrance. According to Leviticus:

> When [Aaron] has finished purging the adytum, the Tent of Meeting, and the altar, he shall bring forward the live goat. Aaron shall lean both of his hands upon the head of the live goat and confess over it all of the iniquities and transgressions of the Israelites, including all of their sins, and put them on the head of the goat; and it shall be sent off to the wilderness by a man in waiting. Thus the goat shall carry upon it all of their iniquities to an inaccessible region.[17]

---

literature. For Asaʾel/Azazel in *1 Enoch* and the *Apocalypse of Abraham*, see the discussion in the next chapter.

16. Nihan, *From Priestly Torah to Pentateuch*, 374. Emphasis in original.

17. Leviticus 16:20–22, as translated by Milgrom, *Leviticus 1-16*, 1010.

There are multiple actions described in this passage, but they can be subsumed into two major categories: (1) transfer and (2) removal. Under the first category, the high priest leans both hands on the goat, confesses sins, and transfers them. Under the second category, the goat is sent from the tabernacle to the "inaccessible region."

In an earlier footnote, I discussed the issue of hand leaning. It could be said that the nexus of leaning hands and transferring sins, explicitly described in verse 21, has spawned the innumerable (I'd argue, inaccurate) interpretations of the sacrificial rites as wrathful punishments.[18] If you assume that every hand-leaning ritual implies the same thing—transfer of sins—then it may seem that the sacrificial animal's subsequent death is a substitutionary punishment for the imputed sin it now bears. Well aware of this interpretive tradition, Milgrom puts great emphasis on the fact that the high priest is instructed to lean *both hands* on the head of the goat, which is different from the ritual for offerings, which calls for the pressure of one hand.[19] The hand ritual for offerings is about establishing ownership—nothing is said about sins or their transfer in the sacrificial texts—but the two-hand ritual unambiguously describes the transfer of sins. Milgrom insists that it is not accurate to use this verse to interpret the meaning of cultic offerings because (a) the ritual is different in each case (one vs. two hands), and (b) the Azazel-goat ritual is not an example of a sacrificial offering (as we'll see below).

In chapter five, we considered the ʿăvōn and pěšāʿim, the iniquities and transgressions, which Aaron confesses over the goat, and there we defined these terms as deliberate wrongdoing and rebellion. These are the great human horrors: the idolatries and murders, all cruelty and violence, pride, lust and arrogance, hatred and despair.[20] Here we have the full parade of human evil, our selfish acts big and small. It all weighs upon the high priest as he emerges from the tent. In this context, it is fascinating to consider the priest's pivotal role on Yom Kippur in representing Israel: whereas moments before he was light as an angel, a conduit of the selfless life of Abraham and Isaac, the same man now quite truly bears the dead weight of the world.[21] With both hands, Aaron presses his weight on the Azazel-goat's head, and he begins to openly confess the evils of the nation.

18. See footnote 8 above.

19. Cf. Milgrom, *Leviticus 1-16*, 1041–42.

20. It is worth noting once more, as Schwartz has emphasized, that impurities do not appear in this list because ritual impurities dissipate immediately upon contact with the purifying blood. Cf. Schwartz, "The Bearing of Sin," 17–18.

21. Cf. Exodus 28:38, Schwartz, 16–18; Vis, "The Purification Offering," 115–18.

Verbal confession is an important Yom Kippur theme. According to *Mishnah Yoma*, the high priest prayed the following words:

> O Lord, your people, the house of Israel, has committed iniquity, transgressed, and sinned before you. Forgive, O Lord, I pray, the iniquities, transgressions, and sins, which your people, the house of Israel, have committed, transgressed, and sinned before you, as it is written in the Torah of Moses, your servant, *For on this day shall atonement be made for you to clean you. From all your sins shall you be clean before the Lord* (Lv 16:30).[22]

This supplication alternates between affirmations of the honor and the humiliation of Israel before God: this house is both the chosen people of the covenant and a house of insubordination, even outright mutiny. Yet as the priest presses all these disgraces upon the head of the Azazel-goat, and as a humbled nation joins their prayers to his, the words of scripture ring out like joyful bells: "shall you be clean." Then, as he finishes the recitation, the rabbis indicate that a final gift is given to a nation made pure: the divine name is pronounced aloud. "And the priests and the people standing in the courtyard, when they would hear the Expressed Name [of the LORD] come out of the mouth of the high priest, would kneel and bow down and fall on their faces and say, 'Blessed be the name of the glory of his kingdom forever and ever.'"[23] This line, "Blessed be the name. . . ," is the second line of the *Shema*, and it was typically recited silently in daily prayer, but on Yom Kippur, and only on Yom Kippur, it was recited aloud. According to Reuven Hammer, "Legends grew up to explain this anomaly." For example, according to one charming midrash:

> Thus Moses said to Israel, 'All the mitzvoth I have given to you I received from the Torah, but this verse is something which I overheard the angels say when they praise the Holy One. I took it from them, therefore say it in a whisper.' Why then is it said aloud on Yom Kippur? Because then they are like angels, wearing white, not eating or drinking; nor do they have any sins or transgression for the Holy One has forgiven all their transgressions.[24]

This explanation accentuates how, for Jews across the centuries, Yom Kippur is indeed a heavenly reality. The response of the people, to fall

---

22. *mYoma* 6:2, A–B.
23. *mYoma* 6:2, C.
24. Hammer, *Entering the High Holy Days*, 122–23.

down upon hearing the Name, also seems to mirror the theophany described in Leviticus 9 when God first tabernacled among his people; with hearts made pure, God's presence is again affirmed as all knees bend at the sound of the Name.[25]

As Milgrom points out, the verbal confession and the transfer of sins go together.[26] By putting these burdens into contrite words, they are released from Aaron and placed on the head of the goat. At this point, the second movement begins: the goat is driven from the tabernacle. The goat's destination is described in two terms: *midbār* and *'ereṣ gezêrāh* (cf. Lv 16:22). The first word was discussed in chapter four: this is the word usually described as wilderness and desert, the place that represents the polar opposite of holiness, the polar opposite of "life-sustaining order." The second Hebrew term used to describe this region is even more despairing. While Milgrom translates *'ereṣ gezêrāh* as "an inaccessible region," he explains in his commentary that these words literally mean "a land cut off." This is a place wholly distinct from the new Eden of Mount Zion. Perhaps it is no surprise that over time the destination of the Azazel-goat was further glossed as a descent into the pit (another common biblical image of a hopeless place).[27]

Why was it so important for the ancient Jewish imagination that the Azazel-goat carry the sins into the wilderness? According to Milgrom, it's because the blood of purification is unable to fully eradicate the substantive "thing" created by wanton sin. Therefore, the only solution was to drive such sins out of the Promised Land. This strategy was in keeping with ancient Near Eastern precedent. Through elimination rites in these societies, "evil was banished to its place of origin (e.g. netherworld, wil-

---

25. The centrality of the pronunciation of the Name grew in heavenly ascent mysticism after the destruction of the temple. Hekhalot mysticism was heavily influenced by Yom Kippur themes. See Stökl Ben Ezra, *Impact of Yom Kippur*, 135–37. For the often neglected importance of the aural in Jewish apocalyptic, see Andrei Orlov, "A Farewell to the Merkavah Tradition" (The Eighth Enoch Seminar: Apocalypticism and Mysticism, Milan, Villa Cagnola, Italy, June, 22, 2015).

26. Milgrom, *Leviticus 1-16*, 1043. In chapter five, we drew the comparison between "wanton sins" and inadvertent sins in Jewish theology to mortal and venial sins in Catholic theology. See footnote 88 above. As Aquinas notes, venial comes from the word "forgivable," and thus mortal sins become forgivable (venial) when confessed. Milgrom's words are striking in comparison: "The crucial significance of the confession is accurately pinpointed by the rabbinic comment: 'By confessing the iniquities and transgressions, they turn them into inadvertencies' (*Sipra, Aḥare* par. 2:6), thus qualifying them for sacrificial expiation." Milgrom, 1043.

27. Thus, the post-biblical Yom Kippur traditions said that the Azazel-goat was pushed backward into a ravine. *mYoma* 6:6.

derness) or to some place in which its malefic powers could work to benefit its sender (e.g. to enemy territory) or in which it could do no harm at
all (mountains, wilderness)."[28] The goal of the elimination rite on Yom
Kippur seems most related to point one ("return to sender") and/or point
three ("do no harm"). Elaborating on point one, Milgrom explains that
in the ANE the wilderness was a symbol of the netherworld, that is, the
demonic realm. Despite his general emphasis on Jewish monotheism, Milgrom is willing to say that "in Israel, the goat for Azazel bearing the sins
of Israel, though it is bound for the wilderness, is in reality returning evil
to its source, the netherworld."[29]

With that said, Milgrom emphatically states that the goat is not a
gift to Azazel and that the rite has nothing to do with appeasing Azazel
(who, Milgrom continues to insist, has been "devitalized"). For this
reason, we must emphasize that the Azazel goat *is not a sacrifice*. In Milgrom's words, "the goat sent [to Azazel] is not an offering . . . an animal
laden with impurities would not be acceptable as an offering either to
God or to a demon."[30] In the end, this animal's role is fairly mundane:
"Instead of being an offering or a substitute, the goat is simply the vehicle
to dispatch Israel's impurities and sins to the wilderness/netherworld."[31]
If the blood of the YHWH-goat purification offering is symbolic of Israel
most fully "in act"—the Yes! of *hinneni*-life—then, at the other end of
the spectrum, the Azazel-goat is most passive: a mere vehicle led by
another (by "a man in waiting," v. 21). Cut off from all community, from
all civilization, from the source of light, the mountain of peace, this most
singular goat was abandoned to the primal chaos, the world of sin, the
final darkness. It is a place that shrinks into a single word, the one seemingly impossible word in our good creation: Godforsaken.

The Sanctuary and the Israelites: Full, Active Participation

The focus of our investigation in this chapter has mirrored the focus
in the sixteenth chapter of Leviticus itself: the key figure is the high priest,
who performs the sacred liturgy. One might well ask, this many pages in,

28. Milgrom, *Leviticus 1-16*, 1072.
29. Milgrom, 1072.
30. Milgrom, 1021. Again, remember, offerings needed to be "spotless"—the idea of
gaining favor by sending what is most detestable would be incomprehensible. This point
once again undermines any attempt to suggest that, in the course of the usual temple offerings, sin is transferred to the victim through (singular) hand leaning. Such an idea would
completely undermine cultic symbolism.
31. Milgrom, 1021. Wright says the same: *The Disposal of Impurity*, 24.

whether this is a private affair between the priest and God? Does the priest here clean up after the sinful chosen people like a parent cleans up after a messy toddler? In other words, where are "the people" in all of this? Are they engaged in the work of purification? And do these liturgies affect their standing with God, or is the liturgy merely focused on cleansing the pollution in the temple, irrespective of the souls of the sinners themselves?

These are crucial questions, and especially after the Second Vatican directive insisting that "full and active participation by all the people"[32] is a high liturgical priority, these questions will be some of the first that modern readers will bring to the Levitical text. To address the place of Israelite laypeople—that is, those in the "kingdom of priests" (Ex 19:6) who are not themselves ordained—we should approach the topic by turning again to the problem of *who*, or *what* (!), is really being purified on Yom Kippur. Milgrom himself answers this question in a way that many subsequent commentators have found unsatisfying. For him, the "miasma" of impurity and sin takes on a life that is independent of the person from whom it is generated. For this reason, addressing the problem of sin in the individual Israelite and addressing the problem of sin as a pollution in the temple constitute two independent processes. The healing of the individual's (inadvertent) sin is accomplished through feeling guilt, and through repentance and prayer[33]—a process that does not necessarily include direct reference to the sanctuary. Therefore, a separate process is required to deal with the pollution generated by impurity or sin, and this separate process is the *ḥaṭṭāʾt* offering throughout the year, culminating in the Yom Kippur liturgy which deals with any impurity that was not otherwise purged. Milgrom's proposal implies that the purification offerings described in Leviticus 4–5 and Leviticus 16 do not in fact address the cleansing of the wrongdoer herself, but these sacrifices relate *only* to the cleansing of the sanctuary from the effects of her "substantive" sin.

While I agree with the other scholars who have attempted to nuance or reverse Milgrom's approach here, the advantages of Milgrom's proposal should not be overlooked. First, this theory helps to highlight a distinct aspect of priestly morality, which Milgrom labels "the priestly

<hr>

32. *Sacrosanctum Concilium*, paragraph 14.

33. Or, in the case of the most severe intentional sins where the forgiveness of the sinner is not possible, according to the earliest strata of priestly thought (as modern scholars have reconstructed it), the only requirement is the administration of the appropriate punishment—for example—in severe cases—capital punishment or *kārēt*.

doctrine of collective responsibility. Sinners may go about apparently unmarred by their evil, but the sanctuary bears the wounds, and with its destruction, all the sinners will meet their doom."[34] For Milgrom, therefore, each severe impurity, and each sin—intentional or unintentional—endangers not *just* the individual, but the entire nation; there are no truly private sins because the entire covenant people were dependent on God's presence in the temple. When the sanctuary is polluted, everyone is endangered, and thus everyone is responsible for upholding the covenant for the sake of everyone else. Milgrom argues that this conviction anticipates the prophetic approach.[35]

Second, Milgrom's interpretation of the purification offering draws our attention again to the most surprising feature of the rite, and effectively explains it: the purifying blood is not applied to the repentant sinner but to the sanctuary. Recall the surprising explanation of the blood manipulations on Yom Kippur: "Thus he shall purge the Shrine of the uncleanness and transgression of the Israelites, whatever their sins. . ." (v. 16). This text unambiguously states that the blood manipulations purge (*kipper*) the sanctuary itself, implying that the object that receives the blood is the object that receives the purification. Insofar as the blood is always applied to cultic furniture, never to the Israelites, this strongly implies that the goal of this action has more to do with the status of the sacred space and less to do with the status of the offerer.[36]

But while accepting Milgrom's description of priestly theology in its broad outline, numerous commentators in recent years have attempted to soften his rigid claim that *only* the sanctuary is cleansed by purification offerings. Is it indeed true that the *ḥaṭṭā't* played no role in the worshippers' own status before God? If so, why is the offerer declared "forgiven" (*sālaḥ*) upon completion of the offering?[37] Milgrom's explanation seems strained: he must conclude that the person is here being "forgiven"

34. Milgrom, *Leviticus: A Book of Ritual and Ethics*, 32; cf. Milgrom, *Leviticus 1-16*, 260–61.

35. See page 166, above. Cf. Milgrom, *Leviticus 1-16*, 231.

36. In fact, there are places where blood manipulation rites were performed on people—one thinks of Moses sealing the covenant at Exodus 24:8, or the ordination of the priests at Leviticus 8:22–24—and yet when it came to the *ḥaṭṭā't* for impurity or for sin, the blood was never applied to the offerer. Therefore, throughout his career Milgrom argued that it is the sanctuary itself, and not the offerer, that is purified by blood manipulation rites in the sanctuary. See, for example, Milgrom, "Kipper," 1039–40; Milgrom, "The Priestly 'Picture of Dorian Gray,'" 76; Milgrom, *Leviticus 1-16*, 254–58.

37. This refrain, with slight differences, is repeated six times in chapters 4–5: "Thus shall the priest effect purgation on [the sinner's] behalf, that he may be forgiven."

for fouling the sanctuary, but that the sin itself had been pardoned before—separately—when the person felt guilt and repented.[38]

Sensing that Milgrom's theory is incomplete and/or out of step with more straightforward, traditional readings of the texts in question, various alternatives have been articulated, but I'd like to turn immediately to my own proposal, which builds on a fascinating observation that was made by Baruch Schwartz. He says: "It would appear that the priestly writings have developed two distinct conceptions of the outcome of transgression: the idea that the sinner bears (carries about) his sin and the belief that sins accumulate in the sacred realm and need to be borne (carried away) therefrom. . . . How can an object, even a metaphysical one such as an objectified sin, be in two places at once?"[39] This is a pressing question, and it is never clearly answered by Schwartz. Answering this question, though, is the key ingredient in considering how temple purification and personal purification may go hand-in-hand in priestly thought.

---

38. See Milgrom, *Leviticus 1-16*, 256, but then, compare his explanation at 245, which is more ambiguous on the "forgiveness" here being offered. Sklar effectively highlights the weakness of Milgrom's argument on this point: *Sin, Impurity, Sacrifice, Atonement*, 87 n.23. An early example of this critique is N. Kiuchi, *The Purification Offering in the Priestly Literature*. See especially: Joshua M. Vis, "The Purgation of Persons through the Purification Offering," in *Sacrifice, Cult, and Atonement in Early Judaism and Christianity*, ed. Henrietta Wiley and Christian Eberhart (Atlanta: Society of Biblical Literature Press, 2017), 33–57, among others.

If Milgrom's "sancta only" interpretation of Yom Kippur has been critiqued because it mutes the effect of this liturgy on worshipers in one way, James A. Greenberg's approach mutes it in another, even more problematic way. Insofar as Greenberg rejects the idea that sin creates some kind of pollution that needs to be borne away (see chapter five, footnote 61, above), he must come up with a new interpretation of Yom Kippur generally, and the Azazel-goat ritual specifically, because this goat's vocation in Leviticus 16 seems to undermine key elements of Greenberg's theory. Therefore, Greenberg must hypothesize that the "live goat" does not bear sins, but rather is a symbol for bearing away rebellious *people*. He says:

> . . . the live goat can be said to bear the guilt of the rebellious people (16:22) by symbolically carrying the rebellious people and their guilt into the wilderness. . . . The Lev 16 *ḥaṭṭāʾt* and live goat offerings do not produce forgiveness for the people but rather symbolically remove rebellious people, whom Yhwh does not forgive, for the benefit of his presence in the sanctuary, and the remaining non-rebellious people. Greenberg, *New Look*, 176.

This ritual is not about forgiveness, and it doesn't even achieve atonement, as that word is typically understood. It is not that sins are removed to restore relationship, but rather, people are symbolically removed to generate a pure society, and thus to draw the deity back to the sanctuary. It is, in a sense, the very picture of Girardian scapegoating. From my perspective, this reading of Leviticus 16 requires interpretive moves that are not at all obvious only to produce a less theologically profound interpretation of Yom Kippur.

39. Schwartz, "The Bearing of Sin," 19.

I've said it before: it is a bizarre fact that two different literatures have developed over the last century—one focusing on the theology of the temple itself, the other unpacking the meaning of cultic offerings—and that these two fields of research are frequently isolated from one another.[40] Mary Douglas' research helps to break down these barriers by pointing out the aesthetic and analogical nature of priestly theology. Douglas offers us a key that helps unlock this mode of thought, a mode which is, obviously, foreign to the modern Western mind: the idea of microcosm.[41] There is not just one microcosm in ancient Jewish thought, but rich networks of interlocking microcosms. Mount Sinai, the tabernacle, Jerusalem, the high priest, and the human being, each with its own constellation of symbols, each related to one another.

I believe that Douglas's "key" helps us unlock a plausible solution to Milgrom's problem—his dubious claim that the ḥaṭṭā't blood purges only the sanctuary and not the offerer—and it also helps us answer Schwartz's question about how sin could be "in two places at once." Douglas's work prompts us to think more creatively about how everyday Israelites may relate to the temple in priestly thought. If the temple is the microcosm of the world, then what happens in the world must in some sense be copied in the holy places. If our crooked actions create, in Schwartz's words, a "metaphysical" something that weighs down the sinner's spirit, then that unwanted something that burdens the human spirit must concurrently burden the sanctuary.[42] For this reason, there is no need to say that "sin" is in two places at once, since macrocosm and microcosm are always mutually present in each other. For the same reason, purgative actions performed in the temple will affect the wider cosmos. Joshua Vis does an outstanding job emphasizing this very point: ". . . the Israelite and the sanctuary, especially the altars of the sanctuary, are in a reciprocal relationship. The sin of the Israelite can stain the sanctuary and the sanctuary, through sacrifice offered within it and on parts of it, can purge the Israelite of his/her sin."[43] With this concept of a reciprocal relationship in

40. Klawans provides the best counterexample to this trend, and indeed his work is forging the way forward. Also notable in this respect: Margaret Barker, "Atonement: The Rite of Healing," *Scottish Journal of Theology* 49, no. 1 (1996): 1–20.

41. See page 172 above.

42. Just to reiterate, the question of how to justify the idea of sin as "metaphysical" remains an open problem; I will try to address this question in chapter ten, below.

43. Vis, "The Purification Offering," 203; Cf. Vis, "The Purgation of Persons." Even earlier, N. Kiuchi poignantly hypothesized that there is a "relationship between the offerer and the sancta" based on the idea that "the sancta invariably represent the people." Kiuchi, *The Purification Offering in the Priestly Literature*, 162. I argue that the microcosm/macrocosm approach would go a long way toward explaining this relationship.

mind, many of the dichotomies common in the debate over who is affected by the purification offerings (both throughout the year and especially on Yom Kippur) break down. It is not the case that *only* the sanctuary is purified, or *only* the offerer is purified. The ritual in the temple is capable of purging the sacred space and releasing a burden from the sinner's soul in one liturgical act.

This is true for the more private *ḥaṭṭā't* offerings throughout the year, but it is true in a special way on Yom Kippur. What sets the Day of Atonement apart is that it is the atoning work of an entire nation coming before God as a unified covenant people mourning their failure to live as a holy nation, a kingdom of priests. Here we turn again to the question of the personal participation of the nation in these holy rites. At the end of Leviticus 16, there is a short section that most scholars consider a latter addition to the chapter, which is typically ascribed to the author of the "Holiness Code"; whatever its provenance, these words accentuate how each and every Israelite was called to be fully and actively involved in the liturgy that day. The ascetic obligations, the call to turn from the grasping self (Adam, Eve, Nadab, Abihu) and to live openheartedly, is not just the high priest's goal, but everybody's. The purgation of the sanctuary and the purgation of each spirit was a simultaneous action; there was a coincidence between the objective liturgy in the temple and the subjective sanctification of the individual because the temple and the people live together. And so we read:

> In the seventh month, on the tenth day of the month, you shall deny your spirits and shall do no manner of work, neither the native-born nor the alien who resides among you. For on this day [the high priest] shall purge you to purify you of all of your sins; you shall be declared pure before Yhwh. It shall be a sabbath of complete rest for you, and you shall deny your spirits; it is a law for all time.[44]

In the context of sin, which is conceived as a grasping self-centeredness, any recommitment to the way of Life involves a denial of "self" in the mode of Abraham and Isaac. Therefore, it makes perfect sense that on Yom Kippur the entire nation passes through the purging fire of self-denial through fasting and resting as they gather at Mount Moriah to reject sin

---

44. Leviticus 16:29–31 as translated by Vis, "The Purification Offering," 97. Vis's translation accentuates the use of *N-P-Š* in vv. 29 and 31 by translating it "spirit," which is the word that also appears in the centrally important Leviticus 17:11, which, as we've seen, stipulates that blood as spirit/life purges the offerer's spirit/life.

and take up again the covenant mode of being.[45] In this way, the temple liturgy is a microcosm of the universal healing work of the nation as each person enters the holy of holies of their own heart in worship and repentance to make their hearts pure and re-consecrate them to God.

In the introduction to this second part of this book, we began with the words of David Fagerberg; his insight into liturgy is here again illuminating: "In my language game, the structure of the liturgical *lex orandi* I call liturgical theology, and the process of shaping lives I call liturgical asceticism. The liturgy doesn't just make the thinker think doxologically, or theologize prayerfully; it forms a believer whose life is theological."[46] There is not only a liturgical theology unfolding in the ritual movements of Yom Kippur, but this theology also shapes and transforms the lives of the worshipping nation. Fagerberg calls this "liturgical asceticism," and these words perfectly capture the sense of healing transformation enjoyed by Israel on this sacred day. The healing comes through taking up again the "yes," the "readiness" before God that should have characterized the nation from the start, and the truth is that for the closed heart, such openness is felt as affliction and a kind of death. Nevertheless, the "death to self" through which Israel must pass is the only way to "choose life."

Days of Awe

"Now did they not have another sign? There was a crimson thread tied to the door of the sanctuary. When the goat had reached the wilderness, the thread would turn white, as it says, *Though your sins be as scarlet, they shall be as white as snow.*"[47]

Goats, as a species, are not known for their theological subtlety. Our two goats were unlikely to appreciate the profound liturgical meaning in their twin missions. The people of Israel, however, could read the signs. They clearly saw their scarlet lives transformed so that they might shine

45. Later rabbinic tradition elaborated on the ascetic practices performed on Yom Kippur. According to the *mYoma*: "On the Day of Atonement it is forbidden to (1) eat, (2) drink, (3) bathe, (4) put on any sort of oil, (5) put on a sandal, (6) or engage in sexual relations." *mYoma 8:1*. The mournful, ascetic nature of this day is not in doubt. However, even later traditions explained these practices in a way that highlights the heavenly nature of the day. The Jews were not to eat, drink, or engage in sexual relations because, on that day, the Jewish people "are on a different plane of existence, closer to angelic beings than to humans. . ." and thus, like angels, they have no need for such worldly goods. Hammer, *Entering the High Holy Days*, 123.

46. Fagerberg, *Theologia Prima*, 4; cf. Fagerberg, *On Liturgical Asceticism*.

47. *mYoma 6:8, E-F.*

again with the purest light, that the whole world might know the grace and forgiveness of God. This joy is the capstone of the Days of Awe, the great liturgical season that began with the shofar's sounding on Rosh Hashanah—at the world's creation and God's enthronement—finds a restful peace at the close of Yom Kippur—a day of atonement, which is to say, a day of eschatological fulfillment as the chosen people enter the holy of holies and definitively cast out and overcome the curse of sin and death. On these ten most holy days, Israel liturgically recapitulates the entire history of the cosmos.

The daily liturgy on Mount Zion continued again after the thread changed color, but now with increasing freedom and joy. The word of forgiveness had been spoken, purification achieved, and now attention turns fully toward unbridled worship. It begins—as is so often the case—with a change of clothing, signifying a new beginning. Aaron removes the simple linen robe, submerges himself in water, and takes up once more his glorious vestments. Then Aaron begins again where he left off many days earlier, before the deadly encroachment of his sons Nadab and Abihu. On that day, "when the daily sacrifices began . . . *the goal of all creation would be consummated.*"[48] Unfortunately, as soon as creation was consummated, it was desecrated. But God gives Yom Kippur to Israel as the means by which they might begin again, and so now that creation has been made new, the daily burnt offerings pick up once more: Aaron "shall go out and sacrifice his burnt offering and the burnt offering of the people. . ." (v. 24). As Aaron draws near to the indwelling Lord with these two rams—which call to mind the ram caught in the thicket by its horns, and which call to mind the great shofar blast ten days earlier—as Aaron draws near on behalf of the house of Israel, all creation is again full with peace.

48. Repeating the citation from Anderson quoted earlier, *Genesis of Perfection*, 202.

CHAPTER 8

Yom Kippur and the Mystery of the Christ: Retrieving a Neglected, Ancient Christian Theology

"Destroy this temple. . ." (John 2:19)

"Then Jesus cried again with a loud voice and breathed his last. At that moment the curtain of the temple was torn in two, from top to bottom. The earth shook, and the rocks were split. . ." (Matthew 27:50–51)

For Christians, the mystery of the temple and the mystery of Jesus Christ are interconnected. A sizable movement in historical Jesus studies seeks to interpret the life and ministry of Jesus within a second temple Jewish framework: as a first-century Jew, the temple was certainly an unavoidable fixture in Jesus' religious landscape.[1] As a theological claim, however, I intend to say something more than historians do when I say Jesus and the temple are interconnected. Throughout these pages, I have sought to appreciate the theology of priestly writers, whose theological landscape is centered in and oriented around the sanctuary of Yhwh. Through this great sacrament of God's presence in the midst of the chosen people, the priestly theologians contemplated the mysteries of God and creation, with an emphasis on Zion's cascading beauty, goodness, and truth. The first Christians also had a theological landscape, but it was centered on and oriented around the person of Jesus Christ. There are at least two ways of interpreting this fact: you could say that, for the emerging Christian tradition, Jesus replaces the temple as the center of theological focus (the supersessionist option), or you could say that the mystery of the temple and the mystery of Jesus Christ

---

1. For a recent review of the evidence that Jesus' attitude toward the Temple was one of reverence and devotion, see James H. Charlesworth, "Jesus and the Temple" in *Jesus and the Temple* edited by James H. Charlesworth (Minneapolis: Fortress Press, 2014), 145–182.

occupy the same "space": without being simply identical,[2] they are analogically one.

For modern Christian theologians building upon the emerging emphasis on the Jewish roots of Christian theology, the analogical approach certainly has the most promise. It is also deeply rooted in the Christian theological tradition;[3] interest in interpreting the phenomenon of Jesus the Messiah in positive relation to the temple was powerfully supported by early Christian hermeneutical methods, as N. T. Wright has shown. Wright points out that 2 Samuel 7 is a key text for a mature temple theology, and when early Christian readers of scripture turned to this chapter, they were fascinated by the way the author cleverly associates the idea of David building a "house" for God, and God building a (messianic) "house" for David. After posing the incredulous question to David through Nathan—"Are you the one to build a house for Me to dwell in?" (2 Sm 7:5)—God sharply reminds the new king that he never requested such a ponderous structure. Then God reinforces who shall be the true builder of Israel:

> The Lord declares to you that He, the Lord, will establish a house for you. When your days are done and you lie with your fathers, I will raise up your offspring after you, one of your own issue, and I will establish his kingship. He shall build a house for My name, and I will establish his royal throne forever. (2 Sm 7:11–13)

This passage becomes especially attractive to early Christian interpreters in its Greek translation because the writers of the Septuagint use the word "*anasteso*" for "raise up," and *anasteso* is the future tense verbal form of the noun "*anastasis*," the Greek word for resurrection. Therefore, the early Christian reader sees a promise that God will raise up *or resurrect* the seed who will establish a kingdom, a house, a royal throne. Looking at these overlapping ideas in 2 Samuel, Wright says,

> Read this story now with early Christian eyes, and what do we find? That the Temple, for all its huge importance and centrality within Judaism, was after all a signpost to the reality, and the reality was the resurrected son of David, who was the son of God. God, in other words, is not ultimately to dwell in a human-built Temple, a timber-

---

2. After all, Jesus says, "I tell you, something greater than the temple is here" (Matthew 12:6).

3. See chapter three, footnote 101 for a partial bibliography on the connection between Jesus and the temple in the New Testament and the early church.

and-stone house. God will indeed dwell with his people, allowing his glory and mystery to 'tabernacle' in their midst, but the most appropriate way for him to do this will not be through a building but through a human being. And the human being in question will be the Messiah, marked out by resurrection.[4]

Two houses are interwoven in 2 Samuel: the "house" of cedar built by Israel for YHWH, which becomes the (semi-)permanent tabernacling place of the creator God, and the "house" built by YHWH for Israel, the Davidic line which is an icon of peace and unity for the nation Israel.

From the perspective of early Christian hermeneutics, these two "houses" converge in the child of Bethlehem, the one who became the firstborn of the dead, the resurrected seed of David whose own flesh is the dwelling place of God, whose own heart is the holy of holies, whose whole spirit is alive in perfect sacrificial worship, whose own blood brings life to the body of creation. Again, to associate this son of Judah with the house built by Solomon and the house built by God is a move virtually demanded by the logic of early Christian biblical interpretation. To then associate that same "house" with the full sequence of offerings proper to that place, in all their liturgical specificity (Leviticus 1–7), along with the priesthood that brings the liturgical space to life, is also well supported by the early Church's biblical perspective because (as I've argued) the temple and its offerings were theologically inseparable.

With this in mind, we can return to an image I mentioned in chapter three. "Conspiracy" in its most literal sense means "breathing together," thus suggesting a deep harmony of persons. I briefly mentioned that, within the Christian imagination, the temple and Jesus "conspire," and this is especially clear in Matthew's account of Jesus' death. For Matthew, the expiration of Jesus, of the temple, and of the cosmos happen simultaneously: the final exhale of life on the cross corresponds with the tearing and splitting of the cosmos, micro and macro. This strongly suggests that Jesus does not displace the temple, but rather the center of his existence corresponds to the center of the temple's existence, which corresponds again to the center of the cosmos—heart to heart to heart—and thus all three fall and rise together.[5] Therefore, temple theology is a precious resource for approaching the riches of Christ. Furthermore, insofar as Yom Kippur is the fullest liturgical expression of the ritual life of the

---

4. N. T. Wright, *The Challenge of Jesus: Rediscovering Who Jesus Was and Is* (Downers Grove, IL: IVP Books, 1999), 110.

5. Cf. Fletcher-Louis, "Jesus, the Temple and the Dissolution."

temple in the context of sin, it would seem that any "conspiracy" between Jesus and the temple would also involve reflection on the shape of the highest holy day as it pertains to the savior's atoning action.

To reflect on Yom Kippur when developing a theology of atonement is not unheard of. Many contemporary Christian theologians have offered interpretations of the cross with reference to the cultic rituals of Leviticus generally, and the Day of Atonement specifically. Without making a thorough review of these modern works of soteriology, two points can be made. First, in these works, Yom Kippur is cited only in passing, as a small piece of evidence to support an argument constructed on other grounds, despite the (almost literally) central place of Leviticus 16 in the Torah. Even worse, many of these interpretations effectively "conflate" the theological meaning of the two goats, failing to see how, in the Jewish theological tradition, the movements of the two goats are distinct in crucial ways. This fundamental confusion has had a mischievous effect on Christian interpretations of Christ's cross that I intend to untangle in this work.

When we turn our full attention to the earliest Christian sources, we discover that, just as these early Christians associated messianic theology with temple theology, they associated the saving work of Christ with Yom Kippur. Did the New Testament and Church Fathers also themselves tend to conflate the two goats, as we do today? I hope to show that the answer to this is "no." Once we achieve greater clarity about the early Jewish interpretations of Yom Kippur, it is possible to return to the New Testament and patristic texts and find that, as a rule, the distinction between the joyful, uplifting movement of the YHWH-goat and the mournful, substitutionary movement of the Azazel-goat is consistently maintained, and thus any contemporary Yom Kippur soteriology would indeed be more faithful to the biblical tradition if it continued to carefully observe the distinction.

Yom Kippur:
Reconfigurations in Judaism and Christianity

Yom Kippur in Cosmic Scope: Jewish Apocalyptic

While we will find that the New Testament does indeed contain a fair number of texts that allude—more or less explicitly—to the *ḥaṭṭā't* offering and/or Yom Kippur, there is one additional Jewish text from the second temple period that merits attention; this text suggests how Yom Kippur's influence on early Christianity may be more pervasive than it initially seems. One of the most important non-biblical texts for the development of post-biblical Judaism and Christianity is the collection now known as *1 Enoch*, and especially the first tractate, *The Book of the Watchers*. This book, which emerges from a priestly milieu[6] in the third-century BC, takes the theological landscape of Yom Kippur and enlarges it to eschatological proportions. The early chapters of the book inter-weave accounts of the two leaders of the fallen "watchers" (or angels), one named Shemihazah, and the other named Asa'el or Azazel.

The first thread is an expansive retelling of Genesis 6:1–4, the bizarre story of the "divine beings" who take the "daughters of men" as wives, and who together give birth to the Nephilim—the latter are further iden-tified as "the mighty men . . . the men of renown." Enoch parallels the Sep-tuagint in translating Nephilim as *gígantes* (in English, giants[7]) and *The Book of the Watchers* dramatically elaborates on the story of the watchers and their misbegotten children. Shemihazah is introduced as a leader of the lustful watchers, and the giants are depicted as a tragic addition to the world: "They were devouring the labor of all the sons of men. . . . And the giants began to kill men and to devour them. . ." (1 Enoch 7:3–4).[8]

Paul Hanson has argued that this almost-cinematic re-telling of Genesis 6:1–4 has four movements, which are the hallmarks of the "rebellion-in-

---

6. The relationship between the "Book of the Watchers" and the Jerusalem temple—especially the Zadokite priests serving the temple—has generated many debates. Some see evidence of different factions and thus interpret Enochic texts as hostile to the official cult. In contrast, James VanderKam defends the thesis that "the separation into different types of Judaism, the highlighting of oppositions, is too rigid if it does not allow space for the many examples of cross-fertilization attested in the sources." "Mapping Second Temple Judaism," in *The Early Enoch Literature*, ed. Gabriele Boccaccini and John J. Collins (Leiden: Brill, 2007), 20. As we discussed in chapter three, one often finds biblical scholars and historians of ancient Judaism interpreting difference as division, implying that interest in heavenly realities suggests hostility to earthly institutions. Of course this is possible, but if the earthly temple were understood as an icon of the heavenly mysteries—if they were, in Mary Douglas's way of putting things, in analogical or correlative relationship with one another—then re-describing one reality in "higher" terms is not in itself evidence of polemics. That others could later use the "higher" to critique the mundane representation may nevertheless occur. Cf. Lester L. Grabbe, *A History of the Jews and Judaism in the Second Temple Period, Volume 2: The Coming of the Greeks: The Early Hellenistic Period (335-175 BCE)* (London: A&C Black, 2008), 240–42; Himmelfarb, *Ascent to Heaven*, 22–23, 27–28.

7. For more on the Hebrew Nephilim and the Greek giants, see Loren T. Stucken-bruck, "The Origins of Evil in Jewish Apocalyptic Tradition: The Interpretation of Genesis 6: 1-4 in the Second and Third Centuries BCE," in *The Fall of the Angels*, ed. C. Auffarth and L.T. Stuckenbruck (Leiden: Brill, 2004).

8. Translations of *1 Enoch* in this section are from George W. E. Nickelsburg and James C. VanderKam, *1 Enoch: The Hermeneia Translation* (Minneapolis: Fortress Press, 2012), 19–49.

heaven" genre: rebellion, devastation, punishment, and restoration. As to the second movement, Hanson emphasizes that "rebellion against the order of the Most High unleashes the forces of chaos,"[9] which is also exhibited in the Genesis account: "The earth became corrupt before God; the earth was filled with lawlessness" (6:11). But while the story of Shemihazah and the other fallen watchers grounds the narrative of rebellion and devastation, Hanson believes that, in itself, Genesis 6 lacked the threads needed to develop the final two themes: punishment and restoration. For these, he says, the writers turn to the imagery of Leviticus 16, and thus weave in material about another arch-demon: Azazel.[10] This next section of the text, therefore, begins by working Asa'el/Azazel into the story,[11] suggesting that his activities were also integral to the spread of sin in the world. It says that Asa'el introduced instruments of war and lust into human society and that he had illicitly revealed heavenly secrets. All this created immense suffering among humans and caused them to cry out to God for relief. The holy ones of heaven—including Michael, Gabriel, and Raphael—received this complaint and brought it to God. They point out that Asa'el "has taught all iniquity on the earth" (1 Enoch 9:6).

In response, God gives the following command to Raphael: ". . . bind Asa'el hand and foot, and cast him into the darkness; And make an

9. Paul Hanson, "Rebellion in Heaven, Azazel, and Euhemeristic Heroes in 1 Enoch 6-11," *Journal of Biblical Literature* 96, no. 2 (1977): 199.

10. Hanson gives an interesting explanation of how the connection between Genesis 6:1–4 and Leviticus 16 was made. In a list of the twenty names of demons, given in the Shemihazah material, "Asael" is mentioned in passing. Hanson speculates that perhaps the name Asael triggered the association: "the name invited comparison with the scapegoat in the *textus classicus* of *yom kippur* in Leviticus 16 with the like-sounding name of Azazel. Since the main theme of the Shemihazah story was the origin of evil and its eradication from the earth, the appropriateness must have seemed compelling for creating an expository connection with the community's primary rite dealing with purgation..." Hanson, 221. Others have more or less strongly downplayed the connection to Yom Kippur; cf. George W. E. Nickelsburg, "Apocalyptic and Myth in 1 Enoch 6-11," *Journal of Biblical Literature* 96, no. 3 (September 1, 1977): 399–404; Archie T. Wright, *The Origin of Evil Spirits: The Reception of Genesis 6: 1-4 in Early Jewish Literature* (Tübingen: Mohr Siebeck, 2013), 105–20. For defenses of the connection between 1 Enoch 10 and Yom Kippur, see R. Helm, "Azazel in Early Jewish Tradition," *Andrews University Seminary Studies* 32, no. 3 (1994): 217–22; Stökl Ben Ezra, *Impact of Yom Kippur*, 85–90; Andrei Orlov, *The Atoning Dyad: The Two Goats of Yom Kippur in the Apocalypse of Abraham* (Leiden: Brill, 2016), 49–57. For a thorough, up-to-date overview of the debate, see Hans M. Moscicke, "Jesus, Barabbas, and the Crowd as Figures in Matthew's Day of Atonement Typology (Matthew 27:15-26)," *Journal of Biblical Literature* 139, no. 1 (March 2020): 129, footnote 19.

11. The Aramaic manuscript seems to use Asa'el throughout, while the Ethiopic generally uses Azazel. See Wright, *The Origin of Evil Spirits*, 110.

opening in the wilderness that is in Doudael. Throw him there, and lay beneath him sharp and jagged stones. And cover him with darkness, and let him dwell there for an exceedingly long time" (10:4–6). Another nearby passage reads, "And all the earth was made desolate by the deeds of the teaching of Asa'el, and over him write all the sins" (v. 8). After the whole earth had been corrupted by his teaching, *all* sin has been written over Azazel, and he is cast into the darkness of a desert pit. According to the text, the result of this expulsion is a restoration of life to the earth, and the extent of the earth's purification is suggested later in the same section:

> Cleanse the earth from all impurity and from all wrong and from all lawlessness and from all sin, and godlessness and all impurities that have come upon the earth, remove. And all the sons of men will become righteous, and all the peoples will worship (me), and all will bless me and prostrate themselves. And all the earth will be cleansed from all defilement and from all uncleanness, and I shall not again send upon them any wrath or scourge for all the generations of eternity. (10:20–22)

Therefore, after considering various explanations for the advent of sin in the world—seeing it to be the result of teaching illicit knowledge, an illicit sexual union between heaven and earth, or the product of the misbegotten giants—the text turns to the final expulsion of sins and the restoration of creation.

The second half of the *Book of the Watchers* opens with the words, "Before these things, Enoch was taken. . ." (12:1); thus begins the story of the great scribe Enoch. These words are an allusion to the enchanting genealogical note found a chapter earlier in Genesis: "All the days of Enoch came to 365 years. Enoch walked with God; then he was no more, for God took him" (5:23–24). As I briefly mentioned in chapter three, through the keyhole of this passage, many fantastic journeys were taken by later Jewish mystics. When Enoch was "taken" by God, the priestly mystics explained, he was taken up into the heavenly realm and invited to survey the mysteries of time, space, and eternity. Thus, he became the tour guide *par excellence* for those called to higher contemplation. Enoch's great visions of the inner throne room of God helped establish the precedent for all future accounts of heavenly journeys.[12] In this story, Enoch becomes the mediator between God and the fallen watchers; the

---

12. For how *The Book of the Watchers* represents a transition from earlier prophetic literature to later heavenly journeys, see Himmelfarb, *Ascent to Heaven*, 9–28.

latter have asked Enoch to petition God to forgive their sins. To that end, Enoch makes his unforgettable entrance into the divine throne room:

> And look, another open door before me: and a house greater than the former one, and it was all built of tongues of fire. All of it so excelled in glory and splendor and majesty that I am unable to describe for you its glory and majesty. . . . And I was looking and I saw a lofty throne; and its appearance was like ice, and its wheels were like the shining sun. . . . The Great Glory sat upon it; his apparel was like the appearance of the sun and whiter than much snow. No angel could enter into this house and look at his face because of the splendor and glory, and no human could look at him...Until now I had been on my face, prostrate and trembling. And the Lord called me with his mouth and said to me, "Come here, Enoch, and hear my word(s)." (14:15–24)

From inside this great and glorious abode, God gives Enoch instructions on what to say to the watchers. It is Enoch's responsibility to deliver the negative judgment against them, culminating with a haunting line: "You will have no peace" (16:4).

The exact chronology and geography of *1 Enoch* is not always easy to follow; whether this is because it is a composite text or whether it is due to the idiosyncrasies of the genre is debatable. Regardless, Enoch's visions of the heavenly throne room (the holy of holies) are clearly said to have occurred "before" the account of how the rogue watchers and the destructive giants are cast out into the desert wilderness. Therefore, confusing as it is, the overarching narrative is patterned on Yom Kippur's liturgical stage, now depicted as encompassing the highest heaven—the space of splendor, glory, and Presence—and the nethermost abyss—which is depicted as a "chaotic and terrible place" (21:1). God invites Enoch to "draw near" to him in the heavenly holy of holies, and from that space, Enoch receives the responsibility to pronounce judgment on the fiendish spirits who have filled the good creation with all manner of violence and evil.

Some commentators see this narrative as an alternative etiology for the introduction of evil into the world.[13] Rather than the well-known biblical story in which human beings introduce evil through their disobedience (and are called upon to resist evil through cultic rites), here humans are the victims of evil, which has been introduced by rebellious

---

13. For a clear expression of this view, see Gabriele Boccaccini, *Beyond the Essene Hypothesis: The Parting of the Ways Between Qumran and Enochic Judaism* (Grand Rapids, MI: Eerdmans, 1998), 71–74.

angels, and thus they must wait upon God's intervention. After our review of Milgrom's insights into the nature of sin in priestly thought, which is *both* rooted in human misdeeds *and yet* "demonically" vital, I wonder if it is really necessary to read the Enochic approach as an incompatible alternative to the biblical focus on human culpability for evil. Perhaps the *Book of the Watchers* recounts the typical priestly perspective on holiness and sin, but now in a different genre: mythology. Why would priestly theologians turn to mythopoetics to supplement their typical historical and cultic modes of reflection? Drawing on the work of Ian Davie, Stratford Caldecott offers a helpful theory:

> Having distinguished the vertical (ontological) dimension from the horizontal (historical, empirical), [Davie] explains that the "vertical" is always best expressed in poetry and myth. This leads him to deplore the "demythologization" of religion. In a theological context, he says, the word "mythology" means "the horizontal (i.e., spatio-temporal) representation of a vertical (i.e., eternal) truth. . . . The theological method . . . is neither one nor the other; neither mythological nor historical, but a combination of both. Thus it uses history as a critique of myth, and myth as a critique of history; for the whole theological purport of myth is to indicate the limits of history, to elicit from the mythological language (which it necessarily uses in speaking of events which are transhistorical, in the exact sense that they are limits of history) a sense of what lies beyond history, the 'beyond' of all time."[14]

With this in mind, I am reminded of Przywara's noetic rule: "truth in-and-beyond history." Modern scholars have innumerable tools for articulating "truth-in-history"; from scientific theorems to critical historiography, the "horizontal" dimension is well captured. But when it comes to communicating the "beyond," our toolbox is mostly empty. According to Caldecott, this is where our degradation of myth has impoverished us: throughout history, many have turned to myth to articulate "vertical" realities that so vastly exceed the limitations of our ponderous tongues. The legends of Enoch are outstanding examples in this important genre.

Thus, priestly intuitions about the strange ontology of sin—a force that is alien to God's will and God's good creation and yet substantively active in the cosmos—require a gallery of images that exceed the strictly horizontal. When we take into consideration (a) the drama of the

14. Stratford Caldecott, *The Radiance of Being: Dimensions of Cosmic Christianity* (Tacoma, WA: Angelico Press, 2013), 166–67.

watchers, (b) the increasingly bold colors of heaven and hell, and (c) the strange possibility of "giants" that are partially of human origin and yet are not quite human—when we look at all this fantastic material and tilt our heads to the side, it is possible to see *The Book of the Watchers* as a spectacular mythopoetic retelling of Leviticus 1–16. Consider this statement from the *Watchers* on the fate of the giants after the flood:

> But now the giants who were begotten by the spirits and flesh—they will call them evil spirits on the earth, for their dwelling will be on the earth. The spirits that have gone forth from the body of their flesh are evil spirits, for from humans they came into being, and from the holy watchers was the origin of their creation. . . . And the spirits of the giants [lead astray], do violence, make desolate, and attack and wrestle and hurl upon the earth and [cause illnesses]. . . . These spirits (will) rise up against the sons of men and against the women, for they have come forth from them. (15:8–12)

We have seen Milgrom, Schwartz, and Anderson struggle to find a vocabulary for the "reality" of the sins that both weigh down humans and invade the temple. Here the *Book of the Watchers* steps in with the notion of "evil spirits" that are *not* created by God—they are *not* beings independent of or threatening to the one Creator (in a polytheistic sense)—but rather are products of corrupted flesh which seek the destruction of the world. This passage is clear that the misborn "spirits" are at war against humankind, trying to bring the world to desolation, which is precisely the problem that the liturgy of Yom Kippur is intended to confront: to purge the sanctuary (the micro-cosmos) of just such evils! Indeed, *Watchers* and Leviticus 16 agree that the only solution for such evil is expulsion, and so in both cases evil is condemned to the abyss. With this in mind, the idea that Enoch has an etiology that radically diverges from other Hebrew traditions is questionable; perhaps the same "reality" is simply being articulated in different theological genres.[15]

As we move toward the nativity of Jesus Christ, it is helpful to see how the priestly myth of the watchers accentuates the significance of Yom

---

15. Therefore, I agree with Hanson when he speaks of a "mythologization and eschatologization of the *yom kippur* ritual" in 1 Enoch 6-11, although I disagree when he says that this is strong evidence of a "sectarian point of view" because "the normal means provided by the temple cult for dealing with defilement is implicitly judged ineffectual. . . ." Hanson, "Rebellion in Heaven, Azazel, and Euhemeristic Heroes in 1 Enoch 6-11," 226. Is it not possible that *Watchers* was written to provide a window into the mystical realities behind the temple liturgy, thus investing the liturgy with more honor, not less? Cf. Himmelfarb, *Ascent to Heaven*, 27.

Kippur soteriology. Now it is clear that, within early Jewish theology itself, the high priest's actions in this great liturgy anticipate, and perhaps even participate in, the final judgment, when God will cast down the "giants" of our world, the evil spirits that prowl across the earth and through our lives, and how—yet more importantly—God will raise all creation to new life.[16] It is clear in 1 Enoch that violence and chaos have no future, and that, in the end, all will be peace, glory, praise, and delight.

Yom Kippur and the Messiah: The New Covenant

Much has been said about the various appropriations of Yom Kippur themes in the Second Temple period; Daniel Stökl ben Ezra's work is an especially thorough overview of the material.[17] Building on his work, I will review a few New Testament texts that apply Day of Atonement themes to the saving work of Jesus Christ. The one point that I want to especially emphasize—and this point has not been emphasized in previous scholarship—is the need to *clearly distinguish the complementary work of the two goats* in considering how any given passage is drawing on Yom Kippur themes. In other words, I argue that some texts draw on imagery best associated with the YHWH-goat, while other texts draw on imagery best associated with the Azazel-goat. When theologians fail to distinguish the two "goats"—each of whom represents a unique constellation of symbols and imagery—and when they apply the hallmarks of one "goat" to the other, this lack of precision can result in significant theological distortion.

With respect to some of the most well-known contemporary Christian soteriologies, the problem of "conflation" is nearly ubiquitous, and this fundamental mistake has the effect of warping our understanding of Christ's cross more generally. An excellent example of this tendency is found in *The Cross of Christ*, John Stott's classic defense of penal substitutionary atonement. In the section where he reflects on the Day of Atonement, Stott's overall goal is to argue that the phrase "to bear sin" in the Old Testament should be taken to mean "to endure [sins'] penal

16. Cf. Stökl Ben Ezra, *Impact of Yom Kippur*, 89–90.

17. Stökl Ben Ezra, *Impact of Yom Kippur*. For continuing development of Second Temple themes in the Jewish mystical traditions, Orlov, *Heavenly Priesthood in the Apocalypse of Abraham*; Orlov, *Divine Scapegoats*; Orlov, *The Atoning Dyad*. See also the sections in Stökl that deal with the *Apocalypse of Abraham*, the Dead Sea Scrolls, *Jubilees*, and the further transformation/interiorization of Yom Kippur themes in Philo and Josephus.

consequences, to undergo its penalty"[18]—that is, to suffer the penalty of death. The best example of this, he says, is found in Leviticus 16. As opposed to interpretations that drive a "wedge" between the goats, Stott finds T. J. Crawford's approach more acceptable: "each [goat] embodied a different aspect of the same sacrifice, 'the one exhibiting the means, the other the results, of the atonement.'"[19] Stott, therefore, certainly does not drive a wedge between the goats,[20] but to the contrary, he argues instead that both equally express the doctrine of penal substitution, both ultimately bearing punishment on behalf of sinners. The goats are differentiated only insofar as one illustrates the nature of the penalty (death) and the other communicates the result of that penalty (removal of sin).[21] From this perspective, both goats are participants in a single act of (violent) punishment that God requires as a condition of divine forgiveness.

The conflation of the two goats under an umbrella of violent action is not a problem merely for defenders of penal substitutionary atonement. Many of this theory's strongest critics nevertheless agree that ancient Jewish cultic practices have violent roots. For example, René Girard and his followers, who are anything but advocates of penal substitutionary atonement, nevertheless use the words "sacrifice" and "scapegoat" interchangeably, all to designate a violent act of exclusion that helps to create a twisted peace in a broken community. Thus, when S. Mark Heim turns to Leviticus 16, he says:

> At the center of Israel's ritual life, we find an event bearing all the marks we outlined in the last chapter [that is, the key elements of Girard's sacrificial theory]. The community centers its collective violence on a representative sacrifice, which is charged with all the guilt and sins that pollute and threaten the people, and driven out and

18. John Stott, *The Cross of Christ* (Westmont, IL: IVP Books, 2006), 143.

19. Stott, 144.

20. One can agree with Stott that a radical separation of the goats would indeed be inappropriate from the perspective of temple theology (since the goats are, together, one *ḥaṭṭāʾt*). Radical separation would thus be deleterious to Christian soteriology. I will make this argument in chapter eleven.

21. This interpretation is not unique to Stott and Crawford. For example, in another essay defending penal substitutionary atonement, Charles Hill argues that the two goats are "in reality one sacrificial object; the distribution of suffering death and of dismissal into a remote place simply serving the purpose of clearer expression, in visible form, of the removal of sin after expiation had been made, something which the ordinary sacrificial animal could not well express, since it died in the process of expiation." Geerhardus Vos quoted by Charles E. Hill, "Atonement in the Old and New Testaments," in *The Glory of the Atonement: Biblical, Theological & Practical Perspectives*, ed. Charles E. Hill and Frank A. James III (Westmont, IL: IVP Academic, 2004), 25f. Examples could be multiplied.

off a cliff—the very image of mob violence against a human scapegoat. What is striking is that the process is not that it differs from
that model, but that it is so extraordinarily explicit. . . .[22]

The primary difference between penal substitutionary atonement theo-
rists and Girardians with respect to the interpretation of Yom Kippur is
that the former believe that God validates and requires the penalty of
death, while the latter suggest that sacrificial practices are recorded in
the Hebrew Bible not because God endorses them, but to give a vivid
example of the "scapegoating mechanism" that will ultimately be overcome through prophetic critique and the resurrection of Christ.[23]

Therefore, in some of the most prominent modern interpretations of
atonement, the two goats are seen as a single symbol of violent death.
Mount Zion becomes the mountain of penal substitutionary violence, or
the mountain of scapegoating violence, or even the mountain of patriarchal abuse and oppression. An additional consequence of this conflation
is that, when these same interpreters turn to some of the most famous
(and controversial) New Testament texts relating to atonement, and when
they find Paul or Peter or anyone else using cultic imagery, their imprecise
understanding of Yom Kippur skews the reading of the texts. Words associated with one "goat" are imported into a context that is, in fact, focusing on Christ's fulfillment of the work of the other "goat," and thus—I
argue—the original author's meaning is garbled. Therefore, for an adequate contemporary Christian soteriology that is rightly attentive to ancient
Jewish priestly theology and that is simultaneously rooted in the New
Testament's own interpretation of Christ's saving work, it is essential to
draw clear and consistent distinctions.

With that in mind, we should review the leading images and theological concepts associated with each of the two goats, as discussed in

22. S. Mark Heim, *Saved from Sacrifice: A Theology of the Cross* (Grand Rapids,
MI: Eerdmans, 2006), 77. Girard himself reflects on the scapegoat ritual most extensively
in *I See Satan Fall Like Lightning*, trans. James G. Williams (New York: Orbis Books,
2001), 154 ff.

23. What makes Leviticus 16 unique, according to the Girardians, is how explicit it
is about the violence of sacrifice and "scapegoating." From their perspective, sacrificial
violence must be veiled to succeed long term, but on Yom Kippur, the death and expulsion
are vividly depicted. Raymund Schwager, S. J. explains: "According to Girard this rite has
no significance fundamentally different from other cult activities except that the hidden
function of all rites is shown somewhat more clearly." *Must There Be Scapegoats?: Violence
and Redemption in the Bible* (New York: Harper & Row, 1987), 87; Cf. Raymund
Schwager, *Jesus in the Drama of Salvation: Toward a Biblical Doctrine of Redemption*
(New York: Crossroad Publishing Company, 1999), 91, 104–5.

the previous chapters. To start, it is essential to emphasize and emphasize again that, even though the goats are together necessary for final purification, the YHWH-goat *alone* is an offering to God. The Azazel-goat, on the other hand, is *not* an offering in priestly theology, but a vehicle for removing sin. The first goat is spotless, unblemished, while the second goat is fouled with all the world's filth; Milgrom points out that, according to ancient Near Eastern assumptions, the latter goat would not be acceptable as an offering, certainly not to an all-holy God, and not even to a demon.[24] The imagery of the YHWH-goat is active, it is associated with the positive movement of "drawing near," while the imagery of the second goat is passive, it is "led away" by another. In terms of spiritual geography, the first is turned toward the holy of holies, the heart of the world, and the second toward the outer wilderness, the extreme abyss. While heaven and hell are not prominent in the Hebrew Bible, the contrast between Eden and exile is clear. As I have argued, through the Akedah of Abraham and Isaac, the covenant people have a glimpse at the paradise lost in Adam and Eve, and in the Babylonian exile, they endure what could be identified as Godforsaken damnation. Each of the two goats is associated with either this "heaven" or this "hell," a contrast that is subsequently pushed into eschatological dimensions in the *Book of the Watchers.*

We now know that the temple, and the goat associated with the temple, is the place of "life-sustaining order," the source of light, living water, and true freedom. The key word, over and over again, is *life*, and its leading symbol is the flowing blood that vivifies the whole body. We also know that the wilderness, and the goat associated with the wilderness, is the place of chaos, a vast void of darkness, it is desert, it is crushing burden, helpless bondage. The key word here is *death*, and its leading symbol is dust as every vital bond breaks away and scatters. We have seen how—paradoxically from a modern standpoint—the biblical concept of freedom is associated with obedience and heart-to-heart communion with God, while spiritual oppression is associated with rebellion against God and neighbor, a division (*diabolos*) that ends in despair.

Even though the offering of the YHWH-goat is adapted to the context of sin, it is fundamentally rooted in a surpassing joy and peace, it recapitulates the well-ordered creation, and with it, the glory of God shines through once more. Of course, this sharply diverges from the movement of the Azazel-goat, who knows only lamentation, who shoulders the non-

---

24. Milgrom, *Leviticus 1-16*, 1021.

integratable "remainder" of sin, that which can only be mournfully sent away, that which can no longer give glory, but only horror. It is the difference between, on the one side, righteousness and holiness, and on the other side, punishment and loss. Therefore, finally, the first goat is a true sacrament, intended to lift up all creation in its fullness and fruitfulness, and to draw all creation into the movement that it perfects, while the second goat is a true substitute, cast out and cast down, bearing away the suffering we've created, for our sake and for our salvation.

TABLE 1. Distinguishing the Goats

Goat for the Lord	Goat for Azazel
An offering	Not an offering
Spotless	Sin-bearing
"Draws near" (active)	Led away (passive)
Holy of Holies	Wilderness
Edenic (Akedah)	Damned (Babylonian Exile)
Peace	Violence
Order	Chaos
Life	Death
Light	Darkness
Freedom	Burden/Bondage
Blood	Dust
Obedience	Rebellion
(Rooted in) joy	Lamentation
Glory	Horror
Unity	Division
Communion	Enmity
Recapitulation	Remainder
Righteousness	Punishment
Lifted up	Thrown down
Sacramental	Substitutionary

Yes, it is essential to distinguish the goats. Concepts like death, punishment, and hell are incongruous with the theological symbolism of the YHWH-goat, just as concepts like sacrifice/offering, spotlessness, and life are in tension with the imagery of the Azazel-goat. This is not to say that the two goats are wholly divided, but the unity cannot be appreciated until the distinction is drawn. Therefore, as we consider New Testament soteriological texts, we should remember an analogous patristic practice: just as the early church developed a nuanced hermeneutic when considering what was being said regarding Jesus's divine nature and what was being said regarding his human nature, without conceding separation between the two, we should be similarly careful to associate the different aspects of Christ's saving work with the movements of the two goats.

The Book of Hebrews

The New Testament text with the most explicit and sustained use of priestly temple imagery generally, and Yom Kippur imagery specifically, is the ninth and tenth chapters of the book of Hebrews. These chapters focus on how Christ fulfills the pattern set by the high priest's YHWH-goat offering on the Day of Atonement. From the start, one notices that the author of Hebrews, even as he builds his argument for the perfection of Christ's sacrifice, nevertheless affirms the value *and* effectiveness of the ancient Jewish cult.[25] After all, it says, "For if the blood of goats and bulls, with the sprinkling of the ashes of a heifer, sanctifies (*hagiázei*) those who have been defiled so that their flesh is purified (*katharótēta*), *how much more* (*pósōi mâllon*) will the blood of Christ, who through the eternal Spirit offered himself without blemish to God, purify (*kathariêi*) our conscience from dead works to worship the living God!" (Hebrews 9:13–14)[26] The suggestion here seems to be that, even as the Levitical cult succeeded, the crowning work of the high priest Jesus Christ succeeds that much more in sanctifying the whole person. In other words, the underlying Levitical theo-logic remains even as the purification found in Christ is more complete from the author's perspective.[27]

According to the Gospel's calendar, Christ's death corresponded with the Passover, but in Hebrews, the event of the cross encompasses more than temporal reality can contain. Reviewing several other New Testament texts, one scholar has pointed out that "early Christians engaged

25. Cf. Vis, "The Purification Offering," 261–62.

26. The Greek words translated as "purified" are both from the word *katharos*; the same word is used often in the Leviticus LXX passages for ritual purification. An especially striking example comes from the Septuagint translation of Leviticus 16: "And he shall sprinkle some of the blood on [the horns of the altar] with his finger seven times and pronounce it clean (*kathariêi*) and hallow it (or sanctify it, *hagiásei*) from the uncleanness of the sons of Israel" (Lv 16:19–20, NETS). The words sprinkle, blood, sanctify, and purify all also appear here in Hebrews 9:13–14.

27. Mayjee Philip comes to a similar conclusion: "The author's rationale regarding Jesus' sacrifice is governed by the OT in general and Leviticus in particular." Mayjee Philip, *Leviticus in Hebrews* (Frankfurt: Peter Lang, 2011), 59–60. Vis says, "The sacrificial system of Israel is subjected to scrutiny and found wanting. However, the fundamentals of the system are affirmed." Vis, "The Purification Offering," 261. See also Eberhart, "Characteristics of Sacrificial Metaphors in Hebrews," 59.

in a process of Yom Kippuring Passover"[28]; by the time Hebrews was written, the connection between Jesus' Passover death and resurrection and the priestly rites of atonement was apparently well established. Hebrews extends the effort to associate Christ with atonement by performing a complex comparison between the "new" and the "old," structured through a series of sophisticated analogies, here called "parables" or "types" (cf. v. 9). These comparisons have been characterized in various ways,[29] but the main idea is this: just as Yom Kippur (Lv 16) is the epitome of Israel's regular cultic practices (Lv 1–5), so too is the offering of Christ the perfection of Israel's sacred rites overall. This complex comparison has spatial and temporal permutations. Focusing first on the spatial, the ninth chapter opens with a brief blueprint of the "earthly sanctuary," highlighting the furniture of the holy place and the holy of holies. The relationship between these two spheres of holiness—one outer, one inner; one higher, one lower—will serve as the model for the other distinctions made in the chapter. Thus, the author moves right into his first observation about the holy place: "the priests go continually into the first tent to carry out their ritual duties" (Heb 9:6)—notice, that's priests *plural*, duties *plural*. This first tent is the realm of spatial movement and temporal change: people are coming and going, day in and day out. The inner tent (the holy of holies) is different: "only the high priest goes into the second, and he but once a year. . ." (v. 7). Here we find an emphasis on the unity, the oneness of the holy of holies, the place where the one Lord and Creator of the cosmos is enthroned in glory (cf. v. 5). This oneness is symbolically represented by the fact that the high priest *alone* enters, and this only *once* yearly.

Having reflected on the relationship between the one and the many within Leviticus itself,[30] the author of Hebrews shifts to the singularity

28. Jeffrey S. Siker, "Yom Kippuring Passover: Recombinant Sacrifice in Early Christianity," in *Ritual and Metaphor: Sacrifice in the Bible*, ed. Christian A. Eberhart (Atlanta: Society of Biblical Literature, 2011), 65. Similarly, N. T. Wright has said, "Passover was not itself an 'atoning' festival. Conversely, the Day of Atonement, by itself, was not about rescue from slavery, the overthrowing of hostile powers. But the particular situation of Israel, from Babylon to the time of Jesus and indeed beyond, demanded that the hope of Israel should somehow bring these two together." N. T. Wright, *The Day the Revolution Began* (San Francisco: HarperOne, 2016), 332.

29. For example, Luke Timothy Johnson, *Hebrews: A Commentary* (Louisville, KY: Westminster John Knox Press, 2006), 218–19; Steve Stanley, "Hebrews 9: 6–10: The 'Parable' of the Tabernacle," *Novum Testamentum* 37, no. 4 (1995): 385–99.

30. The possible role of Platonic philosophy in these reflections is much discussed. Luke Timothy Johnson himself sees clear Platonic influence, while also showing how the author modifies Platonism in fundamental ways: *Hebrews*, 7–8, 15–21. In chapter three

of Jesus: "But when Christ came as a high priest of the good things that have come, then through the greater and perfect tent (not made with hands, that is, not of this creation), he entered once for all into the Holy Place, not with the blood of goats and calves, but with his own blood, thus obtaining eternal redemption" (9:11–12). There is substantial continuity here: Christ is a high priest, and like any high priest he enters the most holy place, and again like any high priest he draws near through the liturgical symbol of life. It is also clear that the immediate reason for this movement is purification from sin, which is exactly what we would expect if the author were drawing on Levitical YHWH-goat theology. First of all, the positive role of blood is reaffirmed: "Indeed, under the law almost everything is purified with blood. . ." (v. 22).[31] But then, the Levitical sense that the sanctuary *itself* needs purification is also implied: "Thus it was necessary for the sketches of the heavenly things to be purified with these rites, but the heavenly things themselves need better sacrifices than these" (9:23).[32] The presuppositions in this verse about the need for blood to purify the sanctuary are thus identical to the priestly presuppositions identified by Milgrom. It is hard to tell whether the author thinks that *even the heavenly temple* needs purification—which would indeed be a radical expansion of Levitical thought, perhaps the result of mixing microcosmic and mirror-of-heaven modes of reflection[33]—or if he simply reasons that if there is an "offering" in the heavenly temple it must be even more extraordinary than any earthly

---

of this book, we also saw how some concepts that parallel Platonic cosmology could develop organically in the Jewish tradition of temple theology. Similarly, see Stökl Ben Ezra, *Impact of Yom Kippur*, 182–84.

31. For more on the meaning of "blood" in Hebrews according to recent scholarship, see chapter six, footnote 63.

32. The word for "purified" in these two verses is *katharizó*. The word is used often in LXX Leviticus with reference to the purification rites and is prominently featured in the concluding verses of the YHWH-goat ritual of Leviticus 16 (as discussed in footnote 26 above).

33. Interesting possibilities for interpreting this verse are given by Harold W. Attridge, *The Epistle to the Hebrews: A Commentary on the Epistle to the Hebrews* (Philadelphia: Fortress Press, 1989), 260–62. One proposal that he mentions (and which he personally rejects) is that this is a reference to the final expulsion of the fallen angels. Certainly, as we have seen in the analysis of *1 Enoch*, there is precedent for linking Yom Kippur with apocalyptic themes. Cf. Gabriella Gelardini, "The Inauguration of Yom Kippur According To The LXX And Its Cessation Or Perpetuation According To The Book Of Hebrews: A Systematic Comparison," in *The Day of Atonement: Its Interpretations in Early Jewish and Christian Traditions*, ed. Thomas Hieke and Tobias Nicklas (Leiden: Brill, 2011), 230.

offerings. In either case, the relationship between Father and Son in the eternal holy of holies is presented as the highest possible form of inter-personal "drawing near." Therefore, the author again presupposes the continuing importance of the underlying principles found in the priestly theological tradition.

If the differences between traditional Jewish temple theology and the Christian book of Hebrews do not revolve around the problem of whether or not the cult itself is pointless or corrupt, and if the overarching validity of the Levitical perspective is taken for granted, then why does the book take such a seemingly negative tone toward the ancient cult? The dispute here is actually over more and less perfect actualizations within the same theological paradigm, and the main polemical question is whether Levitical offerings can make us "perfect."[34] And so: "Since the law has only a shadow of the good things to come and not the true form of these realities, it can never, by the same sacrifices that are continually offered year after year, make perfect (*teleiōsai*) those who approach" (10:1). Now remember, the author has already acknowledged a measure of sanctification through the blood of goats and bulls (cf. 9:13), but in chapter ten there is a new emphasis on "once for all" *perfection*. This "perfection" is seen in the way that believers have unimpeded access to the holy of holies (in and through the all-purifying blood of Christ the high priest): "we have confidence to enter the sanctuary by the blood of Jesus . . . and since we have a great priest over the house of God, let us approach with a true heart in full assurance of faith, with our hearts sprinkled clean from an evil conscience and our bodies washed with pure water" (10:19–22). Such confidence would indeed have been very chal-lenging for mainstream priestly theology, especially considering the trauma of Nadab and Abihu's shocking deaths.[35] For the author of Hebrews, *this* is the awe-inspiring difference that Christ makes. He enters the Holy Place "once for all," and then—the text famously adds—he "sat down" (10:12).[36] Furthermore, unlike the high priests of old who approached with (quasi-) sacramental signs, the blood of the New Cov-enant is the high priest's very own lifeblood. In other words, the high

34. Cf. Johnson, *Hebrews*, 226.

35. For the relationship between the exalted goal of "perfection" and the hope of entering the Holy of Holies, see Stanley, "Hebrews 9," 394–95.

36. For a fascinating discussion of how this likely means that Jesus "sat down" on the "throne" of the ark of the covenant—which yet again accentuates the unparalleled uniqueness of Christ from the perspective of the author of this text—see Jody A. Barnard, *The Mysticism of Hebrews: Exploring the Role of Jewish Apocalyptic Mysticism in the Epistle to the Hebrews* (Tübingen: Mohr Siebeck, 2012), 144ff.

priest in this case pours himself out (cf. Philippians 2:7–8) with an intimacy that the Levitical priesthood could only intimate.[37]

It is necessary to highlight that, even if the blood of Christ opens the way to a deified life previously seen only in misty outline, this new possibility still assumes a Yom Kippur shape. It is still articulated in terms of the most basic biblical geography, oriented toward the paradisiacal center where the all-holy one dwells, and in terms of the most ancient rites, which focus on drawing near with the sign of life. In other words, the author's goal is to show, in careful detail, that Jesus Christ himself fulfills the positive, unifying movement of the High Priest and the YHWH-goat.

This raises the question: what about the second goat? It has been said that the sin-bearing goat is absent from the Christian Yom Kippur theology of the book of Hebrews,[38] but careful awareness of the terminology associated with each goat makes it possible to catch a glimpse of the fleeting profile of the one destined for Azazel. The text says that "just as it is appointed for mortals to die once, and after that the judgement, so Christ, having been offered once *to bear (anenenkeîn) the sins of many*, will appear a second time. . ." (9:27–28, NRSV). With the key phrase in the NRSV translation—"offered once to bear the sins"—we are confronted here with perhaps the most challenging text for my overall argument. While I claim that the two goats must be clearly distinguished, the author of Hebrews seems to bring the movements so closely together that perhaps they are confused or conflated from a New Testament perspective.

While admitting that this is a difficult verse, it is still appropriate to approach this passage from the perspective of the clear teachings of Leviticus, and when we do, we find that, even here, the two distinct movements are respected. The author of Hebrews is, in this slender passage, linking together two aspects of the high priest's mission on Yom Kippur,

---

37. There is a debate in recent commentaries over whether this reference to Jesus' entering the holy of holies with his own blood is an allusion to his death or to his resurrection/ascension, a debate that also hinges on how we interpret cultic blood. Attridge expresses a traditional scholarly view when he says, "Thus 'blood' could be the life that Christ offers eternally in heaven, or more likely, the sacrificial death that precedes that entry." Attridge, *The Epistle to the Hebrews*, 248; cf. Johnson, *Hebrews*, 237. One of the great virtues of the most recent scholarship on Hebrews is its focus on the priestly theology of blood-as-life, thus tilting interpreters away from associating atonement with death. See Willi-Plein, "Some Remarks on Hebrews," 33; Moffitt, *Atonement and the Logic of Resurrection*, 256 ff; Vis, "The Purification Offering," 291 ff.

38. Luke Timothy Johnson, for example, says that Hebrews "leaves out altogether the ritual involving the 'scapegoat' that bears the sins of the people," *Hebrews*, 217. Similarly, see Willi-Plein, "Some Remarks on Hebrews," 30; Stökl Ben Ezra, *Impact of Yom Kippur*, 193.

which are both intensified in Christ. In being the spotless (self-)offering, Jesus himself fulfills the work of the first goat with his own blood, which *subsequently* makes it possible for him to personally bear away the world's sins, thus fulfilling the work of the second goat. Remember: in Leviticus, the removal of sin is contingent on the application of the "ritual detergent" (in Milgrom's terms), the lifeblood that replaces and releases the sin from the sanctuary. This comes first, and it releases the sins from the holy of holies, thus making it possible to bear them away; the second movement is dependent on the first.

It is striking that the offering comes *before* the sin-bearing, the latter being contingent on the former. A more literal translation of the Greek makes the dependent relationship even more explicit: ". . . Christ has been offered once for all *in order to* bear the sins of many [*eis tò pollōn anenenkeîn hamartías*]. . . ."[39] For those who are inclined to "conflate" the goats, it would make more sense to say that the sacrificial goat receives the sins *first*, and *then* it is "offered" (that is, killed / subjected to just punishment) *because of* the imputed sins. But here, it's the opposite: the sacrificial movement (first) makes possible the removal (second). This reinforces the fact that the two "goats" are distinct, and it further shows how this text is attentive to the fundamental "shape" of the Leviticus ritual, even as it concentrates both movements in a single person: Jesus Christ, the final high priest. Therefore, we can conclude that both goats are present in Hebrews. Even though the second goat is only mentioned in passing, the fact that the distinct movements are represented again reinforces the profound overlap between Yom Kippur theology and the work of Christ as described in Hebrews 9–10.

The Two Goats in Other New Testament Texts

While the book of Hebrews is singular when it comes to sustained scriptural reflection on the relationship between Yom Kippur and Jesus

39. This is Gareth Lee Cockerill's translation of Hebrews 9:28 in *The Epistle to the Hebrews* (Grand Rapids, MI: Eerdmans, 2012), 419. Many commentators, including Cockerill and Attridge, point out that the most direct parallel text for Hebrews 9:28 is the famous suffering servant passage, in which the servant "bore the guilt of the many" (Isaiah 53:12). Cockerill, 426; Attridge, *The Epistle to the Hebrews*, 266. Yet this prophetic text itself may well contain an allusion to the Azazel-goat (see Stökl Ben Ezra, *Impact of Yom Kippur*, 116–17, esp. 117 n.193). Whether the allusion to Leviticus is direct, or by way of Isaiah 53, the concept of sin-bearing for the sake of atonement does trigger Yom Kippur imagery, and that association is made stronger by the fact that Yom Kippur is so prominent in this chapter of Hebrews.

Christ, there are numerous other verses, scattered across the New Testament, which imply a relationship. Others have tracked the New Testament's use of sacrificial language in discussing the saving work of Christ; there is no need to rehash their findings.[40] Building on these previous studies, I will show that attention to the vocabulary associated with each of the two goats (see TABLE 1, above) can help correct some of the dubious interpretations that have appeared from time to time. Therefore, I will briefly review exemplary texts that fall into two major categories: (a) Christ as the "goat for the Lord" and (b) Christ as the "goat for Azazel."[41]

Christ the Goat for YHWH

In the first category, we have verses that imply that the (self-) offering of Jesus can and should be interpreted in continuity with the theology of Levitical purification offerings. Consider the following:

> So if anyone is *in Christ*, there is *a new creation*: everything old has passed away; see, everything has become *new*! All this is from God, who reconciled us to himself *through Christ*, and has given us the ministry of reconciliation; that is, *in Christ* God was *reconciling the world* to himself, not counting their trespasses against them, and entrusting the message of reconciliation to us. So we are ambassadors for Christ, since God is making his appeal through us; we entreat you on behalf of Christ, be reconciled to God. [God] made him who *knew no sin* to be *hamartían* [a "sin" offering[42]]

---

40. See, for example, Eberhart, *The Sacrifice of Jesus*; Vis, "The Purification Offering," 309–38; Stanislas Lyonnet and Leopold Sabourin, *Sin, Redemption, and Sacrifice. A Biblical and Patristic Study* (Rome: Biblical Institute, 1970); Robert J. Daly, *Christian Sacrifice: The Judaeo-Christian Background before Origen* (Washington, DC: The Catholic University of America Press, 1978); Frances Young, *The Use of Sacrificial Ideas in Greek Christian Writers from the New Testament to John Chrysostom* (Cambridge, MA: Philadelphia Patristic Foundation, 1979).

41. In making this inventory, I am identifying texts that exemplify the purification offering/Yom Kippur typology. Certainly, many other New Testament texts articulate a theology of the cross using non-cultic images and metaphors. These images have been usefully categorized by Finlan, *Background and Content*, 5–7; cf. Stephen Finlan, *Options on Atonement in Christian Thought* (Collegeville, MN: Liturgical Press, 2007), 18–42. Therefore, this review of texts will not be comprehensive when it comes to New Testament sacrificial imagery, and it will be even less comprehensive with respect to salvation metaphors generally.

42. The mainstream Catholic tradition has read the noun *hamartia* here as a reference to the "sin offering" of Leviticus 4, and thus Paul is playing with the normal cultic terminology of the Septuagint. See Lyonnet and Sabourin, *Sin, Redemption, and Sacrifice*, 250–53; Daly, *Christian Sacrifice*, 236–40. This translation was most common in the patristic and medieval periods; it became more controversial after the Reformation.

for us,[43] so that *in him* we might become *the righteousness of God.*
(2 Cor 5:17–21)

If we approach this passage from the perspective of temple theology, several things stand out. To be "in Christ" is to be a new creation: throughout this book, we have seen how creation, cosmos, and temple intertwine in ancient Jewish thought. The primordial creation was conceived as a garden sanctuary, the completion of the tabernacle and the inauguration of the cult at Sinai was understood as the capstone of creation, and the Babylonian destruction of the temple represented creation undone. For Paul, those gathered "in" Christ are gathered into a new creation, that is, a renewed, life-giving order. They have "drawn near" to God's new dwelling place among us: Christ himself. The new creation in Christ is characterized by the word "reconciliation," which is the promise of a restored relationship between God and humanity.[44] Recall that in ancient Jewish theology, it is the temple that definitively embodies all-unity. Thus, when it comes time to explain how our relationship with God is restored in Christ, it would be natural for Paul to reach for the technical terminology of the Levitical cult (that is, the language of the purification offering) since cultic offerings were the normal means by which Jews were reconciled to God and creation was made new.[45]

43. I have edited the NRSV here. The NRSV reads, "For our sake he made him to be sin who knew no sin. . . . " The Greek says, "*tòn mè gnónta hamartían hupèr hēmōn hamartían epoíēsen.*"

44. The Greek word, used five times in this passage, is the verb *katallassó* (to reconcile) and the corresponding noun *katallagé* (reconciliation). According to William Barclay, in a secular Greek context the word refers to "the change of enmity into friendship." *New Testament Words* (Philadelphia: Westminster John Knox Press, 1974), 165. The word is rare in the Septuagint, and it is, admittedly, not used in passages related to the temple cult. Nevertheless, Paul primarily uses the word to describe a new relationship between God and humanity (cf. Romans 5:10–11), a new relationship made possible by God himself. Such a concept could call priestly imagery to mind very easily.

45. Several modern commentaries argue against the idea that Paul has the cultic concept of a "sin offering" in mind here. See, for example, Paul Barnett, *The Second Epistle to the Corinthians* (Grand Rapids, MI: Eerdmans, 1997), 314; R. H. Bell, "Sacrifice and Christology in Paul," *Journal of Theological Studies* 53, no. 1 (2002): 13; Frank J. Matera, *II Corinthians: A Commentary* (Louisville, KY: Westminster John Knox Press, 2003), 143; Raymond F. Collins, *Second Corinthians (Paideia: Commentaries on the New Testament)* (Grand Rapids, MI: Baker Academic, 2013), 125–26. A common argument found in these texts is that it seems unlikely to the commentators that Paul would use the same word to mean "sin" in one case ["he knew no sin"] and then, immediately after, "purification offering" in the other ["made him to be a sin offering"]. However, in both the Hebrew and the Greek translation, such oscillation between meanings is rampant in Leviticus 4. As Watts pointed out, the repetitive and evocative use of the word "sin/sin offering" is part of the

In the Greek, Paul puts the sinlessness of Christ first: *the one who knew no sin, he became our purification (sin) offering. . . .* Two things are established by the leading clause: (a) that Jesus needed no purification offering for himself since he was without sin, thus implying that his self-offering is on our behalf, and (b) that he was "unblemished," which is itself the vital requirement for temple offerings. Again, this purification offering by Christ is meant to transform us, "that *we* might become God's righteousness *in him*." It is, in other words, a sacramental event that is intended to draw us into the new, healed, elevated creation which Christ has established through his offering, by his life-blood. This is the movement of God's reconciling love, and it is in perfect continuity with the priestly work of Leviticus, which also sought to realign heaven and earth through the sacred rites which God had given the Jews.

There are many other analogous passages in the New Testament. For example, this Pauline passage is succinct and powerful:

> For in him all the fullness of God was pleased *to dwell*,[46] and through him God was pleased to *reconcile* to himself all things, whether on earth or in heaven, by making peace through *the blood of his cross*. (Col 1:19–20)

Here again is hope for reconciliation,[47] now expanded to include all things in heaven and earth, but now reconciliation is associated specifically with Christ's blood. Although many commentators across the centuries have read the word "blood" quite narrowly as "death," we should consider instead that the word is best associated with the YHWH-goat, and thus with the theme of whole-hearted life.[48] This is the fullness of

---

priestly author's rhetorical strategy. It is not, therefore, a great stretch to think that Paul should be attuned to this peculiarity in Jewish cultic terminology and that he too would draw on it for his own rhetorical purposes.

46. Already, with the use of the word "to dwell"—*katoikēsai*—in association with divinity, temple imagery seems inevitable. In the Septuagint, this word is used often, and mostly with reference to human dwelling. However, when it is a question of divine inhabitation, Zion is generally the identified location. Consider 1 Kings 8:27, 2 Chronicles 6:18, Psalm 9:11, Psalm 135:21, Isaiah 8:18, Isaiah 33:5; cf. Matthew 23:21, Acts 7:48, Acts 17:24. (Some of these passages question the possibility of God dwelling in temples, but the point remains that, when it comes to God, there is an association between the word "dwelling" and the Jerusalem Temple.)

47. The word used in Colossians is the intensified version of *katallassó, apokatallassó*. The idea that the word "reconciliation" was thematically associated with cultic realities in Paul's mind is strengthened by the fact that both here and in Romans 5:9–11 a form of the word is paired with an emphasis on salvation *specifically* through Christ's *blood*.

48. Similarly, see Vis, "The Purification Offering," 327–28.

Life, indeed the fullness of God dwelling among us, which is characterized above all else by the eternal *shalom* of Mount Zion. In this passage, several rich biblical symbols gather around the person of Jesus, including the idea that he is both the new temple and the new purification offering. This is almost to be expected since, as we have seen, these symbols naturally point toward each other in ancient Jewish theology; the purification offering (as an adaptation of the burnt offering in the context of sin) is the dramatic movement—"the Act"—which is the cornerstone of the temple on Mount Moriah. It is by this Act that this great stone structure becomes alive as a glorious icon of God's indwelling presence.

Clearly in Paul, as in Leviticus, cultic blood symbolizes perfect harmony. Thus:

> So then, remember that at one time you Gentiles by birth . . . were at that time without Christ, being aliens from the commonwealth of Israel, and strangers to the covenants of promise, having no hope and without God in the world. But now *in Christ Jesus* you who once were far off have been *brought near* by the *blood of Christ*. For he is our *peace*; in his flesh he has made both groups into one and has broken down the dividing wall, that is, the hostility between us. (Ephesians 2:11–14)

It is the blood of the purification offering on Yom Kippur that draws the nation of Israel together, near to God, unified in peace. Paul sees in Jesus Christ the great culmination of Israel's hope because in him the Day of Atonement expands to cross every boundary, to draw in even those without hope, even those far off in the wilderness of uncircumcision. For Paul, the hope of the Gentiles is to be grafted into the commonwealth of Israel, for all to draw near to the Father together through Jesus' own blood. The theo-logic of Leviticus remains, even as it is extended in Christ.

Many similar ideas are repeated outside of the Pauline epistles. As an example, notice the temple imagery in this passage:

> This is the message we have heard from him and proclaim to you, that *God is light* and in him there is no darkness at all. If we say that we have fellowship with him while we are walking in darkness, we lie and do not do what is true; but if we walk in the light as he himself is in the light, we have fellowship with one another, *and the blood of Jesus his Son cleanses us from all sin*. If we say that we have no sin, we deceive ourselves, and the truth is not in us. If we *confess our sins*, he who is faithful and just will *forgive us our sins and cleanse us* from all unrighteousness. (1 John 1:5–9)

This text, at the beginning of John's first epistle, prompts the listener to make a moral distinction between light and darkness, truth and lies, with God identified as pure light and pure truth. John calls upon believers to walk in the light, but also to sincerely acknowledge and confess their sins. In this context, he brings in unambiguous cultic language: the blood of Jesus cleanses us from all sins, which culminates in forgiveness. Here we see additional New Testament confirmation of one of Milgrom's central claims, that blood is the ritual detergent, and confirmation also of the view of Milgrom's interlocutors, who insist that in cleansing the sacred space, the lifeblood cleanses worshippers from sin as well. Again, the temple principles of confession and purification offerings remain, even as they are recontextualized around Jesus in early Christian theology.

By now it should be no surprise that in the first lines of the Book of Revelation we read:

> To him who loves us and *freed us from our sins by his blood*, and made us to be a kingdom, *priests serving his God and Father*, to him be *glory* and dominion for ever and ever. Amen. (Rv 1:5b–6)[49]

In this opening doxology, the beauty of the Yhwh-goat is celebrated with delight. It is a theology of love, a theology of freedom, and a theology of glory. Those who come to God by means of his blood are elevated into a priesthood ancient and new, and thus they are empowered to joyfully sing praises to God in the eternal holy of holies.

Therefore, throughout the New Testament—from the earliest texts to the latest—reflection on Christ as the purification offering is surrounded by words of rapture and delight. It is a positive movement of love between Father and Son, drawn together in the Spirit, which brings the whole world to salvation and harmony.[50] One does not find, in these

49. For an overview of the textual issues in this passage and for further analysis, see Vis, 333–35.

50. As I mentioned, this section is not exhaustive in its review of possible New Testament allusions to the idea that Christ's self-offering on the cross was a purification offering generally, or that it fulfills the work of the Yhwh-goat specifically. One other passage that has received immense attention and that might have been included here is Romans 3:23–26, which reads: "... since all have sinned and fall short of the glory of God; they are now justified by his grace as a gift, through the redemption that is in Christ Jesus, whom God put forward as a *hilastērion* by his blood, effective through faith." *Hilastērion* is the word used throughout the Septuagint to translate the Hebrew word *kappōret*, which is the cover of the ark upon which the blood was sprinkled on Yom Kippur. For many, Paul is suggesting that, through the "sprinkling" of his blood, Christ himself becomes that "place" where purification occurs and atonement is achieved between God and humanity. See Daniel P. Bailey, "Jesus as the Mercy Seat: The Semantics and Theology of Paul's Use of Hilasterion in

texts, an emphasis on death, and there is not even evidence of punishment or divine violence. Instead, these verses celebrate the new creation, the reconciled world, a new peace, drawing the whole earth together, in freedom, to God's glory. This is the beauty of Zion, recapitulated in the self-giving of Jesus Christ.

Christ the Goat for Azazel

There is a second set of texts, and they contain an implicit affirmation of the fact that Christ, through his saving work, also fulfills the mission of the Azazel-goat. While these passages are less prevalent compared with the texts which identify Christ as a purification offering, they are nevertheless well-known and crucial for a fuller picture of New Testament soteriology. Below we will consider the clearest examples, one from Paul and one from Peter, and then also a more ambiguous reference from the Gospel of John.

First, in one of Paul's earliest epistles, the letter to the Galatians, we find a well-known passage. Writing in the bold colors which are typical of that letter, Paul proclaims:

Romans 3: 25" (Ph.D. diss., Cambridge University, 1999); Bell, "Sacrifice and Christology in Paul," 17–20; Stökl Ben Ezra, *Impact of Yom Kippur*, 197–205; Markus Tiwald, "Christ as Hilasterion (Rom 3:25): Pauline Theology of the Day of Atonement in the Mirror of Early Jewish Thought," in *Day of Atonement*, ed. Thomas Hieke and Tobias Nicklas (Leiden: Brill, 2012), 189–209; Vis, "The Purification Offering," 312–18.

Another text that has received sustained attention in recent years is the scene in Matthew 27 where Pontius Pilate offers to release either Jesus [the son of God] or Jesus Barabbas [notice: bar-abba, son of Abba]. That their names are identical in Matthew is a first clue. The whole story hinges on the notion that one of the two Jesuses will be released to the mob, and the other will be sent to be crucified. The sin-bearing Barabbas is released among the wicked, and the innocent Jesus is sent to be slaughtered. If the logic of Yom Kippur stands behind this story, Jesus is seen as more closely associated with the YHWH-goat, while an entirely different person represents the Azazel-goat. This type of dichotomy is more like *1 Enoch*, where Enoch is destined for the holy of holies while the demon Azazel is destined for the pit. It is significant, in any case, that this story—if Yom Kippur imaginary stands behind it—implicitly accentuates the connection between Christ's cross and the Holy of Holies. For more careful analysis, see Stökl Ben Ezra, *Impact of Yom Kippur*, 165–71; Daniel Stökl Ben Ezra, "Fasting with Jews, Thinking with Scapegoats," in *Day of Atonement* (Leiden: Brill, 2012), 179–87; Orlov, *The Atoning Dyad*, 58–64. Along these lines, Hans Moscicke has recently done important work tracing Yom Kippur imagery in the gospels, beginning with a highly nuanced reading of the Gospel of Matthew (Hans M. Moscicke, *The New Day of Atonement: A Matthean Typology* [Tübingen: Mohr Siebeck, 2020]) and then adding additional evidence from the other three gospel writers (Hans M. Moscicke, *Goat for Yahweh, Goat for Azazel: The Impact of Yom Kippur on the Gospels* [Minneapolis: Fortress Academic, 2021]).

> Christ redeemed us from the curse of the law by becoming a curse
> for us—for it is written, 'Cursed is everyone who hangs on a tree'—
> in order that in Christ Jesus the blessing of Abraham might come to
> the Gentiles, so that we might receive the promise of the Spirit
> through faith. (Galatians 3:13–14)

Christ becomes accursed that we might receive the Spirit. The text Paul
is adapting here is Deuteronomy 21:22–23, a law that specifies that the
criminal who has been impaled on a stake (which would have occurred
after their execution) shall not remain on display overnight.[51] It says,
". . . you shall bury him that same day, for anyone hung on a tree is under
God's curse [*qillat*]. You must not defile the land that the Lord your God
is giving you for possession" (v. 23, NRSV).

Throughout this book, we have encountered ways in which Deuteronomistic theology exhibits different nuances compared with priestly theology, but despite all the differences in detail, there is a similar theological
geography. While the priests worried extensively about defiling the
sanctuary itself, Deuteronomy puts a lot of emphasis on protecting "the
land" from defilement (this difference is not a contradiction, and the
priestly Holiness code also cautions against defiling the land; cf. Lv
18:24–30). The word for "curse" in this verse appears a few times in Deuteronomy, often juxtaposed with the word "blessing." The words "blessing" and "curse" represent contrasting futures: peace with God in the
promised land vs. the wrath of God in exile. In the twenty-ninth chapter
of Deuteronomy, a devastating fate is anticipated for those who break
their covenantal promises: ". . . they turned to the service of other gods
and worshiped them, gods whom they had not experienced and whom
He had not allotted to them. So, the Lord was incensed at that land and
brought upon it all the curses [*haqqelālāh*] recorded in this book. The
Lord uprooted them from their soil in anger, fury, and great wrath, and
cast them into another land, as is still the case" (Dt 29:25–27). This warning is the general context for the famous passage from Deuteronomy,
which we discussed in the last chapter: "I have put before you life and
death, blessing and curse [*wehaqqelālāh*]. Choose life. . ." (Dt 30:19).
Therefore, within Deuteronomistic theology generally, the "curse" is associated with death, exile, and divine wrath, while "blessing" is associated
with life, land, and divine favor. With that in mind, it seems that the crim-

---

51. Cf. J. Louis Martyn, *Galatians* (New Haven, CT: Yale University Press, 2004),
319; Martinus C. de Boer, *Galatians: A Commentary* (Louisville, KY: Westminster John
Knox Press, 2011), 212.

inal who is fastened to the tree *personally* experiences the divine curse that Israel would *communally* experience in the absolute cataclysm of exile. Such a tragic sign is not to linger upon the tree; the law of Deuteronomy requires that the lawbroken body—the one who breaks the law is broken by the law—be removed before nightfall.

Remembering these associations, we can return to Paul's claim that Christ, as one hung on a tree, has become "a curse for us" so that the Gentiles might gain access to the "blessing of Abraham." From the perspective of the sections of Deuteronomy that we quoted above, "the nations," with their "other gods" and grotesque immorality, are a people who know nothing but perpetual exile. This is the very opposite of the freedom which is intended for Abraham and his children, the *hinneni*-life which is the foundation of Israel's joy. Paul seems to suggest that, for Jesus to bring the lost Gentiles in, he must first go out: he too must endure the curse and exile—and implicitly, even the wrath—of those who live the chaos of sin. Unlike the passages in the previous section, which might be called "sacramental" because Jesus seems to draw believers into his redeeming, doxological work, the implication of *this* text is substitution and exchange: Jesus will take the place of the exiled so that the exiled might receive the living Spirit, which is the ultimate blessing of intimacy with God. While it is not obvious that Paul had the Azazel-goat in mind when he drew upon Deuteronomy to describe the saving work of Christ, it remains true that the notion of one who endures the ultimate exile to save the community from God's abandonment in fact describes the vocation of the second goat exactly.[52]

Paul is not the only one to perceive this side of Christ's mission. Consider, for example, these words from the first epistle of Peter:

He himself bore [*anēnenken*] our sins in his body on the cross [tree, *xylon*], so that, free from sins, we might live for righteousness; by his wounds you have been healed. For you were going astray like sheep, but now you have returned to the shepherd and guardian of your souls. (1 Peter 2:24–25)

---

52. Using different lines of evidence, Stökl also finds an allusion to the Azazel-goat in Galatians 3:13–14. See Stökl Ben Ezra, *Impact of Yom Kippur*, 173–76. Emphasis on the idea that Jesus freely enters into Israel's exile is found in the work of N. T. Wright. For example, he says, "The way of the servant was to take upon himself the exile of the nation as a whole. As a would-be Messiah, Jesus identified with Israel; he would therefore go ahead of her, and take upon himself precisely that fate, actual and symbolic, which he had announced for nation, city, and Temple." Wright, *Jesus and the Victory of God*, 608; cf. 133.

The context immediately preceding this passage is an exhortation to pattern oneself after Jesus and to patiently endure even unjust suffering in household relationships. This idea, it seems, brings to the author's mind the imagery of the suffering servant, a comparison he develops in verses 22 and 23, and then he shifts further into what seems to be a more general soteriological affirmation, which is what we have in verses 24 and 25. Drawing on the imagery from Isaiah—"he bore the guilt of the many" (Is 53:12)[53]—verse 24 emphasizes that it is Christ himself who bears (away) sins: it is notable that the imagery here, like the imagery in priestly theology, is quite substantial. Sin is effectively described as a weight, and because the one who is himself sinless (v. 22) now bears this foreign object, sin seems to be a transferrable "something."[54] This passage from 1 Peter also uniquely stresses the "location" of that sin-bearing: it occurs "in his body" and "on the tree." Somehow Jesus bears our burden away, for the sake of our freedom from sin and our freedom for righteousness, all while remaining bound to the wood of the tree. (This is analogous to how the "eyes of faith" perceive Jesus entering the holy of holies with his own blood, even though, according to our earthly perception, he remained pinned on the "altar" of the cross.) In other words, for the author, Christ endures the weight of exile in his own body so that we can again enjoy intimacy with "the shepherd and guardian" of our souls. By carrying away our corruption, the Azazel-goat makes it possible for us to dwell in peace.

There are other possible references to the Azazel-goat that are less certain and less clear. The most well-known example of this is found in the Gospel of John. After John the Baptist announces the presence of the one who is coming after him, it says:

> The next day [John the Baptist] saw Jesus coming towards him and declared, 'Here is the Lamb of God who takes away [*airōn*] the sin of the world! (John 1:29)

Even though the Greek words used in this passage do not closely parallel the central Yom Kippur texts, the fact that the lamb is carrying away "the sin of the world" is conspicuous. Then again, the fact that the sin carrier is a lamb is also remarkable, and perhaps it represents another challenge to my insistence that cultic offerings are not sin bearers. It is likely that a lamb

---

53. See footnote 39, above, for the possible relationship between Isaiah 53 and Leviticus 16.

54. This is also noticed by William Brown, "'In Him All Things Hold Together': An Ecology of Atonement," *Ex Auditu: An International Journal of Theological Interpretation of Scripture* 26 (May 9, 2011): 9–10.

was chosen in this context as an allusion to the Passover lamb, especially given the centrality of that Jewish feast in the book of John. Indeed, Passover is explicitly mentioned in the next chapter: "The Passover of the Jews was near, and Jesus went up to Jerusalem" (John 2:13).[55] But does that mean that, for the author of this gospel, the Passover lamb somehow carries away sins, thus muddling the clear distinction between the two "goats"?

The best explanation for this unusual passage is found in an outstanding article by Jeffrey Siker. He says: "The temporal connection between Jesus' death and Passover is inevitable since Jesus died in close proximity to this crucial festival. But John appears to import into the meaning of Jesus' death the atoning significance typically associated with the observance of Yom Kippur. John thus blurs the distinctions we might make in order to make a larger point about the unparalleled significance of the death of Jesus as the Lamb of God."[56] Siker then concludes,

> In short, early Christians took the other most significant holy day in Jewish tradition, Yom Kippur, and imported its central emphasis on forgiveness of sins into the ritual imagination of Passover. Thus, early Christians engaged in a process of "Yom Kippuring" Passover, a kind of recombinant theologizing of central Jewish rituals in the service of Christian efforts to make sense of Jesus' death in light of Jewish tradition.[57]

In other words, like a pair of bifocals, the Baptizer's concise description brings the image of Jesus into focus by simultaneously using two lenses: Passover and Yom Kippur. Jesus is the lamb of God who makes possible a new Exodus *from* the exile of Egypt and *into* the eschatological promised land, and Jesus is the Azazel-goat who removes sin *from* the world and goes *into* eschatological oblivion. As with other statements we've seen, even though the early Christian eagerness to speak of Jesus using many biblical motifs all at once can make things more confusing, it is not necessary to conclude that the basic coordinates of Yom Kippur are fundamentally confused.

The overall evidence of the New Testament is clear, even if it is not crystal clear. The idea that the saving work of Jesus Christ is positively related to second temple Yom Kippur theology is unambiguous. The book of

---

55 For a Jewish audience, John's emphasis on Jesus as "Lamb of God" might also call to mind the morning and evening Tamid, the most typical Jewish temple offering, which was an 'olah.

56. Siker, "Yom Kippuring Passover," 75.

57. Siker, 76.

Hebrews is alone sufficient to establish this fact. Looking at other notable texts, especially in the various epistles, generally supports this conclusion. First, the general idea that Jesus effects atonement as a purification offering is suggested by numerous texts, and even though the exact Levitical phrase "goat for the Lord" does not appear, for second temple Jews the connection between purifying blood rites and the high holy day of Yom Kippur would be quite secure. Second, a smaller yet not insignificant number of texts associate Christ's death with the continuing conviction, in Jewish theology, that sin must be removed from Israel, and indeed, from the world. The fact that the mission of the Azazel-goat is emphasized less often in the New Testament compared with the Yhwh-goat may be a reflection of the fact that, in the late second temple period, the Aramaic concept of "sin as debt" overshadowed the earlier Hebrew notion of sin as "something"[58]; nevertheless, the concept of the Savior as sin-bearer and curse-bearer is not wholly absent.

The question now is, did the Jewish-Christian affirmation of Jesus as the fulfillment of Yom Kippur remain relevant in the emerging Christian theological tradition? As Christianity spread, venturing further and further from Jerusalem, did Yom Kippur soteriology continue to shape post-apostolic Christian interpretation of Christ's saving work, or was it quickly forgotten?

A Continuing Tradition: Patristic Developments

There need be no cliffhanger here: the answer to these questions is clear. When it comes to the relationship between the saving work of Jesus Christ and the atoning work of the high priest on Yom Kippur, the earliest Christian theologians took up the theological threads from the apostolic generation and continued to weave. Clear statements on this subject can be found in the *Letter of Barnabas*, and in the writing of Tertullian, Justin Martyr, Origen, and Hippolytus, thus representing a significant soteriological model embraced by Eastern and Western fathers alike. Our goal in this section is to consider the shape of these early reflections: are the authors attentive to the different missions represented by the Yhwh-goat and the Azazel-goat? Do they affirm what is broadly suggested in the New Testament, that Christ fulfills the work of *both* goats? And if the answer to each of these questions is "yes," how are they able to maintain the *different* movements in the work of a *single* savior?

What we find in the earliest sources is that theologians were aware of the difference between the Yom Kippur goats, and they do indeed

---

58. This, again, is perhaps the major argument in Anderson, *Sin*.

assert that Christ himself fulfills the work of both. The earliest extra-biblical example is the *Letter of Barnabas*:

> Notice what was commanded: 'Take two goats, beautiful and similar, and offer them, and let the priest take the one as a burnt offering for sins.' But what are they to do with the other? 'The other,' he says, 'is accursed (*epikataratos*).' Notice how the type of Jesus is manifested: 'And do ye all spit on it, and pierce it, and bind the scarlet wool around its head, and so let it be cast into the desert. . . . What does this mean? Notice, 'that the first (goat) is for the altar, but the other is accursed, and that the one that is accursed is crowned.' Because then they will see him on that day with the scarlet (high priestly) robe on his body, and they will say, 'Is not this he whom we once crucified and rejected and pierced and spat upon? Truly it is he who then said that he himself was the Son of God.' But how is he like (to the goat)? For this reason: 'the goats shall be similar, beautiful, and equal,' in order that when they see him come at that time they may be astonished at the similarity of the goat. See then the type of Jesus destined to suffer. . . .[59]

Barnabas is one of the earliest sources for the idea that the two goats are alike in appearance. They are "similar, beautiful, and equal," but paradoxically, this point is so strongly emphasized precisely because the two seem so unalike! The first, he says, is a "burnt offering for sins"—this itself is a notable phrase, worthy of a brief tangent. According to Leviticus, of course, the first goat is not a burnt offering but a purification offering, and yet Barnabas apparently finds it easy to confuse the two. It is similarly interesting that, in an earlier passage, *Barnabas* ties together the themes of Christ's cross, the offering of Yom Kippur, and the Akedah: ". . . [Jesus] himself was going to offer the vessel of the spirit as a sacrifice for our sins, in order that the type established in Isaac, who was offered upon the altar, might be fulfilled. . . ."[60] In this book, I have argued for the theological interconnection of the Akedah, the burnt offering, and

59. The translation of the *Epistle of Barnabas* 7:6–10 is from Stökl Ben Ezra, *The Impact of Yom Kippur on Early Christianity*, 152–153, which is itself an adaptation of Kirsopp Lake, *The Apostolic Fathers* (Cambridge, MA: Harvard University Press, 1919), 365–69. For further analysis of *Barnabas*, see Stökl Ben Ezra, *Impact of Yom Kippur*, 148–55; Orlov, *The Atoning Dyad*, 73–74.

60. Barnabas 7:3c. The broader context here is a dense passage that seems related to the *third* goat (!) of Yom Kippur, which was eaten by the priests. Numbers 29:11 alludes to a third goat, and later rabbinic tradition explains the necessity of eating its flesh. It seems that Barnabas links *this* goat to the Christian Eucharist. See Stökl Ben Ezra, *Impact of Yom Kippur*, 150–51.

the purification offering using ancient and modern Jewish sources. The
confusion in these passages concerning the burnt offering and the purification offing may be a simple matter of imprecision on the author's part.
But it is also possible that *Barnabas* intuited similar theological connections. On the cross, Jesus simultaneously becomes the antitype of both
Yom Kippur and Isaac on Moriah. And then, when discussing the Day
of Atonement, the purification offering becomes a "burnt offering for
sin." Perhaps the theological relationship between the *'olah* and the
ḥaṭṭā't was at least generally apparent to the earliest Christian writers, a
fact that would bolster my interpretation of these offerings in the previous chapter.

Returning from the tangent, as I mentioned: Barnabas highlights the
similarity between the goats precisely because they are so different. While
the one is an offering, the other is "accursed." This word is significant
because *epikatáratos* is the exact word that appears in Galatians: "Cursed
is everyone who hangs on a tree." By using this word, Barnabas reinforces
the connection between the exile of the Azazel-goat and the Deuteronomistic concept of "the curse." When Jesus endures mistreatment, his
humiliation seems to mirror the humiliation of the accursed goat.[61] For
Barnabas, the connection between Jesus and the second goat is quite
straightforward at this point: in the ordeal of the cross, Jesus fulfills this
sorrowful aspect of the Yom Kippur liturgy. But then, Barnabas alludes
to *the second coming* of Jesus: Christ will be seen "on that day" in the
glorious garments of the high priest. This *second* appearance is correlated
with the YHWH-goat in the mind of the author, but onlookers will gasp
when they notice that the coming high priest is identical in appearance
to the mistreated one! As Christ came in humility, and as Christ comes
in glory, he will appear "similar, beautiful, equal," despite the stark differences. The two "goats" are one.

This method of distinguishing between the goats by dividing between
Jesus' first and second "coming" became the leading interpretive move
in the earliest patristic sources. It is repeated by both Justin Martyr and
Tertullian. The former puts it unambiguously:

---

61. As Barnabas spells out the mistreatment Jesus suffered, it resembles the abuse
that later tradition reports against the Azazel-goat as it makes its lonely journey out of
the camp. The *Mishnah Yoma* says, "And they made a causeway for it because of the Babylonians who used to pull its hair, crying to it, 'Bear [our sins] and be gone! Bear [our sins]
and be gone!'" (6:4). Perhaps drawing on the memory of similar activity against the Azazel-
goat in the late second temple period, Barnabas describes how, like the poor goat, Jesus is
pierced and spat upon as he goes.

> And the two goats of the fast were ordered to be similar. One of
> them was the scapegoat, the other was to be an offering. They were
> prophecies for the two appearances of Christ. For the first appear-
> ance, at which the elders of your people and the priests sent him
> away as a scapegoat, laid hands on him and killed him; and for his
> second appearance, since you will recognize at this very place of
> Jerusalem him who was dishonored by you and [made] an offering
> for all those sinners who want to repent and fast. . . .[62]

The comment on the Azazel-goat is easy enough to follow: Jesus has been
effectively sent away by those who "laid hands upon him and killed
him."[63] This is clearly about Christ's first "appearance." As for the YHWH-
goat, the major themes are Jerusalem and recognition. For Justin, Jerusalem will be the site of Christ's second coming and messianic reign.
Therefore, the fact that the YHWH-goat is offered in Jerusalem (indeed,
the purification offering goat is associated with what might be called the
Jerusalem-of-Jerusalems, the holy-of-holies) is highly significant, and it
corresponds to the Second Coming, when Jesus will be recognized by all.

With Tertullian, there is an interpretation that is both similar and different from each of the foregoing theological reflections. He says,

> If I may, moreover, give an interpretation of the two goats, which
> were offered on the fast, do they not also prefigure the two modes of
> Christ? They were alike, and very similar to the appearance of the
> Lord, since he will not come in any other form, having to be recog-
> nized by those by whom he had been wounded. One of these [goats],
> however, was bound with scarlet, cursed, spat upon, pulled around,
> and pierced, and driven by the people out of the city *into perdition*
> [*perditionem*], being thus marked with the visible signs of the Lord's
> passion. Yet the other [goat], by *being offered up* for sin and given
> to the priests of the temple for food, signified indications of the

---

62. Stökl's translation of Justin Martyr's *Dialogue with Trypho* 40:4–5. See Stökl
Ben Ezra, *Impact of Yom Kippur*, 155. For further analysis of this passage, see Stökl Ben
Ezra, 155–56; Orlov, *The Atoning Dyad*, 75–76.

63. It may at first surprise us that the Azazel-goat is associated with death, since in
Leviticus that goat's physical death is not mentioned (though its exile from the temple
would nevertheless be understood as a living death). As I noted above, later Jewish tradition expands the biblical account by instructing that the Azazel-goat be pushed over a
ledge and into a ravine, effectively guaranteeing its death. By linking the death of Christ
very specifically with the Azazel-goat, the author may have this practice in mind. Then
again, I've argued that the Azazel-goat is synonymous with death, irrespective of the
animal's physical fate, because to be exiled from the sanctuary/holy land is to experience
a living death, much in the manner of Adam and Eve.

second appearance, when—after sins have been expiated—the priests of the spiritual temple, i.e. the church—feast as a sort of flesh offering of the Lord's grace, while the others fast from salvation.[64]

Once again, the context for this passage is a reflection on the "two advents" of Jesus Christ, one perceived as lowly, the other as majestic. Beginning with the lowly, Tertullian also, like his predecessors, straightforwardly associates the Azazel-goat with Christ's passion. In this section, he adds a fascinating gloss: this is the goat that is driven to "perdition," or to destruction. Just as Barnabas showed that he understood basic biblical geography by emphasizing that this goat is "accursed," the association of the Azazel-goat with perdition is perceptive. Perhaps you could say that there is, here, a proto-"descent to hell" doctrine that is awaiting theological development.

Then turning to the YHWH-goat, Tertullian emphasizes that he is "offered up," that he is an "oblation" (*oblatus*) intimately associated with the priesthood. Even though the first goat of Leviticus 16 is not eaten by the priests (unlike other purification offerings), Tertullian associates this goat with eating so as to make a eucharistic connection, or perhaps an allusion to a heavenly feast, which occurs "after expiation" (expiation being related to the Christ-the-Azazel-goat in Tertullian's scheme). Again, for Tertullian, the YHWH-goat anticipates Christ's second coming, and thus he is associated with majesty and glory. Speaking of the second coming earlier in the same passage, Tertullian says, "Then indeed He shall have both a glorious form, and an unsullied beauty above the sons of men."[65] Interestingly, *each* of the three commentators associates the YHWH-goat—more or less clearly—with the second coming of Christ in glory. In many recent Christian interpretations, it is claimed that the YHWH-goat undergoes punishment and wrath, and is thus effectively identical to the accursed Azazel-goat. The earliest post-biblical interpreters were probably still too close to the reality of the temple, and to living Jewish theology, to think that way. Instead, for them, the imagery they use for each goat could not be more dissimilar: when it comes to the YHWH-goat, the explicit emphasis in Tertullian (and the implicit emphasis in *Barnabas* and Justin) is on beauty, grace, glory, honor, majesty, and an "everlasting kingdom." The imagery used for the second goat, consistently, is the imagery of suffering, accursedness, and destruction.

64. This is Stökl's translation of Tertullian's *Contre Marcion* 3:7:7–8. See Stökl Ben Ezra, *Impact of Yom Kippur*, 157. For further analysis of this passage, see Stökl Ben Ezra, 156–58.

65. Tertullian, *Against Marcion*, Book 3, Chapter 7.

The advantage of these early interpretations of Christ's relation to Yom Kippur is that they specify the *difference* between the two "movements" which are together fulfilled by the *one* Christ. Christ fulfills the work of both goats, first in his passion, then in his return in glory. The biggest disadvantage, however, is that the powerful theological symbolism associated with the high priest—both the purification offering and the holy of holies—is disassociated from the self-offering of Christ on the cross and deferred to his glorious return. But as we have seen, the conviction that the self-giving of Jesus on the cross is the purification offering of the New Covenant is suggested by numerous biblical passages across the New Testament, and therefore it seems more appropriate to contemplate how, in the mystery of Christ's one crucifixion, the whole theological reality of Yom Kippur is recapitulated.

Stökl identifies a passage from Hippolytus of Rome's commentary on Proverbs which represents a different approach. The book of Proverbs (LXX) includes a list of things that "move easily," and the author mentions "the he-goat leading the herd."[66] Reflecting on this image, Hippolytus says:

> And a goat as leader of the flock
> Since, it says, this is
> who was slaughtered for the sins of the world
> and offered as a sacrifice
> and sent away to the Gentiles as in the desert
> and crowned with scarlet wool on the head by the unbelievers
> and made to be a ransom for the humans
> and manifested as life for all.[67]

In these lines, Hippolytus circles around the image of the ruling goat and finds it to be a multifaceted symbol. Without a doubt, many of these lines relate directly to Yom Kippur. On the first pass, Hippolytus sees the sacred offering, a victim who overcomes the sins of the cosmos (*kosmou*). On the second pass, Hippolytus sees the one sent into the desert, but in this interpretation, there seems to be a missionary impulse. It is the Gentiles who live in the wilderness, and thus Christ must go out to them, as if on a rescue mission. The theme of "rescue" continues on the third pass, when the goat is seen as a "ransom" (*lýtron*), a concept not intrinsically

---

66. Proverbs 30:31 (NETS).

67. Stokl's translation of Hippolytus' *Catenae on Proverbs*, where Hippolytus is commenting on Proverbs 30:31. For translation and commentary, see Stökl Ben Ezra, *Impact of Yom Kippur*, 158–59.

linked to Yom Kippur logic (as I argued in chapter six), but the ransom theme is nevertheless prominent in the New Testament (cf. Mark 10:45). Finally, in fulfilling the work of the two goats of the Day of Atonement, Hippolytus finds that Christ is manifested as "life for all." While in this passage the two goats serve as little more than a jumping-off point for various reflections—Hippolytus certainly is not attuned to Levitical nuance here—notably, he does not use the goats to distinguish a first and second coming, but apparently sees them both reflected in Christ's paschal work. Thus, Hippolytus overcomes one weakness found in earlier Christian reflection by failing to separate the goats according to a first and second advent.

With Origen of Alexandria, we reach the golden age of patristic biblical interpretation. Origen's two sermons on Yom Kippur (Homilies 9 and 10 in his collected *Homilies on Leviticus*) are the most expansive and multifaceted Christian reflections on Leviticus 16 to be found in the patristic period. Such a rich theological work merits a comprehensive analysis, but I will limit myself to a few highlights. The most significant shift that we see in Origen is the way he implicitly incorporates Enochic intuitions into his reflection. According to Stökl, "All of Origen's interpretations have in common that they are 'bipolar'—the scapegoat represents something bad, the sacrificial goat something good."[68] True, awareness of this difference has been evident in every text that we've investigated. But, remember, in the book of Enoch the distinction between the Azazel-goat and the YHWH-goat is, you could say, pushed to its most extreme eschatological limit. As we turn to Origen, we find that his interpretation is influenced by the absolutization of the temple/wilderness landscape which is already so evident in *1 Enoch* and the canonical Book of Revelation.[69] Origen pursues various "historical" and "mystical" interpretations of the priestly text—some more relevant to the work of Christ, some more relevant to the sanctification of the believer's soul—but each reading is undeniably bipolar, with one lot representing holiness and life, the other representing sin and death.

Origen opens his reflection with a brilliant observation: if there were no sin, there would be only one goat, not two. There would only be the "goat for the Lord," there would only be the pure and holy offering; sin-bearing would be unnecessary. This affirmation reinforces the notion that

68. Stökl, 266.

69. Especially in light of the evidence that the grand cartography of the *Book of the Watchers* was influenced by Leviticus 16, it is correlatively possible to trace "eschatological Yom Kippur" imagery in the twelfth chapter of the book of Revelation (cf. 12:9–12).

the orientation vis-à-vis God represented by the 'olah (and the ḥaṭṭā't) is an Edenic posture. It is the human being fully alive, and therefore it is not ultimately rooted in sin. It is clear that in saying this, Origen has no concept of the ḥaṭṭā't as vicarious punishment; the sacrifice is not a death that God demands because of sin. Like other early Christian theologians, Origen knows that such offerings are positive expressions of openhearted love, which is the truth of the world irrespective of sin.[70]

Language quickly shifts from this positive affirmation to something less congenial: the two lots now represent two groups of people. One lot is a heavenly people, the other lot is damned. Origen is abundantly clear about the hellish nature of the second goat's destination: "'the wilderness,' that is, a desolate place—desolate of virtues, desolate of God, desolate of justice, desolate of Christ, desolate of all good."[71] Drawing loosely on Yom Kippur concepts, Origen even says that the latter "lot," when hurled into the wilderness, "take upon their heads the sins of those who have repented. . . ."[72] On the other hand, those "whose 'lot' is 'the Lord'," die daily. Origen makes fascinating observations here. He explains that the sinner *does not* die because he or she "is of this world"—they "live" comfortably in *this* world, while the man or woman who belongs to God "dies" to this world so as to live truly. Although Origen does not make the connection directly, our earlier reflections on the Akedah and the paradox of *hinneni*-life once again comes to mind. Origen brilliantly shows how the imagery of the YHWH-goat is taken to exemplify a mode of being that is, indeed, truly free.

While these reflections are interesting, and while they give insight into the relationship between Yom Kippur and early reflections on heaven and hell, they do not directly address the question of Jesus' own relation to the two goats. Indeed, it must be said that Origen puts less emphasis on this particular issue, and instead associates Jesus with the corresponding humans of Leviticus 16: the high priest on one side, the "prepared man" who led the Azazel-goat to the wilderness on the other.[73] Regarding

70. Origen, *Homilies on Leviticus, 1-16* (Washington, D.C.: The Catholic University of America Press, 2005), 9.3.2, pg. 181.

71. Origen, 9.4.1, pg. 182.

72. Origen, 9.3.3, pg. 181.

73. However, Orlov has recently emphasized the important point that the ritual actors and their corresponding goats were seen as intimately associated. He explains that it is necessary to acknowledge "the intertwining roles of the one who makes the sacrifice and the sacrifice itself—that is, the high priest and the immolated goat." Orlov, *The Atoning Dyad*, 71. On this principle, perhaps there is a similar intertwining between the "ready man" and the Azazel-goat itself.

the YHWH-goat, Origen applies Levitical sacrificial imagery to Jesus in a few places. First, early in the sermon, Origen embraces the interpretation of the Letter to the Hebrews, underlining the singularity of Christ's offering: "For *he did this once* when he offered himself as an offering."[74] Origen also seems to identify Jesus as the paradigmatic recipient of the first lot when he says: "this one indeed, upon whom 'the lot of the Lord' falls, is killed and dies, that by his blood he may purify the people of God."[75] It is remarkable to note that Origen, in full agreement with priestly theology, continues to accentuate the fact that blood is the means of cultic purification. Jesus is the Levitical high priest who enters the holy of holies of heaven with his own blood as the *"hilasmos"* (the atonement) for our sins.[76] The positive connection between Jesus and the YHWH-goat/high priest is, therefore, clearly articulated.

Origen is a little less clear on the relation between Christ and the goat which is sent away, but what he does say is fascinating. In one section of his homily, Origen compares the two goats to the two thieves who flank Jesus on Golgotha. The one who "reviled" Jesus, he notes, was sent to the "'wilderness' of hell."[77] The Alexandrian exegete then loosely quotes Colossians 2:14–15—in his paraphrase, Christ "fastened the principalities and opposing powers upon his cross and he triumphed over them"—and interprets it by saying, "in this he fulfilled 'the lot of the scapegoat' and as 'a prepared man' he led them 'into the wilderness.'" Along similar lines, Origen adds:

> [Christ] would make 'the lot of the scapegoat' the opposing powers, 'the spirits of evil and the rulers of this world of darkness' [cf. Eph. 6:12] which, as the Apostle says, 'he led away with power triumphing over them in himself' [cf. Col. 2:15]. 'He led them away.' Where 'did he lead' them except 'to the wilderness,' to desolate places?[78]

74. Origen, *Homilies on Leviticus, 1-16*, 9.2.1, pg. 178, emphasis added. Cf. Hebrews 7:27b.

75. Origen, 9.3.4, pg. 182.

76. Origen, 9.5.8, pg. 187; cf. 9.10.1, pg. 199. In speaking of Christ as *hilasmos*, Origen is quoting 1 John 2:1. Rufinus' Latin translation of Origin's Greek uses "repropitiatio" to render 1 John 2:1, which in English becomes "propitiation"—at which point the English passage has become rather remote from the priestly theology of purification. For a description of how the Greek *hilasmos* is likely linked with the Hebrew *kipper*, see Lyonnet and Sabourin, *Sin, Redemption, and Sacrifice*, 148ff; cf. Stökl Ben Ezra, *Impact of Yom Kippur*, 205–7.

77. Origen, *Homilies on Leviticus, 1-16*, 9.5.2, pg. 184.

78. Origen, 9.5.2, pg. 184.

In this interpretation, Jesus is very clearly the designated man who is charged with the responsibility of leading the Azazel-goat to the wilderness (and in a later tradition, ultimately pushing the goat into the abyss). It seems that Origen here also depicts the Azazel-goat as the demons themselves—the powers, principalities, and "rulers of this world"—which Jesus both fastens to the cross and overcomes *in himself*. Even though this victory occurs in Christ on the cross, Origen is quick to add that Christ indeed leads the evil powers into the barren wilderness, and in fact, he emphasizes that just as Christ the high priest alone can turn back the flaming swords and bring the repentant thief to paradise, so also Christ alone can lead away the evil spirits to the furthest wilderness.

With this established, Origen continues to surprise. He says: "Therefore, for that reason, it was necessary for my Lord and Savior not only to be born a man among men but also to descend to Hell that as 'a prepared man' he could lead away 'the lot of the scapegoat into the wilderness' of Hell."[79] Here, for the first time, the concept of Christ's descent to hell is associated specifically with Yom Kippur soteriology, and yet more specifically with the crucial movement of the Azazel-goat who bears away sins. It is not that this concept was *entirely* absent from the foregoing tradition, but Origen—who's landscape is bipolar in a way analogous to *Enoch*—stretches the argument to its extreme, including even a descent to Hell that is not exclusively a triumphant harrowing. The most striking difference in Origen, compared to his predecessors, however, is that he seems hesitant in comparing the work of Jesus to the Azazel-goat *itself*, instead comparing Christ to the goat's guide. The reason for this hesitance may be the fact that, as I just noted, Origen associates the second goat with demonic spirits; this goat is no longer a lowly vehicle carrying away the wreckage of sin, but it has instead become synonymous with fallen angels. Perhaps as the Jerusalem temple became a less vivid memory, and as the Church became less attuned to the nuances of Jewish priestly theology, the idea of sin as a vital, substantial, but non-demonic "miasma" that pollutes the sanctuary also became less comprehensible. The concept of sin-bearing was less easily understood, and so the Azazel-goat came to represent actual demons instead.[80] When this happens, a very clear distinction needs to be made between the all-holy Christ and

79. Origen, 9.5.4, pg. 185.

80. Then again, I have also argued that, already in *1 Enoch*, the priestly concept of "substantial" sin becomes once again "demonized" through Enoch's grand mythopoetic imagery. Therefore, perhaps the precedent is more properly to be found in that profoundly Jewish work.

the second goat, and thus the prepared man takes on new importance. Unfortunately, however, this move has the effect of separating the work of the Christian savior from an essential element of Yom Kippur soteriology: personally enduring the weight of sin, and personally experiencing the exile of Israel, for the salvation of the world. When only the YHWH-goat is emphasized, the danger would indeed be a "theology of glory" which overlooks the sheer horror of Christ's cruciform exile.

Nevertheless, by the time of Origen in the third century, there are abundant theological resources available for the development of a rich and profound Christian Yom Kippur soteriology. Of course, with the defeat of Marcionite anti-Judaism, all of the resources of the Hebrew Bible remained available to the early church to better understand the prototypical liturgical means by which YHWH sought to purify the world and draw humanity back into perfect communion so that men and women might again walk peacefully with God in the cool of the day. On this subject specifically, the deep symbolism and theo-logic of the priestly liturgies and rituals remained a remarkable resource for the early Christians as they meditated on the mystery of salvation. The early Christians also took advantage of the endlessly fascinating "inter-testimonial" pseudepigraphal literature—such as the adventures of Enoch—which itself represents an extraordinary commentary on and development of the great biblical mysteries.

But then there are the diverse, non-systematic meditations of the New Testament evangelists and letter writers, whose inspired pens became gushing fountains of theological insight. Hopkins famously said that "Christ plays in ten thousand places," and for the New Testament writers, this is nowhere more true than on the pages of their ancient Jewish Scriptures. Indeed, they could not help but find the playful traces of their Messiah between every line as they pondered the Torah in resurrection light. Therefore, we find in the New Testament a cascade of insights as the excited authors caught glimpses of Jesus—first here, then there—never pausing for long enough to fully unpack any particular symbol or type. This great flood of charismatic insight resulted in vast, fertile fields—sort of like a new Eden which invites all future generations to "till and keep."

That's precisely the task that the earliest generations took up with joy as they continued to draw connections and seek the deeper theo-logic order in this beautiful diversity of images. Still so close to the Jewish roots of Christian theology, these early interpreters immediately saw the crucial importance of Yom Kippur in any interpretation of Christ's "atoning" work on the cross. They pursued interpretations that both remained faithful to Jewish traditions while illuminating the meaning of Jesus's saving action. As a result of their "tilling and keeping," they provided future generations with many brilliant and creative insights. In the rough draft sketches of *Barnabas*, Justin, Tertullian, Hippolytus, and Origen, one finds a soteriology of immense potential, ripe for continued development. However, as Jews and Christians drifted and divided from one another, as the beautiful temple and its profound liturgies fell out of the Church's memory, Christian Yom Kippur soteriology seemed to go dormant as theologians continued to reflect on the work of Christ.[81] For hundreds of years, there was enthusiastic debate around words like ransom, satisfaction, exemplar, substitution, propitiation, expiation, sacrament, even "scapegoat" . . . but the temple logic of the two goats seemed forgotten.

The question for today is, in this period of amiable dialogue between Jews and Christians, in this springtime of nuanced and sympathetic interpretations of ancient Jewish priestly theology, at a time when the insightful "theological interpretations" of early Christians are again winning respect and appreciation, is it possible to take up once more this dormant theological tradition? Is it possible to return to the most ancient sources to again discover the original contours of the glorious word "atonement"? Is it even possible for modern systematic theologians to learn to appreciate the fathomless secrets which have been faithfully kept for millennia by our two humble goats?

81. Of course, given the prominence of Leviticus 16 in the Pentateuch, discussion of Yom Kippur never entirely disappeared. Consider, for example, how interpretations of Yom Kippur factored into the debate between Julian the Apostate (d. 363) and St. Cyril of Alexandria (d. 444). Notably, Cyril continues the tradition of arguing that Jesus, in his death and return, fulfills the work of both goats, though Cyril's interpretation is also strikingly different from his predecessors. For Cyril, the YHWH-goat represents Jesus' kenotic death, and the second goat represents his resurrection, insofar as the second goat is "Sent Away" from death. This surprising association between the second goat and resurrection is based on the LXX translation of "goat for Azazel," which is *apopompaios*, "sent out." See Brad Boswell, "Goats, Gods, and the Mystery of Christ: Exegesis and Narrative Conflict between Julian and Cyril," *Studia Patristica* 129 (2021): 51–69. Cyril's reading still strives to interpret both goats in light of Jesus's one saving work, but when compared to the earlier fathers, his interpretation seems less informed by the distinctive theo-logic of the ancient Jewish liturgy. This fact tends to support the larger point that I am making here: over time, the early potential for a Christian Yom Kippur soteriology, animated by the mature priestly theology of temple and sacrifice, seems to have gone unfulfilled.

PART III

Two Goats, One Savior: A (Modern) Yom Kippur Soteriology

Christian Yom Kippur Soteriology: A Systematic Outline

Two goats: identical, beautiful, perfect. It seems idiosyncratic, or even idiotic, to think that an iron-age ritual could be the hidden map we need to navigate contemporary Christian soteriology. It is even more incredible to assert that these two beasts, who briefly appear in Leviticus, keep between themselves the deepest mysteries of the cosmos. Of course, for Christian theology, it is the Word made flesh who is the mystery of mysteries, the One who embodies the mystery hidden in God from the beginning. But his is a Jewish body, his is Jewish blood, his is a mission which is inseparable from Israel's covenantal romance, and so one cannot entirely understand the atonement he accomplishes apart from the double movement of Yom Kippur. Here in Leviticus, we encounter the most holy hooves that trod a double path—in the temple and in the desert—which will become the good and sorrowful way that the Messiah himself will carefully follow in the fullness of time. *Via Dolorosa*. To know where he is going, to theologically trace his atoning steps, it was necessary that we should see how that very trail was forged over the centuries on the holiest of all holy days. That has been the work of this book until now.

This section will articulate in outline a systematic theology that contemplates how Jesus Christ could fulfill the work of both goats in a single movement of self-giving love. A major thesis here is that the Christian tradition provides the raw materials for a highly nuanced theology of Christ as the goat for the LORD and also a separate highly nuanced theology of Christ as the goat for Azazel. Each of these theological approaches is profound and illuminating, and each is weakened only by its separation from the other. The first goal in a Christian Yom Kippur soteriology, therefore, is to collect the raw materials needed to interpret fully each goat in a Christian context. Thus, in chapters nine and ten, we will explore contemporary theologies of the YHWH-goat and the Azazel-goat in turn. In these two chapters, we will look at two theologies of the cross that are exceptionally profound and challenging, each advanced by a modern theological master. The first is the soteriology of David Bentley

Hart, the second is the soteriology of Hans Urs von Balthasar. Using the framework spelled out in the previous chapters, I will argue that each man's contributions are wholly biblical and profoundly orthodox, and yet incomplete precisely because each develops the theological meaning of one "goat" without fully reflecting on the equally necessary work of the second.[1] After looking at these soteriologies in chapters nine and ten, we'll turn to the second goal, which is the more difficult task: to imagine how the two distinct movements find their fulfillment in a single work, which is to say, to answer the question: how can Christ enter both the holy of holies and the distant wilderness simultaneously? In chapter eleven, therefore, I argue that to see both-movements-in-one requires the type of imaginative and paradoxical thinking that is always the hallmark of robust Christian orthodoxy.

A greater appreciation of the cross as an icon of life—as a *tree of life*—will be the final destination on this journey. It is precisely for this tree that we are made, and now as flaming swords return to their sheaths, now as our eyes become more capable of the Glory who sits amidst the cherubim, we will fix our sight once more on the first mystery, and the last.

---

1. This is especially true for Hart with respect to the Azazel-goat. When it comes to Balthasar, it is true that the themes associated with both goats can be found in his work, but sometimes his soteriology is (I will argue) imbalanced such that the presence of the YHWH-goat is obscured.

CHAPTER 9

The Goat for the Lord in Contemporary Theology: David Bentley Hart

As we saw in part two of this book, the major characteristic of the "goat for the LORD" was that it symbolized life, and thus it is associated with the temple itself and its most holy center, which represents life as it was intended from the beginning. Precisely as the great symbol of "life," this goat is also associated with the ancient Jewish theology of sacrifice; despite the common misunderstanding that imagines sacrifice as being in allegiance with death, Israel's priestly offerings sought to re-establish order and harmony by returning again and again to the wholehearted *hinneni*-way-of-life, embodied most fully by Abraham and Isaac on Mount Moriah. Therefore, a soteriology that is rooted in the symbolic universe of the YHWH-goat will have a fundamentally positive orientation: it will interpret Christ's work as drawing together, restoring, and elevating all things through a genuinely good and meritorious movement, a movement that reiterates and perfects life as it was intended at its origin.

I am not aware of any modern theologian who has captured the essence of this positive Levitical vision more perceptively or eloquently than David Bentley Hart, above all in his magisterial *The Beauty of the Infinite*.[1] Hart directly discusses the theological meaning of Christ's cru-

---

1. Note that I am arguing that Hart's theology especially captures the themes correlated with the goat for the LORD, as identified in the previous chapters, and in that way his approach to the cross can be associated with a "YHWH-goat soteriology" (though, see also my clarification in the introduction; page 10, note 18). Indeed, Hart is explicitly attentive to the shape of Israel's theology of sacrifice (see *Beauty of the Infinite*, 350–54), and he has developed his soteriology specifically with the priestly theology of sacrifice in mind. Succinctly but with great nuance, as we will see, he shows how the theology of "gift" is at the heart of Israel's most mature cultic practices. That said, I am not aware of a place where he speaks explicitly about Yom Kippur or the YHWH-goat. Despite this fact, it is easy to find parallels to and echoes of temple theology and YHWH-goat soteriology throughout Hart's work; I will be highlighting these to argue that he implicitly yet powerfully develops the theological themes associated with this "goat" for contemporary theology.

cifixion in a section entitled "The Economy of Violence"; while this section is relatively short (only fourteen pages), it is particularly dense insofar as Hart here brings together and integrates many of the central themes of his book: the competing narratives of the two "cities" (one of violence and one of peace), the harmonious nature of distance within the Trinity, the importance of the doctrine of divine *apatheia*, the nature of gift, an anthropological vision rooted in *epektasis* and deification, the problem of sin and evil, and the defense of *analogia entis* as the authentic Christian metaphysic. In other words, to fully appreciate what Hart is doing in his climatic section on the cross, one must take into consideration his entire project in that book—which resists summary. The best we can do, therefore, is to highlight areas where there is continuity between Hart's Christian soteriology and the mature Jewish theology we have been exploring in this book. Happily, it is not difficult to identify points of agreement.

The Two Cities

Hart follows John Milbank in identifying an underlying "ontology of violence" in postmodern philosophy, which emerges from the belief that ontological difference always suggests foundational violence, and in fact, that our world of difference inevitably finds itself ensnared in an endless melee of clashing forces. Hart says that this postmodern ontology is "nothing other than a version of an ancient pagan narrative of being as sheer brute event, a chaos of countervailing violences, against which must be deployed the various restraining and prudential violences of the state, reason, law, warfare, retribution, civic order, and the vigilantly sentineled polis."[2] Following Nietzsche, modern philosophy's subliminal conviction is that the forces of Dionysus and Apollo—the god of wine with his "indiscriminate violences" and the god of music and poetry with his "precisely discriminating violences"—must be balanced. Therefore, from the perspective of the postmodern ontology of violence—which once again calls to mind a pagan worldview, like the one depicted in the *Enuma Elish* narrative that we described in an earlier chapter, albeit now recapitulated in a post-Christian variation[3]—if there is to be any kind of peace, it can exist only though suppression of the antecedent and more

2. Hart, 36.

3. For Hart, it is not possible to simply revive pagan metaphysics after the Christ event; in some definitive way, Christ has abolished the gods. See "Christ and Nothing (No Other God)" in David Bentley Hart, *In the Aftermath: Provocations and Laments* (Grand Rapids, MI: Eerdmans, 2008), 1–19.

basic chaos: "all peace, civility, harmony, or beauty is accomplished by limiting a preexisting discord."[4]

To understand Hart's soteriology, it is necessary to consider his use of the terms "totality" and "infinity,"[5] terms which are very much related to the ontology of violence and the ontology of peace:

> By "totality" I mean the attempt to grasp the being of beings as a whole, immanent to and sufficient for itself, and to grasp all things and values—epistemic, moral, aesthetic—within the confines of this immanentism; and by "infinity" I mean what one desires when one seeks to see the totality as the gift of a true transcendence, granting the totality its essences, its existence, its values, and its transcendental properties from beyond itself, by the grace of participation and under the "rule" of analogy.[6]

The totalizing disposition, then, sees the world in terms of a closed circle: it is the world described by univocal ontology, where "being" is an umbrella category that contains all things, including any possible god. Within the circle of "metaphysical totality" we are viciously torn between two poles: "the savage equivalence of univocity and equivocity, Apollo and Dionysus, pure identity and pure difference."[7] Such a world is a perpetual power struggle, with shifting hierarchies of suppression, with the violence of shattering anarchy and the violence of imposed order, with the hot blood of revolution and the cold tears of oppression. It is a constant effort at properly balancing brutal forces. *Conversely*, an ontology of infinity envisions the world as fundamentally open and peacefully suspended, obtaining itself from that which is beyond itself—ultimately, through participation in God.

What we have here, then, is a distinction between a non-analogical "totality"—which tends toward either purely "immanent" eruptions of violence as *being* forever jostles against *being* in a perpetual power strug-

---

4. Hart, *Beauty of the Infinite*, 40.

5. Hart here indicates that he is subversively borrowing the totality/infinity distinction from Emmanuel Levinas, but using them in a way that corresponds with Milbank's observations about the two totalities.

6. Hart, *Beauty of the Infinite*, 14.

7. Hart, 242. This calls to mind the contrast Przywara draws between Heraclitus and Parmenides. Przywara, *Analogia Entis*, 203–7. Even before Hart, along with John Betz, translated Erich Przywara's *Analogia Entis* into English, Hart popularized Przywara's ideas in *Beauty of the Infinite*, enhancing them through a deeper engagement with the (especially Eastern) church fathers, and bringing them into critical conversation with postmodern philosophy.

gle or it tends toward an equally terrifying "transcendent" that violently absorbs all difference into "One"—or you have the Christian alternative, a Trinitarian analogical "infinite" which is the fullness of being and the fullness of peace, where difference is not the enemy of perfect oneness. For the latter, the "beings" of creation are from nothing (affirmation of *creatio ex nihilo* is essential)—they have no ground in themselves, no independent foundation—and each can be understood only in terms of its true participation in the Trinity, but always within the "ever greater dissimilitude" between (Triune) Being and beings. This analogical interval, Hart argues, is the necessary condition for integral peace, deep communion, and perfect intimacy between God and creation.

Throughout his book, therefore, Hart identifies two competing narratives: "one that finds the grammar of violence inscribed upon the foundation stone of every institution and hidden within the syntax of every rhetoric, and another that claims that within history a way of reconciliation has been opened up that leads beyond, and ultimately overcomes, all violence."[8] It is right to say that this affirmation is the precious inheritance of Christian Trinitarian and incarnational theology and that the hope of overcoming all violence depends on that distinctive theological foundation. In the present book, I have also argued that such hope has substantive antecedents in the Hebrew Bible, and most profoundly in temple theology. Through a complex historical process, a single site became (a) the locus of God's presence in creation, with divinity intimately dwelling at the heart of the microcosm, and (b) the mere shadow of a yet greater perfection. In this way, the temple itself becomes an implicit symbol of creation as a "suspended middle"—wholly dependent on the "always greater" Glory in which it participates while making that Glory uniquely present in this most-central liturgical site. Within second temple Jewish thought, it is right to say that "a way of reconciliation has been opened up" which overcomes "all violence," and this way is the way of the YHWH-goat, who re-establishes the original pattern of creation as doxological praise, as genuine self-giving freedom before God, all of which affirms the temple's unique ontology as a "suspended middle." On Yom Kippur, the very presence of true life (symbolized by the lifeblood) releases or eradicates the miasma of death that had sought to suffocate the temple itself. This "life" conquers death by virtue of its own superabundant vitality; death is unable to comprehend it, unable to mount any response at all. The YHWH-goat is the pure reaffirmation of what is most

---

8. Hart, *Beauty of the Infinite*, 2.

ultimate and true, an Edenic work that is victorious by virtue of its own divine vitality.

The Temple and Jesus

With this in mind, it is possible to look at Hart's soteriology and see how effectively he applies temple themes in his Christology and his exegesis of Christ's saving work. In our analysis of the temple, it was possible to distinguish three strands in contemporary research: the temple as the site of God's glory (God's perfect beauty), the temple as the model of right action (where "the good" is seen), and the temple as the symbol through which Israel meditates on the relationship between heaven and earth (or, in other words, the problem of how God's truth and creaturely truth interrelate). Hart's brief Christological treatise covers this same territory, but now centered on the mystery of Christ himself. Hart fills pages with virtual hymnody—at once profound and wonder-full—in praise of Jesus, who is the coincidence of heavenly and earthly perfection. For Hart, Christ is "at once the true form of God and the true shape of humanity. . . ."[9] As true God, he is also the embodied realization of the transcendentals. Thus, the Son is "the infinite beauty of God's eternal utterance,"[10] and in his incarnation, he is "divine beauty that becomes visible again,"[11] and "the measure of all beauty, who restores beauty to what has become formless through sin and death..."[12] In a great crescendo worthy of a full gospel choir, Hart sings of Christ who is "the beauty of the infinite, the shape of God's desire and object of his love, the splendor of his glory."[13]

In addition to his aesthetic brilliance, Hart also affirms Christ as the personification of right action. Jesus is himself "God's supreme rhetoric," who at once "embodies a real and imitable practice, a style of being that conforms to the beauty of divine love, but that is also a way of worldly godliness. . . ."[14] Focusing especially on this "style of being" which encapsulates the creaturely ideal, Hart accentuates what is perhaps the most ancient Christian soteriological model of all: recapitulation (*anakephalaiōsis*). Echoing Paul, Irenaeus, and Athanasius, he affirms that "Christ's life effects a narrative reversal, which unwinds the story of sin and death

9. Hart, 336.
10. Hart, 334.
11. Hart, 338.
12. Hart, 320.
13. Hart, 344.
14. Hart, 320.

and reinaugurates the story that God tells from before the foundation of the world. . . ."[15] In doing so, Jesus at once "reestablish[es] the original pattern after which the human form was crafted"[16] and shows forth God's own "goodness, love, and holiness"[17] in its eternal perfection. For Hart, the absolutely unique form of Christ—the very Word of God, the rhetoric of God in incarnate act—is "repeated endlessly, in the circle of the church, in boundless variety. . . ."[18] To know "the Good" in Christian reflection is not primarily to study tablets of law, it is not a particular approach to ethics, but it is a way of being and seeing shaped by the unique drama of the savior's life, death, and resurrection.

Finally, with equal emphasis, Christ is put forward as the fullness of truth. He is the *Logos* made flesh, which contains every *logoi*, which heals and elevates the innumerable words of the book of creation, "and so restores to the world its truth."[19] This one person is the embodiment of Being-itself and of creaturely being: "the Son is himself, in a sense, the ontological analogy between God and creation. . . ."[20] When the world has fallen into every error and helpless bondage, the Word himself, through the drama of his own life, becomes "the true story of the world,"[21] and at the same time, he makes present Truth eternal. Hart does not shoehorn Greek philosophical categories into his reflection on the Jewish Messiah in any of these three areas. Very much to the contrary, he is taking what is most undeniably central to the cultic life of the Jewish people and applying these Jewish reflections to the Messiah himself.

The Purification Offering and Jesus

Hart adopts the full vocabulary that is proper to Zion—glory, beauty, holiness, perfection, truth, peace, joy, harmony—and he applies this great litany of praises to the Word-made-flesh. Now we must remember that, from the perspective of priestly theology itself, it is none other than the YHWH-goat who, on Israel's holiest day, theologically makes present all the perfections of the cosmos, of Israel, and of Zion. In ancient Jewish theology, as I have interpreted it, the offering of this goat was a recapitulation of the orientation that characterized Israel's life at its sacred

15. Hart, 325.
16. Hart, 325.
17. Hart, 358.
18. Hart, 339.
19. Hart, 329.
20. Hart, 325.
21. Hart, 327.

beginning. On this point especially, Hart shows he deeply understands the logic of the YHWH-goat. He points out (against a possible danger in Girard) that Christian approaches to soteriology must avoid turning to a "Marcionite savior"[22] who is divorced from the way of atonement so elaborately developed in the Hebrew Bible. From Hart's perspective, though, there would be a real concern if the Jewish sacrificial rites were—like pagan political sacrifices—imagined as acts of violence to secure order within the "totality." As Hart says, the pagan or secular "regime" "belongs principally to a sacral order that seeks to contain nature's violence within the stabilizing forms of a more orderly kind of violence. . . . [A]ll secular order as such subsists upon sacrifice, upon the calculus of an economy of violence. . . ."[23] This is the world of Romulus and Remus, of the one brother who slays the other brother for failing to observe the boundary. Sometimes the good of life must be sacrificed to the higher good of extracting order out of chaos.[24] *If* Israel shares this pagan vision of the need to impose a favorable balance within the totality by force, then she is as indebted to the economy of violence as any pagan state.

According to Hart, when Israel is most faithful to its original logic, its sacrificial practices are motivated by a very different ideal, one that follows the logic, not of the totality, but of the "infinite." Thus, Hart offers his read on Genesis 22:

> . . . Israel, for all the multiplicity of its cultus, "fails" to imagine an economy of sacrifice that neatly closes off the cosmos in a cycle of strict equivalence and indemnity. . . . This is evident from the beginning of Israel's story, in the binding of Isaac: a sacrifice, that is, that does not effect a limited transaction with the sublime, in the interest of founding or preserving a city, but that happens apart from and before every city; the offering of Isaac can serve no economy, because all of Israel slumbers in his loins, because he is the child of Sarah's dotage who cannot be replaced, because he is the whole promise and substance of God's covenant; he is manifestly, in his particularity, infinitely other. He is the entire gift, returned before the gift has been truly given; but then God, who is not a God of the indeterminate sublime, feeding upon the destruction of the beautiful, but a God of determinate beauty and love, gives the gift again. . . . Henceforth Israel is doubly given, and can know itself only as gift, imparted by God and offered ceaselessly back to God, in the infinity of love's exchange.[25]

22. Hart, 349.
23. Hart, 346.
24. Hart, 353.
25. Hart, 351–52. We alluded to this quote a few times in chapter two.

With this, Hart is able to perceive in Israel's gifts a movement that fundamentally contradicts the totalizing aspirations of "the world," and which opens a new way of true liberation through non-grasping freedom, openness, and love before the God who created from nothing. In the second chapter of the present book, Hart's brief interpretation of the *Akedah* was confirmed and strengthened through a close reading of the Genesis text itself, with support from contemporary biblical scholarship. Therefore, there is good reason to suppose that Hart's interpretation of the key "act" of Israel is aligned with the intentions of the ancient Jewish priestly authors themselves.

Crucially, the mode of being introduced in the dramatic action of Abraham and Isaac, which is (I have argued) the mode of being re-presented in the Jerusalem cult, is perfected in Christ's own incarnate life. According to Hart, the integrity of the Son's radical self-giving freedom before God was an existential threat to "the totality," which is promoted by the prince of this world. Therefore, just as Babylon once moved to swallow Judah, "the totality" mobilized against the one called the Christ to enclose him within the normal economy of violence, to secure the peace of the state through his death. When the structures of violence mount their attack, the shape of the attack is cruciform: "The cross itself, of course, is of pagan origin, and so the crucifixion in itself expresses perfectly the sacrificial logic of the secular order. . . ."[26] For Hart, the intersecting branches of the cross might be seen as the intersection of the two orders of sacrifice: "From a pagan perspective the cross is a sacrifice in the 'proper' sense: destruction of the agent of social instability in the interest of social order. . . ."[27] But, even as the powers and principalities surround him to close off his open-hearted communion with God, Christ lives more and more fully according to Israel's sacrificial ideals, which is to say, Christ continues to lift up his heart to the Father in the style of the burnt offering/purification offering. He continues to live in the way appropriate to one who dwells in God's presence in the temple. He continues in all things to "choose life" over any alliance with the forces of death and violence. For those who crucified him, Christ's death is a typical political sacrifice, but Jesus himself takes what the world had intended for evil and destroys it by reaffirming the ultimate Good proper to his own divine nature, which is indeed the sacrificial movement of love within which and for which the world itself was created—it is the very sacrificial movement that Israel ritually practiced, morning and night, on Mount Zion. The deformed sacrificial prac-

26. Hart, 351.
27. Hart, 353.

tices of the "totality" confront the true "sacrificial" orientation of the persons of the triune God, and as when darkness encounters light, the former cannot comprehend the latter. The morning glow of Easter Sunday is the great confirmation of what has always been true, the good news known since Moriah: Israel's God is the God of life and not death, and thus to enter the divine movement of mutual self-giving is to find the abundant life which is the heart's original, Edenic bliss.

Clearly, for Hart, to embrace the sacrificial mode of being is to discover the way of deification, because "sacrifice" rightly and analogically understood is proper to divine life. "For Christian thought the true order of sacrifice is that which corresponds to the motion of the divine *perichoresis*, the Father's giving of the Son, the Son's execution of all the Father is and wills, the Spirit's eternal offering back of the gift in endless variety, each person receiving from and giving to each other in infinite love."[28] Such an awareness of God's inner life is the fruit of intimacy with the incarnate (pierced) heart of God, and thus it is a revelation that goes further than the earlier Jewish covenants. But even here, looking at the Old Testament with Christian eyes, one finds this indiscernible mystery hidden in plain sight. Remember: it is God himself who renames the mountain of Abraham's offering YHWH-*yireh*, which can be translated as "the LORD is seen." As I suggested at the end of chapter two, in the mutual self-giving trust of Abraham, Isaac, and YHWH, an early icon of God's own inner life is written, one which is perpetually re-dramatized and reinforced by the sacred liturgy of Zion. That God should be known as kenotic love is truly a "new" revelation of Jesus Christ, but it is a newness of a very particular sort, like that moment when one suddenly knows their life's purpose. The discovery may come as a shock, and yet it hits with strange familiarity. When the truth is known for the first time, it is simultaneously clear that it had been known all along. This is the nature of analogical theology, where the Truth is known in-and-beyond history such that, when Truth and history converge in a single person, it clarifies what has nevertheless been known dimly at every other point, and especially what had been known uniquely and superlatively in symbol and truth by the chosen people through the great covenants.

The Futility of Sin

Hart's account powerfully accentuates the idea that Jesus lives life to the fullest, as it had been intended from the start, despite the surrounding

28. Hart, 353.

chaos of ugliness, evil, and deceit. Evil cannot sway him. Christ cuts through the fray and shows that a different way is both possible, and in him, made present. For Hart, sin is a discordant note, a sun-starved shadowland, a habituated amnesia, and above all, a violence that distorts all that is well-formed by the good and loving Creator.[29] Hart's analogies always reflect his unwavering commitment to the revered philosophical affirmation that sin is a privation of being, and this philosophical truth is itself a corollary of Hart's twin emphasis on creation *ex nihilo* and the *analogia entis*. When speaking about God as creator, Hart says:

> But nothingness does not challenge God, it is not some "thing" with which God becomes creatively involved; he passes nothingness by without regard, it is literally nothing to him, it has no part to play in the way by which he is God or in his desire to create. Nothing is what is overcome, indeed, but this is to say that there is no original overcoming. . . . God's triumph is always already complete; it lies in his being the God he is in eternity, always infinitely "going forth" from and "possessing" himself.[30]

Applying this insight to engagement with "evil," which is "that purely privative nothingness that lies outside creations' motion toward God,"[31]

29. In his own words,

Sin, violence, cruelty, egoism, and despair are the discords that disrupt the surface, but always as privation, a failure of love; they are no part of being's deep music, but only shrill alarms and barren phrasings, apostasies from music altogether. Evil, for all its ineradicable ubiquity, is always originally an absence, a shadow, a false reply, and all violence falls within the interval of a harmony not taken up, within which the true form of being is forgotten, misconstrued, distorted, and belied. (Hart, 208)

30. Hart, 259. In the original context, Hart is responding to Eberhard Jüngel's theology of creation. I would argue that this passage also helps us understand, *mutatis mutandis*, the nature of Christ's engagement (or lack of engagement) with sin, in Hart's soteriology, as Christ brings the new creation to birth on the cross. On the same page, Hart shifts to a reflection on the (so to speak) superficiality of evil, and this supports the application of this quote to a soteriological context: "The expressive beauty of creation conceals no chaotic depth, but only embraces, intensities and complications of surface; and even the most tragic of circumstances points to no deep and abiding truth, but only to disorders and derangements of the surface, wounds to be healed. There is no chaos, but only a will toward chaos, and the violence it inflicts upon being" (Hart, 259).

31. Hart, 194. For a longer defense of the tradition of defining evil as *privatio boni*, which Hart says is "high among Christian tradition's most venerable and most indispensable metaphysical commitments," see David Bentley Hart, *The Doors of the Sea: Where Was God in the Tsunami?* (Grand Rapids, MI: Eerdmans, 2005), 73–78. In this section, Hart effectively links the concept of evil as privation of the good to the doctrine of divine

it is indeed sensible to say that one does not confront the problem "head on" by screaming at the off note or stomping on the shadow, but rather one simply lives harmoniously again, one embraces the light again, despite every barrier created by our current age. It is clear that Hart's approach has an impeccable biblical pedigree: "The Light shines in the darkness, and the darkness did not comprehend it" (John 1:5, NASB).

That verse really is the key to Hart's soteriology. It is an approach where Christ recapitulates the original intention for creation, but very much unlike Adam, he lives out his vocation of perfect, heart-to-heart communion with the Father to the end. His suspension on the cross is his ascension to the holy of holies, where perfect obedience and love are made complete, where the intimacy between Father and Son is consummated. For Hart, reprising Irenaeus, that simply is the essence of Christ's saving work:

> First and foremost, Christ recapitulates humanity's struggle against evil, and in so doing achieves the victory that humanity could not...; he who is from the beginning the head of all things recapitulates the human entirely, in the shape and substance of a whole life lived for the Father, never lapsing into sin, never yielding to the temptation to turn from God, enacting in every instant the divine figure of the human. . . . Thus, as Paul says, the disobedience of Adam, which brings death into the world, is undone by Christ's obedience unto death. . . .[32]

This vision of realized perfection, amid the forces of sin and death which circle like vultures, is exactly the idea behind the priestly goat for YHWH, which recapitulates Israel's icon of restored Edenic life, and overcomes the pollutants of uncleanness, sin, and death with purifying blood. Importantly, for the theology of the YHWH-goat—as articulated in Leviticus, in later rabbinic tradition, and by modern Jewish commentators—there is no great war between life and death in the holy of holies; life conquers death by virtue of its own infinitely superior dynamism, its perfect compatibility with the God of Life who makes Zion his throne. The high priest may be a type of divine warrior, but the imagery of the feast does

---

apatheia; defending the importance of the latter against the hazy and sentimental protests made by modern theologians is a primary objective in many of Hart's works. The emphasis on sin as a privation of the good is found throughout Hart's works; most recently, he reiterates the point in *That All Shall Be Saved: Heaven, Hell, and Universal Salvation* (New Haven, CT: Yale University Press, 2021), 70–71, 165, 175, 190–91.

32. Hart, *Beauty of the Infinite*, 326.

not suggest a head-to-head battle against a chaos-monster or some living demonic force. Violence is not overcome by violence, as Hart so often insists in unison with the church fathers. If anything, the priest's battle is within himself, to faithfully live out the call to remain pure,[33] to stay awake,[34] to not succumb to fear,[35] and to be the very embodiment of the words he bears on his brow: "Holy unto YHWH."[36]

In the sprinkling of his own blood, as he ascends to the holy of holies of his own pierced heart, Christ achieves nothing less than the most perfect intimacy with the Father. In *Beauty of the Infinite*, the affirmation of *both* difference and oneness between Father and Son in the Holy Spirit are mutually necessary. Distinction and perfect unity are non-sublatable themes in Trinitarian theology, and also in soteriology, because at the moment when the man Jesus, who is other than the Father, most nakedly confronts the horror of human violence in the pagan sacrificial symbol of the cross, he simultaneously joins his heart to the Father's in absolute unity, enjoying a bond of love beyond human understanding, thus providing the final icon of Israel's most holy sacrificial work. Ultimately, for Hart, any theology of sacrifice must find its home in the Trinitarian theology of gift: "There is only the gift and the restoration of the gift, the love that the gift declares, the motion of a giving that is infinite, which comprehends every sacrifice made according to love, and which overcomes every sacrifice made for the sake of power."[37] Christ's life is thanksgiving, *eucharistia*, and in his death, he refuses to waver from his identity.

Other Examples of YHWH-goat Soteriology

Of course, Hart is not the first to develop the soteriological themes associated with the YHWH-goat, but he does an exceptional job of articulating this ancient approach to the cross in critical dialogue with more recent perspectives. In addition to his own contributions to contemporary reflection on the work of Christ, one of the great strengths of Hart's chapter on soteriology is that he shows how the much-maligned soteriology

33. Neusner, *The Mishnah*, para. 1:1; page 265.

34. Neusner, para. 1:4, 1:7; page 266.

35. Neusner, para. 1:5; page 266. In the *Mishna Yoma*, the "agents of the court" charge the high priest with faithfully carrying out his liturgical duties. In this context, it says the high priest "turns aside and weeps" and the agents "turn aside and weep" (*M. Yoma 1:4*).

36. Exodus 28:36.

37. Hart, *Beauty of the Infinite*, 351.

of Anselm of Canterbury is itself (in effect) a version of Yʜᴡʜ-goat soteriology,[38] which is ultimately also the soteriology of Irenaeus and his theory
of recapitulation.[39] A full analysis of Anselm's work in light of Levitical
atonement theory will require more space, but in anticipation of that, a
brief comment: the basic conviction behind *Cur Deus Homo* is that the
life of the Son, culminating in his death, is a positive movement of love
and obedience toward the Father. Sin is not confronted *directly*, as it will
be in Azazel-goat soteriologies, but it is effectively overcome, on our
behalf, through the Son's absolute freedom in unwavering self-giving. A
key text for understanding Anselm is this:

> God, therefore, did not force Christ to die, there being no sin in him.
> Rather he underwent death of his own accord, not out of an obe-
> dience consisting in the abandonment of his life, but out of an obe-
> dience consisting in his upholding of righteousness so bravely and
> pertinaciously that as a result he incurred death.[40]

The central idea here is that neither the Son nor the Father enters into
any kind of alliance with death, as if such an evil can be willed for the
sake of good, nor do they promote any other form of violent power,
which would be inimical to the goal of restoring peace to creation.
Rather, the mutual commitment of Father and Son is toward unwavering
life, which is lived out as righteousness.

The Father did not send the Son to die, but *to live to the end*—and
in the context of our sinful world, the awesome power of triune life will
inevitably provoke a challenge from the rebellious powers of death and
despair. In the context of this unavoidable test, the Son is called to be
brave, to be tenacious, to love, come what may. For Anselm, Christ
defeats the ugliness of sin and death and restores the beauty of creation
through his devotion to the way of life,[41] a "way" he knew eternally as

38. On the term "Yʜᴡʜ-goat soteriology," see the clarifying note in the introduction;
page 10, note 18.

39. See Hart, *Beauty of the Infinite*, 360–72.

40. St. Anselm, *Anselm of Canterbury: The Major Works* (Oxford: Oxford University
Press, 1998), 277.

41. The aesthetic aspect of Anselm's thought, and especially his emphasis on 'fitting-
ness,' has lately been emphasized. Anselm says, "When such a being desires what is right,
he is honoring God, not because he is bestowing anything upon God, but because he is
voluntarily subordinating himself to his will and governance, maintaining his own proper
station in life within the natural universe, and, to the best of his ability, maintaining the
beauty of the universe itself. But when a rational being does not wish for what is right, he
dishonors God . . . and is disturbing, as far as he is able, the order and beauty of the

the second person of the Trinity, but also, a way he knew covenantally as a Jewish man who was there on Mount Moriah, slumbering in Isaac's loins, when the son of great promise united his will to his father's. Jesus further knew the way of life liturgically because his whole existence was shaped by the temple, where he lingered as a child and toward which he set his face as a man: "Did you not know that I must be in my Father's house?" (Luke 2:49). For Anselm, in the solution that he gives, ". . . all that is contained in the New Testament and Old has been proved."[42] While using an eleventh-century vocabulary to articulate perennial biblical truths, Anselm has reinforced the Jewish view of sacrifice as "drawing near," and thus he again overcomes the temptation toward *violent* sacrifice, which so often ensnares the human heart.

An Eastern Orthodox theologian like Hart, who is so deeply immersed in patristic thought, is able to understand Anselm rightly where so many post-Enlightenment Westerners have failed. Thus, Hart concludes:

> Even here, then, in the text that most notoriously expounds the sacrificial logic of atonement, the idea of sacrifice is subverted from within: as the story of Christ's sacrifice belongs not to an economy of credit and exchange but to the trinitarian motion of love, it is given entirely as gift—a gift given when it should not have needed to be given again, by God, at a price we imposed upon him. As an entirely divine action, Christ's sacrifice merely draws creation back into the eternal motion of divine love, for which it was fashioned.[43]

When one considers the long development of the "satisfaction" approach in the Catholic tradition, with eyes trained by the movements of the high priest who bears the lifeblood of the YHWH-goat, one finds that mainstream Catholic soteriology since the time of Anselm—including in a special way Thomas Aquinas and his students[44]—has primarily emphasized how, first, Christ restores the beauty, goodness, and truth of creation

---

universe." This sin creates "a certain ugliness, resulting from the violation of the beauty of order" in the universe (Anselm, 288, 289). This emphasis on order and beauty harmonizes with ancient priestly thought.

42. Anselm, 355.

43. Hart, *Beauty of the Infinite*, 371.

44. For an outstanding reflection on Thomas's soteriology with reference to Jewish temple theology, which compellingly expresses the long tradition of Catholic "YHWH-goat soteriology" (so to speak), see Matthew Levering, *Christ's Fulfillment of Torah and Temple: Salvation according to Thomas Aquinas* (Notre Dame, IN: University of Notre Dame Press, 2002), esp. 51–66, 76–79.

though his total self-giving,[45] and second, how human beings are taken up into that work through God's grace operating in the sacraments.[46] The proclamation of this positive movement is the joyful heart of our shared patristic traditions, East and West. It is also certainly to be found in Protestant and Anglican theologies. In modern times, the work of figures like John Milbank,[47] Kathryn Tanner,[48] or Sarah Coakley[49] comes immediately to mind, and this list could certainly be expanded further.

YHWH-goat Soteriology: Beautiful and Incomplete

Hart's soteriology is persuasive, inspiring, and incomplete. Certainly, in the ritual of Leviticus 16, the YHWH-goat is preeminent, and so the Christian tradition is well-calibrated whenever it accentuates this aspect of Christ's work. Hart's theology excels at this. That said, I would put the following question before Hart: what about the "second goat" who is "left standing" at the entrance of the tent? While reestablishing the original glory of creation in the kenotic love of the Son is, liturgically and metaphysically, the priority, to neglect the saving work of the Azazel-goat

45. See Levering, *Christ's Fulfillment of Torah and Temple*, 61.

46. To cite just one recent example of this theme, which is prevalent in Catholic theology: ". . . all aspects of Eucharistic theology receive their intelligibility in light of the requirement of cruciform communion. It is through Christ's sacrifice, participated in sacramentally in the Eucharistic sacrifice and sacrificial meal that fully includes us within Christ's action, that God caused the gift of charitable communion in us." Matthew Levering, *Sacrifice and Community: Jewish Offering and Christian Eucharist* (Hoboken, NJ: Wiley-Blackwell, 2005), 194.

47. John Milbank, *Being Reconciled: Ontology and Pardon* (London: Routledge, 2003), esp. 79–104.

48. Kathryn Tanner, *Christ the Key* (Cambridge: Cambridge University Press, 2010), 247–73. Tanner calls her approach the "incarnational model of atonement." Responding to feminist critiques of typical theories of atonement, Tanner articulates the core of her approach: "Each moment of Jesus' life as it happens is being brought into connection with the life-giving powers of the Word. . . . Here is a God who works unswervingly for our good, who puts no value on death and suffering, and no ultimate value on self-sacrifice for the good, a God of gift-giving abundance struggling against the forces of sin and death in the greatest possible solidarity with us—that of incarnation." Tanner, 261. Tanner's interesting analysis of "sacrifice" itself is at points in agreement, and at other points in tension, with the arguments of this section. Tanner, 262–73.

49. Coakley is developing a theology of sacrifice that does not presuppose divine or ontological violence and which is in conversation with contemporary evolutionary theory. For the inauguration of this project, see Sarah Coakley, *Sacrifice Regained: Reconsidering the Rationality of Religious Belief* (Cambridge: Cambridge University Press, 2012). More recently, Coakley has developed her thoughts in the DuBose Lectures at the University of the South's School of Theology (2015) and the Stob Lectures at Calvin Theological Seminary (2015).

would result in an imbalanced soteriology because, without this goat, Christ's direct engagement with sin "itself" is inadequately appreciated. Thus, if one were to say that Christ, in his perfect kenotic obedience and love, "passes [death] by as though it were nothing,"[50] that would accurately describe Christ the high priest's triumph in bearing his own blood as the final "YHWH-goat," as I emphasized at length in chapter seven; but this same statement forgets that it is simultaneously necessary that the Azazel-goat bear the full weight of sin as "not nothing." Hart would dislike this Balthasarian formula, but I would insist that it contains a biblical insight that still demands our attention, whether or not it forces us to grapple with the (potentially productive) tensions between our philosophical presuppositions and the biblical mysteries.

The potential imbalance in *Beauty of the Infinite* has been observed before, and I believe that it is an imbalance that has persisted in Hart's theology. Shortly after its publication, *Beauty of the Infinite* was enthusiastically engaged by the best theological minds at academic conferences and in esteemed theological journals. The book was universally hailed as a major event in modern theology. Without detracting from this fact, when one looks back at the early reflections on Hart's masterpiece, there is a common note of apprehension. Again and again, reviewers zero in on Hart's treatment of the role of "tragedy" in theology as a place where his theological imagination seemed limited. I'll provide two examples. First, Lois Malcolm, in her review of Hart's book, commends the fact that Hart refuses to follow those excessively "tragic" soteriologies which had become popular among some theologians, especially since the Second World War. She values the way Hart draws on the Jewish awareness of the fact that creation is good and that God is working to redeem the good creation. But then she notes that

> that very Jewish wisdom, especially as expressed in Job, the psalmist's laments, and even in Jesus' quotation of Psalm 22 in Mark 15, also has a place for mourning and lament. Our world—with its hurricanes and earthquakes, senseless wars, bombings, inequalities between the poor and rich, injustices repeated over generations—though it is God's good world is also a world of evil, sin, and suffering.[51]

50. Hart, *Beauty of the Infinite*, 322. Note how Hart's language here parallels the quote we used earlier: "But nothingness does not challenge God, it is not some 'thing' with which God becomes creatively involved; he passes nothingness by without regard, it is literally nothing to him. . . ." Hart, 259.

51. Lois Malcolm, "On David Hart's *The Beauty of the Infinite*," *New Blackfriars* 88, no. 1017 (2007): 598.

Similarly, Gerald Loughlin, after unpacking the main themes in Hart's rhapsodic theology, concludes with a note of caution: "But then I remember that the world does not shine for all, nor all the time for those who have been given to glimpse its light; and that about this darkening of a world made by love, Hart's lengthy book is strangely silent—perhaps properly but also perplexingly for a story that would out-narrate all others."[52]

On the particulars, Hart effectively responds to these critics. For example, in his response to Lois Malcolm, he says that he takes her words to heart, and points her in the direction of his *Doors of the Sea* as a possible corrective to his "theological emphasis" in *Beauty of the Infinite*. That said, he insists that *Beauty* is not "one long, boisterous romp of merry rhapsody,"[53] and that his argument, in its depths, is keenly attentive to the reality of evil as epitomized in the death camps. Similarly, in his response to Francesca Murphy's review, which also raised doubts about Hart's approach to "the tragic" in theology—worrying at one point that he wants to brush suffering and victimization "under the carpet of eschatological joy"[54]—Hart insists that

> One of the book's darker leitmotifs—for want of a better term—is that of the death camps; they constitute a sort of index of theological sanity for me: any theology of the cross that could possibly serve to mitigate our sense of the absolute, pointless and infinitely meaningless evil of what happened there is not a real theology of the cross, but merely a 'tragic theology', which does as much to reconcile us to evil as to wake us to enmity against it.[55]

52. Gerard Loughlin, "Rhetoric and Rhapsody: A Response to David Bentley Hart's 'The Beauty of the Infinite,'" *New Blackfriars* 88, no. 1017, 2007, 608.

53. David Bentley Hart, "Response to James KA Smith, Lois Malcolm and Gerard Loughlin," *New Blackfriars* 88, no. 1017 (2007): 616–17.

54. Francesca Murphy, "David Hart, The Beauty of the Infinite: A Response," *Scottish Journal of Theology* 60, no. 1 (2007): 86.

55. David Bentley Hart, "Response from David Bentley Hart to McGuckin and Murphy," *Scottish Journal of Theology* 60, no. 1 (2007): 98. It is true that, in *Beauty of the Infinite*, Hart references the death camps in numerous places. For example, he notes the danger of responding to Auschwitz with a theology of divine suffering, which could unintentionally become "the metaphysical ground of Auschwitz" (160), and reflection on the demands for "eschatological justice" from the victims of the death camps also helps us to see the dangers of Nicholas Lash's romanticization of tragedy and death in contrast to genuine Christian resurrection (390). Furthermore, the tortured little girl in Ivan Karamazov's famous moral complaint against God and his creation (which will be discussed further below) is already present as an important test case for any theology's ability to adequately face evil and suffering (165). These are just a few of many possible examples.

With all this in mind, it seems to me that Gerald Loughlin has put things too starkly when he says that Hart's book is *silent* when it comes to those who experience a "darkening" in the world made by love. The ability to speak intelligibly and morally about God before such individuals really does seem to be among Hart's motivations for writing the *Beauty of the Infinite.*

And yet, it is interesting that reviewer after reviewer feels a sense of disquiet on this point. The most obvious feature of Hart's text is its overwhelming insistence, its proper insistence, on the metaphysical primacy of delight, beauty, joy, glory, love, on and on, so much so that one almost begins to feel a sense of panic under the surface. At first, the reader is transported by the splendor of it, but an unsettled feeling also creeps in. Like an extravagant military parade before a weary nation, one detects anxiety behind the poetic onslaught. What can account for this feeling? Looking at Hart's writings throughout his career, it is possible to conclude that when David Bentley Hart sits down to write, Ivan Karamazov joins him at the table. One might say that everything is written for him. Ivan haunts Hart's theology, and thus the specter of atheism haunts Hart's theology; it seems that David Hart—one of our greatest contemporary theological minds—is continually writing his way through the acute theological trauma of Ivan's challenge to Alyosha.

Who can forget the soul-shattering account of the unloved little girl—five years old—who was locked in an outhouse, feces smeared over her face by her own mother as punishment for soiling her bed? "Can you understand," Ivan asks, "why a little creature, who can't even understand what's done to her, should beat her little aching heart with her tiny fist in the dark and the cold, and weep her meek unresentful tears to dear, kind God to protect her? . . . Do you understand why this infamy must be and is permitted?"[56] How do we come to terms with the reality of that little girl's suffering? Ivan, for one, can't come to terms. He won't. He imagines that immense joy, when the final trumpet has sounded, and all creation is gathered into a single hymn of praise before the God whose name is Justice, and he imagines the torturer and the tortured reconciled, in tears of joy, and all shall be well, and all shall be well, and . . . *stop*. Ivan must interrupt: "I can't accept that harmony," he says.[57] Ivan rejects the "higher harmony" because none of it—*none of it*—is worth the tears of that lonely, terrified child. The tears, Ivan says, are not atoned for, and no pos-

---

56. Fyodor Dostoevsky, *The Brothers Karamazov*, trans. Constance Garnett (New York: Modern Library, 1996), 219.

57. Dostoevsky, 221.

sible forgiveness could undo what has been done. And God allowed it to happen. Ivan returns his ticket to that happy land; he wants none of this divine harmony.

Again, Hart feels Ivan's protest deeply, and this shows Hart's warmth and integrity. He will not sweep Ivan's critique under the rug; he will face it squarely. One way to read *Beauty of the Infinite* is as an extravagant attempt to establish a theological and metaphysical structure capable of withstanding the prophetic storm unleashed by Ivan. But, perhaps unexpectedly, many reviewers missed this central theme, and they thought Hart was indifferent to the problem of evil and suffering. What can account for the fact that what the author sees as a major theme in his work appears completely absent to so many intelligent readers? In numerous subsequent publications, Hart has sought to underline how seriously he takes this issue, bolster his response to the problem of evil, and more directly address Ivan's dogged challenge. In my assessment, however, Hart has—thus far—failed in his quest, and has in fact made matters worse, precisely because of the fundamental oversight in his work—at least with respect to his soteriology and eschatology: the absence of the Azazel-goat in his theology of the cross.

For example, *The Doors of the Sea* is a powerful argument against the many superficial or outrageous responses to evil that can be found in Christian (or pseudo-Christian) discourse. This little book is a sustained confrontation with the tragedy of evil, and an explanation for why Christianity must not and cannot provide a "total explanation" for evil and suffering.[58] In other words, there is no balancing of accounts when it comes to evil; it cannot be made lovely as part of a larger portrait. The monstrosity is not lessoned by saying that, like *chiaroscuro*, the light is more brilliant due to the shadow. There is no "happy fault"; the good is in no way enhanced by evil. Hart is right that that would be a metaphysical absurdity: God's profile is not enhanced in any way by the existence of evil. Evil is in no sense intelligible, and not everything happens for a reason. Hart, with the explicit help of Ivan Karamazov, magnificently blocks every shortcut away from the problem. But, after ruling out the unacceptable answers, what can be said?

For his positive answer, Hart returns to his rhapsodies. He beautifully shows that what Christianity offers is not a neat and tidy theodicy, but the good news and theological hope. This, Hart says, is the "knowledge central to the gospel":

58. Hart, *The Doors of the Sea*, 68.

the knowledge of the evil of death, its intrinsic falsity, its unjust dominion over the world, its ultimate nullity; the knowledge that God is not pleased or nourished by our deaths, that he is not the secrete architect of evil, that he is the conqueror of hell, that he has condemned all these things by the power of the cross; the knowledge that God is life and light and infinite love, and that the path that leads through nature and history to his Kingdom does not simply follow the contours of either nature or history, or obey the logic immanent to them, but is opened to us by way of the natural and historical absurdity—or outrage—of the empty tomb.[59]

As Hart makes his way back to the poor and desperate child of Ivan's speech at the very end of the book, his language once more takes flight, and goes higher still: "there is in all the things of earth a hidden glory waiting to be revealed, more radiant than a million suns, more beautiful than the most generous imagination or more ardent desire can now conceive."[60] His final word to the little girl is beautiful—God will raise her up, wipe away every tear, and "Behold, I make all things new"—and yet, still seems to miss Ivan's deepest challenge: how does the happy eschatological conclusion alleviate the real historical catastrophe of this innocent life? Is the monstrosity of this world, of even the little girl's world, ever truly addressed in *Doors of the Sea*, or is it simply ignored in a rush toward greener pastures? Again, while Hart's overall argument in this book is highly convincing, the Azazel-goat is still absent; there is no reflection on Christ "bearing" the sins of the world, nor does Hart (returning to one of Malcolm's concerns) address "Jesus' quotation of Psalm 22 in Mark 15."[61] There is still a missing piece.

Even today, Ivan remains a tormenting presence. I suspect that Hart was never fully satisfied with the answers he gave to the problem previously, and in fact, it seems that the difficulty he faced in trying to answer the question has, over time, pushed him to put universalism more and more at the center of his thought. While Hart had discussed universalism in *The Beauty of the Infinite*—and in retrospect, it is obvious that all the lines of his argument pointed in that direction—he was also quick to say that "Orthodox tradition does not authorize me" to "enter a brief in

59. Hart, 100–101.
60. Hart, 102.
61. See Hart, *Beauty of the Infinite*, 360, for a brief attempt, which so quickly shifts from "My God, my God . . ." to "Father, into thy hands I commend my Spirit." This rapid shift illustrates the concern of Hart's critics well.
62. Hart, 410.

behalf of [Gregory of Nyssa's] universalism."[62] Needless to say, all restraint is thrown off by the time of *That All Shall Be Saved*, Hart's recent book in defense of a muscular doctrine of universalism. Perhaps one factor that drove this shift was the fact that Hart becomes convinced that the final elimination of hell is the only way to look Ivan in the eye and not flinch.

Ivan is prominent in Hart's recent essay, "The Devil's March: *Creatio ex Nihilo*, the Problem of Evil, and a Few Dostoyevskian Meditations." In that essay, Hart turns once more to the problem of evil and rehearses the tenets of the philosophical theology that has been the cornerstone of his work since *Beauty*. But Hart now also includes a clear affirmation of total *apokatástasis* (restoration of all); he insists that "within the story of creation, viewed from its final cause, there can be no residue of the pardonably tragic, no irrecuperable or irreconcilable remainder left at the end of the tale; for, if there were, this too God would have done, as a price freely assumed in creating."[63] But before Hart himself can fully accept this universalist vision of "the union of all things with the first good," he must face an obstacle: the problem of evil, and more specifically, the question of whether evil is sufficiently addressed by eschatological harmonization. And of course, for him, that means wrestling with Ivan once again.

Hart suggests that perhaps the answer to Ivan's problem can be found, not in the words of Zosima, not in the words or acts of Alyosha, but in the musings of the devil in the course of his fevered conversation with Ivan at the end of Dostoyevsky's masterpiece. At one point the devil tells the story of a "materialist philosopher" who is forced to undergo a "quadrillion-kilometer march," and who, upon finally reaching his heavenly destination, "within two seconds declared it worth every step of his journey."[64] Now, for Hart, it is of central importance that "the tale he tells is not one regarding a universal harmony somehow necessarily premised upon the unanswered tears of a little girl weeping in misery in the night."[65] Instead, he insists, it is "a salvation graciously granted *altogether beyond history*."[66] But here again, *what about history*? Hart believes that his introduction of universalism has contributed something

---

63. David Bentley Hart, "The Devil's March: Creatio Ex Nihilo, the Problem of Evil, and a Few Dostoyevskian Meditations," in *Theological Territories: A David Bentley Hart Digest* (Notre Dame, IN: University of Notre Dame Press, 2020), 82.

64. Hart, 95.

65. Hart, 95.

66. Hart, 96.

important to his struggle with Ivan. Against all the inadequate theodicies, Hart presents "the tale of the rescue of all creatures from nonbeing, and then also from sin and ignorance . . . so that they may be drawn on to the God who will not abandon even those who abandon him."[67] But eschatological peace seems to come by absconding completely from history. He says, "The time of sin and death, which we call history, cannot be—and this is the truth that Ivan sees so clearly—the foundation of God's Kingdom, as then it would be a final harmony sustained by an unredeemed injustice. Rather, it [history?] is the last residue of the darkness of nonbeing that God conquers in creation and salvation."[68] And so, what becomes of the girl? Hart concludes:

> the question of the price of that victory is not one of the rational calculation of relative goods, but one whose final answer is entirely the province of—and this is Zosima's truth—one who can see the whole of creation with the eyes of perfect love: that same little girl, though now lifted up into the eternity of the Kingdom, divinized, glorified, is capable of a love like God's, which can forgive perfectly and thereby triumph over all evil. Yet even this forgiveness cannot bring the Kingdom to pass unless eternity reduce the price of evil to absolutely nothing. For if anything were to be eternally lost—the least little thing—then the goodness of creation could never be more in the end than a purely conditional goodness, a mere relative evaluation, rather than an essential truth.[69]

Hart appears to say that the eschatological solution to the horrors of our world is that *everyone* will look away from the historical reality, and as long as there is no awkward remnant to remind us, the entire unpleasantness of our lives "down below" can be safely transcended. But how does this in any way satisfy the bold and courageous promise of Ivan to *never* look away, to never forget the child in the outhouse, the one whose heart aches so profoundly, because the higher harmony is "not worth it because those tears are unatoned for? They must be atoned for, or there can be no harmony. But how? How are you going to atone for them? Is it possible?"[70]

By refusing the priestly insight that there is a residue in this world, a demonic energy that we create in our acts of torture, cruelty, greed, neg-

67. Hart, 96.
68. Hart, 96.
69. Hart, 96.
70. Dostoevsky, *The Brothers Karamazov*, 221.

lect, violence, hatred, pride—a mournful residue from our lives that merits the unwavering No of God—by refusing this priestly insight, Hart is left with a theology of the cross that remains curiously otherworldly. And so, to go back again to the initial concern that was felt by the reviewers of *The Beauty of the Infinite*, there is something unsatisfying in the way Hart uses his unparalleled gifts as a writer to overwhelm the reader with lyrics of infinite glories and eternal delights, while the horror of evil *feels* ignored—even as it is an ever-present preoccupation.

All of this brings us to Hart's most recent blockbuster, *That All Shall Be Saved*. Hart believes in the *necessity* of the doctrine of universalism— the salvation and restoration of all, and as a corollary, the ultimate annihilation of the phenomenon known as hell. For Hart, the only "hell" that could exist is a (temporary) condition of the individual's mind and heart. It is "the hatred within each of us that turns the love of others— of God and neighbor—into torment. It is entirely a state we impose upon ourselves."[71] This profound sense of misery that we "impose upon ourselves" is eliminated when all are restored. Returning once more to his rhetorical ebullience, Hart, drawing on St. Gregory of Nyssa, says, "Once it has been exhausted, when every shadow of wickedness—all chaos, duplicity, and violence—has been outstripped by the infinity of God's splendor, beauty, radiance, and delight, God's glory will shine in each creature like the sun in an immaculate mirror, and each soul—born into the freedom of God's image—will turn of its own nature toward divine love."[72] Hart, again building on St. Gregory, argues that our interior, subjective hells, "the lingering effects of a condition of slavery," have been conquered by Christ on the cross, and are being conquered and will be conquered in each individual's soul. It is surprising how little Hart has to say about Christ's work on the cross in this book, but he does say this: "Hell appears in the shadow of the cross as what has *always already been conquered*, as what Easter leaves in ruins, to which we may flee from the transfiguring light of God if we so wish, but where we can never finally come to rest—for, being only a shadow, it provides nothing to cling to. . . ."[73]

Zero in on those words, "always already." Interestingly, these are exactly the words that caught Robert Jenson's attention in his 2005 review of *Beauty of the Infinite*. At the end of his review, Jenson presents the following questions:

71. Hart, *That All Shall Be Saved*, 27; cf. 62.
72. Hart, 144.
73. Hart, 129, emphasis added.

what does 'always already' mean? . . . Hart envisions a God whose serenity simply is what it is, and who manifests his glory in the death and Resurrection of Christ but does not constitute it in them. Is this the way Scripture in fact tells its story of God? Another form of the question: Does Hart relate time and eternity in a way that can accommodate a history that is actually saving?[74]

In my own words, in Hart's theology, is there *a history* that is saving? Is there an incarnation that truly confronts, and therefore saves us from, the reality of our sin, or does Jesus remain strangely removed; even when he is "lifted up," is his head in the clouds?

I argue that the five-year-old girl has the right, Ivan has the right, to see the grotesque evil she suffered addressed with all the seriousness and severity it deserves. It is beautiful that Jesus, in his life, passion, and resurrection, tells again the story that is true from the foundation of the world—"always already"—thus inaugurating a new creation in his movement of perfect and eternal love and joy. Fascinatingly, in *That All Shall Be Saved*, Hart admits that his past writings on "the mystery of evil" seem to "retreat" from the question at "just the right moment, and to seek a somewhat craven refuge in the classical metaphysics of divine transcendence."[75] I respect this confession, yet, by the end of *That All Shall Be Saved*, God's confrontation with the "mystery of evil" still seems remote, as if the incarnation were only partial, or as if "the action" that brings our redemption occurs in some higher realm, some fairyland, some Platonic sphere up above. Even though Hart speaks profoundly and convincingly about how our deepest identities are constituted by our relationships in this life, by the "loves and associations and affinities that shape us"[76]—all contingent things—he does not face what Ivan faces. The little girl, like all of us, is who she is in part because of the evil she has borne. As Ivan knows, and as the ancient priestly writers know, if there is any kind of atonement, the lingering reality of *that* evil cannot be avoided. It must be borne away, it must endure the awesome No of God's love, and its condemnation must be eternal. What "it" *is*, that thing that must be borne away, may not be clear at this stage, but one feels its weight, and knows it must be addressed somehow. What's more, it must be removed absolutely, never to be reintegrated, never to be restored,

74. Robert W. Jenson, "Review: The Beauty of the Infinite: The Aesthetics of Christian Truth," *Pro Ecclesia* XIV, no. 2 (2005): 237.
75. Hart, *That All Shall Be Saved*, 67.
76. Hart, 153.

never to be released, for eternity. Therefore, it is a theological necessity, in light of the world that actually exists, given the brutalities of our real history, that there be a real and eternal hell. Not just a temporary psychological state, but a genuine and eternal reality, a place where the injustices and horrors of this world are sent, never to be released. The details of what that wilderness state consists of, the question of what "it is" that might be deposited there, or of how it is that the blessed in heaven might look upon this reality and rejoice . . . all of these questions (and more) are for the next chapter.

By celebrating what is most real and radiant, by persistently drawing the reader toward the holy of holies where Christ once entered and where he forever sits, Hart's soteriology does not linger on the present trauma of howling exile, the Babylonian terrors that so many humans suffer. The full wonder of Christ's saving act is not appreciated unless we appreciate that Jesus himself *does not* look past this exile. He himself *does not* evade the mournful duty to fulfill also the work of the second-goat. The conquering Messiah is truly a man of sorrows, one who knows the deepest grief. Perhaps it is right to say that, if one is to have an imbalanced soteriology, the imbalance should be on the side of glory rather than wilderness. And yet, the mystery of Yom Kippur, the mystery of Good Friday, encompasses it all, and so we must press forward with Christ, who indeed drank the horrible cup, to the bottom, to the last drop.

CHAPTER 10

The Goat for Azazel in Contemporary Theology: Hans Urs von Balthasar

In the previous chapter, I argued that David Bentley Hart's work exemplifies an especially clear modern articulation of one theological interpretation of Christ's work—an interpretation that might be called the "classical" approach since it is so widely affirmed in the Christian tradition, especially in mainstream Catholic and Eastern Orthodox thought. This approach can be correlated with the theology of the goat for the Lord on Yom Kippur. As we shift our focus now to the theology of the second goat, our guide will be Hans Urs von Balthasar. Balthasar will speak for a minority position within the great tradition, but one that nevertheless has been articulated by Catholic, Orthodox, and Protestant theologians. It might be said that a feeling for the absence of the Azazel-goat in Catholic soteriology was a contributing factor in Luther's critique of the "theology of glory," and Balthasar himself is appreciative of the great "thunderbolt" thrown by the reformer in refocusing our attention on Christ's cruciform encounter with sin.[1] Balthasar's own soteriology across the fifteen volumes in his "trilogy," and then spilling out into the countless other books he wrote, is the fullest and most challenging meditation on Christ's saving action in modern Catholic theology, and it cannot be reduced to the Azazel-goat theme. In truth, most of the ideas expressed by Hart are also found in Balthasar.[2] Furthermore, the entire first part of this book was structured by Balthasar's own reflection on the positive Christological themes of beauty, goodness, and truth; it cannot be emphasized enough that the overall focus of Balthasar's work is a sustained contemplation of the theme of divine love. But the focus in *this* chapter will be on the theme that sets Balthasar apart from Hart and from many in the dominant Catholic theological tradition, and thus my

---

1. Balthasar, *TD4*, 284.
2. Hart himself says that his *Beauty of the Infinite* might be "read as a kind of extended *marginalium* on some page of Balthasar's work." *Beauty of the Infinite*, 29.

goal in this section is to make the following argument: Balthasar's soteriology—and especially his controversial reflections on Christ's descent to hell—is thoroughly biblical and absolutely necessary for Christian soteriology because Balthasar retrieves the work of the Azazel-goat with a clarity and consistency that is unique in the Christian tradition.

In earlier chapters, we developed an understanding of the Azazel-goat's mission with help from modern Jewish biblical commentators, especially Jacob Milgrom and Baruch Schwartz. The key terms associated with this movement within the Yom Kippur liturgy include sin-bearing, exile, darkness, lamentation, horror, and death. Milgrom strongly emphasizes that, in the liturgical symbolism of Yom Kippur, this goat *is not* a sacrifice because, as a beast covered in sin, it would have been unworthy as an offering to a demon, and it would be even more outrageous as a gift to the all-holy God of Israel.[3] Instead, Milgrom says, this goat is a vehicle, a mode of transporting that which cannot be integrated into the "very good" cosmos of Israel—the raw "miasma" of sin—transferring it into the wilderness, which represents the chaos that is outside the field of God's loving vision. Within ancient Jewish mythopoetics, this is the "empty howling waste," the expanse of darkness and death that in every way contrasts the lush, peaceful, luminous space of God's paradise. On Yom Kippur, the pilgrim people Israel together move resolutely toward the promised land, and thus, when the Azazel-goat bears the sins into the demonic desert, it is removing the burden from the chosen ones so that they might rise more easily into God's presence. After sin, it is the selfless substitutionary work of this humble beast that makes it possible for Israel to renew her intimacy with the most holy LORD.

The Problem of Sin

This vision is only possible given ancient Israel's understanding of sin. As I've noted, Gary Anderson's *Sin: A History* is exceptional for tracing the imagery used to understand sin in different periods; his primary observation is that Israel's metaphor shifts from sin as a "weight" that has "a certain 'thingness,'"[4] a burden that must be borne, to sin as a debt that must be paid. This transition from the Hebrew idiom for sin to the

---

3. For a fuller discussion of this, see chapter 7. It is true, and always worth emphasizing, that the two goats together are identified as a single *ḥaṭṭā't* (Leviticus 16:5), certainly because they are mutually necessary for achieving final atonement, even though, properly speaking, only the first goat is a sacrifice while the second goat is part of a disposal ritual.

4. Anderson, *Sin*, x.

Aramaic idiom certainly facilitated the dialogue with Greek philosophical concepts like "privation." The major question for the theologian today, and especially for the theologian who seeks to be attentive to the canonical teachings of ancient Jewish priestly theology, is whether meaningful insights are lost when the "substantive" idea of sin is left behind.

Modern writers are no less reliant on metaphorical imagery when talking about sin. It is therefore necessary to pay attention to the images used because, when we don't, we can fail to notice how these metaphors shape different understandings of salvation (and vice-versa). Thus, as I said in chapter five, to see why a modern theologian depicts the *solution* to sin the way he or she does, one should also survey his or her hamartiology. Looking at the metaphors used for sin in Balthasar, one finds a wide range of images. First, some metaphors correspond especially to particular sections of Balthasar's great trilogy on beauty, goodness, and truth, or specific volumes within the trilogy: in developing a theological aesthetics, Balthasar will speak of sin as ugliness; in the book focusing on the Old Covenant, sin is covenant infidelity; in the volumes grouped under the heading *Theo-Drama*, Balthasar describes sin as a misuse of freedom; when he turns to his *Theo-Logic*, sin is described as "the lie."[5] Second, other metaphors are so common that they cannot be associated with any particular volume or group of volumes. For example, sin is chaos. It is also (false) distance. And, for Balthasar, most importantly, sin is a burden.[6]

Sin as a Burden

Balthasar often speaks of sin as a "reality" that has a weight, density, or thingness. It is a burden that has crushed human beings, but that can also be transferred or "loaded" onto the "sin-bearer." The imagery is highly physical and substantial. For example, ". . . the one who abandoned himself can be utterly and completely determined by the will of the Father, who loads on him the burden of the reality that is 'the sin of the world.'"[7] This is anything but an isolated statement; it is repeated

5. That said, Balthasar feels free to mix and match his metaphors, and thus there are many examples of him speaking of sin as a "lie" within the volumes of the *Theo-Drama*, to give just one example. While it is notable that different metaphors take prominence in different volumes, this should be seen as a general heuristic.

6. For a fuller analysis of Balthasar's hamartiology, especially in terms of the metaphors he uses, see Richard J. Barry, "Retrieving the Goat for Azazel: Balthasar's Biblical Soteriology," *Nova et Vetera* 15, no. 1 (Winter 2017).

7. Hans Urs von Balthasar, *The Glory of the Lord: A Theological Aesthetics, Vol. 7: Theology: The New Covenant* (San Francisco: Ignatius Press, 1990), 208. Hereafter, *GL7*.

over and over again. Balthasar says: "the Father—*cooperante Spiritu Sancto*—loads the Son with the sins of the world. . . ."[8] and adds that "Jesus takes upon himself the entire sin of the world. . . ."[9] Thus, the Father loads what the Son freely and kenotically accepts.

When confronted with statements like these, theologians who rightly accept the Augustinian doctrine that evil or sin is a privation of the good immediately challenge Balthasar on his apparent belief that sin is somehow a substantial reality, capable of being transferred from one person to another.[10] Here's the major question: in what sense could the Son—who as the second person of the Trinity is eternally the perfect fullness of love—personally encounter and bear "sin itself" on the cross *if* sin were *merely* a privation of divine love? Unless Balthasar can find a way to think of sin as *in some sense* substantive, such an encounter would necessarily represent a threat to the eternal perfection, immutability, and unity of the divine persons.

Balthasar is aware of this problem, but he is also unwilling to retreat from the biblical notion of "sin-bearing." Therefore, in a remarkable and bold approach, he wrestles with the possibility that sin is (quasi?) substantive. For example, he says: "Because of the energy that man has invested in it, sin is a reality, it is not 'nothing.'"[11] Later, in the second volume of the *Theo-Logic*, he adds:

> Nevertheless, this "it" [the abomination that is the sin of the world] is not simply nothing. On the other hand, the question concerning the essence of sin cannot be positively answered, for sin is the lie

---

8. *TD4*, 335. Balthasar says this after he had already affirmed that it is *human beings* who load sins upon the willing Son:

> If, once the Incarnation has taken place, we ask who burdens the Son, the 'Lamb of God', the "Lamb as though it had been slain," with the unimaginable load of the world's No to divine love, the answer—a preliminary answer, but nonetheless real—must be: men themselves in their darkness. . . . But it is equally clear that nothing would be achieved by men unloading their sin if the one onto whom they load it were incapable of receiving it in its totality, as *what it is*: it presupposes he is both willing and able to bear sin. Balthasar, 334.

Therefore, it is true to say that the Father loads the sins of the world onto the Son, and it is also true to say that we also load *our* sins onto the Son, and at the same time the Son actively opens himself to receive the burden.

9. Balthasar, *TD4*, 180. Or again, "The surrendered Son, in bearing sin, that is, what is simply alien to God, appears to have lost the Father. . . ." Balthasar, 320.

10. See the discussion below on the challenges raised by Alyssa Lyra Pitstick and Matthew Levering.

11. *Theo-Drama: Theological Dramatic Theory, Vol. 5: The Last Act* (San Francisco: Ignatius Press, 1998), 314.

and, hence, neither truth nor being, and yet men have lent it something of their personal being in order to make it possible. Herein lies the self-contradiction that makes sin at once abstract and concrete, so that it can be experienced only "unrealistically," only "negatively."[12]

In this second quotation, Balthasar admits that sin does not have reality in the same way that creatures have reality. Sin is not "truth," and it is not "being." Nonetheless, both quotations indicate that sin obtains some form of existence *through us*, through our energy or our donation, even if this existence is an absurdity, an ontological anomaly, an impossible possibility. This claim will heavily influence Balthasar's mature soteriology, and so Balthasar's vague comments about the "not 'nothing'" "reality" of sin require much more reflection.

To even propose that sin has some kind of reality—without being completely absurd, incoherent, or mythological—Balthasar must avoid landmines on all sides. He is confronting at least two major problems. First, as a leading advocate of analogical metaphysics, Balthasar is well aware of the fact that there can be no "thing" that does not—somehow—participate in God's Being. There is *one* God, the source of all that is. Balthasar would certainly not fall for any metaphysical dualism, some kind of paganism where there are evil forces that compete with God, beings that can independently give substance to evil. Ever since Irenaeus, such ideas have been exposed and dismissed as heresy. Second, on the other hand, there can be no evil in God. Balthasar's theology absolutely rejects theological dualism, and thus he excludes any Hegelian scheme which entertains the possibility of a "dark side" to God that is in the process of

---

12. *Theo-Logic, Vol. 2: Truth of God* (San Francisco: Ignatius Press, 2004), 350. Balthasar is quoting von Speyr's *Kreuz und Hölle*, vol. 1, in this passage. In one of his last books, Balthasar says something similar in a discussion of the "principalities and powers": "To describe the sort of reality that they have is very difficult, for if the evil that leads the world astray has at first only the form of a black 'smoke like the smoke of a great furnace' with which 'the sun and the air were darkened' ([Rv] 9:2), then the men who are led astray by those powers lend the powers something of their own reality; the sins committed by men are something real, which, as it were, nourishes and concretizes the deceiving powers, and precisely this thing, being both somehow real and invested with that reality by man, is committed to self-destruction along with the deceiving powers when God creates the new world and the holy city of Jerusalem." *Dare We Hope That All Men Be Saved? With a Short Discourse on Hell* (San Francisco: Ignatius Press, 1988), 137. Balthasar acknowledges that, with respect to Revelation, we are dealing with visionary images, not history. Yet that does not mean that these "images" are irrelevant to theological reflection; on the contrary, they are signposts that help the theologian to reflect on truths that cannot be expressed by means of a merely historical, "immanent" vocabulary.

being overcome or synthesized.[13] The eternal goodness of the sole Creator is vigorously affirmed by Balthasar. With these concerns in mind, it seems that, as a metaphysical guideline, "privation theory" remains necessary to avoid disastrous consequences, and Balthasar acknowledges its philosophical truth.[14] And yet: behold, the Lamb of God does indeed bear away the sins of the world. Theologically, the great Swiss theologian must walk an exceptionally fine line so as to not say something metaphysically outrageous but also to meaningfully grapple with *central* New Testament assertions about Christ's saving work. Whether or not he is explicitly aware of it, Balthasar is also following in the footsteps of ancient priestly theology and implicitly responding to the demands of Yom Kippur soteriology, and thus his work is doubly important when it comes to the goal of sympathetically engaging the Jewish theological tradition that gives definition to the word "atonement." There is excellent reason, therefore, to take Balthasar's remarkable claims about sin seriously, attempting to see whether these claims are defensible.

Barth's "Das Nichtige"

In this precarious situation, what can be said? One possible resource for Balthasar was Karl Barth's theory of "*das Nichtige,*" which is generally translated as "nothingness."[15] For Barth, "nothing" has "reality" with reference to God's electing will.[16] In an apparent nod to the Calvinist doctrine of double predestination, Barth says that insofar as God as cre-

---

13. See O'Regan, *Anatomy of Misremembering*, for comprehensive justification of the claim that Balthasar is the "most concretely anti-Hegelian theologian of the 20th century."

14. Balthasar says, "[The Old Testament] understanding of evil is as unique as the divine covenant itself. It is a fully theological understanding that transcends every 'metaphysical' understanding of evil, whether mythical or (in later periods) philosophical. When biblical theology later takes up the Greek concept of the μὴ ὄν [non-being] and στέρησις [privation] in order to come closer conceptually to the essence of evil, this is not an error on the level of metaphysical truth, but it does not reach the distinctive essence of theological guilt. . . ." *GL6*, 216. Balthasar is here able both to acknowledge that an expression can be metaphysically appropriate but also capable of further theological refinement in the light of revelation. He later mentions, with approval, that ". . . traditional Christian theology proceeds from the certain conviction that the God who created the world is good, that the creature's freedom remains subordinate to him and that evil is an instance of the privation of good." *Theo-Drama: Theological Dramatic Theory, Vol. 1: Prolegomena* (San Francisco: Ignatius Press, 1988), 48.

15. On this translation, see the note at Karl Barth, *Church Dogmatics: The Doctrine of Creation. Volume III, Part 3* (New York: T&T Clark, 2004), 289, note 1.

16. He says, "The ontic context in which nothingness is real is that of God's activity as grounded in His election. . . . " Barth, 351.

ator elects and says "yes" to creation, God also rejects and says "no."[17] By virtue of God's rejection, *das Nichtige* obtains a unique form of existence, one that is absolutely distinct from God's own existence, and equally distinct from the good creation which God elects positively. That which is passed over and rejected becomes a "sinister system of elements,"[18] an "alien factor,"[19] an "adversary,"[20] an "antithesis,"[21] which has "no substantive existence within creation"[22] and yet is "real but absolutely negative."[23] Attempting to explain what *das Nichtige* "is," Barth says, "Nothingness is that from which God separates Himself and in the face of which He asserts Himself and exerts His positive will,"[24] and he continues, "[God's] rejection, opposition, negation and dismissal are powerful and effective like all His works because they, too, are grounded in Himself, in the freedom and wisdom of His election...For not only what God wills, but what He does not will, is potent, and must have a real correspondence."[25] When God freely elects a good creation, he implicitly rejects all evil, chaos, sin, and death, and precisely by rejecting those things, *das Nichtige*—in a "third fashion"[26]—obtains its unique reality.[27]

Remarkably, *das Nichtige* is already present at the moment of creation; in Genesis 1:2 it is indicated by the mention of chaos, "which the Creator has already rejected, negated, passed over and abandoned even before He utters His first creative Word, which He has already consigned to the past and to oblivion even before the beginning of time at His command."[28] The implication is that the rejected "nothingness"—which includes evil and sin—has a certain presence before any creaturely fall, whether angelic or human.[29] It is coextensive with God's electing will. That said, even though

17. Barth, 351. Cf. Matthias Grebe, *Election, Atonement, and the Holy Spirit: Through and Beyond Barth's Theological Interpretation of Scripture* (Eugene, OR: Pickwick Publications, 2014), 134–36.

18. Barth, *Church Dogmatics the Doctrine of Creation*, 289.

19. Barth, 289.

20. Barth, 302.

21. Barth, 302.

22. Barth, 302.

23. Barth, 304.

24. Barth, 351.

25. Barth, 352.

26. Barth, 350.

27. As Barth puts it, "Nothingness 'is,' therefore, in its connexion with the activity of God. It 'is' because and as and so long as God is against it." Barth, 353.

28. Barth, 352.

29. In fact, Barth rejects the concept of an angelic fall, that is, traditional Christian demonology. Cf. Barth, 519 ff. For Barth, demons "derive from" nothingness, and thus are not fallen but rejected from the start. Barth, 523.

the bizarre "reality" of nothingness precedes human sin, it is not unrelated to human sin. Much to the contrary, Barth says, "We have called sin the concrete form of nothingness because in sin it becomes man's own act, achievement and guilt."[30] Insofar as the sinner is conforming her will to that which God has *not* willed, she is personally embracing and advancing the nothingness that God has rejected from the first.

This idea of *das Nichtige* is—like all theological truth for Barth—revealed only in Christ, who has become incarnate precisely to confront and overcome this force which has brought such suffering to the earth.[31] On the cross, Christ encounters the full force of nothingness: it rains down on him in all of its cruelty and wretchedness, and in so doing it exhausts itself. One sees in the cross of Jesus Christ that *das Nichtige* has been definitively overcome, and therefore nothingness "has no perpetuity" precisely because it "is not created by God, nor is there any covenant with it. . . . It is from the very first that which is past. It was abandoned at once by God in creation."[32] The theological truth of this absolute rejection of nothingness is revealed and permanently affirmed by the cross.

Balthasar's "Not Nothing"

Even as Balthasar was highly influenced by Barth, it is clear that his harmartiology is distinct from Barth's theory of *das Nichtige*. Although there seems to be a verbal echo when Barth says "nothingness is not nothing"[33] and Balthasar says sin "is not 'nothing'"[34] the differences are important. When directly addressing Barth's *das Nichtige*, Balthasar immediately exonerates his theological mentor and friend of the charge of Manichaeism[35] insofar as Barth is adamant that "nothingness" has no reality independent of God's electing will, that it has "'being' only insofar as God's *non*-willing is also *potent*,"[36] and thus it is not a real threat to God's all-sovereignty. Nevertheless, Balthasar is critical. His major concern seems to be that, even if one emphasizes the potency of God's "no," Barth is still obligated to say that evil has its being directly

30. Barth, *Church Dogmatics the Doctrine of Creation*, 310.
31. See Barth, 302ff.
32. Barth, 360.
33. Barth, 349.
34. Balthasar, *TD5*, 314; Balthasar, *TL2*, 323.
35. Hans Urs Von Balthasar, *The Theology of Karl Barth: Exposition and Interpretation*, trans. Edward T. Oakes (San Francisco: Ignatius Press, 1992), 230.
36. Balthasar, *TD5*, 206.

from God's (non-)electing will, wholly independent of and previous to creaturely freedom. Balthasar says, "The theologoumenon of 'nothingness,' however, which is not explained with reference to creaturely freedom (of choice) but is seen as arising from the mere denial and rejection of what is 'chaotic,' 'alien,' and 'hostile to God', is untenable."[37] In another place, he adds,

> But no ontology could entertain the idea that . . . this kind of pseudo-reality [e.g. *das Nichtige*] could have a ("third") form of "being" on the basis of mere rejection. The only way of coming to grips, concretely, with the problem of this kind of "being" is to enquire about the ontological quality of a sin that has been performed by a concrete, free human person and yet has been forgiven by God.[38]

Here it is clear that Balthasar wants to follow Barth in expanding theological reflection on the possible "ontological quality of a sin," but Balthasar repeatedly insists that the origin of sin or evil must be in creaturely freedom, not in God's electing and creating will.[39] This is a vital qualification for Yom Kippur soteriology. Because for Barth, nothingness and sin have a "third" form of being, one which is always already "rejected, negated, passed over and abandoned,"[40] and because sin, therefore, has no perpetuity, its removal is always a foregone conclusion, and thus the dramatic

37. Balthasar, *TD3*, 483.
38. Balthasar, *TD5*, 207.
39. Balthasar's anxiety about any suggestion that evil could have its foundation in God is, undoubtedly, also driven by his desire to completely avoid the errors of German Idealism—especially those associated with Jakob Böhme and Friedrich Schelling—which posits the origin of evil in the theogony of God. For an outstanding discussion of Balthasar's engagement with these figures, and with the Russian idealists—especially Nicholas Berdyaev—who follow them, see the third chapter of Jennifer Newsome Martin, *Hans Urs von Balthasar and the Critical Appropriation of Russian Religious Thought* (Notre Dame, IN: University of Notre Dame Press, 2015), esp. 83–104. Martin shows that Balthasar shares the broadly Romantic goal—against modern rationalism—of taking sin "seriously," but his way of doing this has absolutely nothing in common with Schelling's non-privative metaphysical evil which originates in the process of God's self-generation. On the contrary, Balthasar re-emphasizes the ancient Jewish-Christian doctrine that evil has its origin in finite freedom, thus preserving the indispensable affirmation of God's eternal perfection against all Valentinian-gnostic speculation about divine becoming, while *simultaneously* imagining the possibility of a direct "confrontation" between God and evil (albeit a passive confrontation, as we'll see in his theology of Holy Saturday) which effectively *casts evil out*. Evil's reality *and* basic impotence are exposed, not through Titanic opposition (or integration, or sublation, or restoration in God), but by means of the incomprehensible freedom-in-obedience of true Love, who judges, removes, saves, and heals.
40. Barth, *Church Dogmatics the Doctrine of Creation*, 352.

work of the Azazel-goat is undermined. This calls to mind a powerful critique leveled by Balthasar against his friend: "Too much in Barth gives the impression that nothing much really *happens* in his theology of event and history, because everything has already happened in eternity. . . ."[41] Balthasar has a different vision, one in which sin as "reality" somehow obtains ontological weight in creation and has a certain eternal quality through our "yes" to evil in history. *We* give sin its twisted existence, and that work of dark creation on our part does have a sort of perpetuity because of the way time participates in eternity, and thus the Azazel-goat must walk the dolorous path to the wilderness, for our sake and for our salvation, to establish the eschatological distance between us and our sin.

But still. What is Balthasar *really* saying when he claims that sin is "not nothing"? In what follows, I will make a couple of attempts at understanding how this might be possible—without truly violating the "rules" of privation theory—using the vivid imagistic language that is so common in Balthasar and von Speyr. It remains true (as I mentioned earlier in this chapter) that this imagery has a metaphorical quality, and maybe even a mythological quality, which is (as I mentioned previously) so appropriate when grappling with "vertical" metaphysical concepts.[42]

41. Balthasar, *The Theology of Karl Barth*, 371. It is a surprising parallel, but I critiqued (and will further critique) David Bentley Hart's soteriology along similar lines.

42. I will leave to future research efforts at articulating how such images relate to more formal philosophical categories.

Relatively few commentators have wrestled with the question of what Balthasar might mean when he says that sin is "not nothing." One partial exception is Anne Hunt, who at least broaches the subject. She points out that Balthasar's "graphic" depiction of sin, though it runs afoul of the privation tradition, also has advantages. Balthasar's theology, first, clearly distinguishes "the sinner" from "the sin." Also, in Balthasar, there is "no evading the dreadful reality of sin and no denying God's condemnation of sin in this theology. . . . Sin is graphically portrayed as a formidable reality, a violent and even seemingly overwhelming presence, a monstrous affliction" Anne Hunt, *The Trinity and the Paschal Mystery: A Development in Recent Catholic Theology* (Liturgical Press, 1997), 73–74. Hunt points out that this concept of sin can be helpfully compared to a modern understanding of "institutionalized sin" (a point I made earlier with reference to priestly theology). Hunt concludes that "this 'reification' of sin also allows von Balthasar in effect to contrast the infinity of God's love, the unimaginable excess of this love, with the finitude of sin." Hunt, 74. These observations are very helpful in identifying some advantages to Balthasar's approach, though without really discussing how this theory could be possible theologically.

Another commentator on Balthasar who has engaged this question is John Saward, who says that the idea of Christ viewing "sin without sinners" is "[p]erhaps the most difficult notion in Balthasar's theology of the Descent." *The Mysteries of March: Hans Urs von Balthasar on the Incarnation and Easter* (Washington, D.C.: Catholic University of America Press, 1990), 130. Saward says that, because sin is privation, Christ's encounter

Recall again the key texts cited above: "*Because of the energy that man has invested in it*, sin is a reality, it is not 'nothing,'"[43] and then, "men have lent [to sin] *something of their personal being* in order to make it possible."[44] The concept here seems to be that sin has its "being" parasitically, that it originates from us, in our God-given capacity to be (co-)creators. God invites humanity to join in his creative activity, and we can use this power in two awe-inspiring ways: to cooperate in creating life (pro-

---

with sin in hell (see below) could not be "ocular," but only "intellectual"—in other words, there was "a recognition by the soul of the dead Jesus of what sin amounts to and where it finally leads to, the second death, eternal perdition." Saward, 130. And yet, this answer also creates additional theological problems: can a privation be an "object of knowledge"? After all, as privation, there is a "defect" of intelligibility in sin. Trying once again to understand this difficult teaching, Saward says, "And yet perhaps that is the point: in Hell the immaculate soul of Jesus looks into the yawning gulf of sin's unmeaning." Through this experience, Christ comes to see that "the lie is exposed, the nothingness unmasked." Saward, 131. The major problem with this explanation is that the soteriological value *pro nobis* of such an experience is not clear. Christ understands something about sin and its defeat in Sheol, but is that in itself relevant to the work of salvation?

More than any other commentator, Alyssa Lyra Pitstick is very attentive to the fact that, for Balthasar, "sin has some real existence." Alyssa Lyra Pitstick, *Light in Darkness: Hans Urs Von Balthasar and the Catholic Doctrine of Christ's Descent into Hell* (Grand Rapids, MI: Eerdmans, 2007), 303; cf. 103ff., 117, 128–29, 140, 197–99, 339–40, 390 nn.64, 395 154, but her engagement with this idea is purely negative. I will briefly address some of her claims below.

Craig Giandomenico recently completed a dissertation entitled "A Disease of Being: The Ontological Status of Sin in the Theology of Hans Urs von Balthasar." So far as I know, this is the first sustained consideration of Balthasar's harmartiology, and specifically, the "ontological status of sin." Giandomenico surveys the passages where Balthasar articulates his view, and he shows how different Balthasar's view is from the typical privation account. Giandomenico concludes that "von Balthasar consistently—if in a fragmentary manner—presents moral evil as a substance of human creation." "A Disease of Being: The Ontological Status of Sin in the Theology of Hans Urs Von Balthasar" (Diss., La Salle University, 2017), 83. Unfortunately, Giandomenico misses the apparent Jewish roots of Balthasar's approach (seemingly downplaying the connection to Old Testament religion with the assistance of Bradley McLean's *The Cursed Christ*; 64–67), and he ends up trying to explain Balthasar's approach to sin by suggesting that it is "a reentrance of the primal chaos from which goodness (creation) was called forth into existence" (140; cf. 97). Giandomenico gets here by effectively combining Jon Levenson's approach to creation as God's struggle over the primordial chaos (*Chaoskampf*) with Barth's theory of *das Nichtige*; I express my (Balthasarian) doubts about Levenson's theodicy in chapter four and offered my (Balthasarian) critique of Barth above. I am not convinced that Balthasar sees sin as "connected to the primordial chaos of creation" (97); indeed, in the quote that allegedly proves this theory, Balthasar specifically calls sin "the 'second chaos' (generated by human liberty)." There is still much work to do on this question.

43. *TD5*, 314, emphasis added.

44. *TL2*, 350, emphasis added.

creation) or to violently create corpses (by taking life). Through sin, in ways big or small, we create a "corpse" of our own still-living soul, or at least, we create lifeless amputations.[45] These severed faculties—intended to be alive with virtue—are now the "not nothing" remnants of what might have been. The brimming potential in us for dynamic prudence, temperance, fortitude, justice—and greater still—faith, hope, and love, lies lifeless now on the battlefield of our own lives. Again, these faculties were meant to enable us to live lightly and gracefully, but now we have the double burden of (a) struggling to get around without the aid of all our God-given faculties, and (b) carrying these spiritual amputations as dead weight. Over time, many find that they are increasingly crushed by the burden. As Balthasar says, we have "lent" our personal being to this hideous thing which is wholly our own, not of God, but nevertheless real.

Let me try to articulate the same thing yet again, perhaps taking advantage of more Przywaraian and Balthasarian concepts: at some level, to be human—*imago Dei*—is *always* to hand oneself over, to pour oneself out. As the type of creature who is ontologically always "becoming," and thus inescapably dynamic, it is simply impossible to truly close ourselves off and remain where we are (try as we might). Thus, we are alive if and when we "die to self" and give ourselves over to the triune God, through the triune God. In that way, we are suspended in the "always-greater" God and thus truly free. In this state of perfect vulnerability, the perfectly vulnerable God lovingly holds us in being. The alternative, however— and this is the gate that is wide and the way that is broad—is that we should pour ourselves out, not through love of God and neighbor, but into the great nothingness of sin. The gift element of the human is unavoidable, but here the problem is we give our being, through our free- dom, over to sin. This is the source of our ontological fragmentation. When the dynamics of "the gift" are properly lived, nothing is truly lost because God is the God of life, and what is given is given again (as we saw in the Akedah and temple theology generally). This is the superabun- dance of divine Life. But when one gives oneself improperly, when the seed falls on rocky ground, we give ourselves in such a way that our being is fragmented, becoming a withered and misbegotten thing. In this case, what we have given or "lent" ourselves to, while it surely does not have a reality like God's, nevertheless becomes real in its own way, in and through our willing. This perverse, demon-like "being," entirely unlike

---

45. Cf. Aidan Nichols, *No Bloodless Myth: A Guide through Balthasar's Dramatics* (Washington, DC: The Catholic University of America Press, 2000), 216–17, who uses the same analogy.

divine Being, never returns the gift, but it only takes and entraps. It is we, in our freedom, who let this twisted other "be," and the God who gave us freedom that we might creatively elaborate on the beauty of creation by serving and protecting the garden, also allows us to hand ourselves over in this very different way. The gargoyle remnants of such an ugly kenosis, stony and grotesque, are now a fact of the old creation's history, and with respect to our freedom, God will not simply un-create them, but he will overcome them.[46]

46. For Balthasar, the very possibility of sin as "false distance" is the good and luminous distance of the Trinity. What I have said here is a play on that idea. Balthasar considers, under the umbrella of Trinitarian kenosis, the options of true vs. false distance, of a God-forsakenness of love vs. the godlessness of sin. All of this builds on a relational ontology where every "to be" is related to some kind of giving, some kind of simultaneous loving-into-existence and letting-be, some kind of *communio*. The (impossible-) possibility of the not-nothing of sin is a perversion of just this dynamic, by which the creature "loves"-into-existence and let's-be a perverse form of being which has its existence by twisting away the human essence, its "life" by draining human vitality. Here is a violent kenoticism of perpetual wasting away. Both Sergei Bulgakov and Balthasar persuasively argue that the "underpinning" of such a damnable motion is the infinitely greater kenotic motion of love, and it is the latter that ensures that the former can and will be overcome.

Before moving forward, it is appropriate to register the fact that this concept has—understandably—attracted rebuke. In this respect, Alyssa Lyra Pitstick is without equal. Reviewing Balthasar's work, she also notes that "The 'God-lessness' of the divine love 'undergirds' sin, 'embrace[s]' it, 'renders it possible and goes beyond it.' The greatest suffering and forsakenness (and so all lesser sufferings) are also embraced by the Trinitarian 'distance' and have their archetype in God. Note that both sin and suffering are conceived here as positive realities." Pitstick, *Light in Darkness*, 121–22. A few pages later, she says, "although Balthasar denies that the Trinitarian 'super-kenosis' is the archetype of sin, it is difficult to see how his assertion (and it is only that) can be consistent with other essential aspects of his own theology, such as his positions that sin is not nothing, but a reality, and that God is the source of all being. . . . If the Trinity is not sin's archetype, what is?" Pitstick, 128. Similarly, see Karen Kilby, *Balthasar: A (Very) Critical Introduction* (Grand Rapids, MI: Eerdmans, 2012), 120–22. Here, Pitstick does not give Balthasar the best possible reading, and I am hopeful that my various reflections have opened the way to alternative interpretations. Balthasar does not say that "sin and suffering are positive realities." Yes, the (warped, unnatural) distance that human beings put between themselves and God is dependent—in a sense—on inter-trinitarian distance. But this is true because it is *only* within a universe in which there is "space" for the other to be other that the advent of self-centered-otherness, or the "wasting kenoticism" I just described, becomes conceivable. If God were a perfect monad, there would be no space for genuine otherness (every distance would be collapsed), and there would be no space for finite freedom (every freedom would be overwhelmed), and thus there would be no sin . . . nor would there be love. The false-distance of sin is in no way a "positive" reality, directly partaking of God's Being—Beauty, Goodness, Truth—though it is a possible reality because of distance within the Trinity and the fact that, created in the image of God, we inevitably pour ourselves forth. That we should "lend" our being—which is created good—to dark purposes, does not at all mean sin and suffering are positive realities!

This interpretation of Balthasar's approach to sin is strengthened by von Speyr's account of the "effigies" in hell. Drawing on the first volume of von Speyr's *Kreuz und Hölle*, Balthasar says:

> In his journey through hell, Christ encountered not only the sin which has already become amorphous, but also figures which Adrienne von Speyr called "effigies" They consist of what a person has loaned from her substance to the sin which she has committed: "The lost piece of the person goes into hell with the sin." The Son replaces that which has been lost through his personal grace. "Therefore the one-time sinner now stands closer to the Lord, but she is also imaged in the negative, as a sinner, in hell. An effigy of her . . . is buried and discarded in hell." The effigies are like a hollow impression, as when a body has been lying in the sand. . . . Through the Lord's passing by, they can be "settled," "extinguished," so that they "sink into anonymity." . . . Many [of the effigies] "cry, as it were, for the presence of the holy one" and are "depersonalized" by the Lord.[47]

There are two categories of sin identified here: the "amorphous sins" and the "effigies." It seems that the latter are linked to sinners who are still in the process of purification. The ultimate goal is that the "effigy" would be wholly and definitively detached from the human person, at which point it is "depersonalized," that is, made amorphous and anonymous. In a beautiful twist, Christ—and here I think of the Y$_{HWH}$-goat—through his grace, substitutes his fully-alive faculties where the sinner's soul has grown dead. As Balthasar put it, "The Son replaces that which has been lost through his personal grace." In other words, he prunes the wilted branches and replaces them with his own limbs of super-abundant fruitfulness. In this way, "where sin increased, grace abounded all the more" (Romans 5:20). But Balthasar continues to explain that the effigies stubbornly remain until the person is completely sanctified—or again, deified—and that all-too-often we sinners "revitalize"[48] the effigies we create in hell. Interestingly, von Speyr claims that "The Lord can really unload sin only when man repents of it."[49] This again calls to mind aspects of Yom Kippur theology discussed in previous chapters. Each Israelite participates in the cleansing of the temple through his or her work of self-

---

47. My translation, adapted from Balthasar, *TL2*, 355–56. Compare Hans Urs Von Balthasar, *Theologik 2 / Wahrheit Gottes* (Einsiedeln: Johannes Verlag Einsiedeln, 1985), 324–25.
48. To speak using a twisted analogy, because sin is, first and foremost, dead "matter."
49. Balthasar, *TL2*, 356.

denial, abstaining, fasting, and repentance, culminating in the High Priest's solemn prayer of confession before the Azazel-goat. What is objectively achieved in the Day of Atonement liturgy—the removal of the world's sins by the Azazel-goat—must be subjectively received by each person; otherwise, they remain bound to their hellish reflection. Nevertheless, the goal is that each "effigy" would be released, not destroying the sin itself (which, for Balthasar, is impossible), but fully detaching the parasitical sin from the person or persons from whom it originated: "Whoever is really redeemed goes to heaven; his effigy in hell is extinguished."[50] When the effigy is extinguished, the sin sinks into anonymity, and the redeemed saint is entirely free.

I would argue that an approach to sin along these lines does not directly or radically violate the metaphysical insights of privation theory, even though it does emblazon those insights with an added flourish to make them more harmonious with the great teachings of the ancient temple priests. This approach also explains how evil is rooted first-and-last in the misuse of creaturely freedom,[51] as opposed to Barth's theory of *das Nichtige*. Most importantly, it starts to clarify the nature of the Azazel-goat's work in a comprehensive theory of atonement. The importance of this harmartiology will be clearer as we further unpack the nuances hidden in Balthasar's Azazel-goat soteriology.[52]

Balthasar's Soteriology of the Sin-bearing Goat

In a radio sermon given on Good Friday, Balthasar asks, "Was [Jesus Christ] the one, great and final scapegoat for mankind? Did mankind load him with all its guilt, and did he, the Lamb of God, carry this guilt away?"[53] The soteriology that he presents throughout his career makes it clear that Balthasar's answer to these questions is, emphatically, Yes. In this section, we will consider how this basic theological conviction thoroughly shapes Balthasar's interpretation of Christ's passion and descent.

Turning to look at Balthasar's most substantive soteriological texts from this perspective, one quickly finds that he continually evokes the idea of the Azazel-goat. For example, he says, "Here the God-man drama

50. Von Speyr quoted in Balthasar, 356, n. 165.

51. In one place, Balthasar refers to our sin as "the darkness [the human] has manufactured. . . ." Balthasar, *TD5*, 265.

52. On the term "Azazel-goat soteriology," see the clarifying note in the introduction; page 10, note 18.

53. Hans Urs von Balthasar, *You Crown the Year with Your Goodness: Radio Sermons* (San Francisco: Ignatius Press, 1989), 82.

reaches its acme: perverse finite freedom casts all its guilt onto God, making him the sole accused, the scapegoat, while God allows himself to be thoroughly affected by this, not only in the humanity of Christ but also in Christ's trinitarian mission."[54] Immediately after Balthasar says this, he again refers to Jesus as the "sin bearing Son." It is precisely this enactment of the Yom Kippur ritual that Balthasar calls the acme of the theo-drama.[55] But Balthasar's description of sin as a burden loaded onto the Son is even more nuanced than has been indicated thus far, and the additional details only strengthen the idea that Balthasar is developing an Azazel-goat soteriology. On the Cross, Balthasar says, Christ experiences the reality of sin *in solidarity* with human beings, but in the savior's descent into hell, he experiences sin "as such," independent of individual human persons. Therefore, in the first moment, on the Cross, "God is solidary with us not only in what is symptomatic of sin, the punishment for sin, but also in co-experiencing sin, in the *peirasmos* [trial] of the very essence of that negation—though without 'committing' (Hebrews 4:15) sin himself."[56] Fifteen years later, Balthasar reinforces this claim: "It is essential to maintain, however, that the Crucified does not bear the burden as something external: he in no way distances himself from those who by rights should have to bear it. (Indeed, he is *in* them eucharistically!)"[57] It seems that Balthasar interprets Christ's cross as an act of solidarity with sinners, where Christ suffers God's covenantal wrath (Leviticus 26, Deuteronomy 28) in union with God's unfaithful people. The Son wishes to be with Israel in all things, even if it means suffering with her in exile.[58]

54. *TD4*, 335.

55. In *Theo-Drama 4*, Balthasar traces the history of Christian soteriology. In his telling, "Rupert [of Deutz (1075–1129)] was the first to apply to Christ the image of the scapegoat, an image that was to have such a long history" (Balthasar, 292). As we have seen, this is inaccurate; *Barnabas*, Justin Martyr, and Tertullian highlight this point long before Rupert. Balthasar then traces the idea through Denys the Carthusian, John Calvin, and Theodore Beza, and also explores the modern adaptation of René Girard and Raymund Schwager.

56. Hans Urs von Balthasar, *Mysterium Paschale: The Mystery of Easter* (San Francisco: Ignatius Press, 2000), 137. Hereafter, *MP*.

57. *TD4*, 338. Again: "The Son bears sinners within himself, together with the hopeless impenetrability of their sin, which prevents the divine light of love from registering in them" (349).

58. N. T. Wright emphasizes this point in his reflections on the cross. Discussing the way Jesus non-verbally relates his vocation to Isaiah 53, Wright says: "He spoke of it in his actions, particularly in the upper room, and in his readiness to go to the eye of the storm, the place where the messianic woes would reach their height, where the *peirasmos*, the time of testing, would become most acute, and in bearing the weight of Israel's exile, dying as her Messiah outside the walls of Jerusalem." Wright, *Jesus and the Victory of God*, 603.

However, turning attention to Holy Saturday,[59] Balthasar pivots from the language of solidarity to the language of substitution. He asks: "what good [would] this solidarity do us if it did not have the potential of being intensified into a true substitution?"[60] This intensification is the descent into hell. Quoting Adrienne von Speyr, Balthasar says

> In this view. . . , hell would be what is finally condemned by God; what is left in it is sin, which has been separated from the sinner by the work of the Cross. . . . Sins "are remitted, separated from us, taken away from us. They are banished to the place where everything God does not want and condemns is hell. That is their place. . . ."[61]

On the Cross, Jesus is united to all human beings and, as a corollary, to their burdensome sin. Through his solidarity with us, it becomes possible for our sin to be separated from us, and for Jesus—the sin-bearer—to bear the sins away into hell. What does Christ (passively) experience on Holy Saturday? In *Mysterium Paschale*, Balthasar says Christ experienced ". . . the second death which, itself, is one with sheer sin as such, no longer sin as attaching to a particular human being, sin incarnate in living existences, but abstracted from that individuation, contemplated in its bare reality as such (for sin *is* a reality!)."[62] Then, in the seventh volume of the *Glory of the Lord*, Balthasar says that in the "*visio (secundae) mortis*" in Hell, Christ sees "the whole fruit of the redeeming Cross. . . . That is to say, sin in its 'pure state' separated from man, 'sin in itself' in the whole formless, chaotic momentum of its reality, was seen by Jesus. . . . "[63] For Jesus, the fruit of the Cross is sin-in-itself, which he has removed from sinners

59. It is important to recognize that, for Balthasar, "Holy Saturday" is not a completely distinct "day," since the entire movement of the Paschal Triduum—the Last Supper, the High Priestly Prayer, the Garden of Gethsemane, Christ's suffering and death, the descent, and Resurrection—are mutually revealing perspectives on a single saving action.

60. Hans von Balthasar and Adrienne von Speyr, *To the Heart of the Mystery of Redemption* (San Francisco: Ignatius Press, 2010), 29. Balthasar originally wrote these words in 1977.

61. Balthasar, *TD5*, 314. Balthasar is quoting Adrienne von Speyr's commentary on the Letter to the Ephesians. For more on this theme in von Speyr, see Matthew Lewis Sutton, *Heaven Opens: The Trinitarian Mysticism of Adrienne von Speyr* (Minneapolis: Fortress Press, 2014), 177–78.

62. *MP*, 173.

63. *GL7*, 233. Similarly, and adding even *more* metaphors to the list, "The object of the *visio mortis* can only be the pure substantiality of 'Hell' which is 'sin in itself'. Plato and Plotinus created for this the expression *borboros* (mud, ordure) which the Church Fathers (and notably the Cappadocians) gratefully took up. Likewise, the image of chaos is a natural one here. In another image still, Eriugena says that, in our redemption, 'all the leprosy of human nature was thrown to the Devil.'" *MP*, 173.

through his blood—just as the blood of the *ḥaṭṭāʾt* releases sins from the temple—to be finally taken away, as far from the Father as East is to West.

It is valuable to pause and emphasize the fact that Balthasar associates Hell with "sin itself" repeatedly throughout the trilogy. In the last years of his life, he insists, "Since [hell's] 'substance' is the sin of the world, become (or becoming) anonymous, there is no community in hell; one simply goes 'missing' there without a trace."[64] Continuing to reflect on this nightmare, he adds, "Here the contradictions emerge with full force. First, there is contradiction in the essence of hell itself, insofar as hell is discarded sin. Hell is and at the same time is not. Consequently, it is ultimately something that is at once atemporal-eternal and self-destroying, perishing, 'dragged down,' 'eddying down.' Being both, hell is only 'dregs.'"[65] Again, the Jewish conception of the wilderness as an "empty howling waste" comes vividly to mind. For Balthasar and von Speyr, the essence of hell is the substance of sin, and the "substance" of sin is necessarily irregular and desolating. Sin's reality is a "formless, chaotic momentum,"[66] it is a "second chaos"[67] introduced by humans, which simply "cannot be assimilated,"[68] which is "the final 'residue and phlegm which it is absolutely impossible to restore to life.'"[69] In the end, hell is the eternal essence of true exile: "Babylon, the chaos produced by sin, is being burned eternally; the devouring pit devours itself eternally."[70] Because sin is not nothing, it is devouring and devour-able, but because it is death-reified, it is never satisfied and is never satisfy-able. It is a swirling, sinking chaos, the heart of madness, the consummation of isolation, the sum of all terror, multiplied by every horror, nameless, faceless, the greatest hunger, the final thirst, screaming silence, breaking again what it has broken before, in an endless cycle.[71] Yes, again, it is true Babylon,

64. Balthasar, *TL2*, 349.

65. Balthasar, 351. Here Balthasar is especially drawing on von Speyr's *Kreuz und Hölle*, Volume 1.

66. Balthasar, *GL7*, 233.

67. Balthasar, *TD5*, 316; cf. Balthasar, *TL2*, 348.

68. Balthasar, *TL2*, 323.

69. Balthasar, *MP*, 174. Balthasar is here quoting the early nineteenth-century Swiss Catholic Romantic theologian Aloysius Gügler.

70. Balthasar, *TD5*, 316. For von Speyr's own thoughts on hell as "the reality of sin separated from the world," see Lois M. Miles, "Obedience of a Corpse: The Key to the Holy Saturday Writings of Adrienne von Speyr" (Ph.D. diss., University of Aberdeen, 2013), 178–80.

71. What can account for the "endlessness" of this state? Perhaps it is the shadow side of Gregory of Nyssa's theory of *epektasis*; it is the capacity to move evermore toward nothingness.

the ultimate abyss known to the Azazel-goat alone. For Balthasar, because the essence of sin *is* the essence of hell, when the sin-bearer carries the "not nothing" of sin away from the sinner, he is both bringing that sin to hell and—in-so-doing—creating hell through the very same act.

Thus far we have been drawing on different volumes in Balthasar's "trilogy" to capture the essence of his Azazel-goat soteriology without too much attention to chronology. But there is at least one area in which Balthasar's thought changes from the earlier books to the later. There is a footnote in the second volume of the *Theo-Logic* in which Balthasar laments that *Mysterium Paschale* was written quickly and that students should now refer to von Speyr's thought directly to better understand his own thinking on Holy Saturday. However, the only retraction Balthasar explicitly makes is when he says, "The term 'solidarity with the dead' was a compromise that no longer appears in what follows."[72] Of all the controversial things Balthasar said in *Mysterium Paschale*, this is the one phrase he made a point to correct. Why? Perhaps because of what we explained above: Balthasar wants to limit *solidarity* with sinners to the Cross; the descent into hell is about bearing away the disconnected, depersonalized "sin itself" to the place that God, in his grace, had prepared—that is, to Hell. This change in terminology late in Balthasar's life, mentioned only in a footnote, further suggests his attentiveness to the pattern of Yom Kippur soteriology.

Drawing on what I have said in earlier chapters, we can explain Balthasar's thought like this: just as the temple is connected to all Israel, and the whole world, as microcosm, so also, if Christ is the temple of the new covenant, he shares a similar relationship with the world. Therefore, just as the world's sins are drawn to the Jerusalem temple according to priestly theology, they similarly target the "sacred space" of Jesus, the new temple. Then, through Christ's purifying blood, sin is released from us through Christ's high priestly action in the holy of holies, and (turning toward the second goat) he bears away the sin-in-itself, the dead weight of disembodied human sin. In his descent, in other words, Christ brings sin into a true wilderness, an infinite distance from the Father.

The Passive Contemplation of Sin Itself

One could say that, as Jesus offers himself on the cross, he mystically allows all sinners across time and space to "lay hands" on him, to confess,

---

72. *TL2*, 345, n. 75.

and thus to transfer their sins to the sin-bearing-goat chosen by God.[73]
In Leviticus, this confession was spoken by the high priest, representing
the nation Israel, in the presence of the people, and later Jewish tradition
recorded the priest's full prayer. The prayer, which I quoted above, reads:

> O Lord, your people, the house of Israel, has committed iniquity,
> transgressed, and sinned before you. Forgive, O Lord, I pray, the
> iniquities, transgressions, and sins, which your people, the house of
> Israel, have committed, transgressed, and sinned before you, as it is
> written in the Torah of Moses, your servant, *For on this day shall
> atonement be made for you to clean you. From all your sins shall
> you be clean before the Lord* (Lev. 16:30).[74]

This prayer emphasizes that every kind of sin is addressed by the atoning
ritual of Yom Kippur. As Israel confesses her sins over the Azazel-goat,
she knows that, by virtue of his lonely mission, she is made clean.
However, the ritual does not end with the confession; after having
received this great burden, the goat for Azazel must bear the sins into the
wilderness.[75] As Gary Anderson put it with reference to the Yom Kippur
liturgy, "It is not enough for Israel to fast and repent; the physical material of the sin that had rested on the shoulder of every Israelite must be
carted away into oblivion."[76] For Balthasar, this is what Jesus does for
Israel, and for all humankind. In a way analogous to Milgrom's interpretation of Leviticus 16, Balthasar depicts Christ as a kind of vehicle for
removing sins that have been detached from us and thus depersonalized,
carrying them out into the furthest wilderness. However, there is an
important difference between Christ and the biblical goats which is relevant to Balthasar and von Speyr's vivid descriptions of Christ in hell.
Unlike the goats—which are liturgical "matter" that have theological efficacy in the context of the ritual "form" and which, seen from the Christian perspective, are types that anticipate the act of the coming
messiah—Jesus Christ is able to add full intentionality to his saving
action. This is true with respect to both movements fulfilled on the cross.
The human Jesus offers himself as a *ḥaṭṭā't* with the fullness of love in

---

73. Commenting on Leviticus 16:8, Milgrom says, "The purpose of the lots is clearly
to leave the selection of the animals to YHWH." Milgrom, *Leviticus: A Book of Ritual and
Ethics*, 168. For Balthasar, it is the Father who loads the sins on Jesus even as sinners also
load the sins on him; the two are not mutually exclusive.

74. Neusner, *The Mishnah*, para. 6:2, page 275.

75. As a reminder, Anderson points out that this was "an area that was thought to
be beyond the reach of God." Anderson, *Sin*, 6.

76. Anderson, 6.

contemplative union with the Father in a way that would have been impossible for the humble YHWH-goat, and he also contemplates the bare reality of sin in utter isolation from the Father in a way that would have been impossible for the lamentable Azazel-goat. For this reason, Balthasar and von Speyr's theology of the Azazel-goat develops the Yom Kippur tradition by meditating deeply on the dark night suffered by the sin-bearing-goat.

The first word for Balthasar and von Speyr, here and everywhere, is "obedience." This word is also applicable to both goats, but in different ways. We have seen that the YHWH-goat, who represents the wholeheartedness of Abraham and Isaac, is the liturgical symbol of Israel's active obedience as she draws near to the Lord in ever-renewed love. The obedience of the second goat, however, is passive; in Leviticus 16, after the sins are put on the Azazel-goat's head, it says, "it shall be sent off to the wilderness through a designated man. . ." (v. 21). This goat is dressed with sins and led where it does not want to go, and for the latter Jewish tradition, it is cast into the abyss by the action of another. According to *Mishnah Yoma*, the designated man "pushed it backward, and it rolled down the ravine. And it did not reach halfway down the mountain before it broke into pieces."[77] For Balthasar, the passivity of this movement is of utmost importance: "Since the momentum of the Father's will, which loaded the world's guilt on to Jesus' kenotic *fiat*, in the truest sense 'crushed' the sufferer (Is 53.10), we have here no active descent—far less, a triumphant descent to take possession, or even only a descent that is a struggle in battle; we have only, in this 'sinking down' into the abyss of death, a passive 'being removed.'"[78] As Christ descends into the grave, and even into the pit of death, he is necessarily stripped of everything, including even the conscious awareness of the Father's adoring presence, and his "obedience unto the end" becomes truly blind. Now he "must obey the Father at the point where the last trace of God seems lost (in pure sin), together with every other communication (in pure solitariness)."[79] This is the exilic reality approached by the author of Lamentations: "He has made me dwell in darkness, Like those long dead. He has walled me in and I cannot break out; He has weighed me down with chains. And when I cry and plead, He shuts out my prayer; He has walled in my ways with hewn blocks, He has made my paths a maze" (3:6–9). For Balthasar, following von Speyr, in his passive descent, the savior of

---

77. Neusner, *The Mishnah*, para. 6.6, page 275.
78. Balthasar, *GL7*, 230.
79. Balthasar, 233.

the world endures the total chaos of sin such that he has no point of reference, no companionship, no imaginable way forward.

At the time of the second temple liturgy, the poor Azazel-goat suffers a physical agony when he is cast into the ravenous abyss, but in the descent of Jesus Christ the experience of "breaking apart" is intensified into a spiritual shattering.

> He is the dead "sin-bearer" of all sins. As such, he passes through what, looked at objectively, is his victory, the sin separated from man on the Cross, which God eternally damns as the second—man-created—chaos. However, because he is dead, he cannot know it subjectively as what he has made it to be. He can only "take cognizance" of it as the fearsome agglomeration of all sins that no longer has the slightest connection with the Father who is the good Creator. . . .[80]

This is the source of the psychological agony of the savior that is so prominent in the descent to hell theology of Balthasar and von Speyr. When the Azazel-goat hits bottom, reaching the far end of hell, his human soul is dashed upon the utter and unspeakable brokenness of the place. Here he is among the fragments and fragmentations generated by his own beloved creation's evil will. The shards of cruel torture, burning hatred, everyday degradation, callous abuse, all the murders, acts of stony indifference, the gnarling greed, the brutish rapes, violence against children—his own precious children!—the unkind thoughts, egotistical pride, the genocides . . . this terrible mountain of inhumanity. . . . Jesus has borne it into the sea, and here he drowns beneath the weight of its madness. He has descended into the great chaos, the one authored by his own beloved, by his own image, but it is all now amorphous, unrecognizable, without logic. He confronts, at last, the abomination of desolation, and in this great cacophony, he is silent, and in his silence, he is evermore the living word: "*Take Lord, and receive all my liberty, my memory, my understanding, and my entire will, all that I have and possess. Thou hast given all to me. To Thee, O lord, I return it. All is Thine, dispose of it wholly according to Thy will. . . .*"[81]

As I've said, an essential aspect of this obedience to the end, this embrace of exile in its most concentrated form, is the fact that the Azazel-goat entirely loses sight of Zion. According to the rabbinic tradition, the

80. Balthasar, *TL2*, 348. For "objective sin" in von Speyr's thought, see Miles, "Obedience of a Corpse," 180–82; Sutton, *Heaven Opens*, 183–84.

81. This is the *Suscipe* of St. Ignatius of Loyola. For the influence of this prayer on von Speyr (and, through her, on Balthasar) see Miles, "Obedience of a Corpse."

cliff over which the second goat is sent is about twelve miles from the temple gate,[82] and thus the glory of the dwelling place of God has dimmed to nothing. For Balthasar, Christ suffers a similar sense of distance insofar as, in that "non-place," the Father is entirely veiled from the Son. This is the meaning of the word "forsaken." "The Son hangs between earth and heaven, forsaken by men and God. The darkness of the world's guilt that he bears within him veils and obscures all sight of a meaning to his suffering."[83] He is now truly stripped, truly alone, in an impossible "distance" that has been fabricated by humanity and which is now endured by God. But according to Balthasar, even in this desperate pit, there is an unseen glimmer of the eternal triune glory: "In fact, since all is obedience, he is moving toward the Father through this utter estrangement, but for the present he must not be allowed to know this."[84] In other words, the Son realizes the unity of the triune persons—in his economic mission—by virtue of the profound depths of his obedience, even suffering the midnight darkness of *this* world by experiencing the apparent loss of the Father's presence. By allowing the triune distance, the *diastasis*, to stretch in such unnatural ways, for the sake of love, the Son actually reinforces the truth and beauty of divine oneness, even amid the world's gravest horrors, by showing that love is deeper still.

The only way it would be possible to say all this, to even begin to imagine the Son performing this act of love for the sake of humankind, is if sin is "not nothing." What could it mean to affirm that a metaphysical deficiency is "loaded" onto the Son? What could it mean to say Christ is "crushed" under a privation of the good? For Azazel-goat soteriology to be coherent, *something*, some kind of nuance or some kind of supplement, would need to be added to the Augustinian philosophical discovery, without denying that that theory retains its philosophical authority. More than anything else, it is the liturgy of Yom Kippur which speaks to a reality that must be faced. The priestly theologians knew sin to be rooted in us and our actions and yet somehow independent and vital, having an existence that cannot be merely negated through a positive movement *towards*, but which must also be "physically" eliminated through a negative movement *away*. It may be that the only language we have to capture this phenomenon is poetic and mythic, as in the great dramas of Enoch, but still, the weakness of our language is not in itself an excuse for theologians to neglect the question entirely. With that in mind, Bal-

82. Neusner, *The Mishnah*, para. 6:4, page 275.
83. Balthasar, *TD4*, 356.
84. Balthasar, 356.

thasar should be lauded for his efforts to grapple with the problem of how sin can have a certain kind of perverse substantiality.

Other Examples of the Azazel-goat in Contemporary Theology

Balthasar's Azazel-goat soteriology is perhaps the most widely discussed, and thus the most frequently critiqued, soteriology in contemporary theological literature. However, it is not unprecedented in every respect. A few words should be said about the Russian Orthodox sophiological theologian Sergius Bulgakov.[85] One thing that is glaring in the section on Christ's high priestly ministry in Bulgakov's famous Christological book, *The Lamb of God*, is how frequently he mentions the fact that Christ bears sins.[86] Indeed, this is the central image used in Bulgakov's soteriology, and thus it immediately provides an opening for analysis from the perspective of Yom Kippur theology. In approaching this theme, the first question to ask is how Bulgakov depicts the "reality" of sin itself. Here we find that Bulgakov nods in the direction of Balthasar's more developed theory, though he does not go as far. He says,

> Sin is just as real as the world and man, insofar as it is their state. To be sure, sin is not created by God; it is a product of creaturely freedom. But this freedom, in all its self-definitions, is real with all the reality of this world and of man; therefore, the sin that envelops the world and man is real. The difference is that the world and man, since they are created by God, are indestructible, whereas sin, which is a product of creaturely freedom, is destructible and must be destroyed.[87]

Then, in another place, he adds that sin "is an illegitimate product of creaturely freedom and thus does not contain the power of being, for God did not create sin, just as He did not create death. . . ."[88] In these

---

85. For a far broader and deeper comparison (positive and negative) of Balthasar and Bulgakov's soteriologies, see the third chapter ("Emptiness vs. Effigies: Christology and the Descent into Hell") of Katy Leamy, *The Holy Trinity: Hans Urs Von Balthasar and His Sources* (Eugene, OR: Pickwick Publications, 2015), 81–118.

86. A partial list of examples: "the only one without sin, bore upon Himself the sin of the world" Sergii Bulgakov, *The Lamb of God* (Grand Rapids, MI: Eerdmans, 2008), 347. "Christ takes upon himself the sin of the world" (347); ". . . as one who bore upon Himself the sin of the entire old Adam," (350); "Having taken sin upon himself. . ." (357); "only the God-Man could take upon Himself all human sin. . . ." (358).

87. Bulgakov, 350–51.

88. Bulgakov, 361.

two quotes, one finds some similarities between Bulgakov and Balthasar. Unlike Barth, he does not ground sin or evil in the rejecting side of God's electing will, but rather he sees it as a product of human freedom. He does say it as somehow "real"—but then the similarities between Balthasar and Bulgakov begin to break down. For the great Russian theologian, sin's reality is more with respect to humanity's *state* than with respect to a perverse "not nothing" that human beings have introduced into the good creation. As something which is not created by God, Bulgakov says, sin does not have "being," and thus it is destructible. We have seen that Barth similarly believes that nothingness or sin "has no perpetuity," and thus Barth anticipates the "destruction of sin,"[89] "its radical eradication, which leads to its annihilation."[90]

These views, however, contrast with the basic priestly intuition that, unlike impurities that pollute the temple, serious intentional sins are of the sort that cannot be eradicated, but only removed to a distant place. The priestly understanding of sin has an impressive parallel in Balthasar's thought insofar as he sees the detached, depersonalized "sin itself" as the eternal substance of hell.[91] The advantage of this view is that it accentuates the fact that sin *is* truly removed, as far as the east is from the west, and thus Christians are completely relieved of the burden. At the same

89. David Lauber, *Barth on the Descent into Hell: God, Atonement, and the Christian Life* (New York: Ashgate Publishing, 2004), 37.

90. Lauber, 36. Barth himself says that the "decisive thing" is that "in the suffering and death of Jesus Christ it has come to pass that in His own person He has made an end of us as sinners and therefore of sin itself by going to death as the One who took our place as sinners. In his person He has delivered up us sinners and sin itself to destruction." Karl Barth, *Church Dogmatics. Vol. 4, Part 1 The Doctrine of Reconciliation.* (Edinburgh: T&T Clark, 2004), 253. He adds that Jesus Christ "willed to make Himself the bearer and Representative of sin, caused sin to be taken and killed on the cross in His own person (as that of the one great sinner). And in that way, not by suffering our punishment as such, but in the deliverance of sinful man and sin itself to destruction, which He accomplished when He suffered our punishment, He has on the other side blocked the source of our destruction. . . ." Barth, 254.

On this theme in Barth, see the book by Matthias Grebe which, in a way that is tantalizingly analogous to the present book, interprets Barth in light of the two Yom Kippur goats: *Election, Atonement, and the Holy Spirit*, 38–45. What's striking about Grebe's book is that, while he is highly attentive to the distinct role of each goat, he insists that the second goat should not be given a place in Christian interpretation of the cross, and thus he attempts to re-frame Barth's thought (which, in its own peculiar way, does include both goats as the two sides of God's election) only in terms of the YHWH-goat. Whether or not this is a desirable way to untangle and reinterpret Barth—by retaining God's electing *Yes* and suppressing God's rejecting *No* in Barth's theology of Christ's saving act—I hope that my work here suggests why I consider this approach to be inadequate for Christian soteriology more generally.

91. Cf. Leamy, *The Holy Trinity*, 104–6.

time, eschatologically, the historical reality of the sin—this mournful misuse of our *creative* freedom—is memorialized, but in the most deeply healing way.[92] As I mentioned above, for Balthasar, creaturely history does not receive a Pollyannaish whitewash, but it is thoroughly redeemed. In other words, Balthasar's view, like the priestly view, takes the concrete and often ragged shape of history seriously; the horrors we create in ourselves and in the world are not swept away like a bad dream, nor are they annihilated in a way suggestive of cheap grace.[93] It is all removed and cast into the pit, but still it remains a kind of tombstone for the old creation that has been overcome.[94]

92. Thomas Aquinas made an argument that is not well-received by modern Christians. Asking whether the "blessed in heaven will see the sufferings of the damned," he answers: "Nothing should be denied the blessed that belongs to the perfection of their beatitude. Now everything is known the more for being compared with its contrary, because when contraries are placed beside one another they become more conspicuous. Wherefore in order that the happiness of the saints may be more delightful to them and that they may render more copious thanks to God for it, they are allowed to see perfectly the sufferings of the damned" (Thomas Aquinas, *Summa Theologica, Supplementum Tertiæ Partis*: 94.1c). When von Speyr suggests that the "substance" of hell is the "sin of the world," disconnected from human beings on the Cross and born away by the Son to this place which has been prepared by the loving Father, perhaps in this context Aquinas's comment can be retrieved. Saints can certainly look at *that* hell and rejoice, because "sin itself" has been so thoroughly removed.

93. Donald MacKinnon points out that Balthasar was a young man at the start of World War II, and thus spent most of his writing career in the shadow of Auschwitz. From this perspective, one might notice that "the nervous tension of [Balthasar's] whole argument bears witness to the author's passionate concern to present the engagement of God with the world in a way that refuses to turn aside from the overwhelming, pervasive reality of evil. . . . [Balthasar] insists on a vision that can only be won through the most strenuous acknowledgement of the cost of human redemption." Quoted in Kilby, *Balthasar*, 121.

94. As O'Regan puts it, "Balthasar insists that the 'all in all' of Christ does not exclude the prospect of waste, of elements of reality that are not reconciled to God's will." O'Regan, *Anatomy of Misremembering*, 391.

Balthasar's view that these sins are not annihilated does not necessarily mean that he gives them more credit than they deserve. In fact, fascinatingly, he approvingly quotes C. S. Lewis's *The Great Divorce* (which he calls a "masterpiece" in Balthasar, *Dare We Hope*, 56) to suggest the pathetic smallness of hell. In Lewis's book, the narrator and George McDonald have the following conversation: "'Do you mean then that Hell—all that infinite empty town—is down in some little crack like this?' 'Yes. All Hell is smaller than one pebble of your earthly world: but it is smaller than one atom of *this* world [heaven], the Real World.'" . . . "'It seems big enough when you're in it, Sir.' 'And yet all loneliness, angers, hatreds, envies and itchings that it contains, if rolled into one single experience and put into the scale against the least moment of joy that is felt by the least in Heaven, would have no weight that could be registered at all. . . . For a damned soul is nearly nothing: it is shrunk, shut up in itself.'" Lewis, *The Great Divorce*, 138–39. Balthasar cites this text at Balthasar, *TD5*, 307 n.12.

Bulgakov's treatment of Christ's experience of hell heavily emphasizes his encounter with God's wrath. He writes:

> Having taken sin upon Himself, the only begotten and beloved Son also took upon Himself God's anger at sin, God's hostility, and this led to a separation, as it were, with the Father. The torment of the only one without sin is caused by sin that became His own sin, as it were, having infected the Creator Himself through His creation. The burden was so heavy that, beneath it, His God-abandoned human essence suffered and became infirm. But only such suffering could overcome the power of sin; this was the price at which the New Adam redeemed the disobedience of the old Adam.[95]

Therefore, for Bulgakov—and this is again something he shares in common with Barth—the descent of Christ to hell is less about removing a pollutant and more about suffering a penalty. Now, granted, Bulgakov does make efforts at distancing himself from what he identifies as the "Reformed" position, especially in arguing that Christ does not exactly suffer the agonies of hell in our place. The God-Man's experience of hell could never be the same as that of true sinners precisely because their agony is driven in part by their "sin-corrupted soul,"[96] which the sinless Christ cannot experience. Bulgakov is attempting a delicate operation here. Any theologian who argues that the incarnate Son experiences the Father's dereliction and/or wrath must explain how Jesus, who was entirely "without sin,"[97] can at the same time experience divine wrath and hell. In a sense, this is *the* looming question that will be directly faced in the next chapter: how can a single savior be both YHWH-goat (morally without blemish) and Azazel-goat (loaded with sin)? In his attempt to put these ideas together, Bulgakov says, "This sin—which He took upon Himself not only ideally but also really, although He lovingly experienced it in a sinless manner—became His burden, and it was now He who answered God for human sin."[98] Bulgakov is right to turn to the theme

---

95. Bulgakov, *The Lamb of God*, 356–57.

96. Bulgakov, 361.

97. Heb 4:15; cf. 1 Pt 2:22, 1 Jn 3:5, etc.

98. Bulgakov, *The Lamb of God*, 350. Bulgakov's view becomes nuanced—perhaps to the point of inconsistency—when he says, "That is, he no longer suffers only from the sins of the world that besiege Him from the outside; He now also *inwardly* assimilates these sins by a 'compassionate love.'. . . And by making them His own, as it were, He identifies His sinless human essence with the sinful essence of the old Adam." Bulgakov, 354. He also says the sin of the world "penetrates" Christ's human essence. Bulgakov, 355. Understanding exactly how Christ can remain sinless while "inwardly" assimilating (!)

of "sin-bearing" while attempting to address the theological problem of simultaneous perfection and abandonment, but as I'll argue in the next section, I find that priestly theology undermines a strong emphasis on God's personal wrath directed toward the Azazel-goat. From Bulgakov's own perspective, insofar as the God-man truly takes up our fallen nature, and truly bears our sins, he must also endure God's wrath against sin; anything less would be docetic.[99]

There is one other important theme in Bulgakov that adds complexity to his concept of divine wrath, and that also makes him an important source for Balthasar. Bulgakov makes a connection between Christ's sin-bearing, his suffering, and Trinitarian kenosis. The reason why Christ is able to receive the load of the world's sins, on Bulgakov's account, is because "He humiliates Himself by emptying Himself of His divinity..."[100] As an isolated statement, this is not the most felicitous formulation; it could suggest a strange variant of the Cerinthian Christological heresy where the "divine Christ" flees before the crucifixion, leaving the "human Jesus" to suffer.[101] Of course, this concern is somewhat mitigated when one remembers that, for Bulgakov, kenoticism is the hallmark of God's eternal nature. Thus, with reference to the Father himself, Bulgakov says: "This begetting power is the ecstasy of a going out of oneself, of a kind of self-emptying, which at the same time is self-actualization through this begetting."[102] As Balthasar reads this, Bulgakov has articulated "an initial 'kenosis' within the Godhead that underpins all subsequent kenosis. For the Father strips himself, without remainder, of his Godhead and hands it over to the Son...."[103]

---

sin, and determining whether this concept is coherent, would require a more extensive analysis than I can here provide.

99. He says, "Christ's taking of sin upon Himself would have been docetic if it were not accompanied by all its consequences, that is, by God's anger and by His abandonment of Christ." Bulgakov, *The Lamb of God*, 361.

100. Bulgakov, 351.

101. Irenaeus says that, for Cerinthus, "after [the human Jesus's] baptism, Christ descended upon him in the form of a dove from the Supreme Ruler, and that then he proclaimed the unknown Father, and performed miracles. But at last Christ departed from Jesus, and that then Jesus suffered and rose again, while Christ remained impassible, inasmuch as he was a spiritual being." Irenaeus, *Against Heresies*, trans. Alexander Roberts and William Rambaut, vol. 1, Ante-Nicene Fathers (Buffalo, NY: Christian Literature Publishing Co., 1885), Book 1, Chapter 26. Cf. Gary A. Anderson, "Mary in the Old Testament," *Pro Ecclesia* 16, no. 1 (2007): 47, for similar concerns about the thought of Theodore of Mopsuestia.

102. Bulgakov, *The Lamb of God*, 98.

103. Balthasar, *TD4*, 323.

This is the context for Bulgakov's increasingly bold language in discussing the relations between the triune persons at the time of the Son's passion. Meditating on the Son's crucifixion, Bulgakov shifts focus to simultaneously introduce the corresponding theme of the "divine co-crucifixion" *of the Father*,[104] which is a suffering that is seen as *"equivalent"* to the Son's.[105] In his descent to the cross, the Son is also surely not divided from the Holy Spirit, and thus we have "the image of the spiritual co-crucifixion of the Love-Spirit with the Son, of the co-passion of the Third hypostasis. . . ."[106] The key here is that the triune God—in oneness and in the distinction of persons—is fully engaged in the God-Man's saving descent. The Father and the Spirit do not sequester themselves from the Son's passion; the kenotic motion of one cannot fail to involve the persons together.[107]

Therefore, when the Father lets go of the Son for the sake of salvation, it is a profound kenotic act, a kind of "co-crucifixion," and the Son (who never does but what he sees the Father doing) responds with his own kenotic "being let go." By mutually handing themselves over—which is the eternal peaceful motion of the Trinity that has now been stretched

---

104. Bulgakov, *The Lamb of God*, 353.

105. Bulgakov, 370. Emphasis in the original. It is interesting that von Speyr has a similar teaching about the mutual abandonment of Father and Son:

> Each word the eternal Word says on earth is likewise spoken by the Father, for the Son is the Word of the Father. This is true wherever the Word of God sounds forth on earth. It is also, and especially, true of the word of the Son on the Cross: My God, my God, why have you forsaken me? If the Son is forsaken by the Father, then no one is to think that the Father in turn is not forsaken by the Son: for, if the Son loses his access to the Father, it is impossible for the Father still to have his access to the Son. The Father too is forsaken on the Cross and is separated from the Son who is separated from him. This is so, because love is a unity, and it is not possible in love for one to be affected without the other being affected too. Thus the Father and Son together bear witness to the one, forsaken love." Adrienne von Speyr, *John, Volume 2: The Discourses on Controversy* (San Francisco: Ignatius Press, 1993), 162–63.

See Lois Miles' illuminating commentary on this passage in Miles, "Obedience of a Corpse," 153–54.

106. Bulgakov, *The Lamb of God*, 370.

107. Here again, Bulgakov needs to walk on eggshells to avoid re-awakening the heresy of theopaschism. He basically says that this early heresy was a failure to recognize the difference between the persons. But to say that there is a "spiritual 'co-crucifixion'" is appropriate insofar as it excludes the absurd notion that there can be "nonparticipation" between the persons in the triune work of salvation, each person participating in a way appropriate to that person given the eternal relations between persons. This is effectively a defense of the Trinitarian doctrine of appropriation. Bulgakov, 372.

out into the broken time of our sinful world—both Father and Son endure the loss of the other, which is a shared motion of Love that cannot fail to involve the Spirit with whom they are one.[108] To risk repetition for emphasis: such a shared movement of handing over and letting be is *not* a crisis innovation for the Triune God, but it is the eternal way of being God, now expressed in an extreme and atypical way in the economic work of bearing away sin. This Trinitarian view provides a unique context for the words "abandonment" and "wrath." Bulgakov does not use these words as a one-way-street of unbalanced fury, but as indicating a co-kenotic work of enduring-to-the-end to radically and definitively undermine sin, all for us humans and for our salvation.

With Bulgakov, therefore, there is an early twentieth-century example of a theologian who emphasizes, again and again, the idea that Christ must bear away sins. He also provides a theologically powerful contextualization for such a "self-emptying" by developing kenotic Trinitarian theology. But his understanding of the "reality" of the burden that the messianic Azazel-goat bears is underdeveloped in this text, and thus his theology of Christ's descent to hell is *relatively* inconspicuous, compared to Balthasar, insofar as Bulgakov's descent simply emphasizes Christ's true experience of the phenomenon of death, this being "the deepest point of His in-humanization."[109] (This is akin to Balthasar's earlier emphasis on "solidarity with the dead.") Also, Bulgakov's theology of the cross features a strong focus on the Son's experience of the Father's wrath. This theme is also present in Balthasar, for better or worse.

The Place of Wrath in Azazel-goat Soteriology? A Critique of Balthasar

I mentioned above that Balthasar's Holy Saturday theology has received widespread attention and, often enough, sharp critique. An important goal of this book has been to outline a scriptural framework for responding to those critiques and for advancing a rich and comprehensive Christian soteriology. I am convinced that, overall, Balthasar has articulated aspects of that soteriology that is ultimately grounded in the biblical priestly atonement tradition, and therefore what is so often dismissed as scandalously innovative should instead be received as a needed

108. Cf. Bulgakov, 370. Powerfully, Bulgakov invokes Abraham and Isaac here, father and son, who both let go of everything in mutual trust and mutual love, thus laying the foundation stone for the temple of life.
109. Bulgakov, 373.

retrieval and a powerful development. And yet, from the perspective of a Christian Yom Kippur soteriology, other aspects of Balthasar's account seem unnecessary, and in any case, it is once again important to emphasize that there are *two* goats. The Azazel-goat alone is inadequate.[110] This final section will reflect on some possible weaknesses in Balthasar's soteriology and make recommendations—inspired by contemporary research into the book of Leviticus—for strengthening his insights.

While it has not been emphasized in the foregoing discussion of Balthasar's soteriology, the fact is that he does embrace the idea that the Son must endure the wrath of God the Father. In assessing this teaching, it is first necessary to appreciate and affirm the reasons why Balthasar insists on including the themes of divine anger and wrath in his soteriology, while many other modern theologians do everything they can to sidestep these themes. To put it simply, Balthasar will not avoid this subject precisely because, again, he is a biblical theologian. In reading the Hebrew Bible, Balthasar cannot miss the fact that the joyful theme of covenant is repeatedly and increasingly matched with the dark clouds of creaturely infidelity and divine judgment, anger, and wrath. Balthasar has no difficulty—none whatsoever—in compiling extensive *catena* of biblical texts that describe the Lord as provoked, stirred, and burning with rage against his own people, this traitorous, idolatrous nation, this beloved people who are called away from Egypt and yet who are always sneaking back. In the *Glory of the Lord* volume on the "Old Covenant," Balthasar says,

> Existence in flight and in catastrophe, since the glory of God has changed to blazing wrath, is one of the fundamental themes of the old covenant. The great lists of maledictions in Leviticus [26:14–16] and Deuteronomy [28:15–68] are already in part the verbal expression of the experience of such catastrophes; the books of the prophets are full of the descriptions of these. Round about Israel too there are more and more descents into hell and 'pursuits into the darkness' (Nahum 1.8). . . .[111]

In that same volume, Balthasar further reflects on how, in addition to the intensifying theme of divine anger, there are the corresponding concepts of pure obedience and divine abandonment, a type of descent that is

---

110. As I have said, and will say again, it is *not* the case that themes associated with the YHWH-goat are missing from Balthasar's theology overall—far from it—though I will argue that some of the moves he makes in his soteriology risk significance imbalance in the direction of Azazel-goat themes.

111. Balthasar, *GL6*, 218–19.

experienced acutely by the prophets, from Abraham down to the grief-stricken "Servant" (Is 53).[112]

Because of the sheer, unrelenting persistence of these themes, Balthasar has no patience for the modern Marcionism that would bowdlerize the Hebrew Bible to make YHWH more acceptable to laissez-faire moderns. On the topic of God's anger, Balthasar is uncompromising: "No doctrine of atonement may ignore this reality, which is attested a thousand times in Scripture. . . ."[113] For Balthasar, what is ultimately at stake, when acknowledging divine wrath, is the perfection of God's love.[114] As discussed in the last chapter, we have the searing example of Ivan Karamazov, whose conscience will not submit to a "higher harmony" that is content with the everlasting abomination of tortured children, these precious little ones, their weak fists beating their breasts, pleading with God through the long night for a rescue that will not come. . . . Is such a reality the necessary cost of a future "paradise"? Does God sit serenely through all this, content with some contemptible, epic sublation of evil, as if suffering is a necessary down-payment for joy? Both Balthasar and Hart would agree that such an idea is an abomination. But now Balthasar presses his point: will God not speak a definitive No? Is God's love so languid that he will not resolutely strike out against these horrors? Love without wrath is the accomplice of history's great torturers, the ferocious monsters who lurk in the dark to ruin poor lives forever. Confronted with such realities, will we have a nonjudgmental god? Such a scoundrel would not be worthy of respect, never mind worship. If the rage of Ivan in the face of these horrors exceeds the wrath of YHWH, well, to hell with Christianity and its god. Thus, Balthasar: "This wrath is no 'pretense,' but fully real: the categorical 'No' of God's reaction to the attitude that the world takes up over against him. God owes it to himself and to his loving covenantal righteousness to utter this 'No' and to maintain it as long as his will is not done on earth as in Heaven."[115] From this perspective, an atonement—an "at-one-ment"—that will not honestly and squarely face the reality of sin, fully suffer it, drinking the cup of wrath to the dregs, is theologically unserious and morally outrageous. It is an insipid fairytale, a pastel whimsy, an opiate escape that destroys every-

---

112. Cf. Balthasar, 215–98; Balthasar, *MP*, 73–74.

113. Balthasar, *TD4*, 55. He adds, "It seems naïve and superficial to me to wish simply to suppress everything that is said about God's *judgment* in the Bible, in the NT as well as in the Old." Balthasar and Speyr, *To the Heart of the Mystery of Redemption*, 33.

114. Balthasar regularly speaks of "the inseparable unity of God's wrath and his love" *TD4*, 55, because "the wrath of God is . . . the reverse side of his love"; *MP*, 139.

115. Balthasar, *GL7*, 206.

thing good and humane. A god without wrath is an idol; a savior who will not bear sin is a pretender and a sop.

The problem that Balthasar is trying to address here has nothing to do with placating, appeasing, or propitiating a god in mythological fashion. Balthasar could sign his name to Hart's declaration that God would himself be directly complicit in the dynamics of creaturely violence "[i]f the language of sacrifice in Christian thought did properly refer to an economy of exchange, such that God were *appeased* in the slaughter of a victim and his wrath were simply *averted* by way of a prudential violence of which he *approved*. . . ."[116] There is also no sense in Balthasar that there is a reservoir of wrath stored up in God that is seeking an outlet. Nor is judicial imagery central for him.[117] God's wrath is very specifically and ineluctably tied to the reality of sin, and thus it cannot be separated from the presence of sin. With this in mind, it is fitting to say, with Balthasar, that an atonement theory that preemptively excludes the question of wrath has not yet fully faced the theological crisis of sin.

Even with such contextualization, though, Balthasar's words are distressing:

> Can we seriously say that God unloaded his wrath upon the Man who wrestled with his destiny on the Mount of Olives and was subsequently crucified? Indeed we must.[118]

> He has diverted onto himself all the anger of God at the world's faithlessness. He himself has drained the cup and experienced the full extent of what, in an inchoate and anticipatory way, the Old Testament prophets underwent.[119]

> Divine anger is transformed "since the Father's wrath is transferred from the nations to his own Son." . . . On the basis of the Incarnation it is possible to distinguish between sin and the sinner; on the Cross 'the Son will divert the scourge of eternal wrath on to himself' in order to spare sinners from it. . . . On the Cross the Son "took all sin upon himself in such a way that God cannot strike the sinner

116. And, as Hart adds, "who can deny that many Christians have imagined their faith in just these terms?" Hart, *Beauty of the Infinite*, 348.

117. Balthasar does provide an extended review of the history of the idea of "vicarious punishment"—Balthasar, *TD4*, 290–98—but his own assessment of such language is ambivalent. He is not deeply committed to it. Balthasar, 337–38. Then again, he is also clear about the fact that juridical language itself is biblical, and thus it is not automatically ruled out. Cf. Balthasar, *TD2*, 152 ff.

118. Balthasar, *TD4*, 345.

119. Balthasar, 343.

without striking him"; so the anger is quieted by the love of the suffering Son.[120]

Is there any sense in which this language of "unloading" and "diverting" and "transferring" wrath can be theologically acceptable? Can Balthasar adequately respond to Matthew Levering's crucial question: "Does his theology fragment, by overstepping the limits of human language, the unity of God?"[121] How could it ever be possible to speak of genuine anger and wrath directed from the Father to the Son without damage to foundational Catholic dogma on the consubstantiality of Father and Son, together with the Spirit?

It would require a longer and more focused study to answer this question fully. But I would like to make a suggestion rooted in the central issues we have been studying in this chapter. The key to understanding the Son's experience of wrath—first on the cross in solidarity with sinners, then in his descent in the place of sinners—is to appreciate once more the radical teaching that sin is "a reality." As I said before, the experience of wrath— which is a mode of God's love—is inseparable from the presence of sin. If it is true that Jesus "bears sin," then it seems right to me that Jesus does *not* experience the "wrath of God" directly, but rather he encounters wrath indirectly through his experience of the "sins themselves."

"Sins themselves" surely have a grotesquely irregular form of being.[122] Because they have *some* kind of "reality," perhaps one could even say they are *somehow* "suspended in being," and thus they must *in some way* be related to Love (Being Itself). *But,* because this relation to Love is fundamentally negative or hostile (they are sins!), to the extent they remain "suspended in being," they must be suspended in Love-as-Wrath. Therefore, when Christ bears sin, and what's more, when he contemplates sin "in its bare reality as such,"[123] the sin that becomes the

---

120. Balthasar, *TD5,* 266–67. In order, Balthasar quotes von Speyr's commentary on Isaiah, her *Objektive Mystik,* and her commentary on Revelation.

121. Levering, *Scripture and Metaphysics,* 132. Certainly, some think the answer to this question is "yes." For example, Gavin D'Costa, "The Descent into Hell as a Solution for the Problem of the Fate of Unevangelized Non-Christians," *International Journal of Systematic Theology* 11, no. 2 (April 1, 2009): 154–55.

122. It is worth re-quoting Balthasar's important statement on sin: ". . . the question concerning the essence of sin *cannot be positively answered,* for sin is the lie and, hence, neither truth nor being, and yet men have lent it something of their personal being in order to make it possible." Balthasar, *TL2,* 350. My stammering attempts in this section to find language for it should not be taken as an effort at "positively" describing the essence of sin. Both the "cannot" and the "and yet" in Balthasar's statement should be respected.

123. Balthasar, *MP,* 173.

object of his "vision" is a being that partakes of Wrath. The ultimate Azazel-goat, therefore, does not personally or directly suffer the wrath of God, as if the Father desired to or was able to "pour" wrath and punishment on an innocent victim out of a "need" to discharge this negative energy (like a psychologically deranged father who beats his children to release his frustrations from work, as so many critics put it), but rather the Azazel-goat encounters "wrath" in a secondary or indirect way by virtue of his mission to bear away the sins *we* have manufactured in the world. The encounter with wrath comes through the encounter with the "second chaos," the "second death." It is, for sure, only an analogous knowledge; Bulgakov is quite right that the Son's experience of Hell cannot be identical to the sinner's experience because the Son remains sinless. Nevertheless, according to von Speyr's teaching, the Son who bears the sins to hell completely enters into that experience, in perfect obedience to God's saving will, and thus sin itself becomes an object of his "vision," and through this encounter, God's eternal wrath against sin is indirectly endured.[124]

My primary thesis for this entire book is that the single atoning *ḥaṭṭā't* of the incarnate Christ fulfills the movements of both the YHWH-goat and the Azazel-goat in a single work on the cross. For that to be at all plausible, there must be a way to reasonably imagine absolute loving intimacy between Father and Son on Zion that is simultaneous to the absolute wilderness distance between Father and Son in sin-bearing. It seems to me that an Azazel-goat soteriology becomes imbalanced, and actually hostile to the YHWH-goat, when it presents the theme of divine anger and wrath in such a way as to (absurdly) introduce, imply, or risk a caesura in the ontological unity of Father and Son. It is clear that this is not Balthasar's intent, but there is one way in which he puts himself in unnecessary danger.[125] For

124. Levering is particularly perceptive when he notices that Balthasar must understand "sin as 'chaff' so that Jesus can engage sin interiorly without perverting his will..." Levering, *Scripture and Metaphysics*, 131. Levering is unsympathetic to this hypothesis, though. He rhetorically asks: "Is [Balthasar's] hypostasizing of 'sin' metaphysically acceptable?" Levering, 132. (Nichols, *No Bloodless Myth*, 217, asks the same question.) This is presented merely as a question, but it is notable that in the previous chapter, St. Thomas Aquinas's teaching that "sin is a non-being" is positively presented. At the very least, Levering suggests that Balthasar is contradicting the Angelic Doctor, which is a position that any Catholic theologian should find uncomfortable. See Levering, *Scripture and Metaphysics*, 93–95, especially n.72. I hope that I have shown that Balthasar's "not nothing" approach to sin is not unbiblical, that it does not fundamentally violate the metaphysics of privation theory, and that it merits further investigation.

125. As we have seen, the concern that Balthasar's theology of divine distance—especially in his theology of the cross—endangers Trinitarian unity has been raised by a number

example, consider his reading of 2 Corinthians 5:21: "For our sake he made him to be sin who knew no sin, so that in him we might become the righteousness of God." In Balthasar's soteriological texts, this may be the single verse he cites most regularly. In the last chapter, I presented an argument for why the key word in this verse—*hamartian*—should be translated "a sin offering" or a "purification offering," which is, in fact, the traditional way of interpreting this passage. Balthasar is aware of this translation option, and he acknowledges the fact that this is the preferred understanding of the text in the Christian West from the early patristic period through the Middle Ages.[126] For Balthasar, though, it is Luther who takes this Pauline verse "more seriously" than anyone else[127] by accentuating the fact that Christ is *made sin*, and thus must suffer hell, and this seems to be a point at which the Swiss Catholic appreciates the great Reformer. After all, there are many places where Balthasar apparently strives to match Luther in "seriousness." For example, he says: "Jesus has to experience from within every sin and ungodly doing that has estranged mankind, without distancing himself from it, so that, as Paul says, he is literally made 'sin' for us (2 Cor 5:21)."[128] Or again, Balthasar uses this verse to claim that the Son "identifies himself" with sin,[129] that he "was made the epitome of sin,"[130] and that on the cross he "now embodies" the sin which receives God's final judgment.[131] Finally, building once more on both 2 Corinthians 5:21 and von Speyr, Balthasar says that the experience of having been "made sin" intensifies to the point where Christ no longer experiences himself as Truth, and he "experiences his suffering as 'something like a destruction of the Trinity. . . .'"[132]

Balthasar will always say that the Son remains sinless throughout his dramatic saving work. But when he simultaneously claims that the Son suffers all sins "from within" and is "literally" made sin, identified with it, epitomizing it, embodying it, even to the point where he experiences something like the destruction of triune Love itself (!), the goat for YHWH

---

of important theologians. See Jennifer Newsome Martin, "The Consubstantial Otherness of God: Divine Simplicity and the Trinity in Hans Urs von Balthasar," *Modern Theology* 35, no. 3 (2019): 555, note 68, for a helpful review of the literature.

126. Balthasar reviews the historical interpretive options for this key word at Balthasar, *TD4*, 248, 252, and 296.

127. Balthasar, 284.

128. Hans Urs von Balthasar, *Life out of Death: Meditations on the Paschal Mystery* (San Francisco: Ignatius Press, 2012), 37. This little book was originally published in 1984.

129. Balthasar, *GL7*, 443; Balthasar, *TD2*, 408.

130. Balthasar, *TD4*, 363.

131. Balthasar, *TD5*, 261.

132. Balthasar, *TL2*, 325. Balthasar is quoting from the second volume of von Speyr's *Erde und Himmel*.

seems very much forgotten. As the YHWH-goat fades from view, a real darkness seems to overwhelm the alleged "good news." The great irony of all this is that the very verse Balthasar uses to support these exceedingly bleak statements is a verse that, I am convinced, *originally* celebrated Jesus Christ as the spotless "purification offering!" A verse that intended to speak of intimacy between us and the Father through the Son has become the proof-text for direct hostility between Father and Son, which is indeed a shocking and gratuitous shift in meaning.

My assessment, therefore, is that Balthasar and von Speyr contribute something invaluable to Catholic theology when they speak of Christ bearing sins, and because of the "not nothing" reality of sin, they are also on solid theological footing when they propose an agonizing contemplative vision of sin on Holy Saturday, and it might even be possible to extend this idea to include an experience of vicarious divine wrath as coextensive with the naked encounter with sin . . . but when they push beyond this to claim that Jesus "becomes" sin, and use this as justification for the Father's wrath being *directly* emptied upon the Son—who is now somehow considered the very embodiment of sin—this is grimly unnecessary. Most objectionably, from my perspective, it both misinterprets the work of the Azazel-goat, who is, after all, a humble vehicle, and runs the risk of forgetting the YHWH-goat, as if the mournful experience of the desert were the ultimate priority for Christian soteriology. In fact, Balthasar's adoption of the Lutheran reading of 2 Corinthians gravely risks conflating the distinctive work of the two goats, which can lead to significant theological errors (as we will see in the next chapter). All of this represents a real danger in contemporary Azazel-goat soteriology. The good news is that there are resources within Balthasar's thought to correct these imbalances; nevertheless, I am convinced that correction is needed.[133]

---

133. As I mentioned earlier, and as Balthasar says repeatedly, wrath is a mode of divine Love. It is God's necessary (fitting) response to sin, grounded ultimately in Love's categorical rejection of violence. If God did not respond to sin with wrath, God would be complicit in violence. Therefore, Balthasar is coherent when he has the Son personally suffer the wrath of the Father *only after* "making" the Son sin. But the price of this coherence, vis-à-vis the Son's *direct* encounter with the Father's wrath, is destabilizing confusion in other aspects of Balthasar's Christology and Trinitarian theology. That's much too high a price to pay. It seems to me that some of the most damaging arguments made against Balthasar by his critics could be mitigated—*without altering the basic shape of his soteriology or vitiating his boldest claims*—by restoring 2 Corinthians 5:21 to its original YHWH-goat setting. Cf. Pitstick, *Light in Darkness*, 103–5, 105–12; Kilby, *Balthasar*, 121–22. I ultimately hope that the reflections in this section, based on other aspects of Balthasar's theology, could provide a safer way forward.

Balthasar is a profoundly rich and sophisticated theologian, and his aesthetic and dramatic method creates a situation where he is almost always more complex than a first reading would suggest. As I mentioned earlier, we have emphasized the presence of the Azazel-goat in Balthasar's soteriology because it is one of his distinctive contributions to modern theology, and because it has been highly controversial. Yet themes associated with the YHWH-goat are not missing in his work (even if, as I just argued, they are excessively overshadowed in places); in the next chapter, we will provide additional evidence that demonstrates how Balthasar, in his unique way, seeks to capture the movement of the YHWH-goat. Given that both goats *are* clearly represented in his symphonic theology overall, it could perhaps be said that Balthasar comes closest, among modern theologians, to presenting a comprehensive, biblical Yom Kippur soteriology.

Nevertheless, Steffen Lösel also makes a striking point: "for Balthasar the notion of sacrifice plays a minor role as a soteriological category."[134] He later elaborates, "Nowhere does Balthasar develop his concept of sacrifice from the various Hebrew sacrifices in the context of the temple cult or even the sacrifice of the Day of Atonement (cf. Lev [16]). Rather, his notion of sacrifice builds on an existential interpretation of the term. For Balthasar, sacrifice is but an aspect of every loving relationship. Love, and certainly divine love, expresses itself as 'self-sacrificial' self-giving for the Other."[135] Lösel's use of the word "nowhere" in this quote is putting it too strongly—there are places where Balthasar reflects on the "cultic point of view."[136] Nevertheless, one does not find an extended sympathetic investigation of priestly theology, which is perhaps one reason why the image of the YHWH-goat occasionally fades from view; that is an area where Balthasar can be supplemented by the work of both Jacob Milgrom and David Bentley Hart. Therefore, in the next chapter, we will contemplate whether Hart and Balthasar can be successfully read together to produce a contemporary Christian Yom Kippur soteriology.

134. Steffen Lösel, "A Plain Account of Christian Salvation? Balthasar on Sacrifice, Solidarity, and Substitution," *Pro Ecclesia* 13, no. 2 (Spring 2004): 164.

135. Lösel, 165, n. 126.

136. For example: Balthasar, *TD3*, 113; Balthasar, *GL6*, 24, 43–44, 154–55, 168–69, 196, 397–401.

CHAPTER 11

The Two Goats and the One Lord, Jesus Christ

Alone. The whole world gathers at the temple on the highest holy day, but only one man—one humble priest, clinging to the blood of life—will stand before God in the holy of holies.

Alone. All have sinned and fallen short of God's glory, but one poor creature, deserted, travels the long road to perdition.

Alone. Flanked by criminals, mourned by mother and friend, Jesus Christ goes where none can follow. Alone. Terribly alone.

There is only one—the singular man—but as the true unity of all, this one is able to embrace the whole world. The high and the low, right and left, day and night. He is the rhythm between extremes, the measure of every proportion, the wholly other that makes all truly one.

In this third part of the book, we have surveyed two contemporary soteriologies, two portraits of the savior, that appear—on the surface—very different. For one, the savior recapitulates the glory of Zion, taking up the full litany of praises associated with that most holy mountain. Here even the stones cry out in exaltation, and the angels join in doxological delight. The Son of Man approaches, the Prince of Peace appears. Yea, though his enemies close all around, yea though the valley of death appears, he lifts up his eyes: "Father, glorify your Son that your Son might glorify you!" It is a story of triumph, the way of life, as he gathers all creation to himself and, lifted up from the earth, restores the cosmos to its original beauty by fully embodying love. "Into your hands I commend my Spirit." This is the one who enters the holy of holies and sits down, everything made whole, everything made new. It is finished.

There is another who is stripped bare in the tradition of the Servant. A man of sorrows, marred were his features, with no form, no beauty, that we should look at him. He is the one who bears our sickness, our burden, our sin. He is the one who is wounded, crushed, bruised. And who could describe his abode? He is cast into the abyss, headlong he falls, and he is definitively cut off and forgotten. Alone in the desert, he thirsts. Now is the time of judgment. Now is the night of wrath. His broken heart cries aloud: "*Eli, Eli, lema sabachthani?*" It is finished.

"I believe in one Lord, Jesus Christ."

For Christian theology, all things are summed up in Christ. Although two goats are brought to the temple, they are one. Our challenge is to see the single face in these clashing portraits. This is the great insight of the earliest Christian theologians as they meditated on the Day of Atonement. Both the beloved spotless offering and the sin-bearing outcast are icons of Jesus the Lord. But how? The solution for the earliest Christians—an appealing solution for all its tidiness—was to have each movement represent a different advent, the first and the second coming. First, he comes as stricken, then he comes in glory. But this misses the deep unity of the Yom Kippur liturgy, for the entire rite is a single movement toward God, with *both* goats encompassing the *single* great *ḥaṭṭā't*, lovingly given to Israel by God as a single liturgical act that restores his chosen people to life.

So shockingly different, and seemingly incompatible, are the two goats that it is understandable that key figures in the tradition have tended to accentuate one movement or the other, or have interpreted them as types of different eras in the history of salvation.[1] Today the context is ripe, however, for a deeper understanding of the word "atonement." That is because, especially since the Second Vatican Council, Catholicism has been invigorated with a more profound appreciation of the Jewish roots of Christian theology, Catholics have been encouraged to embrace and utilize the discoveries of critical Bible scholars, and, through ecumenism, Catholics have more and more opportunities to be directly enriched by contemporary Jewish research and reflection on the Hebrew Bible. Concurrently, conditions have been such that Jewish scholars are now able to overcome negative liberal Protestant presup-

---

1. As mentioned above, the difference between the goats has been underlined by Matthias Grebe, as when he asks, "can (and does) Jesus simultaneously fulfill the role of both goats on Lev 16, the sin-laden Azazel-goat as well as the sinless sin offering, two goats which are entirely separate, serving different functions and experiencing different fates (the Azazel-goat released into the desert bearing away the sins, the sin offering slain in a salvation-bringing and purifying death)?" Grebe, *Election, Atonement, and the Holy Spirit*, 67. Ultimately, for Grebe, the two profiles are too different, and thus he chooses the former over the latter. I will continue to argue, however, that fidelity to the comprehensive understanding of the theo-logic of atonement in Leviticus requires us to find a way to preserve both goats in our interpretation of Christ's saving act. Another scholar who has directly confronted the question, and who has reached a conclusion similar to ours, is L. Michael Morales, who says, "Jesus fulfills the pattern of both goats on the Day of Atonement," though his approach is more like the patristic approach, with Jesus fulfilling the work of the Azazel-goat on the cross, and the work of the YHWH-goat with his resurrection. *Who Shall Ascend?*, 128.

positions about the Hebrew Bible's priestly and temple theology and recover a more sympathetic and holistic understanding of these ancient theological traditions. These factors, along with others, create an opportunity in modern systematic theology that is unparalleled when compared with any period of Christian history since the first century or two: there can now be Christian theological reflection that is indebted to, and thoroughly shaped by, the fact that Jesus Christ was and is unequivocally Jewish, as is his teaching, as is his salvation.

When we speak of Christ's "atonement," then, the *first* place we should go for help in understanding this concept is the great liturgy that gives theological shape to the word. And there we find that the two goats, so radically distinct, are engaged in a single work. Based on this, I conclude that Jesus Christ's saving work—iconically represented by the cross, but encompassing the single liturgy of the paschal triduum—must fulfill both movements concurrently, and with this claim, we encounter a theological paradox. That's good because paradox has been a hallmark of all of the great doctrines of classical theology. Henri de Lubac understood this especially well:

> The whole of dogma is thus but a series of paradoxes, disconcerting to natural reason and requiring not an impossible proof but reflective justification. For if the mind must submit to what is incomprehensible, it cannot admit what is unintelligible, and it is not enough for it to seek refuge in an "absence of contradiction" by an absence of thought. It finds stimulation, then, in its very submission. Despite its natural laziness it is almost obliged to delve beneath these superficial contradictions and to penetrate into those deeper regions where what was hitherto a stumbling-block becomes darkness visible.[2]

In soteriology, though, partly because so many "models" have developed side-by-side, the fundamental paradox of Christ's saving act is sometimes obscured. The Eastern Catholic theologian Khaled Anatolios has recently noted that the enthusiasm for identifying soteriological "models" has sometimes created an impression that this branch of theology lacks dogmatic norms, or that it is impossible to articulate the foundational truths

---

2. Henri de Lubac, *Catholicism: Christ and the Common Destiny of Man* (San Francisco: Ignatius Press, 1988), 327. Balthasar approaches theological mysteries (in this case, the Trinity) in a similar way. Jennifer Newsome Martin has pointed out that Balthasar emphasizes "'countervailing propositions,' [TL2, 132] which are 'statements running in opposite directions' [TL3, 157] that 'resist being welded into a unity" [TL2, 132]." See "The Consubstantial Otherness of God," 549.

of Christian soteriology. In his book *Deification Through the Cross*, Anatolios articulates a "systematic soteriology of doxological contrition" which, he says, "enables us to go beyond the framework of a multiplicity of 'models of salvation' and to specify the dogmatic contents of the Christian doctrine of salvation in terms of the fundamental grammar of trinitarian and christological doctrine."[3] As I will suggest below, there is a wonderful complementarity between Anatolios' soteriology of doxological contrition and the Christian Yom Kippur soteriology that I have defended in this book. That complementarity only emboldens my confidence as I make this statement: with Yom Kippur soteriology, we can go deeper than the models and grapple with the mystery at the heart of Christian soteriology.

In other words, turning to Leviticus 16, we discover a biblical framework for articulating the paradox proper to Christian soteriology—this is my boldest claim—which will, according to de Lubac, stimulate the theological imagination to reflective justification. In this chapter, I hope to show how clearly articulating this paradox, and meditating on it, allows us to augment and improve on many of the soteriological approaches common today. In brief: by reinforcing the idea that the cross is a theological *mystery*, Yom Kippur soteriology is an improvement on modern rationalistic models that see Christ's saving work as a mere goad to human action or as exemplary of some more universal philosophical truth, and by emphasizing how the paradox of the cross prompts *reflective justification*, Yom Kippur soteriology is an improvement on fideistic accounts which depend on the inscrutable movements of God's Sovereign Will. Yom Kippur soteriology is also paradoxical in a way that the pure YHWH-goat and Azazel-goat soteriologies are not, the former tending toward idealist accounts which—unallayed—fail to directly engage the horrors of creaturely evil, thus implying an almost otherworldly salvation that seems incapable of fully facing the mournful reality of this world, and the latter tending toward tragic accounts which—unallayed—suggest that overcoming evil comes at the cost of divine unity, simplicity, and impassibility.

---

3. Khaled Anatolios, *Deification through the Cross: An Eastern Christian Theology of Salvation* (Grand Rapids, MI: Eerdmans, 2020), 229–30. Elsewhere he says, "Modern treatments of soteriology based on the 'models' approach tend to bypass the trinitarian and christological norming of soteriological doctrine. . . . [A]ny legitimate conception of Christian salvation, whatever metaphors or imagery it may choose to employ, must not conflict with this dogmatic core and, more than that, must positively depend on it as the source and goal of its inner logic." Anatolios, 167–68.

Grappling with the Yom Kippur Paradox:
Three Aids to Reflection

A few words, then, prompted by the paradox. The question is this: how is it possible, how is it not a contradiction, to say that the more Jesus fulfills the mission of the YHWH-goat, the more he fulfills the mission of the Azazel-goat? The more he is a spotless offering, the more he bears our sins? The more he goes to the center, the more he is cast to the periphery? As I have deliberated on this question—which has become more and more *the* question, the unavoidable question—I have ascertained three aids to reflection.

The first is a principle that is fundamental to priestly thought, as articulated by Milgrom. Within Levitical theology, this priestly law is the key to understanding the temple and Yom Kippur. As Milgrom puts it, for Israel, "impurity was a physical substance, an aerial miasma which possessed magnetic attraction for the realm of the sacred"[4] and "sancta contamination varies directly with the charge (holiness) of the sanctuary and the charge of the impurity."[5] In other words, the most holy attracts the least. Sin penetrates the temple in proportion to its severity, such that the very most grievous crimes of Israel pierce the center, the heart, the holy of holies.

In a fascinating way, and without reference to temple theology, Balthasar noticed a similar phenomenon in salvation history. He calls this the "theological law of proportionate polarization" where "the more God intervenes, the more he elicits opposition to him."[6] Later in the same book, but in a slightly different language, he repeats this law when he speaks of "the reciprocal escalation of love and sin: ever-greater mercy arouses ever-greater anger."[7] It seems, therefore, that love and sin, intervention and opposition, are indexed to each other in a directly proportional way. What is most holy, what is most pure, will draw to itself—like a magnet—what is least holy, what is least pure. Repeatedly throughout scripture, these opposites find themselves face-to-face. It is a remarkable and shocking fact that within Jewish theology the most holy and sacred place on earth, the "incarnate" dwelling place of God himself, becomes the dumping ground for the world's greatest evils: murders, sexual crimes,

---

4. Milgrom, "The Priestly 'Picture of Dorian Gray,'" 392.
5. Milgrom, *Leviticus 1-16*, 980–81.
6. Balthasar, *TD4*, 51.
7. Balthasar, 342.

and idolatries. These abominations come screaming into the Lord's inner chamber, haunting the place with their filth, blaspheming the Name, endangering the cosmos. The more YHWH draws near to Israel, the more the opposition gathers.

As Jesus Christ draws nearer and nearer to the Father in love and in obedience to his earthly mission, perpetually approaching the Father in the ultimate holy of holies, his own divine heart, and as he simultaneously unites himself to his beloved people Israel, in steadfast solidarity, as their representative (and as microcosm to macrocosm), he makes himself more and more vulnerable to the full army of hell. The more perfectly his love and intimacy with the Father is expressed in his incarnate mission, the more our evils are roused in opposition. It is not possible for Jesus, the great high priest, to pass through the final curtain into the highest unity with the Father in the economy of salvation without at the same time confronting that which is marked for final damnation. With this in mind, we can start to imagine the true extent to which the one Christ is stretched out. He is joyfully called, in communion with Israel and (through her) with the world, to draw near to the Father with his own blood, his own *life*, and thus he is propelled by the true beatific vision. Yet also, *in that very same atoning movement*, he will be—he must be—pressed down by ever-intensifying sin, thrown down to the place bereft of love—and all because his love has surpassed all measure. It is not possible to have the second movement without the first, even as it is also not possible to strictly comprehend how they can occur at once—how his highest vision of perfect beatitude on the cross coexisted with the deepest encounter with hopeless damnation.[8] It is simply necessary to say that each pole of this paradox must respect the unsuppressible and undilutable necessity of the other in the economy of salvation if that economy is to be faithful to the theological shape of Yom Kippur.

Adrienne von Speyr, so typically perceptive, is aware of this dual movement. As she says, "The Son presents to the Father, in his own person, the sin of the world that he has taken away," and at the same time Christ presents to the Father, "in his Body, his Bride, the living sinner now stripped of sin."[9] *At the same time.* This is a wonderfully succinct

---

8. There is more to be said about how, according to Yom Kippur soteriology, Christ might have "simultaneously experienced *fruition beata* while suffering *maximos dolores*," as Aaron Riches puts it. *Ecce Homo: On the Divine Unity of Christ* (Grand Rapids, MI: Eerdmans, 2016), 197. For now, Anatolios points the way forward. See Anatolios, *Deification through the Cross*, 335–38.

9. Balthasar, *TD5*, 314–15. Balthasar is quoting from von Speyr's *Katholische Briefe, II*.

expression of the duality of Christ's single movement, on the one hand performing the heroic act of separating out sins to relieve the world's burden, and on the other hand presenting himself as the Second Adam, perfect in love, alive in worship, free in delight. Balthasar himself puts it in these words:

> Fundamentally, [Christ] goes in two opposite directions: (with the thief on his right) toward paradise and (with the one on his left, in order to fetch him) into deep hell. The contradiction, then, is that he is at once the farthest from hell and, as sin-bearer, the closest to it; that, being this dead man, he has lost his Word-character (hence the silence) and yet, at the same time, is also the Father's loudest and clearest message to the world.[10]

Exactly. A paradox like this frustrates our preference for neat lines, but as a student of theological aesthetics and the drama of salvation, as a master of theo-poetics,[11] Balthasar is highly attentive to how the God-Man turns worldly logic on its head, not ultimately in a destructive way, but in a transfiguring way. How it is possible for the second person of the trinity to go in "two opposite directions" on the cross, especially when those "directions" encompass the cosmic high (paradise) and cosmic low (hell) is a true challenge, a potential stumbling block, but such a paradox may well orient us toward a deeper encounter with God's Wisdom itself.

The second aid to reflection is one articulated by both Balthasar and Hart: the "Trinitarian substructure" of the atoning act.[12] When confronted with the two goats, we are confronted with a set of images that suggest absolute unity and absolute difference, perfect intimacy and perfect distance. According to the standards of creaturely logic, these dichotomies are in acute tension, if not in outright contradiction. But of course,

10. Balthasar, *TL2*, 351–52. Balthasar cites von Speyr's *Kreuz und Hölle, I*, in the footnotes associated with this passage.

11. For an illuminating analysis of how Balthasar "presents us with a *theo-poetic* rather than sheer systematic theology," see Anne M. Carpenter, *Theo-Poetics: Hans Urs von Balthasar and the Risk of Art and Being* (Notre Dame, IN: University of Notre Dame Press, 2015), 3. According to Carpenter, Balthasar's theology is performed according to the "logic of poetry," which "rests in its fragile and powerful ability to resonate. A poem will . . . press its point by its unusual comparison of images. . . ." Carpenter, 139. For Balthasar, this "unusual comparison of images" is not intended to work like a Zen *kōan*, prompting apophatic disturbance, but rather it hopes to encourage a deeper encounter with the concrete form of the crucified Word.

12. "Trinitarian substructure" is Balthasar's phrase. Balthasar, *TD4*, 332. As he says, "Scripture clearly says that the events of the Cross can only be interpreted against the background of the Trinity and through faith. . . ." Balthasar, 319.

from the perspective of trinitarian theology, these "dichotomies" are simply markers of who God is. The theme of infinite distance and difference has its origin in the eternal begetting of the Son, which is the Father's kenotic act whereby he both "makes space" for the other, and hands himself over to the other. Thus:

> It is possible to say, with Bulgakov, that the Father's self-utterance in the generation of the Son is an initial 'kenosis' within the Godhead that underpins all subsequent kenosis. For the Father strips himself, without remainder, of his Godhead and hands it over to the Son; he "imparts" to the Son all that is his. . . . [The Father] is this movement of self-giving that holds nothing back. This divine act that brings forth the Son, that is, the second way of participating in (and of being) the identical Godhead, involves the positing of an absolute, infinite "distance. . . ."[13]

At the very center of what it means to be God, from this perspective, is handing over, pouring out, in love. The Son, who does only what he sees the Father doing, eternally responds with a corresponding act of self-gift, and it is precisely in the joy of realizing self-in-other that, through the Spirit, absolute oneness abides.[14] In a single eternal Act, there is a distance that is unity. Hart puts it succinctly: "God is the distance of the infinite, the *actus* of all distance"[15] and "God is in himself a gift of distance."[16] For the immanent Trinity, such "distance" is never absence, but the fullness of Love.

When we contemplate the saving mission of Jesus Christ, we are considering how the "primal divine drama"[17] of divine love is stretched out upon the world stage, thus healing and elevating creation. That is why any consideration of the possibility of Christ, in "the action," exemplifying

---

13. Balthasar, *TD4*, 323. Cf. Balthasar, *GL7*, 213–14. This quote goes on to reinforce the general relevance of Trinitarian "distance" to Azazel-goat soteriology, because the Trinitarian distance ". . . can contain and embrace all the other distances that are possible within the world of finitude, including the distance of sin." Hart says much the same with reference to Christ's prayer at Gethsemane: "his distance from the Father, which both recapitulates and overcomes humanity's sinful estrangement from God, reveals the intratrinitarian distance. In going into the region of death, which lies over against God in enmity toward him and his creation, Christ shows that the divine infinity surpasses all separations." Hart, *Beauty of the Infinite*, 322.

14. As Balthasar says, "absolute fullness...does not consist of 'having' but of 'being = gift.'" Balthasar, *GL7*, 391.

15. Hart, *Beauty of the Infinite*, 182.

16. Hart, 207.

17. Balthasar, *TD4*, 325.

unity and difference, must circle back to the paradigmatic Christian paradox of trinitarian theology. This is clearly the move that Balthasar is attempting to make. From this perspective, economic concepts like radical "self-surrender" (i.e., obedience-to-the-end) and "abandonment" (analogously conceived), have a suspended foundation in the eternal drama of divine Love, and thus they do not represent a fundamental threat to the triune God. As I mentioned in the previous chapter, Balthasar believes that the condition of the possibility of even sin (unfreedom, false-distance) is the primordial freedom and distance in the Trinity.[18] It is for this reason that the Son can take on, and thus radically undermine, our pathetic and violent attempts at creating an empty-distance, a pride-distance, between us and God. By way of an ever-greater obedience, through carrying sin down to the deepest abyss of human depravity and pushing infinitely further, hell is objectively overcome at the moment of its formation. In other words, as Balthasar often insists, hell is now and is always a Christological reality since it is established in the very movement of removing sins (which are the substance of hell!); insofar as that same movement is the movement of love and obedience, hell is—in a delightful twist—radically undermined from its foundation! Even hell cannot avoid the stamp of love. In this sense it seems right to say, despite Balthasar's hesitations, that Christ *is* victorious over hell, hell is entirely harrowed, even as the final Azazel-goat passively suffers the sins of the world.

Through this obedient kenosis, the Son is not becoming other than divine, but living out his divinity, as incarnate and in the context of sin, with greater transparency than ever. Hence, again, the twist: the more kenotic the Son, the more he images the "ur-kenosis" of the Father, and thus the greater the unity-of-being in the economy of salvation. It is simply the nature of Trinity that the deepest intimacy is within the furthest distance. Balthasar and von Speyr write:

During the Passion the Spirit maintains the internal divine diastasis between Father and Son in its economic form, so that "What seems

---

18. For the most powerful critique of Balthasar's Trinitarian theology, especially insofar as it draws unconventional analogies from the Son's suffering and death, see Bernhard Blankenhorn, "Balthasar's Method of Divine Naming," *Thomist* 64 (2000): 499–519. See also Karen Kilby's careful critique in *Balthasar*, 99–122. For a formidable defense of Balthasar's approach, especially in light of his desire to overcome the scourge of Hegelianism, see Cyril O'Regan, who presents Balthasar's use of these ideas as a justifiable use of "second order" "meta-symbols and/or conceptual ciphers"—or "protocol"—which "unname in the very act of naming, but importantly unname directionally rather than into the agnostic void." *Anatomy of Misremembering*, 228; cf. 227–44.

to us to be the sign of separation of Father and Son is precisely the sign of greatest unification. . . ."[19]

This "absolute paradox" is necessary to make it credible that the Father "does not leave the Son for a moment, even in the final abandonment." The Son is "at the same time united more and more to the Father in this separation, until he is nothing more on the Cross than the revelation of the will of the Father." "What is Two here can be shown only in unity: what is One here can be shown only in duality."[20]

This is all crucially relevant to the question of the possible identity of the YHWH-goat and the Azazel-goat. It shows how the apparently contrasting categories of separation and unity are significantly reshaped when they are read in a Trinitarian context. That said, we need to be careful here and not give this too superficial an interpretation. After all, both "goats" are obedient and kenotic in their own way—one by embodying and (in the case of Jesus) perfecting the Yes of Isaac, the openhearted act of love, the spotless way of life, the other by bearing the No of humanity, contemplating the reality of sin, descending to the pit of death. While the first exemplifies the (for us, deifying) oneness between God and the high priest in the holy of holies, this is not a oneness that obliterates difference (like a Platonic One). And then, while the other exemplifies the (for us, damning) distance between God and the sin-bearer, this is not a separation that obliterates communion (like a polytheistic ontology of violence). Therefore, while Trinitarian theology provides another aid to reflection when wrestling with the unity and difference between these aspects of Christ's saving work, creating opportunities to avoid simplistic contrasts, one must simultaneously avoid an equally simplistic division that sees the goats as respectively representing "De Deo Uno" and "De Deo Trino."

The full extent to which the latter would be a mistake is evident as we turn to the third aid to reflection, which is the theological priority of the YHWH-goat. It is essential to remember that the existence of a godforsaken "wilderness," and thus the very need for the Azazel-goat, is theologically unnecessary, and indeed, tragic. This action is not a necessary stage of creation, and it is even less a necessary stage in divine actualization.[21] That

19. Balthasar, *TD5*, 262. Balthasar is quoting von Speyr's *Commentary on John, Vol. 3: The Farewell Discourses*.

20. Balthasar, 263. Balthasar is quoting von Speyr's *Commentary on John, Vol. 2: The Discourses of Controversy*.

21. Hart highlights this point exceptionally well. Cf. Hart, *The Doors of the Sea*, 73–75.

that creature should have to make that journey is what ought not to be, but nevertheless is. The relevance of this fact to the qualifications in the previous paragraph is hopefully clear: "difference" in the trinity in no way implies hell in the trinity—a grotesque thought and a complete misunderstanding of Balthasar's analogical method. The Son can descend to hell bearing sin without endangering his ontological and volitional unity with the Father because God is triune and infinite distance is therefore compatible with infinite unity. If the world had remained pure Yes, and if the Son had been incarnate in *that* world, he would still be "other" and "one" with the Father. Primordial peace does not depend on an expulsion rite; the Edenic "holy of holies" is both chronologically *and* ontologically prior to any imaginable hell. Eden could be Eden, in spotless joy, forevermore, if sin had never occurred. Would that this had been the case!

With that in mind, this observation from Andrew Louth is illuminating:

> One way of putting this is to think in terms of an arch stretching from creation to deification, representing what is and remains God's intention: the creation of the cosmos that, through humankind, is destined to share in the divine life, to be deified. Progress along this arch has been frustrated by humankind, in Adam, failing to work with God's purposes, leading to the Fall, which needs to be put right by redemption. There is, then, what one might think of as a lesser arch, leading from Fall to redemption, the purpose of which is to restore the function of the greater arch, from creation to deification. The loss of the notion of deification leads to a lack of awareness of the greater arch from creation to deification, and thereby to concentration on the lower arch, from Fall to redemption; it is, I think, not unfair to suggest that such a concentration on the lesser arch at the expense of the greater arch has been characteristic of much Western theology.[22]

Because of the diabolical shadows that have spread across the earth, the movements of both "goats" in Christ's saving work are simultaneously necessary, *but only in this context.* Certainly, by embodying the movement

---

22. Louth, "Place of Theosis," 35. I had earlier alluded to this text in chapter 6, footnote 28. It is not hard for me to grant Louth's critique of Western theology here; to the extent that the theme of deification was ever obscured in Western theological reflection (which does seem to be the case, *especially* in mainstream early-modern Western theology), this has been an impoverishment. At the same time, does the West have gifts to share with the East? Taking the specific case of David Bentley Hart—certainly not the singular representative of Eastern Orthodoxy, but a proud Orthodox all the same—it does seem right to suggest that even a theology beautifully saturated with the truths of the "greater arch" can be meaningfully supplemented with Western insights to deepen our appreciation for the full mystery of Christ and his deifying work.

of the Azazel-goat, Christ is dramatically taking upon himself something that is absolutely unnatural and unnecessary. This is a mighty work, a work of mercy and grace, but it is still rightly considered the "lesser arc." In the broadest biblical perspective, in the overall movement from Genesis to Revelation, it is the movement of the first goat, as true Adam, that is the ultimate truth of the world. Here we have the embodiment of true life, transfiguring light, joy and peace, love and sabbath. This is the story of the glory of God, humanity fully alive. Even here, in temple theology, the form of such abundant life is somewhat contorted insofar as it is being embodied in the context of sin. After all, the YHWH-goat is a purification offering and not a burnt offering (which, as we saw, is more primordial and ideal), and thus it too is ensnared in the realities of this fallen world. Nevertheless, I have argued that the purification offering is an adaptation of the burnt offering to the broken world, and thus it recapitulates the most authentic sacrificial movement in our lamentable condition.

Louth believes that the Eastern Church has kept its eyes trained on this "greater arc" in a way that the Western church has not; that may be. But whatever the relative advantages and disadvantages of East and West, moving forward, Christian Yom Kippur soteriology will continue to struggle with the simultaneous importance of the two movements of Christ's saving act, but in doing so we must remember once more this important qualification: "The light shines in the darkness, and the darkness did not overcome it." Between light and darkness, there is no competition. Thus, it is the first movement that is primary—it is Beauty, Goodness, Truth—and it is the second movement that is merely fitting, entirely to be mourned, even as our hearts swell with gratitude before so great a redeemer.

With these three aids to reflection in place, we can look one more time at the two masters who were central to the argument in this part of the book—Hart and Balthasar—and see why they need each other. To show this, we must return one more time to the problem of Hart's extraordinarily confident universalism. Of course, Balthasar himself has been criticized by many for his openness to the possibility that all shall be saved, and for his conviction that each Christian ought to hope for such a conclusion. Hart is unimpressed by Balthasar's hope. He says:

> . . . I want to make it absolutely clear that I approach these meditations not as a seeker tentatively and timidly groping his way toward some anxious, uncertain, fragile hope. Unlike, say, the great Hans Urs von Balthasar (1905–1988), I would not think it worth the trouble to argue, as he does, that—given the paradoxes and

seemingly irreconcilable pronouncements of scriptures on the final state of all things—Christians *may* be allowed to *dare* to hope for the salvation of all. In fact, I have very small patience for this kind of "hopeful universalism," as it is often called. As far as I am concerned, anyone who hopes for the universal reconciliation of creatures with God must already believe that this would be the best possible ending to the Christian story; and such a person has then no excuse for imagining that God could bring any but the best possible ending to pass without thereby being in some sense a failed creator. The position I want to attempt to argue, therefore, to see how well it holds together, is far more extreme: to wit, that, if Christianity is in any way true, Christians dare not *doubt* the salvation of all, and that any understanding of what God accomplished in Christ that does not include the assurance of a final *apokatastasis* in which all things created are redeemed and joined to God is ultimately entirely incoherent and unworthy of rational faith.[23]

In chapter nine, I argued that Hart's theology doesn't have the resources necessary to sustain a morally acceptable universalism (despite his concerns about the moral imbecility of his opponents) because his theology lacks a place for the Azazel-goat. Now, having looked at Balthasar's own theology of the cross, we can return to the critique of Hart, appreciate Balthasar's contribution (without diminishing Hart's contribution), and suggest why Balthasar's hope remains the only appropriate Christian attitude to the questions raised by Hart.

Looking at Hart's recent work, it seems that he engages the *theological* debate about universalism in an odd way. He does not start by grappling with revelation, or even with the person of Christ. Instead, he starts with "the doctrine of hell" in the abstract and asks whether someone prefers this abstract doctrine or whether they would prefer that no such doctrine or place exist, as if this were a completely context-less debate. Do you prefer to imagine humans being tortured or do you prefer to imagine them in a state of happiness? It seems, for Hart, that that is the whole question, and those who choose the former must really be "morally depraved," or whatever other terms of disapprobation he may use. The problem falls from the sky, with no preface or postscript. This is in stark contrast to Balthasar's careful reflection on the intensification of the divine "no" in the history of Israel, culminating in the saving work of Jesus Christ.[24] In fact, in the opening line of his *Dare We Hope*, Balthasar

23. Hart, *That All Shall Be Saved*, 66.
24. This is painstakingly traced in volumes six and seven of *The Glory of the Lord*.

puts the Christian reader at the center of the Biblical drama: "All of us who practice the Christian faith and, to the extent that its nature as a mystery permits, would also like to understand it are *under* judgement. By no means are we above it, so that we might know its outcome in advance and could proceed from that knowledge to further speculation."[25] Hart's ahistorical, non-covenantal approach risks being flippant in comparison, even as the case is prosecuted with maximal severity.

Hart wrote his outstanding theo-aesthetics; *Beauty of the Infinite* remains a work of towering brilliance. But looking back now, through the lens of *That All Shall Be Saved*, one feels the absence of a corresponding theo-drama, and looking now at so many of the (otherwise laudatory) reviews that followed *Beauty of the Infinite*, as we did in chapter nine, one finds an early awareness of that absence. Ultimately, it comes down to this: Hart's theology, lacking a place for the second goat, suffers a dramatic deficit, and this is connected to his inability to truly confront the problem of sin. As I have argued, there is a certain way in which Hart's Christ bypasses the world in its brokenness; it is a passing-by that apparently has salutary effects, but it seems to be more of a theoretical achievement than a dramatic victory over sin. The lack of drama in Hart's Christ is further extended such that there is a lack of drama for each human life. Nothing is ever actually at stake; in our earthly existence, we are apparently all engaged in a very odd, in fact inexplicable, divine exercise.

I have argued that Balthasar's theology captures something important and true when it wrestles with the "not nothingness" of sin; compare this with Hart, who can find himself speaking—quite shockingly—of sin as "transient dissonance."[26] With these two words, we discover a certain lack of moral seriousness has crept into Hart's own theology. Such language strikes me a sub-biblical; there are moments in Hart's work when one feels that he is presenting to us the philosopher's god, a god known in the cool, rational security of one's study, a god who is safely removed from this world, wholly innocent and wholly untouched, who has concocted an "end" in his eternal decrees that appears wholly indifferent to the "transient dissonance" of the temporal. Balthasar, on the other hand, finds it impossible to be so blithe about the problem of evil. In creating, in letting

---

25. Balthasar, *Dare We Hope*, 5.

26. In context, Hart says that anyone who believes that God would create a world where it would be possible for any soul to be eternally damned must necessarily believe that "[God] has willed the tragedy, not just as a transient dissonance within creation's goodness, leading ultimately to a soul's correction, but as that irreducible quantum of eternal loss that, however small in relation to the whole, still reduces all else to a merely relative value." Hart, *That All Shall Be Saved*, 83.

be, God takes on a certain risk[27]—this may be an anthropomorphic affir-mation, but it still says something true—yes, God suffers a certain vulner-ability, which is the wonder and potential sorrow of love. Balthasar knows that in creating, God's own heart is dramatically opened, such that at cer-tain moments heaven falls silent and leans in to hear whether there will be a whispered yes, or a defiant no. And even then, this God—it is breath-taking to discover—takes on responsibility for the no, he bears it, he suffers it, he drags it to hell to release us from it forever. A transient dis-sonance does not bring forth so great a savior; the true drama of creation does, and even if this cannot metaphysically add to the joy of heaven, that joy is nevertheless textured and intensified in remarkable ways on account of the risk. Balthasar's hell is no passing mental state, but a profound Christological truth, a monument to the grim reality of our history, but even more to the ever-surpassing love of God.

Balthasar brilliantly shows why a full and morally serious soteriol-ogy—and by extension, a full and morally serious eschatology—needs the Azazel-goat, and, thus, he shows why hell, as a Christological achieve-ment, is by necessity an eternal reality. This, given the actual world God chose—for unknown reasons—to create, which in fact is a world that includes sin and death, even if by our lights it might have been more appropriate if God had created a world without such horror. The reality of hell is a miracle of divine love; it could not be anticipated or imagined, but it is apparently true that the God of revelation has loved us to the point where he would allow himself to be crushed under the weight of our iniquities, all to free us from them. All of this has an extraordinarily important consequence: the everlasting reality of hell makes it necessarily thinkable that I myself, stubbornly clinging to my sin, could freely choose and choose again to cling to those cold comforts which Christ in fact bore away for my salvation. In holding fast to these sorrows, it is possible for me to be dragged down with them. And it also means that the deeper I go, clinging to these sins, the deeper I go into this space of Jesus's love, and so I remain firmly in the sphere of hope. But in that state, it is not impossible that I should say "no" one more time—the one-millionth time, the one billionth time, the one trillionth time, against all reason, and there

27. Balthasar: "God takes the risk of creating the world, of giving Adam his kingly freedom; he takes the risk of surrendering his only Son into the hands of sinners; he takes the risk of establishing the hierarchical Church as the sign and the locus of his kingdom among the nations. He entrusts himself to us in all these ways, nor does he manifest any distrust at all, but is faithful forever, imparting to his truth the quality of a daring, faithful love." *Prayer*, trans. Graham Harrison (San Francisco: Ignatius Press, 1986), 36.

is no point at which a "no" inevitably flips to a yes. The drama of creation is never overcome, in this world or the next. Even when we grant every philosophical clarification about freedom for the good, we face the absurdity of the heart. That is why we only have hope; that is why Hart's certainty is misguided.[28]

And so, Hart pins upon us an epithet: "infernalist."[29] What is it to be an infernalist? Taking a cue from the etymology, it seems that the infernalists are those who are content to remain in the "lower regions," the inferior realm; perhaps for the Greeks, they are the fools. The infernalist does not live in the heights, he does not feed on the detached ideal in otherworldly castles, he does not abscond to Neoplatonic tranquility; no, the infernalist confronts the world here below, ambiguous, and terrible, and lovely. Here in this netherworld, the infernalist does not claim knowledge of what is not disclosed, but he trusts and waits and prays for hope; he feels evil closing in and '*behold, I have overcome the world*' and the cry of Rebecca rings in his ears and '*behold, I make all things new*' and the dog returns to its vomit. The infernalist, the poor fool, remains in this liminal space. He remains somewhere between '*depart from me*' and '*come unto me.*' The infernalist chooses not to remove himself from the drama that has been laid out, from the ambiguity of his own heart; he struggles not to grasp for and cling to a beauty and wisdom that has not been given to us, as appealing as that tree is now and always.

Alas, to be Christian, I am convinced, means that we must remain infernalists, and remain in hope and in prayer. None of that, however, takes away from Hart's greater achievement. He has, more profoundly than any other modern theologian I know, articulated the mystery of the "greater arch," has captured the splendor of the Christian evangel, has

---

28. And this, I'd say, is where C. S. Lewis also shows himself more perceptive than Hart on the question of hell. *The Great Divorce* is both serious about the possibility of our "no" but also saturated by the greater hope. Balthasar himself admired Lewis for his profundity in this little book and highlights the passage where Lewis rules out the possibility of knowing universalism. That's because, Balthasar says, we can only "speak from within time, where nothing else stands before you but the choice. . . ." Balthasar, *Dare We Hope*, 71. Lewis's George MacDonald says, "Ye *cannot* know eternal reality by a definition. Time itself, and all acts and events that fill Time, are the definition, and it must be lived." Lewis, *The Great Divorce*, 141; quoted in Balthasar, *Dare We Hope*, 71. "With this wisdom," Balthasar says, "all those candles of *apokatastasis* are now blown out. . . ." Balthasar, 71. In my own temporal experience, I find that I say "no" in countless, ever-more destructive, ever-more self-deceptive ways. By what right do we make assurances about the eternal when God, for whatever reason, has chosen to make us merely temporal, and when my temporal existence gives daily evidence of my tendency toward the no?

29. cf. Hart, *That All Shall Be Saved*, 13.

clarified what it means—and what it cannot mean—to say "God is love" with breathtaking care and sensitivity. Emphasizing again the third "aid to reflection," Hart's consistent, even relentless, YHWH-goat theology is a priceless treasure for the Church. I find it is not sufficient in itself, but to lose any part of the *Beauty of the Infinite* would, for me, be a grave tragedy. His achievement is secure.

Therefore, to conclude: Jesus Christ, in his single passion, fulfills the work of both goats. Much more thought is needed on how this paradox might achieve "reflective justification," but I hope the three aids to reflection, enumerated in this section, along with the final reflections on Hart and Balthasar, can help us move in the direction of those "deeper regions" where the infinite God of revelation is encountered as "darkness visible."

Christian Yom Kippur Soteriology in the Context of Modern Soteriology

There has been no shortage of reflections on the mystery of the cross over the last two millennia. Certainly, much more can and should be said about how Yom Kippur soteriology would correspond with other ways of understanding Christ's work on the cross. This is *especially* true with respect to other biblical ways of talking about the cross, including prominent motifs such as Passover and liberation, the Suffering Servant, the Second Adam, ransom, and redemption. While I do believe that Yom Kippur soteriology has a privileged role to play in shaping our understanding of the theology of atonement and that it uniquely helps us capture the paradox at the heart of Christian soteriology, it is certainly not the only component in a comprehensive biblical theology of the cross. Further work will need to be done in showing how the different biblical images fit together symphonically to draw us deeper and deeper into the unfathomable mystery of Christ's saving act.

In this section, however, we will focus on how Yom Kippur Soteriology might relate to other *contemporary* approaches to soteriology. The only surprise, perhaps, is how lively the discussion about the theology of the cross has been at the beginning of the twenty-first century. After all, there was a time when the theological conversation shifted quite emphatically away from the emphasis on this "tree," away from the question of the atoning or sacrificial nature of Christ's death, and toward the moral teachings articulated by the historical Jesus.[30] But there has been a recent

30. Colin Grant reflected on the changing theological focus in the mid-1980s, "The Abandonment of Atonement," *King's Theological Review* 9, no. 1 (1986): 1–8.

surge in interest in the theology of the cross, and it is fair to wonder how the approach articulated in this book corresponds with, augments, or seeks to correct other prominent approaches to soteriology in contemporary theology. We will focus on modern penal substitution, liberationist critiques of atonement, and the Girardian approach to scapegoating.

But first, there is one very recent theology of salvation that deserves special attention because, as I said earlier in this chapter, this approach is in many ways complementary to ours. This is the soteriology of doxological contrition, which Khaled Anatolios describes and defends in his 2020 book, *Deification Through the Cross: An Eastern Christian Theology of Salvation*. Through a careful study of Byzantine liturgy, the Christian scriptures, and the ecumenical councils, Anatolios finds that the tradition does present a normative soteriology, one that is rooted in the goal and experience of deification, and one that can be summed up with the words "doxological contrition." In an especially clear summary statement, Anatolios says, "*The essential core of the gospel, from the perspective of a soteriology of doxological contrition, is that God marvelously accomplishes both his doxological judgment against sin and humanity's full reintegration into the intra-trinitarian glorification, through Christ's representative and inclusive doxological repentance.*"[31] So many of the key claims from Anatolios's book are found in this passage. First, human beings are made for God, which is to say, the triune God who is revealed as eternally alive in mutual glorification; drawing especially on the Gospel of John, Anatolios shows that "trinitarian being" can rightly be characterized as "a communion of mutual glorification"[32] or a "circle of glory."[33] Second, in creating, God intends human beings to be drawn into this circle of glory. Anatolios develops a "doxological anthropology," showing that we are made for "worshipful adoration and doxological 'friendship.'"[34] While it is not his major point of emphasis, Anatolios connects this vision of human being to temple theology in a few places.[35]

The third point drawn from this quote is that, unfortunately, something has gone wrong that requires our "reintegration" into this doxological glory; obviously, that 'something' is sin. Anatolios' understanding of sin is nuanced and fascinating. Keeping with his general emphasis, he describes sin "from the viewpoint of a doxological soteriology, as a mis-

---

31. Anatolios, *Deification through the Cross*, 312, emphasis in the original.
32. Anatolios, 229.
33. Anatolios, 262.
34. Anatolios, 282.
35. Cf. Anatolios, 266, 270.

representation of divine glory"[36] or as "essentially anti-doxological."[37] Notably, from the title of the chapter on sin ("The Doxological Weight of Human Sin"), and in numerous other places throughout the book,[38] Anatolios alludes to the "weight" of sin, without ever really pausing to consider how seriously that metaphor ought to be taken, what it might mean, and what implications it might have. There does seem to be a fascinating opening to reflection here: how might it be that the life-giving "weight of glory," when twisted, becomes a dead weight of sin? In any case, this particular possibility is not developed; Anatolios' distinctive emphasis is on sin as antidoxological, by which he means: a form of idolatry,[39] a failure to properly "image" God,[40] and a "failure to give an appropriate doxological response to [God's] divine disclosure."[41] The most important thing is that, in the context of sin, we need to be reintegrated into the pattern of trinitarian doxology, and this is what Jesus achieves through his saving work.

Fourth, Jesus' cruciform sacrifice achieves *"representative and inclusive doxological repentance."* In other words, Anatolios argues "that Christ saves us by rendering perfect glory to the Father in the Spirit and by enabling us to glorify the Triune God with him and in him, and that he also saves us by being perfectly contrite in expiation of human sinfulness and thus enabling us to repent with him and in him."[42] In this quote, one can see why Anatolios calls his soteriology "doxological repentance"; Jesus saves, first of all, by perfectly glorifying the Father at all moments, thus drawing creation into the "circle of glory" proper to God's inner life, and by restoring human nature, which was always made to reflect this glory as creatures made in the image of God. As Anatolios acknowledges throughout, this is quite similar to Anselm's theory of satisfaction, with a greater emphasis on worship (which is Nicholas Cabasilas's contribution to the theory of satisfaction, according to Anatolios). But, in part grounded in his appreciation for healing rhythms of Byzantine liturgy, Anatolios also puts a heavy emphasis on repentance, and goes even further to suggest that Jesus himself, so intimately united to

36. Anatolios, 298.

37. Anatolios, 113.

38. See Anatolios, 133 (with reference to the suffering servant), 285 (with reference to Anselm), 302 ("the full weight and horror of sin"), 306 ("the weight of sin is infinite precisely because. . ."), and 330 (where he refers to the "antidoxological weight of sin").

39. Anatolios, *Deification through the Cross*, 104 ff.

40. Anatolios, 301–2.

41. Anatolios, 295.

42. Anatolios, 88.

us in our woundedness, experiences perfect contrition on our behalf, which allows us to experience full "doxological contrition" in and through him.

What does it mean to say that Jesus experiences contrition? In a similar way to our Balthasarian critique of Hart above, Anatolios critiques theologians (such as Matthias Scheeben) who primarily emphasize the "positive aspect of Christ's glorification of God" and who do not "sufficiently take account of the negative aspect of Christ's suffering as a response to human sin and the content of that suffering as a direct engagement with this sin."[43] In other words,

> we can say that Christ's suffering and death were part of his drawing human sin and its consequences into the glorification of God and, as such, constituted Christ's own perfect "doxology of judgment" in which he accepted the consequences of human sin as a means of rejecting and condemning sin itself.[44]

Anatolios bolsters his argument for the claim that Christ suffers vicarious contrition through a careful reading of Thomas Aquinas. He ultimately suggests that contrition is the form that Jesus' glorification of the Father takes in the context of human sin. Insofar as Jesus himself experiences perfect doxological contrition in his saving work, he makes this saving way available to each of us.

As I said at the beginning of this section, in so many ways Anatolios's approach to soteriology corresponds to and complements Yom Kippur soteriology. He and I reach very similar conclusions, traveling by rather different roads. This book is grounded in a sustained and close reading of temple theology, especially in the ancient priestly biblical tradition, with a special focus on the Day of Atonement. While Anatolios does mention priestly sacrificial theology from time to time, and occasionally mentions the importance of the temple to a theology of glory, this is not his primary emphasis, and Yom Kippur itself is never discussed in his book. Instead, he achieves his analogous conclusions, as I said, by another path: through a close reading of the Byzantine Christian liturgy and an extraordinarily close reading of the ecumenical conciliar tradition. Anatolios has, therefore, provided incredibly rich resources for thinking about how Yom Kippur soteriology might correlate with the orthodox trinitarian and christological conciliar tradition.

43. Anatolios, 327.
44. Anatolios, 330.

What is so helpful about Anatolios's book is that he effectively develops the need for the "two goats" through related terms—implicitly speaking of the YHWH-goat by using the term "doxological," and implicitly speaking of the Azazel-goat by using the word "contrition"—and he also sees how and why *both* are necessary simultaneously, hence: "doxological contrition." He sees how Christ must fulfill *both* elements in his one cross. To that extent, his conclusions and ours match up beautifully. In the final analysis, though, I do think there are ways in which a Yom Kippur soteriology brings out issues in a "normative" Christian soteriology even more clearly than Anatolios's approach does. First of all, as mentioned, even though Anatolios refers from time to time to the "weight" of sin, this idea is never developed in *Deification Through the Cross*, and so it is not clear what it means to say that Jesus suffers these sins; how is it possible for Jesus, in his all-purity, to take on this burden? It seems to me that Balthasar's development of the biblical priestly tradition helps us to think through how such sin-bearing is theologically coherent. Furthermore, second, framing this question in terms of the single *kipper* of the "goats" on Yom Kippur helps to accentuate the profoundly difficult, and perhaps therefore profoundly illuminating, paradox at the heart of this mystery. While Anatolios puts the two key words side by side, and while he wants to emphasize the challenging issue of Jesus confronting sin and suffering contrition, more could be said in grappling with the profound theological challenge this presents. Consider this passage:

> As in Anselm so with Scheeben, Christ's honoring of God seems to cancel sin simply by outweighing sin on some great metaphysical scale. But what if we were to say that Christ honors God by truly allowing the antidoxological weight of sin to enter into the very offering of praise and glorification to God? Then we would be speaking of doxological contrition. In that case, we would not have merely one weight (the perfect glorification of Christ) canceling out another (human sin as an affront to divine glory), but rather the very content of sin being transformed in Christ into the glorification of God. In the face of human sin and in solidarity with human sinners, Christ's glorification of the Father would thus include an exemplary and representative repentance for humanity's sinful misrepresentation and desecration of the Father's glory.[45]

This is a lovely passage that effectively points out the problem for Anselm, Scheeben, and other advocates of a pure YHWH-goat soteriology.

---

45. Anatolios, 330.

But the way it is framed here, it is not yet clear that the soteriology of doxological contrition has entirely faced the full horrors that confront the Azazel-goat. The notion of the "content of sin being transformed in Christ into the glorification of God" strikes me as potentially inadequate, depending on what Anatolios means by the idea that sin is "transformed." Nevertheless, despite lingering questions, it does seem that the Christian Yom Kippur soteriology, defended in this book, and the soteriology of doxological contrition, which Anatolios powerfully identifies in the Byzantine and ecumenical Christian tradition, share many common convictions and can be brought into fruitful dialogue with each other.

Having considered Anatolios's distinctive contribution to modern soteriology, we can shift our attention to other approaches that, while making positive contributions, can be critiqued in some substantial ways. The modern literature on Christ's cross could be grouped in any number of ways, but I will focus on three trends.[46] First, there are the modern defenders of penal substitution, those who believe that this doctrine is at the heart of the gospel; these are typically evangelicals with a Reformed background. Then there are those who argue that God does in fact use the cross to transform human beings, but who reject the idea of satisfaction entirely and who promote a nonviolent reading of the cross; this approach is taken by Girard and his disciples. Finally, there is a vocal movement that argues that there is nothing redemptive about the cross whatsoever, that theologies of the cross have had disastrous effects on our understanding of God and human morality, and that the death of Jesus is in no way a divine work; these arguments are promoted by some feminist theologians and liberation theologians. Again, each of these movements—even though they are so radically divided amongst themselves—offers genuinely fruitful insights, but I will argue that, because they collapse the distinction between the "two goats," each also fails to be paradoxical enough to properly express the true shape of biblical atonement theology. In this section, I will underline how the three modern approaches succeed, and then suggest ways in which a Christian Yom Kippur soteriology would be able to integrate their insights while avoiding their weaknesses. I will begin by looking at the positive and negative elements of the two "extremes"—those who defend penal substitutionary atonement, and those who reject atonement theology completely, before looking at Girard's theory on its own.

---

46. Others have also chosen the three trends that I've identified as especially important in the modern soteriological landscape; see, for example, John Dunnill, *Sacrifice and the Body: Biblical Anthropology and Christian Self-Understanding* (Abingdon: Routledge, 2018).

Affirmations

Prominent feminist theologians have issued a bold and challenging denunciation of traditional Christian theologies of the cross, and in the process have brought an important insight to the forefront: in assessing a theology of the cross, one must interrogate its moral implications. Looking at traditional models, these feminist thinkers find that they are all profoundly destructive to women's liberation, and thus morally intolerable. Therefore, traditional theories of atonement must not only be modified, but radically opposed, insofar as they stand on the side of the oppressors against the oppressed. Many approaches to the cross seem to suggest that the road to victory is passive endurance of great suffering. Don't such teachings strengthen the hand of the oppressors?

"Women are acculturated to accept abuse"—these are the first words of an article extraordinary for its clarity and daring. Joanne Carlson Brown is a retired Methodist minister in Seattle, WA, and Rebecca Parker is a professor emerita and past president of Starr King School for the Ministry, a Unitarian Universalist seminary in Berkeley, CA. In the late 1980s, they wrote the breakthrough article in feminist soteriology, "For God So Loved the World?" Their primary claim is that none of the common soteriological models in the Christian tradition are morally acceptable from a feminist perspective, because all of them promote submission to violence—glorifying the lamb that goes silently to slaughter— an agenda that hurts women especially. Brown and Parker say, "The central image of Christ on the cross as the savior of the world communicates the message that suffering is redemptive. If the best person who ever lived gave his life for others, then, to be of value we should likewise sacrifice ourselves."[47] Making matters worse, Christ's death is apparently demanded by, and is in obedience to, the Father, and the Son is praised

---

47. Joanne Carlson Brown and Rebecca Parker, "For God so Loved the World?," in *Christianity, Patriarchy, and Abuse: A Feminist Critique*, by Joanne Carlson Brown and Carole R. Bohn (Cleveland: Pilgrim Press, 1989), 2. This problem is only compounded by the fact that, with reference to Eve, women have sometimes been accused of bearing special guilt for sin. Julie M. Hopkins says, "As a feminist, my particular criticism of a sacrificial interpretation is colored by its historical effect upon women. . . . Women, through virtue of their sex, were considered guilty of the death of Christ. To make satisfaction for their guilt, women were offered two forms of expiation, either in a spirit of passivity and obedience to bear the pain of childbearing and submit to their husbands or to transcend their sex and become men through celibacy and ascetic practices." Julie M Hopkins, *Towards a Feminist Christology: Jesus of Nazareth, European Women, and the Christological Crisis* (Grand Rapids, MI: Eerdmans, 1995), 51; cf. Rosemary Radford Ruether, *Introducing Redemption in Christian Feminism* (Sheffield: Sheffield Academic Press, 1998), 99–100.

for going to his death "without even raising a voice." Therefore, according to Christianity, our salvation is won through "divine child abuse" coupled with the victim's total passivity: patriarchal violence and silent submission. Starting from this powerful manifesto in feminist theology, many feminist theologians have argued that the oppressed must be given the resources needed to concretely resist their tormentors, not a demand to await an (eschatological) "new creation." As a result, Christ's cross must be identified as pure tragedy without any redeeming value. Suffering is not redemptive.[48]

The goal here is not to provide a comprehensive response to these concerns, but to suggest avenues for further dialogue and future research. In fact, from the perspective of Christian Yom Kippur soteriology, we can affirm that much of this critique is wise; it is properly rooted in genuine human concern and Christian insight. The absurd imagery of a temperamental and erratic God egotistically obsessing over his honor and choosing to torment his loving Son to assuage his fury (to the extent that anyone truly holds that view) is outrageous, a grotesque pagan monstrosity, deserving of all the disapprobation it receives. Such a nightmare theology cannot—thank God—be supported by the gospel, or by the great tradition, and it is at best the byproduct of a disastrous period of theological decadence.[49] No Christian, therefore, should hesitate to join those

48. Along these lines, the authors of "For God So Loved the World?" do offer a positive assessment of one figure's theology of the cross: Carter Heyward. Her 1982 book *The Redemption of God* improves on earlier considerations of the cross significantly: "For Heyward, Jesus' death was an evil act done by humans. It was unnecessary, violent, unjust, and final." Brown and Parker, "For God so Loved?," 25. Anything beyond this purely negative assessment of the cross fails, they say, including more modern soteriologies, even if they are relatively less offensive than the traditional models. For example, many in the twentieth century emphasized the notion that the cross reveals a God who suffers *with* us. For Brown and Parker, suffering with someone does not reduce the burden in and of itself. Instead of the view that God must submit to suffering and death, Brown and Parker say that "God must be seen as the one who most fully refuses to relinquish life. Lust for life . . . is what has the power to create community and sustain justice." Brown and Parker, 19; cf. Rita Nakashima Brock and Rebecca Ann Parker, *Proverbs of Ashes: Violence, Redemptive Suffering, and the Search for What Saves Us* (Boston: Beacon Press, 2002), 198. Others, like Martin Luther King, Jr., or Oscar Romero, see suffering as potentially "creative" insofar as it has the power to change the hearts of persecutors. Brown and Parker oppose this as a "martyrdom theology" that shows greater concern for the criminal than for the victim. We must not concede the idea that suffering is a normal part of social change. Brown and Parker, "For God so Loved?," 21; cf. Brock and Parker, *Proverbs of Ashes*, 39 ff.

49. By the same token, it might also be argued that many of the critiques of this misconception of God also emerge from the same decadent thought, and thus these contrasting views are eternally linked in a dialectical relationship.

who are eager to reject such a vision. Similarly, there are genuine questions to be raised about the cult of suffering that has been occasionally prominent in the Catholic tradition.[50] Suffering can become a perverse idol, and there have been those who seem to grow cold to the goodness of creation and the beauty of life through a fixation on self-mortification. Then there is the even greater perversion of those who encounter people trapped in abusive relationships and who counsel these victims to become perpetual sacrifices to their abusers, to silently submit themselves to such evils.[51] Such advice is like a child asking his father for a fish and receiving a serpent instead. How could such guidance be correlated with the Lord who brought healing wherever he went—even when it violated custom— who boldly stepped in to save the adulteress from her accusers, who angrily drove the moneychangers from the temple, who announced a devastating fate to those who would lead the little ones astray?

Insofar as some have used a palette of angry colors to depict the Christian God, and insofar as some have so radically divorced heaven from earth that they could instruct the victim of injustice to prayerfully wait for the next life to find relief from their torments, the liberationist critics have identified real shortcomings in the modern theological tradition. There can be no doubt that oppressors have used this twisted theology to baptize their crimes, and this is blasphemous. It is rightly condemned. Furthermore, the utterly passive anthropology that feminist critics identify as "Christian" cannot find support in the faith which announces that the baptized are called to "be courageous, be strong" (1 Cor 13:16). Again, in all of these areas, the feminist intervention is appropriate.

50. Kilby is concerned that "A proclivity to cast suffering in a positive light, and to link faith, love, and obedience with self-loss, self-abasement, even something like annihilation of the self, is something that constantly makes itself felt" in Balthasar's writings. Kilby, *Balthasar*, 115. It is easy to understand why this would raise red flags, even if Balthasar did not intend to leave this impression.

51. For example, Rebecca Ann Parker retells the disturbing story of Lucia, whose husband beat her, and whose priest told her to "rejoice" in her sufferings because "they bring [her] closer to Jesus." Brock and Parker, *Proverbs of Ashes*, 20–21. Parker adds, "Theology that defines virtue as obedience to God suppresses the virtue of revolt. A woman being battered by her husband will be counseled to be obedient, as Jesus was to God. After all, Eve brought sin into the world by her disobedience. A good woman submits to her husband as he submits to God." Brock and Parker, 31. Darby Kathleen Ray summarizes the study of incest survivors conducted by Annie Imbens and Ineke Jonker, who argue that the traditional Christian doctrines of God as Almighty, sin as disobedience, and the cross as sacrifice work to keep victims submissive, excuse the violence of abusers, and prevent healing for survivors. *Deceiving the Devil: Atonement, Abuse, and Ransom* (Cleveland: Pilgrim Press, 1998), 24, 40, 45.

On the other hand, turning to the opposite pole in the contemporary debate, there is also reason to appreciate and support certain key insights advanced by advocates of penal substitutionary atonement.[52] Thinking about the Day of Atonement, and the theology of the temple which undergirds that most sacred day, there is no doubt that sincere and awe-inspired veneration of God's holiness and God's glory, so strongly emphasized by advocates of substitutionary atonement, is appropriate. Human beings in every generation have attempted to seize God and compel God to serve and bless their own ideologies and self-centered schemes. This is the story of idolatry, illustrated dramatically by Nadab and Abihu, and the only true remedy is a lively awareness of the otherness and holiness of God. The biblical emphasis on the otherness of God is not about dividing us from God, but exactly the opposite: it is about preparing us for true intimacy with God. Even when considering the analogy of other human beings, I can only enter into true and intimate communion with another when I make space for that person "to be," when I make space for her to communicate herself freely, without compulsion, without presumption, open to surprise. So much more so with God, who cannot be truly known until we are stripped of the desire to use, control, and dominate God, and to instead stand with hearts open to the encounter. The whole biblical story, articulated with special beauty in priestly theology, is about "drawing near" (*qorbān*), but that movement always requires a reverence for the holiness and infinity of God.

A second point, very much related, and often repeated by advocates of penal substitution, is that there is indeed an awareness here of the "seriousness of sin."[53] Some insist on God's ability to forgive in a way that suggests a blasé attitude toward the crisis of sin, as if the moral outrage articulated by Ivan is overwrought, as if the crime of brutalized children can be overlooked with bland munificence. We just discussed how those who tell sufferers to be submissively patient with their victimization for the sake of some future heaven effectively divide heaven and earth in a way that is unthinkable from the perspective of temple theology. In fact,

52. For a recent overview of penal substitutionary approaches to atonement, see Anatolios, *Deification through the Cross*, 411 ff.

53. John Stott nicely sums up the first and second points: "That God is holy is foundational to biblical religion. So is the corollary that sin is incompatible with his holiness." John Stott, *The Cross of Christ* (Westmont, IL: IVP Books, 2006), 102. It is in this context that Stott brings in the issue of God's wrath, which is the "steady, unrelenting, unremitting, uncompromising antagonism" of an all-holy God toward evil in its diverse forms. Stott, 172. The two essential planks of true atonement theology, then, are the immense gravity of human sin and the perfect holiness of God. Stott, 110.

those who treat sin in a nonchalant way—"God loves you just the way you are. God forgives all. Just try to do better in the future"—are guilty of the very same thing. They radically divide heaven and earth such that the things that happen here on earth, the acts of violence we commit, both petty and great, are casually set aside and forgotten in heaven, to the point where the two places seem virtually unrelated to each other. Sin is not taken seriously. While it is certainly possible to overemphasize sin— as if the threat of evil is something that keeps God up at night in anxious panic—the unwillingness to see suffering and evil as a grave threat is an attitude that—while congratulating itself for its humanism or its spiritual enlightenment—is, in reality, a cold and heartless thing. It will not recognize the great drama of creation, the solemn significance of freedom, the ways in which we bear each other up or drag each other down. "Cain, where is your brother?" Some cultivate such an insipid and wooden imagination that they cannot now see the fact that this unbelievable story, this human story, demands a culminating Act of great love and great severity to save the shattered cosmos. Nothing less is suitable. Only those who take sin seriously can acknowledge the mortal wound which is so great that God alone can bear it.

Finally, substitutionary theories are right to acknowledge that Christ and Christ alone must act in our place. He is singular. As the second Adam and the true high priest, he is the microcosm that uniquely represents all creation before the Father. As the incarnate Word, he is the perfect "mirror of heaven" who uniquely embodies and completes the indwelling presence of God in creation.[54] Therefore, as the YHWH-goat, he is able to realize the entire theological vision of the true temple—the doxological site of heavenly Beauty, the stage upon which the drama of openhearted love is lived as absolute Goodness, the place where Truth is made manifest in history—through the culminating act that epitomized his entire mission. All of this, though, ought to be seen as a sacramental action that is ordered toward unlimited inclusion, so that we might become by grace what he is by nature (this point is not consistently emphasized by advocates of penal substitution). Simultaneously, though—and this is where the advocates of substitutionary atonement especially highlight something helpful—he also performs a service that is (mercifully) exclusive of our participation by removing our sins and

---

54. This concept from temple theology has been articulated by Balthasar. In the essay "Persönlichkeit und Form," Balthasar "calls Jesus Christ the Father's 'temporal mirror in the flesh' (*zeitlicher Spiegel im Fleisch*), emphasizing that the Son in the unity of his divinity and humanity reveals the Father to us." See Carpenter, *Theo-Poetics*, 56.

bearing them away, thus fulfilling the work of the Azazel-goat so that we would be liberated from the terrible burden we create. This is an act that expresses God's final "No" to sin, evil, suffering, and death. It is a type of exile on our behalf, a kind of divine acknowledgment of proper wrath that is necessary if the whole world is to be made right.

Qualifications

I have argued in this chapter that the unique value of Christian Yom Kippur soteriology is that it can maintain the paradox of the cross more effectively than other theological models. A consistent problem for the other theories is that they disregard or collapse the distinction between the two "goats," and as a result, symbols and concepts proper to one movement are attributed to the other, and vice versa. This creates confusion or imprecision, which results in distorted approaches to Christ's saving work.

First, the thoroughly negative assessment of soteriology that appears in some liberationist writings is open to re-examination. With respect to feminist concerns, it might be said that—despite the misrepresentations of some Christians—the atonement theme of drawing near to God is not inherently linked with suffering and wrath, but it is a positive and assertive movement, a joyful movement, of peace and magnanimity. It is a paradisiacal reality, and Eden is the place where God and humanity were meant to walk together in the cool of the day, where man and women dwell together, side by side, in love. The ancient Israelite theology of cultic offerings, which pursues the renewed Eden on Zion, is meant to train Israel in the way of intimacy, harmony, and mutual faithfulness.

Without a doubt, there is an anthropology implicit in temple practices that has been challenged by feminist theologians. I have summarized the Jewish and Christian understanding of what it means to be fully human and fully alive with the word *hinneni* or "openheartedness," but it is true that the difficult concept of "obedience" is implicit in these words. We can again cite a passage from Cyril O'Regan that illustrates why this vision of *hinneni* is so challenging for many modern readers: since the Enlightenment, the "forms of life" inspired by Christian anthropology—which include obedience and humility—are (according to many post-Enlightenment thinkers) "pathological in that they represent attacks on human integrity, autonomy, and legitimate self-regard."[55] Thus, in

55. O'Regan, *Anatomy of Misremembering*, 7.

response to the pathology (allegedly) inherent in Christian anthropology, the modern approach to "salvation" is a call to self-realization. Women especially are urged to "take responsibility for self-actualization"[56] and to "come to themselves."[57] But this is exactly where a clearer distinction between the "goats" could be helpful. I would argue that a Christian humanism grounded in self-giving perpetuates a culture that benefits the strong over against the weak *only if* the YHWH-goat is interpreted using Azazel-goat concepts like blind passivity, unjust suffering, and eternal forsakenness. When the YHWH-goat is clearly distinguished from the Azazel-goat, the post-Enlightenment critique loses its force.

To clarify this argument, let's start with a quote from Darby Kathleen Ray. She has argued that the Anselmian approach to atonement "defines and valorizes power as absolute, as noncontingent, solidary, unitary—in other words, as devoid of mutuality, relationality, plurality, or partiality."[58] If an absolute and solidary power like this "Anselmian" God (as Ray interprets it) commands "obedience," it does suggest a voluntaristic subjection of one will to another, or in other words, mere subservience before brute power. However, for theologians like Hart and Balthasar,

56. Margaret Daphne Hampson, *Theology and Feminism* (Oxford: Blackwell, 1990), 123. Hampson is quoting Judith Plaskow.

57. Hampson, 127. While this is part of it, Hampson does not intend to depict self-realization as self-enclosed. As she says, "If it is not particularly useful to women to see salvation as a breaking of the self, how then should they envisage it? Perhaps as a healing of the self; as a person coming to be all that she may be *in a network of relationships. . . .* If women's ills have been the result of an undervaluation of the self, then their healing must consist in self-actualization." Hampson, 127, emphasis added. Note that this salvation occurs "in a network of relationships," which builds on Hampson's earlier call for "a modality of the 'self-other *relation* [in which] one aims at mutual realization. One sees the self as relational, not 'atomic.'" Hampson's "On Power and Gender" (1988) quoted by Jennifer Newsome Martin in "The 'Whence' and the 'Whither' of Balthasar's Gendered Theology: Rehabilitating Kenosis for Feminist Theology," *Modern Theology* 31, no. 2 (2015): 233. Hampson later defines the "self" in these terms: "It is only as I am treated as an equal, and conceive of myself as such, that I shall be able to be fully present to others. Our goal must be that persons are centered in themselves and open to one another." Daphne Hampson, ed., *Swallowing a Fishbone?: Feminist Theologians Debate Christianity* (London: Society for Promoting Christian Knowledge Publishing, 1996), 121.

While this is not an Enlightenment-style anthropology of "atomic" self-sufficiency, its emphasis on, and apparent prioritization of, being "centered" seems to be in tension with temple anthropology, which features a theological understanding of the human that is significantly more eccentric without, I will argue below, being pathological and self-destructive. For a fuller critique of Hampson's anthropology, see Aristotle Papanikolaou, "Person, Kenosis and Abuse: Hans Urs von Balthasar and Feminist Theologies in Conversation," *Modern Theology* 19, no. 1 (2003): 57–59.

58. Ray, *Deceiving the Devil*, 39.

the Trinitarian context for Christian atonement theology helps to mitigate these concerns. They both interpret the *triduum mortis* in light of the immanent Trinity: the God revealed in this paradigmatic act in salvation history is the eternal God of love. Along these lines, the confident obedience of the incarnate Son in historical time is not a novel act on the part of Jesus, but it has its ground in the eternal mutual bond of Father, Son, and Holy Spirit.

For critics of the traditional emphasis on obedience, this transition to the relations within the immanent Trinity will hardly assuage their concerns, but rather, it will more likely intensify them. Now the Son not only lacks autonomy and self-possession, but he is *eternally* subservient. But of course, what Hart and Balthasar intend to suggest is that the divine persons enjoy eternal perichoretic mutuality, each person receiving "self" in relation, and thus the entire movement is gift. Therefore, to say the incarnate Son is "radically obedient" to the Father through self-giving / self-abandonment implies a "recapitulation," in the context of sin, of what the Son already "sees" the Father doing from all eternity. In other words, the Father is nothing like a cold and aloof commander who, for whatever capricious reason, insists on blind obedience from afar, but the Father is the one who does as the Son does because the Son is always the one who does as the Father does. The Son's giving reflects the Father's giving. Thus, when we see the loving self-gift of the Son, we see a perfect image of the Father who has already handed himself over. Perhaps it is fair to conclude, then, that all proper obedience is "recapitulation" of the immanent relations between Father and Son. Such relations are the very measure of peace, the ever-greater expression of love, and therefore authentic obedience could never endanger one's authentic integrity.[59]

YHWH-goat soteriology is therefore not a matter of power conceived as "noncontingent, solidary, unitary," but power as "mutuality, relationality, triune oneness." In his obedience, Christ refuses to embrace the way of violence, the temptation of "unitary" power, but rather he gives thanks with greater and greater fidelity. The Father does not respond to this with anger—which would be absurd—but he also gives everything he has with overflowing love; in the economy of salvation, the Father and Son are most fully and indivisibly one in Christ's passion, at which point the second Adam, the great high priest of the new covenant, enters the Holy of Holies. At that moment, through the Holy Spirit, they are

---

59. For an extraordinarily helpful discussion of Balthasar's kenotic theology in light of feminist critiques, see Martin, "The 'Whence' and the 'Whither.'"

in one another. While this may not fit the modern ideal of "*self*-actualization," it simply proposes a different anthropology, a deific-humanity, where the "self" is discovered most truly in overflowing love which is "erotic and ecstatic."[60]

But still, modern critics make an incredibly important point when they show that obedience can easily become oppressive *in our wilderness context*, where human beings rarely miss an opportunity to seek power over each other, and then institutionalize that power. To perpetually give oneself in our present circumstances is often a recipe for abuse, and it is (in different ways) dehumanizing for the abuser and the victim.[61] The need for the Azazel-goat is present here: if there is to be genuine intimacy between persons (and between persons and God), those sins that incline us toward violence against each other must be removed. There must be honest confession, repentance, and radical removal of sin. Only as sin is removed can nascent trust and authentic intimacy form. In the absence of *mutual* openheartedness, and a *mutual* commitment to the way of repentance and forgiveness when persons fall short, it can be prudent to withhold the gift-of-self from another, to protect the pearl of one's own heart from the violence of swine, and this is not merely a matter of self-concern (though it is that, and that's okay), but it is also for the sake of the (would be) abuser, insofar as one should avoid being entangled in his own self-desolation, if possible. To repeat, this is a matter of spiritual discernment, but it seems to me that traditional Christian theology has abundant resources for protecting victims, and encouraging them on the true way of life, without requiring a false post-enlightenment anthropology of autonomy. As mentioned, to follow Jesus the YHWH-goat is to follow the audacious one who radically pursues human flourishing at all times, which (because humans are *imago dei*) is necessarily a kenotic let-

---

60. O'Regan notes that these two words, along with *epektasis* (eternal becoming), are fundamental to Balthasar's anthropology. O'Regan, *Anatomy of Misremembering*, 142. The same could be said for Hart. See Papanikolaou, "Person, Kenosis and Abuse" for helpful reflection on Balthasar's kenotic anthropology.

61. As Sarah Coakley says with reference to kenoticism, "The (rightful) concentration in the literature on the profound, and continuing, damage to women from sexual and physical abuse, even in 'Christian' families and churches, and on the seeming legitimization of this by men otherwise committed to disciplined religious practice and the rhetoric of cruciform redemption, shows what a perilous path we are treading here. An undiscriminating adulation of 'vulnerability' might appear to condone, or even invite, such evils." *Powers and Submissions: Spirituality, Philosophy and Gender* (New York: John Wiley & Sons, 2008), 33. For an interesting analysis of the problem of "Kenotic Personhood and the Reality of Abuse," which features a discussion of the literature on trauma, see Papanikolaou, "Person, Kenosis and Abuse," 52–57.

ting go of "self" to live in God.[62] It is precisely the proper distinction of the goats—by recognizing that sin must be borne away if the way of the YHWH-goat can be fully experienced communally on earth as it is experienced eternally in heaven—that creates the context in which such flourishing can be pursued.

One also finds a "conflation" of the goats in penal substitutionary atonement. Here the argument is more straightforward. In his classic book in defense of penal substitutionary atonement, *The Cross of Christ*, John Stott explicitly critiques those who put "a wedge" between the two goats of Yom Kippur.[63] For Stott, *both goats* bear witness to the reality of penal substitution, the first as the means and the second as the result. According to this interpretation, the key to understanding the theology of the goat for the Lord is to interpret the sacrificial blood as a need for death, and not just that, but violent death. When the animal is slaughtered, it suffers the punishment that we deserve, and thus it is a substitute on our behalf. When this penalty is administered, God is propitiated because God's justice has been satisfied. It is thus necessary for God's "holiness to be directed in judgment upon his substitute."[64] Again, because the judgment against humanity is death (including, more or less clearly depending on the author, the second death of hell), God insists that this penalty be executed, although in his mercy he allows it to be executed vicariously. In that way, the death of the animal is the "means" of our salvation. The second goat, for Azazel, shows us the result. Our

62. This calls to mind Sarah Coakley's own conviction that "to offer a defense of some version of *kenosis* is not only compatible with feminism, but vital to a distinctively Christian manifestation of it, a manifestation which does not eschew, but embraces, the spiritual paradoxes of 'losing one's life in order to save it.'" Coakley, *Powers and Submissions*, 4. I hope I have shown that this notion of human being has its roots in ancient priestly temple theology, which Jesus takes up and transfigures in his own way of being.

63. Stott argues that the phrase "to bear sin" in the Old Testament should be taken to mean "to endure [sins'] penal consequences, to undergo its penalty." *The Cross of Christ*, 143. As mentioned in chapter eight (above), Stott believes that the best example of this is found in Leviticus 16, in the account of the two goats. One goat is sacrificed, while the sins are laid upon the head of the second goat, who carries them off to a "solitary place" (Lv 16:22). Stott says, "Some commentators make the mistake of drawing a wedge between the two goats, the sacrificed goat and the scapegoat, overlooking the fact that the two together are described as 'a sin offering' in the singular (v. 5)." He follows up with a suggestion from T. J. Crawford: "each [goat] embodied a different aspect of the same sacrifice, 'the one exhibiting the means, the other the results, of the atonement'" (144). Stott, therefore, would *not* drive a wedge between the goats, apparently because both symbolize penal substitution. If there is a distinction, it is simply to illustrate the nature of the penalty (death) and the result of that death (removal of sin).

64. Stott, 157.

sins are removed—and, especially, the *penalty* for our sins is removed—when the judgment is carried out upon the substitute. These goats are pedagogical, both communicating the single truth of penal substitution.

The problems with this account, from the perspective of the rich symbolism of the ancient Jewish cult in its historical-critical context, are hopefully now clear. The unwillingness to distinguish the goats—which is common among penal substitutionary advocates—invites a blurring of the lines between the theological concepts unique to each, and with that blurring, significant confusion. An entire cultic liturgy grounded in a commitment to life and peace is re-interpreted as an apparatus for administering death and violence. This tragic transversal is seen most blatantly with reference to the symbolism of blood, which is given an interpretation that is exactly opposite to priestly semiotics, and thus the temple becomes almost indistinguishable from Gehenna as a place of punishment. The distinctness of the Azazel-goat is lost, and thus an air of exile and wrath overtakes the entire landscape, from the holy of holies to the abyss. The real problem here is not simply that it is gloomy, but that it fundamentally distorts our understanding of the triune God by over-accentuating the lesser arc and suppressing the greater arc, allowing the themes of the Azazel-goat—now articulated in the terms of early modern jurisprudence—to drive out the themes of the YHWH-goat, which, despite all positive intentions, ultimately represents a victory of darkness over light. While penal substitution preserves several helpful intuitions, it really is "sub-biblical,"[65] *especially* from the perspective of priestly theology, and thus it must be judged as a well-meaning distortion.

René Girard

Among the theories that we have explored, Girard represents something of a special case. His basic idea, as a descriptor of sociological phenomena, is distressingly successful at explaining social behaviors that play out in our daily lives.[66] There is no Eden in Girard's brilliant *Violence and the Sacred*. There is no "before." From the first chapter, the reader

---

65. This is N. T. Wright's assessment of Jeffery, Ovey, and Sach's *Pierced for Our Transgressions*. N. T. Wright, "The Cross and The Caricatures," *Fulcrum Anglican* (blog), April 23, 2007, https://www.fulcrum-anglican.org.uk/articles/the-cross-and-the-caricatures/.

66. There are many outstanding summaries of Girard's general theory. For a recent example, Anatolios's discussion of Girard is excellent, both in terms of explaining Girard's major ideas and engaging them appreciatively and critically. Anatolios, *Deification through the Cross*, 395 ff.

finds herself ensnared in the rhythm of violence, a pounding that seems to have no beginning and no end. *Sacrifice, crisis, scapegoat. Sacrifice, crisis, scapegoat.* Sunrise, sunset, *sacrifice, crisis, scapegoat,* all across the globe. This is the rhythm of a very human problem and a very human solution, all soaked through with violence. Violence against violence, a house divided, it does not stand, but try again: *sacrifice, crisis, scapegoat.*

As a cartographer of the fallen world, of fallen communities, and even of the fallen human heart, Girard traces the jagged mountains and the desolate valleys with remarkable clarity and insight. From my perspective, it is not Girard's sociology that needs supplementation, but his theology.[67] The problems he identifies are real and devastating, but the canvas upon which he tries to fit his solution is not wide enough to address the challenge in its cosmic scope.

To set up the critique of Girard, it is helpful to look briefly at the work of S. Mark Heim. In *Saved from Sacrifice: A Theology of the Cross*, Heim not only summarizes and creatively develops Girardian soteriology, but he productively applies Girard's insights in various areas, such as ecclesiology and sacramental theology. One area where Heim especially refines Girard's thought is his clarification on in what ways we might say Jesus' death *is* a sacrifice, and in what ways it is *not* a sacrifice. Heim says, "The passion accounts are stereoscopic: they tell two stories, superimposed on each other . . . the same story from two different perspectives."[68] In other words, there is a "double story" behind the Bible's depiction of Christ's death. It is according to the first story—the worldly story, a violent and sinful story—that Christ dies as a sacrifice and substitute. Jesus is indeed a Girardian scapegoat, a person singled out by the community, accused of the worst sins imaginable (like blasphemy and rebellion), and killed to preserve the peace. This is the very old story of violence suppressing violence through sacrificial violence, and Jesus does indeed submit himself to this worldly story. Therefore, those many biblical passages that speak of Jesus's death as a sacrifice, or that use substitutionary or scapegoating images to interpret what happened to him, tell the truth. Jesus *does* sur-

---

67. Of course, Girard was first of all a trained historian and literary critic; his interest in theology, which grew in his later years, was secondary to his primary areas of expertise. It is quite right to say that Girard *as a sociologist* cannot be held responsible for missing the Edenic origins and beatific ends of human nature; such ideas are not immediately available to modern sociologists, given the limitations of the field. Nevertheless, as Girard turned more and more to scripture, he was increasingly nuanced in his theological claims. While recognizing this growing nuance, we will still see that dialogue between Girard, his followers, and a Yom Kippur soteriology can be theologically productive.

68. Heim, *Saved from Sacrifice*, 193.

render himself to the sacrificial mechanisms of this world, but *not* in a way that affirms sacrifice as good or holy. Jesus submits himself to our sacrificial practices to overcome them once and for all.

That brings us to the second story, which is superimposed on the first, and which is a radically non-violent and anti-sacrificial story, sealed by Christ's resurrection. First through his teaching, but finally through his death and resurrection, Jesus unmasks the scapegoating mechanism, which was truly hidden since the foundation of the world. He identifies himself with scapegoats, dies like them as a sacrifice for the sake of others, but then God does something radically new in the resurrection: God shows that he is on the side of the victim, on the side of the marginalized, on the side of those crushed in the wheels of history and "progress." For the first time, the scapegoat returns and forces us to really see the victim and face our violence and abuse. In some ways, Jesus' death is agonizingly ordinary, routine, the kind of thing that has been happening on all four corners of the globe from the beginning. In other ways, it is the most extraordinary death because Jesus is the first fully visible victim, and after the light of his truth and peace shines on the world, the faces of all the other unjustly murdered victims come into focus. Jesus exposes the reality of human sin and violence, and in so doing plunders violence of its most prized possession: secrecy. This second story, in other words, does not suggest that God is pleased with, or complicit in, our sacrificial practices, but to the contrary, that God radically opposes the violence of the majority and affirms the dignity and value of the world's victims.[69]

69. Again, this is Heim's re-presentation of Girard's teaching. Overall, it is obvious that Girard and Heim agree on the points mentioned here, but Girard's language in earlier works was less nuanced. He spoke primarily from the perspective of Heim's "second story," which inclined him toward a dismissive approach to New Testament texts that evoke sacrificial themes—especially the Book of Hebrews: René Girard, *Things Hidden Since the Foundation of the World*, trans. Stephen Bann and Michael Metteer (Redwood City, CA: Stanford University Press, 1987), 182. (Compare Heim, who reads Hebrews more positively within a Girardian framework: *Saved from Sacrifice*, 156 ff. Schwager also attempts to articulate a more positive interpretation of the Letter to the Hebrews, but still with a strong emphasis on the discontinuity between Christ's death and the Jewish cult. *Must There Be Scapegoats?*, 200–205; *Jesus in the Drama of Salvation*, 182–86.) For an overview of the development in Girard's thinking, especially on the Letter to the Hebrews, see Anatolios, *Deification through the Cross*, 400.

As an example of Girard's strong opposition to preserving the idea of sacrifice as an interpretive key, in *Things Hidden Since the Foundation of the World* he says, "There is nothing in the Gospels to suggest that the death of Jesus is a sacrifice. . ." and that any sacrificial reading of Christ's death is an "enormous and paradoxical misunderstanding." Girard, *Things Hidden*, 180. But in the same text, he calls Jesus the "most perfect victim" and "the scapegoat *par excellence*," and then, in *The Scapegoat*, Girard is even clearer

Again, there is much that is profound in Girard's thought, and in Heim's theological appropriation of his thought, but from the perspective of this study, we can also highlight the most obvious challenge: the authentic positive theology of the goat for the Lord is underdeveloped here. That the goats are "conflated" is as obvious in Girard as it was in penal substitutionary theories. The French sociologist oscillates indiscriminately between calling the isolated victim of social violence a "sacrifice" and a "scapegoat." He or she is a scapegoat insofar as the disorders and evils that are dividing the community are ascribed to this person or persons. Such evils are "loaded" onto the victim, and he or she must carry them away for the sake of the remaining community. That same person is a "sacrifice" in the conventional sense that they are violently surrendered in hopes of purchasing a provisional peace. Whether the imagery is exile ("scapegoat") or ritual murder ("sacrifice"), the same phenomenon is being described.[70] Girard's sobering conclusion stands out: "Inevitably the moment comes when violence can only be countered by more violence. Whether we fail or succeed in our effort to subdue it, the real victor is always violence itself."[71]

For Girard, the key words I have associated with the YHWH-goat (peace, unity, order, etc.) are here and now made possible by the words associated with the Azazel-goat (violence, division, chaos, etc.). In other words, social peace is dependent on an original violence, social unity depends on a divisive "othering," and social order is imposed on a more basic chaos. It is certainly true that, in his more mature works, Girard identifies Jesus as the one who unmasks the scapegoat mechanism through his cross and resurrection, thus breaking its "spell," and establishing a new kind of community, one rooted in the fact that God is on the side of the excluded victim, not the violent majority. However, precisely because the goat for the Lord theme is never adequately developed

---

about the fact that "the Gospels say that Jesus is in the same position as all past, present, and future victims." René Girard, *The Scapegoat*, trans. Yvonne Freccero (Baltimore: The Johns Hopkins University Press, 1986), 126. By the time of *I See Satan Fall Like Lightning*, Girard is able to open the book with the affirmation that, "Jesus is the unjustifiably sacrificed *lamb of God*." Girard, *I See Satan Fall*, 1. Nevertheless, Girard remains generally hesitant about calling Christ's death a sacrifice, preferring instead to simply say that it is an example of the "mimetic cycle" (106–107) or the "single victim mechanism" (133, 137). Heim's notion of a "double story" thus helps clarify Girard's apparent intent.

70. This conflation has been noticed before. See, for example, Leithart, *Delivered from the Elements of the World*, 104–5, footnote 27.

71. René Girard, *Violence and the Sacred*, trans. Patrick Gregory (Baltimore: The Johns Hopkins University Press, 1979), 31.

as the more basic and primordial truth of creation, this new community lacks solid ontological or salvation-historical foundations. As Hart so perceptively puts it in his own critique of Girard, Jesus runs the risk of becoming a "gnostic savior bearing tidings of an alien God. . . ," or even "a Marcionite savior"[72] who is in no positive relation to Israel's rich and complex tradition of sacrificial thought. Thus, for a Girardian like Heim, Israel's sacrificial practices simply mirror pagan culture and are present in the scriptures merely to illustrate the type of "religion" that must be overcome.[73] The only positive message in the Hebrew Bible, with respect to sacrifice, is the audacious prophetic critique.

Hart's own subtle reading of Israel's cultic theology in relation to the concept of "gift," and from there in relation to God's triune nature, represents a necessary antidote. Girard is starkly dialectical in his classic works, seeing the human community as ultimately grounded in conflictual mimesis and violent scapegoating. Jesus, through his death and resurrection, thoroughly replaces this old order with a new order, but because there are no apparent grounds for the new order in creation itself, Jesus' own church seems as violent an imposition as anything else. It is

72. Hart, *Beauty of the Infinite*, 349. Balthasar issues a similar critique, but instead of comparing Girard to a gnostic or Marcion, Balthasar critically associates him with the early, highly dialectical, Barth! Both, in their respective ways, claim "religion is the invention of Satan." Balthasar, *TD4*, 308.

73. Heim discusses Jewish cultic practice as relating to the "first story" of his "double story" framework (see above), the story that the cross corrects. There is a kind of continuity between the Testaments, Heim says, insofar as Jesus's death cannot be fully understood without appreciating earlier sacrificial practice—the second story is not heard correctly without knowing the first story. Heim, *Saved from Sacrifice*, 66. Israel, therefore, has sacrificial practices that mirror the practices of other cultures. This is especially clear on the Day of Atonement: "At the center of Israel's ritual life we find an event bearing all the marks we outlined [earlier in the text]. The community centers its collective violence on a representative sacrifice, which is charged with all the guilt and sins that pollute and threaten the people, and driven out and off a cliff—the very image of mob violence against a human scapegoat. What is striking is not that it differs from that model, but that it is so extraordinarily explicit. . . ." Heim, 77. (For Girard's own reflections on the scapegoat ritual, see *I See Satan Fall*, 154 ff.)

Heim suggests that God allows a sacrificial cult so as to ultimately expose and denounce scapegoating. For Heim, when it comes to Israel's sacrificial practices overall, the violence present in the Jewish cult is "telling us the truth, the truth about our human condition . . . and most particularly, the truth about the integral connection between religion and violence." Heim, *Saved from Sacrifice*, 101, cf. 69. Jewish sacrifice is not a positive type that Christ fulfills, but a negative contrast that Christ must overcome. See also Schwager, who analyzes the Jewish cult in a similar way. Schwager favorably quotes Helen Schüngel-Straumann: "The sacrificial regulations do not originate from Yahweh's wishes, but are a human invention." Schwager, *Must There Be Scapegoats?*, 84

not clearly a recapitulation as much as it is a replacement, one order for another. God's preference for the victim, which is announced in the resurrection, ultimately seems as arbitrary as the community's original exclusion of the victim. All of this, I would argue, is because the image of the YHWH-goat, who is the restorer of original peace, is mutilated to the point where he is indistinguishable from the Azazel-goat, and thus the entire cultic system takes on a demonic aura.[74] Such an interpretation of Israel's theology introduces significant theological distortions. Here again, it seems that earth and heaven are fractured from each other. The first is violence all the way down, and the second rejects the first root and branch . . . thus flirting with an apocalyptic violence of its own.

At the same time, now turning to the Azazel-goat, there is also a real question over whether or not Girardians adequately confront the problem of sin in its full cosmic scope.[75] Again, from the Girardian perspective, especially as it is glossed by Heim, the death of Jesus as "scapegoat" is doubly mundane, that is, mundane in two senses of the word. First, as we saw above, his death is mundane as in "ordinary" with respect to Girard's sociological account because, from the perspective of the *polis*, Jesus dies as a substitutionary "sacrifice" for the sake of the social order, like so many others across the centuries. Jesus is a political sacrifice according to the Girardian logic of Caiaphas: "it is better for you to have one man die for the people than to have the whole nation destroyed" (John 11:50). He must die to "save" the Roman order from the turmoil he was creating with his kingdom message. In this sense, he is a true scapegoat. But then, secondly, Jesus' death is mundane as in "worldly" because it was focused on the immanent goal of "raising awareness" (to

74. There is an evolution in Girard's thought on this very important point. Girard is indeed sweepingly negative about mimetic desire in early texts, such as *Violence and the Sacred*, failing to reflect on how mimesis could be a genuinely positive force, part of God's good creation. Soon after *Violence and the Sacred* appeared, Schwager refines Girard's general theory by insisting that violence is rooted in the human heart "without belonging to its essence." *Must There Be Scapegoats?*, 198. James Alison also helpfully builds on Girard's theory of mimesis, arguing that this human inclination is not necessarily violent. Alison therefore coins the term "pacific mimesis." James Alison, *The Joy of Being Wrong: Original Sin through Easter Eyes* (New York: Crossroad Publishing Company, 1998), 7–14. In his latter, more theological work, Girard's theory expanded. He came to recognize that mimesis is a fundamentally positive reality that has been distorted by sin: "Without mimetic desire there would be neither freedom nor humanity. Mimetic desire is intrinsically good." Girard, *I See Satan Fall*, 15. This opens the way for him to advocate a positive, non-conflictual imitation of Jesus, who imitates the Father.

75. This concern has been raised by others; recently, Anatolios, *Deification through the Cross*, 408 f.

use the contemporary nomenclature) about the injustice of scapegoating. It was, from the divine perspective, geared toward giving a (resurrected) human face to the faceless multitude who are crushed for the sake of social stability and progress, and thus, through the scapegoated-and-resurrected Jesus, God radically challenges the typical way of creating social cohesion. God is trying to teach humans a lesson through Christ.

This observation raises the question: while Girard does speak often of "scapegoating," does his teaching really address the work of the *Azazel-goat* as it is described in Leviticus? In other words, while Christ's passion has the effect of challenging a particularly invasive social sin (the "scapegoating mechanism"), the more general problem of "sin itself" and God's final "No" to sin—the problem that animated the priestly theologians in antiquity, and Balthasar today—is largely unaddressed. Balthasar feels that Girard only captures a "psychological unloading"[76] whereby *we* accuse the scapegoat of all sins, and thus "it was not God but men who cast their sins onto the Lamb of God" which "seemed to give men the initiative in the redemptive process, while God, whose part it is always to love and forgive (K. Rahner), simply looked on, failing to measure up to the divine action of self-giving."[77] In other words, the cosmic liturgy of Yom Kippur which is the very heart of the Torah, and the full Trinitarian drama in the economy of salvation that culminates in Christian scripture, is attenuated in favor of a miracle (the resuscitation of the victim) that—blandly—challenges us to reassess our behavior. Without intending to minimize the insidious way in which the "scapegoating mechanism" pollutes everything it touches, it is not itself the root cause of all cosmic disorder. It is not the only burden under which creation groans. Raising awareness about this problem is not sufficient to "make all things new," partly because the sin-bearing here is highly specific and horizontal (without the eschatological Azazel-goat and the dynamic of Trinitarian judgment against sin), and partly because the positive side of the equation (the YHWH-goat, the Trinitarian economy of gift) is underdeveloped in Girard's theory.

In the end, each of these three modern theories suffers from notable imbalances. When looking at penal substitution, the feminist critique of atonement, and Girard's theory of Jesus as scapegoat, all of them share an inability to maintain the paradox between the two "goats" of Yom Kippur; they tend to confuse the characteristic vocabulary associated

76. Balthasar, *TD4*, 309.
77. Balthasar, 317.

with each, and thus they inevitably generate a mix of positive affirmations and unfortunate confusions. The best solution is to understand the unique role of each goat, without confusion and without division, so as to retrieve a more profoundly biblical theology of atonement. A Christian Yom Kippur soteriology is, therefore, uniquely capable of presenting a deeply Trinitarian, biblical, analogical, and traditional theology of Christ's saving work.

Tree of Life, Last and First

We shall not cease from exploration
And the end of all our exploring
Will be to arrive where we started
And know the place for the first time.

—T. S. Eliot, *Little Gidding*[1]

There was a little church nuzzled in the heart of old England. This country chapel had for centuries known the gentle rhythm of baptisms and funerals, then more baptisms and more funerals, until the strange day came when the funerals sharply overtook the baptisms, the Black Death overtaking the town. And so, the little church in its pastoral setting was abandoned as the forlorn villagers fled to the wilderness, hoping for a chance. The Easter candle extinguished, the happy alleluias no longer reverberating within the walls, the chapel itself began its own descent into death—a much slower decline than any human could experience but every bit as unnatural for such a hallowed hall. Dust gathered on the altar, foundation stones cracked and crumbled, vines grew over the windows. The old cursed earth, seizing the opportunity for a quiet coup, greedily sought to swallow the little church just as it had previously received the lifeless remains of the villagers. The hungry grave seeks the last word.

Nicholas Ferrar was seeking a site for a new Christian community he hoped to establish. Reaching Little Gidding in 1625, he saw the cozy chapel and knew he was home. He laid his hand upon the cold stones of the ruined structure and commanded them: "arise!" *Arise.* Few words are as deeply Christian. A Christian's eyes dance with a special magic; seeing *through* the ruins, they cast deeper and deeper, until they catch glimpse of the hidden world within, the new creation, ready to burst forth, waiting for the command. Arise! His eyes trained in Christian hope, Ferrar could already see in this deserted wilderness a warm and lively

---

1. T. S. Eliot, "Little Gidding" in *T. S. Eliot: Collected Poems, 1909–1962* (New York: Ecco, 1991), 208.

shire, a blessed community, a people called forth by love, walking together the ancient way of the saints and mystics. And so Ferrar gathered his most intimate friends and family and retreated to Little Gidding, where they began an experiment in communal life. This was a new kind of monasticism, a village monastery of family and friends, devoting themselves to fellowship, continuous prayer, intellectual conversation, artistic labor, and works of charity in the surrounding communities.

According to any worldly standard, the community did not long endure. Within twenty-seven years the great founders had died and the semi-monastic community dispersed. But something beautiful had begun here, a fruitful tree had been planted, and its leaves were a source of inspiration for many. After all, this village of friendship, nestled around an ancient little church, was a place where "prayer has been valid."[2] Thus, its legend lived on, and it burns more brightly now than ever—in verse. In May 1936, the great poet T. S. Eliot made pilgrimage to Little Gidding, and the site of Ferrar's bold experiment in Christian living became, for Eliot, a stirring icon of the New Jerusalem, a place both now and forever, where the temporal opened into the eternal with unusual translucence. Ferrar's ideal of tender community in peace and prayer only grew more urgent for Eliot during the Second World War, when, along with his compatriots, he endured his own descent to hell: the terror of Germany's blitz. While working as an air raid warden, Eliot wrote "Little Gidding" in 1942, which would become the capstone of his Nobel Prize winning masterpiece, *The Four Quartets*.

Now considered one of his finest achievements, and one of the greatest works of Christian art in the 20th century, "Little Gidding" is (among other things) a remarkable meditation on the shape of biblical atonement that is deeply influenced—even if this is simply the result of deep theo-poetic intuition—by the great journey of the high priest on the Day of Atonement in Leviticus 16, toward the holy of holies, toward this long-anticipated trysting place where the burning love shared between Israel and her LORD will, at last, be consummated. Eliot's "Little Gidding" can also be read as a small-scale, modernized *Divine Comedy*. Dante famously opens his poem "Midway along the journey of our life," when he, after wandering into a "dark wood," comes upon a hill bathed in divine splendor. The beauty of this holy hill, and the desire to ascend it, emboldens the pilgrim to make the terrifying-but-necessary journey through hell. Eliot's own journey begins at Little Gidding in "Midwinter spring"—a

2. Eliot, 201.

time where freeze and thaw daily wrestle—when a renegade sunbeam breaks loose from the winter haze and dazzles the ice; this becomes for Eliot a "pentecostal fire / In the dark time of the year."[3] Little Gidding is the place where the glory of the Spirit breaks through, even in the gloomy seasons of life, and thus it represents a beacon in the night to orient and embolden the pilgrim-poet as he passes through his own living hell.

What brought Eliot to this old monastic village many miles to the north of his London home? This is the question he asks himself, and he realizes that one's true motive for the pilgrimage is often richer and deeper than first realized. To approach this holy place, one must approach with an open heart—one does not come to grasp or to master, but to receive:

> . . . You are here to kneel
> Where prayer has been valid. And prayer is more
> Than an order of words, the conscious occupation
> Of the praying mind, or the sound of the voice praying.
> And what the dead had no speech for, when living,
> They can tell you, being dead: the communication
> Of the dead is tongued with fire beyond the language of the living.
> Here, the intersection of the timeless moment
> Is England and nowhere. Never and always.[4]

For Eliot, when you come to this house of prayer, a house sanctified by prayer, you have come to the place where the communion of saints gathers as one body, dead and alive. In this "timeless moment," with communication much richer than ordinary speech, heart speaks to heart, deep calls unto deep. "You are here to kneel / Where prayer has been valid."

Surely Eliot has found the ever-new Zion in this tiny English village. The humble church at the center of Little Gidding does not have the physical grandeur of Solomon's temple—it would not be possible to count its towers or reflect on its ramparts or tour its palaces (Psalm 48)—but this country parish partakes of all the glory of Zion because the King of kings has chosen to sacramentally dwell within its unassuming walls, because the divine fire has been lit in its narrow sanctuary, because the ancient sacrifice of Moriah here finds its final expression: *this is my body, this is my blood*. When questioned by the Samaritan woman about worship at Zion or Gerizim, Jesus says, ". . . the hour is coming, and is now here, when the true worshippers will worship the Father in spirit and truth, for the Father

3. Eliot, 200.
4. Eliot, 201.

seeks such as these to worship him. God is spirit, and those who worship him must worship in spirit and truth" (John 4:23–24). This should not be read as an anti-Temple saying, but rather, in the context of Jesus' own profound self-identification with the temple. Worship in its most authentic shape—in the New Testament as well as the Hebrew Bible—is temple worship because the temple is the icon of presence and thanksgiving, prayer and truth. True worship always takes form in the human heart as *hinneni*, the word etched on Zion's foundations, it is the sacrificial posture that best communicates the way of the Spirit. All Spirit is from Christ and returns to Christ, who with the Father is himself the temple of the new and eternal Jerusalem (cf. Revelation 21:22). And with the Resurrection, the temple of Christ's body is indestructible and sure, ever-present to those who draw near to him. Therefore, Eliot encountered true Zion in Little Gidding, a place hallowed by the Ferrar community's prayer, where believers indeed gathered in "spirit and truth." This true manifestation of Zion, in all its humility, is—like Zion herself—"at the still point of the turning world."[5] Again: "You are here to kneel / Where prayer has been valid" . . . all must find their way to this place at the world's end to encounter the "fire beyond the language of the living." There is only one such place, and it can be found in millions of places across the earth.

While Little Gidding shapes Eliot's hope, it cannot save the poet from descending through the valley of tears. In the second movement of the poem, Eliot brings the reader on patrol through London after an air raid. This becomes a vision of wilderness, exile, and hell as the poet reflects on how each of the four elements—air, earth, water, and fire—deformed by sin, collude to extend the realm of death. Here Eliot brilliantly connects the devastation of his city and the decay of the country church: "Water and fire shall rot / The marred foundations we forgot, / Of sanctuary and choir, / This is the death of water and fire."[6] Eliot has brought us to the realm of "impurity," the mournful truth of a broken world, which

---

5. This is the famous refrain from the first of the *Four Quartets*, "Burnt Norton": Eliot, 177. Thomas Howard explains: ". . . Little Gidding is, at least for Eliot's purposes in this poem, as close as we get in this mortal life to the Still Point. . . . This 'Now and in England' will serve well enough to remind us that *all* 'nows' have the potentiality to be 'the nearest', and any geographical location will serve as the approach to the Still Point. It is just that Eliot has brought us to Little Gidding, which, because of its very nature, is a particularly explicit and stark approach." *Dove Descending: A Journey into T. S. Eliot's Four Quartets* (San Francisco: Sapienta Classics/Ignatius Press, 2006), 126–27.

6. Eliot, *T. S. Eliot*, 202. Howard says, "We get death under the four aspects of the four elements. In other words, there will be no escaping death, because it pervades the whole of created reality." Howard, *Dove Descending*, 128. Compare this claim to our discussion of impurity laws in chapter five.

the ancient priests had surveyed with such spiritual sensitivity. As the world spins its way further and further from its center—for the Still Point, for Zion, for Little Gidding, is the navel of creation—the fallen elements are emboldened to attempt greater rebellions, hoping to deliver final victory to the prince of this world.

While on his tour through the bombed-out city, the "dead leaves" of shrapnel crunching under his feet, Eliot encounters his own Virgil, a "forgotten, half recalled" master who guides him through the inferno.[7] This guide reveals the three "gifts reserved for age"... and the third is especially important. Eliot identifies a gnawing sense of humiliation as he reviews his life: "the rending pain of re-enactment / Of all that you have done, and been; the shame / Of motives late revealed, and the awareness / Of things ill done and done to others' harm / Which once you took for exercise of virtue."[8] This represents a deep internal hell as the wayfarer confronts the reality of his own sin, the moral deaths we choose for ourselves. Here again, Eliot guides us through a world well known to the age-old Levites: the countless ways we "choose death," then hide the fact from ourselves.

In this desert of devastation, this world in rebellion, this wilderness of iniquity, what will become of us? Wouldn't it have been better to die in the snug ignorance of Egypt than to live in the hell of true self-knowledge? Is it not hopeless? The master finishes his speech: "From wrong to wrong the exasperated spirit / Proceeds, unless restored by that refining fire / Where you must move in measure, like a dancer."[9] There *is* a way forward; temple theology is all about the return to Eden, the neglected and paradoxical way of paradise. The temple is the place where we learn how to live in harmony—to move in measure—gracefully in God. It is the place of perfect freedom, dancing upward like a flame, spirit and body flowing together in peace. But the ancient Jewish thinkers were well aware of the fact that in our exile there are innumerable ways in which folly and failure throw us down toward Babylon, toward a life of slavery and sorrow.[10] Maybe that's why, in the Levitical cultic rites, Israel draws

---

7. Howard suggests that this guide could well be Dante himself. See Howard, *Dove Descending*, 131 ff.

8. Eliot, *T. S. Eliot*, 204.

9. Eliot, 205.

10. Michael Fishbane says it beautifully: "The spiritual life walks this perilous path—through the howl of evil and emptiness in the world, consciously confronting its terrors and tasks, striving for integrity without denials or any evasions." And then:

> For Jewish theological consciousness, just this is the sense of fracture and fatefulness of our human condition since Adam's banishment from Eden.... Spatial dislocation thus symbolizes all our exiles and alienations in the world, both

near to the LORD only through fire. Importantly, though, this is not fire as a source of destruction—the fire that mars the foundations—but the fire of God's own presence. As it says in Leviticus: "Fire came out from the Lord and consumed the burnt-offering and the fat on the altar; and when all the people saw it, they shouted and fell on their faces" (9:24). Within the theological imagination of the priestly writers, it is not possible to reach the holy of holies expect to pass through *this* fire, except to have one's heart pierced and purified by *this* flaming sword. And from the perspective of sacrificial theology, as Eliot seems to understand so well, the way through the fire is the way of *hinneni*, the way of loving truly, selflessly, freely. Everything passes, all is change. The only question is whether this mutability is taken as an opportunity to grow ever-more in Love, especially by receiving the world as gift and freely returning it to God with thanksgiving, or whether one tries to cling to the things of this world, thus choosing the stifling death of self-centeredness.

Nothing is lost for those who love. Eliot's purgative way makes this clear: "See, now they vanish, / The faces and places, with the self which, as it could, loved them, / To become renewed, transfigured, in another pattern."[11] The fire of God, through which all must pass, is—for those whose hearts speak the word *hinneni*—a transfiguring fire.[12] Christ said, "I came to bring fire to the earth, and how I wish it were already kindled!" (Luke 12:49). The Spirit lights the whole earth as a sacrificial pyre, starting with the microcosm on Zion, starting too with his own enflamed sacred heart, with the hope that every soul would come to be a living flame of love, renewed and transfigured according to the divine pattern. And so, Eliot's great discovery, echoing the priestly theologians through

---

historical and mental. It is the deepest of archetypes carried in our hearts and souls, and attests to a primordial anxiety over the nature of our human condition. But this negative valence has its ballast. The recurrent dream of harmony and ingathering in a place of blessing is its counterpoint, the longing of the soul since Abraham. It too is archetypal and primordial. It is older than Sinai, and older than Moses as well, who inherited the ancestral promises of the patriarchs, kept alive from generation to generation as a reiterated divine hope. It is the deep yearning for Eden amid the fractures of life.

Michael Fishbane, *Sacred Attunement: A Jewish Theology* (Chicago: University of Chicago Press, 2010), 175–76.

11. Eliot, *T. S. Eliot*, 205.

12. Abraham's *hinneni* is also the heart of Mary's *fiat*. As Howard explains: "…one stands on this ground only insofar as one's motives have been purified from all hopes and loves of the wrong things. *Fiat mihi*, said the pure Virgin: be it done unto me according to thy word." Howard, *Dove Descending*, 141.

the generations: "The only hope, or else despair / Lies in the choice of pyre or pyre- / To be redeemed from fire by fire. . . . We only live, only suspire / Consumed by either fire or fire."[13] There are those, like the rebellious sons of Leviticus 10, Nadab and Abihu, who choose to be a blazing corpse, dead and ever-more dying within. They are self-consumed, they are empty, they are closed in by greed and lust and pride. Then there are those who choose the way of the burnt offering, dying to self, and truly alive. They are self-giving, they are full, they are opened outward by faith, hope, and love. These are the ways, and there are no others.

Just as Eliot has a Virgil, he also has a saintly hero who, not unlike Beatrice, guides him toward the deep mysteries of God. Julian of Norwich's joyful, childlike words of faith become the poem's great refrain: "All shall be well, and / All manner of thing shall be well." Despite the present struggle to embody self-giving, all shall be well. Despite this bombed-out earth, this expanding hell, all manner of thing shall be well. What could give Julian, who was writing in the midst of the black death, the confidence to offer such a promise against all the evidence of our eyes, against every trend in history? Is it not true that all wonders end as ruins, and everything falls apart in time? Julian speaks with courage, for she herself has been to the holy of holies, the dwelling place of God, as she discovers in her contemplation that Jesus sits enthroned as king at the center of her own heart. And speaking from this "everlasting dwelling" at the very center of her being, Jesus promises her:

> You will not be overcome. . . . He did not say: You will not be troubled, you will not be belabored, you will not be disquieted; but he did say: You will not be overcome. God wants us to pay attention to these words, and always to be strong in faithful trust, in well-being and in woe, for he loves us and delights in us, and so he wishes us to love him and delight in him and trust greatly in him, and all will be well.[14]

Eliot, despite every reasonable doubt, trusts in his guide; he chooses to follow her way, to seek with her the eternal holy of holies. Thus, with renewed faith, he finds himself, in the fifth movement of the poem, at the gate which is at once a sorrowful exit and the joyful return. "What we

13. Eliot, *T. S. Eliot*, 207.

14. Julian of Norwich, *Julian of Norwich: Showings*, trans. Edmund Colledge and James Walsh (New York: Paulist Press, 1977), 315. As Howard perceptively has it: "The Lady Julian, and the *Quartets*, arrive at this astonishing place *only after having canvassed the whole breadth and depth of horror.*" *Dove Descending*, 139.

call the beginning is often the end / And to make an end is to make a beginning. / The end is where we start from."[15]

A tree of life stands at the center, and all history mysteriously spirals round. This is the secret in the midst of the garden, the gift at the heart of the city. The secret is not for keeping, the gift is not for having. When love flows like living water, when the nations come and wash their robes, the secret is not our shame but our joy, the gift is not our possession but our being: uncreated by grace, eternal by adoption, the image of the Thrice Holy, the likeness of the Immortal One. This is our beginning, our deepest and most original truth, and it is our end, our highest and most complete happiness: "And the one who was seated on the throne said, 'See, I am making all things new.' Also, he said, 'Write this, for these words are trustworthy and true.' Then he said to me, 'It is done! I am the Alpha and the Omega, the beginning and the end. . .'" (Rv 21:5).

All things new. Newness is not with reference to chronology, the cycles by which things come and go. Surely history unfolds, and surely there is only Now. Eliot understands the meaning of this "Now," the single "Day" that gives shape to the millennia. Here again, we can perceive a connection to the Day of Atonement, which the ancient rabbis referred to as simply: "the Day." Eliot says, "The moment of the rose [fleeting] and the moment of the yew-tree [more lasting] / Are of equal duration. A people without history / Is not redeemed from time, for history is a pattern / Of timeless moments. . . ."[16] All history plays out, in a million acts, the one pattern, the Day that encapsulates it all, the day of the two goats—the one who enters the holy of holies, the other who descends into exilic hell—the Day eternally fulfilled by Jesus on the cross. This Day, lived now on *this* day, is the day of our triumph: "since we have confidence to enter the sanctuary by the blood of Jesus . . . let us approach with a true heart in full assurance of faith. . ." (Heb 10:19–22). This Day, lived now on *this* day, is the day of our lamentation: "But as for the cowardly, the faithless, the polluted, the murderers, the fornicators, the sorcerers, the idolaters, and all liars, their place will be in the lake that burns with fire and sulfur, which is the second death" (Rv 21:9). The Day is now and forever. In Eliot's words: "And any action / Is a step to the block, to the fire, down the sea's throat / Or to an illegible stone: and that is where we start."[17] Every act of violence is a tombstone, weathered by the centuries until illegible, and yet stubborn in its pres-

15. Eliot, *T. S. Eliot*, 207.
16. Eliot, 208.
17. Eliot, 208.

ence. Something past and eternal. Every act of love is a white stone, a new name given by God, illegible to all but the recipient, persistent in its beauty. Something past and eternal. It is all Now, as we follow Azazel into the sulfuric abyss, as we pass through the divine fire into joy, every act a destiny, every act a beginning, as we add our own embellishments on the historical stage.

I am the alpha and omega. Whichever way we go, Christ goes before, and thus there is never reason for pride or despair. This is the ultimate meaning of the affirmation that Christ fulfills the double work of "the Day," of Yom Kippur, through his singular work of love. As Second Adam, he forges the eschatological paths. If in this action I find myself following after the YHWH-goat, I may not boast. *Hinneni*-life is Christ alive in me: *I live, yet no longer I, but Christ. . . .* If in that action I find myself following after the Azazel-goat, I must not despair. Christ has gone further still, bearing sins to the end, so that I may convert and be liberated: *If we confess our sins, he who is faithful and just will forgive us our sins and cleanse us from all unrighteousness.* This is a story of hope on all sides as we strive now to become who we are, to put into act the gift that makes us unique and irreplaceable. And in the end, we receive the gift of the beginning.

> We shall not cease from our exploration
> And the end of all our exploring
> Will be to arrive where we started
> And know the place for the first time.[18]

All of history is oriented around a tree, beginning and end. This tree alone gives immortality, but immortality is a gift that requires fertile soil to take root. Love alone is the way: the open heart will find the gate open, the closed heart will find it closed. When we arrive at last, we see it for the first time. It is *the tree of life with its twelve kinds of fruit, producing its fruit each month; and the leaves of the tree are for the healing of the nations.* It is the true cross upon which the savior died. The fruit is his body, given for us. The leaves are his graces, which make us whole. As the full expression of life—resurrection life—and love—eternal love—it is the one sign that contains the whole truth. It is the holy of holies where God wishes to dwell most intimately, outside the gates, between two thieves, stretched out and abandoned, making all things new. The mystery of this life and this love was always present, in the hidden origins of the

---

18. Eliot, 208.

human story, as the deep magic that fuels the adventure of our lives, but it is only truly known now at the end of the world.

> Quick now, here, now, always—
> A condition of complete simplicity
> (Costing not less than everything)
> And all shall be well and
> All manner of thing shall be well
> When the tongues of flames are in-folded
> Into the crowned knot of fire
> And the fire and the rose are one.[19]

19. Eliot, 209.

Bibliography

Adams, Rebecca. "Loving Mimesis and Girard's 'Scapegoat of the Text': A Creative Reassessment of Mimetic Desire." In *Violence Renounced: Réne Girard, Biblical Studies, and Peacemaking*, edited by W. M. Swartley, 277–307. Telford: Pandora Press, 2000.

Alexander, P. S. "Jerusalem as the Omphalos of the World: On the History of a Geographical Concept." *Judaism* 46, no. 2 (1997): 147–58.

Alison, James. *The Joy of Being Wrong: Original Sin through Easter Eyes.* New York: Crossroad Publishing Company, 1998.

Alter, Robert. *Genesis.* New York: W. W. Norton & Company, 1997.

Anatolios, Khaled. *Deification through the Cross: An Eastern Christian Theology of Salvation.* Grand Rapids, MI: Eerdmans, 2020.

Andersen, Francis. "2 (Slavonic Apocalypse of) Enoch." In *The Old Testament Pseudepigrapha*, edited by James R. Charlesworth, 1.91–221. 2 vols. New York: Doubleday, 1983–1985.

Anderson, Gary A. "As We Have Heard So We Have Seen." *Conservative Judaism* 54 (2002): 50–59.

———. *Christian Doctrine and the Old Testament: Theology in the Service of Biblical Exegesis.* Grand Rapids, MI: Baker Academic, 2017.

———. *The Genesis of Perfection: Adam and Eve in Jewish and Christian Imagination.* Louisville, KY: Westminster John Knox Press, 2001.

———. "Inauguration of the Tabernacle Service at Sinai." In *The Temple of Jerusalem: From Moses to the Messiah: In Honor of Professor Louis H. Feldman*, edited by Steven Fine, 1–15. Leiden: Brill, 2011.

———. "Introduction to Israelite Religion." In *New Interpreter's Bible*, 1:272–83. Nashville: Abingdon Press, 1994.

———. "Mary in the Old Testament." *Pro Ecclesia* 16, no. 1 (2007): 33–55.

———. "The Praise of God as a Cultic Event." In *Priesthood and Cult in Ancient Israel*, edited by Gary A. Andersen and Saul M. Olyan, 15–33. Sheffield: Sheffield Academic Press, 1991.

———. *Sacrifices and Offerings in Ancient Israel: Studies in Their Social and Political Importance.* Harvard Semitic Monographs 41. Atlanta: Scholars Press, 1987.

———. *Sin: A History.* New Haven, CT: Yale University Press, 2010.

———. "'Through Those Who Are Near to Me, I Will Show Myself Holy': Nadab and Abihu and Apophatic Theology." *Catholic Biblical Quarterly* 77, no. 1 (January 2015).

———. "To See Where God Dwells: The Tabernacle, the Temple, and the Origins of the Christian Mystical Tradition." In *Letter & Spirit* 4 (2008): 15–47.

Anselm. *Anselm of Canterbury: The Major Works*, edited by B. Davies and G. R. Evans. Oxford: Oxford University Press, 1998.

Attridge, Harold W. *The Epistle to the Hebrews: A Commentary on the Epistle to the Hebrews*. Philadelphia: Fortress Press, 1989.

Bailey, Daniel P. "Jesus as the Mercy Seat: The Semantics and Theology of Paul's Use of Hilasterion in Romans 3:25." Ph.D. diss., Cambridge University, 1999.

Balthasar, Hans Urs von. *A Theological Anthropology*. Eugene, OR: Wipf & Stock, 2010.

———. *Dare We Hope That All Men Be Saved? With a Short Discourse on Hell*. Translated by David Kipp and Lothar Krauth. San Francisco: Ignatius Press, 1988.

———. *The Glory of the Lord: A Theological Aesthetics, Vol. 1: Seeing the Form*. Translated by Erasmo Leiva-Merikakis. San Francisco: Ignatius Press, 1982.

———. *The Glory of the Lord: A Theological Aesthetics, Vol. 6: Theology: The Old Covenant*. Translated by Brian McNeil and Erasmo Leiva-Merikakis. San Francisco: Ignatius Press, 1991.

———. *The Glory of the Lord: A Theological Aesthetics, Vol. 7: Theology: The New Covenant*. Translated by Brian McNeil. San Francisco: Ignatius Press, 1990.

———. *Life out of Death: Meditations on the Paschal Mystery*. Translated by Davis Perkins. San Francisco: Ignatius Press, 2012.

———. *Mysterium Paschale: The Mystery of Easter*. Translated by Aidan Nichols. San Francisco: Ignatius Press, 2000.

———. "Nine Propositions on Christian Ethics." In *Principles of Christian Morality*, edited by Heinz Schurmann, Joseph Cardinal Ratzinger, and Hans Urs von Balthasar. San Francisco: Ignatius Press, 1986.

———. *Prayer*. Translated by Graham Harrison. San Francisco: Ignatius Press, 1986.

———. *Theo-Drama: Theological Dramatic Theory, Vol. 1: Prolegomena*. Translated by Graham Harrison. San Francisco: Ignatius Press, 1988.

————. *Theo-Drama: Theological Dramatic Theory, Vol. 2: The Dramatis Personae: Man in God*. Translated by Graham Harrison. San Francisco: Ignatius Press, 1990.

————. *Theo-Drama: Theological Dramatic Theory, Vol. 3: The Dramatis Personae: Persons in Christ*. Translated by Graham Harrison. San Francisco: Ignatius Press, 1993.

————. *Theo-Drama: Theological Dramatic Theory, Vol. 4: The Action*. Translated by Graham Harrison. San Francisco: Ignatius Press, 1994.

————. *Theo-Drama: Theological Dramatic Theory, Vol. 5: The Last Act*. Translated by Graham Harrison. San Francisco: Ignatius Press, 1998.

————. *Theo-Logic, Vol. 1: Truth of the World*. Translated by Adrian J. Walker. San Francisco: Ignatius Press, 2000.

————. *Theo-Logic, Vol. 2: Truth of God*. Translated by Adrian J. Walker. San Francisco: Ignatius Press, 2004.

————. *Theologik 2 / Wahrheit Gottes*. Einsiedeln: Johannes Verlag Einsiedeln, 1985.

————. *The Theology of Karl Barth: Exposition and Interpretation*. Translated by Edward T. Oakes. San Francisco: Ignatius Press, 1992.

————. *You Crown the Year With Your Goodness: Radio Sermons*. Translated by Graham Harrison. San Francisco: Ignatius Press, 1989.

Balthasar, Hans von, and Adrienne von Speyr. *To the Heart of the Mystery of Redemption*. Translated by Anne Englund Nash. San Francisco: Ignatius Press, 2010.

Barclay, William. *New Testament Words*. Philadelphia: Westminster Press, 1974.

Barker, Margaret. "Atonement: The Rite of Healing." *Scottish Journal of Theology* 49, no. 1 (1996): 1–20.

————. *Temple Mysticism: An Introduction*. London: SPCK, 2011.

————. *Temple Theology*. London: SPCK, 2004.

————. *The Great High Priest: The Temple Roots of Christian Liturgy*. Edinburgh: T&T Clark, 2003.

————. "Time and Eternity: The World of the Temple." *Month* 34, no. 1 (2001): 15–22.

Barnard, Jody A. *The Mysticism of Hebrews: Exploring the Role of Jewish Apocalyptic Mysticism in the Epistle to the Hebrews*. Tübingen: Mohr Siebeck, 2012.

Barnett, Paul. *The Second Epistle to the Corinthians*. Grand Rapids, MI: Eerdmans, 1997.

Barry, Richard J. "Retrieving the Goat for Azazel: Balthasar's Biblical Soteriology." *Nova et Vetera* 15, no. 1 (Winter 2017): 13-35.

———. "'They Feasted Their Eyes': Nadab, Abihu, and the Original Sin."
Journal of Theological Interpretation 17, no. 2 (2023): 145–165,
https://doi.org/10.5325/jtheointe.17.2.0145.

Barth, Karl. *Church Dogmatics: The Doctrine of Creation. Volume III, Part
3*, edited by G.W. Bromiley and T. F. Torrance; translated by G.W. Bromiley and R. J. Ehrlich. London: T&T Clark, 2004.

———. *Church Dogmatics. Vol. IV, Part 1 The Doctrine of Reconciliation*,
edited by G.W. Bromiley and T. F. Torrance; translated by G.W. Bromiley.
London: T&T Clark, 2004.

Beale, G. K. *The Temple and the Church's Mission: A Biblical Theology of
the Dwelling Place of God*. Westmont, IL: IVP Academic, 2004.

Bell, R. H. "Sacrifice and Christology in Paul." *Journal of Theological Studies*
53, no. 1 (2002): 1–27.

Berman, Joshua. *The Temple: Its Symbolism and Meaning Then and Now*.
Northvale, NJ: Aronson, 1995.

Bibb, Bryan D. "Nadab and Abihu Attempt to Fill a Gap: Law and Narrative
in Leviticus 10.1-7." *Journal for the Study of the Old Testament* 26, no.
2 (2001): 83–99.

Blankenhorn, Bernhard. "Balthasar's Method of Divine Naming." *Thomist*
64 (2000): 499–519.

Blenkinsopp, Joseph. *Prophecy and Canon: Theology*. Notre Dame, IN.: University of Notre Dame Press, 1986.

———. "Structure of P." *Catholic Biblical Quarterly* 38, no. 3 (1976): 275–92.

Bloch-Smith, Elizabeth. "'Who Is the King of Glory?' Solomon's Temple and
Its Symbolism." In *Scripture and Other Artifacts: Essays on the Bible
and Archaeology in Honor of Philip J. King*, 18–31. Louisville, KY: West-
minster/John Knox Press, 1994.

Boccaccini, Gabriele. *Beyond the Essene Hypothesis: The Parting of the Ways
Between Qumran and Enochic Judaism*. Grand Rapids, MI: Eerdmans,
1998.

Boer, Martinus C. de. *Galatians: A Commentary*. Louisville, KY: Westminster
John Knox Press, 2011.

Boersma, Hans. *Heavenly Participation: The Weaving of a Sacramental Tapestry*. Grand Rapids, MI: Eerdmans, 2011.

Boswell, Brad. "Goats, Gods, and the Mystery of Christ: Exegesis and Narrative Conflict between Julian and Cyril." *Studia Patristica* 129 (2021): 51–
69.

Braude, William G., ed. *Pesikta De-Rab Kahana*. Translated by Israel J. Kapstein. 2nd Revised ed. JPS, 2002.

Briggs, Robert A. *Jewish Temple Imagery in the Book of Revelation*. Studies in Biblical Literature 10. New York: Peter Lang, 1999.

Brock, Rita Nakashima, and Rebecca Ann Parker. *Proverbs of Ashes: Violence, Redemptive Suffering, and the Search for What Saves Us*. Boston: Beacon Press, 2002.

Brown, Joanne Carlson, and Rebecca Parker. "For God so Loved the World?" In *Christianity, Patriarchy, and Abuse: A Feminist Critique*, by Joanne Carlson Brown and Carole R. Bohn. Cleveland: Pilgrim Press, 1989.

Brown, William. "'In Him All Things Hold Together': An Ecology of Atonement." *Ex Auditu: An International Journal of Theological Interpretation of Scripture* 26 (May 9, 2011): 1-20.

Brueggemann, Walter. *Theology of the Old Testament: Testimony, Dispute, Advocacy*. Minneapolis: Fortress Press, 2005.

Bulgakov, Sergii. *The Lamb of God*. Grand Rapids, MI: Eerdmans, 2008.

Caldecott, Stratford. *All Things Made New: The Mysteries of the World in Christ*. Tacoma, WA: Angelico Press, 2011.

———. *The Radiance of Being: Dimensions of Cosmic Christianity*. Tacoma, WA: Angelico Press, 2013.

Carpenter, Anne M. *Theo-Poetics: Hans Urs von Balthasar and the Risk of Art and Being*. Notre Dame, IN: University of Notre Dame Press, 2015.

Carr, David M. "No Return to Wellhausen." *Biblica* 86, no. 1 (2005): 107–14.

Caspi, Mishael, and John T. Greene. "Prolegomenon." In *Unbinding the Binding of Isaac*. University Press of America, 2007.

Chau, Carolyn A. "'What Could Possibly Be Given?': Towards an Exploration of Kenosis as Forgiveness—Continuing the Conversation between Coakley, Hampson, and Papanikolaou." *Modern Theology* 28, no. 1 (2012): 1–24.

Childs, Brevard S. *Introduction to the Old Testament as Scripture*. Philadelphia: Fortress Press, 1979.

Christensen, Duane, and Marcel Narucki. "The Mosaic Authorship of the Pentateuch." *Journal of the Evangelical Theological Society* 32, no. 4 (1989): 465–71.

Clements, R. E. *God and Temple*. Oxford: Blackwell, 1965.

Coakley, Sarah. *Powers and Submissions: Spirituality, Philosophy and Gender*. Hoboken, NJ: John Wiley & Sons, 2008.

Cockerill, Gareth Lee. *The Epistle to the Hebrews*. Grand Rapids, MI: Eerdmans, 2012.

Collins, John J. *Jerusalem and the Temple in Jewish Apocalyptic Literature of the Second Temple Period*. Ramat Gan: Bar Ilan University, 1998.

Collins, Raymond F. *Second Corinthians*. Paideia: Commentaries on the New Testament. Grand Rapids, MI: Baker Academic, 2013.

Coloe, Mary L. "The Dwelling of God among Us: The Symbolic Function of the Temple in the Fourth Gospel." *Pacifica* 12, no. 2 (June 1999): 244–244.

Congar, Yves. *The Mystery of the Temple, or, The Manner of God's Presence to His Creatures from Genesis to the Apocalypse*. Translated by R. F. Trevett. Westminster, MD: Newman Press, 1962.

Cortez, Felix H. "From the Holy to the Most Holy Place: The Period of Hebrews 9: 6-10 and the Day of Atonement as a Metaphor of Transition." *Journal of Biblical Literature*, 2006, 527–47.

Cranz, Isabel. *Atonement and Purification: Priestly and Assyro-Babylonian Perspectives on Sin and Its Consequences*. Tübingen: Mohr Siebeck, 2017.

Curcio, Janice Ann. "Genesis 22 and the Socio-Religious Reforms of Ezra and Nehemiah." Diss., Brunel University, 2010.

Daly, Robert J. *Christian Sacrifice: The Judaeo-Christian Background before Origen*. Washington, DC: Catholic University of America Press, 1978.

Davie, Ian. *Jesus Purusha: A Vedanta-Based Doctrine of Jesus*. New York: Lindisfarne Press, 1985.

Davis, Stephen T., Daniel Kendall, and Gerald O'Collins. *The Incarnation: An Interdisciplinary Symposium on the Incarnation of the Son of God*. Oxford: Oxford University Press, 2004.

D'Costa, Gavin. "The Descent into Hell as a Solution for the Problem of the Fate of Unevangelized Non-Christians: Balthasar's Hell, the Limbo of the Fathers, and Purgatory." *International Journal of Systematic Theology* 11, no. 2 (April 1, 2009): 146–71.

De Lubac, Henri. *Catholicism: Christ and the Common Destiny of Man*. San Francisco: Ignatius Press, 1988.

———. "Internal Causes of the Weakening and Disappearance of the Sense of the Sacred." In *Theology in History*, translated by Englund Nash Anne, 223–40. San Francisco: Ignatius Press, 1996.

DeConick, April D. "What Is Early Jewish and Christian Mysticism?" In *Paradise Now: Essays on Early Jewish and Christian Mysticism*, edited by April D. DeConick. Atlanta: Society of Biblical Literature, 2006.

Dennis, John. "The Function of חטאת Sacrifice in the Priestly Literature." *Ephemerides Theologicae Lovanienses* 78, no. 1 (2002): 108–29.

Dostoevsky, Fyodor. *The Brothers Karamazov*. Translated by Constance Garnett. Modern Library, 1996.

Douglas, Mary. *Leviticus as Literature*. Oxford: Oxford University Press, 1999.

Dunnill, John. *Sacrifice and the Body: Biblical Anthropology and Christian Self-Understanding*. Abingdon, Oxon: Routledge, 2018.

Eberhart, Christian. "Characteristics of Sacrificial Metaphors in Hebrews." In *Hebrews: Contemporary Methods, New Insights*, 37–64. Leiden: Brill, 2005.

———. "Sacrifice? Holy Smokes! Reflections on Cult Terminology for Understanding Sacrifice in the Hebrew Bible." *Ritual and Metaphor: Sacrifice in the Bible*, 17–32. Leiden: Brill, 2011.

———. *The Sacrifice of Jesus: Understanding Atonement Biblically*. Minneapolis: Fortress Press, 2011.

Eliade, Mircea. *The Sacred and the Profane: The Nature of Religion*. Translated by Willard R. Trask. New York: Harcourt Brace Jovanovich, 1987.

Elior, Rachel. *The Three Temples: On the Emergence of Jewish Mysticism in Late Antiquity*. Oxford: Littman Library of Jewish Civilization, 2005.

Eliot, T. S. *Collected Poems, 1909-1962*. New York: Ecco, 1991.

Ephrem. *Ephrem the Syrian: Hymns*. Paulist Press, 1989.

Fagerberg, David W. *On Liturgical Asceticism*. Washington, D.C: The Catholic University of America Press, 2013.

———. *Theologia Prima: What Is Liturgical Theology?* Chicago: Hillenbrand Books, 2012.

Feder, Yitzhaq. *Blood Expiation in Hittite and Biblical Ritual Origins, Context, and Meaning*. Atlanta: Society of Biblical Literature, 2011.

———. "On *Kupparu, Kippēr* and Etymological Sins That Cannot Be Wiped Away." *Vetus Testamentum* 60, no. 4 (January 1, 2010): 535–45.

Feldman, Liane M. *The Story of Sacrifice: Ritual and Narrative in the Priestly Source*. Tübingen: Mohr Siebeck, 2020.

Finlan, Stephen. *Options on Atonement in Christian Thought*. Collegeville, MN: Liturgical Press, 2007.

———. *Problems with Atonement: The Origins of, and Controversy about, the Atonement Doctrine*. Collegeville, MN: Liturgical Press, 2005.

———. *The Background and Content of Paul's Cultic Atonement Metaphors*. Atlanta: Society of Biblical Literature, 2004.

Fishbane, Michael. *Sacred Attunement: A Jewish Theology*. Chicago: University of Chicago Press, 2010.

———. "The Sacred Center: The Symbolic Structure of the Bible." In *Texts and Responses*, edited by M. A. Fishbane and P. R. Flohr, 111–76. Leiden: Brill , 1975.

Fletcher-Louis, Crispin. *All the Glory of Adam: Liturgical Anthropology in the Dead Sea Scrolls*. Leiden: Brill, 2002.

———. "God's Image, His Cosmic Temple and the High Priest: Towards an Historical and Theological Account of the Incarnation." In *Heaven on Earth: The Temple in Biblical Theology*, edited by T. Desmond Alexander and Simon J. Gathercole, 81–99. Carlisle: Paternoster, 2004.

———. "Jesus as the High Priestly Messiah: Part 1." *Journal for the Study of the Historical Jesus* 4, no. 2 (2006): 155–75.

———. "Jesus as the High Priestly Messiah: Part 2." *Journal for the Study of the Historical Jesus* 5, no. 1 (2007): 57–79.

———. "Jesus' Divine Self-Consciousness: A Proposal." Manchester, 2014. https://www.academia.edu/8211442/Jesus_Divine_Self-Consciousness_A_Proposal_British_New_Testament_Conference_2014_.

———. *Jesus Monotheism: Volume 1: Christological Origins: The Emerging Consensus and Beyond*. Eugene, Oregon: Cascade Books, 2015.

———. "Jesus, the Temple and the Dissolution of Heaven and Earth." In *Apocalyptic in History and Tradition*, edited by Christopher Rowland and John Barton, 117–41. Sheffield: Sheffield Academic Press, 2002.

———. "The Cosmology of P and Theological Anthropology in the Wisdom of Jesus Ben Sira." In *Of Scribes and Sages: Early Jewish Interpretation and Transmission of Scripture*, edited by Craig A Evans, 69–113. Sheffield: Sheffield Academic Press, 2004.

———. "The Image of God and the Biblical Roots of Christian Sacramentality." In *The Gestures of God: Explorations in Sacramentality*, edited by Geoffrey Rowell and Christine Hall, 73–89. London: Continuum, 2004.

Fossum, Jarl. "Glory." In *Dictionary of Deities and Demons in the Bible*, edited by Karel van der van der Toorn, Bob Becking, and Pieter Willem van der Horst, 348–52. Grand Rapids, MI: Eerdmans, 1999.

Gane, Roy E. *Cult and Character: Purification Offerings, Day of Atonement, and Theodicy*. Winona Lake, IN: Eisenbrauns, 2005.

———. "Privative Preposition מִן in Purification Offering Pericopes and the Changing Face of 'Dorian Gray.'" *Journal of Biblical Literature* 127, no. 2 (July 1, 2008): 209–22.

Gelardini, Gabriella. "The Inauguration of Yom Kippur According To The LXX And Its Cessation Or Perpetuation According To The Book Of Hebrews: A Systematic Comparison." In *The Day of Atonement: Its Interpretations in Early Jewish and Christian Traditions*, edited by Thomas Hieke and Tobias Nicklas, 225–54. Leiden: Brill, 2011.

Giandomenico, Craig. "A Disease of Being: The Ontological Status of Sin in the Theology of Hans Urs Von Balthasar." Diss., La Salle University, 2017.

Gilders, William K. *Blood Ritual in the Hebrew Bible: Meaning and Power*. Baltimore: The Johns Hopkins University Press, 2004.

Girard, René. *I See Satan Fall Light Lightning*. Translated by James G. Williams. New York: Orbis Books, 2001.

———. *The Scapegoat*. Translated by Yvonne Freccero. Baltimore: The Johns Hopkins University Press, 1986.

———. *Things Hidden Since the Foundation of the World*. Translated by Stephen Bann and Michael Metteer. Redwood City, CA: Stanford University Press, 1987.

Golitzin, Alexander. "Christian Mysticism over Two Millenia." *Scrinium* 3 (2007): xxi–xxxiii.

———. "Theophaneia: Forum on the Jewish Roots of Orthodox Spirituality." *Scrinium* 3 (2007): xvii–xx.

Gorman, Frank. "Priestly Rituals of Founding: Time, Space, and Status." In *History and Interpretation: Essays in Honour of John H. Hayes*, edited by M. Patrick Graham, William P. Brown, and Jeffrey K. Kuan. JSOTSup 173. Sheffield: JSOT 1993.

Grabbe, Lester L. *A History of the Jews and Judaism in the Second Temple Period, Volume 2: The Coming of the Greeks: The Early Hellenistic Period (335–175 BCE)*. Sheffield: Continuum, 2008.

Grant, Colin. "The Abandonment of Atonement." *King's Theological Review* 9, no. 1 (1986): 1–8.

Grebe, Matthias. *Election, Atonement, and the Holy Spirit: Through and Beyond Barth's Theological Interpretation of Scripture*. Eugene, OR: Pickwick Publications, 2014.

Green, Joel B. *The Gospel of Luke*. Grand Rapids, MI: Eerdmans, 1997.

Greenberg, James A. *A New Look at Atonement in Leviticus: The Meaning and Purpose of Kipper Revisited*. Winona Lake, IN: Eisenbrauns, 2020.

Greene, Joseph R. "The Realization of the Heavenly Temple in John's Gospel: Jesus and the Spirit." Diss., Southeastern Baptist Theological Seminary, 2012.

Hamilton, Victor P. *The Book of Genesis: Chapters 18–50*. Grand Rapids, MI: Eerdmans, 1995.

Hammer, Reuven. *Entering the High Holy Days: A Complete Guide to the History, Prayers, and Themes*. Philadelphia: The Jewish Publication Society, 2005.

Hampson, Daphne, ed. *Swallowing a Fishbone?: Feminist Theologians Debate Christianity*. London: SPCK Publishing, 1996.

Hanson, Paul. "Rebellion in Heaven, Azazel, and Euhemeristic Heroes in 1 Enoch 6-11." *Journal of Biblical Literature* 96, no. 2 (1977): 195–233.

Haran, Menahem. *Temples and Temple-Service in Ancient Israel: An Inquiry into the Character of Cult Phenomena and the Historical Setting of the Priestly School*. Oxford: Clarendon Press, 1977.

Hart, David Bentley. *The Beauty of the Infinite: The Aesthetics of Christian Truth*. Grand Rapids, MI: Eerdmans, 2004.

———. "The Devil's March: Creatio Ex Nihilo, the Problem of Evil, and a Few Dostoyevskian Meditations." In *Theological Territories: A David Bentley Hart Digest*, 77–97. Notre Dame, IN: University of Notre Dame Press, 2020.

———. *The Doors of the Sea: Where Was God in the Tsunami?* Grand Rapids, MI: Eerdmans, 2005.

———. *The Experience of God: Being, Consciousness, Bliss*. New Haven, CT: Yale University Press, 2013.

———. *In the Aftermath: Provocations and Laments*. Grand Rapids, MI: Eerdmans, 2008.

———. "Response from David Bentley Hart to McGuckin and Murphy." *Scottish Journal of Theology* 60, no. 1 (2007): 95–101.

———. "Response to James KA Smith, Lois Malcolm and Gerard Loughlin." *New Blackfriars* 88, no. 1017 (2007): 610–623.

———. *That All Shall Be Saved: Heaven, Hell, and Universal Salvation*. New Haven, CT: Yale University Press, 2021.

Hartley, John E. *Word Biblical Commentary: Leviticus*. Word Biblical Commentary 4. Waco, TX: Word Books, 1992.

Hayward, Robert. *The Jewish Temple: A Non-Biblical Sourcebook*. London: Routledge, 2002.

Heim, S. Mark. *Saved from Sacrifice: A Theology of the Cross*. Grand Rapids, MI: Eerdmans, 2006.

Heller, Jan. "Der Name Asasel." *Communia Viatorum* 40 (1998): 126–30.

Helm, R. "Azazel in Early Jewish Tradition." *Andrews University Seminary Studies* 32, no. 3 (1994): 217–26.

Hess, Richard S. "Leviticus 10:1 Strange Fire and an Odd Name." *Bulletin for Biblical Research* 12 (2002): 187–98.

Hieke, Thomas, and Tobias Nicklas. "Introduction." In *The Day of Atonement: Its Interpretations in Early Jewish and Christian Traditions*. Leiden: Brill, 2011.

Hilary of Poitiers. "Homilies on the Psalms." In *Nicene and Post-Nicene Fathers, Second Series*, Vol. 9. Buffalo: Christian Literature Publishing Company, 1899.

Hill, Charles. "Atonement in the Old and New Testaments." In *The Glory of the Atonement: Biblical, Theological & Practical Perspectives*, edited by Charles E. Hill and Frank A. James III, 23–34. Westmont, IL: IVP Academic, 2004.

Himmelfarb, Martha. "Apocalyptic Ascent and the Heavenly Temple." *Society of Biblical Literature Seminar Papers*, no. 26 (January 1, 1987): 210–17.

———. *Ascent to Heaven in Jewish and Christian Apocalypses*. New York: Oxford University Press, 1993.

Hogeterp, A. L. A. *Paul and God's Temple: A Historical Interpretation of Cultic Imagery in the Corinthian Correspondence*. Biblical Tools and Studies 2. Leuven: Peeters, 2006.

Hopkins, Julie M. *Towards a Feminist Christology: Jesus of Nazareth, European Women, and the Christological Crisis*. Grand Rapids, MI: Eerdmans, 1995.

Hoskins, Paul M. *Jesus as the Fulfillment of the Temple in the Gospel of John*. Eugene, OR: Wipf & Stock Publishers, 2007.

Houtman, Cornelis. "On the Function of the Holy Incense (Exodus XXX 34-8) and the Sacred Anointing Oil (Exodus XXX 22-33)." *Vetus Testamentum*, 1992, 458–65.

Howard, Thomas. *Dove Descending: A Journey into T. S. Eliot's* Four Quartets. San Francisco: Sapienta Classics/Ignatius Press, 2006.

Hundley, Michael B. "Before YHWH at the Entrance of the Tent of Meeting: A Study of Spatial and Conceptual Geography in the Priestly Texts." *Zeitschrift für die alttestamentliche Wissenschaft* 123, no. 1 (2011): 15–26.

———. "Divine Fluidity? The Priestly Texts in Their Ancient Near Eastern Contexts." In *Text, Time, and Temple: Literary, Historical and Ritual Studies in Leviticus*, edited by Francis Landy, Leigh M. Trevaskis, and Bryan D. Bibb. Sheffield: Sheffield Phoenix Press, 2015.

———. *Keeping Heaven on Earth: Safeguarding the Divine Presence in the Priestly Tabernacle*. Tübingen: Mohr Siebeck, 2011.

———. "Sacred Spaces, Objects, Offerings, and People in the Priestly Texts: A Reappraisal." *Journal of Biblical Literature* 132, no. 4 (2013): 749–67.

———. "To Be or Not to Be: A Reexamination of Name Language in Deuteronomy and the Deuteronomistic History." *Vetus Testamentum* 59, no. 4 (2009): 533–55.

Hunt, Anne. *The Trinity and the Paschal Mystery: A Development in Recent Catholic Theology*. Liturgical Press, 1997.

Hutcheon, Cyprian Robert. "'God Is with Us': The Temple in Luke-Acts." *St. Vladimir's Theological Quarterly* 44, no. 1 (2000): 3–34.

Imes, Carmen Joy. "Between Two Worlds: The Functional and Symbolic Significance of the High Priestly Regalia." In *Dress and Clothing in the Hebrew Bible*, edited by Antonios Finitsis, 29–62. London: T&T Clark, 2019.

Irenaeus. *Against Heresies*. Translated by Alexander Roberts and William Rambaut. Vol. 1. Ante-Nicene Fathers. Buffalo: Christian Literature Publishing Co., 1885.

Isaac, E. "1 (Ethiopic Apocalypse of) Enoch." In *The Old Testament Pseudepigrapha*, edited by James R. Charlesworth, 1.5–89. 2 vols. New York: Doubleday, 1983–1985.

Janowski, Bernd. "Der Tempel als Kosmos - Zur kosmologischen Bedeutung des Tempels in der Umwelt Israels." In *Egypt — Temple of the Whole World*, 163–86. Leiden: Brill, 2003.

Jenson, Philip Peter. *Graded Holiness: A Key to the Priestly Conception of the World*. Sheffield, England: JSOT Press, 1992.

Jenson, Robert W. "Review: The Beauty of the Infinite: The Aesthetics of Christian Truth." *Pro Ecclesia* XIV, no. 2 (2005): 235–37.

John of Damascus. "An Exposition of the Orthodox Faith." In *Nicene and Post-Nicene Fathers, Second Series*, Vol. 9. Buffalo: Christian Literature Publishing Co., 1899.

Johnson, Luke Timothy. *Hebrews: A Commentary*. Louisville, KY: Westminster John Knox Press, 2006.

Josephus. *Jewish Antiquities, Books I-IV*. Translated by H. St. J. Thackeray. Vol. 4. Loeb Classical Library. Cambridge, MA: Harvard University Press, 1967.

Julian of Norwich. *Julian of Norwich: Showings*. Translated by Edmund Colledge and James Walsh. New York: Paulist Press, 1977.

Kalimi, Isaac. "The Land of Moriah, Mount Moriah, and the Site of Solomon's Temple in Biblical Historiography." *Harvard Theological Review* 83, no. 04 (1990): 345–62.

Kant, Immanuel. *Religion within the Limits of Reason Alone*. New York: Harper Torchbooks, 1960.

Kawashima, Robert S. "The Priestly Tent of Meeting and the Problem of Divine Transcendence: An 'Archaeology' of the Sacred." *The Journal of Religion* 86, no. 2 (2006): 226–57.

Kazen, Thomas. "Dirt and Disgust: Body and Morality in Biblical Purity Laws." In *Perspective on Purity and Purification in the Bible*, 43–64. Library of Hebrew Bible/Old Testament Studies 474. New York: T&T Clark, 2008.

Kearney, Peter J. "Creation and Liturgy: The P Redaction of Ex 25—40." *Zeitschrift für die alttestamentliche Wissenschaft* 89, no. 3 (1977): 375–87.

Kerr, Alan. *The Temple of Jesus' Body: The Temple Theme in the Gospel of John*. Sheffield: Sheffield Academic Press, 2002.

Kessler, Edward. *Bound by the Bible: Jews, Christians and the Sacrifice of Isaac*. Cambridge: Cambridge University Press, 2004.

Kilby, Karen. *Balthasar: A (Very) Critical Introduction*. Grand Rapids, MI: Eerdmans, 2012.

Kim, Lloyd. *Polemic in the Book of Hebrews: Anti-Judaism, Anti-Semitism, Supersessionism?* Eugene, OR: Pickwick Publications, 2006.

Kinzer, Mark. "Temple Christology in the Gospel of John." In *Society of Biblical Literature 1998 Seminar Papers* 37, 447–64, 1988.

Kirschner, Robert. " and Abihu Incident (Lev. 10: 1-6)." *The Jewish Quarterly Review* 73, 1983, 375–93.

Kiuchi, Nobuyoshi. *The Purification Offering in the Priestly Literature: Its Meaning and Function*. Sheffield: JSOT Press, 1988.

Klawans, Jonathan. *Impurity and Sin in Ancient Judaism*. Oxford; New York: Oxford University Press, 2004.

———. *Purity, Sacrifice, and the Temple: Symbolism and Supersessionism in the Study of Ancient Judaism*. Oxford: Oxford University Press, 2006.

———. "Rethinking Leviticus and Rereading 'Purity and Danger.'" *AJS Review* 27, no. 1 (April 1, 2003): 89–101.

Klijn, A. F. J. "2 (Syriac Apocalypse of) Baruch." In *The Old Testament Pseudepigrapha*, edited by James R. Charlesworth, 1.615–52. 2 vols. New York: Doubleday, 1983–1985.

Lake, Kirsopp. *The Apostolic Fathers*. 2 vols. Loeb Classical Library 24–25. Cambridge, MA: Harvard University Press, 1912–1913. Lanfer, Peter Thacher. *Remembering Eden: The Reception History of Genesis 3: 22-24*. Oxford: Oxford University Press, 2012.

Lauber, David. *Barth on the Descent into Hell: God, Atonement, and the Christian Life*. New York: Ashgate Publishing, 2004.

Leal, Robert Barry. "Negativity towards Wilderness in the Biblical Record." *Ecotheology* 10, no. 3 (2005): 364–81.

Leamy, Katy. *The Holy Trinity: Hans Urs Von Balthasar and His Sources*. Eugene, OR: Pickwick Publications, 2015.

Leithart, Peter J. *Delivered from the Elements of the World: Atonement, Justification, Mission*. Downers Grove, IL: IVP Academic, 2016.

———. "'We Saw His Glory': Implications of the Sanctuary Christology in John's Gospel." In *Christology, Ancient and Modern: Explorations in Constructive Dogmatics*, edited by Oliver D. Crisp and Fred Sanders. Grand Rapids, MI: Zondervan Academic, 2013.Lemos, T. M. "Where There Is Dirt, Is There System? Revisiting Biblical Purity Constructions." *Journal for the Study of the Old Testament* 37, no. 3 (March 1, 2013): 265–94.

Levenson, Jon D. *Creation and the Persistence of Evil: The Jewish Drama of Divine Omnipotence*. Princeton, NJ: Princeton University Press, 1988.

———. "Genesis Introduction and Annotations." In *The Jewish Study Bible. Tanakh*, edited by Adele Berlin and Marc Zvi Brettler, 8–101. New York: Oxford University Press, 2004.

———. *Resurrection and the Restoration of Israel: The Ultimate Victory of the God of Life*. New Haven, CT: Yale University Press, 2008.

———. *Sinai and Zion: An Entry into the Jewish Bible*. San Francisco: HarperOne, 1987.

———. *The Death and Resurrection of the Beloved Son: The Transformation of Child Sacrifice in Judaism and Christianity*. New Haven, CT: Yale University Press, 1995.

———. "The Eighth Principle of Judaism and the Literary Simultaneity of Scripture." *The Journal of Religion*, 1988, 205–25.

———. "The Jerusalem Temple in Devotional and Visionary Experience." In *Jewish Spirituality, Vol 1*, 32–61. New York: Crossroad, 1986.

———. "The Temple and the World." *The Journal of Religion* 64, no. 3 (1984): 275–98.

Levenson, Jon D., and Kevin J. Madigan. *Resurrection: The Power of God for Christians and Jews*. New Haven: Yale University Press, 2008.

Levering, Matthew. *Christ's Fulfillment of Torah and Temple: Salvation According to Thomas Aquinas*. Notre Dame, IN: University of Notre Dame Press, 2002.

———. *Sacrifice and Community: Jewish Offering and Christian Eucharist*. Hoboken, NJ: Wiley-Blackwell, 2005.

———. *Scripture and Metaphysics: Aquinas and the Renewal of Trinitarian Theology*. Hoboken, NJ: Wiley-Blackwell, 2004.

Levering, Matthew, and Tom Angier. *The Achievement of David Novak: A Catholic-Jewish Dialogue*. Eugene, OR: Pickwick Publications, 2021.

Levine, Baruch A. *In the Presence of the Lord: A Study of Cult and Some Cultic Terms in Ancient Israel*. Leiden: Brill, 1974.

———. *The JPS Torah Commentary: Leviticus*. Philadelphia: The Jewish Publication Society, 2003.

Levitt Kohn, Risa. "A Prophet Like Moses? Rethinking Ezekiel's Relationship to the Torah." *Zeitschrift für die alttestamentliche Wissenschaft* 114, no. 2 (2006): 236–54.

Lewis, C. S. *God in the Dock: Essays on Theology and Ethics*. Grand Rapids, MI: Eerdmans, 1972.

———. *The Collected Letters of C. S. Lewis, Volume 3: Narnia, Cambridge, and Joy, 1950 - 1963*. New York: HarperCollins, 2007.

———. *The Great Divorce*. San Francisco: HarperOne, 2001.

Long, D. Stephen. *Hebrews*. Belief: A Theological Commentary on the Bible. Louisville, KY: Westminster John Knox Press, 2011.

Lösel, Steffen. "A Plain Account of Christian Salvation? Balthasar on Sacrifice, Solidarity, and Substitution." *Pro Ecclesia* 13, no. 2 (Spring 2004): 141–71.

Loughlin, Gerard. "Rhetoric and Rhapsody: A Response to David Bentley Hart's *The Beauty of the Infinite*," *New Blackfriars* 88, no. 1017, 2007, 600–609.

Louth, Andrew. "The Place of Theosis in Orthodox Theology." In *Partakers of the Divine Nature: The History and Development of Deification in the Christian Traditions*, edited by Jeffery A. Wittung and Michael J. Christensen, 32–44. Grand Rapids, MI: Baker Academic, 2007.

Lyonnet, Stanislas, and Leopold Sabourin. *Sin, Redemption, and Sacrifice. A Biblical and Patristic Study*. Rome: Biblical Institute, 1970.

Maccoby, Hyam. *Ritual and Morality: The Ritual Purity System and Its Place in Judaism*. New York: Cambridge University Press, 1999.

Malcolm, Lois. "On David Hart's *The Beauty of the Infinite*." *New Blackfriars* 88, no. 1017 (2007): 594-599.

Martin, Jennifer Newsome. *Hans Urs von Balthasar and the Critical Appropriation of Russian Religious Thought*. Notre Dame, IN: University of Notre Dame Press, 2015.

———. "The Consubstantial Otherness of God: Divine Simplicity and the Trinity in Hans Urs von Balthasar." *Modern Theology* 35, no. 3 (2019): 542–57.

———. "The 'Whence' and the 'Whither' of Balthasar's Gendered Theology: Rehabilitating Kenosis for Feminist Theology." *Modern Theology* 31, no. 2 (2015): 211–34.

Martyn, J. Louis. *Galatians*. New Haven: Yale University Press, 2004.

Matera, Frank J. *II Corinthians: A Commentary*. Louisville, KY: Westminster John Knox Press, 2003.

Matthews, Victor Harold, and Don C. Benjamin. *Old Testament Parallels: Laws and Stories from the Ancient Near East*. New York: Paulist Press, 2006.

Mettinger, Tryggve N. D. *The Dethronement of Sabaoth: Studies in the Shem and Kabod Theologies*. Lund: CWK Gleerup, 1982.

Milbank, John. *Being Reconciled: Ontology and Pardon*. London: Routledge, 2003.

Miles, Lois M. "Obedience of a Corpse: The Key to the Holy Saturday Writings of Adrienne von Speyr." Ph.D. diss., University of Aberdeen, 2013.

Milgrom, Jacob. *Cult and Conscience: The Asham and the Priestly Doctrine of Repentance*. Leiden: Brill, 1976.

———. "Impurity Is Miasma: A Response to Hyam Maccoby." *Journal of Biblical Literature* 119, no. 4 (January 1, 2000): 729–46.

———. "Israel's Sanctuary: The Priestly 'Picture of Dorian Gray.'" *Revue Biblique* 83 (1976): 390–99.

———. "Kipper." In *Encyclopaedia Judaica*, 10:1039–44, 1971.

———. *Leviticus 1-16. A New Translation with Introduction and Commentary. The Anchor Bible*. New York: Doubleday, 1991.

———. *Leviticus 17-22: A New Translation with Introduction and Commentary*. New York: Doubleday, 2000.

———. *Leviticus: A Book of Ritual and Ethics*. Minneapolis: Augsburg Fortress, 2004.

———. "Rationale for Cultic Law: The Case of Impurity." *Semeia* 45 (1989): 103–9.

———. "Sin-Offering or Purification-Offering." *Vetus Testamentum* 21, no. 2 (April 1, 1971): 237–39.

———. *Studies in Cultic Theology and Terminology*. Leiden: Brill, 1983.

———. "The Preposition מִן in the חטאת Pericopes." *Journal of Biblical Literature* 126, no. 1 (April 1, 2007): 161.

———. "The Priestly Doctrine of Repentance." *Revue Biblique* 82 (1975): 186–205.

Moberly, R. W. L. *The Bible, Theology, and Faith: A Study of Abraham and Jesus*. Cambridge: Cambridge University Press, 2000.

———. *The Theology of the Book of Genesis*. Cambridge; New York: Cambridge University Press, 2009.

Moffitt, David M. *Atonement and the Logic of Resurrection in the Epistle to the Hebrews*. Leiden: Brill, 2011.

———. "Blood, Life, and Atonement: Reassessing Hebrews' Christological Appropriation of Yom Kippur," in *The Day of Atonement: Its Interpretations in Early Jewish and Christian Traditions*, edited by Thomas Hieke, 211–24. Leiden: Brill, 2011.

Morales, L. Michael. "Atonement in Ancient Israel: The Whole Burnt Offering as Central to Israel's Cult." In *So Great a Salvation: A Dialogue on the Atonement in Hebrews*, edited by Jon C. Laansma, George H. Guthrie, and Cynthia Long Westfall. London: T&T Clark, 2019.

———. *Who Shall Ascend the Mountain of the Lord?: A Biblical Theology of the Book of Leviticus*. Downers Grove, IL: IVP Academic, 2015.

Morray-Jones, Christopher RA. "Transformational Mysticism in the Apocalyptic-Merkabah Tradition." *Journal of Jewish Studies* 43, no. 1 (1992): 1–31.

Moscicke, Hans M. *Goat for Yahweh, Goat for Azazel: The Impact of Yom Kippur on the Gospels*. Minneapolis: Fortress Academic, 2021.

———. "Jesus, Barabbas, and the Crowd as Figures in Matthew's Day of Atonement Typology (Matthew 27:15-26)." *Journal of Biblical Literature* 139, no. 1 (March 2020): 125–53.

———. *The New Day of Atonement: A Matthean Typology*. Tübingen: Mohr Siebeck, 2020.

Murphy, Francesca. "David Hart, The Beauty of the Infinite: A Response." *Scottish Journal of Theology* 60, no. 1 (2007): 80–89.

Neusner, Jacob, trans. *The Mishnah: A New Translation*. New Haven, CT: Yale University Press, 1988.

———. *Vanquished Nation, Broken Spirit: The Virtues of the Heart in Formative Judaism*. Cambridge: Cambridge University Press, 1987.

Nichols, Aidan. *A Key to Balthasar: Hans Urs Von Balthasar on Beauty, Goodness, and Truth*. Grand Rapids, MI: Baker Academic, 2011.

————. *No Bloodless Myth: A Guide through Balthasar's Dramatics.* Washington, D.C.: Catholic University of America Press, 2000.

Nickelsburg, George W. E. "Apocalyptic and Myth in 1 Enoch 6-11." *Journal of Biblical Literature* 96, no. 3 (September 1, 1977): 383–405.

Nickelsburg, George W. E., and James C. VanderKam. *1 Enoch: The Hermeneia Translation.* Minneapolis: Fortress Press, 2012.

Nicole, Emile. "Atonement in the Pentateuch." In *The Glory of the Atonement: Biblical, Theological & Practical Perspectives*, edited by Charles E. Hill and Frank A. James III, 35–50. Westmont, IL: IVP Academic, 2004.

Nihan, Christophe. *From Priestly Torah to Pentateuch: A Study in the Composition of the Book of Leviticus.* Tübingen: Coronet Books Inc., 2007.

————. "The Templization of Israel in Leviticus: Some Remarks on Blood Disposal and Kipper in Leviticus 4." In *Text, Time, and Temple: Literary, Historical and Ritual Studies in Leviticus*, edited by Francis Landy, Leigh M. Trevaskis, and Bryan D. Bibb, 96–120. Sheffield: Sheffield Phoenix Press, 2015.

Nihan, Christophe and Julia Rhyder, "Aaron's Vestments in Exodus 28 and Priestly Leadership." In *Debating Authority: Concepts of Leadership in the Pentateuch and the Former Prophets*, edited by Katharina Pyschny and Sarah Schulz, 45–67. Berlin: de Gruyter, 2018.

Novak, David. "Supersessionism Hard and Soft." *First Things* 290 (February 2019): 27–31.

O'Connor, Flannery. *Flannery O'Connor: Spiritual Writings*, edited by Robert Ellsberg. Maryknoll, NY: Orbis Books, 2003.

O'Regan, Cyril. *Anatomy of Misremembering: Von Balthasar's Response to Philosophical Modernity. Volume 1: Hegel.* Chestnut Ridge, NY: The Crossroad Publishing Company, 2014.

————. "Newman and von Balthasar : The Christological Contexting of the Numinous." *Eglise et Théologie* 26, no. 2 (1995): 165–202.

Origen. *Homilies on Leviticus, 1-16.* Washington, DC: The Catholic University of America Press, 2005.

Orlov, Andrei. "A Farewell to the Merkavah Tradition." The Eighth Enoch Seminar: Apocalypticism and Mysticism, Milan, Villa Cagnola, Italy, June, 22, 2015.

————. *Dark Mirrors: Azazel and Satanael in Early Jewish Demonology.* Albany: State University of New York Press, 2011.

————. *Divine Scapegoats: Demonic Mimesis in Early Jewish Mysticism.* Albany: State University of New York Press, 2014.

———. *Heavenly Priesthood in the Apocalypse of Abraham*. Cambridge: Cambridge University Press, 2013.

———. *The Atoning Dyad: The Two Goats of Yom Kippur in the Apocalypse of Abraham*. Leiden: Brill, 2016.

Owiredu, Charles. "Blood and Life in the Old Testament." Durham University, 2004.

Palmer, Christine Elizabeth. "Israelite High Priestly Apparel: Embodying an Identity between Human and Divine." In *Fashioned Selves: Dress and Identity in Antiquity*, edited by Megan Cifarelli, 117–27. London: Oxbow Books, 2019.

———. "The Jerusalem Temple: A Sensory Encounter with the Sacred." In *The Routledge Handbook of the Senses in the Ancient Near East*. London: Routledge, 2021.

Papanikolaou, Aristotle. "Person, Kenosis and Abuse: Hans Urs von Balthasar and Feminist Theologies in Conversation." *Modern Theology* 19, no. 1 (2003): 41–65.

Perrin, Nicholas. *Jesus the Temple*. Grand Rapids, MI: Baker Academic, 2010.

Philip, Mayjee. *Leviticus in Hebrews: A Transtextual Analysis of the Tabernacle Theme in the Letter to the Hebrews*. Frankfurt: Peter Lang, 2011.

Philo. *On Abraham. On Joseph. On Moses*. Translated by F. H. Colson. Loeb Classical Library. Cambridge, MA: Harvard University Press, 1935.

Pitre, Brant. "Jesus, the New Temple, and the New Priesthood." *Letter & Spirit* 4 (2008): 47–83.

Pitstick, Alyssa Lyra. *Light in Darkness: Hans Urs Von Balthasar and the Catholic Doctrine of Christ's Descent into Hell*. Grand Rapids, MI: Eerdmans, 2007.

Przywara, Erich. *Analogia Entis: Metaphysics : Original Structure and Universal Rhythm*. Grand Rapids, MI: Eerdmans, 2013.

Radner, Ephraim. *Leviticus*. Grand Rapids: Brazos Press, 2008.

Rahner, Karl. "The Concept of Mystery in Catholic Theology." *Theological Investigations* 4 (1966): 36–73.

Ray, Darby Kathleen. *Deceiving the Devil: Atonement, Abuse, and Ransom*. Cleveland: Pilgrim Press, 1998.

Rendtorff, Rolf. "Leviticus 16 Als Mitte Der Tora." *Biblical Interpretation* 11 (2003): 252–58.

Rhyder, Julia. *Centralizing the Cult: The Holiness Legislation in Leviticus 17-26*. Tübingen: Mohr Siebeck, 2019.

Riches, Aaron. *Ecce Homo: On the Divine Unity of Christ.* Grand Rapids, MI: Eerdmans, 2016.

Richter, Sandra L. "The Place of the Name in Deuteronomy." *Vetus Testamentum* 57, no. 3 (2007): 342–66.

Ruether, Rosemary Radford. *Introducing Redemption in Christian Feminism.* Sheffield: Sheffield Academic Press, 1998.

Ruiten, J. T. A. G. M. van. "Eden and the Temple: The Rewriting of Genesis 2: 4-3: 24 in The Book of Jubilees." In *Paradise Interpreted: Representations of Biblical Paradise in Judaism and Christianity,* edited by Gerard P. Luttikhuizen, 215–27. Leiden: Brill, 1999.

Sanders, E.P. *Judaism: Practice and Belief, 63 BCE-66 CE.* London: SCM Press; Trinity Press International, 1992.

Sarna, Nahum M. *Genesis: The Traditional Hebrew Text with the New JPS Translation.* Philadelphia: Jewish Publication Society, 1989.

Saward, John. *The Mysteries of March: Hans Urs von Balthasar on the Incarnation and Easter.* Washington, D.C.: Catholic University of America Press, 1990.

Schindler, D. C. *Love and the Postmodern Predicament: Rediscovering the Real in Beauty, Goodness, and Truth.* Eugene, OR: Wipf and Stock Publishers, 2018.

Schmid, Konrad. "Abraham's Sacrifice: Gerhard von Rad's Interpretation of Genesis 22." *Interpretation: A Journal of Bible and Theology* 62, no. 3 (July 1, 2008): 268–76.

———. "Die Rückgabe der Verheißungsgabe: Der 'heilsgeschichtliche' Sinn von Genesis 22 Im Horizont innerbiblischer Exegese." In *Gott und Mensch im Dialog: Festschrift O. Kaiser,* edited by M. Witte, 271–300. Berlin: de Gruyter, 2004.

Schreiner, Thomas R. "Penal Substitution View." In *The Nature of the Atonement: Four Views,* edited by James Beilby and Paul R. Eddy, 67–98. Westmont, IL: IVP Academic, 2006.

Schwager, Raymund. *Jesus in the Drama of Salvation: Toward a Biblical Doctrine of Redemption.* New York: Crossroad Publishing Company, 1999.

———. *Must There Be Scapegoats?: Violence and Redemption in the Bible.* New York: Harper & Row, 1987.

Schwartz, Baruch J. "Leviticus, Introduction and Annotations." In *The Jewish Study Bible. Tanakh,* 8–101. Oxford: Oxford University Press, 2004.

———. "The Bearing of Sin in the Priestly Literature." In *Pomegranates and Golden Bells: Studies in Biblical, Jewish and Near Eastern Ritual, Law, and Literature in Honour of Jacob Milgrom,* edited by David Pearson

Wright, David Noel Freedman, and Avi Hurvitz, 3–22. Winona Lake, IN: Eisenbrauns, 1995.

———. "The Prohibitions Concerning the 'Eating' of Blood in Leviticus 17." In *Priesthood and Cult in Ancient Israel*, 34–66. Sheffield: JSOT Press, 1991.

Seters, John van. *Abraham in History and Tradition*. New Haven, CT: Yale University Press, 1975.

Siker, Jeffrey S. "Yom Kippuring Passover: Recombinant Sacrifice in Early Christianity." In *Ritual and Metaphor: Sacrifice in the Bible*, edited by Christian A. Eberhart, 65–82. Atlanta: Society of Biblical Literature, 2011.

Silberman, Lou H. "Wellhausen and Judaism." *Semeia* 25 (1982): 75–82.

Sklar, Jay. "Sin and Impurity: Atoned or Purified? Yes!" In *Perspectives on Purity and Purification in the Bible*, edited by Baruch J. Schwartz, 18–31. New York: T&T Clark, 2008.

———. *Sin, Impurity, Sacrifice, Atonement: The Priestly Conceptions*. Sheffield: Sheffield Phoenix Press, 2005.

Sommer, Benjamin D. "Dating Pentateuchal Texts and the Perils of Pseudo-Historicism." In *The Pentateuch: International Perspectives on Current Research*, edited by ThomasDozeman, Konrad Schmid, and Baruch J. Schwartz, 85–108. Tübingen: Mohr Siebeck, 2011.

———. "Dialogical Biblical Theology: A Jewish Approach to Reading Scripture Theologically." In *Biblical Theology: Introducing the Conversation*, 1–53. Nashville: Abingdon Press, 2009.

———. *The Bodies of God and the World of Ancient Israel*. Cambridge: Cambridge University Press, 2011.

Speiser, E. A. *Genesis: Introduction, Translation, and Notes*. Garden City, NY: Anchor Bible, 1964.

Speyr, Adrienne von. *John, Volume 2: The Discourses on Controversy*. San Francisco: Ignatius Press, 1993.

Sprinkle, Joe M. "The Rationale of the Laws of Clean and Unclean in the Old Testament." *Journal of the Evangelical Theological Society* 43 (December 1, 2000): 637–57.

Stanley, Steve. "Hebrews 9: 6–10: The 'Parable' of the Tabernacle." *Novum Testamentum* 37, no. 4 (1995): 385–99.

Steinmair-Pösel, Petra. "Original Sin, Grace, and Positive Mimesis." *Contagion: Journal of Violence, Mimesis, and Culture* 14, no. 1 (2008): 1–12.

Stemberger, Günter. "Yom Kippur in Mishnah Yoma." In *The Day of Atonement: Its Interpretations in Early Jewish and Christian Traditions*, edited by Thomas Hieke and Tobias Nicklas, 121–37. Leiden: Brill, 2012.

Stevenson, Gregory. *Power and Place: Temple and Identity in the Book of Revelation*. Berlin: de Gruyter, 2001.

Stökl Ben Ezra, Daniel. "Fasting with Jews, Thinking with Scapegoats: Some Remarks on Yom Kippur in Early Judaism and Christianity, in Particular 4Q541, Barnabas 7, Matthew 27 and Acts 27." In *The Day of Atonement: Its Interpretations in Early Jewish and Christian Traditions*, edited by Thomas Hieke and Tobias Nicklas, 165–87. Leiden: Brill, 2012.

———. *The Impact of Yom Kippur on Early Christianity: The Day of Atonement from Second Temple Judaism to the Fifth Century*. Tübingen: Mohr Siebeck, 2003.

———. "Yom Kippur in the Apocalyptic Imaginaire and the Roots of Jesus' High Priesthood: Yom Kippur in Zechariah 3, 1 Enoch 10, 11QMelkizedeq, Hebrews and the Apocalypse of Abraham 13." In *Transformations of the Inner Self in Ancient Religions*, 349–66. Leiden: Brill, 1999.

Stott, John. *The Cross of Christ*. Westmont, IL: IVP Books, 2006.

Stuckenbruck, Loren T. "The Origins of Evil in Jewish Apocalyptic Tradition: The Interpretation of Genesis 6:1-4 in the Second and Third Centuries BCE." In *The Fall of the Angels*, edited by C. Auffarth and L.T. Stuckenbruck, 86–118. Leiden: Brill, 2004.

Sutton, Matthew Lewis. *Heaven Opens: The Trinitarian Mysticism of Adrienne von Speyr*. Minneapolis: Fortress Press, 2014.

Tawil, Hayim. "Azazel, the Prince of the Steepe: A Comparative Study." *Zeitschrift für die alttestamentliche Wissenschaft* 92, no. 1 (January 1, 1980): 43–59.

Taylor, Charles. *A Secular Age*. Cambridge, MA: The Belknap Press of Harvard University Press, 2007.

Tiwald, Markus. "Christ as Hilasterion (Rom 3:25): Pauline Theology of the Day of Atonement in the Mirror of Early Jewish Thought." In *The Day of Atonement: Its Interpretations in Early Jewish and Christian Traditions*, edited by Thomas Hieke and Tobias Nicklas, 189–209. Leiden: Brill, 2012.

Trevaskis, Leigh M. *Holiness, Ethics and Ritual in Leviticus*. Sheffield: Sheffield Phoenix Press, 2011.

Troost-Cramer, Kathleen. *Jesus as Means and Locus of Worship in the Fourth Gospel*. Eugene, OR: Wipf and Stock, 2017.

Turner, Kenneth J. *The Death of Deaths in the Death of Israel: Deuteronomy's Theology of Exile*. Eugene, OR: Wipf & Stock, 2010.

VanderKam, James. "Mapping Second Temple Judaism." In *The Early Enoch Literature*, edited by Gabriele Boccaccini and John J. Collins, 1–20. Leiden: Brill, 2007.

Vis, Joshua M. "The Purgation of Persons through the Purification Offering." In *Sacrifice, Cult, and Atonement in Early Judaism and Christianity*, edited by Henrietta Wiley and Christian Eberhart, 33–57. Atlanta: Society of Biblical Literature Press, 2017.

———. "The Purification Offering of Leviticus and the Sacrificial Offering of Jesus." Ph.D. diss., Duke University, 2012.

Walters, Stanley. "Wood, Sand and Stars: Structure and Theology." *Toronto Journal of Theology* 3, no. 2 (September 1, 1987): 301–30.

Watts, James W. *Ritual and Rhetoric in Leviticus: From Sacrifice to Scripture.* Cambridge: Cambridge University Press, 2007.

Weaver, J. Denny. *The Nonviolent Atonement.* Grand Rapids, MI: Eerdmans, 2011.

Weinfeld, Moshe. *Deuteronomy and the Deuteronomic School.* Winona Lake, IN: Eisenbrauns, 1972.

———. "Sabbath, Temple, and the Enthronement of the Lord: The Problem of the 'Sitz im Leben' of Genesis 1: 1-2: 3." *Mélanges Bibliques et Orientaux En l'honneur de M. Henri Cazelles*, edited by A. Caquot and M. Delcor, 502–12. Kevelaer: Butzer & Bercker, 1981,

Wenham, Gordon J. "The Akedah: A Paradigm of Sacrifice." In *Pomegranates and Golden Bells: Studies in Biblical, Jewish and Near Eastern Ritual, Law, and Literature in Honour of Jacob Milgrom*, edited by David Pearson Wright, David Noel Freedman, and Avi Hurvitz, 93–102. Winona Lake, IN: Eisenbrauns, 1995.

———. *Genesis 16-50*, Word Biblical Commentary. Dallas: Thomas Nelson, 1994.

———. "Sanctuary Symbolism in the Garden of Eden Story." In *I Studied Inscriptions before the Flood*, 399–404. Winona Lake, IN: Eisenbrauns, 1994.

———. *The Book of Leviticus.* Grand Rapids, MI: Eerdmans, 1979.

Wilde, Oscar. *The Complete Works of Oscar Wilde: Stories, Plays, Poems & Essays.* New York: Harper Perennial Modern Classics, 2008.

Willi-Plein, Ina. "Some Remarks on Hebrews from the Viewpoint of Old Testament Exegesis." In *Hebrews: Contemporary Methods - New Insights*, edited by Gabriella Gelardini, 25–35. Leiden: Brill, 2005.

Wilson, Ian. *Out of the Midst of the Fire: Divine Presence in Deuteronomy.* Atlanta: Scholars Press, 1995.

Wintermute , O.S. "Jubilees." In *The Old Testament Pseudepigrapha*, edited by James R. Charlesworth, 2.35–142. 2 vols. New York: Doubleday, 1983–1985.Wright, Archie T. *The Origin of Evil Spirits: The Reception of Genesis 6: 1-4 in Early Jewish Literature*. Tübingen: Mohr Siebeck, 2013.

Wright, David P. *The Disposal of Impurity: Elimination Rites in the Bible and in Hittite and Mesopotamian Literature*. Society of Biblical Literature Dissertation Series 101. Atlanta: Scholars Press, 1987.

Wright, J. Edward. *The Early History of Heaven*. Oxford: Oxford University Press, 2002.

Wright, N. T. *Jesus and the Victory of God*. Minneapolis: Fortress Press, 1996.

———. *Paul and the Faithfulness of God*. Minneapolis: Fortress Press, 2013.

———. *The Case for the Psalms: Why They Are Essential*. New York: HarperCollins, 2013.

———. *The Challenge of Jesus: Rediscovering Who Jesus Was and Is*. Downers Grove, IL: IVP Books, 1999.

———. *The Day the Revolution Began: Reconsidering the Meaning of Jesus's Crucifixion*. New York: San Francisco: HarperOne, 2016.

———. *The New Testament and the People of God*. Minneapolis: Fortress Press, 1992.

Wyschogrod, Michael. "A Jewish Perspective on Incarnation." *Modern Theology* 12, no. 2 (1996): 195–209.

———. "Incarnation." *Pro Ecclesia* 2, no. 2 (1992): 209–15.

Young, Frances M. *The Use of Sacrificial Ideas in Greek Christian Writers from the New Testament to John Chrysostom*. Cambridge, MA: Philadelphia Patristic Foundation, 1979.

Subject Index

Scripture Index